D1190019

HANDBOOK OF ENVIRONMENTAL ECONOMICS
VOLUME 2

HANDBOOKS
IN
ECONOMICS

20

Series Editors

KENNETH J. ARROW
MICHAEL D. INTRILIGATOR

ELSEVIER
NORTH-HOLLAND

AMSTERDAM · BOSTON · HEIDELBERG · LONDON · NEW YORK · OXFORD
PARIS · SAN DIEGO · SAN FRANCISCO · SINGAPORE · SYDNEY · TOKYO

HANDBOOK OF ENVIRONMENTAL ECONOMICS

VOLUME 2
VALUING ENVIRONMENTAL CHANGES

Edited by

KARL-GÖRAN MÄLER
Swedish Academy of Sciences

and

JEFFREY R. VINCENT
University of California

ELSEVIER
NORTH-HOLLAND

2005

AMSTERDAM · BOSTON · HEIDELBERG · LONDON · NEW YORK · OXFORD
PARIS · SAN DIEGO · SAN FRANCISCO · SINGAPORE · SYDNEY · TOKYO

HC
79
.E5
H32852
2003
VOL. 2

ELSEVIER B.V.   ELSEVIER Inc.   ELSEVIER Ltd   ELSEVIER Ltd
Radarweg 29   525 B Street, Suite 1900   The Boulevard   84 Theobalds Road
P.O. Box 211   San Diego   Langford Lane, Kidlington   London
1000 AE Amsterdam   CA 92101-4495   Oxford OX5 1GB   WC1X 8RR
The Netherlands   USA   UK   UK

First edition 2005

Library of Congress Cataloging in Publication Data
A catalog record is available from the Library of Congress.

British Library Cataloguing in Publication Data
A catalogue record is available from the British Library.

ISBN-10: 0-444-51145-8
ISBN-13: 978-0-444-51145-4
ISSN: 0169-7218 (Handbooks in Economics Series)
ISSN: 1574-0099 (Handbook of Environmental Economics series)

∞ The paper used in this publication meets the requirements of ANSI/NISO Z39.48-1992 (Permanence of Paper).
Printed in The Netherlands.

INTRODUCTION TO THE SERIES

The aim of the *Handbooks in Economics* series is to produce Handbooks for various branches of economics, each of which is a definitive source, reference, and teaching supplement for use by professional researchers and advanced graduate students. Each Handbook provides self-contained surveys of the current state of a branch of economics in the form of chapters prepared by leading specialists on various aspects of this branch of economics. These surveys summarize not only received results but also newer developments, from recent journal articles and discussion papers. Some original material is also included, but the main goal is to provide comprehensive and accessible surveys. The Handbooks are intended to provide not only useful reference volumes for professional collections but also possible supplementary readings for advanced courses for graduate students in economics.

KENNETH J. ARROW and MICHAEL D. INTRILIGATOR

PUBLISHER'S NOTE

For a complete overview of the Handbooks in Economics Series, please refer to the listing at the end of this volume.

CONTENTS OF THE HANDBOOK

DEDICATION

Allen Kneese

If anyone should be called the founding father of environmental economics, it must be Allen Kneese. He was a pioneer as a researcher, and he was a pioneer as a research organizer. He inspired a vast number of younger environmental economists. His studies of water issues in the 1960s induced many, including one of the editors of this handbook, to look at environmental problems through the eyes of an economist. His enduring fight for the use of economic instruments in environmental policy had impacts even outside his own country. He was the first to recognize the need for economists to learn from other disciplines – physics, hydrology, ecology, political science – in order to enable us to produce good and relevant policy recommendations. Allen was an editor of the North-Holland *Handbook of Natural Resource and Energy Economics*. He had promised to write an essay describing his personal perspective on the evolution of environmental economics for this handbook. Unfortunately for all of us, he passed away after a long illness. We dedicate these volumes to his memory.

PREFACE TO THE HANDBOOK

Elsevier published a 3-volume *Handbook of Natural Resource and Energy Economics* in 1985 (the first two volumes) and 1993 (the third volume). Why is it now publishing a 3-volume *Handbook of Environmental Economics*? Is it not true that economic development in Europe and North America during the last thirty years has proved that there is no resource scarcity? After all, prices of minerals have not increased (in real terms), despite the enormous economic expansion that has occurred in these regions. Moreover, air quality has improved substantially in Europe and North America. Are not all environmental problems solved? Many "experts" argue that this is the case, and if they were right, there would be no need for a new handbook!

However, here there is a paradox. On the one hand, aggregate data seem to indicate that we have overcome most environmental problems. On the other hand, if we look at a micro level, it is easy to find contrary evidence.

Most environmental problems share the following two characteristics: they are intertemporal, and they are local. Soil erosion may cause severe economic losses in the future, but a long time might pass before the soil is so much eroded that its productivity is affected. And when its productivity is affected, the economic damage will fall primarily on the nearby village of farmers and might be barely felt on a national or international level. Thus, there will be no sign of economic damage until later, and because of the lack of appropriate information and the lack of appropriate property rights, there will be no immediate impacts on agricultural products and their prices.

This parable about soil erosion possibly applies to most environmental problems, which are often invisible unless we look for them. Human-induced climate change is a case in point. Without knowledge of thermodynamics, humans would not have launched the research that uncovered empirical evidence of global warming.

Of course, there are examples of continued environmental deterioration at the aggregate level. Global climate change is perhaps the most dramatic one. Another is the depletion of the world's marine fisheries. But some problems, e.g., biodiversity, are mainly analysed and discussed from a global perspective when the real problem is arguably on a local level. Reduction of biodiversity implies a reduction in ecological resilience, which increases the risk that local human communities will lose essential ecosystem services.

These points are relevant for both rich and poor countries, but if we focus our interest on the poor countries, the magnitude of welfare losses due to environmental degradation is even greater. Urban pollution, soil erosion, reduction both in the quality and quantity of potable water, etc. are the rule, not the exception, in these countries.

Economics, which is about the management of scarce resources, offers the tools needed for a rational analysis of environmental problems. The rapid development of economic theory and methods as applied to the environment is the first reason a new handbook is needed. Several chapters in the earlier Elsevier handbook are outdated. The most obvious example pertains to valuation methods, which economists use to measure environmental changes in monetary terms. The *Handbook of Natural Resource and Energy Economics* had two chapters on valuation, one on theory and one on methods applicable to recreation demand. In contrast, and as a consequence of the explosion of valuation research since the 1980s, the new handbook devotes an entire volume, Volume 2, "Valuing Environmental Changes," to valuation theory and methods. Valuation research has extended into areas, such as experimental economics, that were scarcely imagined in 1985.

Another example is market-based instruments for controlling pollution. An influential chapter by Peter Bohm and Clifford Russell in the earlier handbook made the case for using economic principles to guide the design of pollution policies. Although examples of economic approaches for controlling pollution, such as effluent charges and emissions trading programs, existed in the 1980s, they were so few and so new that experience with them could barely be evaluated. Now, many countries have experimented with pollution charges of various types, and at least one (the United States) has created emissions trading programs at the national level. Economists have analysed the experience with these programs, and the new handbook presents the lessons of their research.

The more important reason for the new handbook, however, is the emergence of entirely new lines of research that either did not exist 10–20 years ago or were so sparsely investigated as to preclude chapter-length reviews. Economic research on the environment today includes much more than studies that estimate the value of particular nonmarket environment goods or the cost-effectiveness of particular pollution control instruments.

Some of the new research is new because it applies microeconomic theory much more carefully to understand institutional aspects of environmental management (or mismanagement). Volume 1 of this handbook, "Environmental Degradation and Institutional Responses," presents much of the new research in this area, especially as it applies to environmental degradation at a local level. It includes chapters on common property management regimes; population, poverty, and the environment; mechanism design and the environment; and experimental evaluations of environmental policy instruments – chapters that have no counterparts in the earlier handbook.

Other research is new because it examines environmental externalities and public goods at larger economic scales: an entire national economy, several countries in a given region, or all the countries of the world. Volume 3, "Economywide and International Environmental Issues," summarises advances in this area. New areas of research that are covered in it include environmental policy in a second-best economy (the "double dividend" literature), empirical studies on economic growth and the environment (the "environmental Kuznets curve" literature), national income accounts and the environment, international trade and the environment, and international environmental agreements. One chapter in the Volume 3 of the earlier handbook touched on environmental applications of computable general equilibrium models and the economics of climate change, but both topics receive much more extensive coverage in Volume 2 of this handbook.

Due to the expansion of economic research on the environment, in one sense the scope of this handbook is, ironically, narrower than that of its predecessor. This difference is signalled by the change in title: the *Handbook of Environmental Economics*, not volumes 4–6 of the *Handbook of Natural Resource and Energy Economics*. Unlike the earlier handbook, this handbook does *not* include chapters on the supply of and demand for energy resources, minerals, timber, fish, and other commercial natural resources.

Instead, this handbook focuses on environmental goods and services that, due to property rights failures stemming from externalities and public goods, are not allocated efficiently by markets. Indeed, these environmental resources often lack markets altogether. They include air and water quality, hydrological functions of forests and wetlands, soil stability and fertility, the genetic diversity of wild species, natural areas used for recreation, and numerous others. They are in principle renewable, but in practise they are often subject to excessive degradation and depletion, sometimes to an irreversible degree.

Commercial natural resources appear in this new handbook only in an incidental way. For example, the development of comprehensive measures of national income and wealth requires consideration of all forms of capital, including all forms of natural capital. So, the chapter on national accounts and the environment discusses adjustments to conventional measures of national income and wealth for not only the degradation of environmental quality but also the depletion of stocks of commercial natural resources. Commercial extraction and utilisation of natural resources are also sources of many of the environmental externalities discussed throughout the handbook. A prime example is damage from emissions of greenhouse gases, which are released primarily by the burning of fossil fuels.

For these reasons, this handbook is best regarded as a complement to the *Handbook of Natural Resource and Energy Economics*, not a replacement for it. This handbook is intended to be an updated reference on environmental economics, not natural resource economics.

This handbook does share two important features with the earlier one, which we have attempted to accentuate. First, both handbooks draw upon research conducted by not only economists but also natural and social scientists in other disciplines. The chapters in this handbook on common property management regimes and population, poverty, and the environment draw extensively on the anthropological literature, while the chapter on political economy of environmental policy draws on studies by political scientists and legal scholars. Some chapters in this handbook are written by noneconomists, from the earth sciences, ecology, and psychology. External reviewers of chapter drafts were drawn from an even broader range of disciplines.

Second, both handbooks emphasise dynamic considerations. Natural resource economics is inherently about efficient allocations over time, but many textbooks present environmental economics in an entirely static context: the valuation of current use of an environmental resource, or the short-run cost-effectiveness of market-based instruments compared to command-and-control instruments. In fact, environmental economics, properly done, must consider several dynamic issues, which the chapters in this handbook highlight.

One is the dynamics of natural systems. The build-up of greenhouse gases in the atmosphere reminds us that pollution involves stocks as well as flows. The same is true for environmental resources other than air quality. Research by natural scientists has revealed that the dynamics of natural systems can be far from continuous and smooth; they can be nonlinear, complex, and chaotic, subject to abrupt and irreversible (or effectively irreversible) "flips" from one state to another. The first two chapters in Volume 1 highlight the dynamics of natural systems, which economists ignore at the risk of constructing economic models with feet of clay. These chapters complement the excellent chapter on dynamics of natural resources by James Wilen in the earlier handbook.

A second dynamic consideration follows immediately from the stock nature of environmental resources: optimal management of environmental resources is no less intertemporal than the optimal management of commercial natural resources. Indeed, the time frame for economic studies of climate change is much longer – centuries instead of decades – than the time frame typically considered in studies on the optimal management of mineral reserves or timber stocks. Hence, although the same questions arise – what welfare function should we use? what discount rate? – answering these questions is harder and more consequential. Several chapters in Volume 2 address these dynamic welfare issues.

Third, a static perspective could cause environmental economists to overlook important impacts of environmental regulations on technological change – and the impact of environmental degradation on empirical estimates of rates of technological change. Chapters in this handbook address these issues. In particular, a chapter in Volume 1 looks exclusively at the impacts of environmental regulations on technological change. This issue was treated only in passing in the earlier handbook.

A final important dynamic area concerns institutional evolution. Like other fields of economics, environmental economics has been heavily influenced by the "New Institutional Economics." Several chapters in both Volumes 1 and 2 of this handbook examine the forces that shape institutional responses to environmental change at local, national, and international scales. Interactions with fertility decisions are especially important at a local level, and so this handbook contains a chapter on population, poverty, and the environment.

Having noted above a way in which the scope of this handbook is narrower than that of its predecessor, we conclude by noting a way that it is broader. The *Handbook of Environmental Economics* places more emphasis on the application of economics to environmental policy issues in developing countries. Environmental economics was born and raised in universities and research institutes in rich, industrialised countries with well-developed political, legal, and market institutions. Most people in the world live in very different circumstances: poverty, restricted civil and political liberties, and traditional property rights that are backed up only weakly, if at all, by the legal system. By and large, they also live in more degraded natural surroundings – which, as economists might surmise, is no coincidence.

We believe environmental economics can play an especially important role in improving the welfare of this destitute majority. Environmental economists know more about institutional failures than do most economists, so the resources of their discipline should be especially valuable when directed toward the problems of poor countries. For this reason, we commissioned for this handbook chapters specifically on developing country issues. We also asked the authors of all the other chapters to search for examples of studies on developing countries.

The authors were helped by the fact that an increasing share of the pages of leading field journals like the *Journal of Environmental Economics and Management, Environmental and Resource Economics, Land Economics*, and *Resource and Energy Economics* are occupied by articles based on studies conducted in developing countries, and by the relatively recent launch of a new journal, *Environment and Development Economics*, that provides an outlet specifically for such research. We find it heartening that most development economics textbooks – and the latest volume of the North-Holland *Handbook of Development Economics* – now include chapters on the environment, and that most environmental economics textbooks now include chapters on the developing world. We hope the *Handbook of Environmental Economics* will accelerate this integration of development and environmental economics.

In drawing attention to the relevance and significance of environmental economics to developing countries, we are also confirming the prescience of Allen Kneese, who was one of the editors of the *Handbook of Natural Resource and Energy Economics*. More than a decade before the Brundtland Commission popularised the phrase "sustainable development," Allen published a paper with Robert Ayres titled "The sustainable economy" (*Frontiers in Social Thought – Essays in Honor of Kenneth E. Boulding*, Elsevier Science Publishers, 1976). To our knowledge, this paper was the first in the environmental economics literature to include the word "sustainable" in its title, and one of the first to examine the differences between developed and developing countries. As in so many other ways, Allen was a pioneer.

Acknowledgements

Our greatest thanks go to Christina Leijonhufvud, without whose administrative support the handbook project would have foundered. Anna Sjöström stepped in and solved multiple problems related to the figures for one of the chapters. Benjamin Vincent relieved much of the tedious work related to indexing the chapters.

Our institutions – the Beijer Institute of Ecological Economics (Mäler) and the Harvard Institute for International Development, Kennedy School of Government, and Graduate School of International Relations & Pacific Studies at the University of California, San Diego (Vincent) – provided congenial and supportive bases of operation.

Finally, a series of diligent external reviewers – Jack Caldwell, Steve Carpenter, Bill Clark, Larry Goulder, Ted Groves, Daniel Kahneman, Charles Plott, Stef Proost, Steve Schneider, Brian Walker, Jörgen Weibull – helped ensure the relevance, comprehensiveness, and accuracy of the material presented in the chapters. Any shortcomings that remain are, of course, our responsibility.

KARL-GÖRAN MÄLER and JEFFREY R. VINCENT
Stockholm, September 17, 2002

CONTENTS OF VOLUME 2

Chapter 18
Cognitive Processes in Stated Preference Methods
BARUCH FISCHHOFF

Chapter 12

WELFARE THEORY AND VALUATION

NANCY E. BOCKSTAEL

University of Maryland, College Park, MD, USA

A. MYRICK FREEMAN III

Bowdoin College, Brunswick, ME, USA

QS1
D63

Contents

Handbook of Environmental Economics, Volume 2. Edited by K.-G. Mäler and J.R. Vincent
DOI: 10.1016/S1574-0099(05)02012-7

Abstract

Public policies that lead to a reduction in the emissions of air and water pollutants or the protection of sensitive ecosystems presumably increase the well-being of many members of society. Applied welfare economists are accustomed to measuring the welfare effects of policies that invoke price changes. If it is granted that the public good attributes of most dimensions of environmental quality preclude the development of well functioning markets for these service flows, how are the monetary values of changes in environmental quality to be measured? The past twenty to thirty years have seen the rapid development of the economic theory and techniques for measuring the demands for nonmarketed goods, and in this chapter we attempt to sketch out the major results. We review the basic concept of economic welfare and derive measures of welfare change for both changes in prices of market goods and changes in quantities and qualities of nonmarket goods. We then describe the principal economic techniques for estimating the benefits of environmental quality improvements when these improvements either directly affect individuals' well-being or indirectly affect individuals through constraints they face. Perhaps the major class of measurement methods is based on the observation that changes in environmental quality may cause individuals to alter purchases of goods and services that are complements or substitutes for environmental quality in their preference orderings. These *revealed preference* methods are the primary focus of this chapter. A second major approach to obtaining estimates of the benefits and costs of environmental changes, *stated preference* methods, are addressed in detail in later chapters. Our treatment of welfare effects places special emphasis on the connection between the underlying economic theory and practical empirical models.

Keywords

welfare economics, nonmarket valuation, environmental valuation, revealed preference methods

JEL classification: Q51, I12, H43

1. Introduction

Public policies that lead to a reduction in the emissions of air and water pollutants or the protection of sensitive ecosystems presumably increase the well-being of many members of society, but they generally also impose costs which translate into reductions in well-being for other members of society. Choice among policies may therefore depend on the measurement of these benefits and costs, and may also depend on the segments of the population to which they accrue. The concept of benefits and costs in economics hinges on the notion of compensation, that is the compensation in some standard unit of measurement that would be necessary to exactly offset the benefits or costs. Welfare effects of environmental changes are usually and probably most usefully quantified and measured in monetary terms, although in principle other units of measurement are possible.

Applied welfare economists are accustomed to measuring the welfare effects of policies that invoke price changes, and much literature has emerged investigating the means by which behavioral functions in markets can be used to generate exact or approximate measures of these effects. If it is granted that the public good attributes of most dimensions of environmental quality preclude the development of well functioning markets for these service flows, how are the monetary values of changes in environmental quality to be measured? The past twenty to thirty years have seen the rapid development of the economic theory and techniques for measuring the demands for nonmarketed goods, and in this chapter we will attempt to sketch out the major results.

One group of measurement models is quite closely connected to conventional applied welfare economics in that it is based on observations of changes in market prices and quantities that result from changes in environmental quality. For example, if an environmental improvement affects the productivity or production costs of firms, these effects may be reflected in higher outputs, lower prices to consumers, and changes in factor incomes and quasi-rents. Similarly, if a regulation imposes costs on firms, these costs will result in some combination of higher prices to consumers and lower factor incomes and quasi-rents. The theory associated with environmental goods as inputs in production is addressed in Chapter 14 by Kenneth McConnell and Nancy Bockstael in this Handbook.

Perhaps the major class of measurement methods is based on the observation that changes in environmental quality may cause individuals to alter purchases of goods and services that are complements or substitutes for environmental quality in their preference orderings. In this case, models of household choice may make it possible to estimate welfare gains in money terms from observed behavior. These restrictions, which form the basis of *revealed preference* methods of welfare measurement, are the primary focus of this chapter.

There is a second major approach to obtaining estimates of the benefits and costs of environmental changes. It involves *asking* people how they would respond to hypothetical changes in environmental quality. Several models and techniques have been developed to interpret individuals' responses to such questions and to allow the calculation of the benefits of the hypothetical changes in monetary terms. These methods are termed *stated preference* methods and are addressed in detail in later chapters, in particular, Chapter 17 by Richard Carson and Michael Hanemann.

In this chapter we will review the basic concept of economic welfare and derive measures of welfare change for both changes in prices of market goods and changes in quantities and qualities of nonmarket goods. We will then describe the principal economic techniques for estimating the benefits of environmental quality improvements when these improvements either directly affect individuals' well-being or indirectly affect individuals through constraints they face. Our treatment of welfare effects places special emphasis on the connection between the underlying economic theory and the practical empirical models.

2. The nature of economic value

The economic concept of value has its foundation in neoclassical welfare economics. The basic premises of welfare economics are that the purpose of economic activity is to increase the well-being of the individuals in the society, and that each individual is the best judge of how well off he or she is in any given situation. Each individual's welfare depends not only on that individual's consumption of private market goods and of goods and services produced by the government but also on the quantities and qualities each receives of nonmarket goods and service flows from the resource-environment system – for example, health, visual amenities, and opportunities for outdoor recreation.[1] Thus the basis for deriving measures of the economic benefits and costs of changes in natural resource or environmental systems is their effect on human welfare.

The economic theory for measuring changes in individuals' well-being was developed to evaluate the welfare effects of changes in the prices of goods purchased in markets. This theory has been extended in the past 30 years or so to changes in the quantity of publicly supplied goods and to other nonmarket services such as environmental quality and health. The theory is based on the assumptions that people have well-defined preferences among alternative bundles of goods, where bundles consist of various quantities of both market and nonmarket goods; that people know their preferences; and that these preferences have the property of substitutability. By substitutability we mean that if the quantity of one element in an individual's bundle is reduced, it is possible to compensate for that loss in terms of increases in other goods so as to leave the individual no worse or better off because of the change. Thus, the cost of a reduction is measured as the compensating increase in some good (or numeraire) and the benefit of an increase is the compensating reduction in that good.

The property of substitutability is at the core of the economist's concept of value because substitutability establishes trade-off ratios between pairs of goods that matter

---

[1] For a further discussion of ecosystem service flows, see the chapter by Simon Levin and Stephen Pacala in the first volume of this Handbook.

to people. For convenience and so that all trade-offs can be made in a common unit of measurement, the compensating increases and decreases are generally stated in terms of changes in exogenous income.[2] If a good is so broadly defined and so important to an individual that there is no compensation that could make the individual "whole" after the loss of that good, then the good is said to be essential. In those rare cases when the good in question is so important (e.g., a person's life) or so broadly defined (e.g., all ecosystems on the planet), then valuation in terms of compensation is no longer sensible. Usually the policy question involves a discrete but small change rather than a total loss of well-being. For example, it might involve a change in the risk of death rather than a certain death, so that compensation for the change is meaningful.

The anthropocentric focus of economic valuation does not preclude a concern for the survival and well-being of other species. Individuals can value the survival of other species not only because of the uses people make of them (for food and recreation, for example), but also because of ethical concerns. The latter can be the source of the existence or nonuse values discussed in Section 8. Furthermore, this anthropocentric focus does not preclude the valuation of ecosystem services, properties, and processes such as nutrient cycling, decomposition, and biodiversity. To the extent that ecosystems enhance human well-being through these services and processes, they have value. For example, ecosystem services such as pollination and biological control of pests contribute to human well-being by increasing the productivity of resources employed in commercial agriculture and increasing agricultural outputs; improvements in estuarine water quality have similar effects on commercial fisheries. The problem facing economists (and ecologists) is to quantify the links between ecosystems and human well-being. The tools described in Chapter 14 by McConnell and Bockstael could be employed to assess the economic value of these services, provided that the link between the level of the services and agricultural or fisheries outputs is known.[3] The link is not always so easily established, however.

In an applied welfare economics framework, individuals are viewed as having knowledge of and well-defined preferences over alternative bundles of goods that contribute to well-being. Where most of the goods and services that contribute to utility are purchased in markets, well-informed and well-defined preferences are rewarded, as the constraints of prices and limited money income make errors in optimization costly. The theory of economic value as applied to environmental goods has taken off from this point by assuming that the domain of preferences extends to environmental goods not available

---

[2] The usefulness of a common numeraire or standard unit of measurement needs no explanation. The drawbacks include the fact that aggregation over individuals will produce policy prescriptions that are sensitive to the choice of numeraire. Brekke (1997) includes a careful analysis of this. Bockstael and Strand (1985) provide an example in which different policies are preferred depending on whether time or money is used as the numeraire.

[3] For examples of this approach to valuing ecosystem services, see Lynne, Conroy and Prochaska (1981), Kahn and Kemp (1985), Barbier, Strand and Sathirathai (2002), and Narain and Fisher (1994). For a more extended discussion of ecosystem services and their valuation, see Daily (1997).

through markets and that these preferences for nonmarket and environmental goods are also well-defined. The more remote the ecological good, the more difficult it may be for individuals to understand and express their trade-offs for it.

Sen has raised questions as to whether this should indeed be the approach to valuation, saying:

> The basic question that is raised by such a market oriented approach is whether this view of the individual as an operator in a market best captures the problems of environmental valuation. An alternative view is to see the individual as a citizen – an agent who judges the alternatives from a social perspective which includes her own well-being but also, quite possibly, many other considerations [Sen (1995, p. 23)].

This same theme appears in some critiques of benefit–cost analysis of environmental policies by philosophers and others [e.g., Sagoff (1981), Kelman (1981)]. While no systematic alternatives for valuation have been developed, caution needs to be exercised with regard to the application of market analogies to more remote ecological systems and services for which individuals have little knowledge and no experience in making trade-offs.

3. Overview of the environmental valuation problem

The objective of this chapter is to outline the theory and methods needed to measure the welfare gains and losses associated with changes in levels of environmental goods, where these goods are rarely sold directly at market prices. Changes in levels of environmental goods often come about either because of private actions, such as waste disposal or oil spills, or because of public actions, such as new environmental regulations – each of which involves some intervention or disruption to the existing system. What we do not address in this chapter is how to measure the full effect of a regulation, including its cost of implementation. Typically environmental regulations will impose increased costs of production in certain industries, decreasing producer surplus for these firms. This shows up in the ultimate welfare assessment as reductions in nonwage, and possibly also wage, income to individuals in society. Evaluation of these types of social costs, on an individual basis, poses no special methodological problems. The real problems arise in determining where in the economy such social costs are likely to arise. Work such as that by Hazilla and Kopp (1990) attempts to measure the social costs of environmental regulation in a dynamic general equilibrium framework. As these authors have shown, the results may diverge substantially from an approach that assesses only changes in private costs of directly impacted industries, and does so ignoring intertemporal investment decisions. The issues that arise in attempting to account adequately for the social costs of regulation are discussed in a chapter by Raymond Kopp and William Pizer in another volume of this Handbook.

As the domain of environmental considerations expands, the range of types of actions grows as well. At one time, the principal environmental concern would have been point source discharges of specific pollutants into water and air, and the principal pathway by which these pollutants affected humans would have been through human health or recreation. While the health and recreational benefits of reducing traditional sources of pollution remain important public policy targets, interest is growing in broader issues such as ecosystem health. For example, managing storm water run-off in urbanized areas is a concern, not only because it is a nonpoint source of nutrients and toxic discharges into waters used for recreation, but also because the storm water run-off from large amounts of impervious surface alters baseline and peak stream flows, affecting the composition and diversity of species in these hydrological systems. Public actions are increasingly taking the form of protecting areas that are deemed environmentally sensitive, actions that do not fit the usual regulatory paradigm. Often they involve public investment in, or public purchase of, ecologically valuable resources.

Although much of the difficulty of welfare measurement comes in the details, it simplifies the discussion of the theory to characterize the problem in abstract terms. Consider a general case in which an action is taken by the public sector that in some way or another affects the decisions of economic agents regarding their activities. This might involve a regulation or other public action that changes the rate of discharge of a pollutant or the amount of habitat destroyed. In any event, the public action has an effect on the flows of services that the ecosystem can generate. Changes in measures of environmental quality or ecosystem health affect the uses made of the environment by producers and households and affect the services that the environment provides.

To formalize these considerations in the context of benefit estimation, consider the following simple abstraction. Let D represent a scalar or vector measure of physical, human-induced impacts on the environment. This might be, for example, the quantity of a pollutant discharged into the air, a measure of impervious surface introduced into an ecosystem, or the area of wetlands or mangrove swamps destroyed. Now let Q be the vector of environmental outcomes that affect humans in some way. Elements of Q may affect human welfare directly (and thus enter individuals' utility functions) or they may matter to humans because they enter as inputs into some household or firm production process which we will call $Z(Q)$. D might be discharges of DDT into the environment and Q, the abundance of bald eagles. The existence and protection of bald eagles may matter to an individual in its own right. In addition, an individual who enjoys bird watching will benefit through his consumption of higher quality recreational trips, Z. The distinction between D and Q is an artificial one. But it serves to emphasize the difference between relationships that biological or physical scientists can best describe and those that are fundamentally economic in nature. The science of the relationships between D and Q is notably imperfect, but determining the precise pathway by which Q affects humans is also not trivial and is the essence of any applied environmental valuation problem.

A mathematical characterization of this story is simple. Let W represent the level of economic welfare. The model, allowing for both direct utility associated with Q and

Q as an input into the production of Z, can be expressed as:

$$Q = Q(D), \tag{1}$$

$$Z = Z(Q), \tag{2}$$

$$W = W\big(Q, Z(Q)\big). \tag{3}$$

Given the way Q and D are measured, $Q'(D) < 0$ and $W'(Q)$, $W'(Z) > 0$, so that by implication $W = f(D)$, where $f'(D) < 0$.

Estimating the benefit of a proposed regulation entails first predicting the responses of affected dischargers, that is, ΔD, and then tracing the effects of ΔD through the links described by Equations (1)–(3) to calculate the resulting welfare change in monetary terms. Predicting dischargers' responses to regulations is itself a challenging task that raises issues beyond the scope of this chapter.[4] Suffice it to say that both theory and observation suggest that the analyst should not assume perfect compliance with all terms of the regulation.

Of course this simple representation of the problem obscures a number of details and complications that have to be reckoned with. First, most environmental problems have important spatial components. Discharges may come from many sources and at different locations. Thus, D may be interpreted as a vector, where D_i indicates sources by location. Both because D is spatially heterogeneous but also because the function that links D to Q may involve a dispersion or diffusion process, Q may also vary in important ways over space. These spatial characteristics should be reflected in the model. There may be important temporal dimensions to discharges and measures of environmental quality, as well. Some activities may be sensitive primarily to changes in long term averages of pollution levels while others are affected primarily by peaks of pollution causing acute effects. In any event, an analysis of the net benefits of a change in Q, without the link through (1), is of little use in policy analysis.

When Q enters into a firm's production function, the relationship, $Z = Z(Q)$, reflects some physical or biological relationship. For example, it could reflect the impact of ozone on agricultural crop yields or of sulfur compounds on materials corrosion rates. In cases when Q enters a household production function, the relationship may also be one that falls in the province of science, for example, the effect of excessive nutrients in groundwater on human health. However, in all these cases the relationship $Z(Q)$ must also incorporate producers' and individuals' behavioral responses to these physical and biological effects. By changing technologies or substituting different inputs, firms and households can sometimes mitigate adverse effects. Farmers can shift away from pollution sensitive crops and cultivars or change planting times and fertilization regimes; households can purchase water filtration systems or bottled water to avoid contaminants found in their drinking water supplies. Changes in the uses of the environment and the

---

[4] The nature of the behavioral response to regulation is a worthy subject for analysis in its own right, the economics of which are discussed in the chapter by Gloria Helfand, Peter Berck, and Tim Maull in the first volume of this Handbook.

welfare implications of these changes depend in part on the opportunities for, and costs of, mitigating and averting activities. Benefit estimation models applied by economists must attempt to capture the major averting and mitigating activities available to people.

The third stage involves estimating the benefits or losses from the public action or exogenous event, as symbolized in (3). This involves employing concepts from welfare economics, as these concepts have evolved over the past 50 years. While the concepts themselves are well-defined, means of empirically measuring them are not always evident. Finding a means of inferring individuals' benefits and losses either from observations on their behavior or from careful questioning poses the greatest challenge to the economist.

In the rest of the chapter, we focus on the economic dimensions of the problem, those that are encompassed in (2) and (3). In doing so, we assume that the natural and physical science relationships in this system are well understood. This is appropriate for expository purposes, even though in practice the lack of knowledge of many of these links is a major barrier to empirical estimation of the welfare effects of environmental changes.

4. Defining a measure of welfare change

We seek a measure of the effect on an individual's welfare brought about by an environmental change. Consider, first, the standard case in which there is no uncertainty and an individual's utility is a function only of private goods purchased. The individual faces a set of given prices for these privately produced goods and chooses quantities of the goods so as to maximize utility given constraints of prices and fixed money income M,[5] that is:

$$\max U = U(X) \quad \text{subject to } P'X \leqslant M, \tag{4}$$

where X is a vector of n goods and services and P is a corresponding price vector. The solution to this problem leads to a set of n ordinary or Marshallian demand functions:

$$x_i = x_i(P, M), \quad i = 1, \ldots, n. \tag{5}$$

By substitution of (5) into (4), the resulting indirect utility function expresses utility as a function of prices and income:

$$U = V(P, M). \tag{6}$$

Now consider introducing environmental quality Q into the problem. There are three possible ways in which Q might alter the individual's choice problem. Q might enter

---

[5] The assumption of fixed and predetermined money income is somewhat restrictive. However, Just, Hueth and Schmitz (2004, pp. 183–214) have shown that welfare measures can be similarly defined even when income is endogenous.

the utility function in (4) directly. An example is when Q represents the survival of bald eagles or the visibility at the Grand Canyon. In other circumstances Q might more usefully be modeled as entering into a production function for a household produced good, $Z(Q)$, where Z enters the utility function. As an example, Q might be the level of particulates in the air and Z might be the individual's health status. Whether Q enters the utility function directly or only affects individuals through the production of Z, it will show up as an argument in the indirect utility function in (6).

The third way in which Q can affect individuals results in a somewhat different welfare assessment. When Q only enters firms' production processes, Q can alter prices of privately produced goods or factors of production. In these cases, changes in Q can affect one or more elements of P and/or can alter the individual's income M. For example, an improvement in air quality over an agricultural region could lead to higher yields and lower food prices. It could also lead to increases in rents to farmland owners and changes in farm workers' income. If factor supplies are independent of factor prices (inelastic supply), then the resulting income change can be taken as a measure of welfare change. But if factor supplies respond to factor prices, opportunity costs must be taken into account [Freeman (2003, pp. 72–74)].

The measures of welfare change that will be used throughout this chapter are based on the compensation principle.[6] It is well known that utility change, *per se*, is neither measurable nor additive over individuals, and unique money measures of utility change can not be defined.[7] Instead, welfare measures are defined in terms of the amount of money that is required to substitute for the change in question, holding utility constant at some predetermined level. For example, the *marginal* welfare change for a change in Q can be derived by differentiating the indirect utility function and expressing the change in M necessary to compensate (i.e., to keep utility constant) for the change in Q:

$$-\frac{\mathrm{d}M}{\mathrm{d}Q} = \frac{\partial V/\partial Q}{\partial V/\partial M}. \tag{7}$$

Note that the concept expressed in (7) is positive for an improvement in Q and negative for a degradation.[8]

For *nonmarginal* changes, the concepts of compensating and equivalent variation are used to measure welfare effects.[9,10] The first expresses the amount of money that must be taken away from (or given to) an individual to make him as well off after the change

---

[6] The Compensation Principle was articulated by both Hicks (1939) and Kaldor (1939).

[7] For a complete discussion of issues of path dependence and constancy of the marginal utility of income, see Just, Hueth and Schmitz (2004, pp. 98–112).

[8] Note that not all economists use the same signing convention. We use this convention because it makes the direction of the welfare effects transparent.

[9] As Silberberg (1972) has noted, it is not correct to refer to compensating and equivalent variation as measures of utility change. They are measures of income change necessary to keep utility constant.

[10] Many authors still follow Hicks (1943) in distinguishing between compensating variation, where quantities adjust in response to price changes, and compensating surplus, where quantities are held fixed. These authors

in environmental quality as he was before it. Using the indirect utility function, compensating variation (CV) can be defined implicitly as:

$$V\left(P^1, Q^1, M^1 - CV\right) = V\left(P^0, Q^0, M^0\right), \tag{8}$$

where the superscripts 0 and 1 denote initial and subsequent levels of the parameters, respectively. Defined this way, the compensating variation measure has the same sign as the welfare change. For example, if only a change in Q takes place and that change is an improvement in environmental quality, then $Q^1 > Q^0$, while $M^1 = M^0$ and $P^1 = P^0$, and $CV > 0$. The latter is true because a positive amount of money must be taken away from income to leave the individual as well off as he was before the change.

An alternative measure that uses the utility level of the subsequent position as the base case can also be defined. It is the amount of money that must be given to the individual (or taken away from him) in *lieu* of the environmental change in order to make him as well-off as he would have been with the change. Equivalent variation (EV) is given by

$$V\left(P^1, Q^1, M^1\right) = V\left(P^0, Q^0, M^0 + EV\right). \tag{9}$$

As with CV, we choose to sign EV such that it has the same sign as the welfare effect.

The CV and EV measures of an exogenous income change are easily evaluated. Consider the case in which there are no price changes, only changes in exogenous income. The CV and EV measures are defined implicitly by

$$V\left(P^0, Q^0, M^1 - CV\right) = V\left(P^0, Q^0, M^0\right) \tag{10}$$

and

$$V\left(P^0, Q^0, M^1\right) = V\left(P^0, Q^0, M^0 + EV\right). \tag{11}$$

Given these implicit definitions, it is obvious that $CV = EV = M^1 - M^0$. However, it is not true that CV and EV are equal for changes in P or Q.

To develop the mechanism for measuring the compensating and equivalent variation associated with changes in prices and Q, it is often useful to express these measures explicitly in terms of the expenditure function, derived from the dual to the utility maximization problem. Consider the case in which Q enters the utility function directly. The dual to the individual's utility maximization problem is:

$$\min P'X \quad \text{s.t.} \ U(X, Q) \geqslant U^0. \tag{12}$$

Substitution of the cost minimizing demands for X into the objective function yields the expenditure function, which expresses the minimum amount of money necessary to achieve a specified utility level, given market prices and environmental quality,

$$e = e\left(P, Q, U^0\right). \tag{13}$$

---

use the term compensating surplus for exogenous changes in quantities of nonmarket goods as well [e.g., Freeman (2003)]. But the distinction between price and quantity variation seems increasingly artificial; so the term compensating variation will be used throughout this chapter.

Compensating and equivalent variation of a change in prices and Q can now be defined explicitly as:

$$CV = e(P^0, Q^0, U^0) - e(P^1, Q^1, U^0) \tag{14}$$

and

$$EV = e(P^0, Q^0, U^1) - e(P^1, Q^1, U^1), \tag{15}$$

where

$$U^1 = V(P^1, Q^1, M). \tag{16}$$

In what follows, we first consider compensating and equivalent variation measures of price changes. The theory and methodology of this is well worked out and is relevant for environmental quality change when the change affects firms' production and therefore goods prices. We then consider these same welfare measures when environmental quality changes affect the individual directly. In so doing, we discuss how these measures or their approximations can be computed from observed behavior.

4.1. Price changes

Consider first a simple and conventional applied welfare question: how do we measure the benefits or losses associated with a policy that alters *one* price from p_1^0 to p_1^1? For the sake of discussion, we will assume that this is a price fall, $p_1^1 < p_1^0$. The indirect utility function is decreasing in prices, so this change in price will increase utility from U^0 to U^1. As indicated in (15), the expenditure function can be solved to determine the expenditure necessary to sustain U^1 given the original price. EV is the increase in income necessary to sustain this higher expenditure in the absence of the price change. In other words,

$$EV = e(p_1^0, \widehat{P}, Q, U^1) - e(p_1^1, \widehat{P}, Q, U^1), \tag{17}$$

where $\widehat{P}$ is the set of all other prices. Likewise, the compensating variation is that offsetting change in income that would make the individual indifferent between the original price and the new price at the original utility level. The CV for this one price change is defined by

$$CV = e(p_1^0, \widehat{P}, Q, U^0) - e(p_1^1, \widehat{P}, Q, U^0). \tag{18}$$

The expenditure function has a number of useful properties that aid in assessing this type of applied welfare question. By Shepherd's lemma, the partial derivative of the expenditure function with respect to a price p_1 yields the Hicksian or compensated demand for the associated good x_1^c,

$$\frac{\partial e}{\partial p_1} = x_1^c(P, Q, U^0). \tag{19}$$

This relationship is central to much of applied welfare economics. Unfortunately there is no corresponding behavioral relationship associated with changes in Q as we shall see later on.

As a result of Shepherd's lemma, we can obtain a measure of EV by integrating behind the compensated demand function conditioned on utility level U^1, and between the two prices, p_1^0 and p_1^1:

$$EV = -\int_{p_1^0}^{p_1^1} \frac{\partial e}{\partial p_1}(p_1, \widehat{P}, Q, U^1)\, \mathrm{d}p_1 = -\int_{p_1^0}^{p_1^1} x_1^c(p_1, \widehat{P}, Q, U^1)\, \mathrm{d}p_1. \tag{20}$$

Correspondingly, compensating variation can be found by integrating between the two prices, behind the compensated demand function conditioned on utility level U^0:

$$CV = -\int_{p_1^0}^{p_1^1} \frac{\partial e}{\partial p_1}(p_1, \widehat{P}, Q, U^0)\, \mathrm{d}p_1 = -\int_{p_1^0}^{p_1^1} x_1^c(p_1, \widehat{P}, Q, U^0)\, \mathrm{d}p_1. \tag{21}$$

One of the appealing features of the compensating and equivalent variation measures is that, for multiple price changes, they are both path independent. This means that if a policy change has the effect of altering several prices, there is a unique CV and a unique EV measure of these multiple price changes, irrespective of the order of the price changes. To make clear why this is true, consider a change of two prices, p_1^0 to p_1^1 and p_2^0 to p_2^1. Compensating and equivalent variation can always be easily stated as the difference in two expenditure functions. For example, compensating variation is given by

$$CV = e(p_1^0, p_2^0, \widehat{P}, Q, U^0) - e(p_1^1, p_2^1, \widehat{P}, Q, U^0). \tag{22}$$

With two price changes, the CV measure is equivalent to a line integral

$$CV = \int_L \mathrm{d}e, \tag{23}$$

where L denotes a path from (p_1^0, p_2^0) to (p_1^1, p_2^1). Since the integrand is an exact differential, the same answer results irrespective of the order in which we change the prices.

One practical consequence of this is that the CV measure can be obtained by either of the following means:

$$CV = -\left[\int_{p_1^0}^{p_1^1} x_1^c(p_1, p_2^0, \widehat{P}, Q, U^0)\, \mathrm{d}p_1 + \int_{p_2^0}^{p_2^1} x_2^c(p_1^1, p_2, \widehat{P}, Q, U^0)\, \mathrm{d}p_2\right] \tag{24}$$

or

$$CV = -\left[\int_{p_2^0}^{p_2^1} x_2^c(p_1^0, p_2, \widehat{P}, Q, U^0)\, \mathrm{d}p_2 + \int_{p_1^0}^{p_1^1} x_1^c(p_1, p_2^1, \widehat{P}, Q, U^0)\, \mathrm{d}p_1\right]. \tag{25}$$

In each case, the welfare effect is measured as the sum of the areas under two demand functions, each calculated between the initial and ultimate price. However, as a consequence of evaluating this line integral, the price changes must be sequenced. If x_1 and

x_2 are functions of both prices, then the first price change must be evaluated holding the second price at its initial level and the second price change must be conditioned on the first price held at its ultimate level. Path independence implies that the same answer will be obtained no matter the order of the price changes, as long as the price changes are sequenced leading to appropriately conditioned demand functions. Path independence also holds if prices and exogenous income change. The result is trivial since the compensated demands are not functions of income; thus the income change can be added to either the *CV* measure as expressed in either form above or the analogous *EV* measure.

As is well known, the *CV* and *EV* measures yield different values for the welfare change unless the income effect of the price change is zero. If the income effect is zero, the two compensated demand functions will converge and they will be identical to the Marshallian demand function. It is not, of course, possible for demand functions of all goods to have zero income effects, but some subset of demands may exhibit this property. In some actual policy situations, an approximately zero income effect is not only plausible but empirically supported; in others this is not the case and we are left with two alternative measures. On a conceptual basis there is little to choose between the *CV* and *EV* measures unless one wishes to appeal to the property rights of the situation (i.e., an individual's entitlement to the policy change). For further discussion of the property rights perspective in the context of environmental policy, see Mitchell and Carson (1989) and Freeman (2003).

4.1.1. Toward measurement

Suppose that the available demand information covers only those goods whose prices change. Either the *CV* or *EV* can be calculated directly if the demand data are in the form of the compensated demand functions. But the compensated demand functions are not generally derivable from observations of market behavior. In fact, the analyst would be fortunate to have reliable estimates of the ordinary (Marshallian) demand functions for the goods in question. If this is all that is available, what is to be done? There are two possible answers to the question: either use information from the ordinary demand functions to obtain information about the indirect utility function; or use areas behind ordinary rather than compensated demand functions as an approximation to the desired *CV* or *EV*.

Perhaps the best known results on the topic of the relationship between areas behind ordinary demands and compensated measures are those attributable to Willig (1976). Often referred to as Marshallian surplus, ordinary consumer surplus of a price change (which we will call *CS*) is the area behind the ordinary demand curve between the initial and subsequent prices. In other words,

$$S = -\int_{p_1^0}^{p_0^1} x_1\left(p_1, \widehat{P}, Q, M\right) \mathrm{d}p_1. \tag{26}$$

Willig offered exact bounds on *CV* and *EV*, given information on *CS*. His expressions provide a way of calculating the magnitude of the differences among the three measures for changes in prices. These differences depend on the income elasticity of demand for the good in question and consumer surplus as a percentage of income or expenditure. The differences among the measures appear to be small and almost trivial for many realistic cases, and they are probably smaller than the errors in the estimation of the parameters of demand functions by econometric methods.

Willig takes into account the possibility that for finite changes in price and quantity, the income elasticity of demand may vary over the range of the price change. He derives rules of thumb for estimating the maximum percentage error in using *CS* instead of *EV* or *CV*.[11] The analysis is carried out for the case of a single price change, but Willig (1979) subsequently extended the analysis to the case of multiple price changes. Willig's analysis provides a strong justification for using the empirically observable consumer surplus measure for the welfare effect of a price change as a valid approximation for either of the theoretically preferred measures *EV* or *CV*.

In his 1981 paper, Hausman questioned the accuracy of Willig's approximation when measuring deadweight loss and the wisdom of settling for approximations when exact measures could be obtained. If integrability conditions are satisfied, it is in principle possible to recover the indirect utility function, or at least a quasi-indirect utility function omitting a constant of integration, from ordinary demand functions [Hurwicz and Uzawa (1971)]. In the case of a single price change, this is accomplished by solving the differential equation implied by Roy's Identity:

$$x_i(P, Q, M) = -\frac{\partial V/\partial p_i}{\partial V/\partial M}. \tag{27}$$

If the left-hand side of this expression can be estimated, the quasi-indirect utility function can be recovered by integration, and then it is straightforward to compute *EV* and *CV*, implicitly. Hausman (1981) demonstrated this approach where the demand function for one good is assumed known and all other goods are collapsed into a numeraire composite commodity.

An alternative approach to integrating analytically is to use numerical methods. Vartia (1983) developed a numerical algorithm to obtain an approximation of the compensating variation of single or multiple price changes with arbitrarily high levels of accuracy, where higher levels of accuracy are purchased with more iterative steps in the algorithm. Vartia's method requires Marshallian demands as a starting point, but it provides a means of approximating the amount of money necessary to achieve the original level of utility after a price change without needing an explicit parametric form for the utility function.

More recently, Irvine and Sims (1998) have developed a computationally simple approximation to *CV* and *EV* that is much more accurate than the ordinary consumer surplus measure. It is based on the concept of the Slutsky compensated demand curve

---

[11] For further explanation and interpretation of the Willig results, see Just, Hueth and Schmitz (2004, pp. 161–170) or Freeman (2003, pp. 63–68).

in which the individual is compensated not to the original level of utility (in the case of *CV*) but to enable the purchase of the original bundle of goods. Since this bundle is observable, it is straightforward to calculate the required compensation for any price change and to use the parameters of the ordinary demand function to calculate a welfare measure. Irvine and Sims show that the error associated with this measure is typically an order of magnitude smaller than the error associated with *CS*.

Other recent papers focus on the ordinary demand functions upon which all these procedures are based. Since researchers never have information on all demands, empirical studies use either partial or incomplete demand systems.[12] An incomplete demand system is a system of n goods of interest, artificially augmented by a composite numeraire commodity representing the remaining goods. A partial demand system includes only the n demands of interest. Separability is assumed between this group of goods and all others, and only the group's budget allocation is included in the system. LaFrance and Hanemann (1989) developed a means for discovering the necessary restrictions implied by weak integrability to obtain exact welfare measures from an incomplete demand system. LaFrance (1993) illustrated the bias that can occur with the usual practice of treating the group's budget allocation as exogenous. In a related literature, Hanemann and Morey (1992) investigated the relationship between true *CV* and *EV* measures and those produced by partial demand systems, where only the n demands of interest are estimated. While these problems arise most naturally when analyzing the effects of price changes for marketed goods (as in the dairy example provided by LaFrance), they can also arise in some nonmarket settings when demands for goods related to the environmental good help reveal its value.

4.2. Changes in environmental quality

From a conceptual perspective, defining welfare measures for changes in environmental quality is also quite straightforward.[13] If the change in environmental quality (Q) has direct impacts on the individual rather than solely through marketed goods' prices, the *CV* and *EV* of a change in this Q are given implicitly by

$$V\left(P^0, Q^1, M^0 - CV\right) = V\left(P^0, Q^0, M^0\right) \tag{28}$$

and

$$V\left(P^0, Q^1, M^0\right) = V\left(P^0, Q^0, M^0 + EV\right). \tag{29}$$

The same *CV* and *EV* measures can also be expressed in explicit form as:

$$CV = e\left(P^0, Q^0, U^0\right) - e\left(P^0, Q^1, U^0\right) \tag{30}$$

---

[12] For a complete treatment of these issues see Pollak and Wales (1992).

[13] For a more comprehensive treatment that roots this theory in the theory of rationing, see Freeman (2003, pp. 74–87).

and

$$EV = e(P^0, Q^0, U^1) - e(P^0, Q^1, U^1). \tag{31}$$

Finding observable measures of these concepts is much more difficult than for price changes, however. In some cases environmental quality can usefully be viewed as a public good whose quantity rather than price is exogenous to the individual. This leads logically to the welfare literature that considers quantity constraints. Lankford (1988) and Bergland and Randall (1984) have presented techniques for recovering the expenditure function when the individual faces a quantity constraint. What these techniques have in common is the requirement for information that reflects the utility maximizing choices of the individual when only income and price constraints are present. As in the case of market goods, when there are no quantity constraints, marginal rates of substitution can be inferred from observed price ratios. But the presence of quantity constraints means that the relevant marginal rates of substitution are not in general equal to observable price ratios.[14] The Lankford and Bergland and Randall techniques require information on what the individual would choose if he could freely choose Q at exogenous prices. But this information is not likely to be available for environmental goods.

A related set of questions is whether there is an observable counterpart to the Marshallian surplus for changes in Q and, if so, how it is related to the exact measures of CV and EV. Randall and Stoll (1980) have analyzed the difference between CV and EV and their relationship to a form of Marshallian measure. Employing a line of reasoning similar to that of Willig (1976) for price changes, they established error bounds and approximations for using their Marshallian consumer surplus measure (CS) as an approximation to CV and EV. As an example, their approximation for CV is given as:

$$CV \approx CS - \frac{\phi|CS^2|}{2M}, \tag{32}$$

where CS is consumer surplus, M is income and ϕ is the price flexibility of income, which is defined as the percentage change in marginal willingness to pay for a given percentage change in income. The authors argue that under plausible conditions these errors are likely to be small, implying that the difference between CV and EV will also be small if these conditions are satisfied. Randall and Stoll's arguments are not so convincing as Willig's, however, since their approximations are functions not of income elasticities but of price flexibilities of income.[15] Hanemann (1991) focused on this key parameter in Randall and Stoll's analysis, which he defines as

$$\phi \equiv \frac{\partial w^m(P, Q, M)}{\partial M} \cdot \frac{M}{w}, \tag{33}$$

[14] For a more detailed discussion of this issue, see Freeman (2003, pp. 76–85).
[15] For an explanation of this point, see Just, Hueth and Schmitz (2004, pp. 246–252).

where the function $w^m(P, Q, M)$ is the Marshallian implicit value function for Q. Hanemann showed that ϕ can be expressed as the ratio of two other terms:

$$\phi = \frac{\eta_m}{\sigma_\phi}, \tag{34}$$

where η_m is the income elasticity of demand for Q and σ_ϕ is the Allen–Uzawa elasticity of substitution between Q and the composite commodity. If there are no close substitutes to the environmental good – that is, if the indifference curve between Q and the composite good is tightly curved or nearly kinked in the vicinity of the individual's observed consumption bundle, then σ_ϕ can be close to zero leading to a very high value for ϕ and a large difference between CV and EV.[16] While conceptually of interest, this quantity constraint literature is only useful empirically if individuals' behavior reveals something about their inverse demand functions. Yet, as we will see in Section 7, revelations of this behavior can be difficult to find.

4.3. Uncertainty and risk

In this section, we briefly take up the issue of welfare measures for individuals under uncertainty. We take uncertainty to refer to situations in which an individual is uncertain as to which of two or more alternative states of nature will be realized and is not indifferent as to which state actually occurs. We assume here that individuals can assign probabilities to these alternative states of nature and that the probabilities are correct in the sense of summing to one and incorporating all available information. They may be subjective probabilities, reflecting a confidence of belief. In this, we follow the modern practice of making no distinction between uncertainty and risk.

Many risk-reduction and risk-prevention measures are public goods in that they have the characteristics of nonrivalry and nonexcludability. In order to determine whether risk-reduction and risk-prevention measures result in improvements in welfare, it is necessary to define and measure the benefits and costs of changes in risks. Define indirect utility as a function of income and the state of nature, suppressing all other arguments that will not change in the analysis. Let D represent the monetary value of the damage caused by an adverse event, given that it has occurred. D is implicitly defined by

$$V(M, A^*) = V(M - D, 0), \tag{35}$$

where the second argument in V represents that state of nature. When this argument equals A^* an adverse event that reduces utility occurs.

People often must make choices before the state of nature is revealed – in other words, *ex ante* choices. Let us assume that individuals make these choices so as to maximize

---

[16] For a more detailed analysis of the relationship between the CV and EV measures for changes in Q, see Hanemann (1999a).

their expected utility, where expected utility is defined as:

$$E[U] = \pi^0 V(M, A^*) + (1 - \pi^0) V(M, 0) \tag{36}$$

and π^0 is the probability of A^* occurring. The expected utility expression provides a basis for an alternative measure of the value of avoiding A^*, namely, the willingness to pay *ex ante*. This state-independent payment is sometimes referred to as option price (*OP*). In this case, option price is defined as the maximum payment the individual would make, *ex ante*, to ensure that the adverse event did not occur. Put another way, it is the maximum willingness to pay for a change in the probability of the adverse event from π^0 to 0. It is also a form of compensating variation, but one where the reference point is defined in terms of expected utility. *OP* is the solution to

$$\pi^0 V(M, A^*) + (1 - \pi^0) V(M, 0) = V(M - OP, 0). \tag{37}$$

OP and *D* will not in general be equal. This is because they are measuring two different things, or more precisely, measuring the monetary equivalent of two different forms of utility change, the *ex ante* change in $E[V]$ and the *ex post* change in $V(\cdot)$. When individuals have opportunities to adjust to risky positions through transactions in related private goods markets, it will often be possible to use a variation of one of the indirect methods described in Section 7 to infer individuals' *ex ante* values for risk changes.[17,18]

5. Aggregation and social welfare[19]

Before turning to methods for empirically estimating values for individuals, we first take up the question of how measures of individual welfare changes (whether *CV*, *EV*, or consumer surplus) can be aggregated into a measure of social welfare change for purposes of policy evaluation. The fundamental value judgment of welfare economics is that the social ranking of alternative policies should be based on individuals' preferences over these alternatives. The key issue is what to do when individuals have different rankings of the alternatives, as would occur, for example, if alternative *B* brought improvements in welfare to some and decreases to others when compared with alternative *A*. This can occur either because these individuals have different preferences or because they are subjected to different outcomes. One approach is simply to add up the welfare measures for all the affected individuals, as is the practice in applied

---

[17] For a more detailed discussion of this and related matters, see Chapter 13 by Karl-Göran Mäler and Anthony Fisher in this volume, and also Chapter 20 by W. Kip Viscusi and Ted Gayer. See also Freeman (2003, Chapter 7).

[18] A different set of issues arises in welfare measurement when individuals possess incorrect assessments of *Q*. See Foster and Just (1989) and Leggett (2002).

[19] For a more detailed discussion of this set of issues, see an advanced welfare economics text, for example, Boadway and Bruce (1984).

benefit–cost analysis. But this approach has some unattractive ethical implications, as we shall see. So, what are the alternatives?

The Pareto Principle provides a minimum standard for deriving a social ranking from individuals' preferences or rankings. It states that if at least one person prefers alternative A over alternative B and all other individuals rank alternative A at least as high as alternative B, then the social ranking should place A above B. For any pairwise comparison of two alternatives (A and B), one of four possible outcomes will occur:

  (i) alternative A will be ranked above alternative B;
  (ii) alternative B will be ranked above alternative A;
  (iii) alternatives A and B will be ranked as equally preferred; or
  (iv) the alternatives will be deemed Pareto noncomparable.

This last outcome would occur if at least one person preferred A while another person preferred B. As long as it is possible to find one individual who would lose from a move from A to B, B could not be Pareto preferred no matter how many others would gain from that move. The Pareto Principle, as benign as it may seem, is not devoid of ethical judgements. This is because all comparisons are made relative to the *status quo*, which itself may be socially undesirable (e.g., it might embody considerable inequality). Some Pareto improvements may actually worsen the inequality. Even if this were not a drawback, the Pareto Principle would be of limited value, as it is difficult to imagine real world policies – from imposing pollution control requirements on firms, to raising taxes to produce public goods, to breaking up the market power of monopolists – that do not involve losses to some individuals either through higher prices or reduced disposable income.

The *potential* compensation test has been proposed as a way to rank policies that impose costs on some while benefiting others. According to Kaldor's (1939) version of this criterion, a policy involving a move from A to B would be accepted if it were possible in principle for those who gain from the intervention to transfer income to those who would lose so that, taking account of the compensation, the losers would be no worse off while still leaving the gainers better off than in the absence of the project. The required compensation of the losers and the willingness to compensate of the gainers are the sums of their respective CVs. Thus according to Kaldor's version of the test, if the project were undertaken and the compensation actually paid, there would in fact be some gainers and no losers. The act of compensation would convert a potential Pareto improvement (PPI) into a true Pareto improvement policy. A policy would pass this version of the test only if the aggregate of all CVs were greater than zero. Thus the Potential Compensation test provides the rationale for the simple aggregation of individual welfare measures.[20]

---

[20] Alternatively, according to Hicks (1939), the policy would be preferred only if those who would lose from it had an aggregate willingness to pay to prevent the policy that was less than what those who would gain from it would require in order to willingly forgo the policy. The sums of the respective EVs would measure the appropriate willingness to pay and required compensation. Scitovsky (1941) advocated checking both tests to ensure the absence of the "reversal paradox."

Although it expands the set of comparable alternatives, this aggregate net benefit criterion is similar to the Pareto criterion in that it omits any explicit concern for the fairness of the underlying distribution of well-being or for the incidence of benefits and costs across different income levels. One way to incorporate a concern for equity in the distribution of well-being, with roots going back to Bergson (1938), is to weight the measures of value or welfare change for each individual by that person's relative degree of "deservingness". This involves employing a social welfare function that attaches a higher weight to benefits going to those judged to be more deserving – because of their lower level of income, for example. However, the search for a social welfare function has been unsuccessful, and in practice, analysts usually give equal weights to all individuals affected by the policy. Perhaps most important, the potential compensation test allows for policy changes that benefit the impoverished at the cost of the well-off, without requiring the former to compensate the latter. As such, if welfare measures can be calculated by subgroups in the population, then benefit–cost analysis can provide information while leaving effective weighting schemes to decision makers.

The original statement of the Compensation Principle by Kaldor (1939) was silent on whether the potential compensation should actually be paid. The purpose of the potential compensation test was to separate the question of whether the policy should be undertaken from the question of whether compensation should be paid, or in other words, ostensibly to separate the efficiency dimension from the equity dimension of the social choice problem. But a number of economists, most notably Little (1957), have criticized this effort. Little argued that if compensation were not in fact to be paid, the potential Pareto improvement criterion should be amended so that the project would be undertaken only if (a) the Hicks–Kaldor potential compensation test were passed, and if (b) the resulting redistribution of well-being is judged to be satisfactory. Thus, Little argued that the problem of judging equity or income distribution could not be avoided.

The potential compensation test or PPI criterion is one of the most controversial features of standard welfare economics. On the one hand it has been criticized as being incompatible with the Pareto Principle since it allows for a ranking of projects that are Pareto noncomparable. On the other hand, its application has been rationalized on the grounds that if a large enough number of PPI projects are undertaken, benefits and costs will be spread sufficiently widely that everyone will be a net gainer from the set of projects as a whole even though some might be losers on some individual projects.

The problems inherent in benefit–cost analysis have not deterred governments from using it for some kinds of policy choices and economists from advocating greater use of it in a wider range of environmental and resource policy questions. Whether this foundation can take the strain associated with its use in emerging environmental policy issues is an important question.

6. Methods of valuation – overview

The principal distinction among methods for valuing changes in environmental goods is based on the source of the data [Mitchell and Carson (1989, pp. 74–87)]. The data can come either from observations of people acting in real-world settings where people must live with the consequences of their choices or from people's responses to hypothetical questions of the form "what would you do if … ?" or "how much would you be willing to pay for … ?" Based on this characteristic, Mitchell and Carson (1989) and Freeman (2003) distinguished between "observed" methods and "hypothetical" methods. But it has become more common now to refer to these as *revealed preference* and *stated preference* methods.[21]

6.1. Revealed preference methods

Revealed Preference methods are based on actual behavior reflecting utility maximization. It is rarely possible for the researcher to deduce welfare effects from behavior without introducing some added structure to the problem. This is true even when choices are observed in a referendum (take-it or leave-it) setting, unless one is satisfied with crude upper or lower bound estimates. Random utility models have been adopted for the purpose of deriving more precise value measures from discrete choices, but at the cost of having to choose among preference structures and probability distributions. In most instances the environmental service does not have an offering price, but sometimes its quantity does affect the choices people make about other things such as quantities of market goods. In these cases, the value of the environmental service must be inferred through the application of some model of the relationship between market goods and the environmental service. Most such models are based on the assumption of some kind of substitute or complementary relationship between the environmental service and marketed goods and services. Examples of these models include the household production model, which includes models of household spending on cleaning and on repair of materials damaged by air pollution, and the travel cost demand model for visits to a recreation site, as well as hedonic property value and hedonic wage models. Revealed preference methods involve a kind of detective work in which clues about the values individuals place on environmental services are pieced together from the evidence that people leave behind as they respond to prices and other economic signals. The basic properties of these models are discussed in Section 7.

---

[21] Some authors have experimented with combining data from two types of methods and jointly estimating the parameters of the relevant models. See, for example, Cameron (1992) who combined contingent valuation (direct stated preference) data with travel cost (indirect revealed preference) data to estimate the value of a type of recreational fishing. See also Adamowicz, Louviere and Williams (1994) and Kling (1997).

6.2. Stated preference methods

The principal difference between revealed preference and stated preference methods is that the latter draw their data from people's responses to hypothetical questions rather than from observations of real-world choices. The earliest techniques for estimating values using stated preference methods involved asking people directly about the values they place on environmental services by creating, in effect, a hypothetical market. For example, people could be asked what value they place on a specified change in environmental services, or how much of an environmental service they would "purchase" at a given price. Stated preference questions of this type simply ask people what value they place on a specified change in an environmental amenity or the maximum amount they would be willing to pay to have an event occur. The responses, if truthful, are direct expressions of value and would be interpreted as measures of compensating variation. The term contingent valuation method (CVM) is conventionally used to refer to approaches based on this form of questioning.

While a variety of solicitation formats is possible, the most popular today is the referendum format, which asks for a *yes* or *no* answer to the question: "Would you be willing to pay $X for ...?" In their simplest form, referendum type questions reveal only an upper bound (for a *no*) or a lower bound (for a *yes*) on the relevant welfare measure. Questions of this sort are often referred to as referendum questions because of the analogy with voting on such things as bond issues. Discrete choice methods applied to a large sample of individual responses can be used to estimate willingness to pay (WTP) functions or indirect utility functions from data on responses and on the characteristics of the people in the sample.

A second form of stated preference question is known as contingent ranking. Respondents are given a set of hypothetical alternatives, each depicting a different situation with respect to some environmental amenity and other characteristics that are presumed to be arguments in the respondent's preference function. Respondents are asked to rank the alternatives in order of preference. These rankings can then be analyzed to determine, in effect, the marginal rate of substitution between any other characteristic and the level of the environmental amenity. If one of the other characteristics is a monetary price, then it is possible to compute the respondent's willingness to pay for the good on the basis of the ranking of alternatives. Uses of this approach include a study of the value of visibility in national parks Rae (1983), the WTP to avoid diesel odors [Lareau and Rae (1989)], and a study of water quality benefits in a river basin [Smith and Desvousges (1986)].

In the third type of stated preference question – known as contingent activity or contingent behavior questions – individuals are asked how they would change the level of some activity in response to a change in an environmental amenity. If the activity can be interpreted in the context of some behavioral model, such as an averting behavior model or a recreation travel cost demand model, the appropriate indirect valuation method can be used to obtain a measure of willingness to pay. McConnell (1986), for example, applied a recreation travel cost demand model to questions of the form "how often would you visit these beaches if they were free of PCBs?" in order to estimate the damages (resource value lost) from the pollution of the waters of New Bedford Harbor, Massachusetts, with polychlorinated biphenyls. For a more recent example of this approach, see Cameron et al. (1996).

A fourth type of indirect stated preference question asks respondents to rate a set of bundles on some scale. As in the case of contingent ranking, if one of the characteristics of a bundle is a money price, values can be inferred from the ratings. This approach is sometimes referred to as conjoint analysis or "attribute-based" stated choice. For a recent example see Roe, Boyle and Teisl (1996).

Some issues and problems in stated preference methods are specific to the particular form of the question being asked. For example, when people are asked how much they would be willing to pay for something, they might say "zero" because they reject the idea of having to pay for something they consider to be rightfully theirs. Other problems are generic to all methods based on hypothetical questions – for example, problems in scenario specification, sampling, and item non-response. The major questions regarding all stated preference methods concern the validity and reliability of the data, that is, whether the hypothetical nature of the questions asked inevitably leads to some kind of bias or results in so much "noise" that the data are not useful for drawing inferences. These questions are left to Chapters 17 and 18 by Carson and Hanemann and Baruch Fischhoff in this Handbook.

In the next section we discuss methods for estimation based on observed behavior, cases where Q has an effect on individual behavior. Section 8 deals with the special issue of nonuse value, which many believe cannot be deduced from observations on behavior.

7. Revealed preference methods for estimating values

Compensating (or equivalent) variation of a change in the public good, Q, is measured by the corresponding change in the expenditure function conditioned on the appropriate utility level as set out in Equations (30) and (31). If the individual's compensated inverse-demand function for environmental quality could be estimated, compensating (or equivalent) variation could be measured by the area under that curve between the initial and final levels of Q. Alternatively, if a Marshallian counterpart could be observed, then some of the techniques discussed in Section 4.2 could be employed. On most occasions, however, it is not possible to estimate either the compensated or ordinary demand function for Q directly.

The main purpose of this section is to describe the available techniques for revealing these welfare measures or approximations of them, using observable data on related behavior and individual choice. Our strategy will be to explore credible *a priori* assumptions that support restrictions on the form of the utility function and/or demand functions for market goods or household produced goods that, in turn, aid in revealing the individual's preferences for environmental quality. Different types of restrictions have different implications for the measurability of the demand for environmental quality. Developing a careful taxonomy of the methods for teasing out the welfare effects of interest helps reveal the broader and more general basis for the welfare economics of environmental valuation.[22]

Before turning to the taxonomy of methods, we first outline the basic theoretical structure of all revealed preference models of value. Since revealed preference methods for measuring values use data on behavior, some theoretical framework must be developed to model this behavior and to relate the behavior to the desired monetary measures of value and welfare change. A key element in the theoretical framework is the model of individual optimizing behavior that relates the individual's choices to the relevant prices and constraints, including the level of environmental or resource quality Q.

7.1. A taxonomy of models

The relationships between Q and other goods that have been found to be of use involve, broadly speaking, either substitution or complementarity relationships between environmental quality and other goods.[23] Exactly how these relationships work out methodologically, however, depends on a number of other considerations. We first consider cases in which the environmental good is a substitute for a marketed good that enters the utility function. A fundamentally equivalent construct is one in which the environmental good is an input into a household production function and has marketed-good substitutes in the production process. The latter is perhaps the more general and also the more useful way of conceptualizing the problem.

In the second category are those models in which the environmental good is in some way complementary to another good. The complementarity is often most usefully conceived such that the environmental good is a quality characteristic of the related good. The related good may be a single homogeneous marketed good, but such examples turn out to be difficult to imagine. There are two often-used derivatives of this construct. In one, the related good is itself a nonmarket good, produced by the household using a household production process. The second is one in which the related good is marketed, but units of the good are heterogeneous and quality-differentiated. Because the good is marketed, the prices of units with higher levels of quality embodied in them are bid up.

For all of the above constructs, discrete choice versions have been developed. In only one case, the case when the household produces a complementary good, have the discrete choice versions become the rule rather than the exception. In what follows, each of these constructs will be discussed with reference to key papers that have established the means for extracting approximate welfare measures or bounds on those measures.

---

[22] A similar taxonomy can be found in Bockstael and McConnell (1999). For a more complete treatment of revealed preference approaches to environmental valuation, see Bockstael and McConnell (in press).

[23] Mäler (1974) was the first to make this observation.

7.2. Substitution restrictions

Ever since Mäler first explored the question in his seminal book of 1974, several authors have attempted to extract information about preferences for a public good from information about its relationship to a substitute, marketed good. Bartik (1988a) distilled these results for the nonmarginal case, clarifying what we can and cannot deduce from information on these related goods.

7.2.1. Perfect substitution

A useful relationship is one in which Q is a *perfect* substitute for a good that appears in the utility function. The individual maximizes $U(X, Z, Q)$ subject to $M - P'X - p_z Z = 0$, where Z is the good in question and X is a composite of all other goods. Specifying Q and Z as perfect substitutes implies a particular mathematical relationship between Z and Q in the utility function. It also implies that there is some good or service that can be equally well supplied by Z and Q. The only difference is that Z must be purchased, but Q is supplied freely as a public good at a fixed level. It is clear that we could just as easily change the semantics of the problem by redefining the labels of our goods. The good or service that is supplied equally well by Z and Q could be labeled S, and the utility function could be rewritten as $U(X, S)$. Defining S as "produced" by inputs Z and Q according to a production process described by $S(Z, Q)$ completes the recasting of the problem in terms of a household production function. As an example, Q could be the purity of public drinking water and Z could be increasingly effective filtration systems. The two are perfect substitutes in the production of S, the quality of drinking water.

In this context, what would we need to know to measure the compensating variation of a nonmarginal change in Q? For problems in which Z and Q are perfect substitutes, the answer to this usually difficult question can be obtained using only information on the technology of the production process. Consider a case in which the individual currently produces S with the available Q (call it Q^0) and some purchased Z. Now suppose the level of the public good changes to Q^1. If $Q^1 < Q^0$ and if the decrease in Q can be exactly mitigated by an increase in the purchase of Z, then the compensating variation measure of the change in Q is given by the cost of the increased purchases of Z necessary to return the individual to his initial consumption of S. Likewise, if $Q^0 < Q^1$ and if in the resulting situation at least some Z is still purchased, then the compensating variation of the increase in Q is given by how much less the initial S would cost for the household to produce. This is a somewhat startling result. It is one of the few cases in which welfare measures for the household can be deduced without knowing anything about preferences. The only information necessary to compute the compensating variation of a change in Q is information about the price of Z and the technological relationship between Z and Q in the production of S.

The above result is in one way an oversimplification, however. Besides needing Q and Z to be perfect substitutes, we need the extra condition (captured by the second "if" in each of the above statements) that the individual is at an interior solution in terms of his demand for Z before and after the change. In some cases, we may not be able to assume this and would need to know something about preferences to determine whether the individual is likely to continue to purchase Z after the change. Nonetheless, this result is interesting enough to explore a little further, because the moment we allow Q and Z to be other than perfect substitutes, this simple answer no longer holds.

To illustrate the point, assume a sufficiently general household production function that exhibits perfect substitution between inputs: $S = (Q + aZ)^{1/2}$, where $a > 0$. Q is initially set at Q^0 and the individual maximizes the constrained utility problem:

$$\max U\big(X, S(A, Q)\big) + \lambda(M - X - p_z Z), \tag{38}$$

where p_z is the price of Z. The initial optimum for this problem is depicted in Figure 1 at point A^0 with utility level $U^0 = U(X^0, S^0)$. Note that the budget constraint is nonlinear, since the production function for S is nonlinear. The implicit budget constraint is given by

$$X = M - \frac{p_z}{a}\big(S^2 - Q^0\big). \tag{39}$$

The budget constraint begins at a point $(Q^0)^{1/2}$ units from the axis for the numeraire good, because this much S is obtainable for free by using the public good. An increase in Q to Q^1 shifts the budget constraint outward so that it starts at a point $(Q^1)^{1/2}$ from the numeraire's axis, but as it shifts, the slope of the constraint at any given level of S remains the same and the vertical distance between the two constraints is constant. This is because additional amounts of S can only be produced by purchasing more Z at the

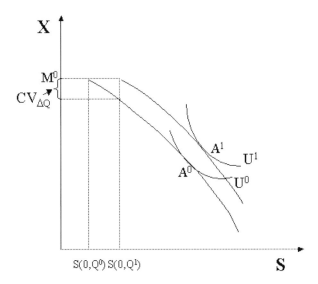

Figure 1. Perfect substitutes in household production.

constant price. The minimum amount of money that needs to be taken away from the individual to move him back to U^0, but with $Q = Q^1$, is the reduction in expenditures on Z necessary to obtain the initial S^0. In the above case this compensating variation measure equals $(p_z/a)\Delta Q$. This is true because price ratios have not changed. In terms of the graph, the CV will be the vertical distance between the two budget constraints. If we take that amount of money away from the individual after the change in Q then he returns to his initial budget constraint (since no prices have changed) and optimizes at A^0 once again. So, in the perfect substitute case, when the individual is at an interior solution both before and after the change in the environmental good, the amount of money necessary to return the individual to his initial level of S is the same amount of money that is necessary to return the individual to his initial level of utility.[24]

7.2.2. Imperfect substitution

Suppose now we have a production technology in which Q and Z are less than perfect substitutes. The precise result obtained earlier for the perfect substitute case no longer holds, although Bartik (1988a) has shown that this concept provides a bound on the welfare measure. It may appear that all we need to know is technology and prices in this case as well, but that result only holds for marginal changes. Reconsider the cost minimization problem that forms the dual of the optimization problem above, but this time for the more general problem, where $S(Q, Z)$ is *any* function for which the isoquants for household production are downward sloping. The individual minimizes

$$\min_{Z, X} X + p_z Z + \mu\big(U - U(X, S(Z, Q))\big), \tag{40}$$

where μ is the Lagrangian multiplier associated with the utility constraint. One of the first order conditions for the expenditure minimization problem is

$$\mu \frac{\partial U}{\partial S}\frac{\partial S}{\partial Z} = p_z. \tag{41}$$

For this problem the marginal willingness to pay for a change in Q, which by definition equals $-\partial e/\partial Q$, is given by $\mu(\partial U/\partial S)(\partial S/\partial Q)$. Combining these two results we have that at the optimum:

$$-\frac{\partial e}{\partial Q} = p_z \frac{\partial S/\partial Q}{\partial S/\partial Z} = -p_z \frac{\mathrm{d}Z}{\mathrm{d}Q}, \tag{42}$$

where the last term is the slope of the isoquant of Q and Z in the production of S. No information on preferences seems needed. This is only true, however, for a marginal change in Q – a case that is rarely very useful in policy analysis. Once we move to a nonmarginal change in Q, the change in the expenditure function must be integrated holding *utility* constant in order to obtain CV and, except in the perfect substitute case, this requires information about preferences as well as technology.

---

[24] When the individual is not at an interior solution in his demand for Z, his indifference curve is not tangent to the budget constraint. Consequently, the equivalence of these two amounts no longer holds.

7.2.3. Defensive expenditures

Bartik (1988a) has shown that the nonmarginal counterpart of (42), the change in the expenditures on Z necessary to achieve the original level of S after the change in Q, is a lower bound on the true compensating variation measure.[25] This result is most easily demonstrated by rewriting the usual compensating variation measure as:

$$CV = e(Q^0, U^0) - e(Q^1, U^0; S^0) + e(Q^1, U^0; S^0) - e(Q^1, U^0). \tag{43}$$

An extra term is both added to and subtracted from the usual CV definition for reasons we will see below. This term, $e(Q^1, U^0; S^0)$, is a restricted expenditure function. It is simply the minimum amount of money needed to achieve a utility level of U^0 when the level of the public good is Q^1 but the consumption of S is constrained to be at the original level of S^0. Define $X(Q^0, U^0)$ as the amount of X consumed in the initial situation when utility equals U^0, S equals S^0, and Q equals Q^0, and define $X(Q^1, U^0; S^0)$ as the amount of X consumed when utility equals U^0, Q equals Q^1, but S is constrained to be at its original level S^0. Finally, define the function $C(S^0, Q^0)$ as Bartik's defensive expenditure function, which equals the amount of money spent on Z (which might be a vector or a scalar) to achieve S^0 given that Q is at level Q^0.

Because the only goods purchased are the numeraire and Z, the first two terms of (43) can be written as:

$$X(Q^0, U^0) + C(S^0, Q^0) - X(Q^1, U^0; S^0) - C(S^0, Q^1)$$
$$= C(S^0, Q^0) - C(S^0, Q^1). \tag{44}$$

By definition $X(Q^1, U^0; S^0)$ must equal $X(Q^0, U^0)$ because utility is a function only of S and X. If U and S are held at their initial levels, then X must also be at its initial level. Equation (43) is now equal to:

$$CV = C(S^0, Q^0) - C(S^0, Q^1) + e(Q^1, U^0; S^0) - e(Q^1, U^0) \tag{45}$$

which equals the change in the costs of producing the original level of S when Q changes, plus a remainder which, by the Le Chatelier principle, must be positive.

The substitutability assumption lies behind the "defensive expenditures" or "averting behavior" technique for estimating benefits of pollution control. These terms generally describe activities undertaken to prevent adverse effects or to counteract the effects of pollution. By appropriately defining S and Z, each of these types of behavior can generally be represented by a household production technology. In attempting to use information about these activities to reveal the value of changes in Q, however, researchers have sometimes calculated the change in *actual* expenditures on defensive or averting activities rather than the measure derived above. Given the substitution relationship, a decrease (increase) in Q is likely to lead to an actual increase (decrease)

---

[25] It is a lower bound along the real number line. Thus, it is a lower bound on the benefits of an improvement and an upper bound on the losses of a degradation.

in spending on the substitute and this change in spending is sometimes viewed as the proper welfare measure.

Is this view correct? Can decreases in *actual* spending on a substitute good be taken as a measure of the benefits of an increase in Q? In general the answer is "No", even in the case when Q and the market good are perfect substitutes. The intuition behind this answer is straightforward. Assume that Q and Z are perfect substitutes. The benefit of an increase in Q is equal to the reduction in the spending on Z that is *required* to keep the individual on the original indifference curve. But in general, the individual will not actually reduce his spending on Z by this amount. There is an income effect as well as a substitution effect. The increase in Q means that the same level of utility can be maintained with a smaller expenditure on Z. As a consequence, the individual will reallocate expenditures among all goods, including Z, so as to maximize the increase in total utility. This may result in increases in the expenditures on other goods.

Bartik (1988a) shows that the actual change in defensive expenditures is always smaller in absolute value than the change in defensive expenditures holding Z constant. This means that the former is a worse lower bound on the true welfare measure of an environmental improvement than is the latter. For degradations, ordering is more difficult and depends on properties of the defensive cost function.[26]

7.2.4. Applications to human health effects

One of the more common applications of the defensive expenditure model is in valuing improvements in human health. The literature on this topic is diverse, but here we give attention to the role that defensive expenditures play in this context. A more complete treatment of the relationship between cost of illness and the bounding results of Bartik can be found in Bockstael and McConnell (in press). Some of the earlier work [e.g., Harrington and Portney (1987)] sought to compare the results from a "cost of illness" approach to the preferred willingness to pay measures. Cost of illness approaches typically measure the wages lost during periods of illness and the medical costs incurred. Much of the early work was restricted to marginal changes, but as usual additional difficulties arise in treating nonmarginal changes in Q.

Taking the simplest case first, let utility depend upon the consumption of a composite good X and the quantity of leisure time L but not on health status. The price of X is normalized to 1. Define the environmental quality variable Q such that improvements in Q result in fewer days of illness, where S will now be defined as sick days, so that $S = S(Q) \geq 0$, $\partial S/\partial Q \leq 0$. We will also assume that $\partial^2 S/\partial Q^2 \geq 0$ and that all days of illness caused by degradation in Q are of equal severity. Sickness reduces the number of days that can be spent in other activities and induces medical expenses $W(S)$ over which the individual has no choice. As specified so far, an increase in Q affects utility

---

[26] Bockstael and McConnell (in press) explore the properties of the defensive expenditure cost function and their implications for bounding more fully.

only through its impact on the budget constraint. The individual faces the following optimization problem:

$$\max_{X,L} U(X, L) + \lambda\big(M + r[T - L - S(Q)] - X - W(S(Q))\big), \tag{46}$$

where r is the daily wage rate, T is the total endowment of time, and M is exogenous, non-labor income. The dual of this problem, which defines the expenditure function, is slightly different from the usual one since a portion of income is determined by the labor choice. In the cost minimizing framework, the individual would minimize the amount of exogenous income necessary to achieve a given level of utility:

$$\min_{X,L} X + W(S(Q)) - r[T - L - S(Q)] + \mu\big(U - U(X, L)\big), \tag{47}$$

where μ is the Lagrangian multiplier associated with the utility constraint. The benefit of an increase in Q is the amount of money that could be taken from the individual leaving him indifferent to the change in Q. Thus, the marginal willingness to pay is given by

$$-\frac{\partial e}{\partial Q} = -r\frac{\partial S}{\partial Q} - \frac{\partial W}{\partial S}\frac{\partial S}{\partial Q}, \tag{48}$$

or the individual's marginal increase in effective income which equals the change in earned income and exogenously determined medical expenses.

In this simple model, obtaining an answer for the nonmarginal case is equally straightforward, since there is no behavior involved in the above expression. This is simply a technical relationship. Increases in Q cause decreases in sick days that cause a change in money income and a change in medical costs. Looked at in another way, the relative prices of the two decision variables X and L do not change when Q changes. Therefore, returning the individual to his original utility level means returning him to his original choice of (X, L). Since in this case a change in Q is directly translated into a change in money income, CV equals EV and the change in the cost of illness exactly equals both of these welfare measures.

This conclusion does not hold if illness causes disutility or if the effect of pollution on health can be mitigated by defensive expenditures. Now let the utility function be $U(X, L, S)$ with $\partial U/\partial S < 0$. Also suppose that sickness can be reduced by defensive expenditures such as air conditioning or asthma medications. Define Z as a purchased input, at price p_z, that can alter sickness, $S = S(Q, Z)$, with $\partial S/Z < 0$. The cost minimization problem now becomes:

$$\min_{X,L} X + p_z Z + W(S(Q, Z)) - r[T - L - S(Q, Z)]$$
$$+ \mu\big(U - U(X, L, S(Q, Z))\big). \tag{49}$$

The willingness to pay for a marginal change in Q is now given by

$$-\frac{\partial e}{\partial Q} = \mu\frac{\partial U}{\partial S}\frac{\partial S}{\partial Q} - \frac{\partial W}{\partial S}\frac{\partial S}{\partial Q} - r\frac{\partial S}{\partial Q} = \left[\mu\frac{\partial U}{\partial S} - \frac{\partial W}{\partial S} - r\right]\frac{\partial S}{\partial Q}. \tag{50}$$

Harrington and Portney (1987) and others have used these results to show that the change in the cost of illness is an underestimate of the benefits of Q. The change in the cost of illness (appropriately signed to make it comparable to the WTP measure) is

$$-r\frac{dS}{dQ} - \frac{\partial W}{\partial S}\frac{dS}{dQ} = -\left(r + \frac{\partial W}{\partial S}\right)\frac{dS}{dQ}, \tag{51}$$

where dS/dQ is the *actual* change in sick days resulting from the initial marginal change in Q. It includes the change in sick days that may come about because of readjustment in the defensive activity, so

$$\frac{dS}{dQ} = \frac{\partial S}{\partial Q} + \frac{\partial S}{\partial Z}\frac{\partial Z}{\partial Q}. \tag{52}$$

The difference between the willingness to pay and cost of illness measures is

$$\mu\frac{\partial U}{\partial S}\frac{\partial S}{\partial Q} + \left(r + \frac{\partial W}{\partial S}\right)\frac{\partial S}{\partial Z}\frac{\partial Z}{\partial Q} > 0. \tag{53}$$

The reduction in cost of illness is smaller than the compensating variation of an improvement in environmental quality. This conclusion would still hold if either sickness did not enter the utility function or defensive activities were impossible. The change in the cost of illness is an exact measure of benefits only in the absence of both.

To relate this to our previous discussion of the defensive expenditure model, it is useful to note that the individual facing the expenditure minimization problem in (49) will choose Z such that

$$\mu\frac{\partial U}{\partial S}\frac{\partial S}{\partial Z} - p_z - \frac{\partial W}{\partial S}\frac{\partial S}{\partial Z} - r\frac{\partial S}{\partial Z} = 0 \tag{54}$$

which implies

$$\mu\frac{\partial U}{\partial S} - \frac{\partial W}{\partial S} - r = \frac{p_z}{\partial S/\partial Z}. \tag{55}$$

It follows that the willingness to pay for a marginal change in Q in (50) can be restated as:

$$-\frac{\partial e}{\partial Q} = \left[\frac{p_z}{\partial S/\partial Z}\right]\frac{\partial S}{\partial Q}. \tag{56}$$

This is the result that we obtained when discussing the defensive expenditure approach. The value of a *marginal* change in Q equals the change in defensive expenditures necessary to keep S at its initial level. As Bartik (1988a) pointed out, this result cannot in general be extended to nonmarginal changes in Q. In addition, in neither the marginal nor the nonmarginal case can the result be interpreted to mean that the change in *actual* expenditures is the appropriate welfare measure.

Even in the presence of costs of illness (such as lost wages and medical costs), however, Bartik's bounds using changes in defensive expenditures still hold. Whether changes in defensive spending are good approximations of benefits or seriously over or underestimate benefits depends on the specific properties of the utility function and the implied relationships between Q and market goods. This analysis illustrates the importance of first developing explicit models of the role of Q in the decision process and how it affects choices of market goods before attempting to draw inferences about the magnitude of benefits from changes in market goods' demands. Murdoch and Thayer (1990) used changes in defensive expenditures holding Z constant to provide a welfare bound in the context of ozone reductions and skin cancer. In their estimation of damages due to drinking water contamination, Abdalla, Roach and Epp (1992) and Harrington, Krupnick and Spofford (1989) use bounds based on actual changes in defensive expenditures.

7.3. Complementary relationships

Perhaps the most common restriction employed to reveal preferences for an environmental good is the weak complementarity restriction, first suggested by Mäler (1974, pp. 183–189). This is a less restrictive assumption than one of perfect complementarity between the environmental good Q and some market good Z but it is far more easily established and yields more useful information about preferences for Q. Weak complementarity between Q and Z implies that if the amount demanded of the market good is zero, then the marginal value of a change in Q is also zero. When such a restriction appears to hold, Q is often playing the role of a quality characteristic of the privately consumed good Z. Weak complementarity implies that the quality of Z does not matter to the individual if she does not choose to consume Z.

Formally, consider the utility function,

$$U(Z, X, Q), \tag{57}$$

where X is the vector of all market goods other than Z. Weak complementarity holds if

$$\frac{\partial U(0, X, Q)}{\partial Q} = 0, \tag{58}$$

that is, if a marginal change in Q is irrelevant when $Z = 0$. The restriction can be restated in terms of the expenditure function, as:

$$\frac{\partial e(\tilde{p}_z, \widehat{P}, Q, U)}{\partial Q} = 0, \tag{59}$$

where $\tilde{p}_z$ is the "choke price" for Z and $\widehat{P}$ is the vector of prices of all other goods. For these definitions to make sense, a further requirement is necessary. The market good Z must be nonessential, which means from a practical standpoint that a choke price exists for the compensated demand function.[27]

---

[27] An inessential good is one for which a finite compensation exists for its complete loss. Mathematically, it must be true that a vector X^1 exists such that $U(Z^0, X^0, \ldots) = U(0, X^1, \ldots)$ for any level of Z^0.

7.3.1. Why the weak complementarity restriction is so useful

Under weak complementarity, the *CV* measure associated with a change in Q can be depicted graphically using Z's compensated demand curves. Label the compensated demand curve for Z conditioned on an initial quality level Q^0 as $Z^h(Q^0)$, depicted in Figure 2. Assume that the price of Z is given at p_z^0 and does not change throughout the analysis. The compensating variation associated with Z (i.e., the *CV* associated with a price change from $\tilde{p}_z$ to p_z^0) is the area *ABC* under the demand curve. Now assume that Q is increased to Q^1. Thinking of Q as a quality characteristic of Z suggests that the compensated demand for Z would shift outward to $Z^h(Q^1)$ as Q is increased. The compensating variation associated with the change can be shown to be area *BCED* ($= ADE - ABC$).

To see why this is the case, write the mathematical expression for the area between these two compensated demand functions. The area behind the initial compensated demand curve is given by

$$\int_{p_z^0}^{\tilde{p}_z} Z(p_z, \widehat{P}, Q^0, U^0)\, \mathrm{d}p_z \tag{60}$$

which can be rewritten as

$$\int_{p_z^0}^{\tilde{p}_z(Q^0)} \frac{\partial e(p_z, \widehat{P}, Q^0, U^0)}{\partial p_z}\, \mathrm{d}p_z = e(\tilde{p}_z, \widehat{P}, Q^0, U^0) - e(p_z^0, \widehat{P}, Q^0, U^0). \tag{61}$$

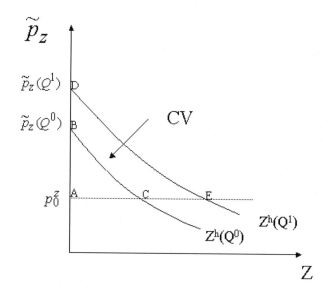

Figure 2. Compensating variation under the weak complementarity assumption.

Note that the choke price is actually conditioned on the level of Q. Likewise, the area behind the new demand curve is given by

$$\int_{p_z^0}^{\tilde{p}_z(Q^1)} \frac{\partial e(p_z, \widehat{P}, Q^1, U^0)}{\partial p_z} \, dp_z = e(\tilde{p}_z, \widehat{P}, Q^1, U^0) - e(p_z^0, \widehat{P}, Q^1, U^0). \quad (62)$$

The difference in these areas is therefore

$$e(\tilde{p}_z, \widehat{P}, Q^1, U^0) - e(p_z^0, \widehat{P}, Q^1, U^0) - e(\tilde{p}_z, \widehat{P}, Q^0, U^0) + e(p_z^0, \widehat{P}, Q^0, U^0). \quad (63)$$

If weak complementarity holds then

$$e(\tilde{p}_z, \widehat{P}, Q^1, U^0) - e(\tilde{p}_z, \widehat{P}, Q^0, U^0) = 0 \quad (64)$$

because a change in Q has no value to the individual if he is not consuming Z. As a result, the difference in the areas behind these compensated demands equals

$$e(p_z^0, \widehat{P}, Q^0, U^0) - e(p_z^0, \widehat{P}, Q^1, U^0) \quad (65)$$

which is the definition of the compensating variation associated with the change in Q. Equivalent variation can be similarly derived using compensated demands for Z conditioned on the *subsequent* utility level.

Admittedly, these precise results are not so easily established in the usual case when we only observe Marshallian demand functions for market goods. In the context of this problem, the Willig bounds referred to earlier are not helpful. For one thing, the measure we seek is not an area defined by an integral over a price change but a difference in two such areas. Second, the bounds of integration are complicated because the subsequent ordinary and compensated demands do not intersect at price p_z^0. This complication is illustrated in Figure 3. The change in the actual Z demanded with a change in Q will differ from the compensated change in Z. To see this note that at point N,

$$Z^h(p_z^0, \widehat{P}, Q^0, U^0) = Z^m(p_z^0, \widehat{P}, Q^0, M(P^0, Q^0, U^0)).$$

A change in Q, however, induces an unequal shift in the Hicksian (Z^h) and the Marshallian (Z^m) functions, so that $\partial Z^h/\partial Q \neq \partial Z^m/\partial Q$. As a result, $Z^h(p_z^0, \widehat{P}, Q^1, U^0) \neq Z^m(p_z^0, \widehat{P}, Q^1, M^0(P^0, Q^1, U^1))$. This is true unless there are zero income effects, in which case the ordinary and compensated demands converge. Otherwise the areas between the compensated and ordinary demands are not directly comparable.

There are additional restrictions that can be placed on preferences to make it possible to compare these areas using the Randall and Stoll bounds. As is suggested by the equations above, Bockstael and McConnell (1993) show that the CV measure in Figure 2 is equivalent to the area between Q^0 and Q^1 beneath a compensated marginal value function for Q. They also show that using the Randall and Stoll results, bounds on the CV measure based on the Marshallian analog to Figure 2 can be obtained. This is possible only if preferences are consistent with a condition set out in Willig (1978).

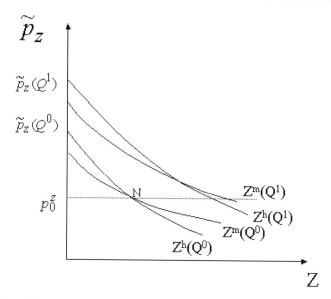

Figure 3. Shifts in Marshallian and Hicksian demands induced by quality changes.

In the context of our problem, this condition requires that

$$\frac{\partial w^m}{\partial p_z} = \frac{\partial Z^m}{\partial Q},$$ (66)

where w^m is a Marshallian counterpart of the implicit value function for Q and Z^m is the Marshallian demand for good. More recently, Smith and Banzhaf (2004) have developed the intuition behind the Willig condition as a restriction on the way income can influence the value of increases in Q at different levels of Z. This condition is equivalent to requiring that the willingness to pay per unit of Z be independent of income. This implies that the choke price is also independent of income.[28] Preference structures that exhibit weak complementarity together with the Willig condition can be found. However, researchers in most applications ignore the problem and proceed assuming that the area between the two ordinary demand curves is an acceptable approximation to the area depicted in Figure 2.

In the price change case, one means of obtaining a compensating variation measure from information on the ordinary demand function is to integrate back from this function to the expenditure function or indirect utility function. It is generally assumed that this is not an option for evaluating quality changes because, while the constant of integration cannot be a function of price, it can be a function of Q, leaving part of the effect of Q

---

[28] For a rigorous treatment and graphical presentation, see Smith and Banzhaf (2004).

unrecoverable.[29] Larson (1991) points out, however, that if it is reasonable to assume weak complementarity (an untestable hypothesis, anyway), one can integrate back from any reasonable and well-fitting demand function and impose weak complementarity by manipulating the constant of integration. In any event, to use the integrability approach in the quality rather than price change case, the researcher needs to be prepared to impose further structure on the problem.

The simplest form of the problem, as presented above, characterizes very few environmental valuation problems. The weak complementarity assumption implies that the public good Q can be interpreted as a quality characteristic of the privately consumed good Z. For the straightforward application to work, the marketed good's price must not change as a reflection of the amount of the Q embodied in it. The hedonic approach to valuation is a means of exploiting weak complementarity for the case in which the market good's price is bid up with rising quality and will be considered later in this chapter. The only obvious cases when the price of a marketed good does not reflect varying quality characteristics are cases in which prices are set administratively. For example, the good Z might be water from an individual's public water supplier and Q, the quality of that water supply.

7.3.2. Weak complementarity in a household model

In most applications of weak complementarity, Z is not really a marketed good at all, but one produced by the household. The best known example occurs in the context of recreation. An improvement in the water quality in a particular lake, for example, is implicitly assumed to be zero for those people who do not use the lake for recreation. So, to make full use of the weak complementarity assumption, let us set it in the context of a household production function. The recreational trip can be conceptualized in just this way. Individuals gain utility from the amounts consumed of a set of marketed goods X, from the amount of a household produced good S, and from the quality level of that good Q. Because S is now produced by the household, it will not have a market price, but it will have a cost of production. If the marginal cost is constant, then the analysis can proceed just as the above, with the constant marginal cost serving as the price of S. The simple travel cost model with constant travel (and possibly time) costs is a common example.

However, in many realistic cases, the marginal cost of production is not constant and no well-defined demand function can be estimated. Nonetheless, an alternative means of extracting information about preferences for Q is sometimes available [Bockstael and McConnell (1983)]. This method draws on results developed by Just, Hueth and Schmitz (2004) in the context of firm production, but it works as well in the household

---

[29] The constant of integration cannot be a function of price, since by Roy's identity, all information about price is captured in the ordinary demand function. However, there is no analog to Roy's identity for Q and no guarantee that the indirect utility function may not include terms in Q that are not reflected in demand.

production function context. Consider how the demand for an input in the production of S changes with changes in Q. First define the production function for S as $S = S(W)$, where W is a vector of inputs and r is the corresponding vector of prices of these inputs. Note that one element of W may be the individual's time, which may or may not have a parametric price. If the individual is paid a fixed wage rate and can choose his work hours (i.e., he is at an interior solution in the labor market), then the corresponding element of r will be the wage rate or a function of the wage rate [see McConnell and Strand (1981), Bockstael, Hanemann and Strand (1986)].

In order to derive a measure of welfare for a change in Q, the concept of an essential input must first be defined; it is an input in whose absence the output cannot be produced. In the context of the theory of the firm, its importance lies in the fact that if circumstances cause the firm not to purchase any of the essential input, then the firm shuts down [Just, Hueth and Schmitz (2004)]. For our purposes, if the individual does not use the essential input, then S is not produced. Consider the case in which Q is weakly complementary to S and W_1 is an essential input into the production of S. The area between the compensated demand curves for W_1 conditioned respectively on Q^1 and Q^0 is given by

$$\int_{r_1^0}^{\tilde{r}_1} W_1\left(r_1, \widehat{R}^0, Q^1, U\right) dr_1 - \int_{r_1^0}^{\tilde{r}_1} W_1\left(r_1, \widehat{R}^0, Q^0, U\right) dr_1, \tag{67}$$

where $\widehat{R}$ is the vector of all other input prices and $\tilde{r}_1$ is the choke price for W_1. Using Shepherd's lemma, this expression can be expanded to the following:

$$e\left(\tilde{r}_1, \widehat{R}^0, Q^1, U\right) - e\left(r_1^0, \widehat{R}^0, Q^1, U\right) - e\left(\tilde{r}_1, \widehat{R}^0, Q^0, U\right) + e\left(r_1^0, \widehat{R}^0, Q^0, U\right), \tag{68}$$

which equals the definition of the compensating (for $U = U^0$) or equivalent (for $U = U^1$) variation:

$$-e\left(r_1^0, \widehat{R}^0, Q^1, U\right) + e\left(r_1^0, \widehat{R}^0, Q^0, U\right). \tag{69}$$

This equivalence follows from the fact that

$$e\left(\tilde{r}_1, \widehat{R}^0, Q^1, U\right) - e\left(\tilde{r}_1, \widehat{R}^0, Q^0, U\right) = 0. \tag{70}$$

At $\tilde{r}_1$, no W_1 is purchased and therefore no S is produced, since W_1 is an essential input. Without the production of S, changes in Q do not matter to the individual if his preferences exhibit weak complementarity. Again, these results hold for the compensated case and are usually assumed to be approximated using Marshallian functions, but depend once again on the Willig condition described earlier.

It is possible to show similar results if the environmental good is weakly complementary to a set of goods rather than just one good.[30] Of course, if weak complementarity

---

[30] The measure in this case involves summing areas over multiple markets, but these areas must be established with the appropriate sequencing of price changes. The problem is often made easier if the prices are collinear. See Bockstael and Kling (1988).

does not hold with respect to a single good or definable group of goods, then the measures obtained above would be incorrect. In cases when the weak complementarity restriction is violated, measures obtained assuming this restriction will usually be underestimates of the true value. Some piece of the expenditure function is essentially missing from our computations.

The augmented weak complementarity model provides more general support for the use of the traditional and familiar Hotelling–Clawson–Knetsch travel cost model. The vast majority of these studies attempt to value changes in water quality, since the benefits from water quality improvements accrue most notably to recreationists. However applications to wildlife, aesthetics, and other recreational activities are also prevalent.

7.4. Exploiting other relationships, including weak neutrality

In principle there are additional ways of extracting information about the value of Q from Marshallian demands, although they have not to date shown much promise. Neill (1988) showed that if one can identify groups of goods that are Hicksian substitutes and/or groups that are Hicksian complements to Q, then lower and/or upper bounds on the marginal value of Q can be obtained. Specifically he proved that

$$\frac{\partial E_s/\partial Q}{\partial E_s/\partial M} < -\frac{\partial e}{\partial Q} < \frac{\partial E_c/\partial Q}{\partial E_c/\partial M}, \tag{71}$$

where M is income, E_s is the sum of expenditures spent on goods that are Hicksian substitutes, and E_c is the sum spent on Hicksian complements. The term in the middle, $-\partial e/\partial Q$, is once again the marginal value of Q. One practical problem with these results is that an upper bound on value is rarely of much use without a lower bound, since an upper bound does not preclude a zero or near-zero marginal value for Q. Also, for the lower bound to be useful, one must be able to identify a set of goods that are Hicksian substitutes, but Marshallian complements, since otherwise the left-hand side of the above equation will be negative which would make for a useless lower bound. This property is not easily testable empirically. Finally, no mention is made of the means by which we would obtain welfare measures for nonmarginal changes in Q.

The above exposition leads naturally to the definition of Hicks neutral goods, ones for which the Hicksian demand is insensitive to changes in Q. Neill mentions that if one were able to identify a group of such goods, then a point estimate of the marginal value of Q could be obtained. Larson (1993) carries this further by noting that if some good x_1 is Hicks-neutral to Q, then

$$-\frac{\partial e}{\partial Q} = \frac{\partial x_1(P, Q, M)/\partial Q}{\partial x_1(P, Q, M)/\partial M}, \tag{72}$$

where the $x_1(P, Q, M)$ is the observable Marshallian demand function. Values of nonmarginal changes in Q could be obtained by integrating back, either analytically or numerically, from this expression.

While these results provide new insights into extracting values from behavioral footprints, we are still left asking how useful they are in actual applications. As with the

Neill results, the answer turns on our ability to identify types of goods on the basis of their Hicksian properties. Since it is ordinary and not compensated behavior that is typically observed, distinguishing types of Hicksian goods may be empirically difficult, and we may have little intuition to aid us.

7.5. Welfare in a discrete choice context

In both the previous sections, Q was viewed as a scalar public good whose level was determined by policy, nature or accident, but outside the choice domain of the individual. The related good Z was viewed as one that could be chosen by the individual at any level along a continuum. But in many circumstances, the behavior that best reveals the value of Q takes the form of a discrete choice among a finite set of alternatives.

In the context of defensive expenditures, the substitute for Q may involve acquisition of one of a number of fixed household investments rather than the purchase of more or less of a variable factor. As an example, imagine an individual who faces a contaminated well water source. In order to "produce" clean water for his household, the individual may make a one-time purchase of a water filtration system or may pay for hook-up charges to a public water system. Applications of this type of averting behavior are not prevalent in the literature.

In contrast, the discrete analog to the weak complementarity case is well explored in the literature. In fact the use of random utility models to model individuals' choices among discrete alternatives in the recreation context has become the rule rather than the exception. In contrast to the defensive expenditure context in which lumpiness or discreteness poses practical problems, quality-differentiated discrete alternatives make welfare assessment of quality changes in the recreational context empirically more manageable.

To see why, consider the difficulty in obtaining observations on demand for trips to a site conditioned on different quality levels. This is the information necessary to estimate the model implicit in Figure 2; we need to know how demand changes with changes in Q. Rarely are data available to estimate the demand for trips at different points in time when the environmental variable Q takes on different values. To solve this problem, researchers have come to exploit information about individuals' choices among many quality-differentiated sites to learn about their willingness to pay for changes in environmental quality. In the process we can also learn more about substitution possibilities.

The individual's decision, cast in a discrete choice framework, involves defining a choice occasion in which the individual chooses among a finite set of alternative actions. To be useful in the context of environmental valuation, these alternatives must embody alternative levels of the environmental good of interest. As the individual chooses which item in the finite set of mutually exclusive commodities to consume, he inherently *chooses* his own ambient environmental quality, even though the *vector* of environmental qualities associated with different quality differentiated goods is exogenous to the individual.

Following McFadden (1973) who first developed the theory of the random utility model, define the individual's conditional indirect utility function for choosing alternative j on a given choice occasion as:

$$\widetilde{V}(p_j, q_j, \widetilde{M}) = \max U(X, z_j, q_j) \quad \text{subject to } \widetilde{M} = X + p_j z_j. \tag{73}$$

In this expression X is a numeraire, j denotes one of a finite set of n alternative commodities, z_j is the quantity of the jth commodity chosen and is usually equal to one on a given choice occasion, p_j is the corresponding price of z_j or the constant marginal cost of producing z_j, q_j is the level of environmental quality associated with alternative j, and $\widetilde{M}$ is income available for this choice occasion. The optimality problem of interest becomes the discrete comparison of the $\widetilde{V}$'s conditioned on each alternative choice. The individual chooses commodity j from the n possible alternative commodities if

$$\widetilde{V}(p_j, q_j, \widetilde{M}) \geqslant \max\left(\widetilde{V}(p_1, q_1, \widetilde{M}), \ldots, \widetilde{V}(p_n, q_n, \widetilde{M})\right). \tag{74}$$

An individual's choice among alternatives with different prices and embodying different qualities reveals something about the trade-offs he is willing to make between money and environmental quality. The results of these models can be used to measure the welfare effect of a change in environmental quality at one or more locations, taking explicit account of the existence of substitutes and their quality levels.

Expressing the conditional indirect utility function as linear in observable arguments, as has been common,

$$\widetilde{V}_j = \alpha q_j + \beta(\widetilde{M} - p_j) + \varepsilon_j, \tag{75}$$

where α and β are parameters of the utility function, and ε incorporates information that is unobservable to the researcher and treated as stochastic. In the simple indirect utility function stated above, indirect utility is linear in income causing income to cancel out in the probability statements. This implies that there are zero income effects in the choice of site – an assumption that in some circumstances has held up empirically. Assuming extreme value distributions for the stochastic terms, the resultant expressions make both estimation and welfare evaluation feasible. Given this error distribution, the probability of the individual selecting alternative j is given by

$$\Pr(j) = \frac{\exp(V_j)}{\sum_{i=1}^{N} \exp(V_i)}. \tag{76}$$

Now consider a change in environmental quality from vector Q^0 to vector Q^1. Using the indirect utility function above, the compensating variation (and equivalent variation, since income effects are zero) associated with this change is given by

$$CV = \frac{1}{\beta}\left[\ln \sum_{i=1}^{N} V_i(Q^1) - \ln \sum_{i=1}^{N} V_i(Q^0)\right]. \tag{77}$$

When $\tilde{V}$ is nonlinear in income, the CV and EV measures necessarily diverge and there is no exact analytical expression for them. Derivations of welfare measures, including alternative approximations, are given in Hanemann (1999b).

Applications of the random utility model to environmental valuation, beginning with Hanemann (1978) are now prevalent. They are too numerous to list, but a summary of some of the earlier ones can be found in Smith and Kaoru (1990). Discussions of some interesting new issues can be found in Train (1999), Herriges, Kling and Phaneuf (1999), Chen, Lupi and Hoehn (1999), and the Handbook Chapter 15 by Daniel Phaneuf and V. Kerry Smith.

7.6. Hedonic models

In the initial development of the weak complementarity restriction, we considered the case in which Q was weakly complementary to a marketed good. Subsequent discussions considered two cases in which the weakly complementary good was one produced by the household instead of purchased. The two cases included the continuous and discrete choice contexts. In the first case, the amount of a single nonmarket good with associated environmental quality was chosen, while in the latter case, the relevant choice was among heterogeneous nonmarket goods, each with a different level of environmental quality. In this latter case, the individual was able to choose environmental quality by selecting among a discrete set of alternatives that embodied different levels of the public good. Now we complete the matrix by considering the case in which the weakly complementary good is again a market good, but the individual can, as in the random utility framework, effectively choose the level of exposure to environmental quality, because heterogeneous alternative goods exist which embody different levels of the quality.

There is another special aspect of this technique which sets it apart from other models of behavior from which willingness to pay can be deduced. In the hedonic case, the market price of the heterogeneous good reflects the level of environmental quality embodied in it. In the housing market – by far the most common application of the hedonic model – houses embodying higher levels of any desirable characteristic (e.g., square footage, scenic vistas, air quality, etc.) will sell for higher prices. This differs from the random utility models discussed in the last section in which the heterogeneous nonmarket goods vary in quality but there is no market mechanism to cause their "prices", which are really costs of production, to vary with the level of quality.

The hedonic technique is a method for estimating the implicit prices of the characteristics which differentiate closely related products in a product class. In principle, if there are enough observations and enough variation in characteristics, it is possible to estimate the relationship between the price of any model of the product and the levels of its various characteristics. The implicit prices of characteristics are given by the partial derivatives of the hedonic price equation with respect to these characteristics.

The three principal types of environmentally-related applications of the hedonic model are the relationship between property values and environmental amenities, the relationship between wages and the risks of accidental death on the job, and the role of differences in amenity levels in explaining interurban wage and property price differences. We take up each of these applications in turn.

7.6.1. Hedonic property value models

Assume that utility is a function of a composite commodity X and housing services consumed, where housing services are defined by levels of attributes embodied in the housing bundle. Let the environmental characteristic of interest (e.g., air quality at the site) be denoted by Q and all other attributes be represented by A, a vector including structural attributes of the house (e.g., number of rooms, square footage of house, etc.) and attributes of the location (e.g., accessibility to employment, surrounding land uses, quality of schools, etc.). The price of any house will depend upon the quantities of the various attributes that it embodies. Let the hedonic price function be denoted $P_H = P_H(A, Q)$, a function that maps bundles of attributes to market prices of houses. The derivative of this function with respect to any attribute, say Q is the marginal implicit price of that attribute. In general, the hedonic price function will be nonlinear, and the marginal implicit price of an attribute will vary over its range and can be a function of all of the attributes of housing.

Assuming that the individual consumes only one house, the individual's choice problem is to:

$$\max U(X, A, Q) \quad \text{s.t. } X + P_H(A, Q) \leqslant M, \tag{78}$$

where the price of the composite good X is normalized to 1. The first-order conditions include:

$$\frac{\partial P_H}{\partial Q} = MRS_{Qx}. \tag{79}$$

This means that the individual locates himself along the nonlinear hedonic price function such that his marginal willingness to trade-off the characteristic Q for the numeraire is just equal to the trade-off required in the housing market – the marginal cost of Q evaluated at the individual's chosen location. The marginal rate of substitution is the slope of what Rosen (1974) called the "bid" function for the characteristic Q. The bid function has embodied in it information about the individual's preferences for Q, and its slope at the tangency to the hedonic price function equals the slope of the hedonic price function. Both are measures of the individual's marginal value, at that point, of the characteristic Q.

The theoretical construct underlying the hedonic model and developed in Rosen's well-known paper is one in which there exists a stock of houses embodying an approximately continuous array of levels of each of the characteristics. The hedonic price function emerges through a bidding process, and the resulting function is an envelope of individuals' bid functions. A few important aspects of this model are worth mentioning here. First, the levels of the characteristics (the elements of A as well as Q) appear as choice variables in this model and not as parameters. Second, the prices are not parameters either, since there is no reason to suspect that the hedonic price function will be linear.

These two features have implications for using the hedonic model to value changes in environmental quality at one or more sites. Welfare analysis is no longer a straightforward prospect of valuing a change in a parameter; the individual's ambient Q is now a choice variable. Welfare analysis now requires making a series of further assumptions about the way in which housing properties are affected, the way in which individuals respond, and the degree to which the nonlinear hedonic price function adjusts. As a further complication, we are generally unable to learn much about the individual's preferences for Q, even if we can estimate a fairly good representation of the hedonic price function, because of econometric identification problems.

Taking this last problem first, estimating the individual bid functions separately from the hedonic price function poses serious problems.[31] The reasons for this are carefully and rigorously laid out in Bartik (1987), Epple (1987), and Chapter 16 by Raymond Palmquist in this Handbook; but can be explained intuitively. The hedonic price function is a locus of equilibrium points with each individual's bid function tangent at one point. Thus we have information about only one point on each of these bid functions. We may have information on the location of different individual's bid functions (e.g., income, age, etc.) but we have no information that helps us learn about the curvature of any one bid function. There is only one situation in which the bid function can be immediately identified – when all individuals have identical incomes and tastes (i.e. utility functions). Then there is only one bid function and the hedonic price function *is* this bid function. Individuals are indifferent as to where they reside along the price function, since changes in characteristics are exactly compensated by changes in house prices.

Since this trivial case never holds, economists have searched for other means of identifying preference parameters, such as imposing additional structure on the problem by invoking *a priori* assumptions about the form of the underlying utility function, or by increasing the quantity of information obtained about the preference parameters by estimating hedonic price functions for multiple markets and then pooling the data on the assumption that the underlying structure of preferences is the same in all markets. The chapter on hedonic methods by Palmquist reviews these approaches.

For a long time, the preoccupation with the identification problem served to confuse the definition of welfare effects. Information about how individuals would choose to trade-off Q for other goods is interesting and sometimes important, but sometimes public agencies want to know the actual welfare consequences for all individuals involved, if Q changes at some set of sites in the housing market. Under some circumstances exact or approximate measures of these welfare changes can be obtained even without knowledge of the underlying preference structure. Ironically, when this is not the case, knowledge of preference parameters is usually insufficient to yield welfare results. At

---

[31] See Brown and Rosen (1982) for the first discussion of this problem.

the heart of this apparent anomaly is that Q is, in essence, a choice variable for the individual, because he can adjust his level of ambient Q by changing his location in the face of changes in the Q schedule (the vector of Q's at different locations). Disasters that lower, or public policies that raise, Q at some or all sites essentially have the effect of moving these sites along the existing hedonic price function. Bartik (1988b) has set out the conditions under which something can be learned from knowledge of the current hedonic price function. If enough sites change, however, the hedonic price function itself changes because of changes in the quantities of sites with different Q's. Even with knowledge of preference parameters, the new location of the hedonic price function is virtually impossible to determine.[32] Thus, the welfare question becomes one associated with a price change, where insufficient information exists to predict the new price schedule.

7.6.2. Hedonic wage models

The basic hedonic wage model has been refined and applied empirically to two important questions of particular interest to environmental and resource economists and policy makers. One question concerns the value of reducing the risk of death, injury, or illness. The hedonic wage model has been used to estimate the wage-risk trade-off as a revealed preference measure of this value.[33] The other question concerns the values of environmental and social amenities that vary across regions. Together with property price differentials, wage differences across regions have been used as indicators of the values of region-specific environmental, cultural, and social amenities.

From a worker's perspective a job can be viewed as a differentiated product. Each job represents a good with a bundle of characteristics such as working conditions, prestige, training and enhancement of skills, and degrees of risk of accidental injury (e.g., from exposure to toxic substances). If workers are free to choose from a menu of differentiated jobs, the hedonic price technique can be applied to the data on wages, job characteristics (including their locations), and worker characteristics to estimate the marginal implicit prices of these job characteristics.

When the hedonic price technique is applied to the study of wage rates, the theory must be modified to take account of an important feature of labor markets. In the typical application of the hedonic theory to differentiated goods, producers are viewed as selling a good embodying a package of characteristics and as being indifferent to the characteristics of the purchaser of the good. In hedonic wage studies, the employer is viewed as selling a package of job characteristics (including environmental quality associated with the job location); but at the same time the employer is purchasing work effort and cannot be indifferent to the productive characteristics of employees. Thus,

---

[32] New work using the equilibrium sorting models of Epple and Sieg (1999) offers some promise in providing an alternative approach that resolves this problem. See Sieg et al. (2004a, 2004b) for an application to an environmental amenity.

[33] These models are discussed in Chapter 20 by W. Kip Viscusi and Ted Gayer in this Handbook.

the hedonic wage equation must be interpreted as a reduced form equation reflecting not only the interaction of supply and demand for job characteristics but also the interaction of supply and demand for worker characteristics [Lucas (1977), Rosen (1979)]. This means that both worker and job characteristics must be included as arguments in the estimated hedonic wage equation.

As in the case of hedonic property values, the derivative of the hedonic wage function with respect to any job characteristic can be interpreted as the marginal implicit price of that characteristic. And if the worker is maximizing utility, the marginal implicit price can be taken as an estimate of the worker's marginal willingness to pay for the characteristic. It gives the change in income necessary to just compensate for a small change in the characteristic. These marginal values may change with levels of the environmental amenity and may be different for different workers.

The interpretation of the hedonic wage function as revealing marginal implicit prices and marginal values requires that all of the transactions that make up the data be undertaken in the same market. In other words, each buyer (seller) in the market must have had the opportunity to match up with any of the other sellers (buyers) and to choose the most preferred prices and other conditions. The market must be in equilibrium and must not be segmented into submarkets with incomplete mobility among segments. If workers are free to move from one urban area to another, then jobs are differentiated, in part, by the environmental and other characteristics of the urban area in which the job is located. Those cities that are more desirable places to work will attract workers from less desirable cities. The inflow of workers will tend to push down wages in the more desirable cities. An equilibrium is reached when wages have fallen to the point, where the marginal worker is indifferent between this city and the next-best alternative location.

Rosen (1979) was apparently the first to provide a formal model for deriving the structural equations relating wages to urban amenities and disamenities. He pointed out that there are really two hedonic markets in which individuals are making choices – one for labor, and one for land or housing. A decision to work in one city is also a decision to purchase housing services in that city. As individuals are drawn toward the more desirable cities and push wages down in those cities, they are also pushing out the demand for land and housing and increasing the prices of land and housing. Not only do compensating wage differentials exist, but compensating land rent and housing price differentials also arise across cities. The labor market model must also provide a coherent explanation for why firms in some cities are able to pay higher wages and still compete in markets for goods traded among cities. A formal model of both sets of markets, such as that set out by Roback (1982), is required in order to draw inferences about amenity values and willingness to pay from data on wage differentials and housing prices. [34]

---

[34] Applications include Roback (1982, 1988), Hoehn, Berger and Blomquist (1987) and Blomquist, Berger and Hoehn (1988).

A very simple model of individual choice of a city in which to live and work illustrates that wage differences alone do not in general measure amenity values. Consider an individual who derives utility from the consumption of a numeraire good X which is traded on a national market, as well as from the quantity of housing consumed, h, at a price of P_h, and the level of an urban-specific amenity, Q. By selecting a city in which to live, the individual determines her annual wage P_w and the level of the urban amenity, Q, which is constant at all locations within the city but varies across cities. The individual selects Q along with a selection of X and h so as to maximize

$$U(X, h, Q) + \lambda [P_w(Q) - P_h(Q)h - X]. \tag{80}$$

Note that both wages and the price of housing vary across cities according to the level of the amenity in each city. The first-order condition with respect to Q makes clear that the marginal value of a change in Q is related to changes in both the wage and the housing price:

$$\text{marginal WTP} = \frac{\partial U / \partial Q}{\lambda} = h \frac{\partial P_h}{\partial Q} - \frac{\partial P_w}{\partial Q}. \tag{81}$$

Thus the marginal willingness to pay for Q is set equal to its marginal cost, which has two components: the marginal change in housing price and the marginal change in wages from living in a higher quality city. Of course, for nonmarginal changes, all the difficulties associated with obtaining accurate welfare measures in the context of a hedonic model still apply.

8. Use and nonuse values

John Krutilla can be credited with first introducing the concept of existence or nonuse values into the mainstream economics literature [Krutilla (1967)]. In his classic article "Conservation Reconsidered," he argued that individuals do not have to be active consumers of a resource, with willingness to pay that can be captured by a price-discriminating monopoly owner, in order to derive value from the continuing existence of unique, irreplaceable environmental resources. He wrote that "when the existence of a grand scenic wonder or a unique and fragile ecosystem is involved, its preservation and continued availability are a significant part of the real income of many individuals" [Krutilla (1967, p. 779)]. The hypothesis that people place values on environmental goods that are independent of their present use of these resources has substantial empirical support.[35] For example, people have expressed willingness to pay to preserve the Grand Canyon even though they do not expect to visit it [Schulze and Brookshire (1983)] and to assure the survival of blue whales [Samples, Dickson and Gowen (1986)],

---

[35] For earlier reviews of this evidence and an extended discussion of conceptual and theoretical issues, see Randall (1991), and Freeman (2003).

eagles and striped shiners [Boyle and Bishop (1987)], and other endangered species even though they never expect to see one of them.

Environmental values that are independent of people's present use of a resource have variously been termed "existence," "intrinsic," "nonuser," and "passive use" values. These values are said to arise from a variety of motives, including but not limited to a desire to bequeath certain environmental resources to one's heirs or future generations, a sense of stewardship or obligation toward nature, and a desire to preserve options for possible future use. Whether motivation needs to be considered in assessing the "appropriateness" of nonuse values has been debated in the literature [see Hanemann (1994), Diamond and Hausman (1994)]. Perhaps the most troubling motivation is altruism, which some have argued can lead to double counting [Madariaga and McConnell (1987)]. In any event, whatever motivations are considered legitimate bases for individuals' values, they need to be empirically obtainable to be useful to policy analysis. If they are large, ignoring them in environmental policymaking could lead to serious resource misallocations.

The starting place for much theoretical and empirical analysis is often the contention that the total value of a change in the quantity or quality of a resource is made up of two *additive* parts – *use* and *nonuse* values. Acting under the assumption that nonuse values leave no behavioral footprints, researchers have typically assumed that the only way to obtain estimates of these values is through stated preference surveys. There are three ways in which stated preference methods could be used to obtain estimates of nonuse values. The first is to use a stated preference question to obtain an estimate of total value and then to deduct from it an estimate of use value obtained with one of the methods of Section 7. The problem with this approach is that the estimate is based on the difference between two other measures, both of which are estimated with unknown errors. The second approach is to ask questions only of those who are known to be nonusers. The problem here is that in principle users can also hold nonuse values, and these would not be counted. The third approach involves asking users to separate their use values and nonuse values. They could be asked to allocate their stated total value to the use value and nonuse value categories. Or they could be asked to state a nonuse value on the assumption that, contrary to their experience, they do not make use of the resource. Many psychologists and economists are skeptical of the ability of respondents to make these allocations; and responses to questions that are inherently counterfactual may not be valid indicators of value. Given these difficulties, many researchers have abandoned attempts to obtain separate estimates for use and nonuse values, and have employed stated preference methods to obtain total value estimates. This philosophy leads to the abandonment of revealed preference methods when nonuse values are thought to be significant.

In attempting to sort out this problem, the precise distinction between *use* and *nonuse* is key. In the earliest discussions, *use* was implicitly defined as a visit to the site or location of the resource in question. And this meant that use value could be captured by something like the travel cost model of recreation demand. If *use* involved the purchase of some other complementary market good, or if there was a market good that was a substitute for the environmental service, then use value could be measured using one of the techniques of Section 7. An alternative is to conceive of use as simply involving physical contact or proximity to the resource. Then use is possible without affecting the demand for a related good. An example is the person who lives within the natural range of an endangered species such as a bald eagle or peregrine falcon and sees members of the species as an incidental part of his daily routine. Another example is the person who drives by a nature refuge or scenic outlook while commuting to work. In both cases, the presence or the absence of the resource may have no effect on the behavior of the individual. Yet this person could have a willingness to pay to preserve the resource.

Given the ambiguity of the concept of use in these cases, an alternative approach, apparently first suggested by Mäler, Gren and Folke (1994), might be more appropriate. From the perspective of measurement of value, the most meaningful distinction is between those cases where changes in the level of Q lead to changes in the behavior of individuals and those where they do not. What sort of preference structure implies no behavioral change? The answer would seem to be a structure incorporating some sort of separability restrictions. Defining X as a vector of all market goods and Q as the environmental good of interest, strong separability in X and Q implies a utility function of the form:

$$U = f(X) + g(Q). \tag{82}$$

If, in addition, Q does not enter any constraints, then Q will not appear in any of the Marshallian demand functions. Larson (1993) has argued that this restrictive form of preferences has some implausible implications. For one thing, (82) implies that the group of marketed goods as a whole is not essential.

A more general form for the utility function, one in which X and Q are only weakly separable, also leads to Marshallian demand functions that are independent of Q, as long as we add the condition that constraints are independent of Q as well. Weak separability takes the form:

$$U = h\big[f(X), Q\big], \tag{83}$$

so that marginal rates of substitution among the elements of X are still independent of Q. If all market goods are in the group that is weakly separable from Q, then no behavioral trail will exist for Q.

Some have argued that it is unrealistic to think that Q can matter to an individual and still have no effect on his behavior. Individuals normally absorb some costs – if only in acquiring information – in order to possess values for the existence of Q [McConnell (1983)]. Larson (1993, p. 381) argues that either changes in Q do affect behavior in ways that can in principle be detected and used to measure values, or such values are likely to be vanishingly small. He points out that, for example, a more realistic model of choice would include a time constraint and that even if Q is not in the demand functions for market goods, changes in Q are likely to affect the allocation of time to different activities. Larson also argues that Hicks-neutral goods can be used, in principle, to reveal existence values. As described in Section 7.4, Hicks-neutral goods are goods whose compensated demands are independent of Q. It is not apparent why this property should be synonymous with the absence of use value. As of this writing, we are unaware of any successful efforts to measure nonuse values for environmental goods using revealed preference methods.

9. Conclusions

The term "value" carries so many diverse connotations that it is important to be precise about the economic definition of environmental valuation. One goal of this chapter has been to show how several popular empirical models used in environmental valuation have in common the same basic theoretical underpinning but are based on different assumed restrictions on the structure of preferences or household technology. Armed with a precise definition of the welfare measures we seek, it is possible to spot methods that produce misleading answers as well as those that can, under some conditions, reveal good approximations.

Carefully articulating the appropriate welfare measure is generally the easiest of our tasks. Teasing out this measure from observations on individuals' behavior or from answers given to interviewers' questions is often exceedingly difficult. The first relies on nature having provided the right configuration of circumstances to allow observation of behavior in response to variation in the relevant parameters. The second relies on the ingenuity of the survey and the cooperation of the respondents. Perhaps the greatest challenge, particularly in the context of environmental concerns of interest in the 21st century, is the most fundamental one. It requires understanding how ecological changes of all sorts translate into outcomes for society.

Acknowledgements

The authors wish to thank Karl-Goran Mäler, Ray Palmquist, V. Kerry Smith, and Jeffrey Vincent for extensive reviews of an earlier draft. The chapter has benefited enormously from their comments and insights.

References

Abdalla, C.W., Roach, B.A., Epp, D.J. (1992). "Valuing environmental quality changes using averting expenditures: an application to groundwater contamination". Land Economics 68, 163–169.
Adamowicz, W., Louviere, J., Williams, M. (1994). "Combining revealed and stated preference methods for valuing environmental amenities". Journal of Environmental Economics and Management 26, 271–292.
Barbier, E., Strand, I., Sathirathai, S. (2002). "Do open access conditions affect the valuation of an externality? Estimating the welfare effects of mangrove-fishery linkages in Thailand". Environmental and Resource Economics 21, 343–367.
Bartik, T.J. (1987). "The estimation of demand parameters in hedonic price models". Journal of Political Economy 95, 81–88.

Bartik, T.J. (1988a). "Evaluating the benefits of nonmarginal reductions in pollution using information on defensive expenditures". Journal of Environmental Economics and Management 15, 111–127.

Bartik, T.J. (1988b). "Measuring the benefits of amenity improvements in hedonic price models". Land Economics 64, 172–183.

Bergland, O., Randall, A. (1984). "Operational techniques for calculating the exact Hicksian variations from observable data". Staff Paper 177, Department of Agricultural Economics, University of Kentucky, Lexington, KY.

Bergson, A. (1938). "A reformulation of certain aspects of welfare economics". Quarterly Journal of Economics 52, 310–334.

Blomquist, G., Berger, M., Hoehn, J. (1988). "New estimates of quality of life in urban areas". American Economic Review 78, 89–107.

Boadway, R., Bruce, N. (1984). Welfare Economics. Basil Blackwell, Oxford, UK.

Bockstael, N.E., Hanemann, W.M., Strand, I.E., Jr. (1986). Measuring the benefits of water quality improvements using recreation demand models. Report to the U.S. Environmental Protection Agency. University of Maryland, College Park, MD.

Bockstael, N.E., Kling, C.L. (1988). "Valuing environmental quality changes when quality is a weak complement to a set of goods". American Journal of Agricultural Economics 70, 654–662.

Bockstael, N.E., McConnell, K.E. (1983). "Welfare measurement in the household production framework". American Economic Review 73, 806–814.

Bockstael, N.E., McConnell, K.E. (1993). "Public goods characteristics of nonmarket commodities". Economic Journal 103, 1244–1257.

Bockstael, N.E., McConnell, K.E. (1999). "The behavioral basis of nonmarket valuation". In: Herriges, J.A., Kling, C.L. (Eds.), Valuing Recreation and the Environment: Revealed Preference Methods in Theory and Practice. Edward Elgar, Cheltenham, UK.

Bockstael, N., McConnell, K. Environmental Valuation with Revealed Preference: A Theoretical Guide to Empirical Models. Springer, Berlin, in press.

Bockstael, N.E., Strand, I.E. (1985). "Distributional issues and nonmarket benefit measurement". Western Journal of Agricultural Economics 10, 162–169.

Boyle, K.J., Bishop, R.C. (1987). "Valuing wildlife in benefit–cost analyses: a case study involving endangered species". Water Resources Research 23, 943–950.

Brekke, K.A. (1997). "The numeraire matters in cost-benefit analysis". Journal of Public Economics 64, 117–123.

Brown, J.N., Rosen, H.S. (1982). "On the estimation of structural hedonic price models". Econometrica 50, 765–768.

Cameron, T.A. (1992). "Combining contingent valuation and travel cost data for the valuation of nonmarket goods". Land Economics 63, 302–317.

Cameron, T.A., Shaw, W., Ragland, S., Calloway, J., Keefe, S. (1996). "Using actual and contingent behavior data with differing levels of time aggregation to model recreation demand". Journal of Agricultural and Resource Economics 21, 130–149.

Chen, H.Z., Lupi, F., Hoehn, J.P. (1999). "An empirical assessment of multinomial probit and logit models for recreation demand". In: Herriges, J.A., Kling, C.L. (Eds.), Valuing Recreation and the Environment: Revealed Preference Methods in Theory and Practice. Edward Elgar, Cheltenham, UK.

Daily, G.C. (Ed.) (1997). Nature's Services: Societal Dependence on Natural Ecosystems. Island Press, Washington.

Diamond, P., Hausman, J. (1994). "Contingent valuation: is some number better than no number?". Journal of Economic Perspectives 8, 45–64.

Epple, D. (1987). "Hedonic prices and implicit markets: estimating demand and supply functions for differentiated products". Journal of Political Economy 87, 59–80.

Epple, D., Sieg, H. (1999). "Estimating equilibrium models of local jurisdictions". Journal of Political Economy 107, 645–681.

Foster, W., Just, R.E. (1989). "Measuring welfare effects of product contamination with consumer uncertainty". Journal of Environmental Economics and Management 17, 266–283.

Freeman, A.M. III. (2003). The Measurement of Environmental and Resources Values: Theory and Methods, 2nd ed. Resources for the Future, Inc., Washington, DC.

Hanemann, W.M. (1978). A methodological and empirical study of the recreation benefits from water quality improvement. Ph.D. Dissertation, Department of Economics, Harvard University, Cambridge, MA.

Hanemann, W.M. (1991). "Willingness to pay and willingness to accept: how much can they differ?". American Economic Review 81, 635–647.

Hanemann, W.M. (1994). "Valuing the environment through contingent valuation". Journal of Economic Perspectives 8, 19–43.

Hanemann, W.M. (1999a). "The economic theory of WTP and WTA". In: Bateman, I.J., Willis, K.G. (Eds.), Valuing Environmental Preferences: Theory and Practice of the Contingent Valuation Method in the U.S., EU, and Developing Countries. Oxford University Press, Oxford, UK.

Hanemann, W.M. (1999b). "Welfare analysis with discrete choice models". In: Herriges, J.A., Kling, C.L. (Eds.), Valuing Recreation and the Environment: Revealed Preference Methods in Theory and Practice. Edward Elgar, Cheltenham, UK.

Hanemann, W.M., Morey, E.R. (1992). "Separability, partial demand systems, and consumer's surplus measures". Journal of Environmental Economics and Management 22, 241–258.

Harrington, W., Krupnick, A., Spofford, W. (1989). "The economic losses of waterborne disease outbreak". Journal of Urban Economics 25, 116–137.

Harrington, W., Portney, P.R. (1987). "Valuing the benefits of health and safety regulations". Journal of Urban Economics 22, 101–112.

Hausman, J.A. (1981). "Exact consumers' surplus and deadweight loss". American Economic Review 71, 662–676.

Hazilla, M., Kopp, R. (1990). "Social cost of environmental quality regulations: a general equilibrium analysis". Journal of Political Economy 98, 853–873.

Herriges, J.A., Kling, C.L., Phaneuf, D.J. (1999). "Corner solution models of recreation demand: a comparison of competing frameworks". In: Herriges, J.A., Kling, C.L. (Eds.), Valuing Recreation and the Environment: Revealed Preference Methods in Theory and Practice. Edward Elgar, Cheltenham, UK.

Hicks, J.R. (1939). "The foundations of welfare economics". Economic Journal 47, 696–712.

Hicks, J.R. (1943). "The four consumer surpluses". Review of Economic Studies 11, 31–41.

Hoehn, J.P., Berger, M.C., Blomquist, G.C. (1987). "A hedonic model of interregional wages, rents, and amenity values". Journal of Regional Science 27, 605–620.

Hurwicz, L., Uzawa, H. (1971). "On the integrability of demand functions". In: Chipman, J., et al. (Eds.), Preferences, Utility and Demand. Harcourt Brace Jovanovich, New York.

Irvine, I.J., Sims, W.A. (1998). "Measuring consumer surplus with unknown Hicksian demands". American Economic Review 88, 314–322.

Just, R.E., Hueth, D.L., Schmitz, A. (2004). The Welfare Economics of Public Policy. Edward Elgar, Northampton, MA.

Kahn, J.R., Kemp, W.M. (1985). "Economic losses associated with the degradation of an ecosystem: the case of submerged aquatic vegetation in Chesapeake Bay". Journal of Environmental Economics and Management 12, 246–263.

Kaldor, N. (1939). "Welfare propositions of economics and interpersonal comparisons of utility". Economic Journal 49, 549–552.

Kelman, S. (1981). "Cost–benefit analysis: an ethical critic". Regulation 5, 33–44.

Kling, C.L. (1997). "The gains from combining travel cost and contingent valuation data to value nonmarket goods". Land Economics 73, 428–439.

Krutilla, J.V. (1967). "Conservation reconsidered". American Economic Review 57, 777–786.

LaFrance, J.T. (1993). "Weak separability in applied welfare analysis". American Journal of Agricultural Economics 75, 770–775.

LaFrance, J.T., Hanemann, W.M. (1989). "The dual structure of incomplete demand systems". American Journal of Agricultural Economics 71, 262–274.

Lankford, R.H. (1988). "Measuring welfare changes in settings with imposed quantities". Journal of Environmental Economics and Management 15, 45–63.

Lareau, T.J., Rae, D.A. (1989). "Valuing WTP for diesel odor reductions: an application of the contingent ranking technique". Southern Economic Journal 55, 728–742.

Larson, D.M. (1991). "Recovering weakly complementary preferences". Journal of Environmental Economics and Management 21, 97–109.

Larson, D.M. (1993). "On measuring existence value". Land Economics 69, 377–388.

Leggett, C. (2002). "Environmental valuation with imperfect information: The case of the random utility model". Environmental and Resource Economics 23, 343–355.

Little, I.M.D. (1957). A Critique of Welfare Economics, 2nd ed. Clarendon Press, Oxford, UK.

Lucas, R.E.B. (1977). "Hedonic wage equations and psychic wages in the returns to schooling". American Economic Review 67, 549–558.

Lynne, G.D., Conroy, P., Prochaska, F.J. (1981). "Economics valuation of marsh areas for marine production processes". Journal of Environmental Economics and Management 8, 175–186.

Madariaga, B., McConnell, K.E. (1987). "Exploring existence value". Water Resources Research 23, 936–942.

Mäler, K.-G. (1974). Environmental Economics: A Theoretical Inquiry. Johns Hopkins University Press for Resources for the Future, Baltimore, MD.

Mäler, K.-G., Gren, I.-M., Folke, C. (1994). "Multiple use of environmental resources: a household production function approach to valuing natural capital". In: Jansson, A.-M., Hammer, M., Folke, C., Costanza, R. (Eds.), Investing in Natural Capital: The Ecological Economics Approach to Sustainability. Island Press, Washington, DC.

McConnell, K.E. (1983). "Existence and bequest value". In: Rowe, R.D., Chestnut, L.G. (Eds.), Managing Air Quality and Scenic Resources at National Parks and Wilderness Areas. Westview Press, Boulder, CO.

McConnell, K.E. (1986). The Damages to Recreational Activities from PCBs in New Bedford Harbor. Industrial Economics, Cambridge, MA.

McConnell, K.E., Strand, I.E. (1981). "Measuring the cost of time in recreation demand analysis". American Journal of Agricultural Economics 63, 153–156.

McFadden, D. (1973). "Conditional logit analysis of discrete choice behavior". In: Zarembka, P. (Ed.), Frontiers of Econometrics. Academic Press, New York.

Mitchell, R.C., Carson, R.T. (1989). Using Surveys to Value Public Goods: The Contingent Valuation Method. Resources for the Future, Washington, DC.

Murdoch, J.C., Thayer, M.A. (1990). "The benefits of reducing the incidence of nonmelanoma skin cancers: a defensive expenditures approach". Journal of Environmental Economics and Management 18, 107–119.

Narain, U., Fisher, A.C. (1994). "Modeling the value of biodiversity using a production function approach: the case of the Anolis lizard in the lesser and greater Antilles". In: Perrings, C.A., et al. (Eds.), Biodiversity Conservation: Problems and Policies. Kluwer Academic, Boston.

Neill, J.R. (1988). "Another theorem on using market demands to determine willingness to pay for non-traded goods". Journal of Environmental Economics and Management 15, 224–232.

Pollak, R.A., Wales, T.J. (1992). Demand System Specification and Estimation. Oxford University Press, Oxford, UK.

Rae, D.A. (1983). "The value to visitors of improving visibility at Mesa Verde and Great Smoky Mountain national parks". In: Rowe, R.D., Chestnut, L.G. (Eds.), Managing Air Quality and Scenic Resources in National Parks and Wilderness Areas. Westview Press, Boulder, CO.

Randall, A. (1991). "Total and nonuse values". In: Braden, J.B., Kolstad, C.D. (Eds.), Measuring the Demand for Environmental Quality. Elsevier, Amsterdam.

Randall, A., Stoll, J.R. (1980). "Consumer's surplus in commodity space". American Economic Review 70, 449–455.

Roback, J. (1982). "Wages, rents, and the quality of life". Journal of Political Economy 90, 1257–1278.

Roback, J. (1988). "Wages, rents, and amenities: differences among workers and regions". Economic Inquiry 26, 23–41.

Roe, B., Boyle, K.J., Teisl, M.F. (1996). "Using conjoint analysis to derive estimates of compensating variation". Journal of Environmental Economics and Management 31, 145–159.

Rosen, S. (1974). "Hedonic prices and implicit markets: product differentiation in perfect competition". Journal of Political Economy 82, 34–55.

Rosen, S. (1979). "Wage-based indices of urban quality of life". In: Mieszkowski, P., Straszheim, M. (Eds.), Current Issues in Urban Economics. Johns Hopkins University Press, Baltimore, MD.

Sagoff, M. (1981). "At the shrine of Our Lady of Fatima or why political questions are not all economic". Arizona Law Review 23, 1283–1298.

Samples, K.C., Dickson, J.A., Gowen, M.M. (1986). "Information disclosure and endangered species valuation". Land Economics 62, 306–312.

Schulze, W.D., Brookshire, D.S. (1983). "The economic benefits of preserving visibility in the national park lands of the Southwest". Natural Resources Journal 23, 149–173.

Scitovsky, T. (1941). "A note on welfare propositions in economics". Review of Economic Studies 9, 77–88.

Sen, A. (1995). "Environmental evaluation and social choice: contingent valuation and the market analogy". Japanese Economic Review 46, 23–37.

Sieg, H., Smith, V., Banzhaf, H., Walsh, R. (2004a). "Estimating the general equilibrium benefits of large changes in spatially delineated public goods". International Economic Review 45, 1047–1077.

Sieg, H., Smith, V., Banzhaf, H., Walsh, R. (2004b). "General equilibrium benefits for environmental improvements: projected ozone reductions under EPA's prospective analysis for the Los Angeles air basin". Journal of Environmental Economics and Management 47, 559–581.

Silberberg, E. (1972). "Duality and the consumer's surpluses". American Economic Review 62, 942–952.

Smith, V.K., Banzhaf, H.S. (2004). "A diagrammatic exposition of weak complementarity and the Willig condition". American Journal of Agricultural Economics 86, 455–466.

Smith, V.K., Desvousges, W.H. (1986). Measuring Water Quality Benefits. Kluwer/Nijhoff, Boston.

Smith, V.K., Kaoru, Y. (1990). "Signals or noise: explaining the variation in recreation benefit estimates". American Journal of Agricultural Economics 72, 419–433.

Train, K.E. (1999). "Mixed legit models for recreation demand". In: Herriges, J.A., Kling, C.L. (Eds.), Valuing Recreation and the Environment: Revealed Preference Methods in Theory and Practice. Edward Elgar, Cheltenham, UK.

Vartia, Y. (1983). "Efficient methods of measuring welfare change and compensated income in terms of ordinary demand functions". Econometrica 51, 79–98.

Willig, R.D. (1976). "Consumer's surplus without apology". American Economic Review 66, 589–597.

Willig, R.D. (1978). "Incremental consumer's surplus and hedonic price adjustment". Journal of Economic Theory 17, 227–253.

Willig, R.D. (1979). "Consumer's without apology: reply". American Economic Review 69, 471–474.

Chapter 13

ENVIRONMENT, UNCERTAINTY, AND OPTION VALUES

KARL-GÖRAN MÄLER

Beijer Institute, Box 50005, 104 05 Stockholm, Sweden

D81

ANTHONY FISHER

Department of Agricultural and Resource Economics, University of California, Berkeley, CA 94 720, USA

Contents

Q51

Handbook of Environmental Economics, Volume 2. Edited by K.-G. Mäler and J.R. Vincent
© 2005 Elsevier B.V. *All rights reserved*
DOI: 10.1016/S1574-0099(05)02013-9

Abstract

We analyze in this chapter decision-making when costs and benefits of an action are uncertain, that is, when future preferences are uncertain. We begin, in Section 2, with the classical analysis by Krutilla et al. (1972) of whether the expected consumer's surplus is a correct measure of the net benefits from the action. It turns out that for one individual, the correct measure is the expected consumer's surplus corrected with one term representing the covariance between the state-contingent consumer's surplus and the state-contingent marginal utility of wealth and a second term representing risk aversion. This corrected measure is what Krutilla et al. (1972) called the option value. Thus the difference between option value and expected consumer's surplus is determined by the covariance between preferences and consumer's surplus and risk aversion. The sign of this difference will therefore depend on these factors. We apply this result to a number of cases in order to derive additional useful results. First we look at the aggregate (over a set of individuals) option value and establish a general result. We then apply this result to the allocation of risk in the context of both public and private goods.

In Section 3, we introduce relevant dynamic elements to the general problem of decisions under uncertainty. We analyze actions that may have irreversible effects, but where the decision-maker can improve her information about the true future preferences. This problem was first studied by Arrow and Fisher (1974) and Henry (1974), who showed (as we do in Section 3.2) that when the decision-maker has to choose between two actions, of which one is irreversible, and future benefits are uncertain in the first time period, maximizing expected value will result in a biased result: the irreversible action will be chosen too often. However, this result is based on assumptions of linearity. In order to study the problem without this restriction, we rely on Epstein's (1980) framework, which we present in some detail. The result is that convexity (concavity) assumptions are essential to establish the direction of the bias. We also use Epstein's framework to look at issues such as uncertainty about cost of restoration and uncertainty about irreversibility.

All of the results to this point are for models with just two time periods. In Section 4, we analyze the many-period case, adopting a somewhat different analytical framework: stochastic dynamic programming, as presented in Dixit and Pindyck (1994). Additional results in continuous time are developed, drawing on the theory of stochastic processes. We look in particular at the "optimal stopping problem," a useful and important special case, and present an empirical application due to Conrad (1997): when, if ever, to cut an old-growth forest that also yields benefits in its natural state.

Keywords

option values, uncertainty, irreversible changes, Bayesian updating, stochastic processes

JEL classification: D800, D810, D830, Q500

1. Introduction

It is trivial to note that the future is uncertain. It is, however, far from trivial to analyze that uncertainty. The environmental field, in particular, is permeated by uncertainty. Besides the usual economic uncertainties, we have major uncertainties characterizing our knowledge of environmental processes. Often, we simply do not know the long run consequences of interventions in the environment. For example, for many new chemicals, we do not know whether they are carcinogenic or not. Our models of ecosystems dynamics are far from precise. Moreover, future preferences for environmental services are uncertain, which means that future benefits from nature preservation today are uncertain. These topics will be addressed in this chapter. In the next section, we will look at an essentially static framework to look at the role of risk aversion in valuing uncertain environmental benefits. The main tool is the use of quadratic approximations of the von Neumann–Morgenstern utility functions, and the main result is that the benefits from environmental policy reforms depend on risk aversion as measured by the Arrow–Pratt measure of absolute risk aversion and on the variance and covariance of the distributions of preferences and the supply of environmental quality and the wealth (or income) of the individuals. When aggregating the benefits over the whole population of households in the economy, some risks will be highly correlated and it is therefore impossible to bring down the cost of risk bearing by pooling risks. On the other hand, it will of course be possible to reduce the cost of risk bearing by diversification (something which is not studied in this chapter). The key issue of whether the difference between total and expected benefits (called option value in the earlier literature[1]) is positive or negative can be much better understood from the point of view of the covariances between environmental uncertainty and preference uncertainty.

The theory of assets with uncertain returns is very well developed in the corporate finance literature. In particular, the capital budgeting decision is from a formal point of view quite similar to the analysis offered here. However, the main problem we face is that for many natural resource assets, there do not exist markets for pooling and sharing risk. Therefore, no models similar to the CAPM can be developed for those assets. However, much of the analytical framework from that literature can be used for an analysis of decision-making on the use of environmental resources when the consequences are risky.

The third part of the chapter looks at the case where information on the state of the world is coming forward with time. Thus, it may be socially profitable to postpone a decision until we know more about the costs and benefits. What's crucial here is that the consequences of a decision, say in the first period of a two-period problem, are difficult or impossible to reverse. There are many examples of this type of problem in the environmental literature, ranging from species loss to climate change. In our analysis of this case, we develop an alternative, dynamic option value concept, called quasi-option value in the initial contribution by Arrow and Fisher (1974); see also Henry

---

[1] Krutilla et al. (1972).

(1974a, 1974b) and Hanemann (1989). Although results here are based on some fairly strong assumptions about the shape of benefit functions and other aspects of the problem, the assumptions are not implausible, at least to a first approximation, in many real-world applications, as we show with an example: whether to develop portions of a tract of land in Central Thailand that is currently part of a national park [Albers, Fisher and Hanemann (1996)]. The rest of the section is devoted to exploring the consequences of relaxing the assumptions, drawing initially on the analytical framework and results of Epstein (1980) and Freixas and Laffont (1984). An interesting question, to our knowledge not treated in the literature, is whether or how it is possible to integrate the two concepts of option value: that arising from the temporal resolution of uncertainty, as in this section, and that based on risk preferences in a static setting, developed in the preceding section. We close with a discussion of this question.

The fourth and final section of the chapter presents a somewhat different approach to the general theory of intertemporal decisions under uncertainty, following closely the treatment in Dixit and Pindyck (1994) and based on the theory of stochastic processes and stochastic calculus. Here we develop first a multi-period model, then continuous time, with special reference to the case of optimal stopping. The latter is important both because a number of environmental and resource problems are appropriately modeled in this way, and also because it is relatively amenable to solution. We illustrate with another example drawn from the literature: the problem of when, if ever, to harvest a stand of old-growth redwood in Northern California that also yields amenity values if left unharvested [Conrad (1997)].

2. Decision-making and risk: a static framework

2.1. The basic framework

As is traditional, we assume that uncertainty can be described by a set of events or states of the world. Each event contains all the information relevant for decision-making and the uncertainty consists of not knowing which event will occur. The particular features characterizing an event we are interested in are income W, supply of environmental resources Q and preferences as measured by utility functions $U(W, Q)$. Note that this means that the individual is not certain what his preferences will be, unless he knows the event that will occur. We will in this section mainly use the indirect utility function, and moreover, we will not, except in the last section consider price uncertainty. One case in which price uncertainty may be quite important is the uncertainty about future interest rates. We will therefore come back to an analysis of that case later. Finally, we will assume that Q is one-dimensional. Generalizations to the case when Q has many but finite dimensions are straightforward.

Let us start by considering one arbitrary individual. For him each event i will describe his income W_i, the supply of environmental services Q_i, and utility function U^i. Let there be a probability measure λ_i over the set of events. The preferences of the individual can then be represented by a von Neumann–Morgenstern expected utility

$$\int U^i(W_i, Q_i)\, d\lambda_i = EU^i(W_i, Q_i). \tag{2.1.1}$$

This means that we simultaneously will study both what has been called supply uncertainty, that is the uncertainty about Q, and demand uncertainty, i.e., uncertainty about the preferences. As usual, we will assume that the individual is risk averse. This is in the simplest case defined as the case when the individual refuses to accept a fair bet, i.e., a bet with expectation zero. It is then easy to prove that risk aversion is equivalent to a concave utility function. However, in our case the utility functions U_i vary from event to event and the situation is slightly more complicated. In view of the confusion about the appropriate definition of risk aversion in this situation, it may be worthwhile to give a brief analysis of the problem.

2.2. Risk aversion

In discussing risk aversion, the focus is on the income or wealth variable, so we assume *for this discussion only*, that the environmental quality variable is constant over all possible events. Then we can as well for simplicity suppress that variable. Assume now the individual has to choose between accepting a fair lottery Y with the price Y_i if event i occurs. The conventional definition of risk aversion is now that if $E(Y) \leq 0$, i.e., if the expected value of the lottery is not positive, then a risk avert individual would not accept a lottery ticket. Based on this definition Schmalensee (1972) found that risk aversion means that the marginal utility of income must be constant over all events. However, in view of the fact that income W varies over events, a risk averter may very well accept a lottery with negative expected value if the lottery is negatively correlated with income. In this case will the lottery act as insurance. Thus we should look at the total lottery $W + Y = Z$. Assume then that

$$E(Z) = \bar{Z}, \tag{2.2.1}$$

if

$$E\big(U(Z)\big) \leq E\big(U(Z)\big), \tag{2.2.2}$$

then we may, for the moment, say that the individual is risk averse (note that the right-hand side is different from $U(\bar{Z})$, since U is dependent on which event that will occur).

Obviously, if the utility functions are independent of states, then risk version would be equivalent to a concave utility function. However, with state dependent utility functions this is no longer so. The reason is that a positive or negative correlation between Z and the marginal utility of income now becomes an important factor. With positive correlation it may happen that

$$E\big(U(Z)\big) > E\big(U(\bar{Z})\big). \tag{2.2.3}$$

However, this possibility of correlation between marginal utility of income and income has hardly anything to do with common sense interpretation of risk aversion. Therefore, our definition of risk aversion is modified as follows.

DEFINITION. An individual is risk averse if

$$E\left(U(Z) - U(\overline{Z})\right) \leqslant 0 \tag{2.2.4}$$

for all distributions of Z and U provided that they are independently distributed.

It is now easy to see that the state contingent utility function of a risk averse individual must be concave in income and conversely, concave state contingent utility functions imply risk aversion.

In fact, with U and Z independently distributed, the definition can be written as a repeated expectation

$$E_U E_Z\left(U(Z) - U(\overline{Z})\right) \leqslant 0 \tag{2.2.5}$$

for all distributions of Z.

A necessary and sufficient condition for this is that for all states

$$E_Z\left(U(Z) - U(\overline{Z})\right) \leqslant Z. \tag{2.2.6}$$

Thus, we have the following theorem:

THEOREM. *An individual is risk averse if and only if his utility function is concave in all events.*

In what follows, we will generally assume that risk aversion characterizes the behavior of the individual and thus we will be using concave utility functions.[2]

We will in the next sections use the expected utility representation of preferences developed above in analyzing some environmental quality decision situation.

2.3. The value of changes in risk

Suppose that the different states are characterized by
- utility functions U^i,
- wealth W_i,
- environmental quality Q_i.

Moreover, there is a probability measure λ_i over the different states. Then, as we have seen, preferences can be represented by the expected utility

$$E_\lambda U^i(W_i, Q_i), \tag{2.3.1}$$

---

[2] Note that is the same result as Bohm (1975) claimed, although the motivation is different.

where E_λ indicates for which distribution the expectation is computed. Let us now consider the case when it is possible to change the probability distribution to λ' by, for example, environmental policy.[3] Then expected utility is

$$E_{\lambda'} U^i(W_i, Q_i). \tag{2.3.2}$$

Different welfare measures for the change in probability distribution can now be defined. The compensating variation CV and the equivalent variation EV are defined by

$$E_\lambda U^i(W_i, Q_i) = E_{\lambda'} U^i(W_i - CV, Q_i), \tag{2.3.3}$$

$$E_\lambda U^i(W_i + EV, Q_i) = E_{\lambda'} U^i(W_i, Q_i). \tag{2.3.4}$$

These measures have the usual interpretations. CV is the amount that can be taken away from the individual when the probability distribution changes. If $CV > 0$, then the change in the distribution has increased expected utility. EV is the amount that would increase expected utility by the same amount as would the change in the probability distribution. Both EV and CV are correct representations of the underlying preference structure and the choice between them is mainly a matter of convenience. Another alternative representation of the environmental change is possible, which implies the one just given, but is more convenient in some applications. Instead of representing the environmental change as a change in the probability distribution, one can look at it as a change in the characterization of each state. Assume then that each state is characterized by environmental quality Q_i so that expected utility is

$$\int U^i(W_i, Q_i) \, d\lambda_i. \tag{2.3.5}$$

Assume now that the environmental quality changes in each state by ΔQ_i so that

$$Q_i' = Q_i + \Delta Q_i. \tag{2.3.6}$$

The expected utility is now

$$\int U^i(W_i, Q_i') \, d\lambda_i. \tag{2.3.7}$$

It can be proved that provided certain conditions hold, there is a probability distribution λ' such that

$$\int U^i(W_i, Q_i + \Delta Q_i) \, d\lambda_i' = \int U^i(W_i, Q_i) \, d\lambda_i. \tag{2.3.8}$$

With this new representation CV and EV are defined by

$$E_\lambda U^i(W_i, Q_i) = E_\lambda U^i(W_i - CV, Q_i'), \tag{2.3.9}$$

---

[3] See Appendix A for a proof that these two representations of changes in environmental policy (that is change in Q and change in λ) are equivalent.

and

$$E_\lambda U^i(W_i + EV, Q_i) = E_\lambda U(W, Q_i'). \tag{2.3.10}$$

The interpretation is exactly the same as the one given above. We will in the sequel only study CV. Define the compensating variation CV_i contingent upon the occurrence of state i as

$$U^i(W_i, Q_i) = U^i(W_i - CV_i, Q_i').$$

We will now try to relate CV to the expected value of CV_i. We have from the definitions

$$E_\lambda U^i(W_i - CV, Q_i') = E_\lambda U^i(W_i, Q_i) = E_\lambda U^i(W_i - CV_i, Q_i'). \tag{2.3.11}$$

By making a quadratic expansion around $\overline{W} - CV$ and Q', where $W = E_\lambda W_i$ and subscripts denote partial derivatives, we have

$$E_\lambda \left\{ U^i + (W_i - \overline{W})U_W^i + \frac{1}{2}(W_i - \overline{W})^2 U_{WW}^i \right\}$$

$$= E_\lambda \left\{ U^i + (W_i - \overline{W} - CV_i + CV)U_W^i \right.$$

$$\left. + \frac{1}{2}(W_i - \overline{W} - CV_i + CV)^2 U_{WW}^i \right\}. \tag{2.3.12}$$

Define
- $\overline{CV} = E_\lambda CV_i$,
- $\mathrm{var}(CV_i) = E_\lambda(CV_i - \overline{CV})^2$,
- $\overline{U}_W = E_\lambda U_W^i(\overline{W} - CV, Q_i')$,
- $\mathrm{cov}(CV_i, U_W^i) = E_\lambda \{(CV_i - \overline{CV})(U_W^i - \overline{U}_W)\}$,
- $\mathrm{cov}(CV_i, W_i) = E_\lambda \{(CV_i - \overline{CV})(W_i - \overline{W})\}$.

Let us for simplicity assume that $(CV_i - \overline{CV})$ is so small that $(CV_i - \overline{CV})^2$ can be neglected in expressions containing $(CV_i - \overline{CV})$ (otherwise we have to solve a quadratic equation yielding complicated messy formulas but essentially the same qualitative conclusions). Then we obtain the desired relation between the expected state contingent compensated variations and the compensated variation CV:

$$CV = \overline{CV} + \frac{\mathrm{cov}(CV_i, U_W^i)}{\overline{U}_W}$$

$$- \frac{1}{2} E_\lambda \left\{ \frac{U_{WW}^i}{\overline{U}_W} [(CV_i - \overline{CV})^2 + 2(CV_i - \overline{CV})(W_i - \overline{W})] \right\}. \tag{2.3.13}$$

If we can assume that U_{WW} is state independent, the factor $-\frac{U_{WW}^i}{\overline{U}_W}$ can be identified as the Arrow–Pratt measure R of absolute risk aversion. Then

$$CV = \overline{CV} + \frac{\mathrm{cov}(CV_i, U_W^i)}{\overline{U}_W} + \frac{1}{2} R\{\mathrm{var}(CV_i) + 2\,\mathrm{cov}(CV_i, W_i)\}. \tag{2.3.14}$$

This is our basic expression for the value of the change in environmental quality. It is based on a set of not too restrictive assumptions.

2.4. Aggregation over individuals

In general, we are not interested, however, in the individual compensating variation but in the aggregate over the relevant population.[4] Let the population be represented by the set H and denote variables for the individual with a superscript h.

It may happen that the individual state contingent values CV_i^h are dependent on the size of the population. If, for example, the total benefits are independent of the population size, then the individual benefits will on average decrease with increasing size. Even if the benefits are of a public goods nature, congestion may decrease the individual benefits if the number of users increases. Only when we have a pure public good without congestion will the individual compensating variations be independent of the size of population sharing the benefits.

Let therefore H be the measure of the set H (this double use of the letter H will not cause any confusion) and assume that CV_i^h is a function of H $CV_i^h(H)$. In general we would expect this to be a decreasing function, but with positive externalities it may in fact be increasing.

The total compensating variation is now (CV will now denote the total compensating variation over the whole population and similarly for $\overline{CV}^h$ and $\overline{CV}$)

$$CV = \int_H CV^h \, dh = \int_H \overline{CV}^h \, dh + \int_H \frac{\mathrm{cov}(CV_i^h, U_W^{ih})}{\overline{U}_W^h} \, dh$$

$$+ \frac{1}{2} \int_H R\{\mathrm{var}(CV_i^h) + 2\,\mathrm{cov}(CV_i^h, W_i^h)\} \, dh. \tag{2.4.1}$$

Let us investigate the three terms in this expression. The first is

$$\int_H \overline{CV}^h \, dh = \overline{CV}, \tag{2.4.2}$$

which obviously is the aggregated expected state contingent benefits. The second term is

$$\int_H \frac{\mathrm{cov}(CV_i^h, U_W^{ih})}{\overline{U}_W^h} \, dh. \tag{2.4.3}$$

The reason for this term is of course that the marginal utility of income is contingent on the state, and the utility value of the monetary benefits CV_i^h depends on the marginal utility of income. If CV_i^h and U_i^h are independently distributed for each individual h,

---

[4] We will not introduce a full fledged social welfare function as it would increase the complexity of the following formulas.

then this term will vanish. We will in the next section see some examples where such an independence assumption may be reasonable.

Let

$$v^{ih} = \frac{U^{hi}}{\overline{U}^h_W},$$
(2.4.4)

$$\overline{CV}_i = \int_H CV_i^h \, dh,$$
(2.4.5)

$$\overline{v}^i = \int_H v^{ih} \, dh,$$
(2.4.6)

and note that $\int v^{ih} \, d\lambda_i = 1$.

The second term can now be written

$$\int_H \frac{\text{cov}(CV_i^h, U_W^{ih})}{\overline{U}^h_W} \, dh = \int_H \int (CV_i^h - \overline{CV}^h)(v^{ih} - 1) \, d\lambda_i \, dh$$

$$= \int\int CV_i^h v^{ih} \, d\lambda_i \, dh - H\overline{CV}$$

$$= \int\int (CV_i^h - \overline{CV}^h)(v^{ih} - \overline{v}^i) \, d\lambda_i \, dh$$

$$+ \int \overline{CV}_i(\overline{v}^i - 1) \, d\lambda_i.$$
(2.4.7)

The mean value theorem gives an i' such that the last term becomes

$$\overline{CV}_i(\overline{v}^{i'} - 1).$$
(2.4.8)

If $\overline{CV}_i$ and $\overline{v}_i$ are distributed sufficiently symmetrically,

$$\overline{v}^{i'} \sim 1,$$
(2.4.9)

and the expression in (2.4.7) becomes

$$H \, \text{cov}(CV_i, v^i).$$
(2.4.10)

This covariance term characterizes for each state the covariance between the benefits and the marginal utility of income over different individuals. If it can be assumed that different individuals are independent of each other in this respect, the covariance becomes zero and the term

$$\int\int \text{cov}(CV_i^h v^{ih}) \, d\lambda_i \, dh$$
(2.4.11)

vanishes although the covariance for each individual may be different from zero.

On the other hand, if there is a nonzero covariance over individuals, the term cannot be neglected. This may happen if the variations in benefits and marginal utility of income have a common cause, for example, random changes in a certain price. We will look into this later.

There remains the third term,

$$\frac{1}{2} \int R^h \left(\text{var}(CV_i^h) + 2 \text{cov}(CV_i^h, W_i^h) \right) dh. \tag{2.4.12}$$

Obviously, this term represents the cost of bearing the risk of variations in CV_i^h. The following factors influence the size and sign of this term: the covariance between CV_i^h and W_i^h, the variance of CV_i^h the degree of risk aversion, and the joint distribution of these variables over states and individuals.

The next section will be devoted to a discussion of the cost of risk bearing and mechanisms for risk sharing.

2.5. The cost of risk bearing

Assume that utility functions are identical in all states. As in the previous section, the cost for individual h of bearing the risk is

$$-\frac{1}{2} \frac{U_{WW}^h}{\overline{U}_W^h} \left\{ \text{var}(CV_i^h) + 2 \text{cov}(CV_i^h, W_i^h) \right\}. \tag{2.5.1}$$

When will this cost be positive, negative or zero?

(i) $R^h = -\frac{U_{WW}^h}{\overline{U}_W^h} = 0$, that if the individual is risk neutral, the cost of risk bearing is zero. However, we will assume this is not the case, that is $R^h > 0$.

(ii) If the bracket $\text{var}(CV_i^h) + 2 \text{cov}(CV_i^h, W_i^h) = 0$ then the cost is also zero. This can happen if the environmental change generates benefits that are essentially independent of income. If the bracket is negative, then the environmental change will act as an insurance and $CV^h < \overline{CV}^h$ and vice versa if the bracket is positive.

Let us now go back to the aggregate cost of risk bearing and consider different mechanisms for allocating the risk.

(A) One mechanism would be to have no risk sharing at all. In that case the social cost of bearing the risk is

$$\frac{1}{2} \int_H R^h \left\{ \text{var } CV_i^h + 2 \text{cov}(CV_i^h, W_i^h) \right\} dh.$$

If all individuals have the same absolute risk aversion and if the joint distribution of benefits and wealth is the product of distributions over individuals and states respectively, i.e., if for all h CV_i^h and W_i^h are independent random variables, the aggregate cost is

$$\frac{1}{2} R \left\{ \overline{CV}_i + 2 \text{cov} \int_H \text{cov}(CV_i^h, W_i^h) \, dh \right\}.$$

Depending on the distribution of covariance over the individuals, this aggregate cost may be positive, zero or negative.

(B) If the risks are "individual risks" in Malinvaud's meaning,[5] the aggregate cost above will be approximately zero because the covariance term vanishes. Thus, society should behave in a risk neutral manner, and could achieve that by implementing an insurance scheme. An insurance scheme which is actuarially fair can be described as a measurable function x^h such that $E_\lambda x^h = 0$. If each consumer chooses the insurance that is best for her, we will have as a result that $\partial U_i / \partial W^h$ is equal across all states. The gain from the optimal insurance $x \bar{x}^h$ for individual h is given by

$$E_\lambda U^h \left(W^h + \bar{x}^h, Q' \right) - E_\lambda U^h \left(W^h, Q' \right) \approx \frac{1}{2} R^h \, \text{var}\left(x^h \right) \bar{U}_W^h.$$

Thus, the variance term in the expression for CV corresponds to the premium an individual is willing to pay for an insurance that will eliminate the uncertainty. However, such a complete insurance system seems unrealistic in view of the serious problems of moral hazard due to the stochastic nature of preferences. Only if the uncertainty of the preferences is due to an objectively measurable variable can the moral hazard problem be overcome. We will in the next section find a case where such an insurance scheme exists, although not completely.

(C) Let us now assume that individual benefits are highly correlated. Suppose for simplicity that the set H is finite $H = \{1, 2, \ldots, H\}$ and that individual benefits CV_i^h are constrained by

$$\sum_{h=1}^{H} CV_i^h = Y_i(H),$$

where $Y_i(H)$ is the total benefits in state i. We will see that the assumption that Y_i depends on H is crucial for the results we will derive. Suppose total welfare can be written[6]

$$\int \sum_{h=1}^{H} \beta^h U^h \left(W_i^h + CV_i^h, Q_i \right) d\lambda_i.$$

Assuming that lump sum transfers are feasible in each state, the optimal allocation of the total benefits in each state among the individuals is given by

$$\max \sum_{h=1}^{H} \beta^h U^h \left(W_i^h + CV_i^h, Q_i \right), \quad \text{s.t.} \quad \sum_{h=1}^{H} CV_i^h = Y_i(H).$$

---

[5] Malinvaud (1972).

[6] This is not necessary for the analysis. Any assumption that keeps the individual small compared to the total income would give the same result, for example, if the total benefits are distributed so that $CV_i^h = \beta^h CV_i$ would yield the same result.

The necessary conditions are

$$\beta^h U^h_{W_i} - \mu = 0,$$

where μ is a Lagrange multiplier. The maximum value of the objective function is denoted $V(Y_i(H), Q_i)$. Note that V will not directly depend on the state. The maximum of the objective function in the original problem can now be written

$$\max \int V\big(Y_i(H), Q_i\big) \, d\lambda_i.$$

Let the Arrow–Pratt measure of absolute risk aversion R_V be defined as

$$R_V = -\frac{V''}{V'}.$$

We know that $V' = \mu$ for all Y and thus,

$$V'' = \frac{d\mu}{dY}.$$

Differentiation of $\beta^h U^h_W = 0$ yields

$$V'' = \frac{U^h_W}{\sum_{h=1}^{H} \frac{1}{\beta^h}}.$$

Thus,

$$R_V = -\frac{U^h_{WW}}{\beta^h \sum_j \frac{1}{\beta^j} U^j_W}.$$

Let $\frac{1}{\beta^k} U^k_W = \min_j \frac{1}{\beta^j} U^j_W$. Then

$$R_V \leqslant -\frac{U^h_{WW}}{\beta^h H \frac{1}{\beta^k} U^k_W} = \frac{1}{H} \frac{\beta^k}{\beta^h} \left[-\frac{U^h_{WW}}{U^k_W} \right] \quad \text{for all } h. \tag{2.5.2}$$

Choose $h = k$ and denote that the individual measure of absolute risk aversion is R_U,

$$R_U = -\frac{U^k_{WW}}{U^k_W}, \tag{2.5.3}$$

and so

$$R_V \leqslant \frac{1}{H} \frac{1}{R_U}. \tag{2.5.4}$$

With increasing size of the population the Arrow–Pratt measure of social risk aversion will therefore go to zero.

The social cost of risk bearing is now

$$\frac{1}{2} \frac{1}{H} \big\{ \mathrm{var}\big(Y_i(H)\big) + 2 \, \mathrm{cov}\big(Y_i(H), W_i(H)\big) \big\}. \tag{2.5.5}$$

(i) If the environmental asset is a pure public good[7] without congestion

$$Y_i(H) = HY_i, \tag{2.5.6}$$

then the social cost of risk bearing is

$$\frac{1}{2} R_U H \{ \text{var}(Y_i) + 2 \, \text{cov}(Y_i, W_i) \}. \tag{2.5.7}$$

In this case, an increase in population will increase the total cost of risk bearing.[7]

(ii) If the asset generates purely private benefits

$$Y_i(H) = Y_i, $$

then the cost of risk bearing is

$$\frac{1}{2} \frac{1}{H} R_U \{ \text{var}(Y_i) + 2 \, \text{cov}(Y_i, W_i) \}. \tag{2.5.8}$$

First, if Y_i and W_i are independent, it follows that the cost of risk tends to zero when the number of individuals sharing the risk increases.[8] If $W_i(H)$ is independent of H, then the cost of risk bearing also tends to zero with the number of individuals sharing the risk. If there are decreasing marginal returns with respect to H, so that $W_i(H)$ is decreasing, the same result obtains.

(iii) In the general case, if both

$$\frac{Y_i(H)}{\sqrt{H}} \quad \text{and} \quad \frac{W_i(H)}{\sqrt{H}}$$

go to zero with increasing H, the cost of risk bearing will be smaller the larger the population is. The importance of this is obvious. Even if insurance markets cannot work because of the correlation of the risks individuals are bearing, it is thus possible to reduce that cost in certain cases by letting more people bear the risk.

2.6. Option prices and option values

Let us apply the theory developed in the last sections to the valuation of a natural asset. Consider the example provided by Schmalensee (1972), i.e., the possible development of Yellowstone National Park which would irreversibly destroy its unique features. The environmental variable Q can in this case assume two values, Q' corresponding to preservation of the National Park and Q'' corresponding to irreversible destruction. Uncertainty comes partly from income uncertainty $\{W_i^h\}$ and partly from preference or utility uncertainty $\{U_i^h\}$.

---

[7] This is due to Fisher (1973).
[8] This result was derived in Arrow and Lind (1972).

CV^h is defined from

$$EU_i^h\left(W_i^h - CV^h, Q'\right) = EU_i^h\left(W_i^h, Q''\right). \tag{2.6.1}$$

CV^h is known as the option price, i.e., the price the individual is willing to pay for keeping the option of going to Yellowstone in the future. The state contingent benefits from preserving the option, CV_i^h, is defined from

$$U_i^h\left(W_i^h - CV_i^h, Q'\right) = U_i^h\left(W_i^h, Q''\right). \tag{2.6.2}$$

From the previous sections we know that

$$CV^h = \overline{CV}^h + \frac{\text{cov}(CV_i^h, U_{i,W}^h)}{\overline{U}_W^h}$$
$$+ \frac{1}{2}R^h\left\{\text{var}\left(CV_i^h\right) + 2\,\text{cov}\left(CV_i^h, W_i^h\right)\right\}. \tag{2.6.3}$$

The difference between CV^h and $\overline{CV}^h$ is known as the option value OV^h,

$$OV^h = CV^h - \overline{CV}^h \tag{2.6.4}$$

and a substantial discussion has taken place in the literature whether the option value is positive or negative.[9] It is clear from the formula above that the option value may be of either sign. However, it is at least possible to outline the factors influencing the size and sign of the option value.

The first term

$$\frac{\text{cov}(CV_i^h, U_{i,W}^h)}{\overline{U}_W^h} \tag{2.6.5}$$

reflects the collinearity between CV_i^h and U_i^h. If the natural asset is not considered of high importance by the individual (i.e., it not would occupy a big share of her budget if she would have to pay for it), it is hard to see why random variations in the marginal utility of income should be of importance. Thus, this term should be small. Moreover, as we saw in the previous section, if we aggregate over individuals and if CV_i^h, and $U_{i,W}^h$ are distributed independently for each state i over individuals, the aggregate will be close to zero. Thus, there seem to be reasons to assume that this term is negligible. The last term

$$\frac{1}{2}R^h\left\{\text{var}\left(CV_i^h\right) + 2\,\text{cov}\left(CV_i^h, W_i^h\right)\right\}$$

is, on the other hand, more interesting. Obviously, it is impossible to say anything in general about the sign and size of this term. However, for some particular cases, some conclusions may be drawn.

[9] See Bohm (1975), Schmalensee (1972), Krutilla et al. (1972).

(i) If the uncertainty about future preferences is in a sense genuine, knowledge about future income would not increase our ability to predict future benefits. Thus CV_i^h and W_i^h will not be correlated for any individual and the term simplifies to

$$\frac{1}{2} R^h \operatorname{var}(CV_i^h),$$

which obviously is positive. In this case risk aversion will imply a positive option value. This is probably the case that corresponds most closely to the problem discussed by Weisbrod (1964) and Cicchetti and Freeman (1971).

(ii) The uncertainty about future preferences may be due to uncertainty about some economic variable not explicitly in the utility function. If the natural asset is a recreational facility and if high future oil prices shift recreational demand from foreign facilities to the domestic asset and vice versa, it is reasonable to assume that CV_i^h and W_i^h are negatively correlated. Thus, the risk premium term for the individual in that case

$$\frac{1}{2} R^h \left\{ \operatorname{var}(CV_i^h) + 2 \operatorname{cov}(CV_i^h, W_i^h) \right\} \tag{2.6.6}$$

may have either sign depending on whether the second term dominates the first or not. It may therefore happen that the individual has a positive option value. However, from the point of view of society, if the recreational asset is such that $\overline{CV}_i$ increases less than in proportion with the size of the population, the term $\frac{1}{H}\overline{CV}$ will be small and the covariance term will dominate.

Thus, even if the individual has a positive option value, society may, in spite of this, have a negative option value. The reason for this is that the risk component corresponding to the variance can be better shared through society and the remaining risk component is essentially an insurance against the future oil prices. In particular, this implies that investments in this facility should be discounted with a negative risk premium. Of course, if the facility is a pure public good with no congestion, then this result does not hold, and the risk term for society is simply the individual risk premium multiplied with the size of the population.

2.7. Price uncertainty

Let us introduce the interest rate r as a variable in the indirect utility function and let us also assume that r is a stochastic variable. We will also neglect the many consumers case and instead assume that the utility represents social utility. The utility function is now

$$U_i(W_i, r, Q_i), \tag{2.7.1}$$

where i as previously represent the state of the world. We can now go through the same kind of exercise as we have done in previous sections in order to derive approximations to the true CV. The result is under essentially the same assumptions as before

$$CV = \overline{CV} + \frac{\text{cov}(CV_i, U_{i,W})}{\overline{U}_W} + \frac{1}{2}R\{\text{var}(CV_i) + 2\,\text{cov}(W_i, CV_i)\}$$

$$- \frac{U_{r,W}}{\overline{U}_W}\,\text{cov}(r, CV_i),\tag{2.7.2}$$

where $U_{r,W} = \partial^2 U/\partial r\,\partial W$ has been assumed state independent. We will assume that $U_{r,W} < 0$, that is, an increase in the price r will reduce the marginal utility of wealth. It is interesting to note that even if the individual is risk neutral so that the utility function is linear in wealth, the last term may be different from zero. In the simple case when preferences are state independent and represent risk neutral behavior we would have

$$CV = \overline{CV} - \frac{U_{r,W}}{\overline{U}_W}\,\text{cov}(r_i, CV_i).\tag{2.7.3}$$

Thus, the possible correlation between on the one hand the state contingent benefits CV_i and the price (or the interest rate) will create a difference between the expected benefits $\overline{CV}$ and the true benefits CV. Is such a correlation to be expected? Should not the covariance between state contingent compensation variations and the interest rate be zero in general? The interest rate will either reflect the desired trade-off between consumption in different time periods or the future marginal productivity of capital. In the latter case, the interpretation is that the interest rate gives an indication of the necessary capital investment today in order to increase consumption with one unit in a future time period. But the future marginal productivity of capital will in general be influenced of the availability of natural resources. An increase in the availability of resources will in general increase the expected future productivity and thereby the interest rate. If we are analyzing a project with large environmental consequences, not only will the cost be large and state contingent benefits small because of that, but the interest rate will be small in the states that correspond to small benefits. Thus we should expect a negative covariance between CV and r. This means that, even in the absence of risk aversion and with state independent preferences, will the true benefit be smaller than the expected compensating variation. The covariance between interest rate and the benefits will thus acts as if the decision maker is risk avert. Another way of seeing that is to look at the following formula for the present value of a current project with future environmental consequences.

$$NB_0 = C_0 - \frac{C_1}{1+r},\tag{2.7.4}$$

where C_0 is the present benefit, C_1 is the future cost from environmental degradation, r is the interest rate, and NB_0 is the present value of the net benefits. Assume C_1 and r are stochastic variables and assume that the decision-maker is risk neutral. The standard procedure is to calculate the number

$$C_0 - \frac{\overline{C}_1}{1+\overline{r}},\tag{2.7.5}$$

where $\bar{C}_1$ and $\bar{r}$ are the expected values of C_1 and r. The expected value of NB_0 is, however,

$$E(NB_0) = C_0 - E\frac{C_1}{1+r} \cong C_0 - E\{C_1(1-r)\}$$

$$\cong C_0 + \frac{\bar{C}_1}{1+\bar{r}} - \text{cov}(r, C_1). \tag{2.7.6}$$

Once again, we see that the covariance between r and C_1 will affect the expected net benefits and with a positive correlation between r and C_1, the expected net benefit will be less that what would be calculated with the conventional practice.

3. Intertemporal resolution of uncertainty

3.1. Introduction

We consider the following situation. Assume a project is designed that will include the use of a particular environmental resource over several time periods. However, the value of this resource in future periods is not known with certainty. There is a possibility that information on these values may be generated over time. What is the appropriate decision-making framework? In most analyses of uncertainty of future environmental resource use, especially empirical applications, the information structure has been very simple. All information is (assumed to be) contained in an a priori probability distribution with no more coming available at a later stage. For some applications, this may be a realistic assumption. Alternatively, if the decision to use a natural asset in a special way can be completely (and costlessly) reversed at a later stage, the prospect of getting more information in the future does not have to be included in the analysis. In this case there are no essential intertemporal connections. In the other extreme when the decision is completely irreversible, the prospect of better information may be quite important, as we shall show in this section. Before proceeding, we need to consider further the concept of irreversibility in the setting of environmental decisions. There are three issues here: (1) are the consequences of a decision irreversible? (2) will information about the environmental values be forthcoming in the future? and (3) how should the prospect of this information be taken into account in a decision to be made in the present, or the first period? We offer a few remarks on the first. On the assumption that the answer to the second may be "yes," the third is the subject of the subsequent analysis in both this section and the next.

As suggested in the introduction to this chapter, environmental impacts of an investment in resource development can be long lasting, or even irreversible. This is a feature of environmental valuation and decision problems that has received a great deal of attention in the literature, based on findings in the natural sciences. For example, there is both scientific and popular concern today about loss of biodiversity, the genetic information that is potentially valuable in medicine, agriculture, and other productive activities. Much of the concern is for endangered species, or the habitats such as tropical moist forests that are subject to more or less irreversible conversion to other uses. But even if species survival is not at issue, biological impacts can be very difficult to reverse over any relevant time span. The clear-cutting of a climax forest species, for example, removes the results of an ecological succession that may represent centuries of natural processes. Regeneration may not lead to the original configuration, as opportunistic species such as hardy grasses come in and preempt the niche otherwise filled by the climax species [Albers and Goldbach (2000)].

Irreversibilities have also been identified as a key feature of the problem of how to respond to potential impacts of climate change. Emissions of greenhouse gases, in particular carbon dioxide, accumulate in the atmosphere and decay only slowly. According to one calculation, assuming business-as-usual use of fossil fuels over the next several decades, after a thousand years carbon dioxide concentrations will still be well over twice the current level, and nearly three times the pre-industrial level – and will remain elevated for many thousands of years [Schultz and Kasting (1997)]. There is also some prospect of essentially irreversible catastrophic impact as would result, for example, from the disintegration of the West Antarctic Ice Sheet and consequent rise in sea level of 15–20 feet. Recent findings suggest that this possibility is more serious, and perhaps closer in time, than economists (and others) have realized [de Angelis and Skvarca (2003)].

On a less grand scale, studies of the dynamics of ecosystems have uncovered positive feedbacks, which give rise to multiple equilibria. Movements from one such equilibrium to another will almost always be characterized by hysteresis and frequently by irreversibility, as illustrated in several cases discussed by Dasgupta and Mäler (2004).

Although we have been speaking of costs and benefits experienced over several periods, the analysis in this section will focus on two-period models. These are sufficient to develop many of the main results on the temporal resolution of uncertainty (though an empirical application we shall discuss is based on a three-period model, a straightforward extension of the two-period model in the next subsection). Section 4 develops more formally the multi-period and continuous-time cases, along with another empirical application based on results there.

3.2. A simple two-period model

Consider the problem, originally studied by Arrow and Fisher (1974) and Henry (1974a, 1974b), as set out in Fisher and Hanemann (1986), of choosing whether to preserve or develop a tract of land in each of two periods, present and future. The development, we assume, is irreversible. Future benefits of development and preservation are uncertain, but we learn about them with the passage of time. In this simplest case, we assume that the uncertainty about future benefits is resolved at the start of the second period.

Let the benefit from first-period development, net of environmental costs (the benefits of preservation), be $B_1(d_1)$, where d_1, the level of development in period 1, can be zero or one. The present value of the benefit from second-period development is $B_2(d_1 +$

d_2, θ), where d_2 can be zero or one and θ is a random variable. Note that, if $d_1 = 1$, $d_2 = 0$.

We want the first-period decision to be consistent with maximization of expected benefits over both periods. If benefits are measured in utility units, then this is equivalent to expected-utility maximization. But we can allow benefits to be measured in money units so that the results we shall obtain do not depend on risk aversion.

Let $\widehat{V}(d_1)$ be the expected value over both periods as a function of the choice of first-period development ($d_1 = 0$ or $d_1 = 1$) given that d_2 is chosen to maximize benefits in the second period. Then, we have, for $d_1 = 0$,

$$\widehat{V}(0) = B_1(0) + E\left[\max_{d_2}\{B_2(0, \theta), B_2(1, \theta)\}\right]. \tag{3.2.1}$$

Second-period development, d_2, is chosen at the start of the second period when we learn whether or not $d_2 = 0$ or $d_2 = 1$ yields greater benefits. At the start of the first period, when d_1 must be chosen, we have only an expectation, $E[\cdot]$, of the maximum.

If $d_1 = 1$, we have

$$\widehat{V}(1) = B_1(1) + E\left[B_2(1, \theta)\right]. \tag{3.2.2}$$

With development in the first period, we are locked into development in the second ($d_1 = 1 \Rightarrow (d_1 + d_2) = 1$). To get the decision rule for the first period, $\hat{d}_1$, compare:

$$\widehat{V}(0) - \widehat{V}(1) = B_1(0) - B_1(1) + E\left[\max_{d_2}\{B_2(0, \theta), B_2(1, \theta)\}\right]$$
$$- E\left[B_2(1, \theta)\right], \tag{3.2.3}$$

and choose

$$\hat{d}_1 = \begin{cases} 0 & \text{if } \widehat{V}(0) - \widehat{V}(1) \geqslant 0, \\ 1 & \text{if } \widehat{V}(0) - \widehat{V}(1) < 0. \end{cases} \tag{3.2.4}$$

Now, let us suppose that, instead of waiting for the resolution of uncertainty about future benefits before choosing d_2, we simply replace the uncertain future benefits by their expected value. This would be appropriate if we did not expect to receive information, over the first period, that would permit us to resolve the uncertainty. In this case, the expected value over both periods, for $d_1 = 0$, is

$$V^*(0) = B_1(0) + \max_{d_2}\{E\left[B_2(0, \theta)\right], E\left[B_2(1, \theta)\right]\}. \tag{3.2.5}$$

Second-period development, d_2, is in effect chosen in the first period, to maximize expected benefits in the second period, because we do not assume that further information about second-period benefits will be forthcoming before the start of the second period. For $d_1 = 1$,

$$V^*(1) = B_1(1) + E\left[B_2(1, \theta)\right]. \tag{3.2.6}$$

As before, development in the first period locks in development in the second.

Comparing (3.2.5) and (3.2.6),

$$V^*(0) - V^*(1) = B_1(0) - B_1(1) + \max_{d_2}\{E[B_2(0, \theta)], E[B_2(1, \theta)]\}$$

$$- E[B_2(1, \theta)], \tag{3.2.7}$$

and

$$d_1^* = \begin{cases} 0 & \text{if } V^*(0) - V^*(1) \geq 0, \\ 1 & \text{if } V^*(0) - V^*(1) < 0. \end{cases} \tag{3.2.8}$$

How do the decision rules in (3.2.4) and (3.2.8) compare? First, notice that

$$[\widehat{V}(0) - \widehat{V}(1)] - [V^*(0) - V^*(1)] = \widehat{V}(0) - V^*(0), \tag{3.2.9}$$

since $\widehat{V}(1) = V^*(1)$. Then,

$$\widehat{V}(0) - V^*(0) = E\left[\max_{d_2}\{B_2(0, \theta), B_2(1, \theta)\}\right]$$

$$- \max_{d_2}\{E[B_2(0, \theta)], E[B_2(1, \theta)]\}. \tag{3.2.10}$$

Finally,

$$\widehat{V}(0) - V^*(0) \geq 0, \tag{3.2.11}$$

from the convexity of the maximum function and Jensen's inequality, which states that the expected value of a convex function of a random variable is greater than or equal to the convex function of the expected value of the random variable.[10]

It is this difference, $\widehat{V}(0) - V^*(0)$, that has been called option value in some of the environmental literature, or as in Arrow and Fisher (1974), quasi-option value. Note that option value in this formulation cannot be negative. It may also be interpreted as a (conditional) value of information: the value of information about future benefits *conditional* on retaining the option to preserve or develop in the future ($d_1 = 0$).

Another important result is that, from Equations (3.2.4), (3.2.8), and (3.2.11), we see that there will be cases in which development is optimally undertaken in the first period in the no-information ("star") scenario, but not in the new-information ("hat") scenario. However, the reverse cannot occur, that is, there will be no cases in which first period development is optimal with the prospect of future information, but not with the prospect of no information. In other words, current development is less likely with the prospect that information about uncertain environmental values will be forthcoming in the future. In the next section this result, along with the potential significance of option value, is illustrated in an empirical application to the choice of development alternatives in a forested region of Thailand.

---

[10] A proof of the convexity of the maximum function is given in Albers, Fisher and Hanemann (1996).

3.3. An empirical application: to develop or to preserve

Most applied benefit-cost analyses of environmental decision problems of course employ the "open-loop" formulation in which random variables are simply replaced by their expected values, the "star" scenario considered above. More sophisticated decision analyses, based on a "closed-loop" approach, in which the agent takes into account the prospect of new information, are however beginning to emerge in the literature (the "hat" scenario). An example is the analysis of implications of uncertainty and irreversibility for valuation and management of a tract of tropical forest land in Thailand, by Albers, Fisher and Hanemann (1996). The problem is specified as one of allocating the forest among three competing uses, P (for preservation), M (for intermediate uses), and D (for development), over three periods, to maximize the expected benefits of use. The pattern of feasible sequences of uses is displayed in Figure 1. Note the greater complexity than in the two-use, two-period model, which involves just three feasible sequences: $P \rightarrow P$, $P \rightarrow D$, and $D \rightarrow D$. The analytical approach, and results, are however exactly analogous to those obtained in the simpler model.

If no information about future benefits is anticipated, the maximum expected present value associated with putting the forest tract to the preservation use in the first period is

$$V_P^* = P_0 + \max\{E[P_1] + \max\{E[P_2], E[M_2], E[D_2]\}, E[M_1]$$
$$+ \max\{E[M_2], E[D_2]\}, E[D_1] + E[D_2]\}, \tag{3.3.1}$$

where P_i, M_i, and D_i represent the benefits from preservation, intermediate uses, and development in period i and the expectation is with respect to the information set available in the first period. This expression is analogous to $V^*(0)$ in the two-period preservation vs. development problem. If, however, better information about future benefits and costs will be forthcoming, this affects not only future decisions that will be made on the basis of the information, but also the current decision, again as in the two-period problem. Specifically, Albers, Fisher and Hanemann (1996) assume that, at the start of each period, the decision-maker learns what the benefits of each of the alternative uses of the tract will be in that period (though not in future periods) and then chooses the highest-yielding alternative. In this formulation, the maximum expected present value associated with preservation in the first period is

$$\widehat{V}_P = P_0 + E\big[\max\{P_1 + \max\{P_2, M_2, D_2\}, M_1 + \max\{M_2, D_2\},$$
$$D_1 + D_2\}\big], \tag{3.3.2}$$

and

$$\widehat{V}_P - V_P^* = E\big[\max\{P_1 + \max\{P_2, M_2, D_2\}, M_1 + \max\{M_2, D_2\}, D_1 + D_2\}\big]$$
$$- \max\{E[P_1] + \max\{E[P_2], E[M_2], E[D_2]\}, E[M_1]\}$$
$$+ \max\{E[M_2], E[D_2], E[D_1] + E[D_2]\}$$
$$\geqslant 0, \tag{3.3.3}$$

again, as in the two-period model, from the convexity of the maximum function and application of Jensen's inequality. The difference, $\widehat{V} - V^*$, is option value. As we shall see, it turns out to be small, relative to the total value of the site, in this application, but to have a dramatic impact on optimal use in the first period.

The area studied is partly included in an existing park, Khao Yai National Park (KYNP), in central Thailand. The analysis divides KYNP into four management units or plots. The outer edge of the park, plot 1, has been encroached and begins in the use M. The inner plots, 2 and 3, begin in the preservation use P. The fourth zone, also in use P, is not currently protected by the park system but is under consideration for annexation.

The preservation benefits include erosion control, hydrologic functions, tourism, and extractive goods. Two states of the world define the uncertainty about future preservation benefits. The high state reflects the additional value that a viable population of Asian elephants creates in KYNP. High-state benefits grow at 2.5 percent per year. The low state reflects the possibility of a large drop-off in tourism revenue in the later periods. The high state occurs with a probability of 0.5 in the second period and 0.25 in the third period.

The intermediate uses, which we do not focus on here, include more intensive extractive activities and small scale shifting cultivation. The irreversible development option generates income through permanent agriculture and eucalyptus plantations. The agricultural values decline over time at a rate that corresponds to erosion-induced productivity declines on the fragile tropical soils. Following Tongpan et al. (1990), a 12-year investment horizon is assumed for the eucalyptus plantations. That 12-year plan, a function of rotation age, defines the length of the planning periods in the analysis.

The open-loop and closed-loop optimizations preserve markedly different amounts of KYNP. Both convert the degraded plot 1 to the development option due to its relatively small returns to preservation; convert plot 4 to intensive extractive goods and small-scale agriculture (the intermediate use M); and preserve plot 2. They differ, however, on plot 3. The open-loop optimization develops this plot and thereby reduces the amount of local parkland by half. The correct, closed-loop approach preserves this area and maintains the opportunity to take advantage of future information about preservation values.

The option value generated in this example constitutes 1.6 percent of the total value over the three periods in the closed-loop calculation. Despite its small size, this additional value creates a dramatic difference in the optimal land-use pattern. Moreover, there are reasons to believe that the option value in the example is understated. Option value will be larger in situations of uncertainty in near periods and in cases of large divergences in possible outcomes [Fisher and Hanemann (1986)]. The latter is probably important in the global valuation of tropical forests, given their potential, though uncertain, significance for biodiversity conservation and global climate control.

3.4. Some extensions of the Arrow–Fisher–Henry–Hanemann analysis

Now let us take up the agenda mentioned in the introduction to the chapter: relaxing implicit or explicit assumptions in a model like that presented in Section 3.2. We consider the following extensions:

- sharper definitions of the meaning of forthcoming information,
- more general benefit functions,
- active search for information instead of passively waiting for it,
- change that can be reversed at a cost,
- uncertainty about irreversibility,
- option value as a risk premium in the sense of Section 2, when there are irreversible changes.

3.5. Bayesian updating[11]

We will consider the following decision-making situation.[12] We are studying two time periods. In time period one a decision has to be made on variable X_1 and in time period two a decision on X_2. X_1 and X_2 can be thought of resource use. Once development has been made, it is impossible to restore the resource and therefore $X_1 \leqslant X_2$ (irreversibility constraint). The pay-off is given by the expected value of the utility function

$$U(X_1, X_2, Z), \tag{3.5.1}$$

where Z is a random variable.

When the decision is made in the first period, the only information on Z is an a priori probability distribution r. We assume that Z only can take a finite number of values, i.e., $Z = (Z_1, \ldots, Z_m)$ and the corresponding probabilities are $r = (r_1, \ldots, r_m)$.

After the decision on x_1 has been made, but before the decision on x_2 is made, the decision-maker gets a signal Y. Y is a random variable taking the values $(Y_1, \ldots, Y_n)$ with probabilities $q = (q_1, \ldots, q_n)$.

If Y and Z are perfectly correlated, the decision-maker knows with probability one which realization of Z will occur, but if Y and Z are independent, the signal Y gives no information at all on Z. In the general case, we know that the decision-maker will revise his probabilities according to Bayes' theorem.[13] Let be the conditional probability distribution of Z given the signal Y be

$$\pi_{i,j} = \Pr(Z = Z_i \mid Y = Y_j) = \frac{\Pr(Y = y_j \mid Z = z_i) r_i}{\sum_{k=1}^{m} \Pr(Y = y_j \mid Z = z_k)}. \tag{3.5.2}$$

---

[11] See Raiffa and Schlaifer (1960) for a very good introduction to Bayesian updating.

[12] This section is based on Epstein (1980).

[13] See Raiffa (1968) for an extremely well-written presentation of Bayesian decision-making. Raiffa and Schlaifer (1960) gives a more advanced discussion.

Let

$$\lambda_{j,i} = \Pr(Y = Y_j \mid Z = Z_i) \tag{3.5.3}$$

be the likelihoods. Then

$$\pi_{j,i} = \frac{r_i \lambda_{i,j}}{\sum_k r_k \lambda_{k,j}}. \tag{3.5.4}$$

Let $\Lambda = [\lambda_{j,i}]$ and $\Pi = [\pi_{i,j}]$.

Then we also have (for any matrix A, A^{T} means the transpose of A)

$$\Pi q = r, \tag{3.5.5}$$

and

$$r^{\mathrm{T}} \Lambda = q^{\mathrm{T}}. \tag{3.5.6}$$

3.6. Information structures

The signal Y is given within a given information structure defined by Y and the probabilities q and Λ. Another information structure, Y', is defined by $(Y'_1, \ldots, Y'_n)$, q', and Λ'. Obviously, if we have the same priors r, $\Pi q = \Pi' q' = r$ and $r^{\mathrm{T}} \Lambda' = q'$. Our decision-making problem can now be written

$$\max_{x_1} \sum_{j=1}^{m} q_j \max_{x_2} \sum_{i=1}^{n} \pi_{i,j} U(X_1, X_2, Z_i), \tag{3.6.1}$$

where X_1 and X_2 must of course be chosen within the feasibility sets. In analyzing this problem we follow Epstein (1980) in introducing a new notation. Let $\xi = [\xi_1, \ldots, \xi_n]$ such that $\xi_i \geqslant 0$ and $\sum_{i=1}^{n} \xi_i = 1$. Define

$$J(X_1, \xi) = \max_{x_2} \sum_i \xi_i U(X_1, X_2, Z_i). \tag{3.6.2}$$

J can be interpreted as the maximum expected utility from using X_1 in the first period, given the probability distribution ξ. We can then formulate the decision problem as follows:

$$\max_{X_1} \sum_j q_j J(X_1, \pi_j), \tag{3.6.3}$$

where π is the $j : t$ column of Π. Following Blackwell (1951) and Marschak and Miyasawa (1968), let us define the concept of "more informative."[14] Consider two information schemes Y and Y' corresponding to the same prior probability distribution. The corresponding posterior probabilities are π and π' and the probabilities for the signals are q and q' respectively. Y is defined to be more informative than Y' if and only

---

[14] See Appendix B for a different but equivalent definition of this concept.

if

$$\sum_j q_j J(X_1, \pi_j) \geqslant \sum_j q'_j J(X_1, \pi'_{i,j}) \tag{3.6.4}$$

for all X_1, all utility functions U, and all feasibility sets. Y more informative than Y' then means that independent of the initial choice of x_1 and the utility functions, Y will give a higher well-being, that is the signal Y enables us to achieve a higher well-being than signal Y'. In order to get a feeling of the meaning of this definition, let us consider two extreme cases:

(i) Y' means that $\pi'_{i,j} = r_i$, $j = 1, \ldots, m$, that is the signal Y' does not carry any new information.

(ii) Y'' implies perfect information, that is $m = n$ and

$$\pi''_{i,j} = \begin{cases} 0 & \text{if } i \neq j, \\ 1 & \text{if } i = j. \end{cases}$$

This shows that the signal reveals with certainty which z that will occur. Obviously $q = r$. If Y is an arbitrary information structure our intuition requires that Y' is more informative than Y which in turn should be more informative than Y'. That this is, indeed, the case is easily proved.

We first have

$$\pi'' q'' = \pi g = \pi' q' = r.$$

Then, from the definition of J it follows that J is convex in ξ (maximum of a linear function in X). Thus,

$$\sum_j q_j J(x_1, \pi_j) \geqslant J\left(x_1, \sum_j q_j \pi_j\right) = J(x_1, r) = J\left(x_1, \sum_j q'_j \pi'_j\right)$$

$$= \sum_j q'_j J(x_1, \pi_j)$$

for all U and X_1. Thus Y is more informative than Y'. Note that in this case, we have

$$\max_{x_1} q_j \max_{x_2} \sum_i \pi'_i U(x_1, x_2, z_i) = \max_{x_1} \sum_j q_j \max_i \sum_i r_i U(x_1, x_2, z)$$

$$= \max_{x_1, x_2} \sum_i r_i U(x_1, x_2, z_i),$$

that is, we maximize the unconditional expectation of the benefits, and no adjustments need to be done with respect to forthcoming information. We also have

$$\sum_{j=1}^m q''_j \max_{x_2} \sum_i \pi''_{i,j} U(x_1, x_2, z_i) = \sum_j q''_j \max U(x_1, x_2, z_j)$$

$$= \sum_i r_i \max_{x_2} U(x_1, x_2, z_i)$$

$$= \sum_j q_j \sum_i \pi_{i,j} \max_{x_2} U(x_1, x_2, z_i)$$

$$\leqslant \sum_j q_j \max_{x_2} \sum_i \pi_{i,j} U(x_1, x_2, z_i)$$

for all U and x_1 and for all feasibility sets. Thus Y'' is more informative than Y.

Another way of understanding the definition of being more informative than is to look at the case when

$$Z = Y + \delta,$$

where δ is the observation error. Assume that δ is normally distributed with zero mean and is independent of Z. It is now easy to demonstrate that if we are comparing two distributions of δ, the one with smaller variance is more informative than the other. Bradford and Keleian (1977) proved the following characterization of Y being more informative than Y'.

THEOREM. *Y is more informative than Y' if and only if for every convex function ρ on S^{m-1} ($S^{m-1} = \{\xi \in R^m; \xi_i \geqslant 0, \sum_i \xi_i = 1\}$)*

$$\sum_j q_j \rho(\pi_j) \leqslant \sum_j q'_j \rho(\pi'_j). \tag{3.6.5}$$

For a proof see Marschak and Miyasawa (1968).

3.7. Irreversibility

Using the characterization given by Marschak and Miyasawa (1968), Epstein (1980) proved the following theorem:

THEOREM. *Let $J(X_1, \xi)$ be concave in X_1. Assume Y is more informative than Y'. Let X_1^* and X_1^{**} maximize $\sum q_j J(x_1, \pi_j)$ resp. $\sum q'_j J(x_1, \pi'_j)$ where (q, π) and (q', π') correspond to information structures Y resp. Y'. If $\partial J/\partial x_1$ is concave (convex) in ξ it follows that $X_1^* \leqslant X_1^{**}$ ($X_1^* \geqslant X_1^{**}$).*

PROOF. The simple proof goes as follows: Let $J_{x_1} = \partial J/\partial x_1$ and let us assume that J_{X_1} is concave in ξ. Then

$$0 = \sum_j q_j J_{X_1}(X_1^*, \pi_j) = \sum_j q'_j J_{X_1}(X_1^{**}, \pi'_j) \leqslant \sum_j q'_j J_{X_1}(X_1^{**}, \pi'_j)$$

because of the assumption that Y is more informative than Y', the Marshak–Miyasawa theorem and that X_1^* and X_1^{**} are maximizers. Then, it follows that X similarly for the case when J_{X_1} is convex in ξ.   □

Note that convexity and concavity conditions are only sufficient conditions for the result! Furthermore, if π is different from π' and J_{X_1} is strictly concave, the weak inequalities will be replaced by strict inequalities. Using this theorem, Epstein further showed that

THEOREM. *Assume that X_1 can take only the values 0 and 1 or that $\sum_j q_j J(X_1, \xi)$ is linear in X_1 and $0 \leqslant X_1 \leqslant X_2 \leqslant 1$. Furthermore, assume the constraint X_1 (irreversibility). Then, if $X_1^{**} = 0$, it follows that $X_1^* = 0$.*

The first condition (X_1 can only take values 0 and 1) is already in Epstein (1980) and the second condition (that $\sum_j q_j J(X_1, \xi)$ is linear in X_1 is in Arrow and Fisher (1974)). Note that in both cases, X_1^* and X_1^{**} are either 0 or 1. As J is concave (convex) in X_1, J_{X_1} is nonincreasing (nondecreasing) and X

$$X_1 \leqslant X_1' \quad (X_1 \geqslant X_1').$$

It is now possible to use this theorem to derive results on the irreversibility effect.

In both cases X_1' and X_1'' are either 0 or 1. Suppose $X_1'' = 0$, and hence

$$\sum_{j=1}^{m} q_j'' J\left(0, \pi_j''\right) > \sum_j q_j'' J\left(1, \pi_j''\right).$$

As Y' is more informative than Y, we have

$$\sum_{j=1}^{m} q_j' J\left(0, \pi_j'\right) \geqslant \sum_j q_j'' J\left(0, \pi''\right).$$

Moreover, as the change is irreversible, that is $x_2 \geqslant x_1$,

$$\sum_j q_j'' J\left(1, \pi_{ij}''\right) = \sum_j \sum_i q_j'' \pi_{ij}'' U(1, 1, z_i)$$

$$= \sum_i r_i U(1, 1, z_i) = \sum_j \sum_i q_j' \pi_{i,j}' U(1, 1, z_i) = \sum_j q_j' J\left(1, \pi_i'\right).$$

Combining the above, we have

$$\sum_j q_j' J\left(0, \pi_j'\right) > \sum_j q_j' J\left(1, \pi_j'\right),$$

and $x_1' = 0$.

Note that the inequality $X_1 \leqslant X_2$ reflects an irreversibility in the decision. If a re-source use equal to x_1 has been decided, future resource use must be equal to or exceed this amount. Thus, if we are going to make an irreversible decision (building a hy-dropower plant, developing Yellowstone National Park to an industrial site, etc.), then the prospect of getting more information in the future on costs and benefits will not increase the benefits of undertaking the development now. However, this theorem was based on the assumption that the optimal value of x_1 is either 0 or 1. The theorem is not necessarily true if the assumptions yielding this are abandoned, unless other restrictions are introduced. Such restrictions apply to the net benefit or utility function. Assuming that the U function takes the special form

$$U(X_1, X_2, z_i) = U(X_1) + V(X_2, z_i),$$

where U and V are strict concave functions of X_1 and X_2 a corresponding result can be derived. We are thus considering the problem

$$\max_{X_1} \left\{ U(X_1) + \sum_j \max_{X_2 \geqslant X_1} \sum_i \pi_{ij} V(X_2, z_i) \right\}.$$

X_1 may be interpreted as the development in period 1, giving net benefits $U(X_1)$ and X_2 is the total development in the next period yielding the present value of the net benefits equal to $V(X_2, z_i)$. The irreversibility is expressed in the condition $X_2 \geqslant X_1$. The J function becomes

$$J(X_1, \xi) = \max_{X_2 \geqslant X_1} \sum_i \xi_i V(X_2, z_i).$$

Assume that $X_2'(X_1)$ solves this maximum problem, where X_2' is continuous and piece-wise differentiable. Then

$$J(X_1, \xi) = \max_{X_2 \geqslant X_1} \sum_i \xi_i V\big(X_2'(X_1), z_i\big).$$

Furthermore,

$$\frac{dX_2'}{dX_1} = \begin{cases} 0 & \text{if } X_2' > X_1, \\ 1 & \text{if } X_2' = X_1, \end{cases}$$

and therefore,

$$\frac{\partial J}{\partial X_1} = \sum_i \frac{\partial V(X_2', z_i)}{\partial X_{2i}} \frac{dX_2'}{dX_1} = \begin{cases} 0 & \text{if } X_2' > X_1, \\ \sum_i \xi_i \dfrac{\partial V}{\partial X_2'} & \text{if } X_2' = X_1. \end{cases}$$

Moreover, $X_2' > X_1$ if and only if

$$\sum_i \xi_i \frac{\partial V(X_2', z_i)}{\partial X_2} > 0.$$

Thus,

$$\frac{\partial J}{\partial X_1} = \min\left\{0, \sum_i \xi_i \frac{\partial V}{\partial X_2}\right\}.$$

As both terms in the bracket are concave, it follows that $\partial J/\partial X_1$ is concave in ξ. Then it follows from Epstein's theorem that

$$X_1' \leqslant X_1''.$$

We then have the following theorem;

THEOREM. *If $U(X_1, X_2, Z_i) = U(X_1) + V(X_2, Z_i)$ and $U(X_1)$ and $V(X_2, Z_i)$ are concave functions of X_1, and X_2, respectively, and if the optimal value for X_1 with information structure Y' is X_1' and with information structure Y is X_1'' where Y is more informative than Y'', then*

$$X_1' \leqslant X_1''.$$

Thus, a fairly general proposition has been established. If more information will be available in the future, "less" irreversible changes should be undertaken now.

3.8. Irreversibility at a cost

Let us now consider the case when it is possible to restore the development but at a cost. This means that we will replace the restriction $X_2 \geqslant X_1$ with a cost function for the measures that are necessary to make $X_1 \geqslant X_2$ feasible. If the decision in the first period is X_1, assume it is possible to restore the resource in the second period to $X_2 < X_1$ but at a cost given by the cost function $c(X_1, X_2)$ defined by

$$c(X_1, X_2) = \begin{cases} 0 & \text{if } X_1 \leqslant X_2, \\ \gamma(X_1 - X_2) & \text{if } X_1 > X_2 \end{cases} \tag{3.8.1}$$

with γ as a constant. Note that with this cost function, cost is a continuous function of the amount of restoration but the marginal cost is discontinuous at zero restoration. We will later look at a different formulation of the cost function. As in the previous section, we define the J-function (making the same intertemporal separability assumption as before) as

$$J(X_1, \xi) = \max_{X_2}\left\{\sum_i \xi_i V(X_2, z_i) - c(X_1, X_2)\right\}. \tag{3.8.2}$$

Define $\overline{X}_2$ from

$$\max_{X_2} \sum_i \xi_i V(X_2, Z_i) = \sum_i \xi_i V(\overline{X}_2, Z_i), \tag{3.8.3}$$

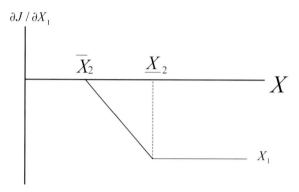

Figure 1.

that is, $\overline{X}_2 = \arg\max \sum_i \xi_i V(X_2, Z_i)$. Assume V is differentiable and define $\underline{X}_2$ from

$$\sum_i \xi_i \frac{\partial V(\underline{X}_2, Z_i)}{\partial X_2} + \frac{\partial c(X_1, \underline{X}_2)}{\partial X_2} = \sum_i \xi_i \frac{\partial V(\underline{X}_2, Z_i)}{\partial X_2} - \gamma = 0. \tag{3.8.4}$$

$\overline{X}_2$ is the upper bound for the set of X_1 at which no restoration will take place and $\underline{X}_2$ is similarly the lower bound for the set of X_1 at which restoration will take place.

As V is concave, it follows that $\underline{X}_2 < \overline{X}_2$. Let us now study the choice of optimal X_2^*, contingent upon the choice of X_1. We have:

(i) If $0 \leqslant X_1 \leqslant \overline{X}_2$, then $X_2^*(X_1) = \overline{X}_2$, and $\partial J/\partial X_1 = 0$, $dX_2^*/dX_1 = 0$;

(ii) If $\overline{X}_2 \leqslant X_1 \leqslant \underline{X}_2$, then $X_2^*(X_1) = X_1$ and $\partial J/\partial X_1 = \sum_i \xi_i \frac{\partial V(X_2^*(X_1),z_i)}{\partial X_2} \frac{dX_2^*}{dX_1}$;

(iii) If $\underline{X}_2 \leqslant X_1$ then $X_2^* = \underline{X}_2$, $\partial J/\partial X_1 = -\gamma$, $\frac{dX_2^*(X_1)}{dX_1} = 0$,

which can be illustrated in a diagram (Figure 1). Obviously, $\partial J/\partial X_1$ is not a concave function, unless $\gamma = -\infty$, but that corresponds to the case we just analyzed, i.e., the pure irreversibility case. As $\partial J/\partial X_1$ is neither convex nor concave as a function of X_1, it follows from Epstein's theorem that there exist information schemes Y, Y', and Y'' and a random variable Z such that both Y' and Y'' are more informative than Y and such that the optimal X_1' for Y' exceeds X_1 (the optimal choice for Y) and the optimal X_1'' for Y'' is less than X_1. Thus, it is impossible to say anything globally on the existence of the "irreversibility effect."

However, if $\partial V/\partial X_2$ is linear in X_2, $\partial J/\partial X_1$ is convex in the interval $[0, X_2]$. Let X_1' be the optimal choice of resource use in period 1 if the information scheme is Y' and let X_1'' be the corresponding choice if the scheme is Y and assume Y' is more informative than Y. Furthermore, assume X_1' belongs to the interval $[0, \overline{X}_2]$. Then, if X_1 would have been restricted to that interval, the optimal choice would still have been X_1. It now follows from Epstein's theorem that

$$X_1' \geqslant X_1''. \tag{3.8.5}$$

Thus, if the initial resource use is small enough, then the prospect of getting more information in the future will increase the initial use.

In the same way, it is seen that $\partial J/\partial X_1$ is concave in the interval so that if X_1' is in this interval,

$$X_1' \leqslant X_1''.$$

Finally, it follows that if X_1' belongs to $[\overline{X}_2, \underline{X}_2]$,

$$X_1' = X_1'',$$

as $X_2^* = X_1$ on that interval.

Thus, if the initial resource use is larger than $\underline{X}_2$, then the prospect of more information will reduce the initial use, while if the initial resource use is smaller than $\overline{X}_2$ the prospect of more information will increase the initial resource use. We can therefore conclude by stating the following theorem.

THEOREM. *If it is possible to restore the resource according to the cost function defined in (3.8.1), then for "small" initial resource use, an increase in expected forthcoming information will increase that initial resource use, while if the initial resource use is "large," more expected information will reduce the initial resource use.*

This result may have an implication for the current discussion on global warming and emissions of greenhouse gases. It has been claimed that the uncertainty about future impacts from climate change should imply that we would reduce the emissions more than would be desirable if no future information is forthcoming. However, the opposite has also been argued, and it may be that this theorem explains why serious scholars have come to such different conclusions.

Now, the theorem is a result of the discontinuity of the cost function. If we modify the cost function, a different result will emerge. Assume then that the cost function can be written

$$C(X_1, X_2) = \omega(X_1 - X_2), \tag{3.8.6}$$

where $\omega(.)$ is strictly concave, $\omega(0) = 0$, $\omega'(0) = 0$, and $\omega(t) = 0$ for $t < 0$. The $\partial J/\partial X_1$ curve will now look like the curve in the diagram (Figure 2).

It is now clear that the curve is concave and that the irreversibility effect is global.

THEOREM. *If the cost function has the properties as illustrated in Figure 2, there will be a global irreversibility effect, that is the prospect of more information will reduce use, regardless of the level of initial use.*

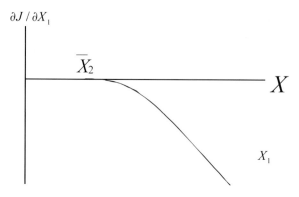

Figure 2.

3.9. The value of information

We can now define the value of one information scheme relative to another, conditional on the decision resource use in the first period as

$$V(X_1, Y'', Y') = \sum_j q_j'' J(X_1, \pi_j'') - \sum_j q_j' J(X_1, \pi_j').$$ (3.9.1)

If Y'' is more informative than Y', we know by definition that $V(X_1, Y', Y'') > 0$. V gives a measure of how much the expected utility from a resource use equal to X_1 will increase, if the forthcoming information changes from Y' to Y''. It is natural to define a zero point for this value by choosing the case of no forthcoming information as a reference point. Thus the value of information Y, conditional on the resource use X_1 in the first period as

$$V(X_1, Y) = \sum_j q_j J(X_1, \pi_j) - \sum_j q_j \max_{X_2} \sum_i r_i U(X_1, X_2, z_i).$$ (3.9.2)

But, as $\sum_j q_j = 1$, we have

$$V(X_1, Y) = \sum_j q_j J(X_1, \pi_j) - \max_{X_2} \sum_i r_i U(X_1, X_2, z_i).$$ (3.9.3)

In particular, the value of perfect information Y, conditional on the resource use X_1 in the first period is

$$\sum_i r_i \max_{X_2} U(X_1, X_2, z_i) - \max_{X_2} \sum_i r_i U(X_1, X_2, z_i).$$ (3.9.4)

The unconditional value of information from the scheme Y is defined as

$$W(Y) = \max_{X_1} \sum_j q_j J(X_1, \pi_j) - \max_{X_2} \sum_i r_i U(X_1, X_2, z_i).$$ (3.9.5)

It is easily seen that $W(Y)$ is always nonnegative and strictly positive whenever Y is strictly more informative than no information at all, and $\sum_j q_j J(X_1, \pi_j)$ has a unique maximum as a function of X_1. Assume now that there is a decision-maker that does not take the possibility of future information into account. He will thus solve

$$\max_{X_1, X_2} \sum_i r_i U(X_1, X_2, z_i). \tag{3.9.6}$$

However, if he would be paid a subsidy equal to the value of the forthcoming information (conditional on his choice of X_1) he would solve

$$\max_{X_1, X_2} \left\{ \sum_i r_i U(X_1, X_2, z_i) + V(X_1, Y) \right\}$$
$$= \max_{X_1} \sum_j q_j \max_{X_2} \sum_i \pi_i U(X_1, X_2, z_i). \tag{3.9.7}$$

Thus, a decision-maker could be made to take forthcoming information into account by being subsidized with an amount equal to the value of information conditional on his choice of resource use in the first period.[15] However, if the decision-maker is rational, he should of course have taken this information into account when he makes the decision and if that is the case, the subsidy would only distort the decision. Basically, there is no need for a subsidy, because the only kind of market failure that would cause an individual from considering the possibility of future information is irrationality. This kind of market failures cannot be solved by subsidies.

3.10. Uncertainty about irreversibility

Assume now that we don't know whether a decision today will have as a consequence an irreversible change in an environmental resource. Let us therefore assume that there is a positive probability p that the change will be irreversible and a corresponding positive probability $1 - p$ that the change is reversible. In terms of the notations used in previous sections, the optimization problem is

$$\max_{X_1} \left\{ U(X_1) + (1 - p) \sum_j q_j \max_{X_2} \sum_i \pi_{i,j} v(X_2, z_i) \right.$$
$$\left. + p \sum_j q_j \max_{X_2 \geqslant X_1} \sum_i \pi_{i,j} v(X_2, z_i) \right\}. \tag{3.10.1}$$

---

[15] The equivalence of option value and the value of information was first suggested by Conrad (1980). Fisher and Hanemann (1986) and Hanemann (1989) subsequently showed that option value is in fact a conditional value of information, as in the text, and that the conditional value is (not strictly) greater than the unconditional value.

The solution to this problem will be compared first, with the solution to the problem when irreversibility is not expected and second with the solution to the problem when it is known for sure that the change is irreversible. The first of these problems is to determine the solution to

$$\max_{X_1}\left\{U(X_1) + \sum_j q_j \max_{X_2} \sum_i \pi_{i,j} v(X_2, z_i)\right\},$$ (3.10.2)

and the second problem is exactly the one we have discussed in previous sections. Denote the solution to the first problem X_1^r and the solution to the second problem X_1. We know that if more information is expected to come forth in the future,

$$X_1^r \geqslant X_1^i.$$

Let $\overline{X}_1$ be the solution to the problem when irreversibility is uncertain. Let us for simplicity assume an interior solution. For any choice of X_1 we have for each j the optimal X_{2j} defined by

$$\max_{X_{2,j} \geqslant X_1} \sum_i \pi_{i,j} v(X_{2,j}, z_i).$$ (3.10.3)

The sum is a linear combination of concave functions and is therefore concave. The optimal X_{2j} will obviously be a function of X_1: $X_{2,j} = X_{2,j}^i(X_1)$. Let $X_{2,j}^r$ be the corresponding solution when there is no irreversibility constraint. If there is no such constraint, $\frac{dX_{2,j}^r}{dX_1} = 0$, otherwise $\frac{dX_{2,j}^r}{dX_1} = 1$. The assumption of an interior solution now yields (suppressing the random variable Z_i)

$$\frac{\partial U(\overline{X}_1)}{\partial X_1} + \sum_j q_j \sum_i \pi_{i,j} \frac{\partial v}{\partial X_2} \frac{dX_2^i}{dX_1} = 0,$$

or

$$\frac{\partial U(X_1^i)}{\partial X_1} = -\sum_j q_j \sum_i \pi_{i,j} \frac{\partial v}{\partial X_2} \frac{dX_2^i}{dX_1}$$

$$\geqslant -p \sum_j q_j \sum_i \pi_{i,j} \frac{\partial v}{\partial X_2} \frac{dX_2^r}{dX_1}$$

$$= \frac{dU(\overline{X}_1)}{dX_1} \geqslant 0 = \frac{dU(x_1^r)}{dX_1}.$$ (3.10.4)

The concavity of the U-function now yields that

$$X_1^i \leqslant \overline{X}_1 \leqslant X_1^r.$$ (3.10.5)

Thus, we have reached the intuitively obvious but very important conclusion that when it is not known for sure that a change is reversible or not, it is better to be cautious and not undertake as much development as would have been optimal if the change had known to be reversible. Note that this conclusion is not dependent on linearity, or a binary choice or even on the possibility of forthcoming information. Whenever one is uncertain about the reversibility of a change, one should be cautious and not undertake as big change one would have had desired if the change had been known with certainty to be reversible.

If it is not known whether a change is going to be irreversible or not, it is still beneficial to be cautious in that one should not undertake as big change as one would have had desired if the change had been known to be reversible. It is easily seen from the inequality above that the optimal amount of development will decrease as the probability of irreversibility goes up.

Finally, it is easily seen that if the utility function is linear or if there is a binary choice, the optimal amount of development will be nonincreasing with the probability of an irreversible change.

3.11. Option values

Let us now try to integrate the model with temporal resolution of uncertainty which we have been discussing in this part with the discussion in the first part on option prices and option values. Consider the situation where Q is the measure of environmental resource use and which can take two values Q', implying that the natural asset is preserved, and Q'' that it is developed and irrevocably lost. The benefits in the present period are known with certainty and are given by the indirect utility function

$$U\left(W^1, Q^1\right),$$
(3.11.1)

where W^1 is wealth in the first period and Q^1 can take the two values Q' or Q''. The present value of future net benefits, given that state i occurs is

$$\frac{v^i\left(W_i, Q^2\right)}{1 + \delta_i},$$
(3.11.2)

where W_i is the future wealth if state i occurs, v^i is the utility function in state i, δ_i is the discount rate in state i, and Q^2 takes the values Q' or Q''. The total present value of benefits, given that state i occurs is

$$U\left(W^1, Q^1\right) + \frac{v^i\left(W_i, Q^2\right)}{1 + \delta_i},$$
(3.11.3)

where $Q^2 = Q^1$ if $Q^1 = Q''$ (the irreversibility assumption). Assuming the same information structure as in the previous section, the decision problem can be formulated

$$\max_{Q^1}\left\{U\left(W^1, Q^1\right) + \sum_j q_j \max_{Q^2} \sum_i \pi_{i,j} v^i\left(W_i, Q^2\right)/(1 + \delta_i)\right\}$$

subject to $Q^2 = Q''$ if $Q^1 = Q''$.
(3.11.4)

The maximum price, CV, the individual would be willing to pay for keeping the option of deciding in the next period the use of the resource is given by

$$U(W^1 - CV, Q') + \sum_j q_j \max_{Q^2} \sum_i \pi_{i,j} v^i (W_i, Q^2)/(1 + \delta_i)$$

$$= U(W, Q'') + \sum_j q_j \sum_i \pi_{i,j} v^i (W_i, Q'')/(1 + \delta_i). \tag{3.11.5}$$

The state contingent benefits CV_i of preserving the asset for at least one period are given by

$$U(W^1 - CV_i, Q') + \max_{Q^2} v^i (W_i, Q)/(1 + \delta_i)$$

$$= U(W^1, Q'') + v^i (W_i, Q'')/(1 + \delta_i). \tag{3.11.6}$$

Thus,

$$v^i (W_i, Q'') = U(W^1 - CV_i, Q') + \max_{Q^2} v^i (W_i, Q)/(1 + \delta_i) - U(W^1, Q''), \tag{3.11.7}$$

and substituting this into (3.11.5) gives

$$U(W^1 - CV, Q') + \sum_j q_j \max_{Q^2} \sum_i \pi_{i,j} v^i (W_i, Q^2)/(1 + \delta_i)$$

$$= \sum_j q_j \sum_i \pi_{i,j} U(W^1 - CV_i, Q')$$

$$+ \sum_j q_j \sum_i \pi_{i,j} \max_{Q^2} v^i (W_i, Q)/(1 + \delta_i). \tag{3.11.8}$$

This simplifies to (remembering that $\sum_j q_j \pi_{i,j} = r_i$)

$$U(W^1 - CV, Q') - \sum_i r_i U(W^1 - CV_i, Q')$$

$$= \sum_j q_j \left\{ \sum_i \pi_{i,j} \max_{Q^2} v^i (W_i, Q)/(1 + \delta_i) \right.$$

$$\left. - \max_{Q^2} \sum_i \pi_{i,j} v^i (W_i, Q^2)/(1 + \delta_i) \right\}, \tag{3.11.9}$$

or

$$U(W^1 - CV, Q') - \sum_i r_i U(W^1 - CV_i, Q') \leqslant 0. \tag{3.11.10}$$

If, as we assume, the utility function U is concave, it follows that

$$\sum_i r_i U(W^1 - CV_i, Q') \leqslant U\left(W^1 - \sum_i r_i CV_i, Q'\right), \tag{3.11.11}$$

and finally

$$U\left(W^1 - CV, Q'\right) \geqslant U\left(W^1 - \sum_i r_i CV_i, Q'\right), \tag{3.11.12}$$

or

$$CV \leqslant \sum_i r_i CV_i.$$

Thus, the option value as defined by Weisbrod (1964), Cicchetti and Freeman (1971) will be positive!

THEOREM. *The option value as defined in Section* 2.6 *will be nonnegative if information is expected to come forward.*

4. Many periods, continuous time, and stochastic processes

In this section we extend the analysis to many periods and continuous time. In doing so we also touch on stochastic processes that underlie the uncertainty we are dealing with. Section 4.1 presents a simple two-period model that forms the foundation for subsequent analysis of the multi-period and continuous cases. The model is a little different from those in the preceding section, but the basic idea is the same: how are first-period or current decisions affected by the presence of uncertainty about future costs and benefits and the prospect of resolution of the uncertainty over time. Section 4.2 extends the model to many periods. Particular attention is given to the "optimal stopping" problem. In each period, the decision-maker is confronted with the alternatives of continuing – say to produce widgets, or to preserve a tract of forest land – and enjoying a flow of benefits, respectively profits or recreation, on the one hand, or stopping and receiving a termination value, respectively the scrap value of the widget plant or the proceeds from a timber harvest, on the other. Section 4.3 extends the multi-period model to treat the case of continuous time, including solution of the optimal stopping problem in this setting. Section 4.4 presents an empirical application: when, if ever, to cut an old-growth redwood forest in Northern California where the recreation values associated with preserving the forest evolve continuously according to a plausible and widely used stochastic specification, a geometric Brownian motion.

4.1. Investment under uncertainty

Let us consider the general problem, as set out in Dixit and Pindyck (1994), of investment under uncertainty. A firm faces a decision of whether or not to make an investment, with a sunk cost of I, in a factory that will produce one widget per period forever. The current price of widgets is P_0 and, in the second period and thereafter, it will be either $(1 + u)P_0$, with probability q, or $(1 - d)P_0$, with probability $(1 - q)$. The expected present value of the return to the investment is then

$$V_0 = P_0 + \frac{q(1+u)P_0 + (1-q)(1-d)P_0}{r}, \qquad (4.1.1)$$

where r is the discount rate. If $V_0 > I$, the investment will be made; otherwise, it will not. Letting Ω_0 denote the net payoff, we have

$$\Omega_0 = \max\{V_0 - I, 0\}. \qquad (4.1.2)$$

This is the standard present-value criterion and, as we shall see, is in fact equivalent to the second decision rule in the last section's model of the decision on environmental preservation.

Implicit in Equation (4.1.2) is that the investment is considered only for the first period. Now, suppose that the opportunity will be available in the second period if it is not taken in the first. The present value of the return to the second-period investment is

$$V_1 = \begin{cases} (1+u)P_0 + \dfrac{(1+u)P_0}{r} & \text{if price } = (1+u)P_0, \\[2mm] (1-d)P_0 + \dfrac{(1-d)P_0}{r} & \text{if price } = (1-d)P_0. \end{cases} \qquad (4.1.3)$$

The net payoff, the outcome of a future optimal decision, called the continuation value, is

$$F_1 = \max\{V_1 - I, 0\}. \qquad (4.1.4)$$

What is the implication for the first-period decision? Notice that, although the second-period decision is made under certainty [by the start of the second period, the firm knows whether price is $(1+u)P_0$ or $(1-d)P_0$ and optimizes accordingly], from the perspective of the first period, V_1 and F_1 are uncertain. Then, the expected continuation value, from the perspective of the first period, is

$$E_0[F_1] = q \max\left\{(1+u)P_0 + \frac{(1+u)P_0}{r} - I, 0\right\}$$
$$+ (1-q) \max\left\{(1-d)P_0 + \frac{(1-d)P_0}{r} - I, 0\right\}. \qquad (4.1.5)$$

The net payoff to the investment opportunity presented in the first period, optimally taken (in the first period or the second), is

$$F_0 = \max\left\{V_0 - I, \frac{1}{1+r}E_0[F_1]\right\}, \qquad (4.1.6)$$

where $V_0 - I$ is the expected present value of the investment made in the first period and $(1/(1+r))E_0[F_1]$ is the (discounted) expected continuation value – what the firm gets if it does not make the investment in the first period.

The difference, $F_0 - \Omega_0$, can be interpreted as option value: the value of the option to postpone the investment decision. As Dixit and Pindyck (1994) point out, the investment opportunity is analogous to a call option on a share of stock. It confers the right to exercise an option to invest at a given price (cost of the investment) to receive an asset (the widget factory) that will yield a stream of uncertain future returns. At first blush this appears somewhat different from the interpretation of option value in the model of Section 3.2 above as a conditional value of information, but in fact is just another side of the same coin. The new information has value only if an option to postpone exists, and the option to postpone has value due to the information that will come available (though, depending on how the problem is formulated, the option to postpone an investment can be valuable even in the absence of new information).

4.2. Multiperiod case

To extend the analysis to many periods [again drawing on the definitive presentation in Dixit and Pindyck (1994, Chapter 4)], we simply repeat the procedure, starting at the next-to-the-last period and working back period by period. We introduce some new notation, which will also be useful when we go to continuous time. A firm's current status is described by the state variable, x, where x_t is known but x_{t+1}, x_{t+2}, etc., are random variables (but all of the relevant information about the probability distribution is in x_t since x is assumed to be a Markov process). The firm's choices are described by the control variable, u. State and control variables affect immediate profit flow, $\pi_t(x_t, u_t)$. Then, using previously defined concepts,

$$F_t(x_t) = \max_{u_t}\left\{\pi_t(x_t, u_t) + \frac{1}{1+r}E_t\big[F_{t+1}(x_{t+1})\big]\right\}, \tag{4.2.1}$$

where $F_t(x_t)$ is the expected net present value of all of the firm's cash flows when all decisions are optimal from t on.

This is the Bellman equation. Bellman's Principle of Optimality is: An optimal policy is such that, whatever the initial action, the remaining choices constitute an optimal policy for the subproblem starting at the state that results from the initial action. In the two-period case, immediate investment ($u_0 = 1$) gave $V_0 - I$ and waiting ($u_0 = 0$) had only a continuation value. The choice was thus a binary one (invest or not at a fixed level). This is a special case of the Bellman equation.

4.2.1. Optimal stopping

Another, more general, example of a binary choice is optimal stopping. In each period either stop and get a termination payoff, Ω, or continue with a current period profit plus an expected continuation value. Then, the Bellman equation becomes

$$F_t(x_t) = \max\left\{\Omega(x_t), \pi(x_t) + \frac{1}{1+r}E_t\big[F_{t+1}(x_{t+1})\big]\right\}. \tag{4.2.2}$$

The two-period investment problem is an optimal stopping problem, where the period 0 termination payoff is $V_0 - I$, and the period 0 profit from continuing (not making the investment) is 0. The control variable, u in the Bellman equation, is implicitly 0 or 1 in an optimal stopping problem, such as the two-period problem. For example, in that problem, choice of u_0 is either 0 (do not make the investment and get only the continuation value, $E_0[F_1]/(1 + r)$) or 1 (make the investment and get the termination payoff, $V_0 - I$).

In the more general optimal stopping problem just above, $u_t = 0 \Rightarrow$ do not stop, i.e., stay in business and get $\pi(x_t) + \frac{E_t[F_{t+1}(x_{t+1})]}{1+r}$, and $u_t = 1 \Rightarrow$ *stop* and get $\Omega(x_t)$. The point is that an optimal stopping problem involves a binary choice, just two alternatives, that we can explicitly specify (and that implicitly correspond to $u = 0$ and $u = 1$). This is often the way problems arise, as in the choice of environmental preservation or development.

4.2.2. Multiperiod solution

To solve the general multiperiod problem, start at the last period, T. The firm gets a termination payoff, $\Omega_T(x_T)$. Then, at period $T - 1$,

$$F_{T-1}(x_{T-1}) = \max_{u_{T-1}} \left\{ \pi(x_{T-1}, u_{T-1}) + \frac{1}{1+r} E_{T-1}\big(\Omega_T(x_T)\big) \right\}. \tag{4.2.3}$$

The decision then moves back to period $T - 2$, where

$$F_{T-2}(x_{T-2}) = \max_{u_{T-2}} \left\{ \pi(x_{T-2}, u_{T-2}) + \frac{1}{1+r} E_{T-2}\big(F_{T-1}(x_{T-1})\big) \right\}. \tag{4.2.4}$$

The essential idea is to split the sequence of decisions into two parts: the immediate choice, and remaining decisions summarized in the continuation value. To find the optimal sequence, work backward. At the last decision point, make the best choice and get the continuation value (F_1 in the two-period case). Then, in the preceding period, we know the expected continuation value ($E_0[F_1]$) and can make the best choice (of the current control variable, here the decision of whether or not to invest).

4.3. Continuous time and stochastic processes

Again drawing on Dixit and Pindyck (1994, Chapters 3 and 4), we now consider the case of continuous time. Many economic and environmental processes do, in fact, evolve continuously rather than in discrete steps. Further, there are mathematical advantages to working in continuous time. Suppose that each period is of length Δt. Now, interpret $\pi(x, u, t)$ as the rate of profit, so profit over the interval Δt is $\pi(x, u, t)\Delta t$. Similarly, r equals the discount rate per unit time, so discounting over Δt is $1/(1 + r\Delta t)$. The Bellman equation becomes

$$F(x, t) = \max_u \left\{ \pi(x, u, t)\Delta t + \frac{1}{1+r\Delta t} E_t\big[F(x_{t+\Delta t}, t + \Delta t) \big] \right\}. \tag{4.3.1}$$

Multiplying both sides by $(1 + r\Delta t)$, dividing by Δt, and letting $\Delta t \to 0$, we obtain

$$rF(x, t) = \max_u \left\{ \pi(x, u, t) + \frac{1}{dt} E[dF] \right\}. \tag{4.3.2}$$

On the left-hand side, we have the opportunity cost of holding the asset for a unit of time, rF; on the right-hand side, the immediate payout or dividend from the asset plus the expected rate of capital gain.

The limit on the right-hand side depends on the expectation corresponding to the random $x_{t+\Delta t}$. One very important and widely used stochastic process (a variable that evolves over time in a way that is at least in part random) that allows such a limit in a form conducive to further analysis is the Ito process, a generalization of the basic Wiener process. If $z(t)$ is a Wiener process, then an increment, dz, can be represented as $dz = \varepsilon_t \sqrt{dt}$, where ε_t is a normally distributed random variable with a mean of zero and a standard deviation of one. Important properties that follow from the definition are that $E(dz) = 0$ and variance $(dz) = dt$. Now, let the random variable, $x(t)$, be an Ito process, defined such that an increment, dx, is represented as

$$dx = a(x, t)\, dt + b(x, t)\, dz, \tag{4.3.3}$$

where $a(x, t)$ and $b(x, t)$ are known (nonrandom) functions and dz is the increment of a Wiener process. Ito's lemma, a Taylor-series expansion of $F(x, t)$, gives

$$dF = \left[F_t(x, t) + a(x, u, t)F_x(x, t) + \frac{1}{2}b^2(x, u, t)F_{xx}(x, t) \right] dt$$
$$\qquad + b(x, u, t)F_x(x, t)\, dz \tag{4.3.4}$$

and

$$E[dF] = \left[F_t(x, t) + a(x, u, t)F_x(x, t) + \frac{1}{2}b^2(x, u, t)F_{xx}(x, t) \right] dt$$

since $E[dz] = 0$. Substituting back in the Bellman equation, we obtain

$$rF(x, t) = \max_u \left\{ \pi(x, u, t) + F_t(x, t) + a(x, u, t)F_x(x, t) \right.$$
$$\left. + \frac{1}{2}b^2(x, u, t)F_{xx}(x, t) \right\}. \tag{4.3.5}$$

We can express the optimal u as a function of x, t, F_t, F_x, and F_{xx} and the various parameters in $\pi(., ., .)$, $a(., ., .)$ and $b(., ., .)$, substitute back into the Bellman equation, and get a partial differential equation of the second order with x and t as the independent variables. If the functions π, a, and b do not depend on time, then F does not either. Then, the Bellman equation becomes

$$rF(x) = \max_u \left\{ \pi(x, u) + a(x, u)F'(x) + \frac{1}{2}b^2(x, u)F''(x) \right\}. \tag{4.3.6}$$

Again, substituting the optimal u in the Bellman equation, we now have an ordinary differential equation with x as the independent variable.

4.3.1. Optimal stopping and boundary conditions

The solution will depend on boundary conditions in specific applications. There is one important class of problems for which we can state boundary conditions: optimal stopping, or binary decisions, with an Ito process.

The Bellman equation (in continuous time) is:

$$F(x,t) = \max\left\{ \Omega(x,t), \pi(x,t)\,dt + \frac{1}{1+r\,dt} E[F(x+dx,t+dt)] \right\}. \qquad (4.3.7)$$

In the continuation region, the second term on the right-hand side is larger. Expanding it by Ito's lemma, as before,

$$rF(x,t) = \pi(x,t) + F_t(x,t) + a(x,t)F_x(x,t) + \frac{1}{2}b^2(x,t)F_{xx}(x,t). \qquad (4.3.8)$$

We have "maximized out" u, choosing to continue, not terminate. This holds for $x > x^*(t)$, where $x^*(t)$ is the critical value of x with continuation optimal on one side ($x > x^*(t)$) and stopping on the other.

There are two boundary conditions for $x^*(t)$. The first is the value matching condition. From the Bellman equation, we know that in the stopping region we have $F(x,t) = \Omega(x,t)$ so, by continuity, we can impose the condition

$$F\big(x^*(t),t\big) = \Omega\big(x^*(t),t\big) \qquad (4.3.9)$$

at the boundary of the stopping region. The second boundary condition is the smooth pasting condition. The values $F(x,t)$ and $\Omega(x,t)$ should meet tangentially at the boundary, so

$$F_x\big(x^*(t),t\big) = \Omega_x\big(x^*(t),t\big). \qquad (4.3.10)$$

This condition is proved by contradiction in Dixit and Pindyck (1994, Chapter 4, Appendix C).

4.4. An application: when to cut an old-growth redwood forest

This is another problem of optimal forest use, here the Headwaters Forest, a large stand of privately owned redwood in Northern California which has been the subject of negotiation between the owner, who has plans to cut, and agencies of both state and federal governments, which would like to see the area preserved. A recent analysis by Conrad (1997) considers the question of when, if ever, it would be optimal (from a social point of view) to cut the Headwaters Forest. Conrad formulates the question as one of optimal stopping in continuous time. We can terminate at any time, harvest and get a payoff N (which corresponds to Ω, but is not in this application a function of a state variable or time) or we can continue and get a flow of amenity services (flood control, erosion control, wildlife habitat, recreation, etc.), $A = A(t)$, where

$$dA = \mu A\,dt + \sigma A\,dz, \qquad (4.4.1)$$

i.e., A is a stochastic process of a particular type: a geometric Brownian motion. Note that this can be considered a special case of the Ito process defined earlier, where μ is the instantaneous drift rate and σ is the instantaneous variance rate. The geometric Brownian motion is very widely assumed in stochastic analysis of environmental and resource problems. It has the virtue of simplicity, and seems plausible, in this case at least, given the upward trend in amenity value, recreational use, etc., and increasing uncertainty about value as we look further into the future [note that $E(dA) = \mu A\,dt$ and variance $dA = \sigma^2 A^2\,dt$].

This is an optimal stopping problem in continuous time. The Bellman equation is

$$V(A) = \max\left\{N,\ A\,dt + \frac{1}{1 + \delta\,dt}\,E\big[V(A + dA, t + dt)\big]\right\}. \tag{4.4.2}$$

Expanding by Ito's lemma, in the continuation region,

$$\delta V(A) = A + \mu A V'(A) + \frac{1}{2}\sigma^2 A^2 V''(A). \tag{4.4.3}$$

This is a special case of the general optimal stopping condition, where the value function V is a function of just one variable A. This is a second-order ordinary differential equation. Conrad shows that the solution is

$$V(A) = kA^{-\alpha} + \frac{A}{\delta - \mu}, \tag{4.4.4}$$

where α is a constant that depends on μ, σ, and δ and $\alpha > 0$ if $\delta > \mu$. If $\delta \leqslant \mu$, it will never be optimal to cut. Therefore, we focus on the case where $\delta > \mu$. The first term on the right-hand side is the value of having an option to cut. As $A \to \infty$, $kA^{-\alpha} \to 0$, as it should. The second term on the right-hand side is the value of never cutting, the flow of benefits A divided by the adjusted discount rate, $\delta - \mu$. The value-matching condition is

$$V\big(A^*\big) = N,$$

and, substituting for $V(A^*)$,

$$kA^{-\alpha} + \frac{A}{\delta - \mu} = N. \tag{4.4.5}$$

The smooth-pasting condition is

$$V'\big(A^*\big) = 0,$$

since N does not depend on A, yielding

$$-\alpha kA^{-(\alpha+1)} + \frac{1}{\delta - \mu} = 0. \tag{4.4.6}$$

These two equations can be solved for the two unknowns, k and A^*. Solving the smooth-pasting condition for k,

$$k = \frac{A^{\alpha+1}}{\alpha(\delta - \mu)}. \tag{4.4.7}$$

Substituting this in the value-matching condition, we obtain

$$A^* = \frac{\alpha(\delta - \mu)N}{\alpha + 1}, \tag{4.4.8}$$

where A^* is the critical amenity value, the level at which the decision maker is indifferent between preserving and cutting.

In order to obtain a numerical solution, we need to estimate μ and σ as specified in Equation (4.4.1); assume something about the discount rate, δ; calculate α [from μ, σ, and δ as given in Conrad (1997, p. 99)]; and substitute the value for N (550×10^6). Conrad estimates μ and σ from data on visitation rates to Redwood National Park, near Headwaters, on the assumption that amenity value, A, is proportional to visitation, R. Visitation data from 1976–1995 are consistent with geometric Brownian motion, with $\mu = 0.05$ and $\sigma = 0.10$. If $\delta = 0.05$, $A^* = 0$ (never cut because $\delta \leqslant \mu$). If $\delta = 0.06$, $A^* = \$5.008 \times 10^6$ – two orders of magnitude less than N (remember, A^* is annual value and N is present value).

Repeated harvests do not add much to the problem, given the great value of old-growth redwood and the length of time required to grow a new, mature stand. Conrad and Ludwig (1994) have estimated elsewhere that the value of future harvests is often less than 2 percent of the value of the old-growth harvest. If $N = \$600 \times 10^6$, $A^* = \$5.463 \times 10^6$, which is very close to the $\$5.008 \times 10^6$ for $N = \$550 \times 10^6$. This is for a nearly 10 percent increase in N, which is much greater than 2 percent.

The impact of a change in the variance can, however, be substantial. The instantaneous variance rate is $\sigma = 0.1$ in the base case. If instead $\sigma = 0.2$, $A^* = \$3.988 \times 10^6$; preserving the old-growth forest is more attractive (requires a lower amenity value) as the amenity value becomes more volatile. The interpretation is that, if the forest is preserved, it is possible to benefit from an above-average increase in amenity value, while retaining the option to cut in the event of a below-average increase, or decline, in amenity value.

Appendix A: on the equivalence of two representations of environmental changes

Assume there is a project that will change the distribution of events from λ to λ'. Assume that λ' is absolutely continuous with respect to. This means that events that have probability zero with λ will also have probability zero with λ'. This may seem a strong assumption. If, however, all events have nonzero probabilities under both λ and λ', the assumption is valid. Let us therefore assume that λ' is absolutely continuous with respect to λ. Then there exists a density $v(i)$, the Radon–Nikodym derivative[16] of λ' with respect to λ so that

$$\int \lambda'_i = \int v(i)\lambda_i.$$

Assume furthermore that Q_i is increasing in i, $U_i(W_i, Q)$ is increasing in Q. We also have the previous made assumption that no event has a zero probability so that $v(i) > 0$.
    Then define

$$Q'_i = U^{i^{-1}}\big(W_i, U^i\big(W_i, Q_i v(i)\big)\big),$$

where $U^{i^{-1}}$ is the inverse function to $\partial U^i / \partial Q$.
    Then it is easily seen that

$$\int U^i(W_i, Q'_i)\, d\lambda_i = \int U^i(W_i, Q_i)\, d\lambda'_i$$

Moreover, assume that the policy change $\lambda \to \lambda'$ means an increase in the probability of states with a high Q, i.e., that $\lambda_i \geqslant \lambda'_i$. This in turn implies that $v(i) \geqslant 1$ and it follows that

$$Q'_i = U^{i^{-1}}\big(W_i, U^i\big(W_i, Q_i v(i)\big)\big) \geqslant U^{i^{-1}}\big(W_i, U^i(W_i, Q_i)\big) = Q_i$$

so that the new Q' variable corresponds to a higher (or unchanged) Q in each state, a result we would demand of an economic reasonable representation.
    The converse proposition follows from a simple variable substitution, i.e., let $Q' = T(Q)$ where T is measurable. Then it follows from Halmos (1965) that

$$\int U^i\big(W_i, T(Q_i)\big)\, d\lambda_i = \int U^i(W_i, Q_i)\, d\big(\lambda_i T^{-1}\big)$$

and we choose $d\lambda'_i = d(\lambda_i T^{-1})$.

Appendix B: a different notion of "more informative"

Epstein's (1980) analysis was based on the notion of "value of information." Freixas and Laffont (1984) developed a parallel and equivalent analysis based on a different notion of "more informative." Let z be as before the random variable characterizing the preferences. Let z be defined on a probability space (Ω, F, μ) (Ω is the set of all outcome, F is the field of subsets on which the probability measure μ is defined). Any partition Δ of Ω (compatible with F, i.e., if $S \in \Delta$ then $S \in F$) corresponds to an information structure, that is the decision-maker knows whether the true state is a point in a set in Δ or not. Briefly, S is an information set. It is now obvious that more

---

[16] See Halmos (1965, p. 128).

informative can be defined by comparing partitions Δ, Δ', etc. The finer the partition is (Δ is finer than Δ' if $\Delta' \subseteq \Delta$), the more information the decision-maker has. Green and Stokey (1978) proved that this definition of "more informative" is equivalent to Blackwell's (1951) definition.

Let us assume that the objective function of the decision-maker is linearly separable between the two time periods:

$$U(X_1) + V(X_2, z).$$

The decision on X_1 will give rise to the feasibility set $X_2(X_1) = \{X_2; X_2 \varepsilon X_1\}$ in the second period. Given X_1, the choice in the second period is determined from

$$\max_{X_2 \in X_2(X_1)} E_\mu\big[V(X_2, z) \mid z \in S\big] = v_2(X_2, S).$$

Let $V_2(X_1, \mathbb{Z})$ be defined as

$$V_2(X_1, \mathbb{Z}) = E_\mu v_2\big(X_2(X_1), S\big).$$

Finally, let X_1^* be the optimal first period choice when the partition is $\mathbb{Z}$, and $X_1'^*$ when the partition is $\mathbb{Z}'$.

We can now state the main theorem derived by Freixas and Laffont:

THEOREM. *Let* $\mathbb{Z}'$ *be a refinement of* $\mathbb{Z}$. *If* V_2 *is quasi-concave in* X_1, *then*

$$X_1^{*'} \leqslant X_1^*.$$

This theorem is very similar to the one Epstein derived, the difference being that here we assume that V_2 is quasi-concave while Epstein assumed U_2 is concave. It is easy to see that if U_2 is concave V_2 must be quasi-concave so that the Freixas and Laffont's theorem is slightly more general.

References

Albers, H.J., Goldbach, M.J. (2000). "Irreversible ecosystem change, species competition, and shifting culti-vation". Resource and Energy Economics 22, 261–280.

Albers, H.J., Fisher, A.C., Hanemann, W.M. (1996). "Valuation and management of tropical forests: Implications of uncertainty and irreversibility". Environmental and Resource Economics 8, 39–61.

Arrow, K.J., Fisher, A.C. (1974). "Environmental preservation, uncertainty, and irreversibility". American Economic Review 88, 312–320.

Arrow, K.J., Lind, R. (1972). "Uncertainty and the evaluation of public investment decisions". American Economic Review 60.

Blackwell, D. (1951). Comparisons of experiments. In: Neyman, J. (Ed.), Proceedings of the Second Berkley Symposium on Mathematical Statistics and Probability.

Bohm, P. (1975). "Option demand and consumer's surplus: A comment". American Economic Review 65.

Bradford, K., Keleian, H. (1977). "The value of information for crop forecasting in a market system". The Review of Economic Studies 44.

Cicchetti, C., Freeman III, A.M. (1971). "Option demand and consumer surplus: Further comment". Quarterly Journal of Economics 85.

Conrad, J.M. (1980). "Quasi-option value and the expected value of information". Quarterly Journal of Economics 95, 813–820.

Conrad, J.M. (1997). "On the option value of old-growth forest". Ecological Economics 22, 97–102.

Conrad, J.M., Ludwig, D. (1994). "Forest land policy: The optimal stock of old-growth forest". Natural Resource Modeling 8, 27–45.

Dasgupta, P., Mäler, K.-G. (Eds.) (2004). The Economics of Non-Convex Ecosystems. Kluwer Academic Publishers, Dordrecht.

de Angelis, H., Skvarca, P. (2003). "Glacier surge after ice shelf collapse". Science.

Dixit, A.K., Pindyck, R.S. (1994). Investment under Uncertainty. Princeton University Press, Princeton, NJ.

Epstein, L. (1980). "Decision making and the temporal resolution of uncertainty". International Economic Review 63.

Fisher, A.C. (1973). "Environmental externalities and the Arrow–Lind public investment theorem". American Economic Review 63.

Fisher, A.C., Hanemann, W.M. (1986). "Option value and the extinction of species". In: Smith, V.K. (Ed.), Advances in Applied Microeconomics. JAI Press, Greenwich, CT, pp. 169–190.

Freixas, X., Laffont, J.-J. (1984). "On the irreversibility effect". In: Boyer, M., Kihlstrom, R.E. (Eds.), Bayesian Models in Economic Theory. North-Holland, pp. 105–114.

Green, J., Stokey, N. (1978). "Two representations of information structures and their comparisons". Technical Report No. 271. IMSS, Stanford University.

Halmos, P. (1965). Measure Theory. Van Nostrand, New York.

Hanemann, W.M. (1989). "Information and the concept of option value". Journal of Environmental Economics and Management 16, 23–37.

Henry, C. (1974a). "Investment decisions under uncertainty: The irreversibility effect". In: Review of Economic Studies: Symposium on the Economics of Exhaustible Resources.

Henry, C. (1974b). "Option values in the economics of irreplaceable assets". In: Review of Economic Studies: Symposium on the Economics of Exhaustible Resources.

Krutilla, J.V., Cicchetti, C.J., Freeman III, A.M., Russel, C.S. (1972). "Observations on the economics of irreplaceable assets". In: Kneese, A., Bower, B. (Eds.), Environmental Quality Analysis: Theory and Method in the Social Sciences. John Hopkins University Press.

Malinvaud, E. (1972). "The allocation of individual risks in large markets". Journal of Economic Theory 4.

Marschak, J., Miyasawa, K. (1968). "Economic comparability of information systems". International Economic Review 9.

Raiffa, H. (1968). Decision Analysis: Introductory Lectures on Choices under Uncertainty. Random House, New York.

Raiffa, H., Schlaifer, R. (1960). Applied Statistical Decision Theory. MIT Press, Cambridge.

Schmalensee, R. (1972). "Option demand and consumer's surplus: Valuing price changes under uncertainty". American Economic Review 62.

Schultz, P.A., Kasting, J.F. (1997). "Optimal reductions on CO_2 emissions". Energy Policy 25, 491–500.

Tongpan, S., Panayotou, T., Jetanavanich, S., Faichampa, K., Mehl, C. (1990). "Deforestation and poverty: Can commercial and social forestry break the vicious circle"? Research Report No. 2, 1990 TDRI Year-End Conference.

Weisbrod, B. (1964). "Collective-consumption services of individual consumption goods". Quarterly Journal of Economics 78, 471–477.

Further reading

Bishop, R. (1982). "Option value: An exposition and extension". Land Economics 58.

Pindyck, R.S. (2000). "Irreversibilities and the timing of environmental policy." Technical report. MIT.

Rod, B.W. (1964). "Collective-consumption services of individual consumption goods". Quarterly Journal of Economics 78.

Scheinkman, J.A., Zariphopoulou, T. "Optimal environmental management in the presence of irreversibilities". Technical Report: Nota di Lavoro 15.96. FEEM, Milan.

Ulph, A.M., Ulph, D. (1997). "Global warming, irreversibility and learning". Economic Journal 107, 636–650.

Chapter 14

VALUING THE ENVIRONMENT AS A FACTOR OF PRODUCTION

KENNETH E. MCCONNELL AND NANCY E. BOCKSTAEL

Department of Agricultural and Resource Economics, University of Maryland, USA

Contents

QS1

Q52

D21

Handbook of Environmental Economics, Volume 2. Edited by K.-G. Mäler and J.R. Vincent
© 2005 Elsevier B.V.   All rights reserved
DOI: 10.1016/S1574-0099(05)02014-0

Abstract

This chapter explores the theory and practice of measuring the economic costs and benefits of environmental changes that influence production, both in the context of firms and of households. The theory uses models of household and firm decision making to map the influence of environmental changes to changes in human welfare. The goal is to measure, by compensating or equivalent changes in incomes, the welfare effects on people, in their roles as owners of firms, owners of factors of production, and consumers. The developing country context is most common for valuing the environment as an input, because agriculture and natural resource extraction are so much more important than in industrialized countries.

When households or firms produce goods for sale on the market, and the environment influences the costs of production, we show the circumstances when one can use information embodied in the supply curve of the marketed good or the demand curve for an input into the production of the good to extract welfare measures for environmental change. When the environment affects the cost of production of goods households produce and consume, we show the restrictions on production technology that will permit welfare measure for changes in the environment. We also look at circumstances that permit the calculations of bounds for the exact welfare measures. We explore welfare measurement under a variety of institutional structures, including government support for agricultural commodities and open-access fisheries. Exact welfare measurement makes extensive demands for data. Because these demands are not often met in practice, researchers resort to a variety of approximations of welfare measures. We assess these approximations, comparing them with the more exact measures.

Keywords

environment as an input in production, household production, applied welfare economics, environmental valuation, revealed preference methods

JEL classification: Q51, Q57, D13

1. Introduction

This chapter explores the theory and practice of measuring the economic costs and benefits of environmental changes that influence production, both in the context of firms and of households. The theory uses models of household and firm decision making to map the influence of environmental changes to changes in human welfare. In best practice, these measures are obtained by exploiting restrictive assumptions about the relationships between production, the state of the environment, and markets. Given the inevitable paucity of data and our limited understanding of the interactions between human activities and ecosystems, approximations to these preferred measures are often needed. In theory, the goal is to measure, by compensating or equivalent changes in incomes, the welfare effects on people, in their roles as owners of firms, owners of factors of production, and consumers. In practice, we often look for approximations to these measures or upper and/or lower bounds on their values.

The environment forms part of the backdrop for all household and firm decisions. These decisions determine the production and the final consumption flows of goods and services. Methods for measuring the benefits and costs of changes in the environment are not as extensively studied when the environment enters production relationships rather than directly affecting consumption. This imbalance is a consequence of the fact that the demand for environmental quality emerged first in the developed world. Because the output of agricultural activities and natural resource extraction are small in comparison to the production of manufactured goods and services in the developed world, and because environmental degradation has had relatively small, diffuse, or localized effects on commercial production, only a relatively small proportion of output has been directly subject to disruption by changes in the environment. The principal losses have been perceived in terms of the final consumption of goods and services – for example, ambient air quality, drinking water quality, or the quality of an outdoor recreational experience. Hence it has been natural to develop techniques for valuing the environment as part of the consumption stream.

Although slight in comparison to valuing the environment as a consumption good, some research has addressed valuing the environment as an input in production. Aspects of the theory are laid out in Freeman (1993), Freeman and Harrington (1990), Mäler (1992), and Point (1994). Applications include the recognition that low-level ozone and acid rain diminish plant growth, which has led to a suite of models designed to measure the economic costs of these types of air pollution for agriculture and forestry [e.g., Garcia et al. (1986), Kopp and Krupnick (1987)]. Ecologists have warned about the potential costs of the loss of spawning habitat, such as wetlands and mangrove swamps, and economists have attempted to measure the production and consumption effects of changes in these habitats [e.g., Ellis and Fisher (1987), Barbier (1994), Barbier and Strand (1998)]. Soil erosion, leading to a cumulative process of land degradation, has generated a number of studies in Africa [Brekke, Iversen and Aune (1999), Bojø

(1996)]. Water pollution has been identified as responsible for the declining productivity of some commercial fish stocks, and attempts to measure these costs can be found in the literature [e.g., Kahn and Kemp (1985), Lynne, Conroy and Prochaska (1981), Hodgson and Dixon (1988)].

Valuation of the environment as an input in production has had a far greater role to play in the developing than the developed world. In developing countries, the demand for environmental quality as a part of the final consumption stream is low because income levels are low, a relationship documented empirically in the environmental Kuznets curve literature [Grossman and Krueger (1993)]. In contrast, the environment has a relatively greater influence on production in developing countries because agriculture and natural resource extraction represent a larger proportion of economic activity and because both the degree and scale of environmental degradation are often large. But there are additional factors. The small scale of agriculture that characterizes many developing economies makes individual enterprises more vulnerable to pollution and less able to internalize environmental externalities. Institutional shortcomings make it more difficult for small-scale agriculture to avert the effects of pollution or seek compensation. Attenuated access to capital markets means that firms and household producers may have limited means for investing in averting techniques, such as terracing agricultural land. And poorly developed pollution liability laws make the recovery of damages from pollution unlikely.

In this chapter, we present the basic models for valuing the environment as an input and then investigate particular practices that have been pursued in the literature. The theoretical basis for valuing the environment as an input does not differ whether one investigates low-level ozone damages to crops in the U.S. or losses of mangrove swamps in Mexico. But the scarcity of data and more tenuous market forces make the practice in developing areas different and more difficult. As a consequence, we pay particular attention to the types of approximations that are often necessary, as well as the implications of these approximations.

Although not part of our analysis, the causes of changes in environmental inputs are worth considering. Changes in environmental inputs are most often the consequence of local and regional economic activity. Logging affects wetlands, which in turn influence fishery production. Emissions from fossil fuels lead to low-level ozone, which retards plant growth. In other cases, the causes are natural, such as the periodic flooding of farmland. But the possibility that the causes of environmental deterioration are in some sense preventable or reversible, at a cost, motivates the search for the damages from the deterioration. Without the possibility of policies that control environmental inputs, there is little to be gained from models that measure the welfare gains and losses associated with the inputs.

As a prelude to presenting the basic models, we consider a set of issues that will sharpen the presentation of these models.

2. The context of the problem

This chapter deals with valuing the environment as an input. It may be an input in a firm's production of a marketed good or an input in a household's "production" of a good that the household itself consumes. It may also be an input in a household's production of a marketed good. The latter relationship characterizes much economic activity in developing countries.

The ways in which the environment can act as an input in production are potentially quite varied. Environmental factors influence output by changing the productivity of inputs, by altering output that has been produced, or by reducing the effective supply of inputs. As long as the price of inputs is not affected, all of these effects can be modeled by including an environmental input in the production function. For example, in the case of low-level ozone, the environmental factor is a one-dimensional variable that can be modeled as an uncontrolled input into the production process. In many cases, however, the environmental effects may be much more diffuse. Flooding of farmlands from watershed degradation alters the production opportunities much more substantially than simply as an uncontrolled input. The loss of productive soil has a long run effect on production opportunities. The loss of wetlands may change the mix of species available for capture, as well as the age distribution of fish, making the change in productive opportunities more than simply a parametric change. Although we will persist in modeling the problem as an input in the production function, it is worth bearing in mind that more complex processes may be at work. This has particular relevance when it comes to obtaining econometric or experimental evidence of injury to production. In a case where the injurious environmental input can be measured, econometric or experimental studies are feasible. But in the more diffuse cases, many of which are important in the developing world, more complicated models or indirect inferences will be required.

In the examples above, the quality of the environmental good is important in making a contribution to production. Implicitly, degradation of the environment shifts production functions such that with the same amount of purchased inputs, less output is possible. There is another way in which to view the environment as an input into production – that is, as a sink for production wastes. Thus pollution can also be viewed as the use of the environment as an input. Some interpretations will change, however. The quality of the environmental resource no longer affects the productivity of the firm, unless the resource reaches saturation. Instead, firm productivity will be sensitive to regulations aimed at restricting this use of the environment. In what follows, most of our examples will relate to the more positive role of the environment in production, but the results will often carry over logically to the pollution case.

In attempting to place economic value on changes in environmental goods and services that enter as inputs into production, we begin with the basic constructs of welfare economics – the concepts of compensating and equivalent variation, as defined in Chapter 12 by Nancy Bockstael and A. Myrick Freeman III in this Handbook. These concepts are now well-understood and broadly accepted within the economics profession as preferable money equivalent welfare measures for individuals. We do not pretend that this is the only way to define value, nor that this way has no ethical drawbacks, but we argue that it is a logically consistent one that allows comparison of alternatives.

Compensating variation is the amount of income (positive or negative) that an individual would need to be paid after an exogenous change, for that individual to be just as well off as he would have been had the change not occurred. Equivalent variation is the amount of income (positive or negative) that the individual would be willing to pay, *in lieu* of the exogenous change, to make him as well-off as he would have been had the change occurred. We have defined compensation in terms of income, and income in terms of money, although in principle compensation could be paid or received in terms of any scarce resource. The choice of money is an obvious one, because it is the natural unit of exchange. However, the results of the application of the compensation principle are not necessarily independent of the units in which the compensation is measured. This is because an individual's willingness to pay or accept payment in terms of some resource will be a function of his endowment of that resource.

Welfare, as we define it here, accrues only to human beings, not to ecosystems directly nor to institutions. Whether the appropriate unit of analysis is the individual or the household is not so easily answered. In principle we are concerned with each and every human being, but both utility and decisions are often interdependent within a household. In this chapter we will use the terms somewhat interchangeably, but there will be many contexts in which one or the other is the more appropriate unit of analysis.

There is an important distinction between compensating or equivalent welfare measures from welfare economics and the empirical magnitudes that are used to supplement market-valued measures of national product to form green net national product. As Weitzman (1976) and Hartwick (1990) both emphasize in their model construction, national product is equivalent to linearized utility, normalized by the marginal utility of income. When environmental services are included in national product, they are priced at their marginal value and added to the market-valued product. This principle is different from nonmarket valuation, which seeks the amount of money that will compensate an individual for a change in the environmental service. This will typically be different from the valuation that goes into green national product, unless preferences are such that marginal values are constant. It is in fact the linearized value of compensation computed from the principles of welfare economics. It is not surprising that these measures should be calculated differently because they fulfill different roles. Nonmarket valuation seeks to measure the amount of income that is equivalent to changes in the environment, while national income accounting of environmental changes incorporates the linearized equivalent consumption.

2.1. The individual or household's decision problem

To set the stage for subsequent discussions, consider the individual's utility maximization problem in a very general context. The individual maximizes utility, which is a function of the purchased goods z_c, household produced goods that are consumed, z_h, and leisure S that she consumes, subject to constraints on her time and on her money income. This problem can be written as:

$$\max U\big(z_c, z_h(L_h, x_h, q), S\big) \tag{1a}$$

subject to

$$\bar{m} + wL_m + p_p z_p(L_p, x_p, q) - p_c z_c - r_h x_h - r_p x_p = 0, \tag{1b}$$

$$T - S - L_h - L_m - L_p = 0. \tag{1c}$$

In (1a) utility depends on purchased goods, household produced goods and leisure. Household produced goods depend on household labor (L_h), market inputs (x_h), and the environmental input q. In (1b), the individual's income constraint requires that non-labor income $\bar{m}$ plus wages received from labor supplied in the market, wL_m, plus income received from selling household produced output, $p_p z_p$, just equal expenditures on market goods, $p_c z_c$, plus expenditures on inputs used in the household production of goods for sale, $r_p x_p$, and expenditures on goods for home consumption, $r_h x_h$. The constraint in (1c) requires that total available time, T, be allocated between leisure or other household activities, S, labor supplied on the market, L_m, and labor used in household production of marketed goods, L_p, and of household consumed goods, L_c. The environmental input may affect goods consumed at home as well as goods that are sold.

Environmental goods can affect individuals directly when changes in their levels affect utility. However, in this chapter we are interested only in their effect through production. Define the indirect utility function as the solution of problem (1) described as a function of the variables exogenous to the individual, $V(\bar{m}, w, p_c, p_p, r_h, r_p, T, q)$. Then, the compensating variation (*CV*) and equivalent variation (*EV*), in money terms, of a change in q from q^0 to q^1 are given implicitly by:

$$V\big(\bar{m} - CV, w, p_c, p_p, r_h, r_p, T, q^1\big) = V\big(\bar{m}, w, p_c, p_p, r_h, r_p, T, q^0\big), \tag{2a}$$

$$V\big(\bar{m}, w, p_c, p_p, r_h, r_p, T, q^1\big) = V\big(\bar{m} + EV, w, p_c, p_p, r_h, r_p, T, q^0\big). \tag{2b}$$

Throughout, we sign the *CV* and *EV* measures according to their welfare effect, such that positive *CV* and *EV* measures imply a welfare improvement.

Expressions analogous to (2) can be derived for any parameter change – whether the parameter is q, some price, or nonwage income. In general, *CV* and *EV* measures are not equal. This is because the parameter changes being valued enter a decision problem in which the objective is to maximize utility. Since the trade-off between utility and money is not constant as one or the other changes, money measures of welfare change differ depending on the base utility level at which the translation is being made (see Chapter 12 by Bockstael and Freeman). The exception is when the parameter change facing the individual is a change in exogenous income. In this case, no translation into money terms is necessary. The amount of money necessary to compensate the individual when facing a decrease (increase) in exogenous income is simply an offsetting increase (decrease) in income.

The welfare measures are stated in the context of individual or household decision making, but we are also interested in welfare effects that arise in the context of firms' production decisions. Welfare always accrues to individuals or households, however, and changes in returns to firms ultimately show up as changes in individuals' nonwage income, denoted $\bar{m}$ in Equation (1). Such changes are direct measures of *CV* and *EV* (which are identical in this case).

For small firms in which most of the labor is supplied by the household or for households that produce for their own consumption and the market, the distinction between firm and household becomes blurred. The important distinction is whether production and consumption decisions can be treated as separable. In the framework of Equation (1), it is clear that when the household is producing for its own consumption, then no separability assumption can be made. Changes in q will be filtered through the utility function, and there may be a difference between the equivalent and compensating variation of a change.[1] For small changes in utility, the distinction between the *CV* and *EV* measures is unlikely to be important. This is useful, because when they diverge, *CV* and *EV* are rarely observable to the researcher. But when the environmental changes are quite disruptive, or the households are very poor, then the distinction between *CV* and *EV* may be significant.

2.2. The firm's decision process

Although all economic welfare accrues to the individual, changes in individuals' welfare that originate in the context of firm production must be analyzed within the decision context of the firm, and it is this context that the researcher will need to explore. There is a vast literature on firms that maximize sales, market shares, or some other criterion, but in this chapter we assume that producers maximize profits unless they face uncertainty. If there is substantial uncertainty in outcomes or prices and if firm owners have preferences over risk, then the problem must, once again, be set in the context of utility maximization. This is most germane for small firms with no internal means of diversifying their risk portfolio. Hence even when consumption and production are separable in small firms, the presence of risk will force us to take into account the owner's preferences over multiple moments of the probability distribution of profits. In the simplest form, preferences for expected profits relative to the variance of profits will affect production decisions and welfare. The tradeoffs between expected profits and risk are implicit in the definition of the utility function of the firm owner leading to the same sort of ambiguities that we normally encounter when measuring welfare in the context of the household. Just, Hueth and Schmitz (2004) and others have shown how firm behavioral functions can be derived in such cases, but the relevant constructs for welfare measurement will now involve compensated output supply and input demand functions. The logical result is that compensating and equivalent variation of changes in the environmental input will no longer be equal when firms have preferences over risks as well

---

[1] Empirically the evidence in support of distinctions between compensating and equivalent variation comes almost exclusively from experimental or contingent valuation studies, and even this evidence is now being challenged. See List (2001).

as profits, although these differences are likely to be small unless the changes in utility are large. For most of this chapter, we will ignore risk and uncertainty, leaving this topic to Chapter 13 by Karl-Göran Mäler and Anthony Fisher in this Handbook.

So as to be clear about the sources of nonwage income arising from the firm, consider the firm's profit maximization problem subject to a technology constraint denoted by the transformation function $t(y, x \mid k^0)$:

$$\max \pi = py - wx - C^0 \quad \text{subject to } t(y, x \mid k^0) = 0 \tag{3}$$

where π denotes profits, y is a scalar or vector of outputs with corresponding price scalar or vector p, x is the vector of inputs, w is the corresponding vector of input prices, k^0 is the vector of fixed factors, and C^0 is fixed cost. The composition of k^0 and therefore C^0 depends on the "length of run" inherent in the analysis. If the context is a short run analysis, then several factors might be considered fixed in that they cannot be altered in the short run. As the time horizon of the analysis lengthens, more and more factors can be altered.

We follow Just, Hueth and Schmitz (2004) in defining the exogenous income arising from the firm to be the quasi-rents generated by that firm's operation. In terms of expression (3), quasi-rents include both pure profit π and returns to fixed factors C^0. If a factor is fixed in the relevant "run", then it has zero opportunity cost and all returns to it are *rent* in that "run". Thus quasi rents (also called producer surplus) equal $\pi + C^0 = py - wx = py - C(w, y, k^0)$, where $C(w, y, k^0)$ is the variable cost function. The quasi-rent or producer surplus of the firm is the total revenue less whatever costs are variable in the relevant "run". Put another way, quasi-rents or producer surplus includes the returns to the owners of the firm and rents to the owners of the fixed factors.

In the usual welfare problem, exogenous changes can occur in any of the prices – the p's and w's. As C^0 is independent of these prices, the resulting change in quasi-rents or producer surplus equals the change in profits, disregarding C^0 which does not change. This makes the profit function a particularly useful construct for welfare evaluation. To illustrate, we introduce an environmental good or service into the firm's problem as an exogenous variable in the production function, so that now profit is maximized subject to a modified constraint:

$$\max \pi = py - wx - C^0 \quad \text{subject to } t(y, x \mid k^0, q) = 0 \tag{4}$$

and quasi-rents are given by $\pi + C^0 = py - C(w, y, k^0, q)$. Now, define the profit function as the solution to the problem in (4) and denote it $\pi(p, w, k^0, q)$. The quasi-rents associated with a change in q, from q^0 to q^1, are simply given by

$$\pi(p, w, k^0, q^1) - \pi(p, w, k^0, q^0), \tag{5}$$

so that knowledge of how the profit function varies with q is sufficient to determine the welfare effect of a change in q.

There is one important case in which using the concept of profits in place of quasi-rents is not correct – that is when the exogenous change causes the firm to shut down.

A firm, forced to shut down by some exogenous change, would lose $\pi + C^0$ if operations ceased. The firm would be willing to pay up to this amount to avoid the change that led to the shut-down.

In any event, changes in quasi-rents translate into changes in income to the owners of the firm and the fixed factors. In the absence of uncertainty about these returns, changes in quasi-rents (producer surplus) equal both the compensating and equivalent variation of an exogenous event, because they affect individuals as changes in exogenous, nonlabor income.

2.3. Issues of scale, interactions, and complexities

Procedures for accurately accounting for the welfare effects of environmental changes depend both on the size of the change and how widespread its effects are. If, for example, the change is a marginal one affecting a single firm, then it might be quite easy to measure the welfare effect. Marginal values are frequently quite easy to obtain empirically and are always available conceptually. To illustrate, consider the case in which the environmental input q, enters the production of a single marketed output y. The welfare effect on the firm is the change in quasi-rents associated with the marginal change in q. Quasi-rents could be written as $py(x, q) - wx$ in which case the change in quasi-rents with a marginal change in q would be given by

$$p\frac{\partial y}{\partial q} + p\frac{\partial y}{\partial x}\frac{\partial x}{\partial q} - w\frac{\partial x}{\partial q} = p\frac{\partial y}{\partial q}. \tag{6}$$

This simplification is implied by the envelope theorem. At the firm's optimum, $p(\partial y/\partial x) - w = 0$. The implication is that a marginal change in q could be valued as output price times the marginal product of q in the production of y. Likewise, we could write quasi-rents as $py - C(w, y, q, k^0)$ and, using the envelope theorem again, see that the marginal change in q could be valued as $-\partial C(w, y, q, k^0)/\partial q$, or the change in costs necessary to obtain the original output level with a marginal change in q.

The use of marginal values, however extrapolated, is least satisfactory when the environmental changes are substantial. Such environmental changes include large and pervasive oil spills such as the Amoco Cadiz, long term degradation of soil quality that might accompany deforestation, or chronic air pollution that affects a firm's output. The most significant welfare measurement challenges arise in these cases, when the extrapolation of marginal changes is inappropriate. With large changes in the environment, a firm may make substantially different production plans. For example, landowners in the vicinity of bauxite extraction facilities in Florida simply switched from growing oranges to raising cattle. Even when there are no price changes to consider, the adjustments in inputs or outputs will alter the damage from the environmental input. Although the marginal value may be all that can be estimated, it may not lead to a close approximation of the total value.

When the environmental change is sufficiently widespread, more than one firm or household will be affected. This causes no added problems in welfare measurement unless the agents are in some way interdependent. In the absence of interdependence we need only add *CV* or *EV* measures (or their approximations) over agents, although one may wish to keep track of the welfare effects on different groups of agents if distribution is an important policy consideration. When interdependencies exist, they can be technological, in which case externalities exist among agents, or they can be strictly pecuniary, in that agents participate in the same markets and their joint actions affect prices. In the first case, the nature of the externality needs to be explicitly accounted for and the optimal behavior of all agents modeled appropriately; in the second, the endogeneity of prices should be incorporated into the analysis.

When the interdependency or externality is the environmental good of interest, for example if q is a pollutant emitted by one firm or industry and affecting other economic agents, then one could attempt to measure the welfare effects of a change in q on the receiving agents, but not the effect on the generating firms, since for them q is a choice variable. As an illustration, consider an agricultural sector whose farming methods cause dramatic downstream sedimentation, thus reducing fish populations and producer surplus to commercial fishermen. With accurate biological and market information, it might be possible to estimate the changes in producer surplus to fishermen from a reduction in sedimentation. A more meaningful and comprehensive study would assess the welfare effects to both parties of a change in regulations or a public investment project that would have the effect of changing the farmers' optimal choice of q.

When the production of marketed goods is affected, a sufficiently extensive environmental change can affect multiple firms in an industry, resulting in price changes. Where markets are localized, price effects are all the more likely. Once prices change, there are additional welfare effects to be taken into account, and these welfare effects will accrue to the firms in the industry, but also to consumers and to firms that buy from this industry. Price changes may also be induced in input markets, if the industry in question is of sufficient size relative to any of these markets. Price changes in factor markets mean changes in producer surplus for factor owners. It is obvious but worth mentioning that the extent of the market, i.e., the total population affected, either directly by the environmental change or indirectly through affected markets, is a critical determinant of the estimate of total gains or losses.[2]

If changes in environmental goods that are inputs in firm production ultimately induce changes in consumer goods' prices or wage rates, then welfare measures developed in the context of the household decision framework, Equation (1) above, will be needed. This is obvious when consumer prices are affected, but perhaps less obvious for wages. However, if labor supply is a relevant decision for the household, changes in wage rates will lead to changes in *endogenous* income. Taking account of the fact that time spent not working may be utility producing, a change in the wage rate translates into a change in the opportunity cost of time spent on leisure or household production, thus changing behavior. Time allocation has been found to be an important decision and one sensitive

---

[2] Just, Hueth and Schmitz (2004) dedicate a significant amount of their book to the analysis of welfare effects in multiple markets.

to changing opportunity costs in the developing as well as developed world [e.g., Cooke (1998), Whittington, Mu and Roche (1990)]. When either consumer prices or wages change, compensating and equivalent variation measures of welfare will diverge. In the case of large changes in prices, this divergence may be important, but for small changes, it probably does not matter.

There are circumstances in which changes best assessed in the context of *household* production can also induce price changes. Consider the effects of economy-wide increases in air pollution, and suppose that these increases in air pollution bring a predictable increase in morbidity. The increased morbidity prevents some individuals from working and causes others to work less effectively. The effects may extend across both home and market supplied labor and may cause the real wage rate for healthy workers to rise, having ultimate effects on firms. These circumstances may be quite prevalent, especially in developing countries. Examples include the high incidence of gastroenteritis from water contamination [Ibáñez (2000)] and the potential effects of air pollution on respiratory illness [Alberini et al. (1997), Chestnut, Whittington and Lauria (1996)].

The way in which welfare effects are assessed depends to a large extent on the size and breadth of the original disturbance. The effects of large or widespread changes cannot be assessed in the same way as localized or marginal changes and then simply scaled up. From the perspective of the economic system, the larger and more widespread the change, the more likely that additional parameters (particularly prices) that are exogenous to individual economic agents will be altered, making for additional sources of welfare effects and bringing in more affected agents and more behavioral adjustments. At the extreme, general equilibrium models may be needed to assess the consequences.

To illustrate the errors that can be made by inappropriate rescaling, consider the recent papers [Costanza et al. (1997), Pimentel et al. (1997) and Ehrlich and Ehrlich (1996)] that have attempted to value the world's ecosystems by extrapolating localized studies of specific resource losses to losses of all such resources on the planet. For example, a localized valuation study that estimated the value of several hectares of lost wetlands at approximately $15,000/hectare would be used to calibrate the value of the world's 330 million hectares of wetlands at about $5 trillion ($15K \cdot 330M$). There are a number of reasons why this approach is incorrect (even if the original localized study were executed properly), in addition to the obvious one that not all wetlands (or beaches or forests) are alike. For one thing, each independent localized study that produces welfare measures does so conditional on the continued health of all other such resources and related ecosystem components. The loss of one wetland when others exist to support similar activities cannot be simply extrapolated to the loss of all wetlands. This is because economic agents will adjust their behavior through substitution, and if this adjustment is not properly accounted for, answers will be incorrect.

Of course, this set of papers offers an extreme example – so extreme that one questions whether there could be a logically meaningful way to answer the question that they pose. When we begin to consider the destruction of all the world's ecosystems, then measuring losses in units of any monetary system is ludicrous. For such extensive changes, the economic system would change completely, generating quite different sets of prices and incomes, since money has no meaning independent of the system in which prices and incomes are determined. Perhaps more fundamentally, what do we mean by the elimination of the world's ecosystems? What is it that arises in the void? What is the alternative? Given a change of such disastrous proportions, there would be no finite compensation that individuals would accept to agree to the loss of the world's ecosystems, and they would pay everything they had to avoid it. In other words, the welfare question may be answerable without reference to empirical studies, and rescaling of results from localized empirical studies misses the point. For critiques of these papers, see Smith (1997), Pearce (1998), Bockstael et al. (2000), and Dasgupta, Levin and Lubchenko (2000).

These criticisms of efforts to value in one stroke the world's ecosystems should not be construed as condemnation of all attempts to value ecosystem services and functions. In fact, it is especially important to document the value of ecosystem services to human well-being as these contributions are critical but often unappreciated because they are indirect and often obscure. It is this very feature that makes valuation so difficult, however. The service flows of ecosystems and their interdependencies are not typically well-understood even by ecologists, nor is the result of perturbations to a system always predictable. Valuations of the global ecosystems, however misguided, may satisfy certain political needs but they do not inform policy decisions, which are typically made on the basis of local, regional or national trade-offs.

As ecologists learn more about ecological system interactions and dynamics, they are finding that ecological production relationships may not always possess the sort of "well behaved" properties often assumed for technological production relationships in economics. The best of the work falling within the rubric of "ecological economics" seeks to document the implications of violations of the smooth, twice differentiable production function [see, for example, Arrow et al. (1995), Carpenter, Brock and Hanson (1999), Ludwig, Walker and Holling (1997)].[3] These irregularities include nonlinearities and discontinuities which suggest that small changes in stimuli can in some circumstances generate large and sometimes catastrophic system effects. They also include nonconvexities, especially in the context of multiple output production functions, so that optimum management solutions may not be characterized by simply equating marginal costs and benefits. Finally, in dynamic systems, these aberrations may take the form of irreversibilities, multiple equilibria and path dependence, such that an action taken at one point in time, may completely preclude certain states of the system in subsequent time periods.

In some sense, these complexities pose a greater challenge to positive than to normative analysis. They tax our abilities to characterize optimum solutions and predict scenario outcomes. In principle, if we know the outcomes that follow each and every action, we can assess the welfare consequences of each action. In practice, since we cannot know these outcomes, we must take into account the level of uncertainty and

---

[3] See the chapter on ecosystem dynamics by Simon Levin and Stephen Pacala in Volume 1 of this Handbook.

the consequences of making a mistake in the welfare analysis. The combination of high levels of uncertainty, path dependence, and the possibility of small changes causing catastrophic events, has led to the desire to obtain, not just the expected value of outcomes, but also the valuation of additional characteristics of the system, such as resilience to perturbations.

The challenges faced by welfare analysts in these complex settings are considerable. As an example, consider the effects of dramatic changes in habitat that lead to reductions in biodiversity and biocomplexity. Scientists have some, but often limited, knowledge of the likelihood of extinction of specific species in the face of such changes, but little knowledge of the long term losses associated with extinction. Much of the literature in this area assesses the value of biodiversity from the perspective of increased potential for pharmaceutical discoveries. More specifically the marginal species is valued as its incremental contribution to the probability of making a commercial discovery times the producer and consumer surpluses of such a discovery [Simpson, Sedjo and Reid (1996), Polasky and Solow (1995), Mendelsohn and Balick (1995)]. In treating only the prospects of pharmaceutical advancements, authors admit to an overly narrow focus, but other pathways by which biodiversity affects humans are even more difficult to define and measure.

In the remainder of this chapter, we will assume a reasonable knowledge of the ecosystem production function and an acceptable means of dealing with the uncertainty. Although ecological systems can be complex, there are numerous cases in which we have a good understanding of the role a natural resource plays in production, such as that of beaches in shoreline stabilization or of forests in nutrient management. In some cases, the resource really acts as a natural asset that provides a flow of services over time. Treatment of q as a natural asset might be viewed as complicating the valuation of changes in its ability to provide service flows, given issues involved with converting the time path of service flows to a current value. We deal solely with valuing the change in service flow in a given period and leave questions of appropriate discounting of long term damage and the treatment of intergenerational tradeoffs to the chapter by Geoffrey M. Heal in a different volume of this Handbook. That the environmental resource is often most usefully viewed as an asset is apparent in the context of fisheries, forestry and soil degradation examples. This way of viewing q affects the character and measurement of welfare by introducing a dynamic element to the underlying production technology. Whether or not the decision process of the firm or household reflects an appreciation of the temporal interdependency often depends on property rights and institutions.

To be relevant welfare analysis needs to be placed in the appropriate institutional setting. Institutions may be informal, such as access to irrigation water, or formal, such as government support of agricultural prices. In two areas of research relating the environment to production, results have been revised considerably as the appropriate role of institutions has been considered. In fisheries, where pollution reduces the productivity of fish stocks, the absence of property rights for harvesting fish may eliminate the impact of environmental changes on net profits to producers [Freeman (1991), McConnell and Strand (1989)]. In studies of the impact of ozone on agriculture, the benefits of ozone

reduction are found to be considerably smaller when the government's role in supporting agricultural prices is taken into account [Kopp and Krupnick (1987), McGartland
(1987), Madariaga (1988)]. Government or community rules on the extraction and sale
of resources can have substantial impacts on the economic costs and gains of environmental changes.

In the ensuing discussion, the time frame that we choose for illustration depends on
the institutional setting. In the initial discussion a competitive, static world is assumed.
The potential for dynamic interactions and/or industry wide effects is ignored in the
interest of getting the basics down clearly. Price effects in multiple markets are then
treated, followed by a discussion of market distortions in the context of agricultural
policy. When we come to the fishery, we will be concerned with steady state analysis, a
particular way of looking at the long run. In order to tell the full story for fisheries, the
industry as a whole must be examined in the long run. For the analysis of the exploitation
of forests, a long run view is essential. Each of these cases differs with respect to the
focus, but the distinctions are essential for understanding the most salient effects of
environmental changes.

The next section of this chapter treats many of these welfare measurement topics
in the context of firm decisions. The final section of the chapter addresses issues in
household production. The goal of both sections is to define the appropriate measure of
welfare change and to uncover a means of inferring the welfare change from observable
data. The theoretical models can help in the estimation of these welfare changes, and
perhaps as important, can expose the approaches that fail to measure changes in human
welfare and illuminate the degree of error from approximation.

3. The environment affects the firm's production opportunities

We begin with the simplest case – a single firm producing for a competitive market,
using inputs purchased in competitive markets.[4] By definition, if the environmental
change affects only one firm in a competitive setting, no prices will change and no further effects will be transmitted through the market. Output depends on the inputs and on
the environmental quality input q. For concreteness, we typically take q to be a "good",
representing in some sense the level of ecological services. There are occasions, however, in which the most natural concept for discussion is a measure of pollution or the
degradation of the environment. Increased pollution or loss of wetlands will be treated
as declines in q. Suppose that the transformation function can be written $t(y, x; q) = 0$
where y is output and maybe a scalar or vector, x is an n-dimensional input vector
$x_1, \ldots, x_n$, and q is the environmental factor.[5] The production relation will be assumed

---

[4] In what follows we draw heavily on Just, Hueth and Schmitz. This book lays out completely the details
of applied welfare analysis in the context of the firm and of markets, although it does not treat environmental
considerations and therefore does not develop the environment as an input case.

[5] Throughout this section we will suppress notation having to do with fixed factors for simplicity.

to be concave and nondecreasing in the inputs including q. Further, given q, there will be nonincreasing returns to scale to proportionate increases in x.[6]

Now suppose that pollution or ecological damage increases so that q decreases from q^0 to q^1. As long as there are no resulting price changes, the welfare effect is the change in the firm's producer surplus or quasi-rents from this environmental degradation. Repeating Equation (5), this is given by

$$\pi\left(p, w, q^1\right) - \pi\left(p, w, q^0\right). \tag{7}$$

If more than one firm is affected by the environmental change, but prices and technology remain unchanged, then the social cost will be the sum of terms such as (7) added across firms. When data on profits are available before and after the change, welfare calculation is purely an accounting exercise. Rarely are such data available, however, making it necessary to look for a means of recovering the essential parts of the profit function and, failing that, to look for approximations.

3.1. Exact measures of the change in producer surplus

The most fundamental, but econometrically most difficult, way of recovering (7) is to estimate a profit function and then simply calculate the difference in the value of the function, evaluated at different levels of the environmental input. Mjelde et al. (1984) and Dixon, Garcia and Mjelde (1985) use this approach to assess welfare effects on U.S. grain farmers of changes in ozone levels.

An alternative approach, more parsimonious than profit function estimation, involves the estimation of an output supply or an input demand function arising from profit maximizing behavior. With certain restrictions on the production function, one or another of these behavioral functions can provide a measure of welfare. In each case, the necessary restriction involves the concept of essentiality which makes it possible to evaluate welfare effects of one or more parameter changes affecting the firm by looking at changes in the area behind only an essential output's supply function or essential input's demand function.

3.2. The single output firm

We begin by imposing the simplest of restrictions – that the firm produces only one output, and if so, that output must be essential. An essential output is defined such that if economic conditions make continued production of this output no longer profitable, then the firm will shut down. To derive the welfare measure of a change in q in this

---

[6] As much as possible, we wish to discuss the intuitive content of production. We provide the basic specifications for production, abatement and cost functions. More general specifications may still satisfy requirements for profit maximization.

setting, note that the profit function is

$$\pi(p, w, q) = \max_{y}\{py - C(y, w, q)\} \tag{8}$$

where the cost function is defined as $C(y, w, q) = \min\{w \cdot x \mid t(y, x, q) = 0\}$. The change in producer surplus with a change in q can be written as

$$\pi(p^0, w^0, q^1) - \pi(p^0, w^0, q^0)$$
$$= [p^0 y(p^0, w^0, q^1) - C(y(p^0, w^0, q^1), w^0, q^1)]$$
$$- [p^0 y(p^0, w^0, q^0) - C(y(p^0, w^0, q^0), w^0, q^0)] \tag{9}$$

where p^0 and w^0 denote existing levels of prices and $y(p^0, w^0, q^i)$ is the optimal value of y given the initial levels of prices and $q = q^i$. The change in profits consists of the change in revenue when output changes in response to the change in the environmental factor and the change in costs when output and the environmental input change. Denoting the marginal cost of y as $C_y(y, w, q)$, (9) can be written as

$$\left[p^0 y(p^0, w^0, q^1) - \int_0^{y(q^1)} C_y(y, w^0, q^1) \, dy \right]$$
$$- \left[p^0 y(p^0, w^0, q^0) - \int_0^{y(q^0)} C_y(y, w^0, q^0) \, dy \right], \tag{10}$$

if $C(0, w, q^0) = C(0, w, q^1)$. This last condition will hold because the firm shuts down when it ceases to produce y, its single output. The only costs remaining are fixed costs, which are equal irrespective of the level of q. Graphically, this measure is represented as area ABCD in Figure 1.

   This same result can be found in a slightly different way, by using the envelope theorem. The partial derivative of the profit function with respect to output price is the supply function:

$$\frac{\partial \pi(p, w, q)}{\partial p} = y(p, w, q). \tag{11}$$

Given this relationship, the producer surplus of a change in q can be written as[7]

$$\int_{\tilde{p}(q^1)}^{p^0} y(p, w^0, q^1) \, dp - \int_{\tilde{p}(q^0)}^{p^0} y(p, w^0, q^0) \, dp$$
$$= \pi(p^0, w^0, q^1) - \pi(\tilde{p}(q^1), w^0, q^1) - \pi(p^0, w^0, q^0) + \pi(\tilde{p}(q^0), w^0, q^0). \tag{12}$$

---

[7] Strictly speaking a constant of integration emerges from these integrals for each $\pi(\cdot)$, which is equal in this case to $-C^0$. But since the constant of integration cannot be a function of the price, it cancels out for each definite integral.

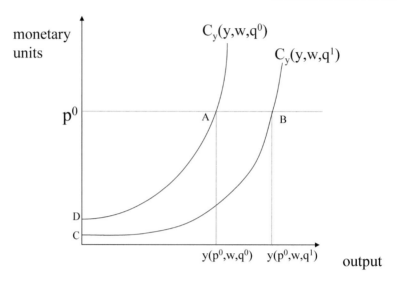

Figure 1. Welfare measure for the single output firm.

In (12), $\tilde{p}$ is the "choke price", i.e., the price below which the firm would cease to produce y. Producer surplus evaluated at the choke price for an essential output is by definition zero, and the remaining expression on the second line of (12), $\pi(p^0, w^0, q^1) - \pi(p^0, w^0, q^0)$, is once again the measure we seek. The first line of (12) is significant because it is the area below price and between the two supply curves, conditioned on the two levels of q – area ABCD in Figure 1.

From an accounting perspective, without knowledge of the supply function, we would need to calculate the change in costs and the change in revenues. The standard model that we have presented shows that it is sufficient to estimate the firm's supply function as it depends on output price and the environmental quality, as well as input prices if they change over the course of the observations. This approach is the best known and most frequently used empirical technique for recovering producer surplus measures in standard welfare analyses of policies that affect prices. However, its use in the context of environmental inputs to production is far more limited. It requires that firms' outputs be observed over a period when prices and environmental quality change. This typically requires panel data, unless there is good reason for cross-sectional variation in prices. Kahn and Kemp (1985) offer an example in which a commercial fishery supply curve (for striped bass in the Chesapeake Bay) is first derived and then estimated as a function of fish stocks, which in turn is modeled as a function of subaquatic vegetation levels.

3.3. The multiple output firm

Now consider the multiproduct firm [see Freeman and Harrington (1990), for a special treatment]. Firms that jointly produce multiple products are perhaps the rule rather than the exception. In fisheries, most vessels catch several species, often simultaneously. In agriculture, especially among small farmers, enterprises may produce some combination of grains, milk, fodder, manure, and livestock. Large farms produce several field crops. Suppose the firm uses, as before, n inputs, but produces m outputs, according to the production technology $t(y, x, q) = 0$. The environmental input is assumed to increase productive capacity. The definition of the social costs of changes in q remains the same – the change in producer surplus or quasi-rents to the firm.

Estimation of a profit function is likely to be an even more difficult task now, although estimation of output supply functions may be possible. But if q enters a multiproduct production function, using supply functions to obtain welfare measures becomes more complicated. The exception is when one of the outputs is essential. The proof is straightforward. Analogous expressions to (11) and (12) hold for each of the m outputs. For the area between the initial and subsequent supply curves of the ith output to measure the entire producer surplus change associated with a change in q, it must be true that

$$\pi\left(\tilde{p}_i\left(q^1\right), p_{(i)}, w^0, q^1\right) = \pi\left(\tilde{p}_i\left(q^0\right), p_{(i)}, w^0, q^0\right) \tag{13}$$

where $\tilde{p}_i$ is the price at which the firm ceases to produce output i and $p_{(i)}$ denotes the vector of prices of other outputs. Expression (13) will hold if, when it is not profitable to produce y_i, the firm shuts down.

In the more general and probably more usual case in which no single output is essential, the welfare measure can still be obtained but with more work. We can illustrate this with an example using two outputs, although it extends directly to m outputs. The change in producer surplus with a change in q is defined as

$$
\begin{aligned}
\pi\left(p^0, w^0, q^1\right) &- \pi\left(p^0, w^0, q^0\right) \\
&= \left\{p_1^0 y_1\left(p^0, w^0, q^1\right) + p_2^0 y_2\left(p^0, w^0, q^1\right)\right. \\
&\quad \left. - C\left(y_1\left(p^0, w^0, q^1\right), y_2\left(p^0, w^0, q^1\right), q^1\right)\right\} \\
&\quad - \left\{p_1^0 y_1\left(p^0, w^0, q^0\right) + p_2^0 y_2\left(p^0, w^0, q^0\right)\right. \\
&\quad \left. - C\left(y_1\left(p^0, w^0, q^0\right), y_2\left(p^0, w^0, q^0\right), q^0\right)\right\}.
\end{aligned}
\tag{14}
$$

In Equation (14), $C(y_1(p, w, q), y_2(p, w, q), q)$ is the joint cost function, defined as $\min\{w \cdot x \mid t(y, x, q) = 0\}$. With accounting information, *ex ante* and *ex post*, (14) could be calculated directly, but such information is unlikely.

The notation in (14) is cumbersome, and the welfare measure is more easily interpreted if one draws on the result that $\partial\pi/\partial p_i = y_i$ but sequences the price changes. The change in profits with a change in q can now be expressed as

$$
\begin{aligned}
\pi\left(p, w, q^1\right) &- \pi\left(p, w, q^0\right) \\
&= \left[\int_{\tilde{p}_1(q^1)}^{p_1^0} y_1\left(p_1, p_2^0, w^0, q^1\right) dp_1 + \int_{\tilde{p}_2(q^1)}^{p_2^0} y_2\left(\tilde{p}_1, p_2, w^0, q^1\right) dp_2\right] \\
&\quad - \left[\int_{\tilde{p}_1(q^0)}^{p_1^0} y_1\left(p_1, p_2^0, w^0, q^0\right) dp_1 + \int_{\tilde{p}_2(q^0)}^{p_2^0} y_2\left(\tilde{p}_1, p_2, w^0, q^0\right) dp_2\right]
\end{aligned}
\tag{15}
$$

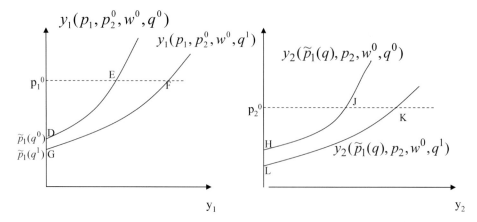

Figure 2. Changes in quasi-rents for a multiproduct firm.

where (15) represents the sum of the areas above each supply curve and below each price. Because the supply functions are exact differentials of the profit function, the line integral will be path independent and any path of integration can be chosen. One of the simplest paths is to condition the first supply function on the initial level of the price of the second and then condition the second supply function on the choke price of the first. Using a path of this sort, we can calculate the producer surplus of a change in q, as areas DEFG + HJKL depicted in Figure 2.

The implications of failing to account for the jointness in production are explored in Freeman (1993, Chapter 9). Whether the error turns out to be severe is an empirical issue. For example, Kopp et al. (1985) do not find any significant difference in the independent marginal cost functions when compared with the joint marginal cost function in a study of the effects of ozone on U.S. agriculture, but this need not be true in other settings.

3.4. Using input demand functions

It is sometimes impossible to estimate supply functions; the output may not be well-defined or easily measured. Suppose, though, that a particular input, say x_1, is essential in production. It is not necessary for x_1 to be linked in any particular way to q. It is only necessary that the input x_1 is such that in its absence the firm cannot produce y (whether y be a scalar or a vector), and so without x_1 quasi-rent will be zero. For example, irrigation water for a very dry climate would be essential for some agricultural production. Fertilizer might be considered essential for some crops on some soils.

Denote the demand function for input x_1 as $x_1(w_1, w_{(1)}, p, q)$, where $w_{(1)}$ is the vector of all other input prices. Let $\widetilde{w}_1$ be the choke price for x_1; that is,

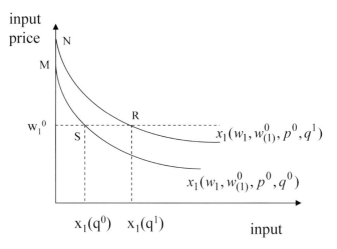

Figure 3. Welfare measurement using an essential input.

$x_1(\widetilde{w}_1, w_{(1)}, p, q) = 0$. Remembering that from the envelope theorem:

$$\frac{\partial \pi(p, w, q)}{\partial w_1} = -x_1\left(w_1, w_{(1)}^0, p^0, q\right),$$ (16)

the change in the area under the input demand function is

$$\int_{\widetilde{w}_1(q^1)}^{w_1^0} x_1\left(w_1, w_{(1)}^0, p^0, q^1\right) dw_1 - \int_{\widetilde{w}_1(q^0)}^{w_1^0} x_1\left(w_1, w_{(1)}^0, p^0, q^0\right) dw_1$$
$$= \pi\left(p^0, w_1^0, w_{(1)}^0, q^1\right) - \pi\left(p^0, \widetilde{w}_1, w_{(1)}^0, q^1\right)$$
$$- \pi\left(p^0, w_1^0, w_{(1)}^0, q^0\right) + \pi\left(p^0, \widetilde{w}_1, w_{(1)}^0, q^0\right).$$ (17)

If x_1 is an essential input, $\pi(p^0, \widetilde{w}_1, w_{(1)}^0, q^1) = \pi(p^0, \widetilde{w}_1, w_{(1)}^0, q^0)$, because both equal zero. As a consequence, the area between the two demand functions can be identified as the change in producer surplus associated with the change in the environmental input as depicted by area MNRS in Figure 3.

There is an alternative production function restriction that can assure that (17) is the proper measure, without appealing to the essentiality argument. For the area between the two demand functions to measure the change in producer surplus, all we really need is that $\pi(p, \widetilde{w}_1, w_{(1)}, q^0) = \pi(p, \widetilde{w}_1, w_{(1)}, q^1)$ even if neither term equals zero. Suppose that the environmental input is a quality dimension of x_1, so that when x_1 is not employed in production, changes in q have no impact on production. The environmental quality only affects the firm's production when x_1 is positive. As an example, now suppose that the firm has two sources of irrigation water, so that no single source is essential. Assume that one source of water is polluted with an industrial effluent. Water quality is the input q, and the producer surplus associated with changes in the effluent can be estimated for the firm as the change in the area under the derived demand for the effluent-contaminated water. The welfare measure is the same as that depicted in Figure 3, but the restriction on technology is different. This case is one of complementarity between the environmental good and a purchased input.

3.5. Implications

The restrictions for welfare measurement require essential outputs or inputs, or that the environmental input be a quality dimension of a purchased input. These restrictions are rarely tested empirically, and in fact it is not clear that econometric tests are available. They are generally established intuitively, from an understanding of the environmental and production processes.

To make use of these results, the researcher needs to be able to estimate supply and/or demand functions that are continuous functions of prices and that incorporate the environmental resource explicitly. There are many examples in the literature where these techniques have been used, especially in agricultural policy analysis, but as we have seen few are in the context of environmental resources as inputs. It is notable that most applications are in developed countries where markets are well-formed and sufficient alternatives exist to make it reasonable to expect supply and demand functions to be approximately continuous functions of prices. In the context of developing country problems practical approaches have been adopted in an attempt to approximate welfare effects.

3.6. Practical approaches to measuring the change in profits from a decline in quality of the environment

The theory provides a guide for practice, but rare is the case when the researcher has access to all the data implied by the theory. This difficulty in obtaining data, especially in developing countries, is at the heart of Mäler (1992) efforts to define welfare measures for changes in output. Here we consider several practices that are used in the absence of more complete data. The assumptions necessary for these practices to produce an accurate approximation are considered, as is the direction of the bias when the assumptions are violated.

3.7. Valuing changes in output using a damage function

The majority of studies that seek to value changes in an environmental resource that serves as an input in production base their estimates in one way or another on the predicted change in output valued at output price. This is akin to the accounting procedures mentioned earlier. If it is possible to predict how output and input use will change, and if prices can be assumed to remain constant, then producer surplus change can be calculated as in (9). But, several pitfalls lie along this path and misleading results can sometimes be generated.

In studies of this sort, the researcher is unable to estimate supply or demand functions but has some information on the nature of the production process. Occasionally, this information is used in a direct estimation of the production function. For example, Acharya (1998) estimates a relationship between crop output in the Hadejia-Nguru Floodplain in Nigeria and the inputs: land, labor, fertilizer and irrigation water. In this study, irrigation water is extracted from aquifers, and pumping costs are affected by groundwater levels that are in turn affected by wetlands. In a quite different example, Lynne, Conroy and Prochaska (1981) estimate a fisheries production function where catch is a function of fishing effort and acreage of marshlands which serves as a natural spawning ground for the blue crab.

In general, direct estimation of production functions is not advisable. If producers have any discretion over the quantity of inputs, then the explanatory variables in such a regression will be endogenous and the estimated coefficients biased. When possible, it is far better to attempt to derive a behavioral function (e.g., supply or demand) from the information about the production relationship and estimate that function, which will typically include only prices as explanatory variables [as in Kahn and Kemp (1985)]. But in the developing country context, prices are often unavailable, making this alternative infeasible.

Occasionally, dose–response or damage functions are available from theoretical or experimental science. They may come from agricultural experiments in which researchers subject different plots of land to different levels of environmental degradation or from engineers who have developed such constructs as the Universal Soil Loss Equation for predicting soil erosion. An example is the use of the Soil Loss Estimation Model by Brekke, Iversen and Aune (1999) who adopt this model in a more complicated, dynamic framework to model soil degradation in Tanzania.

If the agricultural experiments are extensive and include variations in inputs as well as the environmental resource or contaminant, then it may be possible to define a production function from the results, and this production function can then be used to derive a profit function or behavioral functions that describe how producer behavior is likely to change, resulting in accurate welfare measurement. However, the damage functions or dose–response functions most commonly available from natural scientists usually assess the change in output with a change in the environmental input, holding other inputs constant. Agronomic field tests are classic examples. In these tests, a single input such as fertilizer is varied across plots, while other inputs are held constant. In many case studies, such functions have been used to evaluate losses due to environmental degradation or benefits from environmental improvements simply by valuing that loss or gain in output due to a change in the environmental services holding other inputs constant. But the output change thus predicted may not correspond to the actual output change if producers alter inputs. If producers have any discretion over input levels, they will tend to change their use of inputs unless the production function is separable in the environmental resource. In her Nigeria study, Acharya argues that groundwater levels do not become known until after farmers have already committed other inputs, so no adjustment may be possible in such a case. In general, however, the possibility of adjustment causes losses to be less and gains to be greater than estimated by simply pricing the predicted dose–response outcome.

In a good deal of research on the effect of ozone on crop production, researchers have access to experimental data that show the relationship between ozone and yield, with inputs held constant. In this context, the approach would be expected to overestimate the effect of ozone on crop yield because it does not account for the substitution of other factors to mitigate the effects of ozone, or even the possibility of substituting to crops that are less sensitive to ozone. The degree to which input adjustments are possible and likely gives some information as to the accuracy of this type of approximation.

Kopp, Vaughan, Hazilla and Carson exploit the experimental data while imposing some very specific restrictions on the structure of the production function. To begin with, they assume that ozone has only a scale effect on output and does not affect the marginal rate of substitution among inputs. This, together with the assumption that input prices remain constant, means that the only relevant portion of the technology map is a ray from the origin. The effect of increases in ozone is to move the firm along the ray, increasing each of the technical coefficients proportionally: $x_i = ka_i y$ where k increases for increases in ozone, hence increasing the input required to produce a given output. With these restrictions, dose–response data are sufficient to solve for changes in profits, but the realism of the restrictions may be called into question.

A number of studies that have sought to value proposed investment projects have also used the approach of valuing predicted changes in output, often based on assumptions of how land use will change under the project. An example is the analysis of a watershed management project by Fleming, reported in Dixon et al. (1995, pp. 120–132). Assumptions are made about the amount of land that would be used in agriculture, grazing, pasture, scrubland, forest and plantations with and without the management project, and further assumptions are made about "productivity" of the land in these different uses. Valuation of the grazing land component, for example, involves calculating the yield of milk and fertilizer (manure) per hectare of all land assumed to be used for grazing, and valuing this at milk and fertilizer prices, subtracting the cost of feed.

This approach will provide a reasonable approximation if assumptions about land use and productivity are reliable, if technology is so limited that there is little further discretion left to land users, and if prices are good reflections of social costs. With regard to this latter issue, it seems most problematic to estimate the social costs of labor – and not infrequently these costs are omitted entirely. Even in societies without well-developed labor markets, however, the opportunity cost of time can be considerable, as suggested by studies such as Cooke (1998) and Whittington, Mu and Roche (1990). In his study of a soil management project in Lesotho, Bojo (1990) values the project as the crop price times change in yield minus changes in variables costs, and describes the difficulty of pricing labor. In evaluating the benefits of afforestation in Nigeria, Anderson (1987) provides a sensitivity analysis based on different means of calculating the opportunity cost of labor.

The principle of Le Châtelier is useful in assessing the welfare measures that are accomplished with damage functions. This principle states that when constraints are loosened the firm's response to a parametric change will not be smaller than with the constraint. Damage functions essentially restrict the firm to no response at all. When the firm is able to respond, then it will change its input mix to avert some of the damages from a change in the environment or take advantage of an improvement. With this change in input mix, the firm will necessarily be better off. Consequently, the damage function approach will overestimate the welfare losses from an undesirable change in the environment, and underestimate the gains from an improvement in the environment.

The damage function approach is frequently adopted in assessing the damages to agriculture from global warming. In a study of the costs of global warming to agriculture in the USA, Mendelsohn, Nordhaus and Shaw (1994) argue that the damage function approach is equivalent to the "dumb farmer", because it assumes that farmers do not know enough to adjust their inputs. They take the approach that farmers are able to adjust fully and instantaneously to changes in climate, and so estimate global warming damages that are lower than the damage function approach. Quiggin and Horowitz (1999), in commenting on the damage estimates for global warming, note that the damage function approach and the Ricardian or instantaneous adjustment approach are on opposite extremes in terms of adjustment costs. The damage function assumes that adjustment costs are infinite, but instantaneous adjustment assumes that adjustment costs are zero. The truth lies somewhere in between.

3.8. Valuing actual changes in output

On occasion researchers might observe the actual change in output, but *only* the change in output. With this piece of information – actual output changes, it is tempting to try to obtain a bound on the change in producer surplus or to argue that the value of the change in output is a good approximation for the true loss. To investigate this, consider how producer surplus changes with a change in q:

$$\Delta \pi = \left[p \frac{\Delta y}{\Delta q} - C_y \frac{\Delta y}{\Delta q} - C_q \right] \Delta q \tag{18}$$

where Δq is the change in the environmental variable and $\Delta y / \Delta q$ is the optimal response of output to that change in q. The decrease in the environmental input (e.g., fish habitat) will result in a decrease in y, so that $\Delta y / \Delta q$ will be positive. Marginal cost C_y is positive, and C_q is negative because a decrease in the ecological input leads to increases in costs, *ceteris paribus*.

To compare measures, note that in the profit maximizing, perfect competition context, the area under the firm's supply curve is the variable cost of producing any given level of y. Suppose marginal cost curves were as drawn in Figure 4. The correct measure, the change in producer surplus with a decline in the environmental input from q^0 to q^1, equals areas $-(a + b)$. Referring to the expression in (18), the decrease in the value of the output, $p(\Delta y / \Delta q) \Delta q$, is given by areas $-(b + d)$. Roughly speaking,

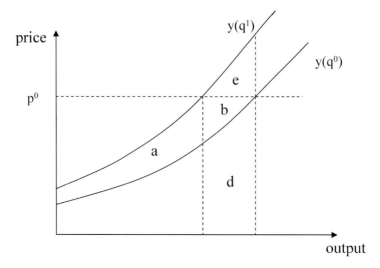

Figure 4. Commonly used measures based on change in output.

$-C_y(\Delta y/\Delta q)\Delta q$, the increase in profits from incurring less costs to produce this diminished output, is given by area (d). The term $-C_q\Delta q$ is represented by area $-a$, the loss in profits due to increased costs of producing y^1 when q is decreased to q^1. The error in using the change in the value of output is areas $(-a) + d$. Since the sign is ambiguous, there is no clear way to use the change in revenues to bound the change in producer surplus without knowing a good bit about the cost structure.

Under some circumstances, pricing actual output changes may be a good approximation to changes in producer surplus. Consider the case in which the only variable input in production is labor, and labor has few alternatives making it not very responsive to changes in productivity. Might artisanal fishermen fish the same number of hours irrespective of catch rates? If so, changes in variable costs are irrelevant, and all the action is in the changes in revenues. Hanayama and Sano [in a study reported by Hufschmidt and Dixon (1986)] appear to make this assumption in valuing a loss in fish habitat, *ex post*, by multiplying the actual decrease in fish catch by fish price and ignoring any changes in inputs. However, in general, if the degradation is significant, we would expect producers to alter their behavior in some way.

In Kopp and Krupnick (1987), an interesting assumption is made that allows this approximation. The authors argue that for any farmer, the variation in yields over time due to weather, pests, etc. is sufficiently great to mask variations due to ozone changes. Therefore, even though the aggregate production may be systematically changing with changes in ozone, individual farmers will not alter their input decisions in response to this change. Thus, costs will remain the same, and the producer surplus change will equal the lost revenue. Whether this is true is an empirical question, but it is an ingenious way to justify this simplification.

3.9. Using changes in costs

Some researchers have attempted to estimate the social losses of ecological damage by calculating how costly it would be to produce the same output levels in the presence of the degraded environment. In the context of our individual firm example, this would be the change in costs with a change in q, holding y constant. In Figure 4, the additional cost is given by areas $-(a + b + e)$ and therefore is an overestimate of the true loss from environmental degradation which equal areas $-(a + b)$. It is not difficult to see that if, alternatively, q were to rise, this change in cost measure would be an underestimate of the gains from environmental improvements. Regulated public utilities that are required to provide a certain level of service might offer one of the few examples in which institutions force firms to remain at a fixed level of output.

Calculating the *actual* change in costs is also incorrect. This ignores the fact that revenues change as well, and will be accurate only if output returns to its original level as in the public utility example. In the usual case the actual, *ex post*, change in costs is given by areas $d - a$, an underestimate (in absolute value terms) of the loss in producer surplus because the decline in revenues (areas $b + d$) is not taken into account. For improvements in q, it is also an underestimate of the gains.

Some of the worst mistakes in environmental valuation are made by attempting to measure the social cost of environmental degradation as the cost of remediating the damage. The only relationship that the cost of an engineering remediation has to the welfare measure we seek is that the former can be no less than the change in producer surplus associated with the degradation. It can however be orders of magnitude more. In a study of the value of a program to reduce soil erosion in Korea, Kim and Dixon (1986) use what is referred to as the "replacement-cost" approach. They calculate the truck rental and spreading costs of retrieving from downstream the sediment loss and take this cost to be the "minimum estimate of the value" of a project that will prevent the damage. Instead, this cost estimate is an upper bound. There is no correspondence between such a cost estimate and the social cost of the soil erosion (or the benefit of a program that prevents the erosion.) Even if this were known to be the least cost mitigation method, the cost calculation would still do nothing to inform our estimate of the value of mitigation.

In contrast, if we were to observe a profit maximizing producer undertaking such a cost, then we would know that the present value of soil loss would not be less than this cost. But this information is revealed by the firm's behavior. In the absence of revealed behavior, engineering costs provide little guidance about welfare costs.

3.10. Further complications

The results so far have related to a single price-taking firm under conditions of certainty and in a competitive, unregulated and unsubsidized economic environment. Relaxing any of these conditions further complicates applied welfare measurement. In the space of this chapter we cannot give substantive treatment to all these complications, but we do suggest the direction in which the previous welfare analysis must be modified.

3.11. Price changes and multiple markets

For the welfare effects of an environmental change to be restricted to the firms that use the environmental input, the output of the firms affected must not be sufficiently large to affect the aggregate supply curve and thus to alter the output price. If output price does change, then the effect on the individual firm can still be measured using the change in area below price and above the supply curve for an essential output (such as Equation (12)), as long as the integral in the after-change case reflects the subsequent price change. The change in producer surplus in such a case is illustrated in Figure 5 as area (p^1AD) − area (p^0BC). Note that consumers lose area (p^0p^1AB).

Likewise, the producer surplus can still be measured as the change in the area above price below the demand curve for an essential input (such as in Equation (17)), as long as the input demand curve after the change is conditioned on the new output price as well as the new environmental quality. Predicting the change in price will, however, require information about aggregate supply and demand.

In a competitive industry, the sum of firms' supply (or marginal cost) curves will equal the aggregate supply function for the industry, and the area below this curve will equal the social costs of production. Likewise the area below price and above the aggregate supply curve will have the same welfare significance for the industry as the analogous area had for the single firm. Areas below aggregate input demands have analogous interpretations to those developed in the single firm case.

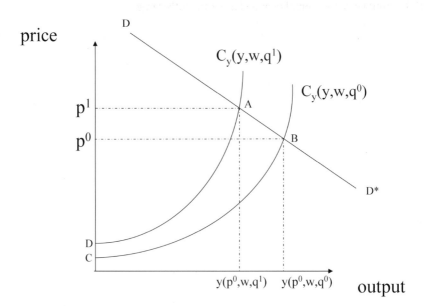

Figure 5. Welfare measure for the single output firm when output price changes.

A change in output price means that the ultimate welfare effect of a change in the environmental input is not restricted to the producers using this input. The consumer (whether household or firm) purchasing this output will also experience welfare effects. When the purchaser is the final consumer (i.e. households), then the change in the area above price and below the aggregate demand function is only an approximation of the sum of consumers' income-compensated welfare measures, but it is often the only measure empirically available. Thus when a price change is likely to occur as a consequence of the change in the environmental input, measurement of welfare effects requires the additional estimation of industry aggregate demand and an assessment of the changes in aggregate consumer and producer surplus. Most applications that value the environment as an input in production ignore the possibility of induced price changes. A notable exception is Kahn and Kemp (1985) who calculate the producer and consumer surplus resulting from shifts in the supply curve for Chesapeake Bay striped bass that come about because of changes in subaquatic vegetation in the Bay.

In developed countries, environmental inputs are most commonly found, not in industries that sell to final consumers, but in primary industries that utilize natural resources and sell to industries that process and distribute the final product. Water pollution is likely to affect fish abundance and therefore the costs to fishermen, but only fresh fish is sold directly to the final consumer. Air pollution may affect tree growth, but harvested timber passes through many production processes before reaching consumers. Soil erosion affects farmers' production functions, but these firms rarely sell their produce directly to households.

If the initial environmental change has sufficiently large impacts on firms' productive capacity to cause a price change in the output market, then other price changes in the marketing chain will be induced, leading to welfare effects on each of at least three distinct groups (primary producers, middlemen, and consuming households). Additional welfare effects can be induced if the affected firms have an appreciable presence in a factor market. What is true in all the above cases, however, is that once the change in the environmental input has been accounted for, any further changes in welfare are the result of induced price changes. This does not make them any less real or any less attributable to the initial environmental change. However, the resulting welfare changes can be measured using standard procedures applicable to *price* changes. Just, Hueth and Schmitz provide an extensive treatment of the different ways in which welfare effects can be captured econometrically in a multimarket framework.

3.12. Instability and uncertainty

Some ecological damage manifests itself in greater climatic or environmental instability. With instability comes greater uncertainty about yields – that is, greater uncertainty about the relationship between inputs and outputs in the production process. For example, great variation in temperatures and rainfall may increase the variability in agricultural harvests from year to year, given the same application of inputs.

Consider how the calculation of producer surplus changes when the firm views outcomes with uncertainty. To begin with, assume that the environmental change only affects a small portion of the market, so that output prices do not change. Also assume that producers are risk neutral. They only care about average returns over the long haul and do not care about the seasonal variability of those returns. In this unrealistic case, firms would maximize their expected profits, which would be a function of the average output, $\bar{y}$, that would be expected given the inputs they employ with certainty. In this case the previous analysis of welfare measurement carries over as long as the mean $\bar{y}$ is substituted for y.

Relaxing any of these conditions adds complexity. Even if firms are risk neutral, if enough firms are affected by the environmental change then prices will change. The price change will be uncertain, but not independent of the changes in output. In fact prices will be negatively correlated with output so that the expected revenue will be smaller than expected price times expected output. In this case, welfare losses to the firm will increase with increasing instability.

Most small firms are unlikely to be risk neutral. Small farmers with little wealth and no borrowing capacity can ill afford downside risk. It is generally assumed that the supply curve of risk-averse producers lies inside that of risk neutral producers, and the welfare significance of the areas behind such curves becomes complicated. For example, the compensating and equivalent variation of parametric changes may no longer be equal for the firm owner who is characterized by risk aversion [Pope, Chavas and Just (1983)].

Earlier we discussed the possibility of small perturbations in ecosystems causing catastrophic outcomes for human production activities. These cases of instability do not fit very well in the standard framework. Very large impacts would be experienced across large sectors of society rather than a single firm or industry and would likely cause firm shut downs rather than simply declines in producer surplus. We leave treatment of these more dramatic outcomes to chapters in volume 3 of this Handbook, which focuses on economywide and international issues.

3.13. Taking the institutional and regulatory environment into account

It would be impossible to investigate here the many institutional and regulatory circumstances in which the firm makes production choices. A few examples that have figured prominently in the literature will serve to illustrate the complications that can occur when distortions to, or other deviations from, the simple, static, perfectly competitive case arise.

3.14. Market distortions

The procedures for welfare measurement outlined above presume that markets clear – that aggregate demand and supply are equal at market price. In some economic sectors (including agriculture in many countries), distortions are introduced into markets by governments attempting to subsidize or tax a sector. When market intervention is prevalent, application of usual welfare procedures can produce misleading results.

An illustration is provided by a series of papers that attempted to measure the benefits from ozone standards in the U.S. [Kopp et al. (1985), McGartland (1987), Madariaga (1988)]. The benefits were assumed to accrue through increased yields for five major agricultural products. In the initial paper demand was assumed to be equal to supply at the price received by farmers. Gains from the reduction of ozone accrued because of the reduction in the social costs of production and the ensuing expansion of consumption at lower prices.

In fact, the price paid by consumers for these agricultural products did not equal the price received by farmers because of price supports and deficiencies payments. The real social gains from the standards equaled the cost savings on the initial production minus the added costs of the expansion in surplus production induced by the increased yields, plus the value of this additional production. We know from the way in which the industry was subsidized that the value of this additional production was far less than the costs of producing it, leading to a deadweight loss. The actual calculation depends on the ultimate use of the surpluses, the magnitude of storage costs, etc. In any event, the net benefits of ozone reduction turned out to be substantially lower when the correct institutional environment was taken into account and, for some crops, may actually have been negative.

3.15. Environmental inputs and open access resources: the case of the fishery

Institutional arrangements, both in market structure and in access to resources, have a critical effect on the social costs of environmental degradation. The fishing industry illustrates the role of institutions, but it is important for its own sake.

Almost all fish stocks are subject to water pollution in some part of their life cycles. Estuaries often fulfill the dual roles of providing spawning grounds and nurseries for various species of fish, and assimilative capacity for water-borne pollutants. Pollution has been blamed for the decline of numerous species, as diverse as Pacific salmon, Chesapeake Bay oysters, Mediterranean swordfish, Amazonian catfish and Indonesian shrimp. Many species are impacted by habitat disruption, particularly in their larval and juvenile stages. In the developing world, timber harvesting and watershed destruction can be harmful to fisheries. The impact of the destruction of mangroves is a widely studied phenomenon in tropical developing countries. The loss of wetlands in general would affect not only fishery production but species diversity. This might occur, for example, if cattle production is substituted for the natural habitat of wetlands. One would expect that environmental improvements that increase the productivity of fish stocks would increase the social returns from fisheries. Yet, whether there are such increases in the social returns from fisheries depends on the institutional structure of the fishery.

To illustrate, we look at the fishery in a steady state framework, ignoring some interesting dynamic issues, but capturing the essence of the fishery in equilibrium. Although this might resemble a static analysis, the kinds of adjustments we analyze are intermediate run rather than short run. Suppose that there is an input, denoted x, that we call effort. It is an aggregate of vessels, workers, captains, electronic gear, equipment and supplies.[8] In our simplified abstraction, the stock of fish is also aggregated, over fish of different ages, so that S, the stock, denotes the biomass in weight or numbers. The harvest or output of the industry depends on effort and stock, which we could crudely represent as

$$y(x) = \alpha x S \qquad (19)$$

where α is the catchability coefficient. The stock of fish, measured as numbers or weight of biomass, grows according to a stock transition equation, where the growth function is assumed to follow the Schaefer model and is conditioned on water quality or quantity of habitat:

$$\frac{dS}{dt} = F(S, q). \qquad (20)$$

Given a level of water quality, the function $F(S, q)$ is concave, with a maximum sustainable yield at the stock S_{msy} that satisfies $F_S(S_{msy}, q) = 0$. Higher water quality enhances the growth of fish, given the stock of fish: $F_q(S, q) > 0$.

The most common institutional arrangement in fisheries is open access, so that commercial enterprises harvest without constraint, imposing externalities on one another and harvesting at greater than socially optimum levels. Even when governments attempt to control access through input regulation, ingenious input choice by fishermen often leads to exploitation of the resource stock that tends to replicate the open access result [see Copes (1986)]. For example, a restriction on the number of vessels can result in larger vessels.

In terms of the current model, open access means that entry of effort into the fishery will continue until there are no excess profits available, leading to the well-known characterization of equilibrium as one in which price equals average (not marginal) cost. Steady state equilibrium in the fishery also requires that harvest equal biological growth, or $F(S, q) = \alpha x S$. The industry equilibrium is reached when the costs and returns of effort are equal. Defining w as the price of effort, p as the price of output, and $y(x)$ as output given by (19), then the industry equilibrium condition is $wx = py(x)$. Equilibrium can be viewed as choosing the amount of effort such that the cost of effort equals the returns to effort or when the average cost of output equals the price of output. We proceed using the industry average cost curve. The industry average cost curve can be computed by defining average costs as $wx/y(x)$, and using the two equilibrium conditions to solve for $y(x)$, the steady state output. Defining the steady state input use as a function of output $x = x(y)$, we can calculate average cost as the cost of inputs divided by output: steady state average costs equal $wx(y)/y$. The "steady state" average cost function is the locus of average cost and output such that output equals production

---

[8] While effort provides a direct and easy way to model the effects of prices and pollution in a fishery, it is not a good way to investigate how behavior responds to incentives or to undertake econometric work. Further, the consistent aggregation of inputs into effort may not always be possible.

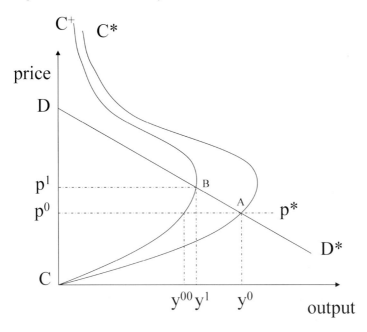

Figure 6. Environmental change in an open access fishery.

and biomass growth equals output. It increases up to the maximum steady state output, and then bends back as costs continue to increase but output declines. Figure 6 shows a typical industry average cost curve in CC^*.

When the environmental change affects localized fisheries that supply larger markets, the output effect may not be substantial enough to affect aggregate market supply. In other words, the local fishermen may face perfectly elastic demand, as is represented by the horizontal schedule $p^0 p^*$ in Figure 6. Initially, industry equilibrium occurs at y^0. At this output, there are no profits in the industry because price equals average cost. Since all the factors of production used by the commercial enterprises are paid their full opportunity cost, the resource itself receives no rents. A decline in the environmental input, because of habitat degradation, for example, shifts the average cost schedule to CC^+. Output decreases to y^{00}, but since this is an open access resource, there are no changes in producer surplus or quasi-rents to fishermen. In the absence of property rights to the resource, no one is able to capture the returns to this fixed factor, and the "rent" to the resource is dissipated. With a decline in the environmental input, commercial fishing firms will continue to cover the opportunity costs of the inputs they employ, but some inputs will be retired from the fishery, presumably employed elsewhere in the economy.

When a significant portion of industry output is affected, price responds to harvest and consumers have a stake in fishery health. Returning to Figure 6 assume that the industry faces the demand curve given by DD^*. Now consider the consequences of a decline in water quality or habitat that shifts the average cost curve to CC^+. The new equilibrium is given by (p^1, y^1). Under the above assumptions of open access, there is no change in producer surplus, but consumer surplus falls by area $(p^0 p^1 AB)$. The environmental change reduces the productivity of the fish stock, reducing steady state consumer surplus by this area.[9]

Empirical studies of the welfare effects of environmental changes in fisheries face an imposing set of difficulties, especially when aggregate data are used. The estimation of gains and losses from changes in productivity of commercial fish stocks calls for the recovery of two functions: the demand function for the commercial harvest and the average cost function as it depends on output and the environmental input, which may be habitat or water quality or other variables that influence fishery health. The demand function estimation is typically accomplished in inverse form, with price a function of quantity and other exogenous covariates, because contemporaneous supply is independent of current price. However, recovering the industry average cost curve as a function of pollution is more difficult. The data requirements, which include time-series of harvest, prices, pollution, and fishing inputs, are substantial. Further, at any point in time fisheries are not likely to be in steady state equilibrium suggesting the need for a more complicated system.

In the unusual case when fisheries are efficiently managed, producer surplus would decline with environmental degradation. The only means yet devised for the efficient management of fisheries provides its own mechanism for measuring the gains or losses from environmental change. Efficient fisheries management seems to occur only when transferable permits, or individual transferable quotas, for harvesting fish are allocated among commercial vessels. The prices of these permits will reflect rents that accrue to the firms that possess rights to the resource. An increase in pollution, for example, would depress permit prices. When these permit prices are observable, constructing and estimating a structural model in which permit prices depend on pollution, among other important variables, would set the stage for the calculation of the costs of pollution in the fishery.

In this simple setting, we have modeled the fishery as a function of a single environmental input. While this model is difficult to implement, in the real world ecological and environmental changes are likely to be more complex, and influence more economic services than harvested fish. For example, when habitat destruction causes fish stocks to decline one might also expect declines in other economic services, such as populations of birds, and water holding capacity of land. Nonetheless, the measurement of economic damages from habitat destruction is usually pursued in piecemeal fashion, independently for different services. Whether this treatment does serious violence to the essence of the problem must be determined in the context of the problem's particular circumstances.

---

[9] Note that if demand for fish products also depends on the water quality because consumers fear the health consequences of consuming fish from contaminated waters, then further complications arise.

3.16. Environmental influences on forestry productivity

There are many situations in which external effects from human actions reduce the productivity of forests. Changing land cover especially from natural to impervious surface can alter hydrological regimes and ultimately affect forest growth. Air pollution from automobiles and power generation undermines the productivity of forests and has led to declines in forest health in northeastern United States and in Western Europe. Forest productivity changes with climate too, and one concern of global warming is its impact on the health of forests.

In this section we consider the difficulty in measuring the economic gains or losses that accrue as a consequence of changes in the productivity of forests. In one sense the production of trees is analogous to the standard production problem. Land can be taken as an essential input, and the change in the area under the demand curve for land, when converted to an annual equivalent, can give the forgone quasi-rents to the owners of the land. This mechanical approach to valuation assumes that land prices are readily observed, and that the observed land transactions pertain to land in timber. Further, it requires that the demand function for land in timber production be estimated, rather than a hedonic function for the price of land. While conceptually feasible, this approach has little else to offer as a means of assessing the productivity of forests.

The alternative approach of assessing the foregone quasi-rents associated with land in timber is no easy task, however. Consider the landowner who, with a fixed amount of land, seeks to earn the highest returns from his land. We wish to find the loss in those returns from a decline in productivity. For a given quantity of land, let $y = V(t, q)$ be the volume of timber produced by trees of uniform age t; q is the influence of the environment or state of natural resources on tree growth, and y is the output or physical volume measured in units such as board-feet. Volume increases as trees age, up to a point, and so it is reasonable to posit $V(t, q)$ as a concave function in t, given q ($V_t \geqslant 0$, $V_{tt} < 0$). Volume is increased by the improvements in state of the environment, q, so that $V_q > 0$. Let p be the stumpage price per unit of physical output – that is the gross price less the harvesting cost, so that the net returns for harvesting y units is py.

In the standard forestry model, the landowner plans the length of growth of the forest for a fixed quantity of land, assuming the land will remain in forestry in perpetuity and that the optimal cycle of t years will continue indefinitely. The present discounted value of the rotations, which depends on environmental degradation, the stumpage price, and the discount rate, is given by

$$P(q, p, \delta) = \max_t \left\{ \sum_{k=1}^{\infty} pV(t, q)e^{-\delta kt} \right\} \tag{21}$$

where δ is the discount rate and k is the index on the age or rotation. In (21), the stumpage price is assumed constant, so that the rotation lengths should remain the same as the land is managed through time. Natural regeneration is assumed so that there are no fixed costs of replanting. The Faustmann solution [see Clark (1976), for a derivation]

comes from choosing the rotation length or the age of trees to maximize Equation (21)
It satisfies

$$pV_t(t, q) = \delta p V(t, q) + \frac{\delta p V(t, q)e^{-\delta t}}{1 - e^{-\delta t}}. \tag{22}$$

The logic of the optimal rotation is familiar, found in the analysis of the optimal exploitation of other resources over time. The trees are allowed to grow until the net value of growth on the left equals the two opportunity costs on the right: the one period opportunity cost of not selling the timber and the one period opportunity cost of not selling the land.

Improvements in the environment (represented by increases in q) that increase the productivity of the forest also increase the value of the land. By the envelope theorem, the effect of an increase in q on the value of the land is given by

$$P_q(q, p, \delta) = \frac{\delta p V_q(t, q)e^{-\delta t}}{1 - e^{-\delta t}}. \tag{23}$$

The marginal effect on the present discounted value of the land is the marginal physical effect of the natural degradation times the price, with the appropriate discounting. Note that the annual loss to a firm for this quantity of land is $\delta P_q(q, p, \delta)$. Unfortunately this gives us only a marginal value for a change in q. To assess the welfare effects of a non-marginal change requires, as always, more information on the behavioral response of an optimizing firm. But the empirical demands for a nonmarginal analysis are especially severe in this context as a finite change in q would likely induce a different rotation.

For the forestry problem, dose–response information may be available in the form of experimental data that show how stand productivity responds to land degradation. However, once again dose–response data do not reflect how the manager may respond by changing the production regime, which in this simple case of the forest means changing the rotation of the forest. Unfortunately, in the forestry case the determination of the optimum rotation for a stand of timber complicates the derivation of the firm's timber supply function. The long time periods inherent in rotation lengths make empirical evidence about the effect of environmental change or ecosystem functions on the rotation length difficult to determine empirically.

An alternative approach is to recognize that, in equilibrium, the value of land equals the price of land. Hence we may take the expression $P_q(q, p, \delta)$ as the price of land. This opens the problem to hedonic analysis. That is, an econometric analysis of land prices as a function of input and output prices, discount rates, land degradation and other factors influencing the productivity of land in forests can give the effects of increases in q on the economic value of the land. While this requires observations on land prices, it does not require that the demand function for land be recovered from the hedonic analysis. Admitting the limitations of hedonic analysis (see Chapter 16 by Raymond Palmquist in this Handbook), this evidence may still contribute to our knowledge of the economic costs of land degradation.

4. The environment affects output produced by the household

In this section we explore the measurement of the costs of environmental degradation when the household produces output dependent on environmental inputs. We begin with the most general case in which the environmental resource is an input into the household production of a commodity, some of which is sold on the market and the rest is consumed by the household. This is a common story for small scale agriculture in developing countries, where a household might grow feed for cows, sell part of the feed and milk, and use cow manure for fertilizer. We then consider more and more restrictive cases, ending with the case encountered most often in the developed country literature in which the environment is treated as an input in the household production of goods such as health, food, clean water, or general environmental ambience.

4.1. The case of household production for consumption and exchange

In many parts of the developing world, especially where market penetration is limited, households produce much of what they consume, although they may sell some of their output if markets for these goods exist. An analogous situation prevails with respect to household labor; some is used in household production of fuelwood, water collection or farming, while some may be sold on the labor market if such a market exists. Models of this type of household behavior are prevalent in the developing country literature [see, for example, Singh, Squire and Strauss (1986a), De Janvry, Fafchamps and Sadoulet (1991)]. However, far less literature can be found that deals with welfare measurement in this context. In this section we first develop the household production model. Then we ask, as we have in previous sections: under what circumstances can we recover a measure of the welfare effects of a change in an environmental resource that serves as an input into production from observations on this type of household behavior?

Introducing consumption and production in the same decision-unit, the household, involves more complications than one might initially expect. In this context, we evaluate changes based on the household's utility, not the firm's profits. When commodities have value both in consumption and sale, subtle issues arise in sorting out the welfare effects of changes in production opportunities. Further, substantial changes in the environment may cause very large changes in household welfare, and may reverse utility-constant comparative static results. In the following section we develop the feasible measures for welfare effects under production and consumption decisions and mention some of these difficulties in welfare analysis.

4.2. Separable production and consumption

We could begin with the problem as we set it up in (1) at the beginning of the chapter. To relate the discussion to the standard models of household behavior, however, we alter that model slightly so that it is similar to Singh, Squire and Strauss (1986b). The household derives utility from the consumption of goods produced by the household, z_p, goods purchased on the market, z_m, and leisure, $T - F$ where T is total time and F is household labor. Instead of leisure, the household may use $T - F$ in other household production activities, but we state the problem this way for simplification. The production relationship for the good produced by the household is $y(L, x, q)$ where y is the output, L is labor used in production – whether purchased or household labor, x is purchased inputs, and q is the environmental input. Corresponding market prices are p_y for output, w for labor, r for other inputs, and p_m for other consumption goods. If there are markets for both the produced good and labor, then the household behaves as though it is maximizing the following problem:

$$\max U(z_p, z_m, T - F) + \lambda\{p_y[y(L, x, q) - z_p] - w(L - F) - rx - p_m z_m\}.$$
$$(24)$$

Stated this way, both the output and labor can be bought or sold at constant prices and, as a result, the production decision is separable from the utility maximization decision. The household chooses the optimal amount of labor and nonlabor inputs to use, as well as the optimal amount of y to produce, by setting the value of the marginal product of each input equal to the price of the input. This is a typical production decision. Once output y, labor L, and market-purchased inputs x are determined, the household maximizes utility as a function of home-produced commodities z_p, market commodities z_m and labor F. The welfare effects of a change in q can be evaluated identically to the theory of the firm and all of the results from the last section carry over straightforwardly. In fact, many of the examples given in that section might alternatively have been set in this framework.

4.3. When production and utility maximization are nonseparable

Some researchers have argued, however, that circumstances in developing countries rarely provide smoothly operating markets, or constant wage rates and output prices [De Janvry, Fafchamps and Sadoulet (1991)]. Equation (24) may deviate from reality for other reasons as well. Household labor may be more productive than purchased labor, or households may prefer to supply labor for household production rather than sell it on the labor market [Lopez (1991)]. In any of these events, the production and utility maximization decisions will be nonseparable. As a result, models of behavior and of welfare measurement will be more complex.

For the firm, we found that areas between supply functions for essential outputs and areas between demand functions for essential inputs provide exact measures of the welfare effects of changes in q. The household context offers some parallels but not exact ones. For one thing, the objective function of the household (i.e., utility) differs from that of the firm (i.e., profit or quasi-rent) which leads to somewhat different results. To illustrate, consider a case in which labor markets are not well developed so that the household can neither sell its labor, nor buy additional labor, at a market price. We will restate the problem as one in which all labor used in the production of y must come from the household:

$$\max U(z_p, z_m, T - F) + \lambda\big\{p_y\big[y(F, x, q) - z_p\big] - rx - p_m z_m\big\}. \tag{25}$$

The production and utility maximization decisions are no longer separable since F must be determined before production levels are chosen.

We can still define a measure of welfare associated with a change in q, but it is no longer a change in producer surplus. Before doing so, note that implicit in (25) is that q matters to individuals only in its effect on the production of y. If y is not produced, then q does not matter. To define the appropriate measure, write the dual of (25) – the expenditure minimization problem:

$$\min p_y\big[y(F, x, q) - z_p\big] - rx - p_m z_m + \mu\big(U - U(z_p, z_m, T - F)\big). \tag{26}$$

Define the expenditure function, $e(p_y, p_m, r, q, T, U)$, as the solution to (26). Then the compensating and equivalent variation measures of a change in q are given by:

$$CV = e\big(p_y, p_m, r, q^0, T, U^0\big) - e\big(p_y, p_m, r, q^1, T, U^0\big), \tag{27a}$$

$$EV = e\big(p_y, p_m, r, q^0, T, U^1\big) - e\big(p_y, p_m, r, q^1, T, U^1\big) \tag{27b}$$

which are clearly a reparameterized version of Equations (2a) and (2b).

To recover either of these measures directly would involve a full accounting of the household's activities, including estimates of the production and utility functions. The usual procedure in the price change case – that of using the area under a demand curve for the good whose price changes – does not work here. Unlike the price change case, where the partial of the expenditure function with respective to a good's price is equal to its demand function, there is no behavioral function related to $\partial e/\partial q$ (for a fuller discussion see Chapter 12 by Bockstael and Freeman). We need to identify further the restrictions that allow us to capture (27a), (27b), either exactly or approximately, using observable behavior.

Attempts to find welfare measures using behavioral functions related to y are problematic since y is both consumed and sold on the market. An alternative way, which follows directly from the theory of the firm, is to use information on a purchased and essential input into the production of y, if such information is available. To demonstrate that this construct can work, even in some household production cases, consider the demand function for x to see whether any restrictions can endow this function with welfare significance. Applying the envelope theorem to (26), it is clear that

$$\frac{\partial e(p_y, p_m, r, q, T, U^0)}{\partial r} = -x\big(p_y, p_m, r, q, T, U^0\big). \tag{28}$$

The change in the area behind the (Hicksian) demand function for x as q changes from q^0 to q^1 is given by:

$$\int_{r^0}^{\tilde{r}(q^1)} x\left(p_y, p_m, r, q^1, T, U^0\right) dr - \int_{r^0}^{\tilde{r}(q^0)} x\left(p_y, p_m, r, q^0, T, U^0\right) dr$$

$$= e\left(p_y, p_m, \tilde{r}(q^1), q^1, T, U^0\right) - e\left(p_y, p_m, r^0, q^1, T, U^0\right)$$

$$- e\left(p_y, p_m, \tilde{r}(q^0), q^0, T, U^0\right) + e\left(p_y, p_m, r^0, q^0, T, U^0\right) \qquad (29)$$

where $\tilde{r}$ is the choke price of the demand function for input x. When x is essential to the production of y, not purchasing x means that y cannot be produced and that the expenditure function does not change when q changes. Hence

$$e\left(p_y, p_m, \tilde{r}(q^0), q^0, T, U^0\right) = e\left(p_y, p_m, \tilde{r}(q^1), q^1, T, U^0\right).$$

So, when x is essential in the production of y, the change in the area under the input demand function for x equals the compensating variation associated with a reduction in environmental degradation.

This procedure should be implemented with some caution. First, one must be sure that the production function has the sort of relationship between the purchased input and the environmental quality that will cause the demand function for the purchased input to shift backward when the quality of the environment is degraded. The reliance on the correct comparative static result holds for all such uses of input demand functions. Second, one must beware of changes in the environmental quality of such magnitude that the income effect becomes relevant. The results derived above are for utility constant demand functions. Large changes in utility might in fact reverse the utility-constant comparative static results, as households buy more of an input to keep their income from falling.

An example frequently exploited in the environmental valuation literature applies the essential input construct to advantage. Consider the case in which z_1 is fish catch at a certain recreational fishing site. Water quality alters fish abundance and therefore catch rates. Transportation or travel to the site is an essential input into the production of these fish. Thus the demand for travel or trips to the site represents the demand for an essential input. The price of this travel is just the travel cost. This leads logically to a familiar travel cost model where the demand for trips will shift with a change in the fish catch. This simple case works because the comparative statics result holds and the change in utility is small.

As we saw earlier, one can use the demand function for an essential input into the production of y when the decision-making unit is a firm and there is no utility maximization involved. The approach works as well in the consumption and production case, as well as the pure consumption case – that is when y is produced for household consumption only and not sold on the market. In all these cases, the only practical difference is that input demand will be a function of a different set of arguments. There is an additional theoretical difference, however. Whenever utility maximization is part of the problem (i.e., in all but the firm case), the demand function in (28) arises from the household's minimum expenditure function in (26) and is a compensated (or Hicksian) demand. But rare is the occasion when compensated demand functions are revealed to the empiricist. Because Hicksian curves are not generally observable, areas behind these curves are generally approximated with areas behind Marshallian (or ordinary) demand functions. For price changes, well-known results exist that show that compensating and equivalent variation will bound the consumer surplus measure and that differences among the three measures will often be proportionately small [Willig (1976)]. However, when the welfare effect we seek equals the area between two compensated curves, we cannot always be so sanguine that areas between the corresponding uncompensated curves will yield good approximations [Bockstael and McConnell (1993)]. Nonetheless, little in the way of alternatives exists and so most researchers proceed by making the substitution of uncompensated for compensated demand functions when the latter are not empirically observable.

4.4. The case of pure household production

This is the most common case found in the literature, the case in which the household is viewed as producing a commodity that enters its utility function, but no market exists for this commodity because it generally cannot be easily exchanged. It is common in the literature, because it is a construct often used to value environmental amenities in developed countries. The principal applications are to recreation, where the environmental resource is treated as an input into the household production of a recreational experience, or to health, where the environmental resource is an input into the household production of longevity or wellness.

Now the household problem might be set out as

$$\max U\{a(x, T_a, q), z_m, S\} + \lambda(\bar{m} + wL_w - rx - p_m z_m) + \mu(T - S - L_w - T_a).$$
(30)

In this problem, the household produced good is indicated by a and is a function of purchased inputs, x, household time spent on production of a, T_a, and the environmental resource, q. Income includes nonwage income, $\bar{m}$, and wage income wL_w; and, we set out the time constraint explicitly where S is leisure.

4.5. Can the demand for the household produced good be estimated?

In the pure theory of the firm, q is valued because it enters into the production of some good, which in turn is sold on the market. In the pure consumption case, q enters the production of a and is valued because a contributes directly to utility. Consequently, there is no direct analogy to estimating the value of q by measuring the change in the area above the supply function for the produced good. However one might be tempted to seek a representation of the *demand* function for a, since changes in q can be expected to change the implicit price of a.

Where production technology is simple so that constant marginal costs prevail, this is by far the most straightforward means of obtaining a welfare measure. As an example consider the household's production technology for providing water in a small village in a developing country setting. The marginal cost of delivering each additional bucket full of water from a distant well may be nearly constant. It equals the opportunity cost of the time and energy it takes to carry the water bucket to and from the well site. Now assume that an ecological disturbance affects groundwater levels and lowers the water level in the well. The household may now have to travel to a farther well for water, changing the marginal cost of water collection. In this story, the environmental change acts as a price change and welfare analysis can proceed accordingly.

Most environmental changes have a more complex effect on household production leading to a cost function that is nonlinear in output. Whenever the marginal cost of a is not constant, there will be no parametric price for a and the demand for a will be difficult to define and estimate. In such cases we must resort to more complex approaches.

4.6. Averting behavior by the household

In the section on nonseparable production and consumption, we saw that if one of the purchased inputs is an essential input into the production of the household produced good, then its demand function can be used to reveal welfare effects of changes in q. This holds whether the household produced good is marketed or not. There is an alternative restriction on technology that can help us recover welfare measures in the pure consumption case. If an input that is a substitute for q in the production of a can be identified, then bounds on the welfare measures can sometimes be obtained. The literature in which this last restriction is explored generally refers to averting behavior or defensive expenditures, because the household is viewed as undertaking averting behavior to mitigate the negative effect of environmental degradation.

When averting behavior is possible, it is not surprising that economists have asked how these pollution abatement expenditures might be used to measure the willingness to pay for environmental improvements. Bartik (1988) has shown how to derive exact compensating and equivalent variation measures under some circumstances, and bounds on these measures in others. The bounds reduce the data requirements.

Averting behavior can easily be cast in the household production function framework. To adapt the Bartik analysis to our notation, suppose that z_m is a composite bundle of purchased commodities, as before, but a is now the household's ambient environment quality which is a function of q and purchased inputs. Increases in the environmental factor q increase the household's ambient environment quality in some way, but the household can purchase goods x (including potentially its own time) to mitigate declines in q. For example, a might be the quality of home drinking water. The quality of the public water supply would be q, and households would be able to mitigate degradation in this public water supply through a variety of defensive actions such as by purchasing filters or bottled water. In other examples, the household produced good may itself be an input into the production of health or recreational experiences, so that the problem might more usefully be recast as one in which q and x enter a health production or recreation production function. As an example, q might be the thickness of the ozone layer and x the consumption of sunblock, both of which are inputs into the health production function for the individual at risk of skin cancer. In either type of case, variables can be appropriately renamed such that a enters utility directly, and q and x are inputs into a.

Define the household's cost function for a as the minimum cost of obtaining a given level of ambient environmental quality, subject to the externally fixed level of q:

$$D(a, q, r) = \min\{rx \mid a = f(x, q)\}. \tag{31}$$

Often termed "defensive expenditures," D is increasing in a and decreasing in q. The household maximizes utility subject to a budget constraint:

$$U(z_m, a) + \lambda(\bar{m} - p_m z_m - D(a, q, r)). \tag{32}$$

The measure that we seek, compensating variation of a change in q, is given by

$$CV = e(p_m, r, q^0, U) - e(p_m, r, q^1, U), \tag{33}$$

where $e(\cdot)$ is the expenditure function associated with the problem in (32). In contrast, the change in "defensive expenditures" is given by

$$\Delta D = D(a^0, q^0, r) - D(a^0, q^1, r), \tag{34}$$

where we define this as the change in the amount of money needed to attain the same ambient environmental quality a^0 as before the change in q and sign it according to the sign of the welfare effect.

To compare these, first define the restricted expenditure function as the amount of income required to reach the initial utility level, given the changed level of q, but holding the ambient environmental quality at its initial level. We denote this restricted expenditure function as $\tilde{e}(p_m, r, q^1, U \mid a^0)$. At the new level of q and the initial level of environmental quality the restricted expenditure function equals:

$$\tilde{e}(p_m, r, q^1, U \mid a^0) = D(a^0, q^1, r) + p_m z_m(q^1, U \mid a^0). \tag{35}$$

It is easy to show that $z_m(q^0, U) = z_m(q^1, U \mid a^0)$. Utility depends only on z_m and a, and the numeraire commodity z_m depends on q only through the effect of q on the ambient environmental quality a. In order to hold utility constant at its initial level while a is held constant at its initial level z_m must also be at its initial level. So, we can write

$$\begin{aligned} e(p_m, r, q^0, U) &- \tilde{e}(p_m, r, q^1, U \mid a^0) \\ &= D(a^0, q^0, r) + p_m z_m(q^0, U) - (D(a^0, q^1, r) + p_m z_m(q^1, U \mid a^0)) \\ &= D(a^0, q^0, r) - D(a^0, q^1, r), \end{aligned} \tag{36}$$

which equals the change in defensive expenditures with a change in q, holding a constant.

Now rewrite the compensating variation measure by adding and subtracting the same quantity:

$$e(p_m, r, q^0, U) - \tilde{e}(p_m, r, q^1, U \mid a^0) + \tilde{e}(p_m, r, q^1, U \mid a^0) - e(p_m, r, q^1, U). \tag{37}$$

The first two terms equal defensive expenditures and the last two must be positive from Le Châtelier's principle (i.e., a restricted expenditure function must be greater than an unrestricted one that is conditioned on the same values of the exogenous variables). Hence we know that compensating variation will always be greater than the change in defensive expenditures, along the real number line. That is, the change in defensive expenditures will underestimate gains from improvements and overstate the losses from degradation.

Bartik also shows that, for the household case, when q and some input x are perfect substitutes in the production of a, it may be possible to extract the exact compensating variation measure. As a concrete example, represent the household production function as $a = f(bx + q)$ to reflect that the isoquant between x and q in the production of a is linear. The individual's constrained utility maximization problem will now be:

$$\max U(z_m, a) + \lambda \left(\bar{m} - p_m z_m + \frac{r}{b} q - \frac{r}{b} f^{-1}(a) \right). \tag{38}$$

From the form of the budget constraint, we can see that a change in q acts to augment income rather than change the terms of trade between z_m and a, although this part of income can only be used to "purchase" a. As long as the individual is not at a corner solution with respect to x (i.e., the price of x cannot be so high relative to preferences for a that no x is purchased) and as long as changes in q can be mitigated by changes in x, then the term $\Delta q r / b$ equals the compensating variation of that change in q where b is the rate of technical substitution between x and q in the production of a.

Both these results are useful – the bounding result and the exact result when perfect substitution holds, because they do not require information about preferences. If indeed there is a way to mitigate the environmental degradation caused by a decline in q, we may know something about that technology. That is, we may be able to represent how x and q are traded-off in the production of a. Murdoch and Thayer (1990) use these results in a study that estimates the benefits of reducing predicted increases in rates of non-melanoma skin cancers due to ozone layer deterioration for a 60 year time horizon.

Some studies use *actual* (i.e., observed) changes in defensive expenditures as bounds rather than changes in the defensive expenditures necessary to hold a, the level of the household produced good, constant. Bartik shows that the change in actual defensive expenditures is always smaller in absolute value than the change in defensive expenditures holding a constant. As a result, the actual change represents a worse lower bound on CV when the environment improves. When it degrades, the ordering of CV and actual change in defensive expenditures depends on properties of the defensive expenditure cost function.[10] Papers that have used observed (i.e., actual) changes in defensive expenditures as bounds include Abdalla, Roach and Epp (1989) and Harrington, Krupnick and Spofford (1989) both of which seek to value the losses associated with drinking

---

[10] Chapter 8 of Bockstael and McConnell (in press) supplies a more complete discussion of the bounding results and the likely properties of the defensive behavior cost function.

water contamination incidents. Although most applications that use some form of defensive expenditures as information for valuation can be found in the health literature, the potential usefulness of the approach is much broader. For example, Jakus (1994) used it to assess the costs of gypsy moth infestations.

4.7. Some further considerations

Implicit in all of the above expressions is that q matters to individuals *only* because it is an input in the production of some good (specifically a in the above formulations). If a is not consumed, then q does not matter. This definition sounds like the definition of weak complementarity (see Chapter 12 by Bockstael and Freeman), although it is motivated differently. Generally, the weak complementarity story is told such that q appears as a quality characteristic of a. For example, a might be fishing trips to a given lake, and q may be the catch rate at that lake.

While the distinction is important in interpretation and critical when attempting to employ a defensive expenditure story, most of the methods for revealing the welfare effects of a change in q hold in either case. For example, if q is interpreted as a quality characteristic of a instead of an input into the production of a, then the change in the area below the demand function for a, if such a demand function could be estimated, could still be used as an approximate welfare measure. Likewise, if an essential input into the production of a can be identified, then the welfare effect of a change in q can still be approximated by the change in the area behind the demand for that essential input, whether q is interpreted as a quality characteristic of a or an input into its production.

Problems arise however if q enters independently into the utility function. Suppose that people value the state of the environment for itself, as well as a vehicle for altering the costs of producing a household good or the quality of such a good. Then the welfare measures obtained by the above revealed preference means will typically understate the true value of the environmental resource. In such cases revealed preference methods might inform the analysis but will not be conclusive, and dependence on more direct methods of eliciting value may be necessary.

5. Conclusions

In this chapter we have concentrated our efforts on constructing models of economic behavior by firms and households. These models facilitate the estimation of the welfare consequences of environmental and ecological changes that affect production. Some of the models discussed in this chapter are well established in the literature, and some are less widely exploited. The area of welfare estimation when the environment serves as an uncontrolled input is not nearly so well developed as when the environment is valued for its contribution to a consumer's utility. The conceptual challenges are especially great when the household is also a producer in a variety of markets.

Conceptually the task of valuing the environment as an input is similar to valuing non-market services for consumption, but empirically more difficult. The empirical task of nonmarket valuation for the household's direct consumption of environmental services has been eased by exploiting cross-sectional variation in the implicit price of access to resources, or by resorting to contingent valuation. For welfare measurement for firms, literal application of the models explored in this chapter would require simultaneous observations on firm behavior, input and output prices, and environmental quality. It seems unlikely that strategies for exploiting systematic variation in cross-sectional data for production will emerge in quite the fortuitous way they have developed for households. In effect, then, what is wanted are panel data for firms. A panel of firms or farms over time would be the most likely source of good data for valuing the environment as an input.

Given the time required for construction of panels, as well as the cost, it is reasonable to consider other strategies for valuing the environment, such as contingent valuation. This approach seems feasible when the household is the producer, so that one is not enmeshed in a corporate decision-making structure. Contingent valuation methods have been successfully applied to the valuation of water supply circumstances in Nigeria by Whittington et al. (1992) and Ahuja et al. (2003) to access to veterinarian care by small farmers in India. For welfare evaluation involving larger firms, the collection and analysis of panel data may be the only viable alternative.

Acknowledgements

We thank the editors Karl-Göran Mäler and Jeffrey Vincent and several anonymous reviewers for helping us with the chapter, and in particular to guiding us to relevant applications.

References

Ahuja, V., McConnell, K.E., Umali-Deninger, D., de Haan, C. (2003). "Are the poor willing to pay for live-stock services? Evidence from rural India". Indian Journal of Agricultural Economics 58, 84–99.

Abdalla, C.W., Roach, B.A., Epp, D.J. (1989). "Valuing environmental quality changes using averting expenditures: an application to groundwater contamination". Land Economics 68, 163–169.

Acharya, G. (1998). "Valuing the environment as an input: the production function approach". In: Acutt, M., Mason, P. (Eds.), Environmental Valuation, Economic Policy and Sustainability. Edward Elgar, Cheltenham, UK.

Alberini, A., Cropper, M., Fu, T.-T., Krupnick, A., Liu, J.-T., Shaw, D., Harrington, W. (1997). "Valuing health effects of air pollution in developing countries: the case of Taiwan". Journal of Environmental Economics and Management 34, 107–126.

Anderson, D. (1987). The Economics of Afforestation. Johns Hopkins University Press, Baltimore, MD.

Arrow, K., Bolin, B., Costanza, R., Dasgupta, P., Folke, C., Holling, C., Janson, B., Levin, S., Mäler, K.G., Perrings, C., Pimentel, D. (1995). "Economic-growth, carrying-capacity, and the environment". Science 268, 520–521.

Barbier, E.B. (1994). "Valuing environmental functions: tropical wetlands". Land Economics 70, 155–173.

Barbier, E.B., Strand, I.E. (1998). "Valuing mangrove-fishery linkages: a case study of Campeche, Mexico". Environmental and Resource Economics 12, 151–166.

Bartik, T.J. (1988). "Evaluating the benefits of nonmarginal reductions in pollution using information on defensive expenditures". Journal of Environmental Economics and Management 15, 111–127.

Bockstael, N.E., McConnell, K.E. (1993). "Public goods as characteristics of nonmarketed commodities". Economic Journal 103, 1244–1257.

Bockstael, N., McConnell, K. Environmental Valuation with Revealed Preference: A Theoretical Guide to Empirical Models. Springer, Berlin, in press.

Bockstael, N., Freeman, A., Kopp, R., Portney, P., Smith, V.K. (2000). "On valuing nature". Journal of Environmental Science and Technology 34, 1384–1389.

Bojø, J. (1996). "The costs of land degradation in Sub-Saharian Africa". Ecological Economics 16, 161–173.

Brekke, K.A., Iversen, V., Aune, J.B. (1999). "Tanzania's soil wealth". Environment and Development Economics 4, 333–356.

Carpenter, S., Brock, W., Hanson, P. (1999). "Ecological and social dynamics in simple models of ecosystem management". Conservation Ecology 3.

Chestnut, L.G., Whittington, D., Lauria, D. (1996). "The economic benefits of surface water quality improvements in developing countries: a case study of Davao, Philippines". Land Economics 72, 519–537.

Clark, C.W. (1976). Mathematical Bioeconomics: The Optimal Management of Renewable Resources. Wiley, New York.

Cooke, P. (1998). "The effect of environmental good scarcity on own-farm labor allocation: the case of agricultural households in rural Nepal". Environment and Development Economics 3, 443–470.

Copes, P. (1986). "A critical review of the individual quota as a device in fisheries management". Land Economics 62, 278–291.

Costanza, R., d'Arge, R., de Groot, R., Farber, S., Grasso, M., Hannon, B., Limburg, K., Naeem, S., O'Neill, R., Paruelo, J., Raskin, R., Sutton, P., van den Belt, M. (1997). "The value of the world's ecosystem services and natural capital". Nature 387, 253–260.

Dasgupta, P., Levin, S., Lubchenko, J. (2000). "Economic pathways to ecological sustainability: challenges for the new millennium". Bioscience 50, 339–345.

De Janvry, A., Fafchamps, M., Sadoulet, E. (1991). "Peasant household behavior with missing markets: some paradoxes explained". Economic Journal 101, 1400–1417.

Dixon, B.L., Garcia, P., Mjelde, J.W. (1985). "Primal versus dual methods measuring the impacts of ozone on cash grain farms". American Journal of Agricultural Economics 67, 402–406.

Dixon, J.A., Scura, L.F., Carpenter, R.A., Sherman, P.B. (1995). Economic Analysis of Environmental Impacts. Earthscan Publications, London.

Ellis, G.M., Fisher, A.C. (1987). "Valuing the environment as input". Journal of Environmental Management 25, 149–156.

Ehrlich, P., Ehrlich, A. (1996). Betrayal of Science and Reason. Island Press, Washington, DC.

Freeman, A.M. (1991). "Valuing environmental resources under alternative management regimes". Ecological Economics 3, 247–256.

Freeman, A.M. III (1993). The Measurement of Environmental and Resources Values: Theory and Methods. Resources for the Future, Washington.

Freeman, A.M., Harrington, W. (1990). "Measuring welfare values of productivity changes". Southern Economic Journal 56, 892–904.

Garcia, P., Dixon, B.L., Mjelde, J.W., Adams, R.M. (1986). "Measuring the benefits of environmental change using a duality approach: the case of ozone and Illinois cash grain farms". Journal of Environmental Economics and Management 13, 69–80.

Grossman, G., Krueger, A. (1993). "Environmental impacts of a North American free trade agreement". In: Garber, P. (Ed.), The Mexico–U.S. Free Trade Agreement. MIT Press, Cambridge, MA.

Harrington, W., Krupnick, A.J., Spofford, W.O. (1989). "The economic losses of a waterborne disease outbreak". Journal of Urban Economics 23, 116–137.

Hartwick, J.M. (1990). "Natural resources, national accounting and economic depreciation". Journal of Public Economics 43, 291–304.

Hodgson, G., Dixon, J.A. (1988). "Logging vs fisheries and tourism in Palawan", East–West Environment and Policy Institute, Occasional Paper #7.

Hufschmidt, M., Dixon, J.A. (1986). "Valuation of losses of marine product resources caused by coastal development of Tokyo bay". In: Dixon, J.A., Hufschmidt, J.A. (Eds.), Economic Valuation Techniques for the Environment: A Case Study Workbook. Johns Hopkins University Press, Baltimore, MD.

Ibáñez, A.I. (2000). The random utility model for recreation: incorporating uncertainty and the costs of imperfect information. Ph.D. Dissertation, University of Maryland.

Jakus, P.M. (1994). "Averting behavior in the presence of public spillovers: household control of nuisance pest". Land Economics 70, 273–275.

Just, R.E., Hueth, D.L., Schmitz, A. (2004). The Welfare Economics of Public Policy. Edward Elgar, Northampton, MA.

Kahn, J.R., Kemp, W.M. (1985). "Economic losses associated with the degradation of an ecosystem: the case of submerged aquatic vegetation in Chesapeake Bay". Journal of Environmental Economics and Management 12, 246–263.

Kim, S.-H., Dixon, J.A. (1986). "Economic valuation of environmental quality aspects of upland agricultural projects in Korea". In: Dixon, J.A., Hufschmidt, M.M. (Eds.), Economic Valuation Techniques for the Environment: A Case Study Workbook. Johns Hopkins University Press, Baltimore, MD.

Kopp, R.J., Krupnick, A.J. (1987). "Agricultural policy and the benefits of ozone control". American Agricultural Economics Association 69, 956–962.

Kopp, R.J., Vaughan, W.J., Hazilla, M., Carson, R. (1985). "Implications of environmental policy for U.S. agriculture: the case of ambient ozone standards". Journal of Environmental Management 20, 321–331.

List, J.A. (2001). "The effect of market experience on WTA/WTP disparity: evidence from the field". University of Arizona Working Paper.

Lopez, R. (1991). "Structural models of the farm household that allow for interdependent utility and profit-maximization decisions". In: Singh, I., Squire, L., Strauss, J. (Eds.), Agricultural Household Models. Johns Hopkins University Press, Baltimore, MD.

Ludwig, D., Walker, B.H., Holling, C.S. (1997). "Sustainability, stability and resilience". Conservation Ecology 1, 7.

Lynne, G.D., Conroy, P., Prochaska, F.J. (1981). "Economic valuation of marsh areas for marine production processes". Journal of Environmental Economics and Management 8, 175–186.

Madariaga, B. (1988). "Ambient air quality standards for U.S. agriculture: the correct welfare measure revisited". Journal of Environmental Management 27, 421–427.

Mäler, K.-G. (1992). "Production function approach in developing countries", In: J.R. Vincent, E.W. Crawford, J.P. Hoehn, (Eds.), Valuing Environmental Benefits in Developing Countries, Special Report 29, Michigan State University.

McConnell, K.E., Strand, I.E. (1989). "Benefits from commercial fisheries when demand and supply depend on water quality". Journal of Environmental Economics and Management 17, 284–292.

McGartland, A.M. (1987). "The implications of ambient ozone standards for U.S. agriculture: a comment and some further evidence". Journal of Environmental Management 24, 139–146.

Mendelsohn, R., Balick, M.J. (1995). "The value of undiscovered pharmaceuticals in tropical forests". Economic Botany 49, 223–228.

Mendelsohn, R., Nordhaus, W., Shaw, D. (1994). "The impact of global warming on agriculture: a Ricardian analysis". American Economic Review 84, 753–771.

Mjelde, J.W., Adams, R.M., Dixon, B.L., Garcia, P. (1984). "Using farmers' actions to measure crop loss due to air pollution". Journal of Air Pollution Control Association 31, 360–364.

Murdoch, J.C., Thayer, M.A. (1990). "The benefits of reducing the incidence of non-melanoma skin cancers: a defensive expenditures approach". Journal of Environmental Economics and Management 18, 107–119.

Pearce, D. (1998). "Auditing the earth". Environment 40, 23–28.

Pimentel, D., Wilson, C., McCullum, C., Huang, R., Dwen, P., Flack, J., Tran, Q., Saltman, T., Cliff, B. (1997). "Economic and environmental benefits of biodiversity". BioScience 47, 747–757.

Point, P. (1994). "The value of nonmarket natural assets as production factor". In: Pethig, R. (Ed.), Valuing the Environment: Methodological and Measurement Issues. Kluwer, Dordrecht.

Polasky, S., Solow, A. (1995). "On the value of a collection of species". Journal of Environmental Economics and Management 29, 298–303.

Pope, R., Chavas, J.-P., Just, R.E. (1983). "Economic welfare evaluations for producers under uncertainty". American Journal of Agricultural Economics 65, 98–107.

Quiggin, J., Horowitz, J.K. (1999). "The impact of global warming on agriculture: a Ricardian analysis: comment". American Economic Review 89, 1044–1045.

Simpson, R.D., Sedjo, R.A., Reid, J.W. (1996). "Valuing biodiversity for use in pharmaceutical research". Journal of Political Economy 104, 163–185.

Singh, I., Squire, L., Strauss, J. (Eds.) (1986a). Agricultural Household Models. Johns Hopkins University Press, Baltimore, MD.

Singh, I., Squire, L., Strauss, J. (1986b). "The basic model: theory, empirical results and policy conclusions". In: Singh, I., Squire, L., Strauss, J. (Eds.), Agricultural Household Models. Johns Hopkins University Press, Baltimore, MD.

Smith, V.K. (1997). "Mispriced planet". Regulation 3, 16–17.

Weitzman, M. (1976). "Welfare significance of national product in a dynamic economy". Quarterly Journal of Economics 90.

Whittington, D., Mu, X., Roche, R. (1990). "Calculating the value of time spent collecting water: some estimates for Ukundu, Kenya". World Development 18, 269–280.

Whittington, D., Smith, V.K., Okorafor, A., Okore, A., Liu, J.-L., McPhail, A. (1992). "Giving respondents time to think in contingent valuation studies: a developing country application". Journal of Environmental Economics and Management 22, 205–225.

Willig, R.D. (1976). "Consumer surplus without apology". American Economic Review 66, 589–597.

Chapter 15

RECREATION DEMAND MODELS

DANIEL J. PHANEUF and V. KERRY SMITH

Department of Agricultural and Resource Economics, North Carolina State University, USA

Contents

Q 26

Handbook of Environmental Economics, Volume 2. Edited by K.-G. Mäler and J.R. Vincent
© 2005 Elsevier B.V. All rights reserved
DOI: 10.1016/S1574-0099(05)02015-2

Abstract

Travel cost recreation demand models stem from a simple, but penetrating, insight. Consumption of an outdoor recreation site's services requires the user to incur the costs of a trip to that site. Travel costs serve as implicit prices. These costs reflect both people's distances from recreation sites visited and their specific opportunity costs of time. Today, economic analyses of recreation choices are among the most advanced examples of microeconometric modeling of consumer behavior in economics.

The primary focus of this chapter is on the methods used to describe individuals' recreation choices. We are interested in the economic assumptions made in descriptions of behavior and measures of the economic value of amenities. Before developing this summary, in Section 2 we discuss how outdoor recreation fits within consumers' overall expenditures. Section 3 describes how we might ideally like to estimate consumers' preferences for recreation resources and the compromises implied by the models currently being used. Econometric details are deferred until Section 5, after a discussion of the features of recreation data in Section 4. In Section 6 we turn to conceptual issues in welfare measurement. We close in Section 7 with a discussion of a few research opportunities that seem especially important for the future.

Keywords

recreation demand, random utility models, opportunity cost of time, corner solution models, travel cost

JEL classification: Q51, Q26, L83

1. Introduction

Travel cost recreation demand models stem from Hotelling's (1947) simple, but penetrating, insight. Consumption of an outdoor recreation site's services requires the user to incur the costs of a trip to that site. Travel costs serve as implicit prices. These costs reflect both people's distances from recreation sites visited and their specific opportunity costs of time. Today, economic analyses of recreation choices are among the most advanced examples of microeconometric modeling of consumer behavior in economics.

The literature has gone through three stages. From Clawson (1959) and Trice and Wood's (1958) initial work, the first set of applications can be divided into two types: travel cost demand models estimated with zonal data (i.e., aggregate visit rates from population zones at varying distances from recreation sites) and activity participation models that are best interpreted as reduced form models. The first set of studies focused on the difficulties posed by using aggregate data, without specific socio-economic information about the recreationists involved, to measure recreation demand when the visit rates reflected both the participation and the use decisions.

To our knowledge, Burt and Brewer (1971) provided the first application of the travel cost method to micro-data, estimating a system of demand equations for lake recreation. Their study initiated in the second stage of research with attention shifted to the opportunity cost of travel time, role of substitute sites, trip length, and site attributes in recreation demand.

Two subsequent contributions transformed recreation demand analysis in the third and contemporary stage. The first of these was Hanemann's dissertation and subsequent publications [Hanemann (1978, 1984, 1985)] introducing the random utility model as a theoretically consistent method for resolving the mixed discrete/continuous choice problem he used to describe recreation demand. This research outlined the theoretical landscape. However, the transformation would not have occurred without an unpublished EPA report by Bockstael, Hanemann and Strand (1987) that bridged the early work developed from a demand orientation to the new RUM and mixed discrete/continuous perspective on consumer choice.[1] These two research efforts ushered in the modern era in recreation demand modeling.

The primary focus of this chapter is on the methods used to describe individuals' recreation choices. We are interested in the economic assumptions made in descriptions of behavior and measures of the economic value of amenities. Before developing this summary, we discuss how outdoor recreation fits within consumers' overall expenditures.

Section 3 describes how we might ideally like to estimate consumers' preferences for recreation resources and the compromises implied by the models currently being

---

[1] Several other researchers were recognized as contributing to this report and were co-authors on subsequent papers. They were C.L. Kling, K.E. McConnell, and T.P. Smith.

used.[2] Econometric details are deferred until Section 5, after a discussion of the features of recreation data in Section 4. In Section 6 we turn to conceptual issues in welfare measurement. We close in Section 7 with a discussion of a few research opportunities that seem especially important for the future.

2. What do we know about preferences for outdoorrecreation after 50+ years?

For most environmental economists research on the demand for outdoor recreation is motivated by the need to provide measures of the economic values for the services of recreation sites (and the effects of changes in amenities on them) as part of informing regulatory policy and resource management decisions. Few analysts consider the overall importance of outdoor recreation in relation to consumers' other economic choices, and there is a reason. Evaluating outdoor recreation's role from this perspective is not an easy task.

While outdoor recreation often involves significant expenditures on complementary goods and services, comprehensive summaries of all of the time and travel resources allocated to outdoor recreation are difficult to develop. For the expenditures that can be measured, there is a fairly general argument supporting their use as indirect gauges of the importance of recreation, but no specific theoretical analysis suggesting a direct empirical relationship. As a result, our assessment is a collection of indirect measures, with a summary of what we know about consumer preferences for recreation, including value measures.

2.1. Recreation and consumer expenditures

Clawson and Knetsch (1966) used two different expenditure measures to gauge the importance of outdoor recreation in consumers' economic decisions. The first involved the fraction of recreation expenditures in all of personal consumption expenditures. These expenditures consist primarily of commodities associated with leisure time. While the components have changed dramatically over the 71 years of available data, the overall intent of the category appears to be an effort to identify expenditures on commodities or services that are associated with uses of one's leisure time. Between 1929 and 1959 recreation expenditures as a fraction of personal consumption increased from 5.89 to 6.53 percent.[3] Clawson and Knetsch's (1966) Figure 18 indicates that with the exception of the period 1930–1944 the pattern of growth in all recreation and outdoor recreation

---

[2] Parsons (2003) has developed an excellent and more detailed hands-on description of travel cost methods that nicely complements our chapter's emphasis on model development and assumptions.

[3] These estimates use Clawson and Knetsch's reports in Appendix Table 1 for personal consumption expenditures on recreation and expenditures for sports equipment relative to the total consumption expenditures from *Historical Statistics of the United States* for these two years.

as a share of disposable personal income has exhibited a steady upward trend. This conclusion is consistent with Costa's (1999) evaluation using the historical record from the more detailed consumer expenditure surveys periodically available over the period 1888 to 1991. She finds that:

> The share of household expenditure devoted to recreation rose from less than 2 percent in 1888 to 3 percent in 1917, 4 percent in the mid-thirties, 5 percent in 1950 and 6 percent in 1991 (p. 10).

Because she argues that this pattern indicates improving living conditions, it seems appropriate to use her general reasoning for other developing countries and conclude that increased income will likely lead to increased leisure and to expenditures on recreation related goods and services becoming a larger share of their consumers' budgets. Of course, this does not necessarily mean the increases in leisure are associated with outdoor recreation.

This question brings us to the second indicator suggested by Clawson and Knetsch (1966). They examine the trends in fees paid for hunting licenses, fishing licenses, duck stamps, entrance fees at national and state parks, receipts from federal and state concessors and parks as well as personal consumption expenditures for sports equipment. Comparing these expenditures to disposal income yields a budget share (in percent terms) that nearly doubles over the period they consider from 0.38 in 1941 to 0.73 in 1959. While it is not possible to exactly replicate the components they assemble, using the National Survey of Fishing, Hunting and Wildlife Associated Recreation we can combine trip-related expenses (including equipment) for fishing, hunting and wildlife related activities in 2001. These amount to $179.4 billion dollars for the US population 16 years old and older in this year. Compared to personal consumption expenditures (by type of expenditure) in that year, this amounts to 2.57 percent of that total – over three times Clawson and Knetsch's (1966) estimate for 1959. Thus, these data clearly support the conclusion that participation in outdoor recreation in the US is associated with the overall increasing expenditures for leisure related activities.

Another way of measuring the expenditures motivated in part by environmental amenities is through a broad category of goods usually associated with travel. This category is often labeled tourism. Travel and tourism expenditures are somewhat different from the recreation expenditures identified earlier in the decomposition of the National Income and Product Accounts. In the case of tourism we are focusing more directly on expenditures away from home. Thus, to the extent travel and tourism are motivated by using environmental resources – recreation sites, national parks, etc. – these expenditures are more likely to be directly complementary to the uses of recreation sites. The Bureau of Economic Analysis developed satellite accounts for US travel and tourism for 1992, 1996, and 1997. Their estimates indicate that this sector increased from 3.3 to 3.5 percent of gross domestic product (GDP) form 1992 to 1997. From 1992 to 1997 domestic tourism final demand increased at an average annual rate of 6.9 percent, while gross domestic product increased by 5.6 percent.[4] Recreation and entertainment was the second fastest growing component of this aggregate, rising at an annual rate of 15.7 percent. These estimates do not include the time expended by tourists or the resources associated with maintaining the national parks, beaches, and other environmental resources that motivate the complementary expenditures on related goods and services.

Overall these indirect measures suggest that the importance of outdoor recreation activities in household consumption choices has grown over the past fifty years. By any measure, whether using complementary activities or the costs for access and equipment related expenditures, outdoor recreation is responsible for 2 to 6 percent of consumer expenditures and, very likely, accounts for at least as large a portion of an individual's leisure time.

2.2. Preferences for recreation

Our title for this sub-section is deliberately vague. Applications of the travel cost logic can involve studies of specific recreation sites, recreational activities, or changes in the characteristics of recreation sites. In practice, this distinction is somewhat artificial because studies of recreation demand implicitly address all of these features. That is, when data are collected on recreation activities, the process involves recording the location, level of use, and usually the activities involved. How the findings are reported often depends on whether specific aspects of the experiences varied across sampled recreationists and the end uses for the analysis. These features limit our ability to generally characterize consumer preferences for outdoor recreation.

The recreation literature has grouped sites and activities into some broad composites. Water based recreation sites are divided into fresh- and salt-water locations, with activities such as sport fishing, boating, and swimming treated separately. Sport fishing is often further separated based on mode (boat or shore), use of charter services and, in some cases, whether a species is targeted. For recreation using land based sites (except those involving unique national parks, such as the Grand Canyon) the character of the site in describing the study is often considered secondary and the activity (e.g., hunting or hiking) used as the primary focus.

Based on this broad classification scheme, we construct Table 1 using what is best described as a convenience sample of estimates for price and income elasticities and per day measures of the benefits from access to the site supporting the activity. Virtually all we know about price elasticity of demand is from research that is now nearly 30 years old.[5] A reviewer of an earlier draft of this chapter suggested that price and income

---

[4] Domestic tourism final demand is defined as total tourism demand, less travel by US residents abroad, and less business tourism demand [see Kass and Okubo (2000)].

[5] Smith and Kaoru's (1990b) meta analysis of price elasticity estimates from travel cost studies is somewhat more recent, but is also largely summarizing older research. They found that, in general, sites classified as rivers and forests were more likely to have price elastic demands, while state parks tended to have inelastic demands (each compared to coastal and wetlands). Perhaps the most relevant aspect of their analysis was the

Table 1
Summary estimates of price, income elasticities and consumer surplus per day

Type of site activity	"Early" estimates		Recent estimates		Consumer surplus per day	
	Own price	Income	Own price	Income		
Fresh-water sites	−0.45[a]	–	–	–	–	
	−1.63 to − 1.71	–	–	–	–	
Fishing	−0.27[b]	0.47	–	–	36.52[d]	
Cold water	−0.38 to − 0.97	–	−0.43[c]	–	–	
Warm water	−0.31 to − 0.85	–	–	–	–	
Boating	–	0.34	–	–	39.25	
Sailing	−0.11	–	–	–	–	
Canoeing	−0.19	–	–	–	–	
Swimming	–	–	–	–	31.34	
Salt-water sites	–	–	−1.39[e]	0.24	–	
Sport fishing	–	–	−0.80[f]	–	Salmon/River	13.69[g]
					Salmon/Lake	76.57
					Salmon/GL	114.78
					Bass/River	84.46
					Bass/Lake	34.11
					Bass/GL	27.84
Beach recreation	−0.20	–	−0.33 to − 0.50[h]	0.17	–	
Land based sites	–	–	–	–	–	
Camping	–	0.42	–	–	31.43	
Developed camps	−0.15	–	–	–	–	
Remote camps	−0.18	–	–	–	–	
Hunting	–	–	−1.76 to − 2.40[i]	–	–	
Deer	−0.21 to − 0.87	–	–	–	–	
Small game	−0.36 to − 1.06	–	–	–	42.83	
Big game	−0.23 to − 0.62	–	−1.03	–	45.41	
Waterfowl	–	–	–	–	30.73	
Hiking	−0.18	–	−3.38	–	40.47	
Wilderness	−1.59[j]	2.45	−1.10 to − 6.28[k]	–	–	
Rock climbing	–	–	–	–	Rocky Mtns.	42.04
Wildlife viewing	−0.32	–	–	–	31.07	

(*continued on next page*)

Table 1
(*Continued*)

Type of site activity	"Early" estimates		Recent estimates		Consumer surplus per day
	Own price	Income	Own price	Income	
Skiing	−0.70	0.50	–	–	–
Downhill	–	–	–	–	27.91
Cross country	–	–	–	–	26.19

[a]The price elasticities are taken from Smith and Kaoru's (1990a) Appendix summarizing the results they were able to compute from the primary sources. The sources are identified in their Appendix. Point estimates for specific sites or activities were selected here to fill in categories based on the objectives of the original studies compiled in Smith and Kaoru (1990a).

[b]These estimates are taken from Walsh (1985, Tables 9.3, 9.4 and 9.6). In the case of the price elasticities he cites Adams, Lewis and Drake (1973) as his primary source for all but fishing, hunting and skiing. The hunting and fishing are taken from Gum and Martin (1975). He does not cite his source for the skiing price elasticity. For the income elasticities he cites Kalter and Gosse (1970).

[c]Derived by combining demand model reported in Englin, Lambert and Shaw (1997) with summary statistics in Englin and Lambert (1995) for the same sample. Analysis involves coldwater trout fishery in New York State excluding New York City, New Hampshire, Vermont and Maine.

[d]The values per day in Rosenberger and Loomis (2000a, 2000b) are in 1996 dollars. They combine travel cost demand, random utility and contingent valuation estimates converted to a per day basis. When they were not summarized as overall averages, we computed the means from this table of disaggregate means.

[e]These results are for trips to the Albemarle-Pamlico Sounds in North Carolina and can involve swimming, fishing, camping, hunting, water-skiing and a variety of water related activities. They are taken from Whitehead, Haab and Huang (2000) from their revealed preference model with existing quality conditions. Using a stated preference question, joint estimates of trip participation and demand with 60% improvement in catch and 25% increase in shellfish beds lead to more inelastic demands, both in price and income. Income elasticity was not significantly different from zero. These estimates for the same area were −1.05 for price and 0.06 for income.

[f]These estimates are for Alaska and are taken from the Hausman, Leonard and McFadden (1995) linked RUM/count demand model. Smith (1996) has argued the price index proposed for their demand analysis does not meet the requirements for a consistent price index. Moreover, one of their estimated demand models used for these elasticity estimates has positive price effects (hiking). Given the estimation procedure the authors describe, the positive estimated parameter must be regarded as a type setting error. Otherwise, the elasticity would not be negative.

[g]The sport fishing unit values are in 1996 dollars on a per day basis. They also report per trip estimates. These means are based on the travel cost studies. This summary is from Boyle et al. (1999). GL designates Great Lakes.

[h]These estimates are a composite of those developed by Leeworthy and Wiley (1993) and subsequent reanalysis of their data by Dunford (1999).

[i]These estimates are from Herriges and Phaneuf (2002) for wetlands recreation in Iowa and are computed using the repeated mixed logit specification.

[j]Price and income elasticities are from Smith and Kopp (1980).

[k]Based on Lutz, Englin and Shonkwiler's (2000) comparison of disaggregate versus aggregate travel cost demand for backcountry and wilderness hiking. This range of estimates is across different sites including Hoover, Ansil Adams, John Muir, Lasser, Sequoia-Kings and Golden Trout in Inzo and Lasser National Forest Area. Their models include income but they do not report the means, so it was not possible to compute income elasticities.

elasticities from contemporary models may not serve the same role as in earlier studies. With micro level data, there is likely to be great variability in the estimated demand elasticities due to individual heterogeneity in tastes and opportunities. Differences in spatially delineated substitutes within a region condition the demand structure for sites in that region. When considered across studies, they introduce a source of variation in demand structures that may reduce the value of using elasticities as a summary measure of preferences. For example, the price and income elasticities of demand for fresh-water recreation trips in Minnesota, where there is a large array of alternative lakes, may be quite different than in the Southwest where, even if the recreationists could be assumed relatively homogeneous, the substitutes are distinctively different.

In this respect the spatial delineation in substitutes for recreation is different from market goods in most developed economies, where the existing supply network assures access to a comparable array of substitutes in most areas. Rather than serving as a reason to reconsider the use of elasticities, this seems to offer opportunities for research. Sensitivity of elasticity estimates to the features of the substitutes available, including the numbers of alternatives, their proximity, and attributes raises potentially interesting questions about adaptation. That is, we might consider how individuals adapt to these constraints. Do they substitute longer trips for day trips when there is limited access to a particular type of recreation site in their region? Alternatively, are there substitution patterns across classes of recreational activities that can only be detected by studying cross-region demand patterns? Finally, it is important to acknowledge that the same difficulties arise in comparing welfare measures across regions. Thus, the challenges posed by heterogeneity in taste and opportunity at the micro level of analysis do not necessarily change the value of considering the summary parameters beyond welfare measures that characterize preferences. They do, however, alter the way we interpret and use this information to understand behavior.

Meta summaries of the benefits reported in the recreation literature generally have followed Walsh, Johnson and McKean (1990) and Smith and Kaoru (1990a), focusing on the per-day or per-trip consumer surplus estimates. Rosenberger and Loomis (2000a, 2000b) offer the most complete summary, based on 682 estimates for a range of recreation activities in Canada and the United States reported in the literature between 1967 and 1998. Their Table 1 provides a summary of the raw data for their analysis, based on average 1996 recreation values per person, per day for several categories of recreation.[6] In Table 1 we report the average values from their summary for the activities that match our classification. For example, fishing is represented by 118 observations, with an average surplus of $34.74. Swimming is represented by only seven observations, with an

---

sensitivity of the estimates to the modeling judgments used in developing them. The presence of substitute price measures and the treatment of the opportunity cost of time were especially important choices. To our knowledge, no one has pursued this line of research in subsequent updates to the meta statistical summaries of empirical studies of recreation demand.

[6] Rosenberger and Loomis (2003) provide a nice discussion, summarizing the characteristics of these meta studies as part of evaluating their potential role for benefits transfer.

average surplus of $31.66. Finally, big game hunting has an average surplus of $44.39 based on 170 reported surplus measures.[7]

A few recent papers have discussed preference characterizations beyond benefits measures, including Englin and Lambert (1995), Leeworthy and Wiley (1993), Hausman, Leonard and McFadden (1995), and Herriges and Phaneuf (2002). The first study combined a count data demand model with a catch equation and jointly estimated both relationships, taking account of the role of the expected catch in the trip demand. The primary focus of the paper is in recovering consumer surplus measures for site quality improvements as reflected through enhanced expected catch measures. The second paper uses a single equation travel cost demand model, based on data from the NOAA Public Area Recreation Visitors Survey, to estimate the demand for three California beaches. The initial specification considered only travel costs in demand models for individual beaches and implied own price elasticities ranging from −0.365 to −0.501. Re-analysis of a subset of the beach use data indicated statistically significant price and income elasticities, with an income elasticity estimate of 0.17.

The third study focused on using a random utility model to describe single trip behavior, which is then used to develop a price index for a seasonal demand model for recreation in Alaska. The authors report price elasticities as a gauge of the economic plausibility of their second step trip demand model for different types of trips in the area, finding own price effects from −0.80 to −3.38. The last study uses estimates of the own price and cross price elasticities to summarize the implied substitution patterns associated with different specifications of random utility models applied to the use of Iowa wetlands. Before presenting the estimates, Herriges and Phaneuf (2002) decompose the determinants of own and cross price elasticities for several popular specifications. This process offers general insight into how specification influences substitution. For example, they note in the case of the repeated nested logit (RNL) model cross price elasticities are constrained to be positive, and greater within nested groups than across groups. By contrast, the repeated mixed logit (RXL) model allows unconditional cross price elasticities to vary substantially with the mixing distribution. Within and between nest responses vary dramatically as the magnitude of the standard deviation for the mixing error varies from 0.1 to 10. In practice, these differences can be pronounced. For example, their application compares the RNL to the RXL frameworks and finds there are substantial differences with the RNL exhibiting larger (in absolute magnitude) price elasticities, but smaller cross price elasticities.

At least two conclusions and a note of caution emerge from this summary. First, it is clear that over the past fifty years we have accumulated considerable information about unit values of recreation activities and sites being used for these activities but

---

[7] A concern with their approach arises because they combine Marshallian and Hicksian measures of consumer surplus without adjustment for the differences. Smith and Pattanayak (2002) discuss the implicit assumptions underlying this practice. For our purpose here there is little alternative but to assume that the income effects are inconsequential and their composite estimates indicative of the relative importance of the activities.

relatively little about the structure of consumer demand. The early work suggests that most recreation demands are price inelastic. In a few of the recent studies water based and wilderness demands appear to have quite elastic demands, suggesting considerable sensitivity to pricing policy. This is also consistent with the Herriges and Phaneuf (2002) wetlands work.

This issue seems worthy of further investigation for at least two reasons. From a methodological perspective, modern travel cost studies have paid much greater attention to the time costs of travel. Smith and Kaoru (1990b) found that these decisions were important to the price elasticity estimates in the early work. This impact needs to be distinguished from one that suggests that increases in the implicit price of recreation have heightened the sensitivity of users to further price increases.

Second, we know very little about income elasticities. Costa's (1999) arguments were developed from the premise that the overall responsiveness of all recreation expenditures to income can be used to gauge rising standards of living. Estimates of income elasticities provide information on what individual preferences imply will be the types of recreation most likely to be affected by continued increases in real income.

Finally, it is worth noting that the elasticity concept in recreation is quite different than in other, more homogeneous commodities, and thus we should not be surprised by the range of estimates. The commodity definition itself between studies is highly variable, ranging over different activities and spatial definitions of "sites," and is typically based on the specific needs of the analysis. It is likely that these decisions (combined with the use of micro level data) contribute to the large and varying price elasticities found in recent studies. Likewise income impacts are less easily defined for recreation than other commodities, even when it is possible to estimate income elasticities. Income changes may in fact cause discrete changes in recreation behavior, such as moving to more luxurious or exotic activity/destination combinations, rather than the marginal effects captured by typical income response measures. Finally, efforts to estimate Hicksian surplus measures from incomplete Marshallian demand models have, as we develop below, forced analysts to impose restrictions that limit what can be learned about substitution and income effects in the interest of recovering a consistent measure for Hicksian consumer surplus [see LaFrance (1985, 1990) and von Haefen (2002)].

2.3. Policy impacts

Policy uses of travel cost models have been extensive in the US for at least the past thirty years. Three types of uses are especially noteworthy: project evaluation, resource management, and, most recently, damage assessment.

The first of these was the earliest and has continued. Generally it involves a public investment project, initially developed for hydroelectric dams with a mixture of outputs including power, flood control, and recreation. Sometimes a travel cost demand model for a site providing comparable recreation would be used to estimate the benefits from the new lakes created by the hydroelectric dam. Cicchetti, Fisher and Smith's (1976) early analysis of downhill skiing in California was motivated by the larger task of evaluating the likely development benefits from Walt Disney Enterprise's proposed (at the time) development of a commercial ski resort at Mineral King, requiring access roads through the Sequoia National Park. More recently, the analysis requirements for federal re-licensing of hydro dams in the US (under the Electric Consumers Protection Act of 2002) has generated interest among private power producers in the use of travel cost demand models to evaluate the recreation benefits from reservoir and downstream recreation.

Another recent area with direct policy application is EPA's proposed rulemaking associated with Section 316b of the Clean Water Act. This rule would establish national requirements that affect the location, design capacity, and construction of cooling water intake structures at power plants. A recent description of the economic analysis underlying the proposed Phase II regulations estimates recreational benefits from the improvements in catch associated with reduced losses to fish stocks through reduced entrainment and increased survival from cooling water facilities. The proposed rule uses a random utility model developed for the Ohio River and for several coastal regions. Measures of the per trip benefits from reducing impingement and entrainment were developed to estimate the recreational benefits of the regulations (relying on their impact on catch rates).

These policy uses are not exclusively confined to recent decisions. Indeed, the earlier benefit estimates for improving the catch of striped bass had a role in restricting the striped bass season to allow the stock to recover. Direct evidence for these uses can be found in the simple benefit–cost analysis of a moratorium on striped bass fishing that was presented and discussed as part of the Maryland legislative hearings leading to the Emergency Striped Bass Act.[8]

Somewhat surprisingly, travel cost demand models have not had an especially big impact in evaluating national water quality policies. Random utility models have been used to evaluate more site specific or regional policy issues, such as the reduction in sulfur dioxide emissions and associated acidic deposition [see Morey and Shaw (1990)] and nonpoint source pollution [Feather and Hellerstein (1997)]. Travel cost (and contingent valuation) estimates have provided an important source of the monetary values for the recreation uses evaluated in the Forest Service's multiple use planning framework. Under the legislation defining the standards for forest management, recreation is to be given equal weight with sustainable harvesting of forest products.

Finally, the single most important recent role for travel cost models has been in natural resource damage assessments. Random utility models have played a key role in evaluating the effects of contamination and fish consumption advisories on the benefits associated with restoration. While much of this literature has not appeared in journals, it has nonetheless had a marked influence on the methodological issues associated with designing a random utility model.[9]

---

[8] The history of the process was confirmed via private correspondence with Ivar Strand. Some of the early results are discussed in Norton, Smith and Strand (1983).

[9] Notable examples include the evaluation of damages in the Clark Fork River case in Montana [see Desvousges and Waters (1995)] and a component of the damages attribute to the Green Bay case in Wis-

It is not clear that travel cost recreation demand models are having as large a policy impact outside the US. Pearce's (2000) review of environmental decision making in Europe identifies the travel cost method in his schematic outline of methods but does not provide specific examples where it has been used.

3. Modeling recreation behavior

Our summary of travel cost models follows the evolution of the literature. We begin with a general description of models for individual choice and the assumptions that condition how restrictions on preferences and constraints influence what is learned from observable behavior. This section is developed independent of specific recreation models and is intended to motivate an evaluation of how modeling decisions constrain what can be learned about preferences. After this general overview, we outline the features of an ideal model and introduce the specific types of existing models. A detailed discussion of each class of model used in current recreation analysis then follows.

3.1. Modeling preferences

The basic model for consumer choice used in recreation models begins with a general preference statement $u = u(\mathbf{x}, q)$ and simple version of the budget constraint $m = \mathbf{p}'\mathbf{x}$, where $\mathbf{x}$ is an n-vector of commodities, $\mathbf{p}$ is the corresponding price vector, m is household income, and q is some measure of environmental quality or a public good. When the analysis considers how q influences choice, the framework usually considers only one quality-differentiated, private good that is designated by one of the x's. When this static version of the consumer choice problem is adopted for outdoor recreation, prices do not result from a market exchange process. In the United States most site entrance fees are nominal charges, and the dominant component of price arises from the cost of traveling to a site.

This simple specification abstracts from time. In some consumer choice applications it is justified by arguing that $\mathbf{x}$, q, and m are rates – quantities consumed by the individual per unit of time. This logic is inappropriate with outdoor recreation since the choice variables measure the use of recreation sites, requiring time to be introduced to characterize both the activities undertaken and the full costs of resource utilization. This need is accommodated by introducing a second constraint, the time budget, to the basic problem. The new constraint links a person's endowment of time to income via hours at work and activities involving time costs. Formally we can state the time constraint as $T = t_\mathrm{L} + \sum t_i$, where T is total time available, t_L is time spent working, and t_i denotes

consin [see Breffle et al. (1999)]. The Parsons, Plantinga and Boyle (2000) discussion of "surgical" choice sets was also motivated in part by the discussion in these cases in this context. A surgical choice set presumably implies a decision to select the specific sites used in a RUM analysis to highlight a subset of particular interest for a policy evaluation or damage assessment.

the units of time allocated to the ith activity. Income is then given by $m = wt_L + R$ where w is the wage rate and R is nonwage earnings.

Clearly something is still missing from this basic story. Although time has been added to the model it will not affect choices because it has not been related to x, p, or q. One approach to provide a connection is to identify the time costs associated with each of the choice variables x and consider simultaneously the allocation of time to leisure and earning income needed to sustain market consumption. This extension necessarily implies we confront the tradeoffs between consumption of goods versus leisure time. Data restrictions have generally required most studies to assume some type of separability between the labor–leisure choices and goods consumption, or make simplifying assumptions concerning how individuals exchange time for money. This may in fact unrealistically constrain estimated preferences. When we consider the role of leisure, we often focus on time allocated to trips and not leisure as an argument of utility. Separability of labor/leisure choices from commodity choices implies that all goods are average substitutes for leisure. In the case of recreation trips we might argue that the relationship is more likely to be one of complementarity. Thus, the separability restriction is important in limiting the relationship between goods and time consumption, and in the implied nature of the budget allocation process.

Becker's (1965) early description of the household production function (HPF) model and its role in how people allocate time is a useful pedagogical tool for summarizing how constraints on behavior are combined to structure implicit prices of each consumption choice. As specific examples of structural assumptions we consider ideas set forth by Bockstael and McConnell (1983), Larson and Shaikh (2001), Provencher and Bishop (1997), and Blundell and Robin (2000) using the HPF framework. In each case our goal is to demonstrate how the different structures imply different implicit prices for recreation, which in turn condition what observed behavior can reveal about preferences.

In a simple HPF model an n-vector of final consumption goods z is produced in the household by combining time and purchased inputs. Suppose technology is given by the linear relationships

$$z_i = a_i x_i,$$
$$z_i = b_i t_i. \tag{3.1}$$

The preference function is now a function of z given by $u(z, q)$, where q is in this case linked to one of the z_i's. With other assumptions (e.g., weak complementarity and essentiality in production) Bockstael and McConnell (1983) demonstrate how some aspects of the amenity contribution to consumer values can be isolated.[10] Under the HPF model the consumer choice problem becomes

$$\max_z \iota(z, q) \text{ s.t. } wT + R = \sum_i \pi_i z_i, \quad \pi_i = \frac{w}{b_i} + \frac{p_i}{a_i}. \tag{3.2}$$

---

[10] Bockstael and McConnell (1983) did not require a fixed coefficient production technology. We have also taken the simple route by assuming the same number of z's as x's. Altering this restriction adds complexity to the notation but does not change the basic point.

The π_i's can be thought of as exogenous implicit prices for a unit of z_i dependent upon the market prices p_i and w of the two inputs – market inputs (x_i) and time (t_i). However, if we replace the fixed coefficient HPF with a neoclassical specification, the budget constraint becomes a more familiar looking cost function $wT + R = C(\mathbf{z}, w, \mathbf{p})$, and Pollak and Wachter's (1975) argument on the limitations in the framework becomes more apparent. Prices may not be constants and may be functions of multiple z's. While it is possible to argue for local linearization of the cost function, the key point is that we don't escape the need to impose structure on the technology to identify the features of preferences and construct the implicit prices for recreation. Also, this structure implies that time can be valued using the wage rate and that the income constraint corresponds to "full" income where all potentially saleable time is monetized.

In contrast Larson and Shaikh (2001) present a two-constraint version of the model that implies a different time/good complementary relationship, and thus a different structure of the implicit prices for the recreation services. In their model the two constraints are separately maintained, with time and income budgets pre-determined from a non-modeled first stage allocation. The dual constraint consumer problem is formally given by:

$$V(m, T, q, p, a, b) = \max_x u(z, q)$$
$$+ \lambda \left[m - \sum_i \frac{p_i}{a_i} z_i \right] + \mu \left[T - \sum_i \frac{1}{b_i} z_i \right], \tag{3.3}$$

where λ and μ are the money and time constraint Lagrange multipliers and, for comparison, we maintain the technology structure from Equation (3.1). We can recover the demand for recreation services z_i using the two forms of Roy's identity:

$$z_i = \frac{-V_{p_i/a_i}}{V_m} = \frac{-V_{1/b_i}}{V_T}. \tag{3.4}$$

The two constraints imply there are two Slutsky symmetry conditions: one each for the equality of cross money–price and cross time–price effects. These conditions suggest a specific structure on how choices respond to the relative scarcity of time and money. The implicit price of recreation is a function of the market price of the purchased input, and an endogenously determined marginal cost of time given by the ratio of the Lagrange multipliers.

These two structures offer examples of mechanisms that control income and substitution effects in empirical models based on them. In the extreme of the Leontief technology of the first structure there is no substitution between goods and time in production. As a result, marginal costs of produced services are fixed multiples of prices and wages. Larson and Shaikh (2001) relax the link between commodity prices and wages and the opportunity cost of time, yet here too potentially relevant constraints are not considered. Both models assume that each unit of the good consumed is temporally exchangeable with the other units (and independent of the past stock of experiences). However, a key feature of recreation behavior is its dependence on both the amount and the timing of available time. Time cannot be directly stored, although time can be indirectly transferred between periods by shuffling commitments. In addition, in any particular interval there are limits to how time can be used. For example, there are only so many hours of daylight. Bresnahan and Gordon (1997) provide an interesting discussion of how artificial light has changed the nature of this constraint. Furthermore free time is often available only in discrete bunches due to fixed work schedules and other commitments. This constrains the feasible choice set for allocation in a given interval. Each of these examples suggest that time is not the perfectly fungible commodity implied by the static and linear time budget constraint.

It is possible to spell out these temporal details in a dynamic framework as proposed by Provencher and Bishop (1997), following the Rust (1987) stochastic, discrete, dynamic optimization structure. However, to do so requires extensive information about how time constraints differ among people. In the Provencher and Bishop (1997) analysis, recreation consumers maximize the sum of expected current and discounted future utility subject to inter-temporal constraints. Preferences are time separable and stochastic due to the assumption of unobserved heterogeneity. Both the preference function and budget constraint are linear and defined over each day of the season. While their conceptual approach is clearly relevant to concerns about how conventional models treat time, the framework's ability to deal with them depends on whether the analyst can specify sufficiently rich time-related constraints to capture the effects of substitution through time. That is, does the available information and temporal structure yield implicit prices for recreation that are significantly different from the static models in their ability to capture the temporal effects limiting choice?

Related to this question, there are situations in which it is unreasonable to assume that people have time separable preference functions consistent with discounting. Instead, they behave in a choice context that "brackets" choices in time. Current choices are influenced only by contemporaneous or relatively near term alternatives. Read, Loewenstein and Rabin (1999) describe choice bracketing based on a wide array of simple psychological "experiments" that examine choice behavior. They observe that bracketing effects are most likely cases of temporal bracketing. If their conjecture is plausible, it does not necessarily require we discard constrained utility maximization. Rather, it implies future research should investigate alternatives to the simple discounted, time separable specifications for preferences.

Our final example on the role of structural assumptions is based on Blundell and Robin's (2000) latent separability. This restriction is a generalization of weak separability, and serves to demonstrate how separability assumptions condition what can be learned from static behavior. Latent separability implies that purchased commodities can contribute to multiple household activities, provided at least one good is exclusive to each activity. For example, in water recreation boat ownership can be used to produce both fishing and water skiing experiences and thus can be expected to enter both production technologies. Nonetheless, the specific gear used in each activity is exclusive. This restriction (e.g., exclusivity of gear), together with homotheticity, can be used to recover price indexes for each household activity.

To illustrate how this impacts the pattern of substitution relationships, define $\tilde{x}^1$ as the demand for the exclusive good in one of these activities. Under latent separability the demand structure is given by

$$\tilde{x}^1 = g\left[p_{x_1}, \bar{p}, s_1\left(p_{x_1}, \bar{p}_x, \bar{p}, m, q\right)\right],$$ (3.5)

where p_{x_1} is own price, $\bar{p}$ is a vector of prices of the goods used in other activities as well as in this first activity, $\bar{p}_x$ is a vector of prices of goods exclusive to other activities, and s_1 is expenditures for the activity. Notice that p_{x_1} and $\bar{p}$ enter the demand function directly while $\bar{p}_x$ enters only the function $s_1(\cdot)$ describing the expenditures on goods contributing to the first activity. This relationship allows the cross price effect of any $\bar{p}_x$ and income m on the demand for $\tilde{x}^1$ to be used to recover how prices affect the allocations to activities as distinct from the demand for specific goods. This is illustrated for the jth element in the set of exclusive goods ($j \neq 1$) by the following equations:

$$\frac{\partial \tilde{x}^1}{\partial \bar{p}_{x_j}} = \frac{\partial g}{\partial s_1} \frac{\partial s_1}{\partial \bar{p}_{x_j}},$$ (3.6a)

$$\frac{\partial \tilde{x}^1}{\partial m} = \frac{\partial g}{\partial s_1} \frac{\partial s_1}{\partial m}.$$ (3.6b)

The ratio of these two partial derivatives provides information about the allocation process among activities as distinct from the properties of the individual demands. Repeating this for each exclusive good and using the second derivative properties of these ratios, we have sufficient restrictions to identify and re-construct the pattern of substitutions among goods.[11]

Weak separability is useful in cases where we can itemize a set of goods and services always used together. Blundell and Robin's (2000) logic shows that separability requirements need not be this limiting. One exclusive good (or service) per activity is often sufficient to inform (and restrict) the pattern of cross price elasticities in a set of demand functions. When combined with homotheticity, this restriction allows the definition of aggregate price indexes and does not impose the strong restrictions on income elasticities associated with homothetic weak separability. In the recreation context we can consider the impacts of this structure for how time and monetary constraints combine. For example, under this view the implicit price of a trip would be a latent variable that is not determined by a process exogenous to the individual's choices but rather as a reflection of those choices. This was Randall's (1994) basic point and provides a rationale for the Englin and Shonkwiler's (1995) proposal to treat travel cost as unobserved.

---

[11] The logic parallels directly the work of Chiappori (1988) in a different context. See Smith and Van Houtven (2004) for further discussion. In this context, it can be seen as an extension to the early work of Bockstael and McConnell (1983) demonstrating that within a household production framework, if one input is essential to all production activities it is possible to use the demand for that input to recover measures of the value for changes in public goods that are weak complements to one or more of the final service flows. If we assume that q is a weak complement to one (or more) of the activities identified as satisfying latent separability, then with the exclusive input to that activity an essential input we have the same result.

To this point we have said little about the modeling issues concerning the vector of amenities q, usually interpreted as attributes of recreation sites. The conceptual literature has focused primarily on the role of quality with a single private good [Bockstael and McConnell (1993, 1999a, 1999b)] or treated the quality attributes of each site as being linked to that site.[12] The linchpin of most travel cost demand approaches for linking quality attributes to preferences is weak complementarity. Introduced by Mäler (1974), this preference restriction maintains that the only means of deriving satisfaction from quality follows from consumption of the private, weakly complementary good. Thus, if x_j is related to q via weak complementarity the marginal value of q is zero when x_j is zero:

$$\frac{\partial}{\partial q}\left[u(x_1, x_2, \ldots, x_{j-1}, 0, x_{j+1}, \ldots, x_n, q)\right] = 0. \tag{3.7}$$

This can be represented in equivalent terms with either the indirect utility function or the Hicksian expenditure function

$$\frac{\partial}{\partial q}\left[V\left(p_1, p_2, \ldots, p_j^c, \ldots, p_n, m, q\right)\right]$$

$$= \frac{\partial}{\partial q}\left[e\left(p_1, p_2, \ldots, \tilde{p}_j^c, \ldots, p_n, u, q\right)\right] = 0, \tag{3.8}$$

where p_j^c and $\tilde{p}_j^c$ are the choke prices for the Marshallian and Hicksian demand respectively. These definitions assume that the choke prices exist or, equivalently, that the private good x_j is not essential.

The formal definition of weak complementarity can be explained further with Figure 1. In this graph the indifference curves relate the recreation good x on the horizontal axis to spending on all other goods z on the vertical axis. The curves are drawn to represent the same level of utility but each corresponds to a different level of the amenity q. That is, in this case each group of indifference curves varies the amenity while holding utility constant (e.g., $q_0 < q_1 < q_2$ and $\bar{U} = \bar{U}(q_0) = \bar{U}(q_1) = \bar{U}(q_2)$ and $\tilde{U} = \tilde{U}(q_0) = \tilde{U}(q_1) = \tilde{U}(q_2)$ with $\bar{U} < \tilde{U}$). Increases in the level of the amenity reduce the amount of x_j and z needed to reach the reference utility level. The "fanning" property of the graph arises from the nonessentiality of x and its weakly complementary relationship with q.[13] Thus, all curves meet at the point $x = 0$. Movements between the curves in each group therefore do not reflect changes in income or wellbeing (all the

---

[12] An exception to this general form was offered by Bockstael and Kling (1988) who assumed that quality was linked to a set of goods as a weak complement. Their structure was analogous to forming a Hicksian composite commodity in the linked goods.

[13] Weak complementarity does not necessarily imply the smooth shape in the fan, only the intersection of these quality distinguished indifference curves at the same point. Thanks are due to Michael Hanemann for pointing out that this description adds information in specifying a shape for each indifference curve beyond what is actually implied for weak complementarity. We use these forms here because they embody conventional assumptions about preferences.

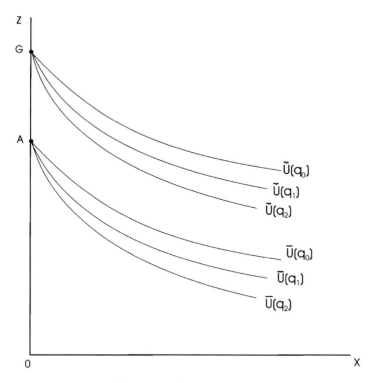

Figure 1. Weak complementarity.

curves intersect at one income level on the vertical axis), but rather the substitutability between trips, the amenity, and spending on other goods. This property allows us to describe how changes in the amenity level, conditional on the pictured level of income, affects the tradeoff between the private goods x and z.

Weak complementarity restricts preferences such that a change in quality (or the public good) can be converted into an exact equivalent change in the price of the weak complement. As we discuss in Section 6, this is a necessary condition for welfare analysis in recreation models. Smith and Banzhaf (2004) illustrate this preference restriction by showing that consumer surplus for a price change in general can be depicted using the spacing of the pivoted budget constraints describing the price change. For example, Figure 2 shows an indifference map between two private goods with no quality dimension. For the case of a price increase for x the average of the distances CD and BA gives a first order approximation to the Marshallian surplus for the implied price change.

The indifference map in Figure 3 shows how weak complementarity allows definition of the price change for the private good serving as the weak complement that is a Hicksian equivalent to the quality change. Utility is held fixed in the fanned indifference curves $\bar{U}$ as quality increases from q_0 to q_1. The quality change is represented as a price change by finding the price lines that are tangent to the two curves corresponding

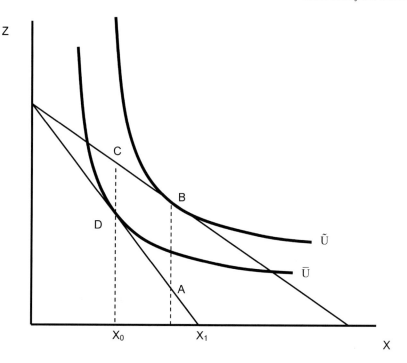

Figure 2. Marshallian consumer surplus for a price change.

to q_0 and q_1. Since the utility level is fixed, the price change is a Hicksian equivalent change. That is, the price change is the amount by which the price of the weak comple-ment would need to rise to maintain utility at the same reference level when there is a quality increase. A first order approximation to the Hicksian surplus for the price (and equivalently, the quality) change is given by the average of the vertical distances DC and AB.

Since we are not able to observe the Hicksian demand for the weak complement we must consider how the quality change is equivalent to an observable Marshallian price change leading to a new level of utility. This is shown in Figure 3, where the price line tangency with $\widetilde{U}(q_1)$ is for the higher quality but a new level of utility. The analysis of the average implied change in consumption of z at these two levels of the weak complement for the same price change is observable with a Marshallian demand. By including one further assumption restricting the size of income effects, it is possible to also recover the Hicksian welfare measure for the change in q. Typically this requires the Willig (1978) condition, discussed by Bockstael and McConnell (1993) and Palmquist (2005). We develop this role for weak complementarity and the Willig condition in the context of welfare measurement in further detail in Section 6.

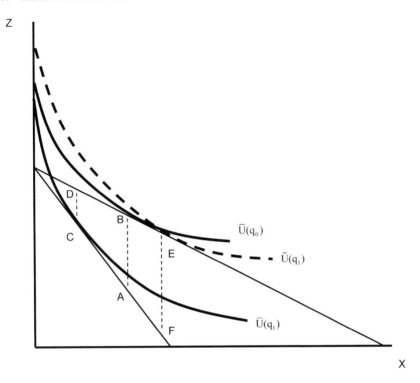

Figure 3. Weak complementarity: price change and quality change.

3.2. An "ideal" implementation of the basic model

The prices for recreation goods are best interpreted as implicit prices that reflect a combination of monetary and nonmonetary constraints limiting the consumer's choice at a point in time and over time. Each of the models in the literature constructs these implicit prices with different judgments on what are the most important monetary and nonmonetary aspects to include. Thus, we begin with a baseline for comparison and specify a wish list of the most desirable features to include in a model of recreation choice.

Nearly all economic approaches for describing recreation behavior seek to estimate the Hicksian consumer surplus for some change in the access conditions or quality of recreation sites. Thus, an ideal model should allow Hicksian surplus measures to be recovered. This goal requires that we estimate structural parameters. Equally important, a desirable modeling strategy is one that recognizes a wide array of substitutes, including both substitute recreation sites and other uses of money and time. Since each individual is unlikely to be observed consuming all available substitutes during a single time horizon the model must allow for nonconsumption or corner solutions, with the further possibility of changes that would imply a switch from nonconsumption to positive consumption if one or more attributes change. Related to this feature, a consistent description of the participation decision requires some limitation on the use of separability. The model should describe the tradeoffs between outside goods and the recreation sites of interest, and allow changes in this tradeoff when access and quality conditions of the recreation sites change.

The model should consistently link site characteristics to site choices. Some site conditions, such as congestion, cannot be known in advance. Others are learned with experience. The process linking *ex ante* site quality perceptions and how these are modified with experience could be an important part of explaining some types of recreation behavior. These connections reflect a temporal learning process that may influence subsequent decisions. Related to this, short-term disruptions to a site's quality conditions can lead to inter-temporal substitution.

This is a long and demanding list of requirements and none of the available modeling frameworks can deal with all of them. Nonetheless, the literature has made impressive progress. For our description we identify five approaches to recreation demand modeling. The earliest of these are the single equation demand studies for individual recreation sites. These have largely disappeared from the literature, except in applications involving joint estimation with stated preference data or when they are used to illustrate some new econometric or modeling twist posed by available data, such as the work motivated by count data methods.

Recognition that a single, independent recreation site rarely exists led early researchers to consider demand system models for recreation sites [e.g., Burt and Brewer (1971)]. Current literature focuses on the theory underlying incomplete and partial demand models to consistently recover preference functions appropriate for calculating Hicksian welfare measures [see LaFrance (1985, 1986, 1990) and von Haefen (2002)]. Recent efforts have used these insights in extending single equation count data methods to multiple equations [Ozuna and Gomez (1994), Shonkwiler (1999), von Haefen and Phaneuf (2003a)].

By almost any reckoning McFadden's (1974) random utility maximization (RUM) model has become the workhorse of modern recreation demand modeling. One reason for this widespread adoption is the ability of the model to consistently deal with substitution, nonconsumption, and nonmarket quality attributes in ways that offer measures of Hicksian consumer surplus. Nonetheless, limitations in the ability of random utility models to estimate seasonal benefits measures have led to research in Kuhn–Tucker (KT) models of recreation demand [e.g., Phaneuf, Kling and Herriges (2000), Phaneuf (1999)]. These models attempt to combine the desirable aspects of both the systems approach and the RUM model by adopting the generalized corner solution framework as the organizing principle. The last category of models can be loosely organized under the category of price index frameworks and uses the idea that with a quality-adjusted price index, the choice from a set of heterogeneous sites requires finding the one with the smallest quality adjusted price. Models in this category range from some ad hoc models of the demand for recreation sites or site characteristics to behavioral models comparable to the corner solution models.

3.3. Structure of the primary empirical models describing recreation demand

In this section we describe the critical features of each category of model identified above. We focus primarily on the economic issues outlining each model and discuss briefly the most important econometric issues that can arise in implementation. Later in the review we deal more specifically with econometric issues.

3.3.1. Single equation and demand system travel cost models

The earliest travel cost research used single equation models with aggregate, zonal data; more recent applications have almost exclusively used individual or household level data.[14] Single equation demand models have a simple specification $x = f(c, m, S)$ where x is total trips specified as a function of travel cost (c), income (m), and group or individual characteristics (S). Measures of recreation site quality are generally omitted because there is little ability to observe variations in site quality for a single site over a season.[15] Implementation of this model involves two classes of economic judgments: variable definition and measurement along with demand function specification and estimation. In the first class the most important decisions involve the opportunity costs of time, the role of on-site time [Shaw (1992), McConnell (1992)], and trip cost and multiple objective trips [Haspel and Johnson (1982), Mendelsohn et al. (1992), Parsons and Wilson (1997)]. Judgments on specification and estimation relate to the evolution of single site models to system models. Included in this class are issues such as the treatment of substitutes and the role of on-site and substitute site quality, as well as restrictions necessary to recover estimates of preference functions from both single and multiple site models. We consider each of these decisions in turn.

   Time, its opportunity costs, and its role in the demand for trips remain unresolved questions in recreation modeling. The most common practice is to value travel time at the wage rate or some fraction thereof. There has been and continues to be criticism of this practice [see Smith, Desvousges and McGivney (1983), Shaw and Feather (1999)], as well as alternative suggestions [e.g., Bockstael, Strand and Hanemann (1987), Feather and Shaw (1999)], but little consensus on how this practice should be replaced.

   Other sources provide more complete overviews of the development of the literature on the opportunity cost of time. We limit attention to two proposals for measuring these opportunity costs as a latent variable. First, Englin and Shonkwiler (1995) treat the various determinants of site visitation costs as components of a latent variable. The latent cost variable is estimated using distance converted to money travel costs, travel time, and the wages lost in travel as indicator variables. The approach uses factor analysis to

---

[14] Reviews of this early work can be found in Ward and Loomis (1986), Fletcher, Adamowicz and Graham-Tomasi (1990) and Smith (1989).

[15] The Loomis, Song and Donnelly (1986) regional demand model pools recreation sites described by a single model and is discussed further below.

estimate travel costs. These latent travel costs are measured with error that is assumed independent of the trip demand. Their proposal could be generalized with consideration given to variables describing time availability (e.g., vacation days), nonwage income, household composition, or any other demographics characteristics. However, it requires sufficient restrictions to identify the parameters of the latent cost function that are typically not available from theory.

Second, Feather and Shaw (1999) adapt Heckman's (1974) strategy for estimating the shadow wage by using contingent behavior questions about respondents' willingness to work additional hours along with actual working decisions. Individuals have either a flexible work schedule or are over or under employed in a fixed work schedule. Stochastic wage and shadow wage functions are specified as functions of exogenous variables, and, in the case of the shadow wage, hours worked. The relationship between the wage and shadow wage is determined by categorizing each individual's work schedule. With flexible work schedules hours are adjusted until the shadow wage is equal to the market wage. For over-employed individuals the fixed hours constraint implies the market wage is bounded from below by the shadow wage at zero hours worked and from above by shadow wage at current work hours. The relationship between the shadow and actual wages is then translated to a probability statement, and with contingent choice data, it is possible to use a maximum likelihood estimator to recover the structural parameters of the shadow wage equation. Feather and Shaw (1999) use predictions for each individual's hourly opportunity cost of time to construct the time cost component of prices to recreation sites.

Both approaches find results close to the simpler strategies. With Englin and Shonkwiler (1995) the estimates for opportunity cost of time are close to one-third of the wage rate. For Feather and Shaw (1999) the shadow values are closer to the market wage. Although formal tests were not conducted, the results for both studies seem to imply that welfare estimates from either method would fall within the ninety-five percent confidence interval of the other more approximate methods based on the use of one-third of the wage rate. Thus, although some progress has been made in estimating individual's opportunity costs of time, we still lack a compelling replacement for the ad hoc strategies that dominate most recreation demand applications.

On-site time also remains controversial. For conceptual purposes we can think of the challenges posed in modeling the role of on-site time as consisting of two related components: addressing the endogenous nature of trip length and accounting for the opportunity cost of time spent on site. The latter issue is closely related to our previous discussion, although little work exists addressing specifically the measurement of the opportunity cost of on-site time as distinct from travel time. The former issue is extremely difficult to deal with conceptually in that the distinction between the price and quantity of the recreation good blurs, resulting in a nonlinear budget constraint and endogenous prices. Most recreation studies avoid the issue completely by assuming there is a constant (and exogenously given) amount of on-site time necessary to produce the recreation experience. Alternatively, one might assume, as McConnell (1992) argues, that traditionally estimated demand equations can produce valid welfare measures in the face of endogenous on-site time if there is an exogenously given "price" of on-site time.[16]

The premise of the travel cost model is that the value of access to a site can be developed using the costs associated with getting to the site. This strategy requires that the resources given up in travel are for the single purpose of visiting the site of interest. Haspel and Johnson's (1982) early research identified concerns over violations of this assumption due to multiple purpose trips. If multiple objectives are satisfied in a given trip, then we can not attribute all resource costs to the site of interest for analysis. More recent research from Mendelsohn et al. (1992) has followed up on this by suggesting that multiple objective trips involving a set of recreation sites be defined as one commodity and included in the demand structure. This strategy precludes measuring benefit changes in aspects of the individual sites and does not describe why these composites were selected. Parsons and Wilson (1997) suggest treating the incidental activities as weak complements to the main activity of interest and allowing these benefits to be folded into the value of the main activity. This strategy involves making judgments on the importance of the collateral activities. It is unlikely to be appropriate when a primary activity cannot be identified or if there are substantial resource costs with the bundle of activities being considered. One future direction in this research will be to expand the definition of commodities modeled by including a recreation site as an individual objective and perhaps the same site as a component of a bundled objective containing other sites, with the appropriately defined prices for each.

The travel cost demand literature recognized early on that a single recreation site rarely exists in isolation from alternatives and that usually there are substitutes available. This motivates our second class of economic decisions, centered on judgments about specification and estimation. Concern about the effects of substitute sites motivated the first system of demand equations work. Early examples of this include Burt and Brewer (1971) and Cicchetti, Fisher and Smith (1976). Enthusiasm for the systems models waned due to estimation and conceptual issues. Moreover, Hof and King (1982) and Caulkins, Bishop and Bouwes (1985) argued that it is not necessary to estimate a systems model to account for the effects of substitute site prices and quality measures in benefit estimates when interest centers on a single site.

Because there are often no measures of differences in the site quality conditions during the course of a season, a common practice has been to combine results experienced

---

[16] McConnell's (1992) creative solution suggests specifying the budget constraint by $m = x(p_x + p_t t) + p_z z$, where x is the number of trips, p_x is the money price of trips, p_t is the price of on-site time, t is the amount of on-site time, and z and p_z are the numeraire and price of the numeraire good, respectively. Roy's identity in this case leads to a behavioral function for trips given by

$$x(p_x, p_t, p_z, m) = \frac{V_{p_x}}{V_m},$$

which can be estimated as a function of the price of on-site time. McConnell (1992) further shows that the area behind this curve approximates the true welfare effect of a price change.

by different people at different sites. Two approaches can be found in the literature. Both are ad hoc. The varying parameter model [Vaughan and Russell (1982), Smith and Desvousges (1985)] assumes the parameters of individual site demand models are functions of site characteristics. A second group of studies uses regional demand models [Loomis, Song and Donnelly (1986)] where recreation trip information for multiple sites is pooled and a simple demand model is estimated. The model can include site characteristics and has been specified with ad hoc measures of substitutes. Neither approach provides a consistent or utility theoretical link from choice to empirical demand analysis.

The emphasis on a utility theoretic link between the choice of specific recreation sites and their characteristics has motivated renewed attention to system estimation in recent literature [e.g., Shonkwiler (1999), Englin, Boxall and Watson (1998), von Haefen and Phaneuf (2003a)]. These studies employ the incomplete (or, more accurately, complete with an asymmetric structure) demand system strategy [LaFrance and Hanemann (1989)] to recover estimates of consumer preferences from a system of recreation demand equations by imposing the so-called "integrability conditions" on the functional form of the demand system. As LaFrance (1985, 1986, 1990) points out, these conditions essentially require a choice between allowing income effects or Marshallian cross price effects. LaFrance and Hanemann (1989, p. 272) suggest "... it is generally impossible to measure unequivocally welfare changes from nonmarket effects using incomplete systems of market demand functions." This may in fact be too harsh a judgment. By specifying prices as quality-adjusted repackaging functions [Willig (1978)], von Haefen and Phaneuf (2003a, 2003b) show it is possible to link the nonmarket good to the private good in a utility consistent manner. Nonetheless these models are limited in their ability to parametrically capture substitution and income effects, and further investigation of utility-consistent techniques for linking the private and public goods is needed.

3.3.2. Random utility and related models

Introduced by McFadden (1974) and first applied to recreation models by Hanemann (1978), random utility maximization (RUM) models have become the dominant approach for describing consumer preferences for recreation.[17] Research in this area is so extensive that it is impossible to do justice to all of it, so we focus on four issues: the structure of the choice process, including the impact of error distribution and commodity definition decisions on preference estimates; the choice set definition, including the impact of expansive versus limited approaches to defining the available sites; nonlinearities in income, including discussion of the technical and conceptual challenges of allowing income effects in RUM models; and the link to seasonal demand.

---

[17] Two excellent sources for the derivation and assumptions of simple and nested RUM structures in a recreation context are Morey (1999) and Herriges and Kling (2003). Ben-Akiva and Lerman (1985) provide an excellent general review.

The random utility model describes extreme corner solution decisions – a choice of only one of a finite number of alternatives within a limited time horizon. Hanemann (1984, 1999) provides a careful description of the economic and institutional assumptions that link the RUM choice process to conventional demand and welfare analysis. Preferences are assumed to include a random component reflecting unobserved heterogeneity (from the analyst's perspective) in individual tastes.[18] The model begins with the specification of an individual's conditional indirect utility function for choice alternative k, in period t:

$$v_{kt} = V(m_t, p_k, q_k, \varepsilon_{kt}), \tag{3.9}$$

where m_t is the person's income or budget relevant for period t, p_k is the person's price to acquire alternative k (a recreation site visit), q_k is the vector of characteristics for site k and ε_{kt} is the error. Price and quality can also be assumed to change with the time period of choice; typically, however, data have not been available to make this distinction.[19]

The RUM structure treats site choice as a separable process that is unaffected by other consumption decisions, except indirectly through the definition of choice occasion income. The decision rule is therefore simple: the consumer selects the choice alternative k that has the maximum utility for a given choice occasion. Formally this is given by

$$\underset{k \varepsilon K}{\text{Max}} \left[V(m_t, p_k, q_k, \varepsilon_{kt}) \right], \tag{3.10}$$

where K is the set of all choice alternative available. The analyst cannot observe ε_{kt} and must also make assumptions about the form of the conditional indirect utility function. Empirical implementations of the framework rely on modeling the probabilities that each choice alternative is selected.

McFadden's development of the model assumes either a type I extreme value or a generalized extreme value distribution to describe the error. When the errors are assumed to be additively separable in Equation (3.10), both specifications yield closed form expressions for the choice probabilities and permit maximum likelihood estimation. In the case of linear, separable, and independent type I extreme value errors these probabilities are given by

$$\pi_{kt} = \frac{\exp(\overline{V}(m_t, p_k, q_k)/\tau)}{\sum_{k \varepsilon K} \exp(\overline{V}(m_t, p_k, q_k)/\tau)}, \tag{3.11}$$

where $V(m_t, p_k, q_k) = \overline{V}(\cdot) + \varepsilon_{kt}$ and τ is the scale parameter for the type I error.

---

[18] The standard assumption is that choice is deterministic from the individual's perspective and random only to the analyst. In contrast one could assume, as Hausman and Wise (1978) suggest, that random errors reflect a changing state of mind for the consumer or they reflect errors in measurement for the independent variables affecting choices.

[19] Schwabe et al. (2001) is one notable exception in a study of the effects of seasonal attributes in the context of hunting site choice.

The choice of error distribution in the RUM model constrains the substitution relationships among choice alternatives and the role of unobserved heterogeneity. The correlation structure among the random utilities that derives from similarities between the choice alternatives plays a role akin to what the restrictions on functional structure and constraints did in our description of the basic recreation model. In that case they reduce the dimensionality of the Slutsky matrix and restrict substitution relationships. Here, the assumptions about the error control the degree of substitutability between choice alternatives.

The independent and identical type I extreme value errors model is the simplest version of the RUM and implies the unobserved heterogeneity is independent across choice alternatives. This formulation maintains a person's choice process contains no unobserved elements that are common to each of the alternatives available; hence the random utilities realized are uncorrelated and do not reflect any stochastic substitution. This specification requires behavior consistent with the independence of irrelevant alternatives (IIA) condition, which arises when the ratio of an individual's choice probabilities for any two alternatives is unaffected by the systematic utilities associated with any of the other possible selections in the choice set.[20] As Ben-Akiva and Lerman (1985) suggest, IIA should be evaluated based on whether the specification adequately describes the unobserved heterogeneity of the individuals being modeled. For IIA to hold, all systematic relations between choice alternatives must be captured in the deterministic component of the random utility function.

Nested logit models employ the generalized extreme value distribution. They allow for correlation among the alternative utilities and hence nonzero stochastic substitution. This process requires grouping the available choice options into "nests" containing alternatives considered more similar. The extent of the correlation for the utilities of alternatives within a group is related to the relative size of the dissimilarity coefficient θ_L. As the coefficient approaches one, the model collapses to a conventional multinomial logit, while values approaching zero imply higher levels of correlation. For example, a nested logit model with a two-level nest has probabilities of the form:

$$
\pi_L = \frac{\left[\sum_{j \varepsilon J_L} \exp(V_{L_j}/\theta_L)\right]^{\theta_L}}{\sum_{m \varepsilon M}\left[\sum_{j \varepsilon J_m} \exp(V_{mj}/\theta_m)\right]^{\theta_m}},
$$
$$
\pi_{i|L} = \frac{\exp(V_{L_i}/\theta_L)}{\sum_{j \varepsilon J_L} \exp(V_{L_j}/\theta_L)},
$$

(3.12)

where π_L denotes the probability of being in nest L, J_m denotes the set of alternatives in nest m, and $\pi_{i|L}$ is the probability of choosing alternative i conditional on nest L

---

[20] The IIA property arises from the structure of the multinomial logit probability. Note from Equation (3.11) that the odds of choosing alternative k over alternative j on occasion t is $\pi_{kt}/\pi_{jt} = \exp(\overline{V}_{kt})/\exp(\overline{V}_{jt})$. Thus, the ratio does not depend on alternatives other than k and j, and the odds are the same regardless of the availability of other alternatives. Train (2003) provides an excellent discussion on IIA and its impacts on substitution patterns in the logit model.

selected. The unconditional probability of choosing an alternative is given by $\pi_{iL} = \pi_L \cdot \pi_{i|L}$. Considering two sites within the mth nest, Ben-Akiva and Lerman (1985, pp. 287–290) demonstrate the correlation between their utilities is controlled by the size of the dissimilarity coefficient.

The nested logit is a restrictive model. As Morey (1999) points out, changing the error assumption to a generalized extreme value distribution does not eliminate IIA. It controls the patterns of interaction among alternatives. The ratio of an individual's choice probabilities for two alternatives will exhibit IIA for alternatives within the same group, and for alternatives in different groups if the alternative changing is not in either of the two groups represented by the pair. Of course, changes in alternatives in groups represented by the pair will impact the ratio of choice probabilities and thus do not adhere to IIA. It is important to recognize Morey's point as a conceptual one. We never actually observe information that would be necessary to test IIA for these nested components of the choice model. From the perspective of what we can observe – the choices among alternatives – the nested specification does relax the IIA assumption.

Correlation among random utilities is one of the motivations of Train's (1998) random parameter, or mixed logit model. Because the parameters of the deterministic proportion of the model are replaced with random coefficients that incorporate individual heterogeneity, the random component of each parameter will be shared across choice alternatives and very general patterns of correlation (and, as a result, substitution) will be possible. Herriges and Phaneuf (2002) use this insight to propose specific patterns of correlation by including random coefficients for dummy variables that vary by individual but are shared across choice alternatives. Allowing parameters to change is a more direct approach to controlling how the analyst specifies correlation (and thus ex ante substitution) in this framework.

The second dimension of the choice process incorporated in the random utility framework involves the link between choices through time in multiple choice occasion applications. As a rule, this is handled by assuming each choice occasion is independent. Income is arbitrarily distributed across these occasions. The income per choice occasion is important because it reflects how the prices of nonmodeled goods impact choice. For repeated choice occasion random utility models there is no mechanism to introduce diminishing marginal rates of substitution. This is an important limitation because we normally expect that diminishing marginal utility of commodities is a key element in the explanation for substitution.

The last choice process issue is the definition of a choice alternative, which overlaps with issues of choice set definition discussed next. Definition of the choice alternative is equivalent to the specification of the commodity in ordinary demand analysis, and contributes to whether IIA or some nesting structure adequately describes substitution. Most studies use individual sites, aggregations of sites, or spatially defined areas as the choice alternatives. Kaoru and Smith (1990) first raised the issue of the effects of site aggregation on RUM models and their valuation measures. Subsequent work by Parsons and Needelman (1992), Feather (1994), Lupi and Feather (1998) and Kaoru, Smith and Liu (1995) has been interpreted in some of the literature as yielding conflicting results, with the Kaoru, Smith and Liu (1995) work typically found to be in conflict with the other findings. This view is somewhat misleading in that the different studies employ different aggregation strategies: simple and statistical aggregation.

Consider first the statistical aggregation approaches. Here the aggregate site arises as an average of the conditional indirect utility functions of the elemental alternatives. Trips, prices, and site characteristics are recorded for the individual sites, but are aggregated for the purposes of modeling and estimation. Implicit in this definition is the assumption that the elemental sites represent the correct commodity definition. This general structure describes Parsons and Needelman (1992), Feather (1994), and Lupi and Feather (1998). The results suggest aggregation without accounting for heterogeneity parameters (i.e., the number of alternatives in each aggregate and the diversity in site attributes) can lead to substantial biases in estimates relative to estimating the model with the commodities defined as the individual sites.

Simple averages, by contrast, collect sites into spatial aggregates and do not assume information about the diversity in the values of attributes across elemental sites is known. Trips, prices, and site characteristics are recorded or measured for the spatial aggregate as if it were the true commodity being considered by the individual. Studies have typically compared welfare effects for specific applications and presented these as case studies. Some observations are possible from these, although without knowledge of the true commodity definition is it is difficult to know the best strategy in general.[21]

The consensus in the literature seems to suggest that welfare estimates from aggregated models exceed those from disaggregated models for quality changes that are constrained to be comparable across versions of the model. This popular view is probably too simple. Feather (1994), using simple averages, finds aggregate estimates to be about sixty percent of the compensating variation from the full model. This result is in agreement with Kaoru, Smith and Liu (1995) but in contrast to Parsons and Needelman (1992). Looking closer at the details of these studies, however, we find important distinctions in the aggregation of quality measures that can have direct implications for the possibility of constructing comparable policy changes across models.

For example, in the Parsons and Needelman disaggregate model, the fish species and water quality variables are all qualitative values indicating presence or absence of a species and extreme water conditions at individual lakes. These measures become proportions in the aggregate model. In the policy scenario proportions are set to zero to mimic the loss at the disaggregate level. In contrast, the Feather (1994), Lupi and Feather (1998), and Kaoru, Smith and Liu (1995) studies use quality measures that

---

[21] Comparing welfare effects from estimated models is the common metric for judging the impacts of modeling decisions in recreation demand in general. This presents a perennial difficulty, however, in that the comparison is based on an unobservable baseline and appeals to intuition are needed to differentiate results. This feature of the literature to date suggests that greater efforts to specify more objective measures of comparison between models would be worthwhile. Specific to the question of aggregation, Kaoru, Smith and Liu (1995) propose using the Hausman and McFadden (1984) test for IIA as one appropriate basis of gauging a proposed aggregation.

are continuous. The translation from disaggregate to aggregate variables depends upon what each study assumes is known by the analyst. Thus, the policy scenarios need not be numerically equivalent.

The main message from these comparisons is one of caution. The majority of comparisons include substantial doses of judgment on the part of the researcher to arrive at the overall results. As a consequence of this, at this point we probably can not conclude unequivocally how the choice alternative aggregation affects welfare measurement, nor can we say much in general about the appropriateness of aggregate versus individual site commodity definitions. These decisions will likely continue to be based on the specific application and needs of the study.

In an innovative twist, Lupi and Feather (1998) consider partial aggregation as an alternative to complete disaggregate or aggregate models within a nested framework. Their approach treats popular and policy relevant sites as distinct alternatives with other sites treated in a variety of different aggregates. It parallels distinctions in ordinary demand models where price aggregates are used to represent a class of substitutes.

Their argument fits nicely into our suggestion that preference restrictions and constraints can be thought of as implying different implicit prices. Here the inclusive values associated with each of the nests in the various aggregation strategies can be thought of as different strategies for collapsing the information relevant to the individual's choice. Moreover, the extent of each model's stochastic substitution captured by the nesting of aggregate alternatives can be judged by the size of the square of the estimated dissimilarity parameters. Overall, this comparison suggests modest differences in implied substitution across the alternatives. Nonetheless, some of their findings suggest measures for the most aggregate models are smaller than the disaggregate and others the reverse outcome, implying the specific details of the aggregation of quality attributes and travel costs are likely to be important to interpreting any overall conclusions on site aggregation.[22]

Table 2 provides a detailed overview of the features and conclusions of studies evaluating the effects of analyst-imposed restrictions on the choice set. As in the case of the site commodity definition, it is difficult to extract many general conclusions from these studies because the evaluations are case studies and the points of comparison are the unobservable benefit measures. The evaluations focus on the sensitivity of estimated benefits to the choice set decisions, typically in relation to a broad or general choice set that could be defined for each application.

With these caveats, it appears choice set definitions reducing effective substitutes lead to increases in per trip welfare measures of quality changes or site losses.[23] This ten-

---

[22] No one has specifically discussed the potential implications of differences in the measurement of travel costs across aggregations in each of these studies. Some examples indicate there were clear differences in practices used. Parsons and Needelman (1992) alter their measures of travel cost to consider the centroid of the aggregate site. Kaoru, Smith and Liu (1995) use the measured travel cost to the disaggregated site selected and the average of the travel costs to the sites in an aggregate for the substitute sites that were not visited.

[23] The Hauber and Parsons (2000) comparison of choice sets defined through distance contours found that benefit measures were invariant outside the equivalent of 1.6 hours. This finding is also consistent with our

dency includes nesting structure or other decisions that affect the correlation in random utilities for choice alternatives. The Parsons, Plantinga and Boyle (2000) comparison of alternative "surgical" definitions of choice sets (in which the choice set is reduced by aggregating what are judged by the analysts to be policy irrelevant sites, while keeping sites of direct policy interest and their close substitutes as individual choice alternatives) also conforms to this general tendency. Indeed the only notable exception can be found in Kling and Thomson (1996). Their nested models exhibit large differences in benefit measures for all the policies considered across the different nesting specifications. Hauber and Parsons (2000) and Jones and Lupi (1997) have contrasting results.

Three factors may help to explain these discrepancies. First, the most outlying welfare estimates for Kling and Thompson arise from models whose estimated dissimilarity parameters are likely to be outside the Börsch-Supan (1990) range for utility theory consistency, as developed by Herriges and Kling (1996). Indeed, the authors acknowledge this issue. Second, their salt-water fishing application has direct implications for the interpretation of their choice set. For private boat and charter boat models, the actual site alternatives are extensive. The identified sites are in some cases launch points.[24] This discrepancy between what can be observed and the actual site alternatives may be less dramatic for some of the fresh-water applications considered by Parsons and his collaborators. Finally, the sites in Kling and Thomson (1996) have substantial differences in costs largely independent of travel distance that arise from mode (e.g., boat fees and fuel costs) that would not be as different across the alternatives in other studies. Each of these may imply the commodity is more diverse across choice alternatives than in other applications. Taken in this light, the Kling and Thomson (1996) results appear more consistent with our substitution argument. Their nest A is judged to have the greatest substitution, followed by B and finally C. The size of their benefit estimates where mode and policy scenario do not interact conforms in several cases to this ordering.

Several recent papers have suggested employing user provided information in the construction of the choice set. In addition to the Parsons, Plantinga and Boyle (2000) surgical choice set, Peters, Adamowicz and Boxall (1995) and Hicks and Strand (2000) use survey respondent reports on sites they were aware of to eliminate different alternatives for each user depending on their responses. Not surprisingly, the Parsons, Plantinga and Boyle (2000) study shows the implications for benefit measurement depend on how the model characterizes available substitutes as well as how the definition of the policy scenario impacts the number of affected users.

Haab and Hicks (1997) specify an endogenous choice set model, treating the probability a site is in a person's choice set as independent of whether it is selected. Their

---

summary because progressive increases in travel costs with distance imply that the set of sites added at greater distances contribute less and less to what might be termed effective substitutes because they are all priced out of consideration.

[24] There are also a smaller number of site alternatives in the Kling–Thompson choice set (26 mode/site alternatives) than in any of the evaluations conducted by Parsons' applications. The later are typically in the hundreds, and often involve a randomization scheme to compose the choice set for estimation [as in Hauber and Parsons (2000)].

Table 2
Evaluations of choice set specification in recreation context

Authors	Structure of choice set	Total number of alternatives	Type of recreation	Model	Environmental quality measures	Policy considered	Welfare computation	Findings for benefit measures
Parsons and Kealy (1992)	3, 6, 12 and 24 lakes randomly drawn from within 180 miles of person's home	1,133	Fresh-water recreation at Wisconsin lakes	Nested logit two levels; North and South Wisconsin, then lakes in each group	Dissolved oxygen (DO) and secchi disk discrete readings; site attributes	Improve all lakes to a low DO standard; improve all lakes to high DO standard	Uses all sites in 180 miles and all visited by at least one person and within 180 miles	Large variation in per trip Hicksian welfare measure; larger number of sites generally but not always smaller benefit measure; difference as large as 9 times across models
Feather (1994)	6, 12, 24 simple and importance sampling	286	Fresh-water at Minnesota lakes	Simple RUM	Water quality measured using secchi disk	10% increase in lake size	All alternatives	Importance sampling close to model based on full choice set yields differences in welfare measures under 20% over range of models; simple random sampling of site alternatives understates full model's benefit measure, has more instability at a given sample size of choice alternatives; its difference with full model declines with number of sites

(continued on next page)

Table 2
(*Continued*)

Authors	Structure of choice set	Total number of alternatives	Type of recreation	Model	Environmental quality measures	Policy considered	Welfare computation	Findings for benefit measures
Kling and Thomson (1996)	Five near shore site aggregates supporting each of four modes (beach, pier, charter boat, private boat) and three offshore supporting two modes (charter and private boat); four site/mode nesting structures	26	Sport fishing in California	Nested logit two levels	Average catch rate for all species	Eliminate site alternatives in various combinations	All alternatives	Evaluate sensitivity to restrictions on catch coefficient and to nesting structure; welfare estimates for all policy scenarios sensitive to nesting structures and restrictions on catch coefficient; values differ by 3 to 4 times from lowest to highest per trip for all policy scenarios; test favors model with largest welfare measures
Parsons and Hauber (1998)	Choice set defined by distance pre-measured in terms of travel time 0.8 to 4.0 hours	1,899	Recreational fishing Maine	Nested logit three levels; site type of fish	Water quality fish species presence and abundance; level of toxic pollution	Clean to EPA attainment; clean toxins; salmon absent	Choice set defined by distance boundary	Outside 1.6 hours travel time little change in per trip benefit measures across all three scenarios; dramatic differences inside this boundary; on average benefit measure 6 to 7 times larger for smallest to largest choice set

(*continued on next page*)

Table 2
(Continued)

Authors	Structure of choice set	Total number of alternatives	Type of recreation	Model	Environmental quality measures	Policy considered	Welfare computation	Findings for benefit measures
Shaw and Ozog (1999)	Examined two nesting structures: A – participation, stay overnight, the site choice (8 alternatives); B – participation, site choice first day and stay overnight	Sites aggregated from 13 rivers to 8 river group defined as site alternatives; Atlantic salmon fishing	Five sites in Maine, three in Nova Scotia, New Brunswick, and Quebec, Canada	Nested logit three levels; nonlinear income effect	Catch rates	Double salmon catch rates at Penobscot River	All alternatives	Use quadratic loss function to solve for per trip consumer surplus; only model A could be solved for benefit measure; B could not be solved; per period Hicksian consumer surplus lower for those users with one day trips than those staying overnight; no conclusion on alternative nests based on welfare measures; model A preferred on consistency conditions of dissimilarity parameters

(continued on next page)

Table 2
(Continued)

Authors	Structure of choice set	Total number of alternatives	Type of recreation	Model	Environmental quality measures	Policy considered	Welfare computation	Findings for benefit measures
Parsons, Plantinga and Boyle (2000)	Combination of aggregation and distance based definitions – regional aggregate, popular sites, policy region, composite commodity for all outside sites	814	Fishing lakes in Maine	Nested logit in study area and outside	Measure of expected cold water fish catch rate and qualitative variable indicating importance of site for cold water species	Loss of five sites in China Lakes region	Compares nested with random sample of all sites to different "surgical" aggregates: regional aggregate of alternatives, alternatives as popular sites and no consideration of outside alternatives – simple RUM focused on region	Definition of alternatives impacts substitution effect and extent of market; latter arises because expansion of sites considered as substitutes has number of individuals "unaffected" by loss increased when more substitutes; treatment of substitutes included in model affects per recreationist benefits; substitution works as expected – less substitutes, measures for loss larger; extent of market tends to reduce discrimination between alternatives
Jones and Lupi (1997)	Examine eight different nesting structures to describe choice sets that include	2,029 fishing sites and up to four fish species at each site	Recreational fishing in Maine	Nested logit	Qualitative variables for elevated toxics and fish consumption	Three scenarios: cleanup of nonattainment sites	Median estimate of 20 random draws from each model – using average across	

(continued on next page)

Table 2
(Continued)

Authors	Structure of choice set	Total number of alternatives	Type of recreation	Model	Environmental quality measures	Policy considered	Welfare computation	Findings for benefit measures
	species–site and site–species combinations in 2, 3 and 4 level nests				advisories, nonattainment of EPA water quality standards due to nonpoint source pollution and for species abundance (salmon, trout, bass and other)	based on water quality; cleanup based on toxics; eliminate salmon as available species	all sample individuals of per trip consumer surplus	
Parsons, Massey and Tomasi (2000)	Compares simple RUM with full choice set to: nested with only familiar and unfamiliar; simple RUM with only "favorite" sites; simple RUM with only familiar and favorite (labeled Peters et al.); and	62 beach sites from Sandy Hook, NJ, to Assateague Island, VA	Beach recreation in Delaware, New Jersey, Maryland, and Virginia	Nested logit two levels; simple RUM with full and variety of smaller choice sets; over number of site familiar = 11.5 sites, favorite = 9.4 sites and visited = 4.1 sites	Length of beach, dummy variables for: width of beach, boardwalk, amusements, park inside, presence of surfing	Beach closures and loss in beach width	Uses choice set relevant to each model	Full choice set has smallest Hicksian welfare measure per trip for most beach closures; full choice set welfare measure in the middle of the range of values across models; variation in estimated per trip consumer surplus can be large

(continued on next page)

Table 2
(Continued)

Authors	Structure of choice set	Total number of alternatives	Type of recreation	Model	Environmental quality measures	Policy considered	Welfare computation	Findings for benefit measures
	simple RUM with only familiar (labeled Hicks and Strand)							
Peters, Adamowicz and Boxall (1995)	Compares full choice set, random selection with 5 alternatives, and individually defined consideration based choice set	67	Fresh-water fishing in Southern Alberta, Canada	Simple RUM	General catch rate, trout catch rate, index of effort for large fish; qualitative variables for pristine lake, trees stocking; measures of stability of water flow and length of stream	Site closures (four alternatives) increase tree cover at a site, introduce trout stocking	Appears to be all sites for full model and random selection and individually defined choice set for consideration based choice set	Full and random choice set very close estimates of per trip Hicksian surplus measures; individual consideration set large differences; relationship depends on policy considered; always agrees in direction of effect; magnitude of estimates varies from 4 times larger to 1/10 as larger

(continued on next page)

Table 2
(*Continued*)

Authors	Structure of choice set	Total number of alternatives	Type of recreation	Model	Environmental quality measures	Policy considered	Welfare computation	Findings for benefit measures
Hicks and Strand (2000)	Compares full choice set with distance based choice set (6 different alternatives) and set defined as familiar to individual	10	Publicly accessible recreation beaches along the western shore of Chesapeake Bay in Maryland	Simple RUM	Measure of bacterial contamination (fecal coliform in water), measure of presence of both facilities, boat docks, and pools	Reduction in fecal coliform, closure of sites (including well-known site)	Uses all sites for full site model, distance (or time) based and familiarity based definitions	Distance based measures of choice set stabilize to approximate the full choice set for all Hicksian welfare computations (based on mean for per trip values) at approximately 2.5 hours (set ranges from 1 to 3.5 hours); full set is about 4 hours travel time; familiar set very different for all three welfare scenarios; estimates especially different for loss of familiar site (five times larger then conventional estimates); otherwise smaller than full site and distance based measures (60 to 84 percent of their values)

estimates of the value of a quality change are smaller than what was estimated for the same quality improvements using a conventional multinominal specification. This finding is hard to evaluate because it seems unlikely that the probability a site would be in a user's choice set would be independent of the likelihood it would be chosen for a trip. Parsons, Massey and Tomasi (2000) exploit this potential for correlation by defining familiar and favorite sites. They conjecture that not all sites contribute equally as effective substitutes and conventional approaches making this assumption may understate welfare gains or losses.

All our discussion of random utility models thus far has maintained the standard assumption of constant marginal utility of income. As noted above, this implies that the choice process is independent of income (and that Hicksian and Marshallian benefits measures are equivalent) under the standard logit and nested logit models, since income does not vary over alternatives and therefore drops out of the probability calculations. Many researchers have considered this assumption to be overly restrictive and have pursued alternatives allowing the marginal utility of income to vary. Ideally, the random utility model would allow income to influence the choice among alternatives, and would provide a consistent definition of the choice occasion income relevant to the decision being modeled. The literature has not realized this overall goal. As a result, we divide our discussion on this topic into two parts, considering first the technical challenges associated with employing models with income effects, and then noting the conceptual challenges in interpreting them.

The majority of the literature to date has focused on the technical challenges associated with estimation and welfare calculations in the nonlinear nested logit model. Examples of this include Morey, Rowe and Watson (1993), Herriges and Kling (1999), Karlström (1999) and Dagsvik and Karlström (2005). These papers suggest techniques for calculating welfare measures given the absence of the closed form formula available in the linear case. Herriges and Kling offer the most comprehensive comparison of the effects on benefit measures of nonlinear income models. They compare three functional forms – linear RUM, generalized Leontief, and translog specifications – for the conditional indirect utility function and several nesting structures for the error distribution. Each is used to estimate sport fishing choices in southern California, using the Kling and Thomson (1996) data with an emphasis on mode choice (beach, pier, private or charter boat). Three measures each of the compensating variation for a price change, a quality change, and a choice set change were evaluated. The first uses the simulation method proposed by McFadden (1999), which estimates the expected value of the compensating variation for a given vector of observed characteristics by generating pseudo-random numbers from the assumed error structure, solving for the income compensation, and constructing the mean over the set of draws of vectors of pseudo-random numbers. This technique is computationally intense due the inability to directly resample pseudo-random numbers from the GEV distribution.

The second approach, labeled the representative consumer method, exploits the closed form for the expected value of the maximum function for a set of choice alternatives with common error distribution. While the compensating variation itself can not be expressed as a closed form expression in terms of site alternatives, the task of numerical approximation is less demanding than with the first method. The last method corresponds to bounds proposed by McFadden (1999) as simpler alternative to using the simulation method. While the Herriges and Kling (1999) findings are limited to one application, they seem to suggest greater sensitivity in the welfare estimates to the error distribution (i.e., nesting structure) than to nonlinearity in income, especially when quality changes were being evaluated.

Recently, Morey, Sharma and Karlström (2003) have proposed a simpler strategy based on using a piece wise linear spline function for income. In this case, the expected willingness to pay is readily approximated without addressing the challenges considered by Herriges and Kling (1999). Their approximation is not an exact relation because any policy being evaluated could, in principle, cause an individual to move between income categories. Their application finds the simple approximation works well, provided the policy is small in relation to the income categories. This result brings us to a central issue, largely relegated to footnotes in discussions of preferences assumed to be nonlinear in income, namely, what is the relevant income measure?

There is very little research examining the process by which choice occasion income is defined. Nearly all studies to date define choice occasion income by some ad hoc division of annual income into choice occasion expenditures. In models that impose zero income effects this is innocuous. However, as our technical knowledge on nonlinear income effects evolves and applications seek to employ the more general model, the question of choice occasion income will be more important. Benefits estimates in these cases will directly depend not only on the functional form for utility, but also on the way that choice occasion income is defined. This aspect of the nonlinear income RUM model deserves further investigation.

We conclude our discussion by considering the links between choice occasion models and seasonal demand. Bockstael, Hanemann and Kling (1987) first identified the need to develop consistent measures of season benefits from choice occasion models. They used a participation equation, specified as a function of the expected level of choice occasion maximum utility (i.e., inclusive value) estimated from the choice occasion model. Aggregate benefit measures were approximated as the product of RUM per trip benefit measures and estimates of the number of trips based on these models.

The intervening decade has seen the development of four alternative models closely related to this suggestion. Morey, Rowe and Watson (1993) expand the random utility model framework to the season by including a no-trip alternative along with the available sites. Seasonal benefits estimates are calculated as the product of choice occasions (which is assumed to be fixed and exogenous) and the per trip consumer surplus estimate. Proposals by Parsons and Kealy (1995) and Feather, Hellerstein and Tomasi (1995) also begin with the RUM and use it to estimate the predicted probabilities of trips to different choice alternatives. In Parsons and Kealy (1995) the predicted probabilities weight alternative specific prices and site attributes. These price and attribute indexes are then used as explanatory variables in an aggregate trip "demand" equation. Feather, Hellerstein and Tomasi (1995) use the same aggregate price but replace the expected value of the index of site attributes with the expected value of each index for the seasonal demand. Both approaches acknowledge the link to the trip demands to be ad hoc.

Hausman, Leonard and McFadden (1995) take a different strategy in explaining their measure. Like Bockstael, Hanemann and Kling (1987), they use a function of the inclusive value in their participation model, but they argue it offers a theoretically consistent price index. As a result, they suggest the analyst can begin with the RUM, derive the price index from the inclusive value, and then develop a consistent demand function that allows welfare measurement directly from the trip or participation model. Unfortunately this argument is incorrect. The reason follows directly from the logic of developing price indexes.

The economic approach for defining a price index must rely on an optimizing model of behavior and, generally, some form of homothetic separability as we discussed in describing the distinction between weak and latent separability [for early discussions of these issues see Samuelson and Swamy (1974)]. A consistent price index follows from these assumptions. The associated quantity index cannot be defined independently from it. In the case of seasonal recreation demand, total expenditure on the set of site alternatives, described as an aggregate, must equal the sum of expenditures on each alternative over the season. When the aggregate quantity index is not derived from the price index, this condition will not hold. Consider the price index for Parsons and Kealy (1995) and Feather, Hellerstein and Tomasi (1995) and divide it into the total expenditure of recreation trips during the season. The process does not yield the aggregate quantity measure they propose – trips during a season. The same is true for Hausman, Leonard and McFadden (1995) and their use of the inclusive value [Smith (1996)].

While none of these models is fully consistent, it may be the distinctions we are drawing are unimportant for some classes of problems. Unfortunately, this is not what the results to date suggest. Parsons, Jakus and Tomasi (1999) found fairly close consistency in mean benefit measures derived from the Bockstael, Hanemann and Kling (1987), Hausman, Leonard and McFadden (1995), and Morey, Rowe and Watson (1993) models. However, both the Parsons and Kealy (1995) and Feather, Hellerstein and Tomasi (1995) approaches were sensitive to the types of policy analyses considered and were generally different from the other estimates. Herriges, Kling and Phaneuf (1999) add further questions for the more stable of these approaches. Using a different application (fishing in the Wisconsin Great Lakes), they found the Hausman, Leonard and McFadden (1995) strategy was sensitive to the preference specifications used and the form of the participation equation, with extremely large variations in the average value of seasonal benefits for a given policy scenario.

3.3.3. Corner solution models

The limitations of the random utility model for estimating seasonal benefits have motivated research on the Kuhn–Tucker demand models. Based on the work of Wales and Woodland (1983) and Lee and Pitt (1986), these models have been applied in primal and dual form by Phaneuf, Kling and Herriges (2000) and Phaneuf (1999), respectively. Corner solution models derive demand relationships from the specification of the consumer's choice problem. A key feature of the model is that binding nonnegativity constraints or corner solutions are handled in a theoretically consistent way. The primal version of the model uses the individual's Kuhn–Tucker utility maximization conditions to derive directly the probability of observing a set of observed choices. In the dual model the virtual prices implied by corner solutions are compared to actual prices to derive the probabilities of observing the person's site visitation pattern.

To illustrate the basic logic, consider the primal problem. The consumer's maximization problem for the n-vector of recreation site visits $\mathbf{x}$ is given by

$$\underset{\mathbf{x},z}{\text{Max}}\{U(\mathbf{x}, z, \mathbf{q}, \boldsymbol{\varepsilon}; \gamma)\} \quad \text{s.t. } \mathbf{p}'\mathbf{x} + z = m, \ \mathbf{x} \geqslant \mathbf{0}, \tag{3.13}$$

where $\boldsymbol{\varepsilon}$ is an n-vector of random errors, γ is a vector of utility function parameters to be estimated, z is spending on all other goods (with the price normalized to unity), and the remaining notation follows from the previous section. Assuming spending on all other goods z is strictly positive the Kuhn–Tucker first order conditions can be written as

$$\frac{U_{x_i}(\mathbf{x}, \mathbf{z}, \mathbf{q}, \boldsymbol{\varepsilon}; \gamma)}{U_z(\mathbf{x}, \mathbf{z}, \mathbf{q}, \boldsymbol{\varepsilon}; \gamma)} \leqslant p_i,$$

$$x_i \geqslant 0, \tag{3.14}$$

$$x_i\left(U_{x_i}(\mathbf{x}, \mathbf{z}, \mathbf{q}, \boldsymbol{\varepsilon}) - p_i U_z(\mathbf{x}, \mathbf{z}, \mathbf{q}, \boldsymbol{\varepsilon})\right) = 0, \quad \forall i,$$

where U_x and U_z denote the derivatives of utility with respect to x_i and z, respectively. A link is made to estimation by assuming the utility function allows the first order conditions to be restated as

$$\varepsilon_i \leqslant g_i(\mathbf{x}, \mathbf{z}, \mathbf{q}, \mathbf{p}; \gamma),$$

$$x_i \geqslant 0, \tag{3.15}$$

$$x_i\left(\varepsilon_i - g(\mathbf{x}, \mathbf{z}, \mathbf{q}, \mathbf{p}; \gamma)\right) = 0.$$

The form of g_i depends on the specific function used to describe individual preferences. Given an assumption on the distribution for $\boldsymbol{\varepsilon}$, the probability of observing the revealed outcomes for each individual in the sample can be stated. For the case where the first K goods are positively consumed the probability is given by

$$\text{pr}(x_1, \ldots, x_K, 0_{K+1}, \ldots, 0_N)$$

$$= \text{prob}(\varepsilon_1 = g_1, \ldots, \varepsilon_K = g_K, \varepsilon_{K+1} \leqslant g_{K+1}, \ldots, \varepsilon_N \leqslant g_N). \tag{3.16}$$

Maximization of the likelihood function, defined using these probabilities, allows recovery of estimates of the parameter vector γ and characterization of preferences up to the unobserved error term.

Most applications of the primal and dual versions of corner solutions model have been limited to relatively small choice sets. For example, the Phaneuf, Kling and Herriges (2000) primal study uses a modified Stone–Geary utility function and generalized extreme value (GEV) error structure in a four-site model. In this case two sources of site substitution are included: one due to the parametric form of utility and the other due to the GEV nesting structure assumed. Phaneuf and Herriges (1999) estimate a larger dimension model (fifteen sites) but assume the errors are independent extreme value. The Phaneuf (1999) dual study uses multivariate normal errors and a homogeneous translog indirect utility function, which limits income effects in the model but permits relatively general substitution patterns.

Both models are computationally demanding and have thus far seen limited application. However, von Haefen, Phaneuf and Parsons (2004) have demonstrated that with strategic separability assumptions and random parameters in the primal model it is possible to expand the choice set to larger dimensions, allow relatively rich patterns of stochastic substitution, and compute the required welfare calculations. These developments suggest the model can be used for a wider array of policy relevant applications. Von Haefen, Phaneuf and Parsons (2004) rely on an innovative and efficient sorting rule based on the numeraire good that uses separability and quasi-concavity of preferences when each set of discrete choices is made.

Two extensions in their logic would expand the potential range of policy applications. First, it would be desirable to consider relaxing their additive separability assumption using latent separability along with exclusive goods to evaluate whether large sets of goods could be accommodated. We believe this line of inquiry might pay off. Second, an appealing feature of the corner solution model is the ability to exploit discontinuities as information. In the applications to this point the discontinuities have been confined to restrictions implied by zero consumption of a subset of the goods available. Restrictions on the role of quality as imposing information at discontinuities offer another potential extension. For example, water quality must exceed a threshold to support game fish. Below that level it does not contribute to enhancing game fishing activities. Another higher level is required for swimming. Past specifications of recreation models have tended to focus on continuous effects of quality or to consider only recreation sites that serve a dominate activity. When we use sites that can support multiple activities, it may be possible to specify exogenously restrictions that imply quality has an exclusive role in some recreation activities at different quality levels. Corner solution models, generalized to describe how these types of quality influences specific activities in discontinuous ways offer another area for future research.

Expanding the model to allow more general error assumptions and parametric forms for utility raises comparable dimensionality issues that have been discussed in the context of the multivariate probit model and flexible functional form issues, respectively. Nonetheless, this class of models consistently integrates choice at the extensive margin among many sites with conditional usage decisions and is at the frontier of recreation demand modeling. Overall, the primary limitation on these models remains at the stage of implementation. We can relax some of the early dimensionality constraints, but too do so requires restricting preferences. What remains is to accumulate experience with the tradeoff in terms of the impact of these restrictions (and some of the alternatives we have suggested) versus the simpler but less consistent alternatives. At this stage, this modeling framework seems to offer payoffs worth the effort of strategic simplifications in the choice complexity it accommodates.

3.3.4. Price index models

Our last category of models is a mixed set that includes a class with ad hoc connections to a consistent behavioral model and others more directly linked. What unifies them is that each is organized around the assumption of a price index that captures the full effects of variations in site attributes.

The first is the hedonic travel cost model, introduced by Brown and Mendelsohn (1984), and adapted by several authors for a range of applications. The hedonic travel cost model attempts to draw an analogy with hedonic price models but was subject to considerable criticism when explained in these terms [see Bockstael, Hanemann and Kling (1987), Bockstael and McConnell (1999a, 1999b), Smith and Kaoru (1987)]. While Englin and Mendelsohn (1991) and Pendleton and Mendelsohn (2000) have proposed answers to some of the criticisms, basic issues remain unanswered.

The hedonic cost framework begins with the assumption that there exists a price frontier linking travel costs to the characteristics of the recreation site, usually the measures of quality attributes or disamenities considered in the site selection models of a RUM analysis. The slope of this function, with respect to each attribute, is interpreted as a marginal price. Each individual, in principle, is assumed to face a different price locus so that the variation in marginal prices along with differences in site choices and selected levels of characteristics are used to estimate inverse demand function for characteristics.

In contrast to applications of hedonic methods for housing prices or wage rates, one must ask what process leads to the hedonic cost function in travel cost applications, since there is no market equilibrium at work. While one might argue the specification of this function is simply one way to characterize the locus of alternatives available to recreationists [see Smith, Palmquist and Jakus (1991)], this does not answer how one composes the set of sites that defines the locus.[25] Moreover, in practice most authors have estimated the locus for each of a set of origin zones, rather than an individual user. Using a set of origin zones leaves the hedonic cost function without a clear economic

---

[25] The Smith, Palmquist and Jakus (1991) application proposes interpreting the cost function as a frontier – the locus of least cost ways (sites) of acquiring the desirable characteristics are restricted to be positive. The use of regression methods to estimate the hedonic cost function does not preclude negative marginal prices for attributes [see Bockstael, Hanemann and Kling (1987) and Smith and Kaoru (1990a, 1990b]. Englin and Mendelsohn (1991) suggest that such prices can reflect satiation and do not, as other authors have argued, invalidate the method. Bockstael and McConnell (1999a, 1999b) have observed this explanation raises the prospect that the consumer choice problem is not well defined. Allowing for satiation implies that the set of sites defining the locus cannot preclude situations where less of a site characteristic actually costs more.

interpretation. Pendleton and Mendelsohn (2000) have argued that the choice between a RUM and the hedonic travel cost boils down to econometric considerations. Unfortunately, the focus of their attention is on differences in the functional form used to describe consumer preferences and not the source of the cost function.

Smith, Palmquist and Jakus (1991) offered a strategy for estimating these cost functions that precludes negative prices and treats the function as an efficient locus describing the "prices" of obtaining attributes. However, they do not explain how the analyst is to determine for each individual which sites define this locus or the economic rationale for describing choice alternatives as a continuous cost locus. Until these concerns are explained benefit measures derived from the model are unlikely to be considered as an economically meaningful alternative to the RUM framework.

The second approach is theoretically consistent but also relies on a price index. Introduced by von Haefen (1999), it adapts the Chiang and Lee (1992) framework for discrete–continuous choices. Trips are augmented by a function of a site's quality characteristics (q_k) along with an error to reflect individual heterogeneity. Maximizing a utility function that assumes trips can be converted into equivalent units, after adjusting for observed and unobserved heterogeneity, yields (with the appropriate preference function) a site selection rule based on the quality adjusted prices for each site. Like the RUM model, an individual is assumed to select a best site. In this case, however, the selection applies for the full time period assumed relevant to individual decisions. With only one application to recreation site choice, it is too early to judge whether the framework will be competitive to RUMs or the other more popular models.

3.3.5. Overall prognosis on the modeling strategies

A few specific conclusions have emerged from our overview of the primary recreation models. First, the current and dominant modeling strategy is some form of the random utility model. While RUMs will almost certainly always have a place in recreation due to their simplicity and flexibility to work with many different data types, the framework will always have limitations in describing seasonal behavior. As such some variation of the incomplete demand or corner solution models is likely to become the preferred candidate for future applications in this area.

Second, as recreation has become an incubator area for many microeconometric innovations research has tilted toward a focus on econometric and other technical issues in estimation and welfare measurement. This process has redirected attention away from what might be termed the fundamental economic issues in the choice process. This tendency is best seen in the sophisticated approaches to incorporating unobserved heterogeneity and dealing with corner solutions, while ad hoc assumptions on the opportunity cost of time are maintained.

Finally, there are topics identified as research areas that have received little current attention. For example, the impacts of separability and time horizon decisions have not been fully explored. Models based on the RUM strategy have focused considerable effort on nonlinear effects of income on utility without considering how the relevant income is determined in relation to other consumption choices. The importance of separability and the time horizon relevant for inter-temporal choices clearly are relevant to progress on this issue. Also, the issue of multiple purpose trips and activity bundling has received little recent attention. For example, in most popular beaches 40 to 50 percent of the recreationists are children. Are their gains from improved conditions (or losses from a beach closure) adequately represented in conventional models? There are also stark differences in the outdoor recreation patterns by gender. Dual earner households must balance a complex set of work, housework, and leisure tradeoffs. One would think that recreation choices would offer a clear set of opportunities for understanding household behavior. To our knowledge, only one application has begun to consider this issue [McConnell (1999)].

4. Recreation data

The data available for describing outdoor recreation behavior in the past fifteen years have transformed the practice of recreation demand modeling. Early applications relied on visitor counts at a site that provided only limited information on the visitor's origin, usually in the form of aggregate zones.[26] These counts were normalized by the population of the zone and treated as measures of the overall population's use rate, or as the product of the rate of use of recreationists and the participation rate among the population as a whole. Nothing was observed about users' income or socio-economic characteristics.

The availability of micro-data reporting individuals' recreation behavior changed everything. It became possible to consider differences in the opportunity cost of time and other variables across individuals. Past experience, equipment ownership, and a host of economic and demographic factors could, in principle, be exploited to specify more precise demand models. With this opportunity came new problems of analyzing demand at an individual level. Consistent economic models needed to take into account zero or infrequent consumption, quantity measures that were discrete count variables, incomplete records of the consumption of other goods, as well as an array of other features.

Three types of recreation data sources are now available: household surveys, user group surveys, and on site surveys. In addition to national surveys, many states conduct periodic specialized surveys of fishing or hunting activities.[27] Moreover, in recent years,

---

[26] See Clawson and Knetsch (1966), Cesario and Knetsch (1970), and Cicchetti, Fisher and Smith (1976) as examples of demand analyses relying on these data.

[27] The Public Area Recreation Visitors Survey (PARVS) is an example of a long term effort coordinated by H. Ken Cordell of the US Forest Service to collect on-site recreation surveys for forest service areas and in coordination with NOAA, for beaches around the US, Vernon R. Leeworthy has been especially active in developing well-documented recreation databases relevant to NOAA's activities. Daniel Hellerstein has focused efforts at the Economic Research Service on related activities for recreation sites relevant to agricultural policy.

natural resource damage assessments have prompted efforts to collect both one-time surveys of recreationists and panel surveys of behavior over time.

There are few examples of comparisons of the characteristics of respondents or the results from these different sources of data. One notable exception by Teisl and Boyle (1997) compared the results derived from three samples corresponding to our classification: a general population survey, an intercept of marine anglers, and a sample of licensed inland anglers who indicated they also participated in marine fishing. The objective was to evaluate the effectiveness of each approach in developing a representative sample of marine anglers. They conclude that the use of a population of licensed anglers for another type of fishing yields a sample equivalent to the group of interest in terms of tests comparing groups' socio-economic characteristics and fishing activities. Such comparisons are potentially important because of the cost of developing samples of recreation site users using general population surveys.

In the remainder of this section we consider four aspects of recreation data. These include data collection as an economic process, combining revealed and stated preference data, linking site characteristics to behavioral data, and measuring distances for travel cost estimation.

4.1. Data collection as an economic process

Data collection should be viewed as an economic process of information gathering subject to two types of constraints: the resource constraints of the study and constraints on the time individuals will devote to survey responses. There is increasing recognition among economists that many of the issues raised in designing effective contingent valuation surveys are also relevant to the collection of revealed preference information. In short, respondents may not interpret questions asking for reports of their activities as intended by the analysts who use those responses. As a result, focus groups and cognitive interviews have become a part of the design of special purpose recreation surveys. Unfortunately, there have been few systematic comparisons of the effects of different approaches for asking about recreation behavior. Three related aspects have been studied: the effects of time span on the accuracy of reports of past recreation activity, the advantages of diaries versus one-time surveys for recreation expenditures, and the extent to which econometrics can correct for on-site sample selection problems.

As part of an evaluation of the design of the Fishing, Hunting and Wildlife Recreation Survey, Westat Inc. [see Westat (1989)] evaluated alternative time periods for reporting past activities. The analysis concluded that information collected for a three-month period was more accurate than annual summaries of both the level and timing of activity.

There is little direct experience with the degree of cooperation and accuracy of panels in publicly available recreation surveys. Early general discussions of panel data construction, such as Sudman and Ferber (1979), provide detailed accounts of the difficulties of getting and sustaining cooperation and accuracy.[28] They note that requesting

---

[28] For a more recent summary of the issues in implementation see Tourangeau, Rips and Rasinski (2000).

written records can reduce initial cooperation. Their early discussion argues that accuracy issues are most serious for diary studies, where panel members record purchases or activities daily. A time-in-sample bias is also noted by Bailar (1989). He suggests that respondents are "trained" by their exposure to the survey. They may also learn that some responses will lead to additional questions. This learning may lead to responses intended to avoid the added questions. Hanemann (1995) used this background together with evidence from one-time surveys to critique the Montana Outdoor Recreation Survey conducted by RTI from July/August 1992 through July/August 1993 in seven waves. Respondents were asked to record all recreation trips taken every two months during this time span. These data were used as part of the Upper Clark Fork Basin natural resource damage case. While there is some evidence of a time-in-survey bias discussed in Hanemann's critique, this is not a controlled experiment evaluating panels and diaries.[29] Overall, these general warnings and the example cited suggest that modeling efforts to develop dynamic models that seek to describe the temporal pattern of recreation use must devote equal attention to the challenges in collecting accurate temporal records on recreationists' behavior.

Choice-based samples provide a different type of challenge. Manski and Lerman (1977) study the econometric treatment of these choice-based samples for RUM analyses. The primary issue arises in this case because on-site samples are used to collect information about site usage. The authors conclude that sample exogenous maximum likelihood estimation can be used for these types of data, treating the sample as exogenous but allowing for adjustment of the alternative specific constants, using knowledge of the relative size of the sampling fraction in comparison to the population fraction with each choice alternative. This adjustment will yield maximum likelihood estimates for the multinomial logit [Cosslett (1981)]. More generally, Manski and Lerman (1977) have also shown that consistent estimates can be derived for a wider array of choice models by weighting the sample likelihood function in inverse proportion to the ratio used to adjust the alternative specific constants (i.e., using the population fraction relative to the sample fraction for each choice alternative).[30]

4.2. Combining revealed and stated preference data

Two lines of applications have developed from Cameron (1992) and Morikawa's (1989) independent proposal to use revealed and stated preference data jointly in estimating

---

[29] Hanemann (1995) notes that of 224 individuals who reported participating in fishing in the first wave, only 64 reported participating during the last wave. While this change seems like a large decline, the paucity of temporal records on recreation use makes it difficult to judge in unambiguous terms.

[30] McFadden (1996) has recently considered the relevance of this result for intercept and follow-up samples. He concludes from simulation experiments that simple adaptations to the weighted maximum likelihood, or including selection effects to account for the follow-up success rate, result in substantial errors in both the parameter estimates and the estimates of willingness to pay when compared with the correct intercept and follow-up likelihood function.

individual preferences.[31] The first uses the restrictions implied by constrained utility maximization to combine revealed and stated preference responses, which provide
complementary pieces of information for recovering preference estimates. The second
"stacks" data from the different sources and seeks to estimate a single model using the
two types of observations, which represent two different ways of getting the same type
of information necessary to recover preference estimates. We focus on the first strategy as a vehicle for illustrating how survey question format influences and conditions
microeconometric modeling using the resulting data. We then conclude with a brief
discussion of cases where stated preference surveys are designed to provide data that
address issues in the available revealed preference information, such as collinearity or a
limited range of variation in important quality attributes.

To illustrate the first situation, consider the Cameron (1992) framework. Using data
available from a sport fishing survey, she combined a conventional travel cost trip-
demand model with responses to the following discrete response contingent valuation
question: "If the total cost of all your salt-water fishing last year was T more, would
you have quit fishing?" The bid amounts included one of eleven different values ranging form $200 to $20,000 (the average expenditures for the season were estimated to
be $507). Her analysis models the response to this question by allowing the number of
trips to optimally adjust to the added fixed cost T. Under this interpretation respondents
are assumed to solve the following optimization problem:

$$\max_{x,z} U(x, z) \quad \text{s.t. } m = px + z + T, \tag{4.1}$$

where x is the number of recreation trips priced at p, income is given by m, and z
represents all other spending. The solution to this problem is compared to the solution
when trips are constrained to be equal to zero. This implies the binary choice problem
based on a utility difference is given by

$$\Delta V = U\big[m - T - p \cdot x(p, m, T), x(p, m, T)\big] - U(m, 0). \tag{4.2}$$

This is certainly a reasonable way to interpret the economic behavior underlying
responses to the stated preference question. However, other interpretations are possible,
which would suggest different model estimation. Respondents could have interpreted
the question to imply that they could not adjust the number of trips taken during the
year and were offered an all or nothing choice costing T dollars more. In this case, the
behavioral model underlying the discrete response CV would be different, given by

$$\Delta V = U\big[m - T - p\bar{x}, \bar{x}\big] - U[m, 0], \tag{4.3}$$

---

[31] Cameron's (1992) research was actually completed in 1989 and was circulating as a discussion paper
for some time prior to publication. There are important differences in the two studies. Cameron combines
a continuous travel cost demand with a discrete response contingent valuation question. Morikawa's (1989)
analysis focuses on random utility models applied to model choice in transportation, using both revealed and
stated preference choice data.

where $\bar{x} = x(p, m)$, the level of consumption fixed at the original level of price and income.

A second example of the issues associated with how we use revealed and stated questions arises with the two Haab, Huang, and Whitehead applications [Huang, Haab and Whitehead (1997) and Whitehead, Haab and Huang (2000)]. They combine reports on past participation and level of use responses under current conditions with expected use without a quality change and with a program to improve quality. By using this design they can test for differences between revealed and stated preference responses before considering a quality change. They found no difference in travel cost, substitute price or income coefficients in their models for past and expected trips with current quality.

A quality improvement is found to increase expected demand. It appears both papers consider the same survey and the comparison of methods used raises another issue. In the initial paper [Huang, Haab and Whitehead (1997)], they consider the use questions along with a binary choice contingent valuation question on improved quality. In the subsequent paper they focus on demand (both revealed and stated) without the payment for the program. As a result, they implicitly raise the issue of how many stated preference questions should be used in a single model of preferences. The financing of the program could be deducted from income available for recreation and never explicitly modeled. The authors do not raise this issue, but it is clearly one for further consideration as the stated preference approach moves toward adapting the multiple question conjoint framework to meet the needs of economic models.

These two examples are not criticisms of past work. Rather, they serve to highlight the general issue that the questions asked in any data collection effort (RP/SP or RP alone) need to be both clear to the survey respondents and link in as unambiguous terms as possible to a specific description of a consumer's choice.

Adamowicz, Louviere and Williams (1994) provide an example of the second type of RP/SP joint model, where a stated preference choice survey is designed to expand the range of variation in site characteristics. In contrast to other applications of the joint estimation logic, data combinations in the RUM framework usually focus on specific policy problems requiring an expansion in the attribute set beyond what can be observed in nature. In this study the objective is to evaluate alternative flow regimes for specific rivers in the study area of southwestern Alberta, Canada. A conjoint choice survey is administered to a subset of the sample contacted for the RP information about water based recreation. A wider range of flow conditions and water quality can be considered with the expanded attribute set. As a rule, these applications apply fairly standard linear RUM specifications and do not consider the issues posed by explaining both the site choice and level of use. The only methodological issue typically addressed is the relative size of the scale parameter in the RUM logit models, which can be identified by restricting structural parameters in the jointly estimated choice models to be equal. As we note below, this focus could certainly expand as we consider how to evaluate the ways individuals simplify complex choice tasks. For example, it is possible to conceive of SP models helping to inform the process of organizing complex decision processes that might underlie RP data on behavior.

4.3. Linking site characteristics to behavioral data

One of the most important uses of travel cost models has been to estimate consumers' willingness to pay for improvements in the quality of recreation sites. Several aspects of quality have been considered, including pollution related amenities (i.e., water pollution measured with technical or perception based indexes), resource management related quality (including congestion), catch measures for fishing, and tree cover and site conditions related to hiking and low density recreation.

There are behavioral modeling and data issues that arise in each of these examples. We consider three aspects of the data issues. The first concerns whether pollution measures are based on technical or subjective indicators. Technical measures of quality include chemical or biological measures, while subjective measures often collapse multiple chemical measures into one variable. In other cases subjective measures involve the use of qualitative variables such as the water quality ladder.

Evaluations of which approach is best have led to mixed results. Bockstael, McConnell and Strand (1987) found that subjective perceptions of water quality were often based on features of water bodies that were not closely aligned with the pollution related quality indexes. Only in the case of water clarity (where secchi disk readings may be used to measure turbidity) is there likely be a reasonable level of consistency. More recently McDaniels, Axelrod and Cavanagh (1998) report survey results also suggesting that water quality perceptions by individuals differ from technical measures of water quality. By contrast, in the case of landscape amenities, including visibility [Stewart, Middleton and Ely (1983), Rowe and Chestnut (1982), Chestnut and Rowe (1990)] and marine debris [Smith, Zhang and Palmquist (1997)], there appears to be good correspondence between people's subjective ratings and technical indexes of quality. [32]

Common sense suggests that site users focus on observable attributes directly related to their activities. Thus, to the extent algae blooms and fish kills are closely linked to nutrient loadings, water recreationists will be likely to consistently identify extreme conditions by observing these outcomes. For acidity, fecal coliform, or hazardous materials there are unlikely to be observable measures that people can use to gauge quality conditions. In these cases, public warnings (a type of subjective quality measure) are the only sources of information. For example, one of the most widely used information

---

[32] In an unpublished Ph.D. thesis Egan (2004) uses a mixed logit random utility model to investigate the factors influencing site choices for one-day trips to fresh-water lakes in Iowa. He finds direct support (e.g., statistically significant parameter estimates) and plausibly signed effects for technical indexes of water quality as factors influencing site choice with fresh-water lakes in Iowa. The model includes measures of lake size, facilities, boat ramps, and regulations on boat wakes (that might disturb angling) as well as a large array of physical indexes for water quality. Estimates for travel cost and the other site characteristics are quite stable for two models that differ in the number of characteristics. However, the estimated parameters for income, gender, and age are not. While the author does consider how recreationists "learned about" the water quality features, his results imply this issue is definitely worthy of further consideration.

measures has been public fish consumption advisories. Jakus et al. (1997) is the first published study to evaluate if these advisories influenced recreationists' choice of sites. Most studies since this initial work have evaluated model specifications including warnings by examining benefit measures associated with removing warnings from affected sites. A simpler strategy is to ask how large the imputed price increase would need to be for an equivalent effect on the likelihood of visiting a site with advisories.[33]

The literature suggests per-trip consumer surplus measures for removing advisories between $1.46 and $7.40 (in 1998 dollars), with most estimates in the lower part of this range. By contrast, the equivalent price measure would attach greater importance to the advisories, suggesting they are equivalent to an increase of about $5.00 per trip. Unfortunately, there has been little direct information collected about what recreationists actually do when faced with consumption advisories. Both of these comparisons rely on interpreting the estimated coefficients as if the fishing parties know about the advisories for the sites they are using.

These examples illustrate the challenges in specifying models and interpreting estimates based on both technical and subjective measures of recreation amenities. Bockstael and McConnell (1999a, 1999b) challenge analysts to go beyond a strategy that stops after finding significant and properly signed coefficient estimates on quality measures and think further about the construct validity of models with respect to the specification of quality variables. This task may involve the use of cognitive interviews or focus groups to determine what types of measures are expected to provide a behavioral footprint, as well as further research investigating proper strategies for defining amenity levels entering preference functions.

Our second quality data issue concerns the relationship between an amenity level and recreation behavior. We assume and observe that people respond to quality differences across sites. However, they can also respond to heterogeneity in quality at a given site. These adjustments arise by changing how they use a site. For example, people may visit on weekdays rather than weekends, purchase larger and more powerful fishing boats to allow consideration of a larger range of areas for fishing from a given access point, or select more difficult trails to avoid the congestion effects associated with meeting other recreational parties. Most of our information on these types of adjustments stems from sport fishing and the estimation of catch models as examples of produced quality [Smith, Liu and Palmquist (1993), McConnell, Strand and Blake-Hedges (1995), Schuhmann (1998)]. However, there is some evidence of these types of responses in selecting the timing of use for fishing in Alaska [Carson, Hanemann and Wegge (1989)], trails for rock climbing [Jakus and Shaw (1997), Grijalva et al. (2002)] and location and timing in deer hunting [Schwabe et al. (2001)].

Our last issue concerns the linking of quality measures to recreation sites. Often the monitoring of variables related to quality does not directly overlap with the recreation

---

[33] This approach is analogous to the rationale we have argued accounts for weak complementarity's effectiveness in recovering Hicksian measures of quality change. The restriction allows quality changes to be represented as Hicksian equivalent price changes.

alternatives we wish to consider. For example, catch rate estimates are based on ex post creel surveys. Similarly, pollution concentration may be measured for locations different than the areas where people recreate. This is particularly troublesome in the case of water quality applications, since transport models describing the inter-connections between spatially separate locations are not well developed.

Faced with these issues and the variety of different technical measures available the analyst must decide how to impute and attach the characteristics thought to influence behavior to the recreation commodities defined. This decision overlaps substantially with the commodity definition issue discussed above. There are few studies examining the implications of these decisions. The most complete is von Haefen (1998), who studies the issue as it relates to water quality impacts on recreation. He finds that defining the recreation commodities based on hydrological boundaries (watersheds) and linking water quality measures originating in the watershed to trips to that watershed, provides a more consistent link than geographical boundaries such as counties. Phaneuf (2002) provides an application of this logic to the issue of TMDL regulation design in North Carolina.

4.4. Measuring travel distances and costs

A key element in all travel cost models is the distance assumed relevant for each individual's trip to a recreation site. The actual practice of measuring distance has changed dramatically with access to modern micro computer based software such as GIS packages (i.e., ARCVIEW) or routing software used in planning trucking routes (e.g., PC Miler). On the whole, most analysts believe respondents are reasonably accurate about the distance to the recreation site they recently visited (or where they were interviewed, if the data are collected in an intercept survey). Bateman et al.'s (1996) study (and, more recently, Bell and Strand (2003)) confirmed this conclusion, suggesting that the highest resolution GIS computations are quite close (on average) to respondent reports.

There are, however, two aspects of distance measurement that have not been explicitly discussed in the literature. First, respondents' reports of the distance to the sites they visit will not provide information about the alternatives they considered but did not visit. This is also closely related to the definition of the commodity and the set of alternatives discussed in the previous section. The issue here concerns what is the correct measure of distance to the alternative sites. Should we assume people know the technical distance measures if they have not visited the site? And what distance measure should be used when we typically only know the respondent's zip code? Answers to these questions are especially important to RUM and hedonic travel cost models where the substitute site distances can be very influential in estimating the choice model.

The second question concerns the appropriateness of distance in the construction of imputed prices.[34] Distance measures generally rely on travel by auto to the site. This

---

[34] The eco-tourism literature has considered this issue in developing countries, but there have been few attempts to apply travel cost models in this context. Most of this work has relied on contingent valuation.

strategy generally means that the nature of the commodity is different for local recreationists, with one-day visits, in comparison to those coming from a greater distance. Certainly the early results of Smith and Kopp (1980) and Haspel and Johnson (1982) support this argument. Parsons and Hauber (1998) have offered a detailed comparison across distance zones that indicates the analysis should distinguish visitors who travel great distances from local users. These concerns are especially important as applications consider prominent national and international recreation and eco-tourism sites, where for larger distances, airline fares are not systematically related to distance and multiple objective trips are more likely to be dominant considerations for modeling.

Distance also becomes a concern for the case of very local recreation. Deyak and Parliament (1975) noted over twenty-five years ago that time costs are more likely to be a constraint in this case. In these cases, it is not simply an issue of the marginal value of additional time, but the availability of discrete blocks of time to complete activities – a short hike or jog, game of golf, or bike ride. Thus, it would seem that activities at great distance from one's residence and those very close that support local (e.g., day to day) activities set boundaries on the plausibility of the use of distance related costs as the implicit price in travel cost models for recreation demand. The reasons underlying these limitations both stem from the way time constraints and the value of time influence individuals' decisions about how to allocate leisure to different types of recreation (see Palmquist, Phaneuf and Smith (2005) for a recent example).

5. Econometric issues in recreation demand modeling

The econometric issues identified as part of recreation demand modeling are too extensive to do justice to all of them. Our discussion in this section focuses on the interaction between econometric and economic issues.[35] A particular area we consider is how error terms enter each econometric model and how they are interpreted. One common strategy holds that the errors represent unobserved heterogeneity in preferences, while a second considers them as measurement errors that are unimportant to preferences.[36] We examine this issue as it relates to single equation, multiple equations, and RUM models. The section concludes with discussion of temporal models and nonparametric methods as they relate to recreation.

5.1. Single site demand models

The earliest single site models relied on ordinary least squares with aggregate zonal data. Two early econometric issues have persisted in generic terms in the current literature on single site demand models. The first concerns the extent of the market, and

---

[35] Haab and McConnell (2002) provide a more complete overview of econometric models used in recreation demand analysis.

[36] Bockstael and Strand (1987) provide an intuitive discussion of this distinction in the context of single site demand models.

the second is associated with the interpretation of visitation decisions as the product of an average seasonal usage for recreation participants and a probability of participating. Smith and Kopp (1980) raised the first issue by using a test for the stability of a simple travel cost model as the origin zones used to estimate that model are expanded to progressively further distances. The logic underlying the economic question posed in their test parallels recent work on single equation, pooled site models of demand [Loomis, Song and Donnelly (1986)] as well as the composition of the choice set in the RUM framework (see Table 2 and the related discussion). This early work concerns the definition of a recreation site and substitute alternatives and the conditions when trips to the site could be considered homogeneous measures of quantity demand. These concerns parallel the definition of a choice alternative and the choice set in random utility models. Bowes and Loomis (1980) raised the second issue and address it as an adjustment for heteroscedasticity. Their discussion of the relationship between the decision to participate in recreation and the level of use parallels recent work comparing repeated discrete choices versus various forms of the linked RUM and trip equations discussed earlier [see Parsons, Jakus and Tomasi (1999)].

The development of count models for use in recreation analysis evolved from these issues based on the characteristics of contemporary, individual-based recreation data, which typically provide trip counts in nonnegative integers, often with "excess zeros" if the survey contains nonparticipants. Combinations of probability models were designed first to account for these characteristics of the data.

This perspective is illustrated by using the count data model as a starting point for a discussion of hurdle models.[37] For the Poisson model the probability that individual i makes y_i visits to a recreation site is given by

$$\text{pr}(Y_i = y_i) = \frac{e^{\lambda_i} \lambda_i^{y_i}}{y_i!},\tag{5.1}$$

where Y_i is an integer outcome reflecting the fact that trips must be taken in nonnegative whole number increments, λ_i is the expected number of trips that is typically parameterized as $\lambda_i = E(Y_i) = \exp(X_i \beta)$, X_i is a vector of individual characteristics thought to affect the expected demand for trips (i.e., travel cost, income, site quality variables, etc.) and β is a vector of unknown parameters to be estimated. A restrictive characteristic of this model is that the conditional mean and variance are equal (although estimates of the parameters of the conditional mean are robust to mis-specification of the higher moments). Thus, over-dispersion, a common empirical observation in many recreation data sets, is not consistent with the assumptions of the statistical model. In response to this limitation, many analysts have employed the negative binomial generalization in place of the Poisson. This formulation allows inequality of the conditional mean and variance.

---

[37] Shonkwiler and Shaw (1996) provide an excellent overview of count models, zero inflated adaptations and hurdle specifications.

Nonetheless, the simple Poisson and negative binomial distributions typically do not place enough probability mass at zero to account for the empirical regularity of excess zeros in many types of recreation data set. Hurdle models address this by using multiple data generating processes to explain the likelihood of individuals being one of three types: nonusers, potential users, and users. Nonusers will never visit a site, even if the price is sufficiently low. Potential users' utility functions contain trips to the sites, but they are assumed to face a price at or above their choke price. In the double hurdle model the recreation decision is assumed to depend on two sets of explanatory variables (X, Z) such that the demand for trips y_i is given by $y_i(X_i, Z_i)$. It is further assumed that the latent (unobserved) variable D_i summarizes the individual's decision to recreate such that the number of trips to the site is zero if $D_i \leqslant 0$. A convenient assumption is that $\Pr(D_i = 0) = \exp(\phi_i)$, where $\phi_i = \exp(-Z_i\gamma)$ and γ is a vector of parameters to be estimated. If consumption is positive, then observed consumption equals desired consumption such that $y_i = y_i^*$. The probability of not making a trip is thus given by

$$\mathrm{pr}\left(y_i^* \leqslant 0\right) + \mathrm{pr}\left(y_i^* > 0\right) \times \mathrm{pr}(D_i \leqslant 0). \tag{5.2}$$

The first term is the probability of being a nonuser and the second term is the probability of being a potential user; that is, someone with positive desired consumption, who faces an additional hurdle that may prevent consumption. Correspondingly, the probability of taking a positive number of trips is given by

$$\mathrm{pr}\left(y_i^* > 0\right) \times \mathrm{pr}\left(y_i^* \mid y_i^* > 0\right) \times \mathrm{pr}(D_i > 0). \tag{5.3}$$

The functional form of these probabilities is derived from the probability statements for D_i and Y_i.

Count data models and their generalizations to include hurdles and excess zero corrections adopt our second error interpretation that the stochastic components in recreation demand models are incidental to the economic description of behavior. Rather than explicitly modeling the presence of unobserved heterogeneity in the form of an additive error, count data models parameterize the first moment of a distribution that is assumed to generate individual trip realizations so it matches the form of the reports provided in available micro-data. Estimation recovers a characterization of the conditional mean of the distribution that generates the (unobserved) actual trip taking behavior, and should therefore be interpreted a representative consumer's behavioral function rather than the result of individual optimizing behavior [see von Haefen and Phaneuf (2003a)].

Taking this further, one might ask if the underlying process could be derived from a single consistent constrained optimization framework. Haab and McConnell (1996) implicitly raise this issue by asking whether consistent welfare measures can be derived from count and zero inflated models. A few observations suggest this is not strictly the case. First, one cannot distinguish user/nonuser status from the identification of an individual as a nonparticipant at a specific site without assuming the people involved (i.e., users and nonusers) have different preference functions. This outcome can arise with restrictions on a model's parameters, its functional form or through observed heterogeneity. But these people must be different – the same neoclassical constrained optimization problem will not deliver the three-part distinction outlined with a double hurdle model. Second, the division of explanatory variables determining participation and consumption can only arise from an interpretation of the underlying behavioral functions as approximations. In a fully consistent model with nonparticipation, a comparison between the market price and the individual's reservation price, derived from all arguments in the utility problem, implies an extensive margin of choice between conditional utilities representing participation and nonparticipation. Importantly, the same factors determine participation and consumption. Thus, the only argument for separate determinants of participation and demand must stem from interpreting the two functions as local approximations at different points and as such they appear to arise from different preference functions.

This discussion is not a criticism of the count or the hurdle framework. These models were originally designed to improve the fit of reduced form demand equations to the types of micro-data available for specific recreation sites, and have subsequently proven useful in a variety of contexts. The point is simply that in the absence of further behavioral information we do not know if the relative importance of a hurdle function intended to take account of excess zeros (relative to what would be implied by the error distribution) is due to a measurement issue or an underlying feature of behavior. This question in fact hints at a larger issue. Beyond hurdle models, contemporary recreation analysis has had little to say about the behavioral process in which individuals acquaint themselves with recreation opportunities that they may decide to use in the future. While it is intuitive that some sites are not part of individuals' decision sets, little conceptual research exists on how to model this process in a utility-consistent manner.

5.2. Systems of recreation demand equations

Early applications of demand systems used zonal data and assumed multivariate normal errors. With micro-data the primary challenge has been how to deal with the requirement that trips must be positive or zero.[38] We discuss how three systems approaches have evolved in the literature to address this issue: count demand, share, and Kuhn–Tucker models.

Count data demand system models grew naturally from their single equation counterparts. Ozuna and Gomez (1994) were the first to apply a seemingly unrelated Poisson regression model in a recreation context. Unfortunately, the specification of their incomplete demand system does not adequately account for the restrictions required to develop consistent Hicksian welfare measures [see LaFrance and Hanemann (1989)]. More importantly in terms of future applications, generalization of their estimator beyond the two-site model represents a nontrivial challenge. Later applications such as Englin, Boxall and Watson (1998) use specifications for the system of expected demands that are consistent with integrability conditions and simplified the error structure

---

[38] See Morey et al. (1995) for an overview of multiple site demand models that allow interior and corner solutions.

(via assuming independent Poisson distributions for each equation) to allow estimation of a larger dimension problem. Shonkwiler (1999) further addresses these issues in the context of a multivariate generalization to a count model that allows for both positive and negative correlation and incorporates the parametric restrictions for consistent welfare measures from an incomplete demand system.

All of these generalizations should be considered statistical approaches to accommodating count data within a system of demand equations, in that while they provide distributions that allow a nonzero probability of observing zeros, they do not explain the source of the zeros as corner solutions. Indeed, in applying the integrability conditions to the sets of demand models we are implicitly relying on interior solutions with some measurement issue responsible for the zeros. When excess zeros confound our ability to estimate these models it seems reasonable to ask whether the data are suggesting the decision of whether or not to participate is an important part of the process.

An early alternative to this approach was Morey's (1981, 1984, 1985) share model, which sought to describe the share of total trips across sites. The total seasonal number of trips for each individual was assumed to be determined outside the model. The modeling strategy involves choosing a utility function and deriving the associated trip share equations, which are then used to parameterize the location parameters of a multinomial distribution. Morey argues that the multinomial is an appropriate distribution for shares, since it allows positive probability for shares only in the unit interval, including the endpoints, which allows for corner solutions. In a recent update to this idea, Morey, Breffle and Greene (2001) employ a nested CES indirect utility function along with the multinomial distribution to estimate models based on shares of trips and shares of expenditures for Atlantic salmon fishing. The structure of the nested CES function divides the seasonal recreation decision into steps captured through price aggregates for each "nest." The first nest determines whether or not to participate in salmon fishing, subsequent nests determine the area (i.e., Maine versus Canada) and then, conditional on the area, the final nest determines the site. The structure uses the ability to define price aggregations from each homogeneous of degree one CES sub-function to sequence the structure describing the share parameters. For example, the indirect utility function (and top level nest) for the alternatives model is given by

$$V = -\frac{1}{B}\left(P_{\mathrm{NF}}^{1-\sigma} + P_{\mathrm{F}}^{1-\sigma}\right)^{1/(1-\sigma)}, \tag{5.4}$$

where P_{NF} and P_{F} are the price aggregates for the nonfishing and fishing options, σ is the elasticity of substitution between fishing and nonfishing, and B is a utility function parameter. The upper level nest implies price aggregates

$$P_{\mathrm{F}} = \left(P_{\mathrm{M}}^{1-\sigma_{\mathrm{F}}} + P_{\mathrm{C}}^{1-\sigma_{\mathrm{F}}}\right)^{1/(1-\sigma_{\mathrm{F}})}, \tag{5.5}$$

where P_{M} and P_{C} are the price aggregates for the Maine and Canada areas and σ_{F} is the elasticity of substitution between fishing areas. Finally, the area price aggregates are

$$P_{\mathrm{M}} = \left(\sum_{j=1}^{L_{\mathrm{M}}} h_j^{\sigma_{\mathrm{M}}} P_j^{1-\sigma_{\mathrm{M}}}\right)^{1/(1-\sigma_{\mathrm{M}})}, \tag{5.6a}$$

$$P_C = \left(\sum_{j=1}^{L_C} h_j^{\sigma_C} P_j^{1-\sigma_C} \right)^{1/(1-\sigma_C)}, \qquad\qquad (5.6b)$$

where L_M and L_C denote the number of sites in Maine and Canada, the h_j's are site quality measures, the P_j's are travel costs, and σ_M and σ_C are the elasticities of substitution between sites. The preference specification yields a multiplicative form for the share of choice occasions to a site as given by

$$s_{Ml} = \frac{(1/P_F)^\sigma}{(1/P_F)^\sigma + (1/P_{NF})^\sigma} \frac{(1/P_M)^{\sigma_A}}{(1/P_M)^{\sigma_A} + (1/P_C)^{\sigma_A}} \frac{(h_l/p_l)^{\sigma_M}}{\sum_{k=1}^{L_M} (h_k/p_k)^{\sigma_M}}. \qquad (5.7)$$

This share is then used to parameterize the multinomial distribution.

The model assumes the site choice is made from a seasonal perspective. However, we do not avoid an important conditioning factor: the number of choices between fishing and nonfishing alternatives is determined outside the model. Thus, as in the case of the repeated random utility framework, we fall short of a full utility-consistent model linking site choice, level of use of each site, and total amount of use in relation to prices and income. While the nested CES utility function allows substantial flexibility in characterizing a wide array of substitution patterns, it seems unlikely to overcome the limitations that have prevented share models from offering a compelling basis for describing seasonal recreation demands for multiple sites. As demonstrated by von Haefen and Phaneuf (2003a) however, the Morey, Breffle and Greene (2001) nested CES model may be useful when applied in the count data demand system framework.

The only currently available system model that interprets the stochastic components as unobserved heterogeneity and allows a behaviorally consistent description of corner solutions is the Kuhn–Tucker model in either its primal or dual form. These features, however, come at a cost in that this class of model is conceptually and computationally more complex than the competing count data and share model frameworks. Estimation requires the integration of multiple dimension probability integrals, while welfare calculation involves solving for each respondent's demand levels given simulated realizations of the unobserved heterogeneity. Von Haefen, Phaneuf and Parsons (2004) discuss how these tasks increase in complexity, requiring sophisticated computational techniques, as the number of sites and the flexibility of the deterministic and stochastic components of the model increases.

As described in Section 3 Kuhn–Tucker models can be specified beginning with either a direct or indirect utility function. The two approaches are conceptually dual to each other but empirically unique in how the error specification is exploited to provide the link between the econometric and behavioral models. Both, however, allow preferences to exhibit substitutability through the functional and stochastic components of the model. Econometric issues in this area center on striking a balance between increasing functional and stochastic flexibility to more realistically model preferences, and maintaining the tractability necessary for practical estimation. Related to this, the practical advantages of the consistent Kuhn–Tucker specification over computationally less demanding system models are not yet fully understood. In one application evaluating this von Haefen and Phaneuf (2003a) find that welfare measurement is more sensitive to model fit and other factors than the choice of count data versus Kuhn–Tucker model estimation.

5.3. Random utility models

In the random utility framework the errors in the model are interpreted as unobserved heterogeneity and, given the relative sparseness of the parametric specification, play a large role in determining the amount of substitution that can be captured. The distributional assumptions restrict the correlations between the random utilities associated with choice alternatives. In the simple multinomial logit this correlation is zero. For the nested logit model the utilities of alternatives have nonzero correlations, consistent with common elements affecting how each individual makes choices. These correlations can be related to the dissimilarity parameters across nests [see Ben-Akiva and Lerman (1985)]. Aside from the heuristic parallel between substitution relationships there is little explicit guidance from economic theory that can be offered for selecting among nesting structures.

In recognition of this limitation the multinomial probit model is often mentioned as a replacement for the nested logit specification. It would relax restrictions limiting the types of substitution relationships that can be accommodated. Historically, the model has imposed significant computational burdens. Simulation estimation [see Stern (1997)] has helped to increase its feasibility and led to a few applications in the area of recreation demand [see Chen and Cosslett (1998)]. Nonetheless use of the probit model for practical applications remains rare.

One alternative to the nested logit adopts a statistical approach to incorporating heterogeneity, arguing that individuals fall into one of a discrete set of latent classes, determined by their attitudes or perceptions. Boxall and Adamowicz (2002) describe an application involving past wilderness users (in a conjoint setting) where a simple RUM describes choice among a discrete set of site alternatives and then a multinomial logit characterizes the probability of membership in one of a discrete set of types of groups of individuals, each with different preference and scale parameters for the choice model. In this setting the probability of selecting a site is the product of the site choice probability (given the unique preference parameters associated with membership in one of the latent classes) and the probability an individual is a member of that class given her characteristics, attitudes, or perceptions. Thus the probability that person n chooses site i is given by

$$\pi_n(i) = \sum_{s=1}^{S} \pi_{ns} \cdot \pi_{n|s}(i), \tag{5.8}$$

where π_{ns} is the probability that person n is in group s, $\pi_{n|s}(i)$ is the probability that person n chooses site i given membership in s, and S is the number of potential "preference" groups. The framework usually describes the determination of preference or membership groups as a statistical approach to preference discrimination because the number of groups must be determined from fitting criteria, rather than as a maintained assumption about the form of preference heterogeneity.

Provencher, Baerenklau and Bishop (2002) have recently applied this model to allow for temporal correlation in trips. They compare the results with a mixed logit model (described next) and find that the benefit estimates from latent class models evaluated for different membership groups generally bracket the mixed logit average estimate for the scenarios considered. A choice between the models rests in part on whether the analyst is prepared to use a finite set of alternative types of individuals (preference groups) to describe unobserved heterogeneity. With the mixed logit, each individual is assumed to have different preference parameters and, using the Herriges and Phaneuf (2002) suggestions, could be used to represent the extent of substitution among choice alternatives. Substitution patterns are also altered with the latent class model but the outcomes will depend on the statistical decision rule used to select the number of groups and thus cannot be easily interpreted a priori.

A second alternative to the nested logit model that has received significant recent attention in recreation demand is the mixed, or random parameter, logit model [McFadden and Train (2000), Train (2003)]. This approach mixes additional source of randomness into the basic logit format. It can be used to approximate any discrete choice model derived from random utility maximization.

Train (1998) outlines the basic logic as a variation on the multinomial logit model. The setup of the model is the same as was described in Section 3, where the errors enter linearly and are assumed to follow independent type I extreme value distributions. In Train's (1998) generalization the parameters of the utility function are random variables with known distribution. This formulation can be interpreted as introducing unobserved heterogeneity in preferences. The probability a person chooses site i on choice occasion t, conditional on the utility function parameters β and the explanatory variables x_{it} is

$$L_{it}(\beta) = \frac{\exp(\beta x_{it})}{\sum_{j=1}^{J} \exp(\beta x_{jt})}. \tag{5.9}$$

When β is a random variable, drawn from the distribution $f(\beta; \theta)$ where θ is a parameter vector, the researcher can only form an expectation of the probability in Equation (5.9):

$$P_{it}(\theta) = \int L_{it}(\beta) \cdot f(\beta; \theta) \, d\beta. \tag{5.10}$$

If the data includes multiple choice occasions $L_{it}(\beta)$ in Equation (5.10) is replaced by the product of the conditional probabilities of the observed site selections, and the unconditional probability of the sequence of choices is defined. By restricting the values of the random parameters to be constant across choice occasions for each individual, the mixed logit model allows for a cross-choice occasion stochastic relationship that is absent in the simpler repeated choice models.

The likelihood function is defined in terms of these expected probabilities. As a practical matter, estimation requires simulation since no closed form exists for the probability in Equation (5.10). Train (2003) describes this process in detail. Heuristically, multiple realizations of the vector β are drawn from the distribution defined by a candidate set of values of θ. P_{it} is computed for each draw. A simulated estimate of the expected probability, $\widetilde{P}_{it}$, is then given by

$$\widetilde{P}_{it}(\theta) = \frac{1}{R} \sum_{r=1}^{R} P_{it}(\beta^r; \theta), \tag{5.11}$$

where R is the number of repetitions. The simulated probabilities are then used in place of the probabilities in (5.10) to form to likelihood function. Standard maximum likelihood search routines are then employed to estimate the parameter vector θ.

The mixed logit model is attractive under the error components interpretation of the random parameters, fitting into our first interpretation of the errors as reflecting an unobserved component of preferences. It also provides a bridge between the nested logit model and the multivariate probit model in specifying more general patterns of error correlation and stochastic substitution. Recently Herriges and Phaneuf (2002) have examined the implications of defining the mixed logit random parameters, interpreted as error components, to capture a diverse pattern of stochastic substitution among the available sites. Comparing price elasticity matrices from the multinomial logit, nested logit, and mixed logit they find dramatic improvements in the richness of elasticity estimates that can be characterized using the most general mixed logit models. Herriges and Phaneuf (2002) conclude from their application that, in spite of the increased computational burden, mixed logit models are worth the added cost when compared to the benefit of the increased realism they add to preference estimates.

Of course, in general uses of the model it is important to select distributions for the β's consistent with the economic interpretation of the parameters. This is clear in some cases and not in others. We might, for example, be willing to select a distribution that restricts the parameter on travel cost to be negative such as the log-normal, but will be less clear about sign restrictions for parameters associated with quality attributes. It is clear, however, that simulation techniques provide important flexibility and offer the prospect for more complex interrelated decision models. What is less clear is the economic basis for selecting among the alternatives. It may well be that composite strategies exploiting jointly estimated models with revealed and stated preference data, where the latter focus is on the choice process rather than site attributes, offers the best short term basis for reducing the dimensionality of the problem. That is, this approach would select alternatives that are now technically feasible based on what appears to correspond to the decision rules people use to bracket choice alternatives or otherwise simplify complex choice sets.[39]

---

[39] Thanks are due to J.R. DeShazo for discussing aspects of his unpublished research relevant to this strategy.

5.4. Dynamic models

The models used in recreation analysis nearly always assume temporal exchangeability, although common sense suggests this is not in reality true. Provencher and Bishop (1997) offer the first attempt to use Rust's (1987) integrated discrete dynamic programming framework to describe dynamic trip decisions over a season. Observed choice results from the maximization of the expected present value of utility, subject to a budget constraint defined over the season. Following Rust (1987) they assume independent type I extreme value errors, which implies the probability of taking a trip depends on the current value of the utility function with additional terms added to each choice alternative to reflect the discounted contribution of the next period's utility, conditional on the current decision. Backward recursion allows the discrete dynamic programming model to be solved for each potential set of preference parameters. Maximum likelihood estimation of the model's parameters requires that all the possible solutions be evaluated. Intuitively the estimation task requires that the different possible use profiles (for alternative values of the model's parameters) be compared with the observed record for each person. The estimator selects the vector of parameters with the highest value of the log likelihood function.

Provencher and Bishop (1997) assume a linear utility function and a simple daily budget constraint, avoiding a labor/leisure choice or other specific time constraints.[40] The angler's choice problem is whether to take a salmon-fishing trip each day at the application site (Lake Michigan). Weather, expected catch, exogenous features of each person's constraints (interacted with a dummy variable that identifies weekdays throughout the solution time span) and the out-of-pocket costs of a trip influence these choices.

Empirical tractability requires their application to consider only participation choices and not site selection decisions. Most of the specific time related variables and out-of-the-pocket costs are exogenous for each respondent. While the model does allow for some learning with experience and the exogenous characteristics of specific days to influence individuals' participation decisions, these characteristics suggest changes in spending or in the work/leisure allocation and numerous other adjustments (e.g., re-allocating existing income) cannot be accommodated in a computationally tractable model. Thus, one might ask whether there are gains from this more complex, but temporally consistent, formulation over simpler alternatives.

Adamowicz's (1994) adaptation of Pollak's (1970, 1976) habit formation model offers one such alternative. By assuming consumer's choices can be described in terms of stocks of visits to recreation sites, his framework demonstrates that a random utility model can be reformulated in terms of "dynamic prices" to reflect habit formation or variety seeking. These prices reflect the role of accumulating consumption into a stock measure and its implications for the budget constraint. To illustrate, consider a simple

---

[40] Differential time costs are reflected in the expected cost of a trip through dummy variables for full employment, weekdays and length of workweek. However, they are not treated as choice variables.

two-good model. In the Adamowicz (1994) framework the terms entering the utility function are stocks of recreation goods consumed over T time periods. Utility is therefore given by $U(W_{11}, W_{21}, \ldots, W_{1T}, W_{2T})$ where W_{it} is the stock of the ith good at time t, determined by the equation of motion $W_{it} = d_i W_{it-1} + X_{it}$ with X_{it} being the current period consumption of good i and d_i reflecting the durability of the stock. The sign of d_i determines if good i is a variety seeking (d_i positive) or habit formation (d_i negative) good. Maximization of this utility function subject to the equations of motion and an intertemporal budget constraint implies the demands for current period consumption are functions of temporally adjusted prices, given by $\widetilde{P}_{it} = P_{it} - d_i P_{it+1}$. If preferences are assumed to be separable over time, attention can focus on the demand for current period consumption as a function of the temporally adjusted prices and income. For good 1 in our example this is given by

$$X_{1t} = f\left(\widetilde{P}_{1t}, \widetilde{P}_{2t}, \widetilde{m}_t\right) - d_1 W_{1t-1}, \tag{5.12}$$

where $\widetilde{m}_t = \sum \widetilde{P}_{jt} X_{jt}$.

Adamowicz uses this framework to motivate an empirical discrete choice problem for multiple choice occasions. The model is an approximation reflecting the general spirit of the habit formation model. For the linear conditional indirect utility specification, site choice decisions are based on dynamic prices and the stocks of all past consumption for the different sites. In our two-good model this implies conditional indirect utility functions of the form

$$V_{1t} = \alpha_1\left(\widetilde{m}_t - \widetilde{P}_{1t}\right) + \alpha_2(d_1 W_{1t-1}) + \alpha_3(d_2 W_{2t-1}) + \varepsilon_1,$$

$$V_{2t} = \alpha_1\left(\widetilde{m}_t - \widetilde{P}_{2t}\right) + \alpha_2(d_2 W_{2t-1}) + \alpha_3(d_1 W_{2t-1}) + \varepsilon_2. \tag{5.13}$$

Re-arranging terms and substituting for $\widetilde{P}_{1t}$ and $\widetilde{P}_{2t}$ we have the final form of the empirical model:

$$V_{1t} = \alpha_1\left(\widetilde{m}_t - P_{1t}\right) + d_1\left[\alpha_2 W_{1t-1} + \alpha_1 P_{1t+1} + \alpha_3 \frac{d_2}{d_1} W_{2t-1}\right] + \varepsilon_1,$$

$$V_{2t} = \alpha_1\left(\widetilde{m}_t - P_{2t}\right) + d_2\left[\alpha_2 W_{2t-1} + \alpha_1 P_{2t+1} + \alpha_3 \frac{d_1}{d_2} W_{1t-1}\right] + \varepsilon_2. \tag{5.14}$$

The distinction between this approach and the Provencher–Bishop formulation depends on the distinctions between the added terms to reflect forward-looking behavior. In our simple example, where prices are travel costs including vehicle and time costs, we expect that the primary changes in P_{it+1} will depend on how the time constraints vary over the course of the proposed inter-temporal planning horizon. Weekdays and weekends can have distinctive effects based on each person's decisions about whether and how much to work. Predefined fishing tournaments and weather can also be allowed to displace the net costs of a trip.

Provencher, Baerenklau and Bishop's (2002) latent class application also offers another way of dealing with inter-temporal linkages by describing trip decisions as part of a Markov process and specifying seasonal trip taking behavior using the simulated likelihood associated with the product of the integrals for all the trips that can be taken in a season by each recreationist. The correlation structure for the errors, together with the evolution of the state of exogenous variables is the way dynamics are represented in these models. In their application, the authors find correlation in unobserved heterogeneity occurs when potential trip occasions are small. Thus, the overall effect of assuming temporal independence for welfare measurement was small in their application. It did appear to be quite different across the groups described as their latent classes.

To some extent, all of these efforts overlook another key element in the dynamics, which motivated early discussions of preservation versus development [Krutilla (1967) and Krutilla and Fisher (1975)]. In these theoretical analyses, individuals' demands for some types of recreation changed with experience. Learning by doing created intertemporal effects akin to adjacent complementarity as discussed by Becker (1992) in distinguishing habits from addiction.[41] There has been very little empirical work on this dynamic process. It is implicit in the Adamowicz (1994) specification, but is a part of the hypothesized stock effects in preferences and is maintained, not explained, by the model. Thus, future research could seek to more accurately specify the temporal constraints facing individuals and the internal production (to the individual) of experience capital and its effect on leisure time choices.

Finally, we would expect that different individuals would select into jobs with more or less discretion. This argument suggests the introduction of unobserved heterogeneity in model parameters of the Adamowicz model might be more effective in capturing these types of differences than in generalizing the time constraints (for everyone) in the Provencher–Bishop model. Given its significant computational demands, future efforts might focus on how large the differences between ad hoc adjustments to static choices need to be in order to warrant full scale dynamic optimization models.[42] They might also consider the importance of learning and behavioral choices that would allow the analyst to evaluate the importance of experience capital for choice over time.

5.5. Nonparametric methods and models

There have been two primary strands of research on nonparametric methods in recreation modeling. The first seeks to relax the distributional and parametric restrictions associated with random utility models. The second adapts Varian's (1982, 1983) tests for the predictions of revealed preference theory to evaluate individual choices in the context of neoclassical demand theory. The basic logic associated with these two disparate applications is similar. They acknowledge that parametric models will include additional restrictions associated with features of the functional form or the assumed

---

[41] See McConnell, Strand and Bockstael (1990) and Munley and Smith (1976) for early empirical analysis in simpler models.

[42] Provencher and Bishop (1997) also highlight this issue in their closing comments.

error distribution that do not arise from the choice process. As a result, it is reasonable to ask how sensitive the results are to these restrictions by considering approaches that limit the restrictions imposed on the data to a set of conditions implied by economic theory.

We begin with a discussion of nonparametric econometrics in recreation demand. While there has been some interest in applying nonparametric and semi-nonparametric methods in contingent valuation applications [see Haab and McConnell (1997)] and in micro demand analysis [see Hausman and Newey (1995)], to our knowledge there have been no applications to demand system recreation models. Huang and Nychka (2000) have developed a nonparametric multiple choice method for applications in a choice occasion setting. Their analysis extends Wahba's (1990) continuous spline smoothing to the discrete choice setting. Using river recreation sites, they found large discrepancies in the Hicksian per trip consumer surplus for the loss of access to one of seven sites from what was estimated with a simple logit.[43] The mean nonparametric estimate for the WTP to retain a site was 60% of the RUM measure, and simple confidence intervals did not overlap.

These results contrast with the Herriges and Kling (1999) study discussed earlier. Both relax the constancy of the marginal utility of income. The Herriges and Kling (1999) parametric model found little difference in welfare estimates for a variety of types of changes. Their study involved a more comprehensive comparison of model specifications, distributional assumptions, and welfare scenarios. Given the difficulties in dealing with a large number of variables in the framework of a cubic smoothing spline, it seems likely that generalizations of the linear in income RUM model will continue to be based on parametric models combined with generalized error structures. In the context of demand models, where the deterministic component carries a proportionately heavier weight, there may be opportunities to consider whether the sensitivity found by Hausman and Newey (1995) in estimates of the equivalent variation for price changes for gasoline is paralleled in recreation demand models.

The second type of nonparametric methods involves Varian's (1982) algorithms for detecting violations of the strong axioms of revealed preference theory.[44] His approach requires at least two sets of price and quantity choices. With two goods the revealed preference responses should, given different sets of relative prices, be consistent with convex indifference curves. If we observe two selections of the two goods at different prices it should never be the case that one combination of goods is selected when the second is feasible, followed by the choice of the second at the new prices when the first remains affordable. The logic implies that when the vector of consumption goods

---

[43] The simple RUM framework yields a closed form solution for the willingness to pay. The nonparametric does not, and requires an approximation of the marginal utility of income. This is estimated as the negative of the derivative with respect to travel cost for each individual evaluated at the travel cost for the site to be maintained.

[44] Varian (1982) formalized the concept of a generalized axiom of revealed preference that allows for multi-valued demand functions.

$x_1 = [x_2^0, x_1^0]$ selected under one price set is superior to another vector of consumption goods x_2 we should expect to find $P_1^0 x_1^0 + P_2^0 x_2^0 \geqslant P_1^0 x_1^1 + P_2^0 x_2^1$. Varian (1982) defines a constant e such that $e(P_1^0 x_1^0 + P_2^0 x_2^0) \geqslant (P_1^0 x_1^1 + P_2^0 x_2^1)$ when $e = 1$. If we let e be the amount of budget reduction that will just satisfy the inequality, then e can be used as an index of efficiency and is the basis of the subsequent tests of revealed preference models.

Adamowicz and Graham-Tomasi (1991) were the first to propose using this idea with travel cost models. Their initial study compared the performance of travel cost and contingent valuation responses in terms of their consistency with revealed preference. The travel cost analysis treated each of the trip choices (for hunting bighorn sheep) made by an individual as independent. They evaluated the revealed preference axioms for each individual by comparing the price and quantity, travel, lodging, food, and other hunting related items for people with multiple trips. A key consideration in applying these nonparametric indexes for market goods is the exogeneity of prices. For the travel cost model, one of the most important components of the price – the travel cost (including the opportunity cost of travel time) is determined by individuals' time constraints, labor/leisure choices, and a host of other unobservable factors. Given this qualification, it should not be surprising that the percentage of observations with violations of the axioms is sensitive to the treatment of the opportunity cost of time, with the largest number of violations when it is ignored.

A subsequent analysis of the same survey by Boxall, Adamowicz and Tomasi (1996) considers the same tests applied to the prices for each of ten sites, comparing the results for the season across respondents (rather than across trips for each of the multiple trip takers). Conclusions about consistency depend on the treatment of the opportunity cost of time. Nonetheless, comparisons across people reveal a much larger number of violations, on the order of 76% of the comparisons.

It is hard to judge how these results should be interpreted. If we assume people act rationally, then the results offer evidence of the limitations in conventional imputation practices with travel costs measurement and modeling, confirming Randall's (1994) critique of the method on conceptual grounds. If we accept the notion of the appropriateness of our price imputation, then we have a strong critique of conventional demand analysis applied to a representative individual and potential support for dealing explicitly with individual heterogeneity.[45] Of course, interpretation is not free of qualifications. The tests build in maintained assumptions including: simple cost-sharing rules among party members, separability of recreation from all other goods (which makes little sense for the labor/leisure choice), and comparability in the goods purchased in broad categories (across trips).

---

[45] This is especially true when we contrast the findings between Adamowicz and Graham-Tomasi (1991) that find a small number of violations evaluating expenditures across trips for the same individual with the cross-individual comparisons in Boxall, Adamowicz and Tomasi (1996).

6. Measuring consumer surplus with travel cost models

Models of recreation behavior have primarily been used to estimate the welfare impacts of changes in the resources that support recreation. The early literature focused on the resources themselves (e.g., the benefits of opening a new hiking trail or the loss from closing a fishing site). During the last decade attention has shifted to measuring the benefits associated with changes in quality attributes of recreation sites, including water quality, fish or other species abundance involved in consumptive use, and scenic attributes of recreation sites. Other chapters in the handbook deal with the theoretical issues associated with welfare measurement in nonmarket valuation. In the following two sub-sections we consider the issues that arise specifically in attempting to recover estimates of these measures with recreation demand models. We first discuss the restrictions needed to relate Hicksian and Marshallian benefits measures. This is followed by a discussion of welfare measurement in extensive margin models with unobserved heterogeneity.

6.1. Price versus quality changes

Substantial discussion has been dedicated to understanding how Hicksian measures of the monetary value of a price or quality change can be measured when Hicksian demands are not observed. Willig (1976, 1978), Hausman (1981), Small and Rosen (1981), LaFrance and Hanemann (1989), and Bockstael and McConnell (1993) have helped to clarify most of the basic concepts. Techniques for price changes by and large have paralleled the development in other areas of applied welfare analysis [see Just, Hueth and Schmitz (2004) for an overview of this literature], while quality changes have presented more unique challenges.

Two approaches have typically been used in demand models to relate Hicksian and Marshallian measures of benefits from price and quality changes: bounding and integration conditions. The first involves developing bounds on the size of the discrepancy between the observable Marshallian and unobservable Hicksian values for price and quality changes. For price changes, these conditions follow directly from Willig (1976) and formalize the intuition that the discrepancy depends on the magnitude of the change in relation to income, and the importance of income effects on demand.[46] For quality (quantity) changes, bounding the discrepancy requires some careful adaptation. Randall and Stoll (1980) outlined the bounds, but two further considerations are important – the income elasticity of the marginal willingness to pay [Hanemann (1993, 1999)] and the ability to connect quality changes to a private commodity [see Willig (1978) and Bockstael and McConnell (1993)].

Most of the attention in travel cost demand models has implicitly or explicitly focused on integration as a means of relating Hicksian and Marshallian surplus measures. The

---

[46] See Freeman (1993) and Chapter 12 by Bockstael and Freeman in this volume.

central insight follows from the recognition of Roy's identity as a differential equation relating the expenditure function to ordinary demand:

$$\frac{\mathrm{d}y}{\mathrm{d}p} = -\frac{V_p}{V_y} = x(p, y), \tag{6.1}$$

where p is the travel cost (price), and y is income. For single equation demand models satisfying the integrability conditions we can recover Hicksian consumer surplus for price changes from the analytical or numerical integral of equations such as (6.1). When we move from a single equation to an incomplete demand system, the conditions for integrability restrict the form of the demand functions more directly [see LaFrance and Hanemann (1989), LaFrance (1990), and von Haefen (2002)], but still allow recovery of the preference function. Direct specification of the direct or indirect utility function, and estimation of the implied demand equations to recover the parameters of the utility function, are also consistent with the integration logic described here.

   Measurement of the Hicksian surplus for a quality change is more demanding, requiring both weak complementarity and the Willig condition. In Section 3 we used a fanning of constant-utility indifference curves around zero consumption of the private good to illustrate how weak complementarity directly simplifies the treatment of a change in quality. It allows the quality change to be converted to a price change for the private good serving as the weak complement. This price change is the one that holds utility constant with a quality improvement. In practice, we cannot measure it. So, the challenge applied analyses must face is to assess whether a Marshallian consumer surplus measure of the benefits attributed to the quality change can be used to approximate the desired Hicksian price change. The answer lies in adding the Willig (1978) condition. Under weak complementarity and the Willig restriction, the Marshallian surplus per unit of the private good will, in the limit, exactly measure the equivalent price change with a quality change. The Willig condition does so by restricting the way changes in income can influence the marginal value of quality changes.

   Figure 4 taken from Smith and Banzhaf (2003) illustrates the effects of weak complementarity and the Willig condition. This figure repeats their graphical interpretation of how weak complementarity allows quality changes to be expressed as equivalent price changes. Here the Marshallian consumer surplus for the quality change from q_0 to q_1 measured at income level T corresponds to the average of CD and FE. The Willig condition allows higher incomes to increase the consumer surplus a person realizes from the same quality increase. However, it restricts the size of the increase in consumer surplus to be proportional to the increase in the demand for the private good from the increased income. In Figure 4 the Willig condition implies that

$$\frac{X_1 - X_0}{X_0} = \frac{(E'F' + C'D') - (EF + CD)}{EF + CD} \tag{6.2}$$

must hold, where the average of $E'F'$ and $C'D'$ is the Marshallian surplus for the quality change at income level T'.

Said another way, calculating quality change welfare measures requires we integrate over both price and quality, and defining a line integral to the differential equation requires restrictions consistent with path independence. Palmquist (2005) suggests that the Willig condition restrictions are equivalent to requiring that the elasticity of the marginal willingness to pay for quality with respect to income (e.g., the price flexibility of income) will equal the income elasticity of demand of the weak complement.

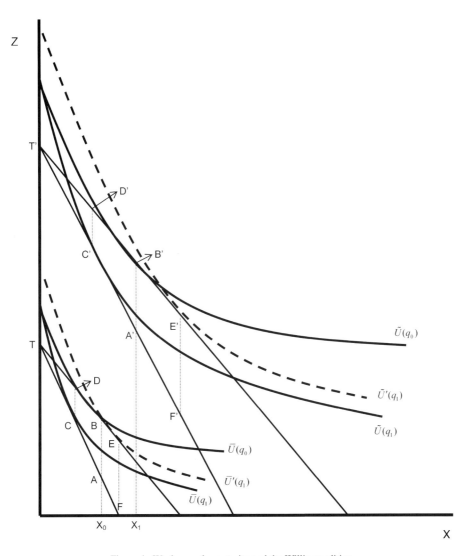

Figure 4. Weak complementarity and the Willig condition.

Analytically this relationship plays a role similar to Hausman's logic for price changes. In general, the integral over price does not allow the analyst to determine how the constant of integration for the indefinite integral in Equation (6.1), with quality included in the demand function, will change. Without this information we don't know enough about the quasi-expenditure function to recover the Hicksian willingness to pay for the quality change. Larson's (1991) adaptation of the Hausman logic for quality changes with linear demands implicitly uses the Willig condition to remove the quality term from the constant of integration. Ebert's (1998) integration of the Hausman, LaFrance, and Hanemann work [with the implicit logic from Larson (1991)] argues that the integrability problem with multiple incomplete demand functions and associated quality can be resolved if we have consistent estimates of the marginal willingness to pay functions for each nonmarket quality attribute. His argument suggests replacing the Willig condition with additional information akin to additional differential equations relating expenditures required to hold utility constant to quality change.

6.2. Valuation measures with extensive margin choices and unobserved heterogeneity

Random utility models as discussed in Section 3 rely on a different set of techniques to arrive at measures of Hicksian welfare measures, since the decision rule is based on the extensive margin and is explicitly influenced by unobserved heterogeneity that must be accounted for. In particular, following the notation from Section 3, the individual's unconditional indirect utility function on a given choice occasion t is defined by the maximum function $V_t(\mathbf{p}, \mathbf{q}, m, \varepsilon) = \max\{V_{1t}(p_1, q_1, m, \varepsilon_1), \ldots, V_{Kt}(p_K, q_K, m, \varepsilon_K)\}$, where K is the number of choice alternatives. Given this form of the preference function, the choice occasion Hicksian willingness to pay measure cv is implicitly defined by

$$\max\{V_{1t}(p_1^0, q_1^0, m, \varepsilon_1), \ldots, V_{Kt}(p_K^0, q_K^0, m, \varepsilon_K)\}$$
$$= \max\{V_{1t}(p_1^1, q_1^1, m - cv, \varepsilon_1), \ldots, V_{K't}(p_{K'}^1, q_{K'}^1, m - cv, \varepsilon_{K'})\}, \qquad (6.3)$$

where superscripts 0 and 1 denote initial and changed prices, respectively, and K' denotes the number of alternatives under changed conditions. Inspection of Equation (6.3) suggests the willingness to pay measure will be a function of the unobserved heterogeneity, and thus a random variable from the perspective of the analyst. Once the parameters of the model are estimated, welfare calculation in the random utility model involves computing the expectation of willingness to pay for each individual in the sample. How this is done depends critically on the specific assumptions of the model.

If the conditional indirect utility function is linear in income and the errors type I extreme value, resulting in the multinomial logit model, the choice occasion welfare measure is given by the familiar difference in log-sums formula

$$E(cv) = \frac{\ln\left[\sum_{k=1}^K \exp(\overline{V}_k(p_k^0, q_k^1))\right] - \ln\left[\sum_{k=1}^{K'} \exp(\overline{V}_k(p_k^1, q_k^1))\right]}{\beta}, \qquad (6.4)$$

where $\overline{V}_k$ is the deterministic component of utility evaluated at the estimated coefficients, and β is the (constant) marginal utility of income.[47] This form makes clear the fact that the Hicksian welfare measure we estimate in simple RUM models assumes constant marginal utility of income to monetize a utility difference. In this respect, it is similar to the Marshallian consumer surplus measure that has been criticized in other contexts. Since the log-sum expression is the expectation of maximum utility under the extreme value distribution, the numerator in Equation (6.4) is simply a measure of the expectation of the change in utility resulting from a change in prices or quality levels. Dividing by the marginal utility of income converts the change in utility into a money-metric measure of the utility change.

In contrast to the simple linear in income logit and nested logit models, a closed form expression for willingness to pay is not available when we generalize the random utility model to mixed logit and probit error distributions, or specify nonlinear income models. Herriges and Kling (1999) provide a detailed discussion of welfare measurement in these models. For the case of the more general error distributions it becomes necessary to use Monte Carlo integration to calculate the expectation of maximum utility under initial and changed conditions. For each individual in the sample this is accomplished by simulating pseudo-random values from the error distribution and calculating the utility levels (as a function of the errors) under initial and changed conditions. Repeating this for several draws of the error, and taking the average of utility levels over all the draws, provides simulated measures of the expectation of maximum utility under initial and changed conditions. Dividing the difference between these measures by the marginal utility of income provides an estimate of the individual's choice occasion willingness to pay.

Nonlinear income models present an additional level of complexity as we noted earlier. In these models, willingness to pay is no longer defined as a money-metric measure of utility difference. Rather, as a true Hicksian measure, it is necessary to compute the level of income that equates realized utility under initial and changed conditions. This implies that not only must the errors be simulated, but for each draw of the error the income differential cv defined in Equation (6.3) must be solved that equates the indirect utility functions under initial and changed conditions. Typically this will require numerical methods. The expectation of an individual's willingness to pay is calculated by averaging the income differentials over all draws of the error.

The measures of willingness to pay discussed thus far in this sub-section can be considered unconditional, since the expectation of willingness to pay is calculated based on the unconditional distribution of an individual's unobserved heterogeneity. However, as suggested by von Haefen (2003), it is also possible to compute the expectation of willingness to pay based on the conditional distribution of unobserved heterogeneity. This strategy relies on the notion that, once the model is estimated, an individual's

---

[47] Linear in income nested logit models have a similar closed form expression for choice occasion willingness to pay. See Morey (1999) for details.

observed choice provides limitations on the support of the distribution that generated the person's behavior. Conditional welfare measures are calculated using Monte Carlo integration by first simulating the errors subject to these limitations such that the realized values are consistent with the choices observed in the sample at baseline prices and quality. This is followed by calculation of the utility levels under initial and changed conditions. As previously, the simulated expected utility levels are given by the average of utility levels over several draws of the error, and the welfare calculation computed by dividing the difference in utility by the marginal utility of income.

The RUM framework, regardless of the error assumptions and welfare calculation technique, delivers choice occasion willingness to pay measures. Calculation of seasonal benefit measures requires an assumption on the relationship between choice occasion selections among alternatives, and the amount of use over the course of a season. For example, Bockstael, Hanemann and Kling (1987) assume that the quantity response to changes in price or quality is zero, and calculate the seasonal measure by multiplying the initial use by the WTP per trip. Morey, Rowe and Watson (1993) divide the season into a fixed number of choice occasions, during each of which respondents choose to participate in recreation or not, and if so, which site to visit. In this case the seasonal measure is the choice occasion WTP times the number of choice occasions.

An advantage of the Kuhn–Tucker class of models is that it avoids this issue by characterizing behavior over the course of an entire season. Welfare analysis, however, presents technical challenges similar to those described above for nonlinear income RUM models. Phaneuf and Syderalis (2003) provide an intuitive overview of the steps necessary to compute willingness to pay for price or quality changes in KT models. Heuristically the process is as follows. With estimates of the utility function parameters, the solution to a consumer's problem (consisting of the combination of visited sites, the level of visits to these sites, and utility obtained) can be solved given a realization of the error in the model. Thus, we begin by simulating pseudo-random values for the errors and solving the consumer's problem under initial and changed levels of price or quality. Following this, an iterative process adjusting income in the consumer's problem under changed conditions is used to arrive at the income differential that equates the utility levels under the initial and changed prices and qualities. This income differential represents willingness to pay for the individual for the current draw of the error. Repeating this process for several draws of the error, and averaging the income differentials, provides an estimate of the individual's expected willingness to pay for the price or quality change.

Welfare measurement in mixed logit and nonlinear income RUMs, Kuhn–Tucker models, and all uses of conditional welfare measurement highlight the importance and influence of unobserved heterogeneity in contemporary recreation demand models. This is consistent with other areas of applied economics, where accounting for unobserved heterogeneity in applications has taken on greater importance as computer power and micro-data sets have become increasingly available. Welfare analysis in these models also highlights the different ways that contemporary approaches address the extensive and intensive margins of choice and the relevant income constraining decisions. The modeling alternatives at the frontier of recreation analysis are generally nonnested and employ different strategies for dealing with these three dimensions. The details of these decisions matter for how behavior is characterized.

Nowhere is this point more apparent than in attempts to compare the welfare measures derived from each model. Ideally, one would like to conclude that for certain classes of problems a particular modeling approach employing particular strategies for unobserved heterogeneity, the extensive and intensive margin, and income constraints will be most effective. Experience with each line of research in applications and controlled simulation evaluation has not been sufficient to offer this type of summary judgment. In fact, the complexity of the models themselves presents challenges for model comparisons that have not been fully addressed in the literature.

One simple proposal that would advance our understanding is to call for meta summaries of the measures from each application. Here, we are not suggesting a summary across approaches, but instead within a modeling alternative across the welfare scenarios and dimensions of heterogeneity [see Banzhaf and Smith (2003)]. This approach might offer a simplifying first step to help analysts understand how each feature of the modeling alternatives is influencing the outcomes for specific types of uses of the model.

7. Research ahead

Recreation demand analysis has evolved over the last fifty years from its beginning as a practical proposal to help a beleaguered Director of the National Park Service [Hotelling (1947)] to prominence in a recent Nobel lecture [McFadden (2001)]. The years between have witnessed the evolution of techniques from simple aggregate demand models to sophisticated analyses of individual level choices. The latter blend economic theory and microeconometrics to describe mixed discrete/continuous demands for multiple sites. While the progress in the last fifteen years has been particularly rapid, it is nonetheless possible to close with a few comments on future research challenges that seem especially relevant given the accumulated experience of the past nearly sixty years.

Table 3 provides groundwork for our suggestions by outlining previous reviewers' suggestions for research needs. Many of these recommendations remain relevant today. A few of the most important in our view include accounting for the opportunity cost of time, the role of inter-temporal constraints (and opportunities) in individual choice, the definition and measurement of the amount of recreation produced and consumed by each individual, the problems associated with multi-purpose trips, and the treatment of the quality attributes of recreation experiences.

To this list we add some further issues centered on four themes. First, there is a need to evaluate the importance of what might be labeled the "balancing judgments" that inevitably accompany empirical research. These arise in many areas but are not usually acknowledged as a general class of decisions needed in the face of multiple competing goals. For example, contemporary microeconometrics has emphasized the importance of individual heterogeneity and incorporating explicit recognition of its influence in modeling and estimation. Recreation demand models certainly face these issues. The challenge arises in matching the modeling choices with the available information and needs of each application. Most models favor treating individual diversity in tastes, knowledge, and constraints as unobserved heterogeneity, characterized with random parameters. The prospect of using observed characteristics of individuals as indicators of latent variables (or classes) is usually regarded as less desirable because it is more restrictive. However, the random parameter models may also be regarded as restrictive by some analysts. They generally assume heterogeneity is captured with specific (and arbitrary) continuous distributions.

Some methods are selected because they represent methodological innovations rather than important features of a problem. This highlights the importance of understanding how a decision on method balances the ultimate use of results, the character of the information available to meet those needs, the sensitivity of findings to how each approach uses available information, and the objectives facing the analyst who undertakes the research.

Similarly, in another example, the data available for recreation trips is often reported as counts rather than as continuous measures of use. A consistent model allowing for multiple corner solutions might require (for tractability) assuming continuity in the measures of use for interior choices. A statistical model of counts might have difficulty in characterizing the role of unobserved heterogeneity motivating the diverse consumption patterns across individuals. Balance in this example might require ignoring one aspect of model implementation, given theory and data, in order to assure another can be met with the practical demands of a research project. Sometimes the literature appears to favor complexity in technique over what might be termed "face value" or plausibility of the resulting economic characterization of choice.

Certainly we feel recreation modeling has served an important role as an incubator for microeconometric research. However, complexity should not outpace the ability to assure that new techniques in fact enhance understanding of choice behavior. This observation is not in itself a research issue. The task of designing methods to evaluate research outcomes is. It requires delineating the objectives of a class of research and designing measures that allow comparison of the key assumptions and results of each model and estimation specification in these terms. What assumptions are consequential to the objectives? And how do modeling and specification judgments influence the robustness of the results?

Our second theme centers on temporal issues. Our review has suggested several examples of how recreation choice and behavior involve time in a number of different ways. Time intervals are not fully exchangeable. Different time intervals convey attributes such as daylight, temperature, seasons, or even order (i.e., first thing in the morning, late in the evening, beginning of a season, etc.). Both the attributes of time and its order can be important to economic models.

Most recreation models have been based on static behavior. This strategy stems from the large conceptual, computational, and data collection burdens of working with fully temporal models. Future research might be directed not only at developing tractable dy-

Table 3

Alternative perspectives on the research challenges for the travel cost method

Author	Research issues
Ward and Loomis (1986)	*Valuation of travel time* Need continued research to evaluate effects of assumptions and establish greater consensus on best practices. *Treatment of on-site time* Develop consistent framework for role of on-site time in trip demand models. *Research issues in matching variant of travel cost model to management issue to be addressed.*
Smith (1989)	*What is a site?* Aggregations and disaggregations of land-based sites have been developed without regard to attachment of site characteristics, travel cost measurement, etc.; we do not understand implications in RUM for choice set in estimation and welfare measurement. *Supply and demand* Modeling of congestion, measures of scarcity of recreation resources, resource management of existing sites require we begin to model sorting of recreationists among sites and define what supply means in this context. *Perceptions versus technical measures of quality* Most site demands include technical measures of quality or warnings (fish consumption advisories); we know little about how people form perceptions about the quality of recreation sites at any point in time or with changing quality over time. *Demand for recreation activities* Classification of studies and results in early literature mixed site demand with activity demand; issue of whether we can consistently interpret and measure them; can we move the modeling of activities for stories to identifiable analytical models capable of empirical implementation?
Fletcher, Adamowicz and Graham-Tomasi (1990)	*Primary data collection* On-site, intercept, and user group surveys with limited information on perceptions, time allocation and choices among activities for using time; limit ability to address fundamental issues in travel cost models; need more primary data. *Evaluation of modeling performance, especially benefit measures and transfer* Recommend comparison of estimates for comparable activities across geographic areas and evaluate sources of differences. *Aggregation* More attention to aggregation over time, quality conditions for trips, individuals and sites. *Welfare measurement* Selection of functional forms for demand/preference models and welfare measures.
Bockstael, McConnell and Strand (1991)	*Modeling range of recreation decisions* Consider the relative strengths and weaknesses in discrete choice and continuous demand models. Integrate models of participation decisions. *Dealing with multiple price/quality changes* Evaluate how effects of price and quality changes on demand and welfare measures can be consistently aggregated over different sites and activities.

(continued on next page)

Table 3
(*Continued*)

Author	Research issues
	Dynamic behavior and welfare measurement Repeated visits reduce site attribute uncertainty and lead to increased skills. Develop models for the effects of these changes over time in a consistent framework. *Aggregate welfare measurement* Reconciling needs for individual welfare measures, consistent aggregation, and evaluation of distributional effects implied by heterogeneity in preferences and income.
Parsons (2003)	*Measuring trip cost* Consider how we measure travel and time costs, access fees, equipment costs, lodging, time on site in integrated model. *Perceived versus objective quality measures* Perceived measures are preferred to describe behavior, but may be able to short circuit the need to know them if objective measures are a consistent proxy across people. *Multiple destination trips* Cost allocation is key issue when trip has multiple objectives; portfolio of sites used as a choice alternative needs to be investigated in RUM framework. *Site and choice set definitions* Need to evaluate approaches to defining sites and choice sets in a RUM framework; evaluate sensitivity to their definition; potential in considering choice set formation as an endogenous process. *Time interdependence* The role of experience and habitats in some types of recreation potentially important; also RUM often assumes independence across choice occasions; influence of season and timing of use important.
Herriges and Kling (2003)	*Opportunity cost of time* Multiple influences on the full opportunity costs of time; despite extensive research empirically tractable, theoretically consistent, encompassing, solutions remain to be developed. *Dynamic aspects of recreation choices* Potential for individuals to substitute inter-temporally between current and future trips has significant implications for welfare measurement. Experience with discrete dynamic optimization models is limited and needs to expand. *Multiple site trips* Consider evaluation of multiple objective trips as portfolios or trip combinations. Limited research using this strategy – it is worthy of further study. *General modeling issues* Continuing need to evaluate selection criteria to discriminate among alternative functional forms for demand and indirect utility functions; issues with site aggregation and extent of the market lack clear-cut resolution; scope for using combined revealed/stated preference data in recreation as a validity gauge for each method, especially if stated preference includes nonuse values.

namic methods for recreation, but also at understanding the degree to which behavior characterized by static approaches can approximate behavior that is influenced by the attributes and order in which time is used. A particularly important area in this dimension is to more fully consider the impacts of a richer set of time constraints, recognizing that time is only partially fungible and often is available only in discrete blocks.

Related to this, most studies of choice set determination and extent of the market are based on cases studies of researcher-defined choice boundaries. Introspection suggests, however, that an individual's choice set is in fact endogenous and based on a dynamic information gathering process. Today's endogenous choice set and spike models with adjustments inflating the probability of zero use are statistical approaches to addressing the fact that many individuals may never consider a recreation site included by the analyst in the choice set. Utility consistent conceptual and empirical models that account for the effects of the search costs on the process of determining individual choice sets have been lacking in recreation analysis and offer a topic for future research.

Over longer times people learn and change their behavior. This learning can be through formal education, direct recreational experiences, and indirect experiences that are acquired by reading or viewing materials related to potential interests. Changes in the availability of time over time and in experiences are what Krutilla (1967) argued would be likely to change the relative importance of amenities to produced goods. Recently Costa and Kahn (2003) suggest there have been increases in the value of climate amenities. While expenditures for desirable climate conditions have not changed (based on their hedonic models) the price to purchase preferred climatic conditions (controlling for other locational attributes) increased by sixfold in their example, rising from $1,288 to $7,547 to purchase San Francisco's climate over that of Chicago. Some meta analyses of benefit measures suggest time trends in these models that display similar changes in broad terms. Time plays many different roles in the analysis of market choice. It should not be surprising that the challenges in reflecting the multiple roles for time and distinguishing the impact of changes on other dimensions of constraints are great.

Our third and forth themes are related, and center on the role that data and policy analysis can play in recreation applications. On the data side, research on combining revealed and stated preference data should continue, both from the perspective of study and model design. Likewise revealed preference data collection should adopt the construct validity criteria used in contingent valuation. Finally, methods need to be developed that allow practitioners to readily draw on multiple sources of existing publicly available data, either alone or combined with small purpose-generated survey data, to address specific policy questions.

This suggestion stems from Heckman's (2001) call for parsimonious models. If we begin with the premise that travel cost models are developed primarily for use in the evaluation of policy, then the research challenge involves developing models that allow public policy analysts to tailor the available results (based on these data) so that they can be used to address their specific questions.

This latter suggestion overlaps with the role that policy demands play in recreation analysis. There are two ways in which policy can and should play a role in recreation modeling. The first has received a fair amount of attention and involves benefit transfer. The second is relatively new and relates to the opportunities created by policy experiments.

Benefits transfer – the use of results from one study to inform a decision in another area – is a large and increasing use of recreation results in policy analysis. It is certainly not surprising to suggest that research on consistent methods for benefits transfer should continue. Our proposal calls for a change in orientation. Why not stress the development of models and data that can be consistently augmented with special purpose information relevant for each problem? Under this view, the ideal would not be one large multi-purpose survey and model to address all problems. Rather, it would be a platform with a sufficiently detailed structure to permit special purpose issues to be addressed by using targeted data collection efforts that could be linked to the base model and data. The goal would be adapting the methods of sample matching developed by Rosenbaum and Rubin (1983) and evaluated extensively by Heckman and his collaborators to meet the challenges posed in developing information for policy on the demand for and value of recreation resources.

This strategy would combine matching methods with joint estimation. Samples might include both revealed preference and stated preference information, linked through a description of behavior and tailored to the policy issue of interest. Multiple data sources could be used to estimate consumer preferences using joint estimation/matched samples estimators. With joint estimation we can take advantage of the scale of a larger set of background information and yet tailor the model to address details of the potentially smaller policy case. This strategy combines the structural features of joint estimation [as introduced by Cameron (1992)] with the lessons from meta analysis [Walsh, Johnson and McKean (1990), Smith and Kaoru (1990a, 1990b, Smith and Pattanayak (2002)] and preference calibration [Smith, Van Houtven and Pattanayak (2002)] to assure that consistent structures are imposed in using past results to estimate consumer demand and measure benefits of policy interventions.

The literature in environmental economics has begun to explore the advantages of quasi-random experiments [see Chay and Greenstone (2003) and Greenstone (2002) as examples], our second role for policy activities in research design. Recreation models may also benefit from linking data collection to policy. The National Park Service changed fee schedules at a number of its major parks without adequate effort to collect and evaluate the responses. The Grand Canyon has an ambitious management plan to alter the role of automobiles within the park and no specific plans to track attendance and usage. Recent concerns about snowmobiles in Yellowstone prompted calls for evaluations ex ante of regulations, but no specific proposals for data collection and evaluation ex post.

Several national databases together with differences in state regulations provide opportunities for using these differences to evaluate recreation behavior. Snyder, Stavins and Wagner (2003) have done this recently with fishing licenses. Restrictions on timing of hunting and the design of lotteries for access to some specialty hunting are other examples [see Scrogin and Berrens (2003)]. Some of these studies have exploited insights from the quasi-experimental design literature. Our point is that many more opportunities abound.

In many respects an important lesson from the recreation demand literature is that the diversity of opportunities in the US and around the world has created opportunities to use nonmarket choices among these alternatives to learn about individual preferences for environmental quality. Economists working in this area have certainly seized them. The result has been a rich harvest of insights that extend greatly beyond the domain of recreation demand. Contributions to this literature have addressed some of the most interesting modeling issues in describing and understanding consumer choice. As the access to micro level data increases, we expect the lessons being learned in modeling recreation behavior will be of increasing interest to environmental and mainstream economists alike.

Acknowledgements

Thanks are due to Wiktor Adamowicz, Ted McConnell, and Roger von Haefen for detailed and very constructive comments on an earlier draft as well as to the editors for their comments and patience with us in responding to them. Partial support to both authors for completion of revisions to an earlier draft of this research was provided through EPA Star Grant No. R-82950801.

References

Adamowicz, W. (1994). "Habit formation and variety seeking in a discrete choice model of recreation demand". Journal of Agricultural and Resource Economics 19, 19–31.

Adamowicz, W., Graham-Tomasi, T. (1991). "Revealed preference tests of nonmarket goods valuation methods". Journal of Environmental Economics and Management 20 (1), 29–45.

Adamowicz, W.L., Louviere, J., Williams, M. (1994). "Combining revealed and stated preference methods for valuing environmental amenities". Journal of Environmental Economics and Management 26 (May), 271–292.

Adams, R.L., Lewis, R.C., Drake, B.H. (1973). "Outdoor recreation in America: an economic analysis". Appendix A, Bureau of Outdoor Recreation, US Department of the Interior, Washington, DC.

Bailar, B.A. (1989). "Information needs, surveys, and measurement error". In: Kasprzyk, D. (Ed.), Panel Surveys. Wiley, New York.

Banzhaf, H.S., Smith, V.K. (2003). "Meta analysis in model implementation: choice sets and the valuation of air quality improvements". Discussion Paper. Resources for the Future, Washington, DC, August.

Bateman, I.J., Garrod, G.D., Brainard, J.S., Lovett, A.A. (1996). "Measurement issues in the travel cost method: a geographical information systems approach". Journal of Agricultural Economics 47 (2), 191–205.

Becker, G.S. (1965). "A theory of the allocation of time". Economic Journal 75 (September), 493–517.

Becker, G.S. (1992). "Habits, addictions, and traditions". Kyklos 45 (3), 327–345.

Bell, K.P., Strand, I.E. (2003). "Reconciling models of recreational route and site choices". Land Economics 79 (August), 440–454.

Ben-Akiva, M., Lerman, S. (1985). Discrete Choice Analysis: Theory and Application to Travel Demand. MIT Press, Cambridge.

Blundell, R., Robin, J.-M. (2000). "Latent separability: grouping goods without weak separability". Econometrica 68 (January), 53–84.

Bockstael, N., Kling, C. (1988). "Valuing environmental quality: weak complementarity with sets of goods". American Journal of Agricultural Economics 70 (3), 652–654.

Bockstael, N.E., McConnell, K. (1983). "Welfare measurement in the household production framework". American Economic Review 73, 806–814.

Bockstael, N., McConnell, K. (1993). "Public goods as characteristics of nonmarket commodities". Economic Journal 103 (420), 1244–1257.

Bockstael, N., McConnell, K. (1999a). "Revisiting the hedonic travel cost model". Working Paper. Department of Agricultural and Resource Economics, University of Maryland.

Bockstael, N., McConnell, K. (1999b). "The behavioral basis of nonmarket valuation". In: Herriges, J.A., Kling, C.L. (Eds.), Valuing Recreation and the Environment. Edward Elgar, Northampton, MA.

Bockstael, N., Strand, I. (1987). "The effects of common sources of regression error on benefit estimates". Land Economics 63 (1), 11–20.

Bockstael, N., Hanemann, W.M., Kling, C. (1987). "Estimating the value of water quality improvements in a recreational demand framework". Water Resources Research 23 (5), 951–960.

Bockstael, N., Hanemann, W.M., Strand, I. (1987). Measuring the benefits of water quality improvements using recreation demand models. Draft Report presented to the US Environmental Protection Agency under Cooperative Agreement CR-811043-01-0. Washington, DC.

Bockstael, N.E., McConnell, K.E., Strand, I.E. (1987). Benefits from Improvements in Chesapeake Water Quality, vol. II. Report to US Environmental Protection Agency. Department of Agricultural and Resource Economics, University of Maryland, March.

Bockstael, N., McConnell, K., Strand, I. (1991). "Recreation". In: Braden, J., Kolstad, C. (Eds.), Measuring the Demand for Environmental Quality. North-Holland, Amsterdam.

Bockstael, N., Strand, I., Hanemann, W.M. (1987). "Time and the recreational demand model". American Journal of Agricultural Economics 69 (2), 293–302.

Börsch-Supan, A. (1990). "On the compatibility of nested logit models with utility maximization". Journal of Econometrics 43 (2), 373–388.

Bowes, M.D., Loomis, J.B. (1980). "A note on the use of travel cost models with unequal zonal populations". Land Economics 56 (4), 465–470.

Boxall, P.C., Adamowicz, W.L. (2002). "Understanding heterogeneous preferences in random utility models: a latent class approach". Environmental and Resource Economics 23 (December), 421–446.

Boxall, P., Adamowicz, W., Tomasi, T. (1996). "A nonparametric test of the traditional travel cost model". Canadian Journal of Agricultural Economics 44, 183–193.

Boyle, K. et al. (1999). "A meta analysis of sport fishing values". Prepared for Economics Division, US Dept. of the Interior Fish and Wildlife Service, April.

Breffle, W., Morey, E., Rowe, R.D., Waldman, D.M., Wytinck, S.M. (1999). "Recreational fishing damages from fish consumption advisories in the waters of Green Bay". Prepared for US Fish and Wildlife Service, November.

Bresnahan, T., Gordon, R. (1997). "The economics of new goods: introduction". In: Bresnhan, T., Gordon, R. (Eds.), The Economics of New Goods: NBER Studies in Income and Wealth. University of Chicago Press, Chicago.

Brown, G., Mendelsohn, R. (1984). "The hedonic travel cost method". Review of Economics and Statistics 66, 427–433.

Burt, O., Brewer, D. (1971). "Estimation of net social benefits from outdoor recreation". Econometrica 39 (5), 813–827.

Cameron, T.A. (1992). "Combining contingent valuation and travel cost data for the valuation of nonmarket goods". Land Economics 68 (3), 302–317.

Carson, R., Hanemann, W.M., Wegge, T. (1989). "A nested logit model of recreation demand in Alaska". Working Paper. University of California, San Diego.

Caulkins, P., Bishop, R., Bouwes, N. (1985). "Omitted cross-price variable bias in the linear travel cost model: correcting common misperceptions". Land Economics 61 (2), 182–187.

Cesario, F.J., Knetsch, J.L. (1970). "Time bias in recreation benefit estimates". Water Resources Research 6 (June), 700–704.

Chay, K., Greenstone, M. (2003). "The impact of air pollution on infant mortality: evidence from geographic variation in pollution shocks induced by a recession". Quarterly Journal of Economics (August), 1121–1167.

Chen, H., Cosslett, S. (1998). "Preference and benefit estimation in multinomial probit models". American Journal of Agricultural Economics 80 (3), 512–520.

Chestnut, L.G., Rowe, R.D. (1990). "Preservation value for visibility protection at the national parks". Draft Final Report to US Environmental Protection Agency. RCG/Hagler Bailley.

Chiang, J., Lee, L.-F. (1992). "Discrete/continuous models of consumer demand with binding nonnegativity constraints". Journal of Econometrics 54 (1–3), 79–93.

Chiappori, P.-A. (1988). "Rational household labor supply". Econometrica 56 (January), 63–89.

Cicchetti, C., Fisher, A., Smith, V.K. (1976). "An econometric evaluation of a generalized consumer surplus measure: the mineral king controversy". Econometrica 44 (6), 1259–1276.

Clawson, M. (1959). "Methods of measuring the demand for and value of outdoor recreation". Reprint No. 10, Resources for the Future. Washington, DC.

Clawson, M., Knetsch, J.L. (1966). Economics of Outdoor Recreation. Resources for the Future, Washington, DC.

Cosslett, S. (1981). "Maximum likelihood estimator for choice based samples". Econometrica 49 (5), 1289–1316.

Costa, D. (1999). "American living standards: evidence from recreational expenditures". Working Paper 7148. National Bureau of Economic Research, July.

Costa, D.L., Kahn, M.E. (2003). "The rising price of nonmarket goods". American Economic Review, Proceedings 93 (May), 227–232.

Dagsvik, J.K., Karlström, A. (2005). "Compensating variation and Hicksian choice probabilities in random utility models that are nonlinear in income". Review of Economic Studies 72 (January), 57–76.

Desvousges, W., Waters, S. (1995). "Report on potential economic losses associated with recreation services in the Upper Clark Fork River basin, vol. III". Report submitted to the US District Court, District of Montana, in relation to pending litigation between the State of Montana and the Atlantic Richfield Company.

Deyak, T.A., Parliament, T.J. (1975). "An analysis of youth participation at urban recreation". Land Economics LI (May), 172–176.

Dunford, R.W. (1999). "The American trader oil spill: an alternative view of recreation use damages". Association of Environmental and Resource Economists Newsletter 19 (1), 12–20.

Ebert, U. (1998). "Evaluation of nonmarket goods: recovering unconditional preferences". American Journal of Agricultural Economics 80 (2), 241–254.

Egan, K. (2004). "Recreation demand: on-site sampling and responsiveness of trip behavior to physical water quality measures". Unpublished Ph.D. Thesis. Iowa State University.

Englin, J., Lambert, D. (1995). "Measuring angling quality in count data models of recreational fishing: a nonnested test of three approaches". Environmental and Resource Economics 6, 389–399.

Englin, J., Mendelsohn, R. (1991). "A hedonic travel cost analysis for valuation of multiple components of site quality: the recreation value of forest management". Journal of Environmental Economics and Management 21 (3), 275–290.

Englin, J., Shonkwiler, J.S. (1995). "Modeling recreation demand in the presence of unobservable travel costs: toward a travel price model". Journal of Environmental Economics and Management 29 (November), 368–377.

Englin, J., Boxall, P., Watson, D. (1998). "Modeling recreation demand in a Poisson system of equations: an analysis of the impact of international exchange rates". American Journal of Agricultural Economics 80 (2), 255–263.

Englin, J., Lambert, D., Shaw, W.D. (1997). "A structural equations approach to modeling consumptive recreation demand". Journal of Environmental Economics and Management 33 (1), 33–43.

Feather, P. (1994). "Sampling and aggregation issues in random utility model estimation". American Journal of Agricultural Economics 76 (4), 772–780.

Feather, P., Hellerstein, D. (1997). "Calibrating benefit function transfer to assess the conservation reserve program". American Journal of Agricultural Economics 79 (1), 80–88.

Feather, P., Shaw, W.D. (1999). "Estimating the cost of leisure time for recreation demand models". Journal of Environmental Economics and Management 38, 49–65.

Feather, P., Hellerstein, D., Tomasi, T. (1995). "A discrete-count model of recreation demand". Journal of Environmental Economics and Management 29 (2), 214–227.

Fletcher, J., Adamowicz, W., Graham-Tomasi, T. (1990). "The travel cost model of recreation demand: theoretical and empirical issues". Leisure Sciences 12, 119–147.

Freeman III, A.M. (1993). The Measurement of Environmental and Resource Values: Theory and Models. Resources for the Future, Washington, DC.

Greenstone, M. (2002). "The impacts of environmental regulations on industrial activity: evidence from the 1970 and 1977 clean air act amendments and the census of manufactures". Journal of Political Economy 110 (December), 1175–1219.

Grijalva, T., Berrens, R.P., Bohara, A.K., Jakus, P.M., Shaw, W.D. (2002). "Valuing the loss of rock climbing access in wilderness areas". Land Economics 78 (February), 103–120.

Gum, R.L., Martin, W.E. (1975). "Problems and solutions in estimating demand for and value of rural outdoor recreation". American Journal of Agricultural Economics 57 (November), 558–566.

Haab, T.C., Hicks, R.L. (1997). "Accounting for choice set endogeneity in random models of recreation demand". Journal of Environmental Economics and Management 34, 127–147.

Haab, T.C., McConnell, K.E. (1996). "Count data models and recreation demand". American Journal of Agricultural Economics 78 (1), 89–102.

Haab, T.C., McConnell, K.E. (1997). "Referendum models and negative willingness to pay: alternative solutions". Journal of Environmental Economics and Management 32 (February), 251–270.

Haab, T.C., McConnell, K.E. (2002). Valuing Environmental and Natural Resources: The Econometrics of Non-market Valuation. Edward Elgar, Northampton, MA.

Hanemann, W.M. (1978). A Methodological and Empirical Study of the Recreation Benefits from Water Quality Improvement. Ph.D. Dissertation (Economics). Harvard University.

Hanemann, W.M. (1984). "Discrete–continuous models of consumer demand". Econometrica 52 (2), 541–561.

Hanemann, W.M. (1985). "Welfare analysis with discrete choice models". Working Paper. Department of Agricultural Economics, University of California, Berkeley. Reprinted in Kling, C., Herriges, J. (Eds.), Valuing Recreation and the Environment. Edward Elgar, Northampton, MA.

Hanemann, M. (1993). "Willingness to pay vs. willingness to sell: who much can they differ?". American Economic Review 81, 635–647.

Hanemann, W.M. (1995). "Review of triangle economic research report on economic loss to recreational fishing in the Upper Clark Fork River". Unpublished, October 27.

Hanemann, W.M. (1999). "The economic theory of WTP and WTA". In: Bateman, I.J., Willis, K.G. (Eds.), Valuing Environmental Preferences: Theory and Practice of the Contingent Valuation Methods in the US, EU and Developing Countries. Oxford University Press, Oxford.

Haspel, A.E., Johnson, F.R. (1982). "Multiple destination trip bias in recreation benefit estimation". Land Economics 58 (August), 364–372.

Hauber, A.B., Parsons, G. (2000). "The effect of nesting structure specification on welfare estimation in a random utility model of recreation demand: an application to the demand for recreation fishing". American Journal of Agricultural Economics 82, 501–514.

Hausman, J. (1981). "Exact consumer's surplus and deadweight loss". American Economic Review 71 (4), 662–676.

Hausman, J., McFadden, D. (1984). "Specification tests for the multinomial logit model". Econometrica 52 (5), 1219–1240.

Hausman, J.A., Newey, W.K. (1995). "Nonparametric estimation of exact consumer surplus and deadweight loss". Econometrica 63 (November), 1445–1476.

Hausman, J., Wise, D. (1978). "A conditional probit model for qualitative choice: discrete decisions recognizing interdependence and heterogeneous preferences". Econometrica 46 (2), 403–426.

Hausman, J., Leonard, G., McFadden, D. (1995). "A utility-consistent, combined discrete choice and count data model: assessing recreational use losses due to natural resource damage". Journal of Public Economics 56 (1), 1–30.

Heckman, J.J. (1974). "Shadow prices, market wages, and labor supply". Econometrica 42 (4), 679–694.

Heckman, J.J. (2001). "Microdata, heterogeneity, and the evaluation of public policy: Nobel lecture". Journal of Political Economy 109 (4), 673–748.

Herriges, J.A., Kling, C.L. (1996). "Testing the consistency of nested logit models with utility maximization". Economics Letters 50 (1), 33–40.

Herriges, J., Kling, C. (1999). "Nonlinear income effects in random utility models". Review of Economics and Statistics 81 (1), 62–72.

Herriges, J., Kling, C.L. (2003). "Recreation demand models". In: Folmer, J., Tietenberg, T. (Eds.), International Yearbook of Environmental and Resource Economics 2003/2004. Edward Elgar, Cheltenham, UK, pp. 331–372.

Herriges, J.A., Phaneuf, D. (2002). "Introducing patterns of correlation and substitution in repeated logit models of recreation demand". American Journal of Agricultural Economics 84 (4), 1076–1090.

Herriges, J.A., Kling, C.L., Phaneuf, D.J. (1999). "Corner solution models of recreation demand: a comparison of competing frameworks". In: Herriges, J.A., Kling, C.L. (Eds.), Valuing Recreation and the Environment. Edward Elgar, Northampton, MA.

Hicks, R., Strand, I. (2000). "The extent of information: its relevance for random utility models". Land Economics 76 (3), 374–385.

Hof, J., King, D. (1982). "On the necessity of simultaneous recreation demand equation estimation". Land Economics 58 (4), 547–552.

Hotelling, H. (1947). "Letter to the National Park Service". Reprinted in An Economic Study of the Monetary Evaluation of Recreation in the National Parks (1949). US Department of the Interior, National Park Service and Recreational Planning Division, Washington, DC.

Huang, J.-C., Nychka, D.W. (2000). "A nonparametric multiple choice method within the random utility framework". Journal of Econometrics 97 (August), 207–226.

Huang, J.-C., Haab, T.C., Whitehead, J.C. (1997). "Willingness to pay for quality improvements: should revealed and stated preference data be combined?". Journal of Environmental Economics and Management 34 (3), 240–255.

Jakus, P., Shaw, W.D. (1997). "Congestion at recreation areas: empirical evidence on perceptions, mitigating behavior and management practices". Journal of Environmental Management 50 (4), 389–401.

Jakus, P., Downing, M., Bevelheimer, M., Fly, J.M. (1997). "Do sportfish consumption advisories affect reservoir anglers' site choice?". Agricultural and Resource Economics Review (October), 196–204.

Jones, C., Lupi, F. (1997). "The effect of modeling substitute activities on recreation benefit estimates". Working Paper. Damage Assessment Center, National Oceanic and Atmospheric Administration.

Just, R., Hueth, D., Schmitz, A. (2004). The Welfare Economics of Public Policy. Edward Elgar, Cheltenham, UK (in press).

Kalter, R.J., Gosse, L.E. (1970). "Recreation demand functions and the identification problem". Journal of Leisure Research 2 (Winter), 43–53.

Kaoru, Y., Smith, V.K. (1990). "Black mayonnaise and marine recreation". Unpublished. North Carolina State University.

Kaoru, Y., Smith, V.K., Liu, J.-L. (1995). "Using random utility models to estimate the recreational value of estuarine resources". American Journal of Agricultural Economics 77 (1), 141–151.

Karlström, A. (1999). "Four essays on spatial modeling and welfare analysis". Ph.D. Thesis. Department of Infrastructure and Planning, Royal Institute of Technology, Stockholm, Sweden.

Kass, D.I., Okubo, S. (2000). "US travel and tourism satellite accounts for 1996 and 1997". Survey of Current Business (July), 8–24.

Kling, C.L., Thomson, C.J. (1996). "The implications for model specification for welfare estimation in nested logit models". American Journal of Agricultural Economics 78, 103–114.

Krutilla, J. (1967). "Conservation reconsidered". American Economic Review 57 (4), 777–786.

Krutilla, J.V., Fisher, A.C. (1975). The Economics of Natural Environments: Studies in the Valuation of Commodity and Amenity Resources. Johns Hopkins, Baltimore.

LaFrance, J.T. (1985). "Linear demand functions in theory and practice". Journal of Economic Theory 37, 147–166.

LaFrance, J.T. (1986). "The structure of constant elasticity demand models". American Journal of Agricultural Economics (August), 543–552.

LaFrance, J.T. (1990). "Incomplete demand systems and semilogarithmic demand models". Australian Journal of Agricultural Economics (August), 118–131.

LaFrance, J., Hanemann, M. (1989). "The dual structure of incomplete demand systems". American Journal of Agricultural Economics 71 (2), 262–274.

Larson, D. (1991). "Recovering weakly complementary preferences". Journal of Environmental Economics and Management 21 (2), 97–108.

Larson, D., Shaikh, S. (2001). "Empirical specification considerations for two-constraint models of recreation demand". American Journal of Agricultural Economics 83 (May), 428–440.

Lee, L.-F., Pitt, M.M. (1986). "Microeconometric demand system with binding nonnegativity constraints: the dual approach". Econometrica 54 (5), 1237–1242.

Leeworthy, V.R., Wiley, P.C. (1993). "Recreation use value for three Southern California beaches". Unpublished Paper. Strategic Environmental Assessments Division, National Oceanic and Atmospheric Administration, Rockville, Maryland, March.

Loomis, J.B., Song, C.F., Donnelly, D.M. (1986). "Evaluating regional demand models for estimating recreational use and economic benefits: a case study". Water Resources Research 22 (April), 431–438.

Lupi, F., Feather, P. (1998). "Using partial site aggregation to reduce bias in random utility travel cost models". Water Resources Research 34 (12), 3595–3603.

Lutz, J., Englin, J., Shonkwiler, J.S. (2000). "On the aggregate value of recreational activities". Environmental and Resource Economics 15, 217–226.

Mäler, K.-G. (1974). Environmental Economics: A Theoretical Inquiry. Johns Hopkins University Press for Resources for the Future, Baltimore, MD.

Manski, C., Lerman, S. (1977). "The estimation of choice probabilities from choice-based samples". Econometrica 45 (November), 1977–1988.

McConnell, K. (1992). "On-site time in the demand for recreation". American Journal of Agricultural Economics 74 (4), 918–924.

McConnell, K.E. (1999). "Household labor market choices and the demand for recreation". Land Economics 75 (3), 467–477.

McConnell, K., Strand, I., Blake-Hedges, L. (1995). "Random utility models of recreational fishing: catching fish using a Poisson process". Marine Resource Economics 10 (3), 247–261.

McConnell, K., Strand, I., Bockstael, N. (1990). "Habit formation and the demand for recreation: issues and a case study". In: Smith, V.K., Link, A. (Eds.), Advances in Applied Microeconomics, vol. 5. JAI Press, Greenwich, CT.

McDaniels, T.L., Axelrod, L.J., Cavanagh, N. (1998). "Public perceptions regarding water quality and attitudes toward water conservation in the Lower Fraser Basin". Water Resources Research 34 (May), 1299–1306.

McFadden, D. (1974). "Conditional logit analysis of qualitative choice behavior". In: Zarembka, P. (Ed.), Frontiers in Econometrics. Academic Press, New York.

McFadden, D. (1996). "On the analysis of 'Intercept & Follow' surveys". Working Paper. Department of Economics, University of California, Berkeley.

McFadden, D. (1999). "Computing willingness-to-pay in random utility models". In: Moore, J., Riezman, R., Melvin, J. (Eds.), Trade, Theory, and Econometrics: Essays in Honour of John S. Chipman. Routledge.

McFadden, D. (2001). "Economic choices". American Economic Review 91 (3), 351–378.

McFadden, D., Train, K. (2000). "Mixed MNL models for discrete response". Journal of Applied Econometrics 15 (September/October), 447–470.

Mendelsohn, R., Hof, J., Peterson, G., Johnson, R. (1992). "Measuring recreation values with multiple-destination trips". American Journal of Agricultural Economics 74, 926–933.

Morey, E. (1981). "The demand for site-specific recreation activities: a characteristics approach". Journal of Environmental Economics and Management 8 (4), 345–371.

Morey, E. (1984). "The choice of ski areas: estimation of a generalized CES preference ordering with characteristics". Review of Economics and Statistics 66 (4), 584–590.

Morey, E. (1985). "Characteristics, consumer surplus, and new activities: a proposed ski area". Journal of Public Economics 26 (2), 221–236.

Morey, E.R. (1999). "Two RUMs unCLOAKED: nested logit models of participation and site choice". In: Herriges, J.A., Kling, C.L. (Eds.), Valuing Recreation and the Environment. Edward Elgar, Cheltenham, UK.

Morey, E.R., Shaw, W.D. (1990). "An economic model to assess the impact of acid rain: a characteristics approach to estimating the demand for and benefits from recreational fishing". In: Smith, V.K., Link, A.N. (Eds.), Advances in Applied Micro Economics, vol. 5. JAI Press, Greenwich, CT.

Morey, E., Breffle, W., Greene, P. (2001). "Two nested CES models of recreational participation and site choice: an 'alternatives' model and an 'expenditures' model". American Journal of Agricultural Economics 83 (May), 414–427.

Morey, E., Rowe, R., Watson, M. (1993). "A repeated nested-logit model of Atlantic salmon fishing". American Journal of Agricultural Economics 75 (3), 578–592.

Morey, E.R., Sharma, V.R., Karlström, A. (2003). "A simple method of incorporating income effects into logit and nested logit models: theory and application". American Journal of Agricultural Economics 85 (February), 248–253.

Morey, E., Waldman, D., Assane, D., Shaw, W.D. (1995). "Searching for a model of multiple-site recreation demand that admits interior and boundary solutions". American Journal of Agricultural Economics 77 (1), 129–140.

Morikawa, T. (1989). "Incorporating stated preference data in travel demand analysis". Unpublished Ph.D. Thesis. Department of Civil Engineering, Massachusetts Institute of Technology.

Munley, V.G., Smith, V.K. (1976). "Learning by doing and experience: the case of whitewater recreation". Land Economics 52 (November), 545–553.

Norton, V.J., Smith, T.P., Strand, I.E. (1983). Stripers: The Economic Value of the Atlantic Coast Commercial and Recreational Striped Bass Fisheries. UM-SG-TS-83-12. University of Maryland Sea Grant, College Park, MD.

Ozuna, T., Gomez, I.A. (1994). "Estimating a system of recreation demand function using a seemingly unrelated Poisson regression approach". Review of Economics and Statistics 76, 356–360.

Palmquist, R.B. (2005). "Weak complementarity, path independence and the intuition of the Willig condition". Journal of Environmental Economics and Management 49 (January), 103–115.

Palmquist, R.B., Phaneuf, D.J., Smith, V.K. (2005). "Short run constraints and the increasing marginal value of time". CEnREP Working Paper. North Carolina State University, October.

Parsons, G.R. (2003). "The travel cost model". In: Boyle, K., Peterson, G. (Eds.), A Primer on Non-Market Valuation. Kluwer Academic Publishers, Dordrecht.

Parsons, G.R., Hauber, A.B. (1998). "Spatial boundaries and choice set definition in a random utility model of recreation demand". Land Economics 74 (February), 32–48.

Parsons, G., Kealy, M.J. (1992). "Randomly drawn opportunity sets in a random utility model of lake recreation". Land Economics 68 (1), 93–106.

Parsons, G., Kealy, M.J. (1995). "A demand theory for number of trips in a random utility model of recreation". Journal of Environmental Economics and Management 29 (3), 357–367.

Parsons, G., Needelman, M. (1992). "Site aggregation in a random utility model of recreation". Land Economics 68 (4), 418–433.

Parsons, G., Wilson, A. (1997). "Incidental and joint consumption in recreation demand". Agricultural and Resource Economics Review (April), 1–6.

Parsons, G., Jakus, P., Tomasi, T. (1999). "A comparison of welfare estimates from four models for linking seasonal recreation trips to multinomial logit models of choice". Journal of Environmental Economics and Management 38 (2), 143–157.

Parsons, G., Massey, D.M., Tomasi, T. (2000). "Familiar and favorite sites in a random utility model of beach recreation". Marine Resource Economics 14, 299–315.

Parsons, G., Plantinga, A., Boyle, K. (2000). "Narrow choice sets in a random utility model of recreation demand". Land Economics 76 (1), 86–99.

Pearce, D. (2000). "Cost benefit analysis and environmental policy". In: Helm, D. (Ed.), Environmental Policy in the UK. Blackwell, Oxford.

Pendleton, L., Mendelsohn, R. (2000). "Estimating recreation preferences using hedonic travel cost and random utility models". Environmental and Resource Economics 17, 89–108.

Peters, T., Adamowicz, W., Boxall, P. (1995). "Influence of choice set considerations in modeling the benefits from improved water quality". Water Resources Research 31 (7), 1781–1787.

Phaneuf, D.J. (1999). "A dual approach to modeling corner solutions in recreation demand". Journal of Environmental Economics and Management 37 (1), 85–105.

Phaneuf, D.J. (2002). "A random utility model for TMDLs: estimating the benefits of watershed based ambient water quality improvements". Water Resources Research 38 (11), 36.1–36.11.

Phaneuf, D.J., Herriges, J.A. (1999). "Choice set definition in a Kuhn–Tucker model of recreation demand". Marine Resource Economics 14, 343–355.

Phaneuf, D.J., Syderalis, C. (2003). "An application of the Kuhn–Tucker demand model to the demand for water trail trips in North Carolina". Marine Resource Economics 18 (1), 1–14.

Phaneuf, D.J., Kling, C.L., Herriges, J.A. (2000). "Estimation and welfare calculations in a generalized corner solution model with an application to recreation demand". Review of Economics and Statistics 82 (2), 83–92.

Pollak, R.A. (1970). "Habit formation and dynamic demand functions". Journal of Political Economy 67 (July/August), 745–763.

Pollak, R.A. (1976). "Habit formation and long run utility functions". Journal of Economic Theory 13 (October), 272–297.

Pollak, R.A., Wachter, M. (1975). "The relevance of the household production function and its implications for the allocation of time". Journal of Political Economy 85, 255–277.

Provencher, B., Bishop, R. (1997). "An estimable dynamic model of recreation behavior with an application to Great Lakes angling". Journal of Environmental Economics and Management 33 (2), 107–127.

Provencher, B., Baerenklau, K.A., Bishop, R.C. (2002). "A finite mixture logit model of recreational angling with serially correlated random utility". American Journal of Agricultural Economics 84 (November), 1066–1075.

Randall, A. (1994). "A difficulty with the travel cost method". Land Economics 70 (1), 88–96.

Randall, A., Stoll, J. (1980). "Consumer's surplus in commodity space". American Economic Review 70 (3), 449–455.

Read, D., Loewenstein, G., Rabin, M. (1999). "Choice bracketing". Journal of Risk and Uncertainty 19 (1), 171–197.

Rosenbaum, P.R., Rubin, D.B. (1983). "The central role of the propensity score in observational studies for causal effects". Biometrika 70 (April), 41–55.

Rosenberger, R.S., Loomis, J.B. (2000a). "Using meta analysis for benefit transfer: in-sample convergent validity tests of an outdoor recreation database". Water Resources Research 36 (April), 1097–1107.

Rosenberger, R.S., Loomis, J.B. (2000b). "Panel stratification in meta analysis of economic studies: an investigation of its effects in the recreation valuation literature". Journal of Agricultural and Applied Economics 32 (December), 459–470.

Rosenberger, R.S., Loomis, J.B. (2003). "Benefits transfer". In: Champ, P.A., Boyle, K.J., Brown, T.C. (Eds.), A Primer on Nonmarket Valuation. Kluwer Academic Publishers, Dordrecht.

Rowe, R.D., Chestnut, L.G. (1982). The Value of Visibility: Theory and Application. Abt Books, Cambridge, MA.

Rust, J. (1987). "Optimal replace of GMC bus engines: an empirical model of Harold Zurcher". Econometrica 55 (5), 999–1033.

Samuelson, P., Swamy, S. (1974). "Invariant economic index numbers and canonical duality: survey and synthesis". American Economic Review 64 (August), 566–593.

Schuhmann, P. (1998). "Deriving species-specific benefits measures for expected catch improvements in a random utility framework". Marine Resource Economics 13, 1–21.

Schwabe, K.A., Schuhmann, P.W., Boyd, R., Doroodian, K. (2001). "The value of changes in deer season length: an application of the nested multinomial logit model". Environmental and Resource Economics 19 (2), 131–147.

Scrogin, D., Berrens, R. (2003). "Rationed access and welfare: case of public resource lotteries". Land Economics 79 (2), 137–148.

Shaw, W.D. (1992). "Opportunity cost of time". Land Economics 68 (1), 107–115.

Shaw, W.D., Feather, P. (1999). "Possibilities for including the opportunity cost of time in recreation demand systems". Land Economics 75 (4), 592–602.

Shaw, W.D., Ozog, M. (1999). "Modeling overnight recreation trip choice: application of a repeated nested multinomial logit model". Environmental and Resource Economics 00, 1–18.

Shonkwiler, J.S. (1999). "Recreation demand systems for multiple site count data travel cost models". In: Herriges, J.A., Kling, C.L. (Eds.), Valuing Recreation and the Environment. Edward Elgar, Northampton, MA.

Shonkwiler, J.S., Shaw, W.D. (1996). "Hurdle count-data models in recreation demand analysis". Journal of Agricultural and Resource Economics 21 (2), 210–219.

Small, K., Rosen, H. (1981). "Applied welfare economics with discrete choice models". Econometrica 49 (1), 105–130.

Smith, V.K. (1989). "Taking stock of progress with travel cost recreation demand methods: theory and implementation". Marine Resource Economics 6 (4), 279–310.

Smith, V.K. (1996). "Combining discrete choice and count data models". Working Paper. Department of Economics, Duke University.

Smith, V.K., Banzhaf, H.S. (2003). "Quality adjusted price indexes and the Willig condition in one graph". Unpublished Paper. Department of Agricultural and Resource Economics, North Carolina State University, October.

Smith, V.K., Banzhaf, H.S. (2004). "A diagrammatic exposition of weak complementarity and the Willig condition". American Journal of Agricultural Economics 86 (2), 455–466.

Smith, V.K., Desvousges, W.H. (1985). "The generalized travel cost model and water quality benefits: a reconsideration". Southern Economics Journal 51, 371–381.

Smith, V.K., Kaoru, Y. (1987). "The hedonic travel cost model: a view from the trenches". Land Economics 63 (May), 179–192.

Smith, V.K., Kaoru, Y. (1990a). "Signals or noise? Explaining the variation in recreation benefit estimates". American Journal of Agricultural Economics 72 (2), 419–433.

Smith, V.K., Kaoru, Y. (1990b). "What have we learned since Hotelling's letter? A meta analysis". Economics Letters 32 (3), 267–272.

Smith, V.K., Kopp, R.J. (1980). "The spatial limits of the travel cost recreational demand model". Land Economics 56 (February).

Smith, V.K., Pattanayak, S.K. (2002). "Is meta analysis a Noah's Ark for nonmarket valuation?". Environmental and Resource Economics 22 (1–2), 271–296.

Smith, V.K., Van Houtven, G. (2004). "Recovering Hicksian consumer surplus within a collective model: Hausman's method for the household". Environmental and Resource Economics 28, 153–167.

Smith, V.K., Desvousges, W., McGivney, M. (1983). "The opportunity cost of travel time in recreation demand models". Land Economics 59, 259–278.

Smith, V.K., Liu, J.-L., Palmquist, R. (1993). "Marine pollution and sport fishing: using Poisson models as household production functions". Economics Letters 42 (1), 111–116.

Smith, V.K., Palmquist, R.B., Jakus, P. (1991). "Combining Farrell frontier and hedonic travel cost models for valuing estuarine quality". Review of Economics and Statistics 73 (November), 694–699.

Smith, V.K., Van Houtven, G., Pattanayak, S.K. (2002). "Benefit transfer via preference calibration: 'prudential algebra' for policy". Land Economics 78 (1), 132–152.

Smith, V.K., Zhang, X., Palmquist, R.B. (1997). "Marine debris, beach quality, and nonmarket values". Environmental and Resource Economics 10, 223–247.

Snyder, L.D., Stavins, R.N., Wagner, A.F. (2003). "Private options to use public goods". Unpublished Paper. Harvard University, March.

Stern, S. (1997). "Simulation based estimation". Journal of Economic Literature 35 (4), 2006–2039.

Stewart, T.K., Middleton, P., Ely, D. (1983). "Judgments of visual air quality: reliability and validity". Journal of Environmental Management 3, 129–145.

Sudman, S., Ferber, R. (1979). Consumer Panels. American Marketing Association, Chicago.

Teisl, M., Boyle, K. (1997). "Needles in a haystack: cost effective sampling of marine sport anglers". Marine Resources Research 12, 1–10.

Tourangeau, R., Rips, L.J., Rasinski, K. (2000). The Psychology of Survey Response. Wiley, New York.

Train, K.E. (1998). "Recreation demand models with taste differences over people". Land Economics 74 (2), 230–239.

Train, K.E. (2003). Discrete Choice Methods with Simulation. Cambridge University Press, New York.

Trice, A.H., Wood, S.E. (1958). "Measurement of recreation benefits". Land Economics 34 (February), 195–207.

Varian, H.R. (1982). "The nonparametric approach to demand analysis". Econometrica 50 (4), 945–973.

Varian, H.R. (1983). "Nonparametric tests of consumer behavior". Review of Economic Studies 50 (1), 99–110.

Vaughan, W., Russell, C. (1982). "Valuing a fishing day: an application of a systematic varying parameter model". Land Economics 58 (4), 451–463.

von Haefen, R.H. (1998). "The welfare implications of environmental integrity for recreation site definition". Unpublished Paper. Department of Economics, Duke University.

von Haefen, R.H. (1999). Valuing Environmental Quality in a Repeated Discrete–Continuous Framework. Ph.D. Dissertation. Duke University, September.

von Haefen, R.H. (2002). "A complete characterization of the implications of Slutsky symmetry for the linear, log-linear, and semi-log incomplete demand system models". Journal of Agricultural and Resource Economics 27 (2), 281–319.

von Haefen, R.H. (2003). "Incorporating observed choice into the construction of welfare measures from random utility models". Journal of Environmental Economics and Management 45 (March), 145–165.

von Haefen, R., Phaneuf, D.J. (2003a). "Estimating preferences for outdoor recreation: a comparison of continuous and count data demand systems". Journal of Environmental Economics and Management 45 (May), 612–630.

von Haefen, R.H., Phaneuf, D.J. (2003b). "A note on estimating nested constant elasticity of substitution preferences for outdoor recreation". American Journal of Agricultural Economics 85 (May), 406–413.

von Haefen, R., Phaneuf, D., Parsons, G. (2004). "Estimation and welfare analyses with large demand systems". Journal of Business and Economic Statistics 22, 194–205.

Wahba, G. (1990). Spline Models for Observational Data. Society for Industrial and Applied Mathematics, Philadelphia, PA.

Wales, T., Woodland, A. (1983). "Estimation of consumer demand with binding nonnegativity constraints". Journal of Econometrics 21 (3), 263–285.

Walsh, R.G. (1985). Recreation Economic Decision. Department of Agricultural and Natural Resource Economics, Colorado State University, Fort Collins, CO.

Walsh, R.G., Johnson, D.M., McKean, J.R. (1990). "Nonmarket values from two decades of research on recreation demand". In: Smith, V.K., Link, A.N. (Eds.), Advances in Applied Microeconomics, vol. 5. JAI Press, Greenwich, CT, pp. 167–193.

Ward, F., Loomis, J. (1986). "The travel cost demand model as an environmental policy assessment tool: a review of literature". Western Journal of Agricultural Economics 11 (2), 164–178.

Westat, Inc. (1989). "Investigation of possible recall/reference period bias in national surveys of fishing, hunting and wildlife-associated recreation". Final Report presented to the US Fish and Wildlife Service under Cooperative Agreement 14-16-009-87-008. Washington, DC.

Whitehead, J.C., Haab, T.C., Huang, J.-C. (2000). "Measuring recreation benefits of quality improvements with revealed and stated behavior data". Resource and Energy Economics 22 (4), 339–354.

Willig, R. (1976). "Consumer's surplus without apology". American Economic Review 66 (4), 589–597.
Willig, R. (1978). "Incremental consumer's surplus and hedonic price adjustment". Journal of Economic Theory 17 (2), 227–253.

Chapter 16

PROPERTY VALUE MODELS

RAYMOND B. PALMQUIST

Department of Economics, North Carolina State University, Raleigh, NC 27695-8110, USA

Contents

Handbook of Environmental Economics, Volume 2. Edited by K.-G. Mäler and J.R. Vincent
© 2005 Elsevier B.V. All rights reserved
DOI: 10.1016/S1574-0099(05)02016-4

Abstract

One of the only places where environmental quality is traded on explicit markets is real estate. There are several techniques that can be used to study the effects of environmental quality on property values and infer willingness to pay for improvements. The most commonly used method is the hedonic model. In environmental economics the hedonic model has mainly been applied to the prices of real property and to wages. It assumes that there is a schedule of prices for the differentiated product (i.e., houses) that can be estimated. An alternative set of models postulates that consumers' choices are discrete between houses rather than continuous in characteristics as in the hedonic model. Discrete choice models are applied to estimate consumer preferences. Recently a model has been developed that mixes discrete and continuous decisions and emphasizes the locational equilibrium.

This chapter reviews these techniques, with an emphasis on methodological issues and recent developments. Section 2 describes the theoretical models that underlie these techniques. The theoretical hedonic model is developed first, and then the theoretical modifications that are necessary for the discrete choice models are described. The main models are developed for residential properties, but differentiated factors of production are discussed briefly. Section 3 is devoted to the empirical issues involved in estimating a hedonic price schedule. This is the most common type of estimation in property value models. Section 4 discusses the empirical application of the second stage of the hedonic model, the estimation of the underlying preferences. Section 5 covers the two types of discrete choice models that are used in environmental economics, random utility models and random bidding models. Section 6 briefly discusses the new locational equilibrium models, and the final section is devoted to conclusions and directions for further research.

Keywords

property value, hedonic, revealed preference, benefit measurement, differentiated product

JEL classification: Q51, R21, C31

1. Introduction

Valuing environmental goods is often difficult because they are usually non-market goods. One of the only places where environmental quality is traded on explicit markets is real estate. Yet even here, extracting information on environmental values is often quite complex. Housing and other types of real property are differentiated products, and virtually every unit is different. This results in the complexity, but it also is the reason we can observe environmental quality being sold. Property value studies are one of the most frequently applied techniques for benefit measurement.[1]

There are several techniques that can be used to study the effects of environmental quality on property values and infer willingness to pay for improvements. The spatial nature of almost all environmental problems is crucial for each of the techniques. The most commonly used method is the hedonic model. The somewhat misleading name was coined by Court (1939) in a study of automobiles, and the technique was popularized by Griliches (1971) with the same product. One of the earliest applications was Waugh (1928) on vegetables, although Colwell and Dilmore (1999) uncovered a 1922 Masters thesis by G.C. Haas that used similar techniques on farmland. The technique has been applied to a wide variety of goods and used in many different fields since those early studies. However, in environmental economics the hedonic model has mainly been applied to the prices of real property and to wages. The hedonic model assumes that there is a schedule of prices for the differentiated product (i.e., houses) that can be estimated. Estimation of this hedonic price schedule can provide some information on valuing public environmental goods. However, often it is necessary to go further and learn about individual behavior in the market, the second stage of the hedonic model. An alternative set of models postulates that consumers' choices are discrete between houses rather than continuous in characteristics as in the hedonic model. Discrete choice models are applied to estimate consumer preferences. Finally, recently a model has been developed that mixes discrete and continuous decisions and emphasizes the locational equilibrium.

This chapter is organized as follows. The next section describes the theoretical models that underlie these techniques. The theoretical hedonic model is developed first, and then the theoretical modifications that are necessary for the discrete choice models are described. This section also has a detailed theoretical discussion of welfare measurement in these models under the different circumstances that arise. The main models are developed for residential properties, but differentiated factors of production are discussed briefly at the end of the section. Section 3 is devoted to the empirical issues involved in estimating a hedonic price schedule. This is the most common type of estimation in property value models, and there is a wide range of issues that must be considered. Section 4 discusses the empirical application of the second stage of the hedonic model, the estimation of the underlying preferences. Section 5 covers the two

---

[1] While these techniques are widely accepted, it is worthwhile to consider the cautionary note expressed by Mäler (1977). Some of the issues raised there are discussed throughout this chapter.

types of discrete choice models that are used in environmental economics, random utility models and random bidding models. Section 6 briefly discusses the new locational
equilibrium models, and the final section is devoted to conclusions and directions for
further research.

There have been a number of thorough reviews of property value models previously
[see Bartik and Smith (1987), Palmquist (1991), Freeman (1993)]. While the current
chapter attempts to provide a fairly complete overview, the emphasis has been on more
recent developments. Those interested in more details on the earlier literature will find
these other surveys complementary. The emphasis here is on methodological issues and
innovations. There is a vast literature of applications of the techniques to a wide range
of issues. Examples of the empirical applications are discussed by Smith and Huang
(1993, 1995) and Palmquist and Smith (2002).

2. Theoretical models and welfare measurement

2.1. The theory of consumer behavior in markets for differentiated products

Most property value models deal with residential housing. Housing is a differentiated
product. A differentiated product is one where there are obvious differences between
units of the product, yet the various types of units are traded in a single market.[2] Since
each unit differs, there will not be a single, uniform price in the market even if the market
is competitive. The price for which a house sells will depend on consumers' preferences
for the characteristics that house embodies. If one is modeling new construction, the
price would also depend on the cost of producing a house with those characteristics and
firms' profit maximizing decisions. However, the stock of existing houses dominates the
market in most areas. Researchers generally assume that the supply of houses is fixed
in the short-run. The prices of existing houses are demand determined. For that reason,
the models discussed here will concentrate on the market equilibrium and the consumer
side of the market and take the supply of houses to be fixed.

Following Rosen (1974), let $\mathbf{z} = (z_1, \ldots, z_n)$ represent the n characteristics of
houses. All of the models discussed here assume that the price of a house is related
to the characteristics it contains. The hedonic models are the most explicit about this
relationship and will be followed here initially. The equilibrium price of a house is a
function of the characteristics it contains, $P = P(\mathbf{z}) = P(z_1, \ldots, z_n)$. This function is
the hedonic price function or hedonic price schedule. It is the equilibrium price schedule in a given market and holds for all the houses in that market. Individual consumers
can affect the price they pay for a house by the characteristics they choose. However,

---

[2] One can say that the units are traded in a single market without implying that every consumer is a potential
customer for every unit sold in the market. A given consumer may only be interested in a segment of the
market. However, all that is required for the market to be integrated is that segments for different consumers
overlap.

they cannot affect the equilibrium price schedule in a competitive market. They are price-schedule-takers.

The hedonic price schedule may or may not be linear. If it were possible to move characteristics between houses easily (costless repackaging in Rosen's terminology), arbitrage would force a linear price schedule. Since it would be very costly or impossible to move characteristics between houses, the hedonic price schedule need not be linear, although it can be. The functional form is determined in the market with few theoretical restrictions.[3]

The consumers and their preferences and the variety of houses that are available underlie the equilibrium price schedule. Consumers are assumed to purchase one house. If a consumer purchases more than one house, the houses are assumed to be purchased for different purposes (i.e., a primary residence and a vacation home) and to enter the utility function separately. Following Rosen (1974) consumer js decision involves maximizing a utility function,

$$u^j = U^j(z_1, \ldots, z_n, x, \alpha^j), \tag{1}$$

subject to a budget constraint,

$$m^j = P(\mathbf{z}) + x. \tag{2}$$

The z_i ($i = 1, \ldots, n$) are the characteristics of the house as before, x is the nonhousing numeraire good, and m^j is consumer j's normalized income. All prices and income have been normalized by dividing by the price of x, and x is a Hicksian composite good representing all the other goods. The utility function is assumed to be strictly concave as well as conforming to the usual assumptions. Socio-economic variables that vary across individuals are included in the vector α^j. The first-order conditions are:

$$U_{z_i}^j = \lambda^j p_i, \quad i = 1, \ldots, n, \tag{3}$$

$$U_x^j = \lambda^j, \tag{4}$$

$$m^j = P(z) + x \tag{5}$$

where subscripts on functions denote partial derivatives, p_i is the marginal price of characteristic i (the partial derivative of $P(\mathbf{z})$ with respect to z_i), and λ^j is the Lagrange multiplier. Thus, the marginal rate of substitution between a characteristic and the numeraire is equated to the marginal price of the characteristic

$$\frac{U_{z_i}^j}{U_x^j} = p_i. \tag{6}$$

---

[3] In the hedonic model, if a characteristic i is desirable to consumers, then $\partial P/\partial z_i \geqslant 0$. The degree of curvature in preferences places a limit on the degree of concavity of the hedonic function (for interior solutions), but the former concept is not known *a priori*.

It is important to remember that the i equations in Equation (6) are simply the result of manipulating Equations (3) and (4) and do not incorporate the budget constraint.[4] If one minimized expenditure subject to achieving a given level of utility, one would also derive Equation (6). Which constraint is used determines the nature of the demand equations derived.

It is useful to consider how much an individual would be willing to pay for a house with a particular set of characteristics. This would depend on the characteristics of the house, the income the individual had, the preferences of the individual, and the level of utility attained. This is Rosen's bid function θ^j which is defined implicitly by

$$U^j\left(z, m^j - \theta^j, \alpha^j\right) = u^j \tag{7}$$

where $\theta^j = \theta^j(\mathbf{z}, u^j, m^j, \boldsymbol{\alpha}^j)$. Implicitly differentiating Equation (7) (dropping, for the moment, the j superscript and the $\boldsymbol{\alpha}$ vector) yields insights into the function:

$$\theta_{z_i} = \frac{U_{z_i}}{U_x} > 0, \tag{8}$$

$$\theta_u = -\frac{1}{U_x} < 0, \tag{9}$$

$$\theta_m = \frac{U_x}{U_x} = 1, \tag{10}$$

$$\theta_{z_i z_i} = U_{z_i z_i} U_x^2 - 2U_{z_i x} U_{z_i} U_x + U_{xx} U_{z_i}^2 < 0. \tag{11}$$

Most of these make intuitive sense. If the quantity of one of the characteristics increases, holding constant income and satisfaction, the bid increases (Equation (8)). If the characteristics and income are held constant, an increase in utility is obtained by consuming more x which means the bid has to be lower (Equation (9)). Equation (11) shows that the marginal bid for z_i is less as the quantity of z_i increases. The partial derivative with respect to income (Equation (10)) is slightly less intuitive. However, holding constant the characteristics and utility also means that x is being held constant. This means that all additional income must be used in the bid for the house. Since $\theta_m = 1$, we can rewrite θ as

$$\theta(z, u, m) = \theta^*(z, u) + m. \tag{12}$$

$\theta^*(\mathbf{z}, u)$ will be negative, so it is not a bid function. It is introduced to provide intuition for some of the results to come. For example, the marginal bid function, $\partial\theta/\partial z_i$, depends only on $\mathbf{z}$, u, and $\boldsymbol{\alpha}$, but not m. Also, if characteristics change, the difference in the bids does not depend on income (as long as income does not change).

Rosen's familiar diagram is shown in the upper part of Figure 1. The diagram shows one characteristic z_i[5] and holds the other characteristics constant. The equilibrium hedonic price schedule is represented by the darker line and could also be convex or linear.

---

[4] McConnell and Phipps (1987) have called this function a marginal rate of substitution function.
[5] In the figures the subscript i is omitted to simplify the labels.

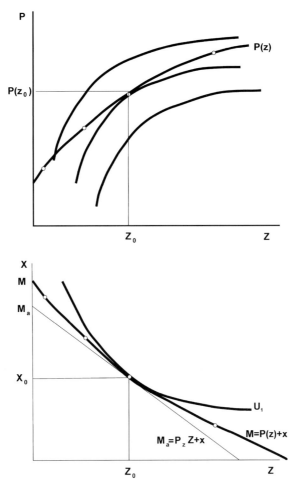

Figure 1. Bid contours and the equilibrium hedonic price schedule.

For the moment, the small circles on the price schedule can be ignored. Level curves for the bid function (or bid contours) for one individual are shown. The contours differ by the level of utility, with increasing subscripts on θ representing higher levels of satisfaction. Other individuals would have other families of bid contours (and tangencies) depending on their income and socio-economic attributes. The individual shown would choose to locate where z_0 units of the characteristic were available and pay $P(z_0)$ for the house.

Since the utility function is monotonically increasing in x, $u = U(z_1, \ldots, z_n, x)$ can be inverted to get

$$x = W(z_1, \ldots, z_n, u). \tag{13}$$

This gives the quantity of the numeraire necessary to reach u for given quantities of the characteristics z. Thus, the numeraire is a function of the characteristics and the level of utility. For a given level of utility, this is the equation for an indifference surface in terms of the numeraire. It is also true that

$$x = W(\mathbf{z}, u) = m - \theta(\mathbf{z}, u, m) = -\theta^*(\mathbf{z}, u). \tag{14}$$

Thus, there is a close relationship between changes in the bid function and changes in the numeraire that will hold the level of utility constant. This will be useful in developing welfare measures.

The derivative of the bid function with respect to a characteristic, $\theta_{z_i}(z, u)$, is called the marginal bid function. The first-order conditions for the utility maximization problem imply that $\theta_{z_i}(z, u) = p_i$ for all i and $P(\mathbf{z}) = \theta(\mathbf{z}, u, m)$ from the budget constraint. Each individual's utility function depends on the vector $\boldsymbol{\alpha}^j$ of that individual's socio-economic variables. As long as there are these differences in the individuals' utility functions and income, the bid functions will also differ between individuals. This results in the house characteristics, house prices, and marginal characteristic prices differing between individuals.

The consumers bidding for the houses establish a short-run equilibrium in a market. In equilibrium, each individual has the winning bid for one house.[6] No one could improve their level of satisfaction by increasing their bid for some other house above the current resident's bid. The hedonic model assumes that the resulting winning bids can be modeled as a continuous equilibrium hedonic price schedule depending on the characteristics. On the other hand, the discrete choice models assume the distributions of winning bids and the underlying characteristics are discontinuous. Such models will be discussed subsequently.

Because of the potential nonlinearity of the hedonic price schedule, the consumers may face nonlinear budget constraints. In this case the marginal prices of the characteristics are not parameters, but rather are determined by the choices consumers make. The theory of the comparative statics in the presence of nonlinear budget constraints has been developed by Blomquist (1989) and Edlefsen (1981). A few of the results (Engel and Cournot aggregation, Slutsky decomposition) for demand systems with linear budget constraints continue to hold with nonlinear budget constraints after natural generalizations. However, this is not true for homogeneity, negative semidefiniteness, and symmetry. In addition, the wealth of econometric tools that have been developed with linear constraints may not be useful with nonlinear constraints.

Fortunately, the complexities of nonlinear budget constraints can be avoided in most environmental property value studies. With knowledge of the nonlinear hedonic price

---

[6] It would be possible that two or more consumers with different $\boldsymbol{\alpha}^j$'s might have equivalent winning bids for identical houses (although given the spatial nature of housing, since two houses cannot be in exactly the same location, they cannot be exactly identical). It would be possible that an individual could be indifferent between making the winning bid on two or more houses. Neither of these possibilities substantively changes the discussion that follows and will not be pursue here.

function and the house where an individual chooses to locate, one can infer the marginal prices that an individual faces. We know from Equation (6) that the individual's marginal rate of substitution between a characteristic and the numeraire will be equal to that marginal price:

$$p_i^j = \frac{U_{z_i}^j(z, x)}{U_x^j(z, x)}. \tag{15}$$

By linearizing the budget constraint, an uncompensated inverse demand for characteristic i, $P_i^j(\mathbf{z}, x)$, can be derived in the following way.

In environmental economics we are interested in learning about the underlying utility function. An individual would choose the same house with a linearized budget constraint where the prices for the characteristics are parameters equal to the marginal prices at the chosen house and income has been adjusted to allow the same bundle of goods to be purchased [Palmquist (1988)]. Income has to be adjusted because the actual expenditure on housing with the true equilibrium price schedule will differ from the expenditure if the price of each unit of a characteristic were equal to the marginal price

$$m_a = m - P(\mathbf{z}) + \sum p_i z_i \tag{16}$$

where m_a is adjusted income.

These parametric prices and adjusted income are closely related to the concepts of virtual prices and virtual income used in the rationing literature. By using virtual prices and income, much of the existing literature on demand systems can be used. For welfare measurement when there are changes in quantities of characteristics, knowledge of the direct utility function is quite useful even without forecasting how the equilibrium price schedule will change.

The information in the upper part of Figure 1 can also be shown in a typical indifference curve diagram that will be useful later. The lower part of Figure 1 again features characteristic z_i and holds the other characteristics constant, but now the numeraire is measured on the vertical axis. The true budget constraint (Equation (2)) is shown with the darker line. An indifference curve with the usual properties represents the maximum attained level of satisfaction, u_1, at (z_0, x_0). The marginal price or virtual price p_z is the slope of the indifference curve at that point. The virtual income m_a is also shown, as is the linearized budget constraint.

In estimating inverse demands, prices are usually normalized by income because a linear budget constraint is unchanged if all prices and income are multiplied by a constant. The Hotelling–Wold Theorem yields uncompensated inverse demands. In contrast, for the hedonic model prices and income are normalized by the price of the numeraire x. Nevertheless, Equation (15) and the linearized budget constraint can yield an analogous Hotelling–Wold identity. The linearized budget constraint is

$$m_a = \sum p_i z_i + x \tag{17}$$

where m_a is the virtual income. Substituting Equation (15) in the budget constraint yields

$$m_a = \sum \frac{U_{z_i}}{U_x} z_i + \frac{U_x}{U_x} x = \frac{\sum U_{z_i} z_i + U_x x}{U_x}, \tag{18}$$

so

$$U_x = \frac{\sum U_{z_i} z_i + U_x x}{m_a}. \tag{19}$$

Substituting Equation (15) and reorganizing yields

$$P_i^j (z, x) = \frac{m_a \cdot U_{z_i}}{\sum U_{z_i} z_i + U_x x} \tag{20}$$

the uncompensated inverse demand for characteristic z_i. The researcher could specify the utility function and derive the estimating equations using Equation (20). Because of the linearization of the budget constraint the estimated demands would have limited usefulness on their own, but they could be used to recover the parameters of the utility function and evaluate changes in characteristics.

Empirically, first the equilibrium price schedule is estimated using data on the prices of houses and their characteristics.[7] From this, the marginal prices of the characteristics are calculated for each individual and the relevant characteristics. Then the quantities of the characteristics and the marginal prices of the characteristics are combined with data on income and other socio-economic variables to estimate the inverse demands for the characteristics generated from Equation (20). Ideally, the inverse demands for all characteristics would be estimated simultaneously as a system. However, because of the large number of characteristics this usually is not possible, and separability assumptions may have to be invoked to reduce the dimensionality of the problem. System methods such as the direct translog [e.g., Palmquist and Israngkura (1999)] and single equation estimation [e.g., Boyle, Poor and Taylor (1999, 2000)] have been used.

2.1.1. Discrete choice models

The random utility models view the consumer's decision in a somewhat different light. The consumer still cares about the characteristics of the houses but makes a discrete choice between houses rather than a continuous choice about the levels of the characteristics. The utility function and the bid function are identical to those in the hedonic model. The difference is in the choices the market presents to the consumer and the way in which the stochastic elements are assumed to enter.

The hedonic model seeks to predict house prices and assumes that there is a stochastic element that the researcher cannot observe. This may be due to omitted characteristics (which might introduce bias in the coefficient estimates), or it might be due to aspects of

---

[7] Details of the various estimation techniques are discussed below.

the negotiations between the buyer and seller that diverge from the competitive model because of search costs, etc. (which might be uncorrelated with the observed characteristics). The hedonic regression reveals an estimate of the expected value of the house given the characteristics and the expected contribution of each of the characteristics to that value. These expected marginal prices are used in the second stage.

The random utility models, on the other hand, take the sales prices as representative of market prices available to all consumers. This makes sense if the error in the hedonic equation is due to omitted characteristics, but may be less appropriate if search costs account for the unexplained part of prices. A given consumer makes a discrete choice among houses to maximize utility. The individual perceives the satisfaction he or she would receive from each of the N houses that is available. For example, house k would provide $u^k = U(\mathbf{z}^{*k}, x^k) = U(\mathbf{z}^{*k}, m - P^k)$, where U is the individual's true utility function, z^* is a vector of all the characteristics of the house that are important to the consumer, and P^k is the market price of that house. The randomness is introduced because the researcher does not know the true utility function or all of the characteristics. The consumer selects the house that provides the highest level of satisfaction, and receives $u = \max(u^1, \ldots, u^N)$.

This can be visualized in the context of the diagrams used earlier. In the top diagram of Figure 1, ignore $P(z)$ and assume instead that the only houses available are at the little circles. The individual considers each of the houses before choosing the one at z_0. Each of the other houses lies on a higher bid contour, which implies a lower level of satisfaction. The same concept is shown by the little circles in the lower diagram in Figure 1. The budget constraint only exists at those circles, and one can see that all but the chosen house would be on lower indifference curves. In actuality, the price-characteristics combinations would not all be on the hedonic price schedule but rather would be scattered in the neighborhood of it because of the error term in the hedonic regression. The hedonic model assumes the utility function is tangent to the hedonic price schedule, while the random utility model uses the actual prices. If the prices are truly available to all consumers, the prices that lie below the hedonic price schedule provide information on the shape of the bid contours in the random utility model that would not be available in the hedonic model. On the other hand, if transactions and search costs mean that each potential buyer only considers a subset of the houses used in the hedonic, then the curvature of the bid functions may be exaggerated in the random utility model if all the houses are consider to be alternative choices.[8]

The theory of the random bidding model, which was developed by Ellickson (1981) and modified by Lerman and Kern (1983), is quite different from the models discussed so far. It uses econometric techniques that are very similar to random utility models, but the theory is not based on an individual maximizing utility by choosing the best house as the previous models are. Rather it models the equilibrium in the housing market. It seeks to predict the type of individual who will have the winning bid for a house

---

[8] Discrete choice models are discussed further in Section 5 below.

with given characteristics in an equilibrium allocation. In fact, as originally proposed by Elickson, the model could not be used for welfare measurement. Lerman and Kern modified the model to utilize the information in the observed price (which would be equal to the winning bid), so that welfare measurement would be possible.

2.2. Theory of hedonic welfare measurement

The goal of most hedonic estimation in environmental economics is welfare measurement when there are changes in the quantities of some of the environmental characteristics. However, the techniques that must be used differ greatly depending on the type of environmental change, the transaction costs in the housing market, and the time period considered. The environmental change might affect only a small number of properties relative to the size of the market. This is the case of a localized externality [Palmquist (1992a)], and the hedonic price schedule will not be changed. On the other hand, the environmental change may affect a large part of the market, resulting in a change in the price schedule. The other dimension in which the welfare measurement techniques will differ is whether or not households move in response to the environmental change. They may not move because of the costs involved in moving or the short time period considered. Depending on the assumptions, the effect on consumers may be a change in quantities or prices.[9]

2.2.1. Localized externalities

If the hedonic price schedule does not change because of the limited scope of the environmental change and there are no transactions or moving costs, the consumers of housing services are able to get exactly the same bundle of characteristics in a house for the same price as before. Thus, their level of utility will be unchanged, and their willingness to pay or accept will be zero. However, the owners of the houses with the environmental changes will experience capital gains or losses, and this would represent the amount the owners would be willing to pay or accept for the change. The capital gains or losses can be forecast from the unchanging hedonic price schedule. This is the simplest case for hedonic welfare measurement.

The analysis can also be done for a localized externality when there are transactions and moving costs without estimating the bid functions in some cases [Palmquist (1992b)]. If those costs are low enough, the consumer will move to a house providing the original characteristics, the consumer's welfare cost will be equal to the transactions and moving costs. This will partially offset the gain to the owner. If the transactions and moving costs are high enough that the resident chooses not to move, these costs still provide an upper-bound to the welfare cost. If the costs cannot be quantified, then one must estimate the underlying bid functions [Bartik (1986)].

---

[9] In all these cases the property value models are only capturing the benefits associated with the place of residence. Benefits occurring away from home must be measured separately.

2.2.2. Nonlocalized externalities without moving

If there is a major environmental change, the localized techniques above are not appropriate. However, there may be reasons that the consumers do not move in response to the environmental change. For example, the transactions and moving costs may be substantial compared to the benefits of relocating because of the environmental change. Under such circumstances, the welfare measure must be based on the preference structure of the consumers and deal with quantity changes. A vast majority of the research on welfare measurement has dealt the welfare effects of changes in prices. In that case there is an intuitive metric for the gains or losses, the change in income that would leave the individual at a given utility level. These measures can be defined implicitly using the indirect utility function or explicitly using the expenditure function. For example, if a price falls, income can be reduced to maintain the original level of satisfaction. If prices are normalized by income, then effectively all normalized prices are scaled up to maintain the utility level. This maintains the new relative prices, changes income, and allows the consumer to optimize.

In quantity space, the analogous operations would involve the direct utility function and the distance function.[10] An increase in the quantity of one or more of the characteristics would allow the consumer to reach a higher level of satisfaction. This consumption bundle could be scaled back to return the individual to the initial level of satisfaction. This is the welfare measure for quantity changes proposed in Palmquist (1988) and Kim (1997). However, compensating by scaling the consumption bundle is only one way of returning to a given utility level. The duality between the expenditure function and the distance function is mathematically elegant, but it doesn't lead to the most useful welfare measures. In the short-run, if one or more of the environmental characteristics of a house change, the resident will not move. The bundle of characteristics cannot be scaled back proportionally to return the individual to a level of satisfaction the way normalized prices can be if income is changed.

The compensation returning the individual to a level of utility can be done in an infinite number of ways. Luenberger (1992) introduced a new dual form for the utility function, the benefit function. The benefit function selects a reference bundle of goods, $\mathbf{g}$. Any vector of goods $\mathbf{X}$ (not to be confused with the numeraire x used here) could be increased or decreased by some multiple of $\mathbf{g}$ to reach a reference level of utility. Chambers, Chung and Färe (1996) have extended Luenberger's benefit function to a production context and introduced an alternative name for it, a directional distance function. Formally, the benefit function $b(\mathbf{X}, u; \mathbf{g})$ is defined as

$$b(\mathbf{X}, u; \mathbf{g}) = \sup_{\beta} \{\beta \in \mathbb{R}^1 \colon (\mathbf{X} - \beta\mathbf{g}) \in \mathbb{R}^n_+, \ U(X - \beta\mathbf{g}) \geqslant u\}. \tag{21}$$

---

[10] The distance function (also called the transformation function) is a representation of a consumer's preferences that is dual to the more common direct and indirect utility functions and the expenditure function. Accessible discussions are in Anderson (1980), Weymark (1980), or Cornes (1992).

While this has been called a directional distance function, it should be remembered that it is based on a directional translation **X**, whereas the usual distance function uses scaling to the origin. If **g** is taken to be equal to **X**, then

$$b(\mathbf{X}, u; \mathbf{X}) = 1 - \frac{1}{D(\mathbf{X}, u)} \tag{22}$$

where $D(\mathbf{X}, u)$ is the usual distance function, but for other vectors **g** the two distance functions are very different concepts.

While Luenberger's benefit function achieves generality by not restricting **g**, the benefit function also has little policy relevance unless **g** is selected appropriately. In the hedonic model, the numeraire good x provides the natural choice for **g**: $(0, \ldots, 0, 1)$ where the last element is the x direction. The compensation should be measured in units of x. Because of the normalization, this provides a money measure, and it holds constant the quantities of the characteristics, which is appropriate for the policy changes being analyzed.[11] In what follows **g** always will be taken to be this vector.

Suppose that an initial vector of characteristics, $\mathbf{z}^0$, has one or more of its elements changed to $\mathbf{z}^1$. The initial level of utility is $U(\mathbf{z}^0, x^0) = u^0$, which can be expressed in terms of the bid function as $U(\mathbf{z}^0, m - \theta(\mathbf{z}^0, u^0; m)) = u^0$, and in terms of the indifference surface function as $U(\mathbf{z}^0, W(\mathbf{z}^0, u^0)) = u^0$. The benefit function initially is $b(\mathbf{z}^0, x^0, u^0) = 0$, where **g** is omitted and is understood to be $(0, \ldots, 0, 1)$. After the characteristics change, the utility in terms of the bid function is $U(\mathbf{z}^1, m - \theta(\mathbf{z}^1, u^0; m)) = u^0$, in terms of the indifference surface function it is $U(\mathbf{z}^1, W(\mathbf{z}^1, u^0)) = u^0$, or in terms of the benefit function it is, $U(\mathbf{z}^1, x^0 - b(\mathbf{z}^1, x^0; u^0)) = u^0$. As long as actual income does not change, the monetary welfare measure for the change in the quantity of the characteristics can be expressed in three alternative ways:

$$b\left(z^1, x^0, u^0\right) = \theta\left(\mathbf{z}^1, u^0; m\right) - \theta\left(\mathbf{z}^0, u^0; m\right) = W\left(\mathbf{z}^0, u^0\right) - W\left(\mathbf{z}^1, u^0\right). \tag{23}$$

The use of the benefit function for welfare measurement in a nonhedonic framework is discussed in Luenberger (1996). The use of the bid function is discussed diagrammatically in Palmquist (1991). The use of $W(\mathbf{z}, u)$ has not been previously suggested.

Equation (23) holds utility at its initial level. If one were to follow the nomenclature of Hicks (1956), this would be called "compensating valuation." If utility were held at its new level, this would be "equivalent valuation." In the literature today, the commonly used terms for these quantity welfare measures are compensating and equivalent surplus. However, when Hicks introduced these terms, he was referring to a distinctly different concept that was a welfare measure for changes in prices. Because the use of

---

[11] Madden (1991) in an excellent paper on demand rationing discusses a similar system where one good is unrationed (the numeraire x here) and all the other goods are rationed (the characteristics **z** here). His interest is in the substitute-complement classification in such a system. He shows that his R-classification corresponds to the Hicksian q-classification. Previous literature had incorrectly suggested an equivalence between the q-classification and a classification based on the Antonelli matrix or traditional distance function.

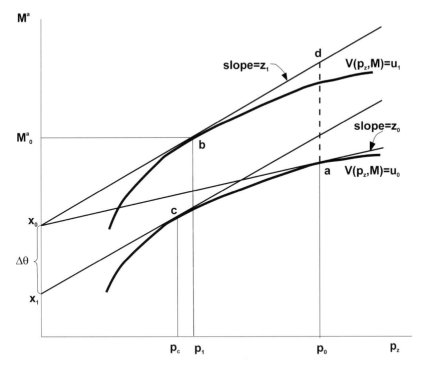

Figure 2. Welfare measurement and the indirect utility function.

the terms compensating and equivalent surplus for quantity changes is so widespread, the valuation and the surplus terms will be taken to be interchangeable. Compensating valuation and equivalent valuation will be denoted by CV_q and EV_q.

A diagram of an indirect utility function provides additional insights into these welfare measures. Figure 2 highlights one of the characteristics, holding the other characteristics constant in the background. The budget constraint has been linearized by using marginal prices and virtual income m_a. Typically prices are normalized by income, so $u = V(r_1, r_2)$ where r_i represents a price normalized by income. In that case, level curves of the indirect utility function would be shown in a diagram with normalized prices on both axes. In the hedonic model we have normalized by the price of the numeraire. The indirect utility is $u = V(p_z, m_a)$. Therefore, Figure 2 has p_z on the horizontal axis and m_a on the vertical axis. The level curves are upward sloping because higher prices would require higher incomes to maintain the level of satisfaction. The level curves are increasing at a decreasing rate because the consumer can substitute away from the characteristic as the price rises. Higher level curves represent higher levels of satisfaction ($u_1 > u_0$ in the diagram).

Linearized budget constraints, $m_a = p_z z + x$, can also be shown in the diagram. For a given level of z and x, as p_z increases, m_a must increase linearly to satisfy the budget constraint, and the slope is equal to z. If $p_z = 0$, then $m_a = x$. Typically, the dual problem is to select income-normalized prices to minimize the indirect utility function subject to the budget constraint. For the hedonic problem, one selects p_z and m_a to minimize $V(p_z, m_a)$ subject to the constraint. Thus given z_0 and x_0 the optimum is at a, the marginal price is p_0, the virtual income is m_a, and the level of utility is u_0. If there is an increase in z to z_1, the budget constraints rotates up, the optimum shifts to b, and the minimum value of the indirect utility function increases to u_1. In order to return to u_0, the quantity of the numeraire must be decreased from x_0 to x_1, and the tangency is at c. This maintains the new level of z and the original level of satisfaction. The amount by which x can be reduced, $W(\mathbf{z}_0, u_0) - W(\mathbf{z}_1, u_0)$, is the monetary welfare measure we are seeking. In terms of the bid function, $m_a = m - \theta + \sum p_i z_i$, so $\theta = m - m_a + \sum p_i z_i$. Since m and m_a do not change, the difference in bids, $\Delta\theta = \theta_1 - \theta_0$, can also be seen in the diagram.

Welfare measurement for changes in prices is often done by integrating to the left of compensated demands. There is no ambiguity because compensation in terms of income is the natural choice. Unfortunately, welfare measurement for changes in quantities using compensated inverse demands is not as clear. In fact, there are a variety of compensated inverse demands that could be used. It depends on what type of compensation is used to return the individual to a given level of satisfaction.

This can be clarified using the diagrams in Figure 3. The top diagram is an indifference curve diagram showing the initial position of the individual at z_0, x_0. The virtual price of z or the marginal willingness to pay for z is represented by the slope of the indifference curve at that point (the slope of the line tangent to the indifference curve at z_0, x_0). In the upper diagram, the various points z_i, x_i are labeled with the number i and the tangent lines are labeled with p_i at each end of the line. In the lower diagram p_i represents the price itself. Now assume that the level of the characteristic changes exogenously to z_1. The virtual price changes to p_1, the slope at the new tangency. The lower diagram shows the uncompensated inverse demand (labeled $p_z(z, x)$). It goes through the two points (z_0, p_0) and (z_1, p_1) where the prices are the slopes of the tangents. If x is normal, it will be downward sloping.

What sort of compensation should be used to return the individual to u_0? The most common compensation leads to Antonelli inverse demands [see Deaton (1979)]. However, note that the compensation using the distance function uniformly scales the commodity bundle to the reference level of utility, moving back towards the origin to point 3. The virtual price there is p_3. However, this associates z_1 with a virtual price at a different level of z. A more intuitive form of compensation is in terms of the numeraire, holding z constant. This takes us to the tangency at point 2 with virtual price p_2. This is exactly the type of compensation in the bid function when z changes and u and m are held constant. Thus, the lower diagram also shows this compensated inverse demand or marginal bid function.[12] It is labeled θ_z. If z is normal, $\theta_z(\mathbf{z}, u)$ will be more steeply sloped than $p_z(\mathbf{z}, x)$. The desired welfare measure can be obtained by integrating under

---

[12] Given the **g** vector discussed earlier, Luenberger (1996) would call this an adjusted price function.

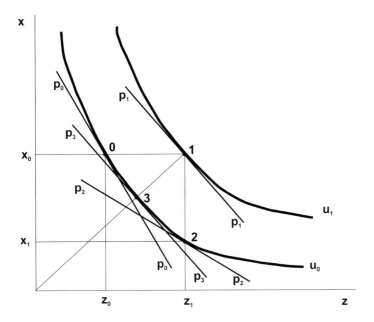

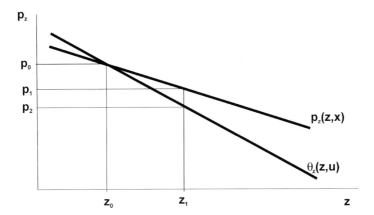

Figure 3. Welfare measurement and inverse demand functions.

this compensated inverse demand between z_0 and z_1 to obtain the compensating valuation CV_q.[13] Now consider the Antonelli compensated demand. The virtual price p_3 is

---

[13] It would be possible to obtain CV_q in terms of the more typical compensating variation. To simplify the notation, let $\theta_{z1}(z_1, z_2, u)$ be denoted as $\pi(z_1, z_2, u)$, the virtual price of z_1. Integrating by parts,

$$CV_q = \int_{z_{10}}^{z_{11}} \pi(z_1, z_2, u) \, dz_1 = \pi(z_{11}, z_2, u) z_{11} - \pi(z_{10}, z_2, u) z_{10} - \int_{\pi_0}^{\pi_1} z_1(\pi, z_2, u) \, d\pi$$

less than p_0 and greater than p_2 if z and x are normal, but we cannot say its relation to p_1. Integrating this demand will yield a higher willingness to pay, but it is based on an odd type of compensation.

The specific techniques for welfare measurement that are appropriate depend on the estimation that is done. One can start with an explicit form for the direct utility or subutility function and derive the estimating equations for a system of uncompensated inverse demands. The specified utility function can be inverted to get $W(\mathbf{z}, u)$ which can be used in developing welfare measurements.[14] An alternative would be to estimate a system of inverse demands that could have been derived from some unspecified direct utility function and use numerical methods to solve for the welfare measures.[15] The third alternative is welfare measurement when only the inverse demand for a single environmental variable is estimated. The techniques for an inverse demand and a quality change are similar to those developed by Hanemann (1980), Hausman (1981), and Bockstael, Hanemann and Strand (1984) for an ordinary demand and a price change.[16]

For example, suppose one estimates an uncompensated inverse demand using marginal prices from hedonic regressions and a log-linear functional form,

$$\frac{\partial P}{\partial z_1} = e^{\alpha} z_1^{\beta_1} z_2^{\beta_2} x^{\gamma} \tag{24}$$

where z_1 is the environmental variable of interest, z_2 represents all other housing characteristics, x is the numeraire (income minus the house price),[17] and the Greek letters are parameters. A standard duality result converts Marshallian demands to Hicksian demands by substituting the expenditure function for income. A similar change is possible here. Using the fact that $P_z = \theta_z$ and by substituting $W(z_1, z_2, u)$ for x and writing this in terms of the bid function, Equation (24) becomes an ordinary differential equation in θ,

$$\frac{\partial \theta}{\partial z_1} = e^{\alpha} z_1^{\beta_1} z_2^{\beta_2} (m - \theta)^{\gamma}. \tag{25}$$

where the last term is a compensating variation measure. However, the compensation must result in the actual quantity changes, so the virtual prices depend on those quantity changes. Also, the calculations are more complex, so it is easier to use CV_q.

[14] While some previous researchers have specified a utility function to derive the estimating equations, they have integrated the uncompensated inverse demands to derive welfare estimates rather than deriving exact welfare measures. Palmquist and Israngkura (1999) return to the utility function to estimate exact welfare measures.

[15] This would be analogous to the procedure of Vartia (1983) developed for integrating ordinary demand systems to an expenditure function. The algorithms would have to be modified for inverse demands integrating to $W(\mathbf{z}, u)$ or $\theta(\mathbf{z}, u, m)$, but conceptually it is possible.

[16] In this theoretical section the stochastic nature of the coefficient estimates is ignored, but the distribution of the welfare measures is discussed in the econometric section.

[17] By using the numeraire, the problems of the nonlinear budget constraint are avoided. The information about both income and inframarginal prices is incorporated. This also distinguishes Equation (24) from the marginal rate of substitution function discussed in footnote 4.

This differential equation is separable, so it can be solved analytically for θ,

$$\theta = m - \left[-(1-\gamma) \frac{e^\alpha z_1^{\beta_1+1} z_2^{\beta_2}}{\beta_1+1} + C \right]^{1/(1-\gamma)} \tag{26}$$

where C is the constant of integration that will depend on u but not z_1. Setting C equal to u, and inverting yields

$$u = (m-\theta)^{1-\gamma} + (1-\gamma) \frac{e^\alpha z_1^{\beta_1+1} z_2^{\beta_2}}{\beta_1+1}. \tag{27}$$

The condition for economic integrability is

$$\frac{\beta_1}{z_1} - \frac{\gamma}{m-\theta} P_z < 0. \tag{28}$$

If β_1 is negative and γ is positive, as would be expected, the integrability condition is fulfilled, although this is not necessary. This provides sufficient information to calculate the compensating valuation and equivalent valuation (compensating and equivalent surplus),

$$CV_q = \theta(z_1, u_0) - \theta(z_0, u_0)$$
$$= m - \left[-\frac{1-\gamma}{\beta_1+1} (e^\alpha z_{11}^{\beta_1+1} z_2^{\beta_2} - e^\alpha z_{10}^{\beta_1+1} z_2^{\beta_2}) + (m-P_0)^{1-\gamma} \right]^{1/(1-\gamma)} - P_0, \tag{29}$$

$$EV_q = \theta(z_1, u_1) - \theta(z_0, u_1)$$
$$= P_0 - m + \left[-\frac{1-\gamma}{\beta_1+1} (e^\alpha z_{10}^{\beta_1+1} z_2^{\beta_2} - e^\alpha z_{11}^{\beta_1+1} z_2^{\beta_2}) + (m-P_0)^{1-\gamma} \right]^{1/(1-\gamma)} \tag{30}$$

where z_{10} is the level of the environmental characteristic before the improvement and z_{11} is its level after the change, and P_0 is the initial price of the house. P_0 appears in both Equations (29) and (30) because the uncompensated change holds x constant, which implies the $m - \theta(z_1, u_1)$ equals $m - \theta(z_0, u_0)$. Since income does not change, this means $\theta(z_1, u_1)$ equals $\theta(z_0, u_0)$ which, in turn, equals P_0 from the consumer's optimization.

The cases of a semi-log and linear functional form are presented in the appendix to this chapter.

In the case of environmental changes where residents do not move, it is also possible to derive welfare measures from discrete choice models. Random utility models estimate the parameters of the utility function, which can be inverted to derive the bid function. Random bidding models derive the parameters of the bid function directly. In either case, once the bid function is estimated, the techniques discussed above can be used to develop the welfare measures.[18]

---

[18] Using discrete choice models to develop welfare measures is easier for housing than it is for recreation as long as residents do not move in response to the environmental change. With recreation models, one

2.2.3. Nonlocalized externalities with moving

The most difficult situation for welfare measurement using property values is when there is a major environmental change, the hedonic price schedule changes, and residents move. Most property value studies are used to develop welfare estimates before the environmental change takes place.[19] This means the researcher must forecast the change in the hedonic price schedule that will result from the environmental change. It is difficult to forecast a change in a scalar price for a homogeneous product, let alone forecasting the change in the entire price schedule for housing. Because of this difficulty, one alternative is to use the measures discussed in the last section as lower bounds to the true welfare measure [Palmquist (1988)]. How tight this bound will be depends on many factors and cannot be known *ex ante*.

Bartik (1988) has shown that the hedonic price schedule might provide an upper bound on the value of an environmental change, although this will not always be true. Because the bid contour is tangent to the hedonic price schedule from below, it is always true that the willingness to pay along that bid contour is necessarily less than the price change predicted by the initial hedonic. However, Bartik is considering the more general case where individuals move and the hedonic price schedule changes. He shows that the initial hedonic schedule may still provide some information about benefits. However, since this is not always an upper bound and we do not know how good an approximation it is, it is important that simulations be done to learn under what circumstances the approximation is accurate. If close approximations are possible using only the initial hedonic schedule, it will greatly reduce data requirements and further enhance the usefulness of hedonic techniques.

There is a promising alternative that has not yet been implemented in a hedonic framework.[20] As discussed earlier, the real estate market price equilibrium is established by a process that allocates each house to the highest bidder. The houses differ in their characteristics, and the consumers differ in their socio-economic attributes. Matching individuals to houses and determining the equilibrium price is a typical assignment problem. Environmental economists do not typically worry about this assignment problem because the market solves it for us. However, in a valuable pair of articles, Cropper

---

has to consider the changes in the sites visited in response to the environmental change. With housing and no moving, this is unnecessary. However, if residents move in response to the change, it is more complex than with recreation. With recreation, the prices (travel costs) do not change. A major environmental change affecting housing will result in a new vector of prices that must be forecast and incorporated into the welfare measures.

[19] Retrospective studies designed to analyze the benefits provided by environmental policies that have already been implemented are rare but not unheard of, for example, the retrospective analysis of the Clean Air Act. In a hedonic context, if the policy has already been implemented, the hedonic price schedule could be estimated both before and after the policy. Then the *ex post* hedonic welfare measures discussed in Palmquist (1988) could be used.

[20] Sieg et al. (2002) have recently used a related technique in a locational equilibrium model. This new technique will be discussed later in this chapter.

et al. (1988, 1993) have used an assignment model developed by Wheaton (1974) to simulate a hedonic market in order to better understand estimation issues. A similar assignment model could be used in a different framework to develop welfare measures.

We can observe the real estate market before the environmental change. Typical techniques can be used to estimate the hedonic equation and, at the second stage, the preferences of the consumers. Once the *ex ante* distribution of houses and individuals is known, a hypothetical environmental change can be introduced. The assignment model can then be used to allocate the consumers to the houses with the new characteristics and estimate the new hedonic price schedule. Now the change in the quantity of the environmental characteristic has been transformed into a change in the prices of houses. With this forecast of the *ex post* hedonic price schedule, techniques such as those discussed in Palmquist (1988) can be used to forecast welfare changes.

If one were using discrete choice models, one would also have to forecast the new prices of houses using the assignment model in order to introduce both price and characteristics changes into the welfare measures.

2.3. Differentiated factors of production and land markets

The models discussed so far deal with residential properties, and most empirical studies have used data on residential properties. However, only a small fraction of land is used for residential purposes, and there is the potential to use other types of land values to reveal some types of environmental benefits or costs. However, this land or property is a differentiated factor of production in this case, and the bids are from firms rather than consumers. The Rosen model can be modified to deal with this case, and the welfare measures are somewhat different [see Palmquist (1989)].

To date most such studies have dealt with agricultural land values.[21] Some of these studies have considered characteristics that have environmental implications, such as erosivity or the drainage of wetlands. Examples include Miranowski and Hammes (1984), Ervin and Mill (1985), Gardner and Barrows (1985), and Palmquist and Danielson (1989). There have been more recent hedonic studies of agricultural lands, but they have followed similar methodologies. An exception is a recent article by Bastian et al. (2002) that has used variables derived from a geographical information system to improve the spatial specification of the characteristics of agricultural lands. They find that nonagricultural characteristics can have a significant effect on rural land prices.

3. Estimating the hedonic price schedule

The most widely used of the property value models is the first stage of the hedonic model. This methodology uses data on sales prices for properties and the characteristics

---

[21] A good overview of agricultural land markets is Miranowski and Cochran (1993). Urban industrial and commercial lands have received considerably less attention in an environmental context. However, Ihlanfeldt and Taylor (2004) have recently studied the effects of Brown fields in such a setting.

of the properties. The type of data necessary for these studies is often readily available. Although some of the initial hedonic studies used census data, which are aggregated spatially and use owner-estimates of prices, today almost all studies use micro data. These are available from a variety of sources, including multiple listing services, assessor's offices, and companies specializing in real estate data. The first-stage does not require information on the individuals living in the houses, which greatly ease the data collection problems. The econometric issues are also simpler for the first stage, although there are some important estimation issues that must be addressed.[22]

3.1. Extent of the market

The hedonic price schedule is the equilibrium price schedule in a market. The researcher must be confident that the observations come from a single market. Early hedonic studies used market areas that varied from separate markets every few square blocks to nationwide.[23] It is difficult to determine the appropriate size of the market using statistical or econometric tests. The usual F-tests assume the equations estimated are correctly specified. As was pointed out earlier, theory provides almost no guidance as to the specification of the hedonic equation. If separate hedonic equations were run for two locations in a city and an F-test rejected the hypothesis that the coefficients were equal, this could be because there were two separate markets. However, it also might be because the functional forms were not appropriate or the equations were otherwise misspecified. Such misspecifications need not be significant economically, even if they are significant statistically.[24] Given the large sample sizes that are typical in hedonic studies today, F-tests will almost always reject combining areas in hedonic regressions.

For this reason, it is more appropriate to think about the types of transactions that are taking place in the area. As discussed in footnote 2, if there are a reasonable number of consumers who would consider the alternative areas, then those areas can be treated as a single market, even if many people only consider one or the other. If there are almost no consumers who would consider the two areas viable substitutes, they can be treated as separate markets. Most researchers today take an urban area to be a single market, although in large, consolidated areas such as Los Angeles one might choose to treat this as several markets. Even if one considers an urban area to be a single market, this does not preclude studying just a subset of that market if that is appropriate for the research question being asked. Problems only arise when separate markets are treated as one. In

[22] Smith and Huang (1993, 1995) have conducted an exhaustive meta-analysis of hedonic studies of air pollution over a 25-year period. While they find that a negative relationship between air pollution and property values is probably well established, the magnitude of the effect is influenced by data and modeling decisions. The meta-analysis provides both guidance on those decisions and an overview of one strand of the hedonic literature.

[23] See Palmquist (1991) for examples of this range.

[24] McCloskey (1985) and McCloskey and Ziliak (1996) strongly advocate shifting from statistical significance to economic significance in exactly such cases.

fact, there are often advantages to using smaller areas if the environmental issue can be addressed within that area (e.g., hazardous waste sites, highway noise, etc.). With more limited areas, one can avoid the complexity of fully specifying all the important characteristics that vary over an urban area but not within a neighborhood.[25]

3.2. Stability over time

Frequently a researcher would like to combine data over time. This may be because there has been an environmental change, or it may be to increase the number of useable observations. Whatever the reason, this is only valid if the contributions of the various characteristics to the value of a house have been relatively stable over that period. Intuitively, one would expect that consumers' tastes for the various characteristics relative to one another would change more slowly than changes in the overall housing price level, which may vary within and between years. It is possible to do statistical tests of aggregation over time, while allowing for changes in the real estate price index. For example, dummy variables for the year of the sale can be included in the hedonic regression where the dependent variable is the natural log of price. Frequently, though, F-tests reject aggregation over more than a very few years. Ohta and Griliches (1975) have suggested a less stringent guide to aggregation over time in hedonic regressions. As with aggregation over space, one would reject most aggregation over time if one used F-tests. An important consideration is the usefulness of the approximations such aggregation allows. They base their decision on comparing the standard errors of the constrained and unconstrained regressions. If the standard error increases by more than ten percent, they reject aggregation. Based on this guideline, aggregation over longer periods is often acceptable. This issue of aggregation over time is relevant both to hedonic applications and to the repeat sale model to be discussed later.

3.3. Functional form

The functional form of the hedonic equation has to be determined from the data. Early hedonic studies sometimes chose among simple functional forms such as linear, semi-log, and log-linear. As computing costs came down, greater flexibility was introduced. In an influential article, Halvorsen and Pollakowski (1981) suggested the use of the quadratic Box–Cox functional form. This allowed considerable flexibility, albeit local flexibility. Most of the commonly used functional forms were nested within the

---

[25] A recent study by Black (1999) on school quality takes this strategy one step further. School quality differs across school boundaries, but the nature of the neighborhood may not. Black focuses on houses within close proximity to boundaries. This natural experiment can control for omitted variables in the specification. This interesting strategy may not be useful for most environmental problems where there is continuous rather than discrete variation, but under the right circumstances it can prove useful. An excellent example of this type of natural experiment in a hedonic environmental context is Poulos and Smith (2002).

quadratic Box–Cox, so testing the restrictions was possible. However, computer limitations usually forced the researcher to have the same Box–Cox transformation applied to all the characteristics. If the interest was in a minor characteristic such as air quality, the transformation might be determined largely by other more important characteristics. The wrong transformation of the environmental variable could have a large impact on the environmental welfare measures. Because of this concern, Cassel and Mendelsohn (1985) advocated the use of simpler functional forms. A more flexible alternative was implemented in Israngkura (1994) where a separate transformation parameter for the environmental variables was introduced.[26]

Another potential problem with the quadratic Box–Cox is the possibility that omitted or misspecified variables in the hedonic equation might reduce the desirability of introducing greater local flexibility. This is exactly what Cropper, Deck and McConnell (1988) found in simulation studies on the accuracy of various functional forms in predicting marginal prices. The quadratic Box–Cox form did well when the estimating equation contained all the characteristics, although not particularly better than the linear Box–Cox. However, when there were omitted or incorrectly measured variables, the quadratic Box–Cox performed poorly. The linear Box–Cox and even simpler forms (linear, semi-log) did best. For the moment, the linear Box–Cox seems to be the best compromise, and having different Box–Cox parameters for the various characteristics is a promising next step.

3.4. Nonparametric and semiparametric estimation

Since neither the functional form of the hedonic equation nor the distribution of the error term can be known *a priori*, there has been some work on using nonparametric methods in the estimation. With nonparametric regression, the researcher need not specify parametric forms, but there are trade-offs. The robustness of the estimators comes at the cost of a reduction in the rate of convergence of the estimators. Larger sample sizes are important with nonparametric regression. This problem is aggravated as the number of independent variables increases. As Yatchew (1998) points out, "100 observations in one dimension would yield the same accuracy as 10,000 observations would in two dimensions and 10 billion would in five dimensions." Obviously, some restrictions are necessary. We will highlight smoothing with kernel estimators and semiparametric regressions.[27]

Suppose the price of a house, P, is hypothesized to be influenced by a vector $\mathbf{z}$ of n characteristics. For a given set of observations of houses, there is an $(n + 1)$-dimensional joint density $f(P, \mathbf{z})$. We are interested in an unspecified function $M(\mathbf{z})$

---

[26] A similar strategy has been implemented in Cheshire and Sheppard (1995), although not in an environmental context. A separate Box–Cox parameter is estimated for land area.

[27] For a more complete discussion of nonparametric estimation, see Ullah (1988), Härdle (1994), and Yatchew (1998). Pace (1993, 1995) has a fairly complete discussion in a housing context.

such that $P = M(\mathbf{z}) + u$ or $E(P \mid \mathbf{z}) = M(\mathbf{z})$. This is equal to

$$M(z) = E(P \mid z) = \int \frac{Pf(P, z)}{f_z(z)} \, dP. \tag{31}$$

Nonparametric estimation of this regression can utilize techniques for nonparametric estimation of a density function. The most commonly used method in the housing literature has been kernel estimation. Given T observations, one wishes to estimate the underlying density function. The estimated density at a point is a function of the observations near that point, with the weight given to an observation declining with distance from the point of interest. The kernel function assigns nonnegative weight to each observation, is usually symmetric and centered on zero, and the weights sum to one. A density function is often used as a kernel function. The normal is a common choice, although there are other possibilities that are used. The particular choice is usually not significant.[28] However, what is important is the dispersion of the kernel, which is referred to as bandwidth or window width.[29] For a univariate distribution let $K(w_j)$ represent the kernel function where $w_j = (x_j - x_0)/h$, x_0 is the point for which the density is to be determined, x_j is a data point ($j = 1, \ldots, J$ where J is the number of observations), and h is the bandwidth. The density function evaluated at x_0 is

$$\hat{f}(x_0) = \frac{1}{hJ} \sum_{j=1}^{J} K(w_j). \tag{32}$$

For a multivariate distribution let $w_{jk} = (x_{jk} - x_{0k})$, and

$$K(w_j) = \prod_{k=1}^{K} K(w_{jk}) \tag{33}$$

where $k = 1, \ldots, K$ is the index of jointly distributed variables, and $K = n + 1$ in our case.

Returning to the regression,

$$\widehat{M}(z) = \int \frac{P\hat{f}(P, z)}{\hat{f}_z(z)} = \sum_{j=1}^{J} P_j r_j(z) \tag{34}$$

where

$$r_j(z) = \frac{K(w_j)}{\sum_{j'=1}^{J} K(w_{j'})}. \tag{35}$$

---

[28] However, Stock (1991) did find it made a difference.
[29] For example, if the normal $N(0, h^2)$ is used as a kernel, h is the bandwidth.

Determining the bandwidth is crucial. There is a trade-off between bias (which decreases with reductions in bandwidth) and variance (which increases with reductions in bandwidth). Usually a bandwidth proportional to $J^{-1/(4+K)}$ is chosen if a uniform bandwidth is used. A variable bandwidth that is wider in the tails of the observed distribution is sometimes used.[30]

Not surprisingly, nonparametric regressions do not generate the usual parameter estimates obtained with parametric regressions. One can define $\beta_{ji} = \partial M/\partial z_i$ at point j as

$$\beta_{ji} = \lim_{h \to 0} \frac{M(z + h/2) - M(z - h/2)}{h} \tag{36}$$

or with an alternative proposed by Ullah (1988) that utilizes the kernels from the estimation. Either of these yields a regression coefficient that varies with the values of the explanatory variables. One can report a single coefficient estimator by evaluating β at the mean of the explanatory variables or by calculating β at each observation and averaging. It is also equivalent to the semiparametric estimates of a single index model, where $z\beta$ is a linear index that is then entered nonparametrically in the regression [see Pace (1995, and the references therein)].

Semiparametric estimators like the single linear index model improve convergence by imposing additional structure. One can use a partially linear model where, for example, $P = z_a\beta + M(z_b) + u$ where z_a is the vector of characteristics entered parametrically and z_b is the vector of characteristics entered nonparametrically. This substantially reduces the dimensionality problems. One can also assume additive separability between groups of explanatory variables to reduce the interactions.

There have been several applications of nonparametric and semiparametric estimation to housing. Pace (1993, 1995) has demonstrated nonparametric estimation with three different data sets and also applied a semiparametric estimator (the single index model) to one of them. Anglin and Gencay (1996) use a partially linear model where the dummy variables are entered parametrically and the continuous or count variables are entered nonparametrically. Stock (1989, 1991) also used a partially linear model with the town dummy variables entered linearly. Of these studies, two consider environmental conditions. Pace (1993) used the Harrison and Rubinfeld (1978) data from their study of air pollution. Using the census tract data he found that the nonparametric estimator was better able to deal with some erroneous observations. The averaged coefficient on the air pollution variable was reduced greatly in magnitude, although it was still significant. Stock (1991) studied hazardous waste sites using indexes based on weighted distances to the sites, size of the sites, and publicity about the sites. He considered the benefits from cleanups and found that the choice of the kernel affects the results.

---

[30] There are alternatives to kernel estimation, such as k nearest neighbor estimation or spline estimation [see Yatchew (1998)], but they have not been used in property value studies very much.

Environmental hedonic regressions must include a substantial number of character-istics of the houses. The environmental variables of interest generally play a minor role in the determination of price, and the equation must be well specified to obtain reliable estimates. This means that completely nonparametric estimation may prove difficult. Fortunately, many years of experience with appraisal techniques provides guidance on the parametric specification with respect to the major characteristics. It is with the en-vironmental variables that such guidance is not available. Entering the environmental variables nonparametrically in a semiparametric specification may yield valuable in-sights.

3.5. Measurement of the environmental variables

An important issue for all characteristics is the appropriate measure of the characteristic that will capture the way consumers view the characteristic. This is particularly relevant for the environmental variables since we are attempting to learn exactly that. Typically objective measures (micrograms per cubic, parts per million, etc.) are the easiest to obtain. However, if property values are to be affected, the pollutants have to be per-ceived by the residents. In some cases (for example, certain air pollutants), the objective measures may be highly correlated with what is perceived. In other cases, some trans-formation of the objective measure may be a better proxy for perceived levels. Often these transformations would suggest increasing marginal damages from the pollutant. However, if residents can take steps to mitigate the damages, marginal damages may not be monotonically increasing. As the level of the pollutant increases, at first the damages would increase at an increasing rate, but once the pollutant levels were high enough to induce averting behavior total damages might increase at a decreasing rate. Transfor-mation that allow such inflection points are sometimes useful but have not often been applied to date. Another technique that may be appropriate in some cases is combining readings on several pollutants into a single index.

A promising alternative to using objective measures is to use surveys to get at the subjective perceptions of the levels of environmental quality. The price of an individual house would not depend very much on the specific perceptions of the resident of that house because the price is the result of a market equilibrium determined by the interac-tions of all potential purchasers, not just the winning bidder.[31] However, knowledge of the relationship between the average perception of residents and the objective measures could be quite useful. The survey does not have to be of the same individuals or even the same area as the hedonic study.

The usual pollution measures focus on a single measure for each pollutant (annual arithmetic or geometric mean, annual second highest reading, etc.). However, the vari-

---

[31] The results in Poor et al. (2001) could be explained by this. They found that objective measures of water quality performed better in a hedonic regression than the subjective measures given by the resident of each house.

ability of the pollutant may be as important in some cases. Murdoch and Thayer (1988) study visibility considering not only annual mean but also variance and also the probability that visual range on a given day will be in each of four categories. While the variance has no explanatory power, using the probabilities instead of the mean is desirable. Further investigation of the distribution of pollution readings over time is desirable for fluctuating pollutants.

3.6. Other specification issues

The issue of multicollinearity is frequently raised in hedonic studies and is often used to explain problems encountered. Concern about these issues led Atkinson and Crocker (1987) to use Bayesian techniques to consider collinearity. They speculate (as do many others) that "(n)umber of rooms, number of bathrooms, house size, and lot size, for example, are highly collinear due to their nearly fixed proportions in housing construction." They are concerned that with collinearity the bias-variance trade-off can lead to substantial coefficient instability and that mismeasurement bias in some variables will be transferred to the variables of interest. They are really concerned about issues of specification and measurement that would be important even in the absence of degrading collinearity. Graves et al. (1988) consider these same issues using a different data set and emphasizing environmental variables.

Both articles use "focus," "free," and "doubtful" variables where focus variables are the variables of interest (environmental variables), free variables are well specified but not of interest (structural variables), and doubtful variables may or may not belong in the equation. They find that altering the specification of the doubtful variables can affect the magnitude and even sign of some focus variables. For example, Graves et al. (1988) find that the coefficient on visibility changed markedly when different combinations of doubtful variables were included, while the coefficient on total suspended particulates did not. Both articles also considered measurement errors in the focus and doubtful variables. An interesting result in Graves et al. (1988) is that measurement error in the environmental variables created problems, while errors in the other variables were less of a problem.

These results on variable choice and measurement are potentially quite significant and deserve further research. These issues would be exacerbated by multicollinearity. However, the question remains, is degrading multicollinearity a significant problem in estimating hedonic regressions. There has been some research on this topic. Using the diagnostic techniques developed by Belsley, Kuh and Welsch (1980), Palmquist (1983) estimated hedonic regressions for 14 cities with an extensive set of variables including four air pollutants. Only in one of the cities was there collinearity between a pair of the pollutants (one out of 39 possible pairs). There was collinearity between a pollutant and a nonpollutant variable in three cases (out of 53 possible cases). There was more frequent collinearity among the neighborhood variables, which were census tract data, but the environmental variables were not involved.

3.7. Spatial econometric techniques

In the past, almost all environmental property value studies assumed that the disturbances were spherical. The possibility of heteroskedasticity was occasionally considered, but the tools necessary to allow spatial autocorrelation were difficult to implement.
Recently, though, exciting progress has been made in spatial econometrics, and there
have been interesting implementations in urban and regional economics and, more recently, in environmental economics.

Allowing for serial correlation with time series data has been common for many
years. This difference in evolution between autocorrelation techniques with time-series
and cross-sectional econometrics is because of the difference in the complexity of the
problem. With time-series data, the autocorrelation is one-dimensional (the time dimension) and it may be uni-directional (the past may influence the present but not vice
versa). With cross-sectional data, the error term for a house can be correlated with the
error terms for houses in any direction. The problem is at least two-dimensional (three-
dimensional in the case of high-rises). To make matters worse, the relationships are
bidirectional. The natural ordering provided by time is not available spatially.

A different econometric issue is also considered in spatial econometrics, autoregression. It is possible that the price for a given house is influenced by the prices of other
houses nearby. If the prices of these other houses are included in the regression, they
are correlated with the error term with all the attendant implications.

Spatial autocorrelation and spatial autoregression are distinct concepts, although they
are often discussed together. Spatial autocorrelation is also referred to as spatial error
dependence or a spatially dependent error term.[32] In contrast, spatial autoregression is
also called spatial lag dependence, structural spatial dependence, or a spatial autoregressive dependent variable process.

With spatial errors there are two major approaches that have been followed. It is
possible to specify the error covariance (or correlation) matrix directly. Anselin and
Bera (1998) refer to this as "direct representation," following the usage in other fields.
Obviously all elements of the correlation matrix cannot be estimated independently, so
the correlation is generally hypothesized to be a function of the distance between the
two observations. This function, the correlogram, is usually assumed to take one of three
forms.[33] For early examples of this method applied to housing see Dubin (1988, 1992)
[see also Dubin (1998a, 1998b)]. Unfortunately, this method cannot yet deal with the
large data sets that are commonly used for property value studies.

The alternative to direct representation is the lattice approach. In this approach the
error for each house is assumed to be influenced by the errors at some neighboring
houses but not all houses in the sample (as is done with direct representation). This

[32] Pace and Barry (1997a) use the term "spatially autoregressive error process," but including the word "autoregressive" might be confusing.

[33] These functions are the negative exponential, Gaussian, and spherical. See, for example, Dubin, Pace and
Thibodeau (1999).

approach is preferable with data that are spatially aggregated (census tract, counties, etc.) because of the discrete observations, but it is also the most common technique used with disaggregated data. The method can be used with much larger data sets than direct representation. With the lattice approach, a spatial weights matrix is used to specify the neighbors and the weights they receive. An example is a spatial weights matrix where element w_{ij} is equal to 1 if observations i and j share a common border or are within a certain distance of each other ($i \neq j$), and 0 otherwise.[34] One can also have the weights decline with distance, reaching zero at a given distance.

More formally, spatial autocorrelation is modeled as

$$P = z\beta + \varepsilon \quad \text{where } \varepsilon = \lambda W \varepsilon + u. \tag{37}$$

In this equation, P is a vector of house prices, z is a matrix of characteristics, β is a vector of coefficients, and ε is vector of random error terms. W is the spatial weights matrix discussed above, λ is a scalar parameter to be estimated, and u is a vector of random error terms with mean equal 0 and variance–covariance matrix $\sigma^2 I$. Rewriting Equation (37) yields

$$P = z\beta + (I - \lambda W)^{-1} u \tag{38}$$

and so

$$E[\varepsilon \varepsilon'] = \sigma^2 [(I - \lambda W)'(I - \lambda W)]^{-1}. \tag{39}$$

Alternatively, the spatial autoregression model is

$$P = \rho W P + z\beta + u \tag{40}$$

where ρ is a parameter to be estimated. Here the prices of some neighboring houses influence the price of any given house. The spatial lag term $W P$ will be correlated with the error term. Equation (40) can be rewritten as

$$P = (I - \rho W)^{-1} z\beta + (I - \rho W)^{-1} u. \tag{41}$$

Comparing Equations (38) and (41) makes clear the similarities and differences in the two models.[35]

The spatial weights matrix must be specified by the researcher, and only λ or ρ is estimated. A good deal of judgment is involved in specifying W, and many articles estimate the models with several versions of W. The researcher must decide which covariances should be nonzero. Sometimes a specific number of nearest neighbors are given a nonzero covariance, while an alternative would be specify some distance where the covariance goes from nonzero to zero. Bell and Bockstael (2000) and Can (1992) use

---

[34] Actually the weights matrix is usually row-standardized so that the sum of the elements in any row is equal to 1. This standardization is useful for the estimation and eases interpretation [see Anselin and Bera (1998)].

[35] Spatial lags and spatial errors can be combined in single equation, but distinctly different weights matrices probably are necessary for successful estimation. This is often referred to as the general spatial model.

the inverse of distance with a cutoff distance (as well as some other specifications). The potential problem with this specification is the discontinuity in the weight at the cutoff distance. The inverse of the square of distance has also been used [Can (1992)], but with a cutoff distance the same problem arises. An alternative that avoids the discontinuity is used by Pace and Gilley (1997). They use the maximum of $1 - (d_{ij}/d_{max})$ and 0 where d_{ij} is the distance between house i and house j and d_{max} is the cutoff distance. Bell and Bockstael (2000) have recently introduced an interesting modification of weights that cutoff at a certain distance. Instead of estimating a single spatial autocorrelation parameter as in Equation (37), they estimate three parameters by introducing three weights matrices. Each of the three weights matrices has nonzero elements for different ranges of distances between the houses. The three spatial correlation parameters decline with distance, as would be expected.

The estimation of these spatial models raises some interesting issues. Most researchers have used maximum likelihood methods. However, the likelihood function involves the Jacobian $\ln \| I - \lambda W \|$. This involves repeatedly taking the determinant of an $N \times N$ matrix (where N is the number of observations) or finding the N eigenvalues of the spatial weights matrix [Ord (1975)]. Either of these can be quite difficult or impossible as N becomes large, although this limit is being relaxed with increased computing power and sparse matrix techniques. Pace and Barry (1997a, 1997b) have been important contributors to the use of sparse matrices for spatial econometrics, and estimation with sample sizes over 100,000 is now feasible.[36]

There are alternatives to maximum likelihood estimation that are used. For the spatial autocorrelation case, if λ were known, familiar generalized least squares techniques could be used. However, the estimation of λ is more complex than with time-series [see Anselin and Bera (1998)]. For spatial lag models, the endogeneity of the prices of neighboring properties can be considered using instrumental variables. Typically, the characteristics of the neighboring houses are used as instruments for their prices. Finally, Kelejian and Prucha (1999) have developed a generalized method of moments estimator for the spatial autocorrelation case. Bell and Bockstael (2000) have applied this estimator. This allows them to specify the three spatial weights matrices discussed above, something that currently would not be possible with maximum likelihood estimation.

There have now been a number of applications of spatial econometrics to urban property value studies, many of which have been cited above. Closer to environmental economics, a series of studies by Nancy Bockstael and her graduate students have used spatial econometrics to model land conversion and property values. Many of these studies have concentrated on open space and landscape indices [see Bockstael (1996), Geoghegan, Wainger and Bockstael (1997), Geoghegan and Bockstael (1995), Bell and Bockstael (2000)].

---

[36] With direct representation, the sample sizes that can be used are still relatively small. In the early article by Dubin (1988), the number of observations was restricted to 80 to allow the estimation to proceed. In Dubin (1998b) the sample was 1,000.

There are a few studies that consider typical environmental variables like air and water pollution. Pace and Gilley (1997) took the Harrison and Rubinfeld (1978) data set and reestimated the model using spatial econometric techniques. These data are at the census tract level and have been used previously by Belsley, Kuh and Welsch (1980). Pace and Gilley found that the spatial techniques reduced the sum-of-squared-errors by about 45%. The coefficient on the age of the house changed from positive to negative and significant, as would be expected. Finally, the coefficient on the air pollution measure fell by about 38% but was still significant.

Kim, Phipps and Anselin (2003) use spatial econometric techniques to study the effects of air pollution on property values in Seoul. They discuss both spatial lag and spatial error models, but the empirical results with the spatial lag model get the most attention. The houses were allocated to subdistricts and houses in the same and adjacent subdistricts were considered neighbors. They used both maximum likelihood and spatial two stage least squares. They prefer the latter because their maximum likelihood estimates impose normality. They also find that considering the spatial nature of the data reduced the coefficient on the air pollutant SO_2. However, because of the spatial lag, a spatial multiplier must be use in determining the marginal effect on a house price of a general marginal improvement in air quality. The marginal effect is $\beta_k[I - \rho W]^{-1}$. After this transformation, the estimated marginal effect with the spatial model was quite close to that with OLS. A final study by Leggett and Bockstael (2000) considers the effect of water quality in Chesapeake Bay on surrounding property values. They use both OLS and spatial error models. The coefficient on the water quality variable is relatively stable between the two models. Because of the importance of spatial considerations in both real estate and the environment, we should see increasing use of these tools.

3.8. Rental prices vs. asset prices

Most of the theoretical hedonic models abstract from the role of houses as an asset with a relatively long lifetime. Yet a majority of the environmental hedonic studies that have been done have used sales prices rather than rental prices. It is important to take this into account when interpreting the meaning of the coefficients on environmental variables.

The sales price (asset price) is the capitalized value of the anticipated future services provided by the house. The rental price is the value of those services over the coming month or other rental contract period. However, the difference between the two can be more than simply a financial calculation. If it is expected that there will be a change in the environmental conditions in the future, this expectation will be reflected in the sales price but not the rental price. The most stark example would be beach front property that is so close to the ocean that it has a beautiful view but is also expected to be washed away in the next storm. Ocean proximity might increase the rental price and reduce the sales price. Less dramatic examples are common.

One must be careful in interpreting the results of a study of hedonic sales prices. The researcher must specify the commonly held view as to the course of environmental change before determining what is being measured. In many cases this is well known, but in others its determination may require a separate research effort.

3.9. Timing of environmental impacts

When there is an environmental change, an important question is when the change is reflected in the property values. This issue also depends on information and expectations. Property values, since they capitalize future rents, provide information on residents' expectations. Property values often react before the environmental change. Property values also will adjust if people revise their expectations. Finally, an effect on property values requires that consumers are aware of the environmental conditions. These considerations can be considered by conducting hedonic studies at different times in the evolution of the changing environmental conditions.

There have been a number of studies that considered the timing of impacts. Many, but not all, have studied hazardous waste sites and related operations. One example is Kohlhase (1991). She studied toxic waste dumps in the Houston area to see when residents became aware of problems and how significant the effect on property values was. Her findings indicated that property values were not affected when the sites were operating but not well publicized. It was only after a site was placed on the National Priorities List of Superfund that significant negative effects on property values were found. A tentative encouraging finding was that after a toxic site was cleaned up, there seemed to be no residual effect.

A second example is Kiel and McClain (1995) where the effects of the construction of a hazardous waste incinerator were studied. They considered five stages starting with pre-rumor and going through rumor, construction, bring on-line, and finally ongoing operation. They ran separate hedonics for each stage and found there was no effect in the first two stages. During construction there was a significant negative effect on property values that became larger when the incinerator started operation. However, after it had been operating a while, the effect, while still negative and significant, returned to the lower level it had had during construction. Presumably, this occurred as the residents gained more information about the operation.

Dale et al. (1999) did a similar study of the impacts in different time periods from a lead smelter that was eventually closed and the site cleaned up. They find that, while there was a significant negative effect on property values while the smelter was operating and immediately after it closed, once the site was cleaned up, property values rebounded. The stigma of the smelter disappeared.

Information may be as important as clean up. Gayer, Hamilton and Viscusi (1999) found that property values surrounding hazardous waste sites were significantly reduced before the U.S. Environmental Protection Agency released its assessment of the sites and this effect was mitigated by the information subsequently released.

3.10. Repeat sales

A typical environmental property value study treats each observation as independent. However, frequently a data set will contain repeat sales of houses, and such data can provide additional information. Between sales, many of the characteristics remain unchanged. For observed characteristics this may or may not allow simplified estimation. For unobserved characteristics, repeat sales provide additional information that should be incorporated in the estimation. Environmental repeat sales studies have the most to contribute when there has been a change in the environmental quality.

Repeat sales real estate price indexes were developed by Bailey, Muth and Nourse (1963), and frequently have been applied in that context. However, the method was modified by Palmquist (1982) to estimate the value residents put on environmental changes. Certain assumptions are necessary for the simplest version. An unspecified general functional form for the hedonic equation is hypothesized except for three restrictions. Geometric depreciation is assumed. The environmental variable must be transformed so it has a linear effect on the natural log of the house price. Finally, the index of the change in real estate prices does not depend on the characteristics of the house. All three assumptions can be relaxed, although the last one is the only one that is very restrictive. With these assumptions the hedonic equation for house i at time t is

$$P_{it} = B_t g(z_i) \exp(\gamma E_{it}) \exp(-\delta A_{it}) \exp \varepsilon_{it} \qquad (42)$$

where B_t is the real estate price index at time t, E_{it} is the environmental variable at house i at time t, A_{it} is the age at the time of the sale, and $\varepsilon \sim N(0, \sigma^2 I)$. With repeat sales at t and t', the ratio of the prices can be formed, and the function $g(z_i)$ will cancel out.[37] The price index and depreciation are perfectly collinear, so if one cares about the price index it is necessary to use external information on the geometric depreciation rate of houses. On the other hand, if the only interest is in the environmental effect, this is not necessary. Taking the natural log of the ratio yields

$$r_{itt'} = -\beta_t + \beta_{t'} + \gamma E_{itt'} + v_{itt'} \qquad (43)$$

where r is the natural log of the price ratio, the β's are the natural logs of the B's, and v is the difference in the error terms in the two hedonic equations. The β's are the coefficients of a vector of dummy variables taking a value of 1 at t', -1 at t, and 0 otherwise. The environmental effect can be estimated without a complete specification of the characteristics or the functional form. If there are more than two sales, the correlation of the error terms must be incorporated in the estimation. Examples of the application of this technique are Palmquist (1982), Parsons (1992), Mendelsohn et al. (1992), and Poulos and Smith (2002).[38]

---

[37] If the characteristics of the house (other than age and environmental quality) have changed between sales, it will be necessary to incorporate those changes in the same manner as the environmental changes.

[38] Poulos and Smith (2002) is an example of how one can allow for changes over time in other hedonic characteristics.

There are some drawbacks to this technique. First, it assumes the hedonic equation $g(z)$ is stable over time. Second, it only uses data where there are two or more sales, which is usually a small fraction of the full data set. These problems have been relaxed recently in the real estate price index literature, and similar modifications will be possible in the environmental area. Case and Quigley (1991) used a stacked regression to combine a hedonic equation for houses that sold only once and resale equations for houses where the characteristics did and did not change between sales. They also allowed the parameters of the characteristics to vary over time. Estimated generalized least squares is used to allow for the three types equations. A later study by Hill, Knight and Sirmans (1997) generalizes Case and Quigley by incorporating serial correlation and using maximum likelihood joint estimation.

The objective of both papers was to develop a real estate price index, not to measure the effects of changes in characteristics. However, similar efforts in the environmental area should be productive. A panel hedonic study will utilize all the data that are available. Since the hedonic equation often changes over time, it will be important to allow for changes in $g(\mathbf{z})$. On the other hand, some of the sources of the error in the estimation relate to the specific house, so it also will be important to utilize this information in developing the error covariance matrix.

3.11. Search costs and time on the market

The basic hedonic model assumes that there is a perfectly competitive market with no significant transactions costs. In actuality, real estate markets are subject to a variety of transactions and moving costs. Some of these were important in developing the welfare measures earlier. The search costs in real estate markets are particularly relevant in determining if environmental conditions are completely captured in real estate prices or if some of the impacts take the form of longer selling times.

In selling a house, the owner determines a reservation price, accepting offers that meet or exceed the reservation price and rejecting others. The reservation price is set to maximize the expected value of the sale to the owner when the costs of waiting are considered. If a house is subject to an adverse environmental effect this may have two effects. The probability of receiving an offer in a given time period may be reduced since there may be fewer potential customers. On the other hand, the reservation price probably will be lower, which will lead to shorter duration on the market. Which effect dominates is an empirical question. The issue is important because waiting costs can be significant.

Real estate search costs and marketing times have been considered by some researchers in real estate [e.g., Miller (1978), Haurin (1988), Kang and Gardner (1989), Asabere and Huffman (1993)]. However, in an environmental context the issue has not received much attention except with respect to highway noise [see Nelson (1982), and the studies discussed there]. Huang and Palmquist (2001) have proposed a model of the impact of environmental disamenities on the duration of sales and used an econometric model to simultaneously estimate the reservation price equation and the duration equation. The results suggest that while highway noise has a significant negative effect on reservation and sale prices, it does not have a significant effect on duration. There is evidence that the reservation price is reduced as duration increases, which is the offsetting effect described above.

4. Estimating the demand for environmental quality

In the theoretical section we saw that some policy questions can be addressed using the information contained in the hedonic price schedule. One can establish whether or not there is a statistically significant marginal willingness to pay for an environmental improvement. For nonmarginal environmental changes it is possible to estimate or at least bound the total willingness to pay if the effects are localized. However, there are important environmental issues that are not localized. A nonmarginal change in environmental quality often will result in changes in the equilibrium price schedule for houses. Knowledge of the underlying preferences will be necessary to develop welfare measures. This is the reason that there has been considerable interest in using the hedonic model to estimate the underlying preferences, even though it is considerably more complex than estimating the hedonic equation.

Estimating preferences or demands for environmental quality in the hedonic model is usually done in two steps.[39] The estimation of the hedonic equation proceeds as described in Section 3. The parameter estimates from the hedonic equation are used to calculate marginal prices for the characteristics. These prices are combined with data on the quantities of the characteristics and socio-economic data on the purchasers to estimate the demands. This sounds like a straightforward procedure, but we now realize that the data and estimation requirements are quite stringent.

4.1. Identification

In his original article Rosen suggested that since a nonlinear hedonic price equation provided varying marginal prices within a single market, it would be possible to estimate the demand and supply functions for a characteristic.[40] However, for any one individual,

---

[39] As in other areas of econometrics, a limited information or two-stage estimator is less efficient than a full information estimator. Simultaneously estimating the hedonic equation and the demand equations has been proposed by Epple (1987). That possibility is also discussed in a recent methodological paper by Tauchen and Witte (2001). A good deal of structure must be assumed in the linear–quadratic structure in Epple model. In important work Ekeland, Heckman and Nesheim (2001) point out short-comings with the linear–quadratic model and are working on relaxing that structure. Their work is promising but only deals with a scalar characteristic, so empirical applications are still quite a ways away.

[40] Rosen was careful to distinguish between marginal bid functions (which hold utility constant) and uncompensated inverse demands which do not. In the literature that followed, that careful distinction has not always been maintained, perhaps because of Rosen's well-known diagram. However, it is the uncompensated demands or inverse demands that are estimated.

we observe only one data point on his or her demand function, the chosen house with a given amount of the characteristic and a given marginal price.[41] There are an infinite number of demand functions that could go through that point. If the demand function is to be identified, additional information must be used. This issue is not just the usual identification problem with the demands and supplies of characteristics, which was discussed by Rosen (1974). It is present even with micro data that are commonly used today, where only the demands and the price schedule often are estimated. Several of the researchers who initially implemented the Rosen model were unaware of this issue and unintentionally achieved identification through functional form restrictions.

The identification issue was demonstrated by Brown and Rosen (1982). They used the simple case where the hedonic price schedule is quadratic in the characteristics and the uncompensated inverse demands are linear in the characteristics. If we estimate the quadratic hedonic, the calculated marginal prices will be linear in the characteristics. If we try to explain the marginal prices with quantities of characteristics and socio-economic data, there will be nothing for the socio-economic data to explain. We just get the same information we got from the hedonic equation and are unable to identify the demands. Brown and Rosen suggest that data from separate markets or restrictions on the functional forms could be used to achieve identification.[42]

In a single market, identification can be achieved in several ways such as by excluding some characteristics from the demand equations, imposing restriction on the parameters, or by nonlinearities in the equations. In a sense, all of these imply *a priori* restrictions on the functional forms of the hedonic equation and the demand equations.[43] If the restrictions are correct, this is quite useful, although one cannot test the restrictions. Quigley (1982) restricted individuals to have identical generalized constant elasticity of substitution utility functions. With a homothetic utility function the varying marginal prices allow identification of the parameters of the utility function. Similarly, Kanemoto and Nakamura (1986) impose the restrictions on the bid function to achieve identification. Recently Chattopadhyay (1999) has shown that the nonlinearities in his functional forms allow him to meet the rank conditions with a linear Box–Cox specification for the hedonic equation and restricted forms of either the Diewert (generalized Leontief) or translog utility functions.

An alternative way of achieving identification is by using data from several markets. The markets could be separate spatially or temporally. It is necessary to assume that

[41] This point is easy to see by thinking about Figures 1 or 2. We observe the chosen point $\{z_0, P(z_0)\}$ or $\{z_0, x_0\}$ and the resulting marginal price at that point. Since we do not observe any other choices the individual would make, we cannot know if the bid function or utility function has the curvature shown. It would be observationally equivalent if these functions had more or less curvature, but that would imply very different demands.

[42] Ekeland, Heckman and Nesheim (2001) have recently pointed out that the Brown and Rosen (1982) identification problem has considerably less generality than is usually supposed.

[43] The discussion here focuses on identification of the demand functions and not the hedonic equation because the hedonic equation can always be identified because it does not include the socio-economic variables that are in the demand equations.

consumers with the same socio-economic profile have the same preferences, regardless of the city in which they live.[44] First, a separate hedonic price schedule is estimated for each market, and marginal prices are calculated for each resident. Then the demand function or system is estimated by combining data across markets. In different markets a particular type of individual would face different prices and make different choices because of that. Thus, we effectively observe as many different points on a demand function as we have markets.[45] If the assumption that an individual would have the same tastes no matter where he or she lived is appropriate, this method of identification is more acceptable than depending on a chosen functional form. However, one must have good data on the individuals' socio-economic characteristics. In some cases, one might want to interact the socio-economic characteristics with an attribute of the city in cases where the demand for the characteristic is influenced by that attribute. A nonenvironmental example would be the demand for central air conditioning being influenced by summer temperatures, but the technique might also be useful with some environmental issues. Separate markets have been used for identification in a nonenvironmental context by Witte, Sumka and Erekson (1979), Palmquist (1984), Parsons (1986), Bartik (1987), and Ohsfeldt (1988). The technique has been used by Palmquist (1983), Palmquist and Israngkura (1999), and Zabel and Kiel (2000) to study the demand for air quality and by Boyle, Poor and Taylor (1999, 2000) to study lake water quality.

4.2. Endogeneity

If the hedonic price schedule is nonlinear, both prices and quantities will be endogenous in the demand equations.[46] For example, for inverse demands the error term represents unexplained variation in the marginal price. If there were different draws from the error distribution, different marginal prices would result. Different marginal prices are associated with different quantities of the characteristics. Thus, both price and quantity are correlated with the error term. Least squares estimation is no longer consistent. Murray (1983) first raised this problem of endogeneity in the hedonic second stage, and Epple

---

[44] One can assume that consumers with the same socio-economic attributes have the same tastes no matter where they live and still expected that the hedonic price schedules will differ between cities. There are substantial frictions in moving firms and individuals between cities. For this reason, the distribution of different types of consumers may differ between cities. Also, because structures are a type of capital that is long lived, the existing stock may differ greatly between cities. These factors will result in different equilibrium price schedules between cities.

[45] Of course, for this to work the hedonic price schedules have to be sufficiently different in the various markets. Markets for a single city over short periods of time might not have sufficient variation. Spatially separated markets might also have this problem, but it seems less likely. Ohsfeldt and Smith (1985) conducted Monte Carlo studies on this issue.

[46] Some studies have used linear hedonic equations in the first stage and then used multiple markets for identification. If the linear functional form is appropriate, this avoids the endogeneity problem. However, it often will not be appropriate, and its use will introduce substantial measurement error in the marginal prices.

(1987) has analyzed it in depth. In addition, while actual income is exogenous, adjusted income or the quantity of the numeraire nonhousing good is also endogenous.

Given the endogeneity, the search for instruments begins.[47] A valid instrument must be uncorrelated with the error (orthogonality condition), correlated with the endogenous variable (relevance condition), and provide additional information or not be redundant (uniqueness condition). The orthogonality condition rules out using any of the other characteristics or marginal prices. If actual income and the demographic traits of the individual are not measured with error, they can serve as instruments.[48] When multiple markets are used, dummy variables for the different locations or times can be used. Finally, transformations of these potential instruments (e.g., powers of the variables or interaction terms) can be used.[49] While there are statistical tests of the orthogonality condition that can be done, one may create pre-test estimator problems.[50] Using theory to select instruments may be more appropriate.

It is not enough to have orthogonal instruments if the instruments explain little of the variation in the endogenous variable. While such weak instruments may provide an unbiased estimator asymptotically, there may be very large standard errors. In addition, for finite samples the estimator will be biased in the same direction as ordinary least squares. Bound, Jaeger and Baker (1995) demonstrate these potential problems. It is important to have instruments that, *a priori*, one would expect to be highly correlated with the endogenous variables. Lacking that, some techniques such as the one in Hall, Rudebusch and Wilcox (1996) have been developed to measure instrument relevance, but they may actually make the finite sample problems worse. However, Hall and Peixe (2003) have recently developed a method for selecting instruments based on their relevance that may avoid the problems of pre-testing. They suggest using Andrews' (1999) method to select orthogonal instruments and then their technique to select instruments that are relevant.

---

[47] It would be possible to avoid the use of instruments if one used full-information maximum likelihood estimation for the entire system including the hedonic equation. Assumptions about the distributions of the error terms (including cross-equation correlations) would be necessary. Such estimation has not yet been implemented.

[48] If the some of the demographics are measured with error, they will be correlated with the error and unacceptable as instruments.

[49] Examples of studies that have used these types of instruments with multiple markets are Bartik (1987), Boyle, Poor and Taylor (1999), and Palmquist (1984). Chattopadhyay (1999) used instruments in a single market. The other empirical studies used linear hedonic regressions. A recent study by Cheshire and Sheppard (1998) has attempted to use a different source for instruments. They use spatial lags in the way temporal lags are used as instruments in time series analysis. Unfortunately, spatial lags are not unidirectional and so cannot serve as valid instruments.

[50] Andrews (1999) has recently developed a method for selecting, from a set of potential moment conditions, the largest vector of moment conditions that is consistent with the data. These moment conditions can then be used in a generalized method of moment (GMM) estimator. The instrumental variable estimator is a GMM estimator. Andrews applies his method to the selection of instruments meeting the orthogonality condition. He shows that asymptotically this method selects all instruments that satisfy the orthogonality condition with probability one, so it may eliminate the potential for data mining.

If only weak instruments are available, one must make a choice between using weak instruments and not using instruments. Nakamura and Nakamura (1998) have argued that a policy of "always instrument" can be a mistake. Indeed, with weak instruments and finite samples, one may be accepting much higher variance for the estimates without eliminating bias. On a mean square error criterion, ordinary least squares may dominate. One must carefully consider the uses to which the results will be applied.

A closely related issue in estimating the second stage of the hedonic model is the fact that the socio-economic characteristics of the residents may be measured with error. This has not been an issue with the empirical applications mentioned above since they have used data on the individual purchasers. However, the difficulty of obtaining such data explains the small number of such studies. One could use aggregate data on socio-economic variables from census blocks or block groups, etc. to greatly expand the number of data sets available for this estimation. However, this measurement error will be correlated with the error term in the equation being estimated, and the same issues discussed above are present. However, the search for instruments will be that much more difficult because the socio-economic variables obviously cannot be used as instruments in this case.[51]

5. Discrete choice models

Discrete choice models represent an alternative approach to modeling consumers' preferences for the characteristics of heterogeneous housing. This topic has been introduced in earlier sections on the theoretical models and welfare measurement. This section provides more detail on the estimation techniques that are available and some of the applications that have been done. There are two types of qualitative models that have been used with property value models: random utility and random bidding models. Random utility models have had their greatest application with recreation demand, and the chapter of this volume on Recreational Demand Models provides much more detail on the technique. While there is a brief overview provided here, this section focuses on the issues that are most important with housing.

5.1. Random utility models

In random utility models each consumer is assumed to make a discrete choice between K houses.[52] The consumer knows all of the characteristics of each house that are relevant to him or her ($\mathbf{z}^{*k}$ for house k) and the exact form of the utility function, $U^k(\mathbf{z}^{*k}, x^k)$. However, the researcher does not know the exact specification of the true

---

[51] A related issue is the possibility that the errors in the behavioral equations are correlated for observations in the same group (e.g., block group). In this case, even small correlations can cause spurious reductions in the standard errors when aggregate data are used. Moulton (1990) has raised this problem.

[52] How the choice set is determined will be discussed below.

utility function, so the perceived utility provided by house k, $V(\mathbf{z}^k, x^k)$ is measured with error. For example, for house k,

$$u_k = U\left(\mathbf{z}^{*k}, x^k\right) = V\left(\mathbf{z}^k, x^k\right) + \varepsilon_k. \tag{44}$$

The individual maximizes utility by selecting the one house that yields the highest level of satisfaction,

$$\max U = \max\{u_1, \ldots, u_K\} = \max\left\{V\left(\mathbf{z}^1, x^1\right) + \varepsilon_1, \ldots, V\left(\mathbf{z}^K, x^K\right) + \varepsilon_K\right\}. \tag{45}$$

The probability of a consumer selecting house k is

$$\text{Prob}(k) = \text{Prob}\left[\varepsilon_{k'} < V^k - V^{k'} + \varepsilon_k \text{ for all } k' \neq k\right]. \tag{46}$$

The distributional assumptions made about ε determine the type of estimation done. The simplest estimation assumes the ε are independently and identically distributed as Type I Extreme Value, which leads to conditional logit. However, because this distributional assumption imposes independence from irrelevant alternatives (IIA), some studies have assumed a special case of the Generalized Extreme Value Distribution, which leads to nested logit.[53] This avoids IIA between nests, although IIA is assumed within nests.

The researcher must choose the functional form for the observed utility function $V(\mathbf{z}, x)$. The numeraire x is replaced by income minus the price of the house, $m - P$. The same coefficient(s) applies to income and the negative of price. The consumer's income does not vary between houses, but price does. One can use the estimated coefficient(s) on price to derive the implicit coefficient(s) on income. If the numeraire enters linearly, the estimated coefficient on price is the negative of the (constant) marginal utility of income. Early studies used a linear form for the utility function because it was easy to estimate. Subsequently, the characteristics were entered nonlinearly, although the $m - P$ term was usually entered linearly. Recently, researchers in the recreation literature have allowed for nonconstant marginal utility income, although this has not yet been done in the property value literature. This is unfortunate because, for most people, housing makes up a large fraction of expenditure. Assuming a constant marginal utility of income may be inappropriate. Modifying the estimation to allow for a varying marginal utility of income will be relatively straight forward, but the welfare measurement in some cases will become considerably more complex [see McFadden (1999), Herriges and Kling (1999)].

The demographics of the individual can be expected to influence the level of utility provided by a house with a particular set of characteristics. However, we are modeling the discrete choice the individual makes, and that person's demographics do not vary with the different choices. This means that demographic variables can only be entered in the estimating equation if they are interacted with one of more of the characteristics of the houses, since these will vary over the choices. By analogy with estimation with

---

[53] It is interesting that the frequently cited article where McFadden introduced GEV (and also sampling of alternatives, to be discussed below) was about the choice of residential housing [McFadden (1978)].

panel data sets, one could refer to this as allowing for fixed effects of the demographics. Random effects are discussed below.

An important difference between most recreational site choice studies and housing choice studies is in number of alternatives available. In estimating a general random utility model, the researcher uses data on the house chosen and all of the houses that could have been chosen but were rejected. Thus, each observation may use data on a large number of houses, making estimation time consuming. Fortunately, with conditional logit and nested logit, McFadden (1978) has shown that one only needs to use the chosen house and a random sample of the houses not chosen. If the sampling gives equal probability to the selection of each house that was not purchased (within a given nest for nested logit), the sampling rule satisfies the uniform conditioning property. Consistent estimates can be obtained with the sample if the uniform conditioning property holds. This sampling is possible because IIA holds within nests.

A closely related issue is the relevant choice set from which to sample. This is a complex issue here, as it is with all random utility models. The researcher wants to know the alternatives available to the individual, and time plays a crucial role in real estate markets. If a house is sold before the purchaser enters the market or comes on the market after the purchaser has closed on a house, it was not in his or her choice set. However, the length of time between entering the market and purchasing a house varies greatly between purchasers. In addition, when a person enters the market, he or she only considers a subset of the houses that are available. Only houses in a certain price range, or with certain characteristics, or in a certain part of the city are considered. Unfortunately, the researcher almost never knows this type of information. Obtaining it would require extensive surveying. For this reason, most studies have sampled from all house sales.[54] These choice set issues deserve further consideration.

Welfare measurement within the random utility models for housing is either simpler or more complex than for recreation, depending on the assumptions made. With recreation, if there is a change in some characteristics, some recreationists will decide to visit a different site because there are no transactions costs to doing so. The welfare measures for the change will require predicting the new site. However, the travel costs of visiting the sites are unaffected by the change. With housing there are substantial transactions costs of moving to a new house. It may be reasonable to assume that an environmental change alone will not result in moving. Then one does not have to predict the new locations and can use the estimated utility function to calculate the willingness to pay for nonmarginal changes. If there is movement, this still provides a lower-bound for willingness to pay for an improvement. However, if the environmental change is significant enough to induce moves, the equilibrium house prices will change, unlike travel costs. The random utility model alone is insufficient to predict those changes. However, the different utility functions estimated for different demographic types could be combined

---

[54] Palmquist and Israngkura (1999) experimented unsuccessfully with using the date of purchase to establish a population of houses that sold near that date from which to sample.

with information about the existing houses in an area using an assignment model similar to that discussed in the hedonic sections above to predict the new equilibrium prices. Then the welfare measurement techniques used for recreation could be applied. (See the chapter on recreation.)

Recently there have been interesting developments in the estimation of discrete choice models that represent potential improvements over logit and nested logit. In the past the errors were assumed to have some type of extreme value distribution because this yielded models that were tractable to estimate. With the advent of greater computing power and techniques such as simulated maximum likelihood and simulated method of moments, using more general distributions became possible. Multinomial probit models were estimate using a Gibbs sampler [e.g., McCulloch and Rossi (1994)] and the GHK simulator [e.g., Chen, Lupi and Hoehn (1999)]. However, while our capabilities are expanding, the number of choices still is somewhat limited, at least by the standards of housing markets. One of the main advantages of using probit is to avoid the restrictive assumptions such as IIA, but it is exactly IIA that allows us to use sampling to reduce the number of choices not selected. Research movement is this direction will probably be slow.

Another recent generalization may be more promising: random parameters logit.[55] It is assumed that individuals differ in unobserved ways and that the parameters in the logit model differ by individual. Since the coefficients cannot be observed for any individual, a density function for the expected value of each parameter is assumed. The probability of choosing a house then involves integrating over these densities. Again, simulated maximum likelihood can be used. The reason this technique may be more promising in the near term is that McFadden and Train (2000) have shown that any random utility model can be approximated arbitrarily closely with a random parameters logit model. With appropriate assumptions, sampling of alternatives not selected may be possible while maintaining the differences in the consumers. Random parameters logit has been used to allow individual differences even when nothing is known about the demographics of the purchasers. If information is available on the individuals, one can combine fixed effects (discussed above) with these random effects. Such techniques may be promising for property value studies.

Two important empirical applications of the random utility model to housing are Quigley (1985) and Chattopadhyay (2000), although only the latter focuses on an environmental issue. Both use nested logit with the nests being referred to as town or city, neighborhood, and dwelling, although each used data from a single metropolitan area. Quigley used about 600 households, while Chattopadhyay had a little over 3,000. Quigley used household income, while Chattopadhyay used income, race, and number of children. Socio-economic characteristics have to be interacted with housing

---

[55] This model has also been called mixed logit, random coefficients logit, and error components logit, often by the same authors. While this plethora of names is unfortunate, they do describe the technique. For an overview, see Train (1998) and the references there.

characteristics since they do not vary by choice otherwise. Quigley found that a linear utility function performed better than logarithmic or income interaction terms. The coefficients on the inclusive value terms were between 0 and 1 and had the correct relative magnitudes (σ higher for the town nest than the neighborhood nest), and were both significantly different than zero thereby rejecting IIA between nests. Chattopadhyay's results were similar using a Cobb–Douglas utility function with a type of demographic translating, although he could not reject IIA between neighborhoods. He also calculated welfare measures and compared them to hedonic results. The RUM welfare measures were generally less than those for the hedonic model and they were sensitive to alternative nesting structures.

There have also been some interesting simulation studies comparing RUM results to hedonic results, although conflicting evidence leaves the issue open. Quigley (1986) and Mason and Quigley (1990) used a generalized CES utility function and a distribution of income to predict a vector of equilibrium prices. They then compared the hedonic model with the discrete choice model when the errors introduced were of varying sizes. When the errors were small, the hedonic tended to underestimate willingness to pay, but the average underestimate was small. The discrete choice model had little bias, but the dispersion of the estimates was much larger. For larger errors, the dispersion with discrete choice was very large. While these studies seem to favor hedonics, the forms of the utility functions for the two techniques may have favored hedonics.

The alternative simulation was done by Cropper et al. (1993). Using the data generation techniques in their functional form simulation discussed earlier, they compared hedonic and discrete choice models. Their specification of the characteristics of the houses and individuals was more complete than in the Quigley studies. They also experimented with more functional forms. For marginal willingness to pay, the errors with the two models are roughly comparable. However, for nonmarginal changes the discrete choice models do much better. The study is well done, but since the results are contrary to those in Chattopadhyay (2000) and the Quigley simulations, further research can probably be justified.

5.2. Random bidding models

An alternative discrete model was proposed and implemented in Ellickson (1981). He suggested that the researcher could form a hypothesis about the form of the bid function rather than the utility function. This bid function would differ from the true bid, which would be known to the individual. As consumers interact in the housing market, each individual would have the winning bid for a house. Ellickson's interest was in predicting the type of household that would occupy different types of houses.[56] This requires that there be a relatively limited number of types of households. Some demographic attributes are naturally discrete (e.g., renting vs. owning and, to a lesser extent, race), but

---

[56] The random utility models, on the other hand, would predict the type of house occupied by a particular individual.

many are continuous (e.g., income). Categories must be established for these latter types of variables (e.g., income ranges), and this is done at a sacrifice of information. Assume that $t = 1, \ldots, T$ indexes the household types that have been created. In the theory section of this chapter, the true bid function for individual j was $\theta^j = \theta^j(\mathbf{z}, u^j, m^j, \alpha^j)$ with the notation defined earlier. Suppose individual j is of type t, and let j be a member of the set of all type t individuals, N_t. The bid function is $\psi_t(\mathbf{z}) + \varepsilon_{tj}$ where ψ_t is the common bid function for type t, and ε_{tj} is a individual-specific error term that subsumes u and m. Houses go to the winning bidder, so the probability that a family of demographic type t will occupy a house with characteristics $\mathbf{z}$ is

$$\text{Prob}(t \mid \mathbf{z}) = \text{Prob}\{\psi_t(\mathbf{z}) + \varepsilon_t > \psi_{t'}(\mathbf{z}) + \varepsilon_{t'} \text{ for all } t' \neq t\}. \tag{47}$$

Because the winning bid on a house is the maximum bid, the Extreme Value Distribution, which is usually used, has a theoretical justification in addition to its ease of estimation. That distribution also allowed Ellickson to estimate the model separately for subsets of the household types, an important consideration at the time of his research.

Ellickson correctly made the point that his model could not be used to estimate willingness to pay for characteristics because the parameter estimates were only indentifiable up to scale factor. Only differences in parameters between types and not absolute estimates were meaningful. If this problem could not be avoided, the random bidding model would have little relevance for environmental economics. Fortunately, Lerman and Kern (1983) modified the model to avoid this shortcoming. The researcher has another piece of information, the price for which the house sold, which can be assumed to equal the winning bid. This allows Equation (47) to be modified,

$$\text{Prob}(t, P \mid \mathbf{z}) = \text{Prob}\{\psi_t(\mathbf{z}) + \varepsilon_t = p \text{ and } \psi_{t'}(\mathbf{z}) + \varepsilon_{t'} \leqslant p \text{ for all } t' \neq t\} \tag{48}$$

so that all parameters are identified. This modification has increased the interest in the model.

Lerman and Kern also point out that the means of the errors depend on the group size and should be accounted for in the estimation unless a full set of alternative-specific constants is included. They also comment on the loss of information in the aggregation into groups of household types. They suggest an alternative where each individual is considered a type. This would use all data on the individual, but it requires that there be as many types as there are individuals in the sample. This introduces an unmanageable dimensionality. To deal with this, they suggest using a sample of the individuals. This is losing information in a different way, although it would allow comparison of the results obtained using different parts of the information contained in the data. In either case, this loss of information is the major drawback with random bidding models.

There has been one environmental application of the random bidding model.[57] Chattopadhyay (1998) used this third technique to go with his hedonic and random

---

[57] There have been a few nonenvironmental applications [see Gross (1988), Gross, Sirmans and Benjamin (1990)].

utility studies discussed earlier. Using the same data, he used a logarithmic specification for the bid function. He divided the households into four types by two categories of income and two categories of family size, and estimated all four sets of bid parameters in a single equation using dummy variables. He then compared the results to those from the hedonic model. They were quite close for both marginal and nonmarginal willingness to pay for characteristics. The random bidding model did seem relatively stable for alternative categorizations of the demographics. Chattopadhyay's conclusion is that the main advantage of the random bidding model would be if the interest were in the willingness to pay of different demographic groups.

6. Locational equilibrium models

The theoretical hedonic model describes an equilibrium, but there has been little formal work on modeling how that equilibrium would change if there were changes in exogenous factors. Empirical work with first-stage hedonic estimation has been limited to estimating a single equilibrium price function or, occasionally, a series of *ex post* equilibrium price functions to trace the shifts. Second-stage hedonic estimation has concentrated on the parameters of utility or bid functions. The discrete choice models have had the same goal. It is only recently that researchers have attempted to incorporate the estimation of preferences into models of the market equilibrium. At the moment there are two main ways in which this is being done. One is motivated by the jurisdictional equilibrium models developed by Dennis Epple and his various colleagues. These models, for example, Sieg et al. (2004), explicitly consider the environment. The other line of research extends the discrete choice models to incorporate equilibrium. Bayer, McMillan and Reuben (2002) develop the methodology and apply it to residential segregation, but the technique could be applied to environmental issues.

Epple and Sieg (1999) and Epple, Romer and Sieg (2001) developed a methodology for empirically implementing models of equilibrium with local jurisdictions and housing markets. The earlier theoretical models [e.g., Epple, Filimon and Romer (1993)] had assumed a stratification of communities by income and a resultant distribution of local public goods. Epple and Sieg introduced an unobservable taste parameter that allows a more general distribution of income within communities while maintaining the earlier theoretical insights. Their model concentrated on local public goods such as school quality and crime. The model is now being used not only for local public goods but also to value environmental goods. The model focuses on the equilibrium that is established by the location choices of the residents and recognizes that both continuous and discrete decisions are involved. Thus, the model builds on elements of the hedonic and discrete choice models but is a new approach. Welfare measurement is possible because the underlying utility function is estimated and a new equilibrium can be simulated. The technique also minimizes the requirement of micro data on the residents. However, these attractive features of the model require that it be tightly parameterized.

Sieg et al. (1999, 2004) are good examples of the work by these authors in this area. They use data from Southern California and focus on air pollution. Following Epple and Sieg (1999), they assume that households are mobile and consider housing market conditions, local public goods, and air quality in their location decisions. The local public goods and air quality are assumed to be the same across a community. The households differ by income and an unobservable taste parameter, and there is a joint density function for the two variables. An individual's utility depends on housing, the location good (which is a linear index of the local public goods and air quality), a composite numeraire, and the taste parameter. The indirect utility function, $V(p, g, y, \alpha)$, depends on the price of housing, the location goods index, income, and the taste parameter, in that order. The specific form of the indirect utility function maintains separability between the public goods index and the market goods, which include housing. The functional form is a variant of the CES.

The slope of an indirect indifference curve between p and g is central to the model. The maintained hypothesis of the single crossing property, introduced by Ellickson (1971), says that the slope of this indifference curve changes monotonically as either income or the taste parameter changes. Thus, a change in income will shift this indifference curve so that it intersects the original indifference curve only once. Preferences that are consistent with the single crossing condition will have three characteristics. The boundary indifference property says that some individuals will be indifferent between two adjacent communities in the hierarchy of communities. Stratification implies that, controlling for tastes, households stratify among communities by income, and controlling for income, they stratify by preferences for the public goods. The ascending bundles property says that ranking communities by housing prices yields the same ranking as ordering communities by local public goods provision.

The estimation of the model involves several steps. In the first step, hedonic techniques are used to generate a housing rental price index for each community.[58] The housing expenditures in each community depend on this index and the distribution of income in the community. The distribution of income within each community is obtained from the Census of Population. Data on schooling, crime, and air quality are used to form the public goods index. Then moment conditions for this index, the quartiles of the income distribution, and the quartiles of the housing expenditure distribution are used in a generalized method of moments estimator. The parameters of the joint distribution of income and tastes, the parameters of the indirect utility function, and the parameters of the locational goods index are obtained.

Since these parameters allow them to predict the locational equilibrium, they can predict the changes in houses price as residents move in response to a significant change in air quality. While conceptually this can be done with the hedonic and random utility models as suggested earlier, it has not been implemented. Thus, Sieg et al. (2004) have taken an important step in modeling the effects of large environmental changes on property values. For example, they are able to estimate the general equilibrium willingness

---

[58] For an expanded treatment of this step, see Sieg et al. (2002).

to pay for the significant improvements in ozone between 1990 and 1995 in Southern California.[59] They find that there are significant differences between the partial equilibrium welfare measures and the general equilibrium measures. For the entire study area, the general equilibrium measure is larger. It is also interesting that when the individual counties within the study area are considered, the general equilibrium measures are sometime larger and sometimes smaller. Since the housing price changes and the pollution changes differ between counties, this divergence is to be expected.

Bayer, McMillan and Reuben (2002) incorporate equilibrium concepts in a different way. They start with McFadden's (1978) random utility model for housing. They modify it by allowing for unobserved quality in each housing unit. They also allow the parameters on the housing characteristics to vary with the characteristics of the household. Finally, they allow for social interactions where a person's utility from a house can depend on the socio-economic characteristics of the neighbors.

The equilibrium concept is incorporated in an interesting way. For the moment, abstract from the varying parameters, social interactions, and unobserved quality. The conditional logit model gives the probability that household *i* selects house *h*. This probability is summed over all households. The assumption they make is that in equilibrium the sum of the probabilities will equal 1 for each house. They solve iteratively for the vector of house prices such that the sum of the probabilities for each house is equal to 1. They describe this as eliminating the excess demand or supply for each type of house, although it is not the same as having one individual have the winning bid for each house.

In the actual implementation, the varying parameters, social interactions, and unobserved quality make the estimation more complex. They use a contraction mapping similar the Berry, Levinsohn and Pakes (1995) and develop instruments for the endogenous characteristics using the characteristics of house that are far enough removed to not be neighbors in the social interactions. Once the model has been estimated, it can be used in simulations of new equilibria.

These two locational equilibrium models and similar models yet to be developed should prove useful in designing property value models for use in environmental economics.

7. Conclusions and directions for future research

This chapter has highlighted the diversity of models and techniques that can be used to study property values as a way of revealing the values individuals put on environmental improvements. In this context, the use of hedonic regressions is well established and widespread. The estimation of the underlying behavioral equations is less common, but recently significant progress has been made here as well. Similarly, the progress on

---

[59] The model can also predict the distribution of benefits among individuals. See Smith et al. (2004).

random utility models in other areas is beginning to have an impact on property value studies. Finally, the new locational equilibrium models are a promising area for further research. Each of these last three areas should grow as more and better data, computing power, and econometric techniques become available.

Throughout this chapter have highlighted areas where future research would be productive. A few can be mentioned here. The spatial nature of environmental problems is central to the use of property value models. The recent availability of geocoded data and spatial econometric techniques should have a major impact on this research area. Significant progress is possible on measuring environmental effects, reconciling subjective and objective perceptions of the effects, and allowing the effects to enter the models in a flexible, perhaps nonparametric, way. We should learn more about the relative strengths and weaknesses of the discrete choice model, the locational equilibrium model, and the hedonic model. A final area that will be very important is refining the welfare measures derived from property value models. This is the goal of the environmental use of these models, and there is still substantial room for improvement.

Acknowledgements

I would like to thank Kerry Smith, Wally Thurman, and Dan Phaneuf for useful discussions of many of the topics in this chapter.

Appendix A

Exact welfare measures using an estimated log-linear uncompensated inverse demand are given above. If the functional form of the estimates were semi-log or linear, the welfare measures are given below.

For a semi-log uncompensated inverse demand,

$$\frac{\partial P}{\partial z_1} = \exp(\alpha + \beta_1 z_1 + \beta_2 z_2 + \gamma x), \tag{A.1}$$

the differential equation is again separable, and the bid function is

$$\theta = \frac{1}{\gamma} \ln\left[\frac{\gamma}{\beta_1} \exp(\alpha + \beta_1 z_1 + \beta_2 z_2 + \gamma m) + \gamma u\right]. \tag{A.2}$$

The direct utility function is

$$u = \frac{1}{\gamma} e^{\gamma P_0} - \frac{1}{\beta_1} \exp(\alpha + \beta_1 z_1 + \beta_2 z_2 + \gamma m), \tag{A.3}$$

and the economic integrability condition is

$$\frac{\beta_1}{\gamma} < P_z. \tag{A.4}$$

The welfare measures are

$$
\begin{aligned}
CV_q = \frac{1}{\gamma} \ln\Bigg[\frac{\gamma}{\beta_1} [& \exp(\alpha + \beta_1 z_{11} + \beta_2 z_2 + \gamma x_0) \\
& - \exp(\alpha + \beta_1 z_{10} + \beta_2 z_2 + \gamma x_0)] + 1 \Bigg],
\end{aligned}
\tag{A.5}
$$

$$
\begin{aligned}
EV_q = -\frac{1}{\gamma} \ln\Bigg[\frac{\gamma}{\beta_1} [& \exp(\alpha + \beta_1 z_{10} + \beta_2 z_2 + \gamma x_0) \\
& - \exp(\alpha + \beta_1 z_{11} + \beta_2 z_2 + \gamma x_0)] + 1 \Bigg].
\end{aligned}
\tag{A.6}
$$

Finally, if the uncompensated inverse demand function is linear,

$$
\frac{\partial P}{\partial z_1} = \alpha + \beta_1 z_1 + \beta_2 z_2 + \gamma x,
\tag{A.7}
$$

the linear ordinary differential equation can be solved for

$$
\theta = \frac{\alpha + \beta_1 z_1 + \beta_2 z_2 + \gamma m}{\gamma} - \frac{\beta_1}{\gamma^2} + e^{-\gamma z_1} u
\tag{A.8}
$$

and

$$
u = \left(P_0 - \frac{\alpha + \beta_1 z_1 + \beta_2 z_2 + \gamma m}{\gamma} + \frac{\beta_1}{\gamma^2} \right) e^{\gamma z_1}.
\tag{A.9}
$$

The condition for economic integrability is

$$
\frac{\beta_1}{\gamma} < P_z
\tag{A.10}
$$

and the welfare measures are

$$
\begin{aligned}
CV_q = \frac{1}{\gamma} & \left(\alpha + \beta_1 z_{11} + \beta_2 z_2 + \gamma x_0 - \frac{\beta_1}{\gamma} \right) \\
& - \frac{1}{\gamma} \exp[\gamma(z_{10} - z_{11})] \left(\alpha + \beta_1 z_{10} + \beta_2 z_2 + \gamma x_0 - \frac{\beta_1}{\gamma} \right),
\end{aligned}
\tag{A.11}
$$

$$
\begin{aligned}
EV_q = \frac{1}{\gamma} & \left(\alpha + \beta_1 z_{10} + \beta_2 z_2 + \gamma x_0 - \frac{\beta_1}{\gamma} \right) \\
& - \frac{1}{\gamma} \exp[\gamma(z_{11} - z_{10})] \left(\alpha + \beta_1 z_{11} + \beta_2 z_2 + \gamma x_0 - \frac{\beta_1}{\gamma} \right).
\end{aligned}
\tag{A.12}
$$

References

Anderson, R.W. (1980). "Some theory of inverse demand for applied demand analysis". European Economic Review 14, 281–290.

Andrews, D.W.K. (1999). "Consistent moment selection procedures for generalized method of moments estimation". Econometrica 67, 543–564.

Anglin, P.M., Gencay, R. (1996). "Semiparametric estimation of a hedonic price function". Journal of Applied Econometrics 11, 633–648.

Anselin, L., Bera, A.K. (1998). "Spatial dependence in linear regression models with an introduction to spatial econometrics". In: Ullah, A., Giles, D.E.A. (Eds.), Handbook of Applied Economic Statistics. Marcel Dekker, New York, pp. 237–289.

Asabere, P.K., Huffman, F.E. (1993). "Price concessions, time on the market, and the actual sale price of homes". Journal of Real Estate Finance and Economics 6, 167–174.

Atkinson, S.E., Crocker, T.D. (1987). "A Bayesian approach to assessing the robustness of hedonic property value studies". Journal of Applied Econometrics 2, 27–45.

Bailey, M.J., Muth, R.F., Nourse, H.O. (1963). "A regression method for real estate price index construction". Journal of the American Statistical Association 58, 933–942.

Bartik, T.J. (1986). "Neighborhood revitalization's effects on tenants and the benefit–cost analysis of government neighborhood programs". Journal of Urban Economics 19, 234–248.

Bartik, T.J. (1987). "The estimation of demand parameters in hedonic price models". Journal of Political Economy 95, 81–88.

Bartik, T.J. (1988). "Measuring the benefits of amenity improvements in hedonic price models". Land Economics 64, 172–183.

Bartik, T.J., Smith, V.K. (1987). "Urban amenities and public policy". In: Mills, E.S. (Ed.), Handbook of Regional and Urban Economics, vol. 2. North-Holland, Amsterdam, pp. 1207–1254.

Bastian, C.T., McLeod, C.M., Germino, M.J., Reiners, W.A., Blasko, B.J. (2002). "Environmental amenities and agricultural land values: a hedonic model using geographic information systems data". Ecological Economics 40, 337–349.

Bayer, P.B., McMillan, R., Reuben, K. (2002). "An equilibrium model of sorting in an urban housing market: a study of the causes and consequences of residential segregation". Working Paper, Yale University.

Bell, K.P., Bockstael, N.E. (2000). "Applying the generalized method of moments approach to spatial problems involving micro-level data". Review of Economics and Statistics 82, 72–82.

Belsley, D.A., Kuh, E., Welsch, R.E. (1980). Regression Diagnostics. Wiley, New York.

Berry, S., Levinsohn, J., Pakes, A. (1995). "Automobile prices in market equilibrium". Econometrica 63, 841–890.

Black, S.E. (1999). "Do better schools matter? Parental valuation of elementary education". Quarterly Journal of Economics 114, 577–599.

Blomquist, N.S. (1989). "Comparative statics for utility maximization models with nonlinear budget constraints". International Economic Review 30, 275–296.

Bockstael, N.E. (1996). "Modeling economics and ecology: the importance of a spatial perspective". American Journal of Agricultural Economics 78, 1168–1180.

Bockstael, N.E., Hanemann, W.M., Strand, I.E. (1984). Measuring the Benefits of Water Quality Improvements Using Recreational Demand Models, vol. II, Benefit Analysis Using Indirect or an Imputed Market Methods. Office of Policy Analysis, U.S. Environmental Protection Agency.

Bound, J., Jaeger, D.A., Baker, R.M. (1995). "Problems with instrumental variables estimation when the correlation between the instruments and the endogenous explanatory variable is weak". Journal of the American Statistical Association 90, 443–450.

Boyle, K.J., Poor, P.J., Taylor, L.O. (1999). "Estimating the demand for protecting freshwater lakes from eutrophication". American Journal of Agricultural Economics 81, 1118–1122.

Boyle, K.J., Poor, P.J., Taylor, L.O. (2000). "Estimating the benefits of reducing non-point source pollution with a second-stage hedonic model". Working Paper, Department of Economics, Georgia State University.

Brown, J.N., Rosen, H.S. (1982). "On the estimation of structural hedonic price models". Econometrica 50, 765–768.

Can, A. (1992). "Specification and estimation of hedonic house price models". Regional Science and Urban Economics 22, 453–474.

Case, B., Quigley, J.M. (1991). "The dynamics of real estate prices". Review of Economics and Statistics 73, 50–58.

Cassel, E., Mendelsohn, R. (1985). "The choice of functional form for hedonic price equations: comment". Journal of Urban Economics 18, 135–142.

Chambers, R.G., Chung, Y., Färe, R. (1996). "Benefit and distance functions". Journal of Economic Theory 70, 407–419.

Chattopadhyay, S. (1998). "An empirical investigation into the performance of Ellickson's random bidding model, with an application to air quality valuation". Journal of Urban Economics 43, 292–314.

Chattopadhyay, S. (1999). "Estimating the demand for air quality: new evidence based on the Chicago housing market". Land Economics 75, 22–38.

Chattopadhyay, S. (2000). "The effectiveness of McFadden's nested logit model in valuing amenity improvement". Regional Science and Urban Economics 30, 23–43.

Chen, H.Z., Lupi, F., Hoehn, J.P. (1999). "An empirical assessment of multinomial probit and logit models for recreation demand". In: Herriges, J.A., Kling, C.L. (Eds.), Valuing Recreation and the Environment. Edward Elgar, Cheltenham, UK, pp. 141–162.

Cheshire, P., Sheppard, S. (1995). "On the price of land and the value of amenities". Economica 62, 247–267.

Cheshire, P., Sheppard, S. (1998). "Estimating the demand for housing, land, and neighborhood characteristics". Oxford Bulletin of Economics and Statistics 60, 357–382.

Colwell, P.F., Dilmore, G. (1999). "Who was first? An examination of an early hedonic study". Land Economics 75, 620–626.

Cornes, R. (1992). Duality and Modern Economics. Cambridge University Press, Cambridge.

Court, A.T. (1939). "Hedonic price indexes with automotive examples". In: The Dynamics of Automobile Demand. General Motors, New York, pp. 98–119.

Cropper, M.L., Deck, L., McConnell, K.E. (1988). "On the choice of functional forms for hedonic price functions". Review of Economics and Statistics 70, 668–675.

Cropper, M.L., Deck, L., Kishor, N., McConnell, K.E. (1993). "Valuing product attributes using single market data: a comparison of hedonic and discrete choice approaches". Review of Economics and Statistics 75, 225–232.

Dale, L., Murdoch, J.C., Thayer, M.A., Waddell, P.A. (1999). "Do property values rebound from environmental stigmas? Evidence from Dallas". Land Economics 75, 311–326.

Deaton, A. (1979). "The distance function in consumer behavior with applications to index numbers and optimal taxation". Review of Economic Studies 46, 391–405.

Dubin, R.A. (1988). "Estimation of regression coefficients in the presence of spatially autocorrelated error terms". Review of Economics and Statistics 70, 466–474.

Dubin, R.A. (1992). "Spatial autocorrelation and neighborhood quality". Regional Science and Urban Economics 22, 433–452.

Dubin, R.A. (1998a). "Spatial autocorrelation: a primer". Journal of Housing Economics 7, 304–327.

Dubin, R.A. (1998b). "Predicting house prices using multiple listings data". Journal of Real Estate Finance and Economics 17, 35–59.

Dubin, R., Pace, R.K., Thibodeau, T.G. (1999). "Spatial autoregression techniques for real estate data". Journal of Real Estate Literature 7, 79–95.

Edlefsen, L.E. (1981). "The comparative statics of hedonic price functions and other nonlinear constraints". Econometrica 49, 1501–1520.

Ekeland, I., Heckman, J.J., Nesheim, L. (2001). "Identification and estimation of hedonic models". Working Paper.

Ellickson, B. (1971). "Jurisdictional fragmentation and residential choice". American Economic Review 61, 334–339.

Ellickson, B. (1981). "An alternative test of the hedonic theory of housing markets". Journal of Urban Economics 9, 56–79.

Epple, D. (1987). "Hedonic prices and implicit markets: estimating demand and supply functions for differentiated products". Journal of Political Economy 95, 59–80.

Epple, D., Filimon, R., Romer, T. (1993). "Existence of voting and housing equilibrium in a system of communities with property taxes". Regional Science and Urban Economics 23, 585–610.

Epple, D., Romer, T., Sieg, H. (2001). "Interjurisdictional sorting and majority rule: an empirical analysis". Econometrica 69, 1437–1465.

Epple, D., Sieg, H. (1999). "Estimating equilibrium models of local jurisdictions". Journal of Political Economy 107, 645–681.

Ervin, D.E., Mill, J.W. (1985). "Agricultural land markets and soil erosion". American Journal of Agricultural Economics 67, 938–942.

Freeman, A.M. III (1993). The Measurement of Environmental and Resource Values. Resources for the Future, Washington.

Gardner, K., Barrows, R. (1985). "The impact of soil conservation investments on land prices". American Journal of Agricultural Economics 67, 943–947.

Gayer, T., Hamilton, J.T., Viscusi, W.K. (1999). "Private values of risk trade-offs at Superfund sites: housing market evidence on learning about risk". Review of Economics and Statistics 82, 439–451.

Geoghegan, J., Bockstael, N.E. (1995). "Economic analysis of spatially disaggregated data: explaining land values in a regional landscape". Presented at the Association of Environmental and Resource Economists meetings, Washington.

Geoghegan, J., Wainger, L.A., Bockstael, N.E. (1997). "Spatial landscape indices in a hedonic framework: an ecological economics analysis using GIS". Ecological Economics 23, 251–264.

Graves, P., Murdoch, J.C., Thayer, M.A., Waldman, D. (1988). "The robustness of hedonic price estimation: urban air quality". Land Economics 64, 220–233.

Griliches, Z. (1971). Price Indexes and Quality Change. Harvard University Press, Cambridge.

Gross, D.J. (1988). "Estimating willingness to pay for housing characteristics: an application of the Ellickson bid-rent model". Journal of Urban Economics 24, 95–112.

Gross, D.J., Sirmans, C.F., Benjamin, J.D. (1990). "An empirical evaluation of the probabilistic bid-rent model: the case of homogeneous households". Regional Science and Urban Economics 20, 103–110.

Hall, A.R., Peixe, F.P.M. (2003). "A consistent method for the selection of relevant instruments". Econometric Reviews 22, 269–287.

Hall, A.R., Rudebusch, G.D., Wilcox, D.W. (1996). "Judging instrument relevance in instrumental variables estimation". International Economic Review 37, 283–298.

Halvorsen, R., Pollakowski, H.O. (1981). "Choice of functional form for hedonic price equations". Journal of Urban Economics 10, 37–49.

Hanemann, W.M. (1980). "Measuring the worth of natural resource facilities: comment". Land Economics 56, 482–486.

Härdle, W. (1994). "Applied nonparametric methods". In: Engle, R.F., McFadden, D.L. (Eds.), Handbook of Econometrics, vol. 4. North-Holland, Amsterdam, pp. 2295–2339.

Harrison Jr., D., Rubinfeld, D.L. (1978). "Hedonic housing prices and the demand for clean air". Journal of Environmental Economics and Management 5, 81–102.

Haurin, D. (1988). "The duration of marketing time of residential housing". AREUEA Journal 16, 396–410.

Hausman, J.A. (1981). "Exact consumer's surplus and deadweight loss". American Economic Review 71, 662–676.

Herriges, J.A., Kling, C.L. (1999). "Nonlinear income effects in random utility models". Review of Economics and Statistics 81, 62–72.

Hicks, J.R. (1956). A Revision of Demand Theory. Oxford University Press, Oxford.

Hill, R.C., Knight, J.R., Sirmans, C.F. (1997). "Estimating capital asset price indexes". Review of Economics and Statistics 79, 226–233.

Huang, J.C., Palmquist, R.B. (2001). "Environmental conditions, reservation prices, and time on the market for housing". Journal of Real Estate Finance and Economics 22, 203–219.

Ihlanfeldt, K.R., Taylor, L.O. (2004). "Estimating the economic impacts of environmentally contaminated properties in an urban area". Journal of Environmental Economics and Management 47, 117–139.

Israngkura, A. (1994). Environmental benefit measures: a comparison between hedonic and discrete choice models. Ph.D. Dissertation, North Carolina State University.

Kanemoto, Y., Nakamura, R. (1986). "A new approach to the estimation of structural equations in hedonic models". Journal of Urban Economics 19, 218–233.

Kang, H.B., Gardner, M.J. (1989). "Selling price and marketing time in the residential real estate market". Journal of Real Estate Research 4, 21–35.

Kelejian, H.H., Prucha, I.R. (1999). "A generalized moments estimator for the autoregressive parameter in a spatial model". International Economic Review 40, 509–533.

Kiel, K.A., McClain, K.T. (1995). "House prices during siting decision stages: the case of an incinerator from rumor through operation". Journal of Environmental Economics and Management 28, 241–255.

Kim, C.W., Phipps, T., Anselin, L. (2003). "Measuring the benefits of air quality improvement: a spatial hedonic approach". Journal of Environmental Economics and Management 45, 24–39.

Kim, H.Y. (1997). "Inverse demand systems and welfare measurement in quantity space". Southern Economic Journal 63, 663–679.

Kohlhase, J.E. (1991). "The impact of toxic waste sites on housing values". Journal of Urban Economics 30, 1–26.

Leggett, C., Bockstael, N.E. (2000). "Evidence of the effects of water quality on residential land prices". Journal of Environmental Economics and Management 39, 121–144.

Lerman, S.R., Kern, C.R. (1983). "Hedonic theory, bid rents, and willingness-to-pay: some extensions of Ellickson's results". Journal of Urban Economics 13, 358–363.

Luenberger, D.G. (1992). "Benefit functions and duality". Journal of Mathematical Economics 21, 461–481.

Luenberger, D.G. (1996). "Welfare from a benefit viewpoint". Economic Theory 7, 445–462.

Madden, P. (1991). "A generalization of Hicksian q substitutes and complements with application to demand rationing". Econometrica 59, 1497–1508.

Mäler, K.-G. (1977). "A note on the use of property values in estimating marginal willingness to pay for environmental quality". Journal of Environmental Economics and Management 4, 355–369.

Mason, C., Quigley, J.M. (1990). "Comparing the performance of discrete choice and hedonic models". In: Fischer, M.M., Nijkamp, P., Papageorgiou, Y.Y. (Eds.), Spatial Choices and Processes. North-Holland, Amsterdam.

McCloskey, D.N. (1985). "The loss function has been mislaid: the rhetoric of significance tests". American Economic Review 75, 201–205.

McCloskey, D.N., Ziliak, S.T. (1996). "The standard error of regressions". Journal of Economic Literature 34, 97–114.

McConnell, K.E., Phipps, T.T. (1987). "Identification of preferences in hedonic models: consumer demands with nonlinear budget constraints". Journal of Urban Economics 22, 35–52.

McCulloch, R., Rossi, P.E. (1994). "An exact likelihood analysis of the multinomial probit model". Journal of Econometrics 64, 207–240.

McFadden, D. (1978). "Modelling the choice of residential location". In: Karlqvist, A., Lundqvist, L., Snickars, F., Weibull, J.W. (Eds.), Spatial Interaction Theory and Planning Models. North-Holland, Amsterdam.

McFadden, D. (1999). "Computing willingness-to-pay in random utility models". In: Moore, J., Reizman, R., Melvin, J. (Eds.), Trade, Theory, and Econometrics: Essays in Honour of John S. Chipman. Routledge, London, pp. 253–274.

McFadden, D., Train, K. (2000). "Mixed MNL models for discrete response". Journal of Applied Econometrics 15, 447–470.

Mendelsohn, R., Hellerstein, D., Huguenin, M., Unsworth, R., Brazee, R. (1992). "Measuring hazardous waste damages with panel models". Journal of Environmental Economics and Management 22, 259–271.

Miller, N.G. (1978). "Time on the market and selling price". AREUEA Journal 6, 164–174.

Miranowski, J., Cochran, M. (1993). "Economics of land in agriculture". In: Carlson, G.A., Zilberman, D., Miranowski, J.A. (Eds.), Agricultural and Environmental Resource Economics. Oxford University Press, New York, pp. 392–440.

Miranowski, J.A., Hammes, B.D. (1984). "Implicit prices of soil characteristics for farmlands in Iowa". American Journal of Agricultural Economics 66, 745–749.

Moulton, B.R. (1990). "An illustration of a pitfall in estimating the effects of aggregate variables on micro units". Review of Economics and Statistics 72, 334–338.

Murdoch, J.C., Thayer, M.A. (1988). "Hedonic price estimation of variable urban air quality". Journal of Environmental Economics and Management 15, 143–146.

Murray, M.P. (1983). "Mythical demands and mythical supplies for proper estimation of Rosen's hedonic price model". Journal of Urban Economics 14, 327–337.

Nakamura, A., Nakamura, M. (1998). "Model specification and endogeneity". Journal of Econometrics 83, 213–237.

Nelson, J.P. (1982). "Highway noise and property values: a survey of recent evidence". Journal of Transport Economics and Policy 16, 117–138.

Ohsfeldt, R.L. (1988). "Implicit markets and the demand for housing characteristics". Regional Science and Urban Economics 18, 321–343.

Ohsfeldt, R.L., Smith, B.A. (1985). "Estimating the demand for heterogeneous goods". Review of Economics and Statistics 67, 165–171.

Ohta, M., Griliches, Z. (1975). "Automobile prices revisited: extensions of the hedonic hypothesis". In: Terleckyj, N.E. (Ed.), Household Production and Consumption. National Bureau of Economic Research, New York.

Ord, J.K. (1975). "Estimation methods for models of spatial interaction". Journal of the American Statistical Association 70, 120–126.

Pace, R.K. (1993). "Nonparametric methods with applications to hedonic models". Journal of Real Estate Finance and Economics 7, 185–204.

Pace, R.K. (1995). "Parametric, semiparametric, and nonparametric estimation of characteristics values with mass assessment and hedonic pricing models". Journal of Real Estate Finance and Economics 11, 195–217.

Pace, R.K., Barry, R. (1997a). "Sparse spatial autoregressions". Statistics and Probability Letters 33, 291–297.

Pace, R.K., Barry, R. (1997b). "Quick computation of spatial autoregressive estimators". Geographical Analysis 29, 232–247.

Pace, R.K., Gilley, O.W. (1997). "Using the spatial configuration of the data to improve estimation". Journal of Real Estate Finance and Economics 14, 333–340.

Palmquist, R.B. (1982). "Measuring environmental effects on property values without hedonic regressions". Journal of Urban Economics 11, 333–347.

Palmquist, R.B. (1983). "Estimating the demand for air quality from property value studies: further results". Report to the Economic Analysis Branch, Office of Air Quality Planning and Standards, U.S. Environmental Protection Agency.

Palmquist, R.B. (1984). "Estimating the demand for the characteristics of housing". Review of Economics and Statistics 66, 394–404.

Palmquist, R.B. (1988). "Welfare measurement for environmental improvements using the hedonic model: the case of nonparametric marginal prices". Journal of Environmental Economics and Management 15, 297–312.

Palmquist, R.B. (1989). "Land as a differentiated factor of production: a hedonic model and its implications for welfare measurement". Land Economics 65, 23–28.

Palmquist, R.B. (1991). "Hedonic methods". In: Braden, J.B., Kolstad, C.D. (Eds.), Measuring the Demand for Environmental Quality. North Holland, Amsterdam, pp. 77–120.

Palmquist, R.B. (1992a). "Valuing localized externalities". Journal of Urban Economics 31, 59–68.

Palmquist, R.B. (1992b). "A note on transactions costs, moving costs, and benefit measures". Journal of Urban Economics 32, 40–44.

Palmquist, R.B., Danielson, L.E. (1989). "A hedonic study of the effects of erosion control and drainage on farmland values". American Journal of Agricultural Economics 71, 55–62.

Palmquist, R.B., Israngkura, A. (1999). "Valuing air quality with hedonic and discrete choice models". American Journal of Agricultural Economics 81, 1128–1133.

Palmquist, R.B., Smith, V.K. (2002). "The use of hedonic property value techniques for policy and litigation". In: Tietenberg, T., Folmer, H. (Eds.), The International Yearbook of Environmental and Resource Economics 2002/2003. Edward Elgar, Cheltenham, UK, pp. 115–164.

Parsons, G.R. (1986). "An almost ideal demand system for housing attributes". Southern Economic Journal 53, 347–363.

Parsons, G.R. (1992). "The effect of coastal land use restrictions on housing prices: a repeat sales analysis". Journal of Environmental Economics and Management 22, 25–37.

Poor, P.J., Boyle, K.J., Taylor, L.O., Bouchard, R. (2001). "Objective versus subjective measures of water clarity in hedonic property value models". Land Economics 77, 482–493.

Poulos, C., Smith, V.K. (2002). "Transparency and takings: applying an RD design to measure compensation". Working Paper, North Carolina State University.

Quigley, J.M. (1982). "Nonlinear budget constraints and consumer demand: an application to public programs for residential housing". Journal of Urban Economics 12, 177–201.

Quigley, J.M. (1985). "Consumer choice of dwelling, neighborhood and public services". Regional Science and Urban Economics 15, 41–63.

Quigley, J.M. (1986). "The evaluation of complex urban policies: simulating the willingness to pay for the benefits of subsidy programs". Regional Science and Urban Economics 16, 31–42.

Rosen, R. (1974). "Hedonic prices and implicit markets: product differentiation in pure competition". Journal of Political Economy 82, 34–55.

Sieg, H., Smith, V.K., Banzhaf, H.S., Walsh, R. (1999). "The role of optimizing behavior in willingness to pay estimates for air quality". American Journal of Agricultural Economics 81, 1112–1117.

Sieg, H., Smith, V.K., Banzhaf, H.S., Walsh, R. (2002). "Interjurisdictional housing prices in locational equilibrium". Journal of Urban Economics 52, 131–153.

Sieg, H., Smith, V.K., Banzhaf, H.S., Walsh, R. (2004). "Estimating the general equilibrium benefits of large changes in spatially delineated public goods". International Economic Review 45, 1047–1077.

Smith, V.K., Huang, J.C. (1993). "Hedonic models and air pollution: twenty-five years and counting". Environmental and Resource Economics 3, 381–394.

Smith, V.K., Huang, J.C. (1995). "Can markets value air quality? A meta-analysis of hedonic property value models". Journal of Political Economy 103, 209–227.

Smith, V.K., Sieg, H., Banzhaf, H.S., Walsh, R. (2004). "General equilibrium benefits for environmental improvements: projected ozone reduction under EPA's prospective analysis for the Los Angeles air basin". Journal of Environmental Economics and Management 47, 559–584.

Stock, J.H. (1989). "Nonparametric policy analysis". Journal of the American Statistical Association 84, 567–575.

Stock, J.H. (1991). "Nonparametric policy analysis: an application to estimating hazardous waste cleanup benefits". In: Barnett, W.A., Powell, J., Tauchen, G.E. (Eds.), Nonparametric and Semiparametric Methods in Econometrics and Statistics. Cambridge University Press, Cambridge, pp. 77–98.

Tauchen, H., Witte, A.D. (2001). "Estimating hedonic models: implications of the theory". Technical Working Paper 271, National Bureau of Economic Research.

Train, K.E. (1998). "Recreation demand models with taste differences over people". Land Economics 74, 230–239.

Ullah, A. (1988). "Non-parametric estimation of economic functional". Canadian Journal of Economics 21, 625–658.

Vartia, Y.O. (1983). "Efficient methods of measuring welfare change and compensated income in terms of ordinary demand functions". Econometrica 51, 79–98.

Waugh, F.V. (1928). "Quality factors influencing vegetable prices". Journal of Farm Economics 10, 185–196.

Weymark, J.A. (1980). "Duality results in demand theory". European Economic Review 14, 377–395.

Wheaton, W. (1974). "Linear programming and locational equilibrium: the Herbert–Stevens model revisited". Journal of Urban Economics 1, 278–287.

Witte, A.D., Sumka, H.J., Erekson, H. (1979). "An estimate of a structural hedonic price model of the housing market; an application of Rosen's theory of implicit markets". Econometrica 47, 1151–1173.

Yatchew, A. (1998). "Nonparametric regression techniques in economics". Journal of Economic Literature 36, 669–721.

Zabel, J.E., Kiel, K.A. (2000). "Estimating the demand for air quality in four United States cities". Land Economics 76, 174–194.

Chapter 17

CONTINGENT VALUATION

RICHARD T. CARSON

University of California, San Diego, USA

Q 5 1

D 6 1

W. MICHAEL HANEMANN

University of California, Berkeley, USA

Contents

Handbook of Environmental Economics, Volume 2. Edited by K.-G. Mäler and J.R. Vincent
© 2005 Elsevier B.V. All rights reserved
DOI: 10.1016/S1574-0099(05)02017-6

Abstract

Value estimates for environmental goods can be obtained by either estimating preference parameters as "revealed" through behavior related to some aspect of the amenity
or using "stated" information concerning preferences for the good. In the environmental
economics literature the stated preference approach has come to be known as "contingent valuation" as the "valuation" estimated obtained from preference information given
the respondent is said to be "contingent" on the details of the "constructed market" for
the environmental good put forth in the survey.

Work on contingent valuation now typically comprises the largest single group of
papers at major environmental economics conferences and in several of the leading
journals in the field. As such, it is impossible to "review" the literature *per se* or even
cover all of the major papers in the area in some detail. Instead, in this chapter we seek
to provide a coherent overview of the main issues and how they fit together.

The organization of the chapter is as follows. First, we provide an overview of the history of contingent valuation starting with its antecedents and foundational papers and then trace its subsequent development using several broad themes. Second, we put forth the theoretical foundations of contingent valuation with particular emphasis on ties to standard measures of economic welfare. Third, we look at the issue of existence/passive use considerations. Fourth, we consider the relationship of contingent valuation to information on preferences that can be obtained by observing revealed behavior and how the two sources of information might be combined. Fifth, we look at different ways in which preference information can be elicited in a CV survey, paying particular attention to the incentive structure posed by different elicitation formats. Sixth, we turn to econometric issues associated with these different elicitation formats. Seventh, we briefly consider survey design issues. Eighth, we look at issues related to survey administration and extrapolating the results obtained to the population of interest. Ninth, we describe the major controversies related to the use of contingent valuation and summarize the evidence. Finally, we provide some thoughts on where we think contingent valuation is headed in the future.

Keywords

contingent valuation, nonmarket valuation, consumer decision making, public goods, environmental economics

JEL classification: Q510, D610, D120, H400

1. Introduction[1]

Few environmental goods are bought and sold in the marketplace. For economists to move beyond an analysis of the cost-effectiveness of providing a specified level of a particular environmental good it is necessary to have some way of estimating the value of providing different levels of the amenity relative to its cost. Such values are most naturally expressed in monetary terms although other metrics are possible. These value estimates can be obtained by either estimating preference parameters as "revealed" through behavior related to some aspect of the amenity or using "stated" information concerning preferences for the good. In the environmental economics literature the stated preference approach has come to be known as "contingent valuation," as the "valuation" estimate obtained from preference information given that the respondent is said to be "contingent" on the details of the "constructed market" for the environmental good put forth in the survey.[2] The focus of this chapter is on contingent valuation (CV).

Contingent valuation is an inherently more flexible tool than revealed preference techniques such as hedonic pricing and the household production function approach. This is because it is possible in principle to use CV to examine environmental goods and terms for providing them that are different from what has been observed now or in the past. It is also possible in principle to create CV scenario experiments that avoid many of the economic modeling problems that are common to most observational data. Contingent valuation is also the only approach that can generally be used to include what is usually referred to as the existence or passive use component of the economic value of an environmental good. Offsetting these advantages are the problems that can arise with surveys and the reluctance by some economists to rely on information obtained from surveys. Such reluctance, however, is not neutral in terms of its consequences for policymaking.

Rather than seeing an inherent conflict between revealed and stated preference techniques, it is more productive to view the two approaches as complementary but having different strengths and weaknesses. Indeed, it is sometimes possible and useful to combine the two approaches.

The great advantage of the revealed preference approach is, of course, that it is based on actual behavior. The difficulty is that the tie between that behavior and the environmental good of interest is often complex and estimation of the implied economic value

---

[1] This work draws heavily upon our earlier work, and in particular: Carson (1991, 1997a, 1997b, 2000, in press), Carson, Flores and Mitchell (1999), Carson, Flores and Meade (2001), Carson, Groves and Machina (2000), Hanemann (1992, 1994, 1995, 1999), Hanemann and Kanninen (1999) and Mitchell and Carson (1989).

[2] A number of other terms have been used for deriving economic values from stated preference information in surveys. These terms often refer to the specific format in which the preference information is elicited and include among others: binary discrete choice, bidding game, direct (open-ended) question, (multinomial) choice experiment, choice-based conjoint analysis, contingent ranking, double-bounded dichotomous choice, paired comparison, payment card, and referendum question.

placed on a change in the environmental good is highly dependent upon both the underlying theoretical model postulated and the nature of the econometric assumptions made.
Less frequently recognized is that the observed behavior takes place in the context of
a particular market structure that may be substantially different from that in which the
policy change is going to occur.

Contingent valuation has the opposite set of characteristics. The tie between the underlying theoretical model and the information on preferences obtained in the survey is
usually quite close. There are, of course, econometric assumptions to be made but these
tend to be different in nature and relate to aspects of the distribution of economic values
and the nature of the survey data collection effort.

CV surveys differ from other surveys on public policy issues in several important
ways. First, a major portion of the survey is devoted to a description of the public good
(or goods) of interest. Second, the elicitation of preference for the good is more extensive and nuanced than in a typical opinion survey. Moreover, it involves the elicitation of
monetary (Hicksian) measure of welfare: maximum willingness-to-pay (WTP) to obtain
a desired good not currently possessed, or minimum compensation (WTA) to voluntarily
give up a good currently possessed. CV surveys have been used to value large discrete
changes such as the introduction of a new public good, the value associated with substituting one good for another, or the marginal value associated with changing one or
more attributes of an existing good. CV surveys are generally organized in the following manner which reflects current practice: (1) an introductory section identifying the
sponsor and general topic, (2) a section asking questions concerning prior knowledge
about the good and attitudes toward it, (3) the presentation of the CV scenario including
what the project was designed to accomplish, how it would be implemented and paid
for, and what will happen under the current *status quo* situation if the project were not
implemented, (4) question(s) asking for information about the respondent's WTP/WTA
for the good, (5) debriefing questions to help ascertain how well respondents understood the scenario, and (6) demographic questions. Mitchell and Carson (1989) provide
a comprehensive overview of the issues involved in the design and analysis of CV surveys, and Bateman et al. (2002) provide a useful manual for the practitioner.

In spite of the apparent simplicity that some see in asking people whether they would
be willing to pay some specific amount for a given item, contingent valuation has its
drawbacks with regard to providing useful information for policymakers. Much of this
stems from the fact that economists are not generally trained in the design and administration of surveys. Indeed, much of the usefulness of conducting a CV study has nothing
to do with explicitly obtaining an estimate of monetary value.

There is often not adequate awareness among policymakers and many economists
that the choice of the characteristics of the market constructed in the survey can, and
generally does, influence the nature of the economic valuation estimates obtained. In
this sense, the flexibility of contingent valuation is both a blessing and a curse in that,
unless adequate attention is paid, it is possible to obtain estimates that are not directly
tied to the relevant policy changes being considered by decision makers. A good CV
survey lays out the current *status quo* level of the good of interest and the potential

change in that level, the manner in which that change could be supplied, and how it would be paid for by the agent if supplied. It does so in a way that is both acceptable to the technical experts at governmental agencies and understandable to the general public. This brief description of the initial product of a CV study should also make clear that what is typically being valued is a program to provide the environmental good and not the environmental good alone.

The empirical results from a CV study provide a wealth of information about the population of interest's value of the program. Some of this is in the form of aggregate information, such as the aggregate of WTP used in neoclassical benefit–cost analysis or a summary statistic like median WTP (which has a well-known voting interpretation). Contingent valuation itself is agnostic as to the appropriate summary measure that decision makers should use. Contingent valuation studies generally generate information about the broad shape of the WTP (or WTA) distribution and typically information on how that distribution varies with respondent characteristics such as, income, geographic location, and the nature of the use of the environmental good. The nature of this heterogeneity in economic values is often of great importance to decision makers and explaining it is a key task in a CV study.

It is hard to overestimate the central importance of contingent valuation to modern environmental economics. Work on contingent valuation now typically comprises the largest single group of papers at major environmental economics conferences and in several of the leading journals in the field. Carson (in press) provides a bibliography spanning fifty years with over six thousand CV papers and studies from over one hundred countries. As such, it is impossible to "review" the literature *per se* or even cover all of the major papers in the area in any detail. Instead, we seek to provide a coherent overview of the main issues and how they fit together.

The vastness of the literature on contingent valuation also suggests another point that cannot be made too strongly. Contingent valuation is a generic approach to collecting survey information about agents' preferences in the context of a constructed market situation. It is impossible to make any valid general statement about the properties of contingent valuation without specifying more completely the nature of the application and the quality of its implementation. And, it is impossible for a single experiment or statistical test to say anything of substantial generality concerning contingent valuation [Randall (1998)]. Such tests, however, may be quite informative as to the properties of a particular type of CV application in a particular context.

The organization of this chapter is as follows. First, we provide a historical overview of contingent valuation starting with its antecedents and foundational papers and then trace its subsequent development using several broad themes. Second, we put forth the theoretical foundations of contingent valuation with particular emphasis on ties to standard measures of economic welfare and specification of models. Third, we look at types of value including issues concerning existence/passive use considerations and consider the relationship of CV to information on preferences that can be obtained by observing revealed behavior. Fourth, we look at different ways in which preference information can be elicited in a CV survey, paying particular attention to the incentive structure posed by different elicitation formats. Fifth, we turn to econometric issues associated with these different elicitation formats. Sixth, we briefly consider survey design issues. Seventh, we look at issues related to survey administration and extrapolating the results obtained to the population of interest. Eighth, we describe the major controversies related to the use of contingent valuation and summarize the evidence. Ninth, we look at the consistent of CV results with actual behavior. Finally, we provide some thoughts on where we think contingent valuation is headed in the future.

2. History of contingent valuation

2.1. Antecedents and beginnings

Even though economists have largely focused on market prices as the indicator of economic value, earlier writers such as Clark (1915) and Hines (1951) clearly saw that much of an individual's utility was driven by unpaid costs and uncollected benefits and that "market prices" did not exist for many of the more interesting quantities to economists. A theory of public goods developed through the work of economists such as Lindahl helped formalize the notion of an equilibrium set of shadow prices for public goods and the difficulties involved in obtaining them. Other economists such as Pigou began to articulate environmental harm as unpriced externalities that drove a wedge between social cost and private cost making market prices suspect for some purposes.

Bowen (1943) and Ciriacy-Wantrup (1947) were the first to propose the use of specially structured public opinion surveys to value what Bowen called "social goods" and Ciriacy-Wantrup "collective, extra-market goods" – goods such as "beautification of the landscape" (Bowen) or soil conservation (Ciriacy-Wantrup) that "cannot easily be sold to individual consumers and the quantities available to different individuals cannot be adjusted according to their respective tastes" (Bowen). Both Bowen and Ciriacy-Wantrup saw that a distinctive feature of these goods was that, while individuals would have their own distinctive demand curves for these goods, the aggregate demand curve is "obtained by adding the marginal rate of substitution (expressed in money) of the various individuals at each possible quantity of the social good (vertical addition)" (Bowen). The practical problem was to estimate the individual marginal rate of substitution curve "since it requires the measurement of preference for goods which, by their nature, cannot be subject to individual consumer choice." Bowen suggested voting as "the closest substitute for consumer choice" and he noted the possibility of using "polls, questionnaires, interviews" as a means to implement this: "If polls are based on a representative sample of the population, and if questions are put in the same way as if the entire citizenry were voting, the results can, of course, be interpreted in exactly the same way." Ciriacy-Wantrup (1947) covers the same ground and develops the same argument in the context of addressing the difficulties of measuring the benefits of soil conservation programs, and he reiterated his call for the use of the "direct interview method" in his influential book *Resource Conservation: Economics and Policy* (1952), which is often considered the first text book on environmental and resource economics. One major obstacle to Bowen and Ciriacy-Wantrup's calls for the use of surveys to measure benefits of public goods was that they soon clashed with Samuelson's seminal paper [Samuelson (1954)]. In this paper, Samuelson points out the problem of potential strategic behavior when aggregating over individual agents to get the benefit of providing a public good. Samuelson notes: "It is in the selfish interest of each person to give false signals, to pretend to have less interest in a given collective activity than he really has." In the penultimate paragraph of the paper, Samuelson pursues this point further with specific reference to the use of surveys:

> One could imagine every person in the community being indoctrinated to behave like a "parametric decentralized bureaucrat" who reveals his preferences by signaling in response to price parameters or Lagrangian multipliers, or to questionnaires or to other devices. Alas, by departing from his indoctrinated rules, one person can hope to snatch some selfish benefit in a way not possible under the self-policing competitive pricing of private goods.[3]

At roughly the same time a different debate played out between Lester (1946) and Machlup (1946) over whether companies were fully profit maximizing and pricing at marginal cost. Lester's work drew heavily on survey responses from businesses in interviews which suggested that they were *not* consciously maximizing profit in the neo-classical fashion. Machlup's attack relied heavily on disparaging the credibility of survey responses. Milton Friedman later weighed in with an instrumental view that people may effectively act like the rational maximizer of economic theory but did not realize they were doing so. As such, survey responses might be meaningless; and Friedman's analogy of the professional pool player not knowing the underlying physics behind the shot has long become part of the folklore of economists.[4]

Samuelson and Friedman's distrust of surveys played itself out in a variety of different areas of economics and to distance applied economic fields such as marketing and transportation from the economic mainstream.[5] What has always driven economists back to the idea of trying to collect nonfactual information for individual agents

---

[3] In this regard, the early experiment of Bohm (1972) played a key role by suggesting that strategic behavior might not play as large a role as once feared. The concept of strategic behavior was to become a major theme in the use of CV but not one that ultimately blocked its use [Mitchell and Carson (1989)] as economic theorists [e.g., Groves (1973)] started to explore the incentives faced by economic agents in different situations in a much more nuanced manner.

[4] Boulier and Goldfarb (1998) provide an interesting account of this part of the debate on the use of surveys by economists. Even though Machlup's view prevailed at the time, Lester might well be judged the ultimate victor, as a substantial amount of the research in industrial organization in recent years has gone toward explaining the "anomalies" he first identified.

[5] There is, of course, some irony in that almost all of applied microeconomics relies heavily on the use of data collected with survey instruments, typically by government agencies or in the form of large panel data sets like the Panel Study on Income Dynamics. Little attention is currently given by economists to the design of surveys to collect such data even though this was once an active area of research [e.g., Lansing and Morgan (1971)].

is the pressing need for it and lack of any other good way to get the data.[6] Nowhere has this need been more pressing than with public goods, where the major impediment to performing a benefit–cost analysis in many fields of applied economics is the lack of monetary values for the outputs of government policies.

2.2. Early empirical development

The first area where the lack of monetary numbers for a key output of government projects was considered to be a major problem was outdoor recreation. Here, there were two driving forces. The first was land based and involved the U.S. National Park Service and the U.S. Forest Service. The number of people seeking to recreate on government land exploded in the post World War II era, leading policymakers to recognize the need to know what people wanted and how much they were willing to pay for it. The obvious way to do this was to survey the public. The National Park Service engaged Audience Research Inc., a well-known marketing firm (associated with Gallup surveys) that specialized in determining the market value of products (such as movies that had not yet been released), to find out what the public wanted with respect to its national parks. These surveys were instrumental in developing the U.S. national park system in the 1950s and 1960s. Money to run the National Parks was always tight and to explore this issue Audience Research (1958) asked one set of survey respondents about their willingness to pay a day use fee. This question can be seen as the immediate precursor to the use of contingent valuation as an input to the economic evaluation of a project.

The second driving force was water based and involved the U.S. Army Corp of Engineers and other agencies building the major water projects of the 1950s and 1960s. It was on these projects that benefit–cost analysis evolved into its modern form and became institutionalized as a key component of government decision making.[7] Water based recreation along with electricity and flood control were the key outputs of many water projects. Such projects looked considerably less attractive if recreation was unpriced. This led to considerable interest in developing methods to reliably place a monetary value on different types of outdoor recreation.

Davis (1963a) was the first economist to empirically implement a CV survey in his Harvard dissertation entitled "The value of outdoor recreation: an economic study of the Maine woods."[8] Surprisingly, Davis was unaware of Ciriacy-Wantrup's suggestion

---

[6] See, for instance, Arrow (1958), Schelling (1968), Mishan (1976), McFadden (1986), Blinder (1991), and Manski and Straub (2000).

[7] In particular, see U.S. Congress, Senate Committee on Public Works (1957), Eckstein (1958), and Krutilla and Eckstein (1958). Hanemann (1992) provides an interesting account of the key role of water projects in driving developments in benefit–cost analysis.

[8] Davis notes as earlier antecedents the 1958 Audience Research study noted above, a master's thesis by Bruce Stewart (1961) at the University of Maine that asked about willingness to pay for improvements respondents thought desirable, and unpublished work by Ullman and Volk (1961) at Washington University (St. Louis) that asked respondents about their willingness to travel farther to recreate at a new lake. None of these studies bears much resemblance to the Davis dissertation which even today seems remarkably "modern" in its conceptualization of many of the major issues involving the use of CV.

to interview people to measure values associated with natural resources.[9] Davis was, however, strongly influenced by Stanley Stouffer, one of the country's leading academic survey researchers, who at the time was teaching a course in survey methods in Harvard's Social Relations Department. After sitting in on Stouffer's course, Davis reasoned that it should be possible to "approximate a market" in a survey by describing alternative kinds of areas and facilities to make available to the public, and then simulate market bidding behavior."[10] This method he later wrote (1963b), "would put the interviewer in the position of a seller who elicits the highest possible bid from the user for the services being offered."

Davis's dissertation sparked considerable interest in the technique. His dissertation is remarkable from several perspectives. It is comprehensive in terms of its treatment of theoretical economic issues, survey design and sampling issues, as well as statistical issues related to the analysis and interpretation of the data collected. Davis foresaw many of the key issues that later CV researchers would grapple with and researchers currently working on CV studies can still benefit from the insights in his dissertation.

Davis approached contingent valuation from a public finance perspective and was concerned with the need, in the context of a benefit–cost analysis, to measure all of the benefits and costs in monetary terms.[11] To quote Davis (1963a, p. 3):

> The temptations to patch up a benefit–cost statement for recreation in federal projects notwithstanding, the conclusions about our inability to do this in the absence of market prices or their surrogates are incontrovertible. Indeed, if there are no market valuations available, then the outdoor recreation services produced by an investment must be lumped with the intangible results and subjected to the non-quantitative, verbal analysis. At best a marginal production cost can be assigned to outdoor recreation facilities and the valuation of benefits arrived through administrative and political process.

Davis later compared a CV estimate to a corresponding estimate based on the travel cost method [an indirect approach developed at roughly the same time at Resources for the Future by Clawson and Knetsch (1966)] and found the two approaches produced similar estimates [Knetsch and Davis (1966)]. This was to be the first test of "convergent validity" whereby, the estimates from two different valuation techniques expected to produce similar estimates are compared.

---

[9] Davis was aware of Ciriacy-Wantrup's view that public natural resource problems involved issues of external benefits and costs and cites a chapter by him in an edited volume to this effect.

[10] Davis, personal communication, June 16, 1986.

[11] Otto Eckstein was Davis's dissertation adviser. Davis credits John Kenneth Gailbraith with being "instrumental in getting the study launched as a thesis topic." Resources for the Future provided Davis with a dissertation grant in 1961 and employed him in Washington during the final year of working on his dissertation. While at Resources for the Future, Davis was influenced by Marion Clawson, Irving Fox, John Krutilla, Allen Kneese, and Jack Knetsch.

Influenced by Davis, Ronald Ridker (1967) used the CV method in several studies of air pollution benefits. Although the primary thrust of Ridker's work was to value reducing dirty and soot from air pollution by using the hedonic pricing approach [Ridker (1967), Ridker and Henning (1967)], it was his recognition that people might value air pollution because of its "psychic costs" that led him to include a couple of WTP questions in two different surveys he conducted in Philadelphia and Syracuse in 1965. These questions, which asked people how much they would be willing to pay to avoid "dirt and soot" from air pollution, lacked many of the refinements that were later developed for CV surveys. In reflecting on his experience with the survey questions, including the WTP questions, Ridker made an observation that prefigured the later developments in CV research:

> It now seems evident that a much narrower, deeper, and psychologically sophisticated questionnaire is required to measure and untangle the various determinants of cleaning costs. Such a questionnaire would require substantially more time and expenditure-perhaps three to four times greater-than went into this essentially exploratory study. Even then the probability of success may not be very high, for such a project would raise problems in survey design that have not yet been solved. [Ridker (1967, p. 84)]

Over the next few years several other economists associated with Resources for the Future followed Davis's lead and used the CV approach to value various recreational amenities. In 1969, Brown and Hammack (1972), [Hammack and Brown (1974)] sent a mail questionnaire to a large sample of western hunters that asked them how much they would be willing to pay for and willing to accept to give up their rights to hunt waterfowl.[12] The $30 price tag from this work was eventually adopted by state and federal fish and game agencies for determining the value of a waterfowl kill and for estimating the benefits of habitat purchases. This study is also noteworthy for its ecosystem orientation. Next, in 1970 survey, Cicchetti and Smith (1973, 1976a, 1976b) asked individuals who were hiking in a wilderness area how much they would be willing to pay to reduce congestion in the area from other hikers. Influenced by Davis and other work at Resources for the Future, the Department of the Interior's Fish and Wildlife Survey of 1975 contained a question that asked respondents how much costs would have to increase before outdoor recreation would be given up [Brown, Charbonneau and Hay (1978)].

Work was also beginning outside of Resources for the Future's direct sphere of influence. A number of researchers including Miles (1967), LaPage (1968), Sarja (1969), Pattison (1970), Beardsley (1971), Randall (1973), Berry (1974), Meyer (1974), Shechter, Enis and Baron (1974), Gluck (1974) all used some variant of CV techniques

---

[12] In 1967, Mathews and Brown (1970) had undertaken an earlier study to value sport fishing using a simple survey based approach.

to value recreation.[13] Perhaps the most noteworthy of these studies was Darling (1973). Darling, influenced by Davis's work, used personal interviews to ask about willingness to pay for the amenities of three urban parks in California. He compared these estimates to those derived from a property value model and found the estimates from the survey to be on average lower than those estimated using property values. Jack Sinden (1974) also began his work on placing monetary values on recreational amenities at about this time and endeavored to trace out indifference curves. This work later resulted in one of the first books on nonmarket valuation focused on outdoor recreation [Sinden and Worrell (1979)].

Turning back to valuing the amenities of pollution control pioneered by Ridker, in the summer of 1972 Alan Randall and his colleagues used CV to study air visibility benefits in the Four Corners area in the southwest [Eastman, Randall and Hoffer (1974), Randall, Ives and Eastman (1974)].[14] This study, which built directly upon the bidding game approach put forth by Davis, plays a central role in the development of contingent valuation and is discussed in more detail in the next section. Hanemann also studied pollution, this time water pollution, by asking a sample of people in 1974 how much they were willing to pay for improved water quality at beaches in the Boston area [Hanemann (1978), Binkley and Hanemann (1978)]. Hanemann compared his findings with those obtained by a generalized travel cost model based on a random utility model, again finding reasonable correspondence.

Accompanying all of this empirical work was substantial advances on the theoretical side. Weisbrod (1964) had shown the potential importance of option value, Krutilla (1967) the potential importance of existence value and Arrow and Fisher (1974) the potential importance of quasi-option value. The import of all three papers was to suggest that there were many potential economic effects that were not adequately, if at all, reflected in market prices. These effects were thought by many to be particularly important in environmental decisions where irreversibility, a growing information basis, and uncertainty were nearly always present. Currie, Murphy and Schmitz (1971) put forth a coherent view of Hicksian consumer surplus measures while Mäler's (1974) seminal book provided a coherent theoretical view of environmental economics as a whole and the key role environmental externalities played. Freeman's widely used 1979 text on measuring environmental benefits was moving toward the now standard triumvirate of hedonic pricing, travel cost models, and willingness to pay surveys as the approaches to

---

[13] Sarja (1969), a Finnish study on lake recreation, appears to have been the first European CV study, Pattison (1970), a University of Alberta's master's thesis appears to have been Canada's first CV study, Gluck appears to have been the first CV study from Oceania, while Shechter, Enis and Baron (1974), an Israeli study, appears to have been the first study done outside of an OECD country.

[14] The pace of European CV studies also starts to increase during this time period. The original British studies looked at noise [i.e., Plowden (1970), Roskill (1970), Plowden and Sinnott (1977)] took place during this time. There is also a Dutch study by Jansen and Opschoor (1973) that looks at airport noise. Other early American studies looking at pollution were Barrett and Waddell (1973) and Reizenstein, Hills and Philpot (1974) who focused on urban air pollution while Oster (1977) and Gramlich (1977) focused on water pollution in the Merrimack and Charles Rivers, respectively.

obtaining values for nonmarketed goods.[15] Hanemann's work on random utility models (1984a, 1984b) was to have a substantial influence on both contingent valuation and travel cost models and made it clear that both approaches shared the same underlying theoretical framework.

2.3. Health, transportation, and the allocation of public budgets

Outside of the environmental arena, there were two other areas where surveys began to be used for the purpose of evaluating economic policies: health and transportation.[16] Interest in health applications stemmed from dissatisfaction with the human-capital approach to valuing health programs that placed little value on programs that saved mainly old people or young children. Acton (1973) was the first to undertake a serious empirical application here.[17] Acton applied the method to valuing programs such as improving ambulance services that reduced the risk of dying from a heart attack. It appears he did not know about Davis's work, but rather, was influenced by the work of the 1950s and 1960s on choice under uncertainty. Like Davis, Acton had enormous insights into the problems faced in setting up a situation whereby respondents could give up money to reduce low-level risks. Acton realized the difficulties in getting across such risks and notes that his own approach "is to state each probability calculation in several equivalent forms for each person so that he can choose the form most meaningful to him." Many of Acton's findings carry over to today's health risk studies.

Michael Jones-Lee in a seminal theoretical paper (1974) derived many of the properties that consumer surplus measures with respect to risk reductions. Jones-Lee, influenced like Acton, by Schelling and Mishan's call to use surveys to look at willingness to pay for reducing risk to human life, did so in his book [Jones-Lee (1976)]. Activity on valuing health risk using surveys was slow after this, in part due to the opposition of health policymakers to the concept of making decisions on the basis of willingness to pay. Maximizing quality adjusted life years (QUALY) subject to a budget constraint became the dominant paradigm in health policy, in spite of the dubious nature of its ties

---

[15] This process would be completed by the time of Freeman's (1993) book on the same topic. The well-known advanced text on welfare economics by Just, Hueth and Schmitz (1982) was perhaps the first to effectively take this position from a consistent theoretical stance.

[16] There was also relevant early work in marketing, such as Fiedler (1972) and Johnson (1974). Marketing research, however, turned in a more *ad hoc* psychological direction until developments in random utility theory [McFadden (1986)] provided a firmer economic foundation. Louviere (1994) and Louviere, Hensher and Swait (2000) provide an account of later developments in this area.

[17] The use of surveys to value reductions in risks gained a boost from articles by two well-known economists [Schelling (1968), Mishan (1971)], who noted that the other techniques for measuring benefits in these situation were either unavailable or necessitated a large number of implausible assumptions. They concluded that there was everything to gain and nothing to lose from trying the survey approach of asking people for their willingness to pay. Acton notes as the only predecessors to his survey work a draft survey instrument by Schelling and an unpublished paper by a University of Southern California master's student [Palmatier (1969)]. See Melinek (1974), another early study looking at willingness to pay for risk reductions.

to standard welfare economics.[18] Opposition by economists to both the human capital and QUALY approaches led to an interest in estimating risk premiums (and the statistical value of life) from hedonic wage equations. This approach was pioneered by Thaler and Rosen (1976).[19] On the health valuation side, further CV advances were stalled until the 1980s when interest in morbidity effects [e.g., Loehman and De (1982), Berger et al. (1987), Magat, Viscusi and Huber (1988)] and growing recognition of the difficulties involved in hedonic wage equations to value some types of mortality risks, fueled renewed interest in the use of surveys [e.g., Jones-Lee, Hammerton and Philips (1985), Gerking, de Haan and Schulze (1988), Eastaugh (1991)].[20]

In later years, the stated preference research in the area of health economics would encompass a wide variety of other areas of interest to policy ranging from various drug therapy options [Johannesson and Fagerberg (1992)] and discount rates for treatment options [Ganiats et al. (2000)] to the valuation of pharmacy services [Reardon and Pathak (1988)] and willingness to pay to reduce time on waiting lists [Propper (1990)].

In transportation, Jordan Louviere was the primary initiator of using stated preference data to look at transportation issues. Louviere was a geographer with a background in psychology. His first work (1974) dealt with the choice of trout fishing location as a function of the site attributes.[21] In many ways this application can be seen as one of the early outdoor recreation examples with the focus on investigating how distance (travel time) and stream quality (trout per quarter mile) influence stream preference rather than valuing a fishing day per se. Louviere's later work shifted to modeling the determinants of transportation mode choice (e.g., bus versus car) and to a random utility framework [Meyer, Levin and Louviere (1978)].[22] While the original focus of Louviere's work was not on valuation, the shift to a random utility framework [Louviere and Hensher (1983)] made the valuation of marginal changes in attributes straightforward. Later work in transportation would concentrate on the value of time [Hensher and Truong

---

[18] Ironically, an economist played an important role in the early development of the QUALY concept, since Zeckhauser and Shepard (1976) was one of the seminal papers on QUALY. This work grew out of the interest in multi-attribute utility assessment (MAUT), which breaks the elicitation of a multivariate utility function down through the elicitation of a set of separate univariate utility functions for individual outcomes such as health status [Keeney and Raiffa (1976)].

[19] See Viscusi (1993) survey article in the *Journal of Economic Literature* for a discussion of estimating the statistical value of life from hedonic wage regressions.

[20] For a comprehensive review of the issues involved in measuring health impacts see Johansson (1995).

[21] The other early stated preference study in transportation was by Davidson (1973) who undertook a survey aimed at forecasting potential traffic on short takeoff and landing aircraft. While Davidson's work did not have the influence that Louviere would have on modeling stated preferences, it did highlight one of the major issues in transportation, the almost complete lack of information on the impacts of introducing a new form of transportation in a data set on revealed behavior concerning transportation choices.

[22] In this, Louviere followed his dissertation advisor's footsteps with revealed preference data [Rushton (1969)]. Stated preference data proved to be better suited for this task when introducing new transportation modes or substantial changes from existing conditions. In part this was due to being able to control the attributes of choices that respondents saw through experimental design. Louviere and Woodworth (1983) is the seminal contribution with respect to the experimental design of such choice experiments.

(1985)] and the valuation of new forms of transportation such as alternative fuel vehicles [Brownstone, Bunch and Train (2000)].[23]

There was a third strand of work involving the use of surveys to elicit information about preferences for public goods. This involves asking respondents about how they would make trade-offs between multiple goods by allocating a budget. Some of the earliest work in this area was done by Peterson and Worrall (1970) who looked at trade-offs involving access to different neighborhood services. Hoinville and Berthoud (1970) gave respondents a hypothetical budget and asked them to make tradeoffs involving travel time, road safety, vehicle pollution and vehicle congestion in London; and Pendse and Wyckoff (1972) looked at tradeoffs between different water resources.[24] The allocation game concept saw its full realization in Beardsley, Kovenock and Reynolds (1974) who looked at allocating resources to different national priorities, Strauss and Hughes (1976) who looked at substitution effects among budget categories, and Hardie and Strand (1979) who looked at how respondents would reallocate parts of the U.S. Forest Service's budget. Unfortunately, there were several reasons why this line of work never really took off. First, specification of a complete set of all the options was very tedious if done in sufficient detail for respondents to understand. Second, while calculation of marginal rates of substitution at the individual level was straightforward, aggregation across agents or calculation of willingness to pay measures was problematic. Third, the theoretical framework for this type of modeling never found the acceptance that the random utility approach that came to dominate most contingent valuation work did. From a theoretical perspective, Carson, Flores and Hanemann (1998) show that the valuation of a good is dependent upon the sequence in which it is valued (due to both substitution and income effects) making it difficult to meaningfully aggregate the independent budget allocations of different agents.

2.4. The existence value revolution

CV surveys were initially seen as having three distinct advantages. First, CV can obtain useful information where data on past consumer behavior had not been collected. Second, CV permits the creation and presentation of scenarios that provide new goods or changes in existing goods that were substantially outside the range of current consumer experience. Third, CV allows measurement of the desired Hicksian consumer surplus measure rather than its Marshallian approximation. For most economists, the major drawback to CV-based estimates was that they were based upon stated preferences rather than observed behavior.

The existence value revolution occurred when it was shown that willingness to pay, as measured in a CV survey, would include Krutilla's (1967) existence value. As such,

---

[23] See Hensher (1994) for a review of the stated preference work in transportation through the mid-1990s.

[24] Other studies in this vein were Mierheim (1974), an early German stated preference study which looked at parks, and O'Hanlon and Sinden (1978), one of the first studies to look at existence values associated with preserving an area (in New South Wales).

in many instances, non-CV measures of the value of an environmental amenity could be seen as defective because they did not include existence value, which might be a significant component of total value.

The most influential of the early studies that encompassed existence was the study by Randall, Ives and Eastman (1974) valuing visibility in the Four Corners area. Their effort was notable for, among other things, its theoretical rigor, its valuation of a good which could not be valued by alternative methods (such as travel cost and hedonic pricing), its use of photographs to depict the visibility levels being valued, and its experimental design whereby certain aspects of the bidding game (such as the payment vehicle) were varied systematically to see if they affected the WTP amount. Perhaps even more significant, the timely publication of their article on the study in the first volume of the new *Journal of Environmental Economics and Management* brought the method to the attention of a broader audience.

Randall, Ives and Eastman valued changes in air quality necessary to maintain scenic vistas in the Southwest. In this instance, however, the indirect valuation approach was not capable of being applied because all people in the area share the good equally (and hence, not bundled differentially into housing prices) and no expenditure of time or money is needed to enjoy it.

Randall, Ives and Eastman estimated what had been termed "existence value" by Krutilla (1967) in an influential paper. The novel element in Krutilla's framework was that existence values were not generally revealed by market purchases. He argued that some people care about environmental resources, such as wildernesses areas, irrespective of their desire to visit them. Krutilla had not measured existence values, but rather had recommended determining just how large they would have to be to tilt the decision in the other direction. He contended that the failure to include existence values in policymaking would likely entail too great a loss of existing environmental amenities and the provision of too few new environmental amenities. Other related concepts were soon enumerated (e.g., nonuse value, stewardship value, bequest value, option value) and eventually encompassed into a single term "passive-use value," first used in the 1989 court decision *Ohio v. Department of Interior* (880 F.2d 432, D.C. Cir.), which held that government trustees should include passive-use values in damage claims.[25]

What Krutilla had called existence values was part of what had previously been termed "intangible" values [Smith (1976)]. These were not well integrated into welfare economic theory and they were thought to be unmeasurable. The key to measuring them lies in the recognition that due to scarcity effects, any form of economic value can be assessed by creating a trade-off between money and the consideration in question. Monetary measures of economic value are implicitly defined by choices made subject to an income constraint and CV permits the construction of the appropriate trade-off choice. Economic value can be expressed in terms of any constraints and tradeoffs appearing in a choice scenario including time, other public goods, or private goods (money).

---

[25] A comprehensive review of the concept of passive use and passive use values is provided in Carson, Flores and Mitchell (1999).

2.5. Developments from the mid-1970s through the late 1980s

The period from the mid-1970s through the late 1980s saw a continuation of many of the themes of the early 1970s in terms of the types of goods valued by contingent valuation. Valuing outdoor recreation [e.g., McConnell (1977), Cocheba and Langford (1978)] remained the most popular use of CV. The types of recreation valued expanded considerably and now include such diverse applications as congestion in ski areas [Walsh, Miller and Gilliam (1983)] and diving from offshore oil platforms [Roberts, Thompson and Pawlyk (1985)]. Many studies were undertaken to value improvements in air quality [e.g., Brookshire, Ives and Schulze (1976), Loehman and De (1982), Tolley et al. (1986)] and water quality [e.g., Gramlich (1977), Greenley, Walsh and Young (1981), Mitchell and Carson (1986)].

The range of applications also broadened considerably. These included the benefits of reclaiming surface coal mining areas [Randall et al. (1978)], the value of decreased mortality risk from a nuclear power plant accident [Mulligan (1978)], losses associated with toxic waste dumps [Smith, Desvousges and Freeman (1985)], aesthetic benefits from forgoing construction of a geothermal power plant [Thayer (1981)], the benefits of the public collection and dissemination of grocery store price information [Devine and Marion (1979)], the production of local government statistics [Bohm (1984)], the benefits of government sponsored senior companion programs [Garbacz and Thayer (1983)], protecting endangered species [Samples, Dixon and Gower (1985)], preserving wild and scenic rivers [Walsh, Sander and Loomis (1985)], the willingness of farmers to sell development rights to farmland [Conrad and LeBlanc (1979)], the willingness of citizens to buy those rights [Bergstrom, Dillman and Stoll (1985)], and the benefits of government support for the arts [Throsby (1984)].

Many of these studies were considered exploratory with researchers concentrating on refining the CV method by identifying and testing for the possible biases that arose in its use, and on establishing its credibility by making comparisons between the benefits measured in CV studies and those measured for the same goods by one of the established techniques, such as the travel cost method. Much of the pioneering methodological work was conducted by Randall and his colleagues [e.g., Randall, Ives and Eastman (1974), Randall et al. (1978), Randall, Hoehn and Tolley (1981)] at Oregon State University, New Mexico State University, the University of Kentucky, and the University of Chicago, by Cummings, d'Arge, Brookshire, Rowe, Schulze, and Thayer at the universities of New Mexico and Wyoming and by Robert Mitchell and Richard Carson at Resources for the Future. Parallel theoretical work by many of the same researchers has established that CV data are generated in forms consistent with the theory of welfare change measurement [Randall, Ives and Eastman (1974), Mäler (1974), Freeman (1979), Brookshire, Randall and Stoll (1980), Just, Hueth and Schmitz (1982), Hanemann (1984a, 1984b), Hoehn and Randall (1987)].

The Water Resources Council (1979) published its newly revised "Principles and Standards for Water and Related Land Resources Planning" in the *Federal Register*. This important document set forth the guidelines for federal participation in project evaluation which specified those methods that were acceptable for use in determining project benefits. The inclusion of contingent valuation as one of the three recommended methods (the other two were the travel cost and the unit day value methods) was a sign of contingent valuation's growing respectability.[26] The U.S. Army Corps of Engineers began to extensively use the contingent valuation method to measure project benefits during this time period. By 1986, the Corp had conducted almost twenty CV studies of varying degrees of sophistication and, as a consequence, published for Corp personnel the first government handbook on how to undertake contingent valuation studies [Moser and Dunning (1986)]. Contingent valuation was also recognized as an approved method for measuring benefits and damages under the Comprehensive Environmental Response, Compensation, and Liability Act of 1980 (Superfund), according to the final rule promulgated by the Department of the Interior (1986).

Funding from the U.S. Environmental Protection Agency has played a particularly important role in contingent valuation's development. Agency economists recognized early that the prevailing methods of measuring benefits, such as the surrogate markets and the travel cost method, would be of limited use in valuing the benefits of pollution control regulations they would be responsible for implementing. In the mid-1970s the agency began to fund a program of research with the avowed methodological purpose of determining the promise and problems of the CV method.[27] At first, almost all of the CV studies funded by this program were designed to test various aspects of the method and to establish its theoretical underpinnings. As the method became better understood, and the agency's mandate to subject the proposed regulations to benefit–cost analysis was given sharper focus by the Reagan administration under Executive Order 12291 [Smith (1984)], EPA's interest shifted to ascertaining just how effectively contingent valuation could be used for policy purposes.

As part of this effort, in 1983 the EPA commissioned a state-of-the-art assessment of the CV method as a way to step back and reflect on past achievements, remaining problems, and future possibilities. A notable feature of this assessment was the involvement of a review panel of eminent economists and psychologists, including Nobel Laureate Kenneth Arrow and future Nobel Laureates Daniel Kahneman and Vernon Smith. During a conference at Palo Alto, California, in July 1984, these and other scholars who were actively involved in contingent valuation research offered their views about the method's promise as a means for evaluating environmental goods. The leading authors

---

[26] The Principles and Standards document, which was modified and expanded slightly in 1983, also enshrined the then-prevailing CV practice as the officially prescribed way to conduct CV studies of water project benefits. As late as 1986, contract administrators were known to have required researchers to use the by–then outdated bidding game elicitation technique because the Principles and Standards document had declared it to be the "preferred" elicitation format for CV studies.

[27] The Electric Power Research Institute also sponsored some of the early air visibility studies that used the CV method [Blank et al. (1978)]. EPRI continued to sporadically fund CV research on air quality issues. This led to the first sustained involvement by cognitive psychologists in issues related to the design of CV surveys [Fischhoff and Furby (1988)].

of the state-of-the-art assessment [Cummings, Brookshire and Schulze (1986)] concluded that although the method shows promise, some real challenges remained. They gave the highest priority for future research to the development of an overall framework based on a theory of individual behavior in contingent market settings which could serve as a basis for hypothesis testing.

CV's importance in the United States was raised considerably by presidential executive orders that required an assessment of the benefits and costs of all major new government regulations and reauthorization of existing ones [Smith (1984)]. Outside the U.S., CV was incorporated into OECD reports on measuring the economic value of pollution impacts [Pearce and Markandy (1989)] that in part reflected the rapidly growing use of contingent valuation in Europe, where the number of studies being done started to approach that of the United States. The early leaders in this effort were the Norwegians and Swedes who were later joined by the British.[28]

Near the end of this time period studies in developing countries began to be undertaken. Not surprisingly, the first of these studied outdoor recreation. Grandstaff and Dixon (1986) looked at outdoor recreation in Lumpinee, an urban park in Bangkok, Thailand and found that contingent valuation and travel cost analysis produced similar results, while Abala (1987) looked at the determinants of willingness to pay for Nairobi National Park in Kenya. Interest in this topic has continued ever since with researchers looking at both domestic recreation and foreign tourism with an ecotourism theme.

The major innovation in developing countries, however, was the valuation of basic environmental infrastructure projects. The World Bank [Mitchell (1982), World Bank (1987)], the Interamerican Development Bank [Ducci (1988)], and USAID [Whittington (1988)] began exploring the possibility of using contingent valuation as a tool for helping to evaluate projects. Applications followed involving water supply [e.g., Whittington et al. (1988)] and sewage treatment [e.g., McConnell and Ducci (1989)]. The use of contingent valuation surveys in developing countries was to become the growth area of the 1990s [Georgiou et al. (1997), Whittington (1998)].

2.6. The Mitchell and Carson book

The Mitchell and Carson book (1989) *Using Surveys to Value Public Goods: The Contingent Valuation Method* played a central role in defining the practice of contingent valuation. The book put forth a coherent theoretical framework and a now generally accepted typology of the different types of values potentially associated with the provision of a public good. It showed that they could all be measured in a total value framework using contingent valuation. Different elicitation formats were discussed and the issue of strategic behavior considered at length. The Mitchell and Carson book also put forth a comprehensive typology of all of the different types of biases and misspecifications that could occur in CV studies and showed how most of these could potentially

---

[28] Navrud (1992) provides an overview of early CV studies undertaken in the various European Countries.

be avoided by careful survey design. The book devoted considerable attention to survey design and administration issues and brought a rigorous survey perspective into the CV literature. The Mitchell and Carson book had appendices containing information on conducting CV experiments, the questionnaire from a national water quality study, and a brief review of over one hundred CV studies. By the time the Mitchell and Carson book appeared, contingent valuation had clearly ceased to be an "experimental" methodology. The number of CV studies was rapidly increasing and their use in government decision making was becoming commonplace.

2.7. Exxon Valdez

A major stimulus to the current CV debate was the enactment of U.S. laws that allowed for the recovery of monetary damages for injuries to natural resources. The focal point of this debate was the Exxon Valdez oil spill, where the state of Alaska's claim for damages was largely based upon a claim for the loss of passive use value [Carson et al. (1992, 2003)]. Potential liability for natural resource damages should increase a firm's precautionary activities and environmental restoration efforts. Firms facing such liability have responded by questioning whether passive use values should count and whether CV estimates of them were reliable.

Following the *Exxon Valdez* oil spill, the oil industry mounted an aggressive public relations campaign intended to convince policy makers that contingent valuation in any form was too unreliable to be used for any purpose. An important tool in their campaign was a set of contingent valuation surveys that their consultants conducted – on issues other than the Exxon Valdez oil spill – which showed CV in a poor light; these studies and the related critiques of CV were presented at an Exxon-sponsored conference in Washington DC in March 1992, and subsequently published in Hausman (1993).[29] Among the claims made were that CV results were insensitive to the scope of the good being valued, and were highly dependent on what else was being valued and on the way in which the valuation was elicited. It was also argued that the inclusion of passive use values represented a form of double counting. Essentially, the oil industry critique can be summarized as: (a) if contingent valuation did work it should work *always*, regardless of the circumstances and details of its application, and (b) if violations of economic theory are found in CV studies, there must be a flaw in the CV study rather than any problem with the received theory.[30]

Looking back on the debate after more than a decade, one senses that it had several positive aspects. It forced a much deeper consideration of how contingent valuation should be conducted, a deeper consideration of the underlying economic theory, and a

[29] Also see the American Petroleum Institution report by Cummings and Harrison (1992).

[30] There is, of course, some irony in that many of the key tenets of what is now often referred to as the behavioral economics revolution were first demonstrated in CV studies and declared anomalies of the method rather than of actual economic behavior.

reconsideration of whether some of the violations of economic theory that are commonly found in contingent valuation are also observed in other forms of economic behavior and could be evidence of a systematic shortcoming in the underlying theoretical model of behavior.

Immediately after the Exxon conference in March 1992, in the face of tremendous industry lobbying of the White House, the staff of U.S. National Oceanic and Atmospheric Administration (NOAA) convened a Blue Ribbon Panel co-chaired by two Nobel Prize winners [Arrow et al. (1993)] to consider whether passive use values should be included in natural resource damage assessment and whether they could reliably be measured by contingent valuation. The Panel held hearings in the summer of 1992 and reviewed a large volume of evidence. It concluded that passive use values should be included in natural resource damage assessment and that "CV studies can produce estimates reliable enough to be the starting point for a judicial or administrative determination of natural resource damages-including lost passive-use value." That Panel's report was also influential for the guidelines that it set forth for conducting CV studies in natural resource damage cases and for the methodological issues it identified as requiring further research.

The American Agricultural Economics Association organized a symposium on contingent valuation in its policy journal *Choices* in 1993 [Carson, Meade and Smith (1993), Randall (1993), Desvousges et al. (1993a)] while the American Economic Association organized a symposium on continent valuation in its policy oriented *Journal of Economic Perspectives* in 1994 [Portney (1994), Diamond and Hausman (1994), Hanemann (1994)]. These papers, in conjunction with the NOAA Panel report, set the research agenda for contingent valuation for the next decade.

2.8. Literature production

The CV literature grew rapidly after the NOAA Panel Report. Ironically, most of this growth was a response to the growing demand for more comprehensive benefit–cost assessments rather than having anything to do with natural resource damage assessments. The growth also reflected the increasing use of contingent valuation in other OECD countries as well as in developing countries. It also reflected an ever increasing variety of environmental amenities that were being valued and a growing interest in a wider range of methodological issues.

Figure 1 displays the production of CV literature by year from 1960 through 2000. Before 1960, there are only a few papers such as Ciracy-Wantrup's (1952) original proposal for doing contingent valuation and the 1958 Audience Research study for the National Park Service. For all practical purposes, the CV literature starts in the early 1960s with the work of Davis, and built slowly through the late 1960s and early 1970s. The first spike in the production of CV literature occurs in 1974, the year of the classic Randall, Ives and Eastman (1974) study in the *Journal of Environmental Economics and Management*. The presence of twenty-five papers in that year alone points to the active involvement of a number of different researchers and groups and the start of the

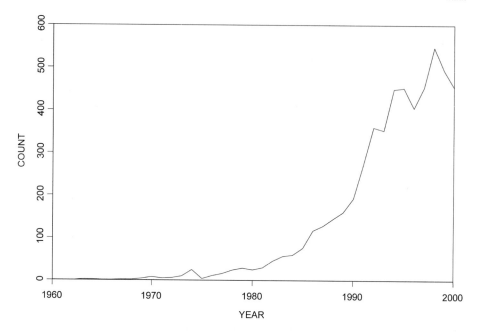

Figure 1. Contingent valuation literature production by year.

use of stated preference techniques in transportation. After a lull in 1975, the output of CV studies grew steadily, indeed at almost an exponential rate up until 1994. By 1994, the production of CV literature reached about 450 papers and studies. Through the end of the decade, the production of CV literature has remained in the 400 to 500 papers per year range.[31] The only exception to this is the upward spike in 1998 to around 550 papers. This appears to be in large part due to the First World Congress of Environmental and Resource Economists in Venice. The Venice World Congress resulted in a substantial increase in the production of papers in environmental economics with nonmarket valuation being one of the most popular themes.

Geographically, CV studies have now been conducted in twenty-nine out of the thirty current OECD members. Luxembourg is the only OECD member country for which a CV study was not found, although there were numerous reports to European Union

---

[31] The Carson (in press) bibliography contains citations to over 6000 papers and studies. There are approximately 250 citations each for the years 2001–2003. The bibliography for these years is more limited than in previous years and mainly lists published journal articles and papers presented at the major environmental economics meetings. The gray literature including government reports and university/research institute working papers and reports is not as well-represented for this time period as in earlier years. A rough comparison in terms of published papers from the 2001–2003 period to the 1994–2000 period suggests that the production of CV literature has remained in the 400 to 500 per year range.

institutions in Luxembourg that were based upon CV results. CV studies have also been conducted in 80 developing countries.[32]

Another indication of the importance of CV can be seen by looking at EVRI (Environmental Valuation Reference Inventory), a large online database currently being assembled for policy making purposes by Environment Canada, as a cooperative venture undertaken with the European Union, the U.S. EPA, the environmental protection agencies of Chile and Mexico, the World Bank, and the Economy and Environment Program for South East Asia. As of January 2005, the EVRI database (http://www.evri.ec.gc.ca/evri/) contained 742 studies based upon stated preferences, 385 studies based upon revealed preferences, and 215 studies based upon actual costs.

2.9. Major issues

One can divide the major issues surrounding contingent valuation into three groups. The first group involves the linkage between the survey response and economic theory. This has involved two key questions: what economic quantity should be measured by different questions and how can one tell whether the response to a CV survey corresponds to the predictions of economic theory. Sections 3, 4, and 5 of this chapter deal with the theory issues while the issue of assessing the congruence of CV results to economic theory has, as one might expect, generated controversies and is dealt with in Sections 9 and 10. To foreshadow some of that discussion, we simply note that CV results have, on several occasions, resulted in a reexamination of the relevant theory from first principles. What was first thought of as an anomaly or violation of economic theory was, instead, what one should have expected to see. Nowhere is this more true than in the current formulation of Section 5 on elicitation formats. In other instances, there are clear anomalies from the perspective of a narrowly defined self-interested maximizing economic agent in CV surveys, but deeper examination shows them to be ubiquitous in actual market transactions.

The second group of issues deals with designing a CV survey, administering it, and analyzing the resulting data. Sections 5 and 6 look at choosing a format for eliciting preference information and econometric estimation of WTP distributions. Sections 7 and 8 look at designing and administering a CV survey. Part of what emerges here is that there is a reasonable consensus about how to do a contingent valuation study if

---

[32] The list includes Argentina, Armenia, Bangladesh, Bahamas, Barbados, Botswana, Brazil, Bulgaria, Burkina Faso, Cambodia, Central African Republic, Chile, China, Columbia, Costa Rica, Cuba, Croatia, Dominica, Dominican Republic, Egypt, El Salvador, Ecuador, Estonia, Ethiopia, Gambia, Ghana, Georgia, Guatemala, Haiti, Honduras, Indonesia, India, Israel, Iran, Ivory Coast, Jamaica, Kenya, Laos, Latvia, Liberia, Lithuania, Madagascar, Malaysia, Mali, Micronesia, Morocco, Mozambique, Myanmar, Namibia, Nepal, Netherlands Antilles, Nicaragua, Niger, Nigeria, Panama, Pakistan, Papua New Guinea, Peru, Philippines, Puerto Rico, Romania, Russia, Sierra Leone, Singapore, South Africa, Sri Lanka, St. Lucia, Taiwan, Tanzania, Thailand, Tunisia, Trinidad and Tobago, Uganda, Ukraine, Uruguay, Vanuatu, Venezuela, Vietnam, Zambia, and Zimbabwe.

there was no serious budget constraint. Disagreement occurs on what is the best way to collect the "appropriate" information at a reasonable cost. Decisions here are often hard because all parts of the policy evaluation need resources to better understand the implications of the choice faced by policy makers; and where time and money to do the analysis are both often quite limited.

The third group of issues related to how to successfully apply contingent valuation to value particular types of goods is not dealt with in this chapter. This at some level is both the "art" of contingent valuation and the specific knowledge that gets passed down. The history of contingent valuation is full of examples of survey scenarios and instruments that just did not work quite right. This continued until some researcher figured out how to explain or visually depict the good to be valued, and how to formulate a provision and/or payment mechanism in such a way that respondents understand what they are getting, believe it could be provided, and are satisfied that the government would enforce the payment if the good were provided.[33] Unfortunately, there is nothing in economic theory per se that provides this information, economists are typically not taught these skills in the course of their graduate education, and the issues involved in designing a CV survey are generally beyond those with which a conventional survey designer has experience. When someone finds an approach that works, it is often replicated and modified for valuing related goods. The best advice that we can offer here is to carefully read the studies (and most importantly their survey instruments) that try to value goods similar to the one of current interest and determine how well those survey instruments are working and where problems are seen to exist. Section 7 provides some guidance on evaluating how well a survey instrument is working.

3. Economic theory of contingent valuation

3.1. Economic welfare measures

Since CV uses surveys to measure an economic concept of value, we begin a brief review of the relevant economic theory (see Chapter 12 by Bockstael and Freeman in this handbook for a more detailed treatment).

The goal of a CV study is to measure an individual's monetary value for some item. We denote the item being valued by q; for now we will treat this as a single item – whether a single commodity or a single program involving some mix of commodities treated as a fixed group – and therefore q is a scalar.[34] Assuming the individual is a consumer and using essentially the same notation as Bockstael and Freeman, we assume

---

[33] For an interesting example involving the valuation of low level risks, one of the most difficult problems faced in environmental valuation, see Corso, Hammitt and Graham (2001).

[34] The valuation of multiple items is covered in Sections 5 and 6 under the discussion of choice experiments.

the individual has a utility function defined over the quantities of various market commodities, denoted by the vector x, and q, $u(x, q)$.[35] Corresponding to this direct utility function, we can write an indirect utility function, $v(p, q, y)$, where p is the vector of the prices of the market commodities and y is the person's income.[36] We make the conventional assumption that $u(x, q)$ is increasing and quasi-concave in x, which implies that $v(p, q, y)$ satisfies the standard properties with respect to p and y;[37] but we make no assumptions regarding q. If the agent regards q as a "good," $u(x, q)$ and $v(p, q, y)$ will both be increasing in q; if she regards it as a "bad," $u(x, q)$ and $v(p, q, y)$ will both be decreasing in q; and if she is indifferent to q, $u(x, q)$ and $v(p, q, y)$ will both be independent of q. We make no assumption regarding quasiconcavity with respect to q.

The act of valuation implies a contrast between two situations – a situation with the item, and one without it. We interpret what is being valued as a change in q.[38] Specifically, suppose that q changes from q^0 to q^1; the person's utility thus changes from $u^0 \equiv v(p, q^0, y)$ to $u^1 \equiv v(p, q^1, y)$. If she regards this change as an improvement, $u^1 > u^0$; if she regards it as a change for the worse, $u^1 < u^0$; and if she is indifferent, $u^1 = u^0$. The value of the change to her in monetary terms is represented by the two Hicksian measures, the compensating variation C which satisfies

$$v\left(p, q^1, y - C\right) = v\left(p, q^0, y\right), \tag{1}$$

and the equivalent variation E which satisfies

$$v\left(p, q^1, y\right) = v\left(p, q^0, y + E\right). \tag{2}$$

Observe that

$$\text{sign}(C) = \text{sign}(E) = \text{sign}\left(u^1 - u^0\right). \tag{3}$$

If the change is regarded as an improvement, $C > 0$ and $E > 0$; in this case, C measures the individuals' maximum WTP to secure the change, while E measures her minimum WTA to forego it. If the change is regarded as being for the worse, $C < 0$ and $E < 0$; in this case, C measures the individuals' WTA to endure the change, while E measures her WTP to avoid it. If she is indifferent to the change, $C = E = 0$.

---

[35] One can develop the theory of a producer's WTP or WTA for a change in using the profit function in place of the indirect utility function, but this will not be pursued here.

[36] The income variable that applies here can be defined in different ways. For example, it could be the supernumerary income that is available to the individual after allowing for certain committed expenditures on market or nonmarket goods.

[37] That is, we assume $v(p, q, y)$ is homogeneous of degree zero in p and y, increasing in y, nonincreasing in p, and quasiconvex in p.

[38] The alternative is to represent it as a change in p. McConnell (1990) adopts this approach for a valuation question of the form. "Would you accept a payment of $\$A$ to give up your right to use this commodity for one year?" Let p^* be the choke price vector (i.e., a price vector such that, at these prices, the individual would choose not to consume the resource), and let p^0 be the baseline price vector. McConnell represents the change as a shift from (p^0, q, y) to (p^*, q, y).

To emphasize the dependence of the compensating and equivalent variation on (i) the starting value of q, (ii) the terminal value of q, and (iii) the value of (p, y) at which the change in q occurs, we sometimes write them as functions: $C = C(q^0, q^1, p, y)$ and $E = E(q^0, q^1, p, y)$. To simplify things, we will define the WTP function,

$$\text{WTP}(q^0, q^1, p, y) = \begin{cases} C(q^0, q^1, p, y) & \text{if } C \geq 0, \\ -E(q^0, q^1, p, y) & \text{if } C \leq 0. \end{cases}$$

The WTA function $\text{WTA}(q^0, q^1, p, y)$ is defined analogously. The goal of a CV study is to measure one or another of these valuation functions – either the entire function, or a particular point on the function. For simplicity, in the remainder of this section we assume that the change is an improvement ($C \geq 0$) and we focus on the measurement of WTP.[39]

Let $y = m(p, q, u)$ be the expenditure function corresponding to the direct utility function $u(x, q)$ and the indirect utility function $v(p, q, y)$; this should be increasing in u, and nondecreasing, concave and homogeneous of degree 1 in p. It is decreasing in q if q is desired, increasing in q if q is a bad, and independent of q if the individual is indifferent to q. In terms of the expenditure function, the compensating and equivalent variations are defined as

$$\begin{aligned} C &= m(p, q^0, u^0) - m(p, q^1, u^0) \\ &= y - m(p, q^1, u^0) \end{aligned} \tag{1'}$$

and

$$\begin{aligned} E &= m(p, q^0, u^1) - m(p, q^1, u^1) \\ &= m(p, q^0, u^1) - y.^{40} \end{aligned} \tag{2'}$$

It is also natural to impose the restriction that

$$\lim_{y \to 0} v(p, q, y) = -\infty \tag{4a}$$

or, equivalently, that, given any q' and any $y' > 0$, there exists no q'' such that

$$v(p, q'', 0) = v(p, q', y'); \tag{4b}$$

that is to say, the market goods x in the underlying direct utility function $u(x, q)$, taken as a group, are essential. This implies that $m(p, q, u) > 0$, and, from (1'), that

$$C < y. \tag{5}$$

---

[39] Note that in the valuation question considered by McConnell (1990), what is being measured is WTA, not WTP. McConnell emphasizes that a correct specification of a WTP or WTA function must *exclude* endogenous variables such as quantity demanded.

[40] McConnell (1990) refers to (1') and (2') as *variation* functions and analyzes their derivatives with respect to p and y. He notes that these results can be used in a nonparametric way to compare predictions implied by a CV response model with actual behavior.

Note that from (2′), the equivalent variation (WTA) is *not* similarly bounded by y. We defer further discussion of the differences between WTP and WTA and the implications for estimation to Section 6.

We illustrate these concepts with a specific example, the Box–Cox indirect utility function:[41]

$$v_q = \alpha_q + \beta_q \left(\frac{y^\lambda - 1}{\lambda} \right), \quad q = 0, 1, \tag{6a}$$

where $\alpha_1 \geqslant \alpha_0$ and $\beta_1 \geqslant \beta_0$. This can be regarded as a form of CES utility function in q and y. The corresponding formulas for C is

$$C = \left(\frac{\beta_0 y^\lambda}{\beta_1} - \frac{\lambda \alpha}{\beta_1} + \frac{\beta_1 - \beta_0}{\beta_1} \right)^{1/\lambda}, \tag{6b}$$

where $\alpha \equiv \alpha_1 - \alpha_0$. McFadden and Leonard (1993) employ a restricted version of this model with $\beta_1 = \beta_0 \equiv \beta > 0$, yielding

$$v_q = \alpha_q + \beta \left(\frac{y^\lambda - 1}{\lambda} \right), \quad q = 0, 1, \tag{7a}$$

$$C = y - \left(y^\lambda - \frac{\alpha}{b} \right)^{1/\lambda}, \tag{7b}$$

where $b \equiv \beta/\lambda$. This nests many of the utility models used in the existing CV literature. It is somewhat flexible in that it permits a variety of income elasticities of WTP; the income elasticity of WTP is negative when $\lambda > 1$, zero when $\lambda = 1$, and positive when $\lambda < 1$.[42] For convenience, we will use (7a,b) to illustrate issues of modeling methodology.

3.2. From WTP to CV response

CV uses a survey to measure people's WTP or WTA for the change in q. The utility theoretic model of consumer preference outlined above provides the framework for interpreting the CV responses. Researchers use several different survey formats that involve asking people different questions; and the way one links the survey responses to the measurement of WTP or WTA is somewhat different in each case. In many cases, the response to the survey question is not itself a direct measure of WTP but yet a measure of WTP can be derived from the survey responses. The derivation typically involves a statistical analysis of the survey responses. In the framework of statistical modeling, it

---

[41] For simplicity, we suppress p and write the indirect utility function as a function of q and y: however, α_q and/or β_q would in fact be functions of p.

[42] It does not, however, satisfy (4a), (4b); this restriction must be imposed separately. Note also that there may be measurement issues with respect to y that may play a role in empirical econometric estimation.

is conventional to treat the survey responses as the realization of a random variable. It is necessary, therefore, to recast the deterministic model of WTP outlined above into a stochastic model that can generate a probability distribution for the survey responses.

The mapping from the deterministic model of WTP to a probabilistic characterization of survey responses involves two steps: (1) the introduction of a stochastic component into the deterministic utility model which leads to what is called a *WTP distribution*; and (2) the formulation of a connection between the WTP distribution and what we call the *survey response probability distribution* based on the assumption of a utility-maximizing response to the survey question. The WTP cumulative distribution function (cdf) will be denoted $G_C(x)$; for a given individual, it specifies the probability that the individual's WTP for item in question is less than x

$$G_C(x) \equiv \Pr(C \leqslant x),$$

where the compensating variation C is now viewed as a random variable.[43] The corresponding density function is denoted $g_C(x)$.

Step (1) above deals with how one goes about the formulation of C as a random variable (more on this later). Step (2) deals with the link between the survey responses and $G_C(x)$, which varies with the form of the survey question. We illustrate this here with two simple examples. The first is the *open-ended* question format: the respondent is asked "How much are you willing to pay for the change from q^0 to q^1?" Suppose the response is A? This means that, for this respondent, his value of C is A. Referring now to the underlying WTP distribution, the probability of obtaining this particular response from the individual is given by

$$\Pr(\text{Response to open-ended CV question is } A) = \Pr(C = A) \equiv g_c(A). \tag{8}$$

The second format is the *closed-ended, single-bound* discrete choice format: the respondent is asked: "Would you vote to support the change from q^0 to q^1 if it would cost you A?" Suppose the response is 'yes'. This means that for this individual, his value of C is some amount more than A. In terms of the underlying WTP distribution, the probability of obtaining a 'yes' response is given by

$$\Pr(\text{Response to closed-ended question is 'yes'}) = \Pr(C \geqslant A) \equiv 1 - G_C(A). \tag{9}$$

With the open-ended format, the response directly reveals the respondent's value of C; with the closed-ended format, it does not reveal the exact value of C but it does provide an interval in which C must lie. In both cases, however, we can forge a link between the WTP distribution and the response probability distribution.

How does one get a WTP distribution? Two approaches have been used in the literature. Historically, the first approach, adopted in the context of the open-ended CV format, was to directly specify a distribution for C. In effect, one writes C as a mean, $E(C) = \mu_C$ together with some white noise ε. The early literature adopted a pragmatic

---

[43] For now, we assume the change is regarded as an improvement, so that C measures WTP.

approach to the specification of μ_C and viewed it as a linear regression involving some covariates Z and their coefficients, $\mu_C = Z\gamma$. If the random term is additive and has a mean of zero, then

$$C = \mu_C + \varepsilon = Z\gamma + \varepsilon, \tag{10}$$

which is a linear regression model.[44] An alternative specification is that the logarithm of C has a mean of $Z\gamma$, or equivalently, that the error term is multiplicative.

$$\ln C = Z\gamma + \varepsilon. \tag{11}$$

If ε is a standard normal variate than (10) implies C is normally distributed. If the random term is multiplicative as in (11), then C is lognormally distributed. As an alternative to these somewhat *ad hoc* specifications for μ_C, one could also employ a utility theoretic specification of the compensating variation function as discussed above. Using an additive error term, this is

$$C = C\left(q^0, q^1, p, y\right) + \varepsilon. \tag{12}$$

In the case of the Box–Cox model (7), for example,

$$C = y - \left(y^\lambda - \frac{\alpha}{b}\right)^{1/\lambda} + \varepsilon. \tag{13}$$

The second approach introduces a random term directly in the utility function, appealing to the notion of random utility maximization (RUM). In a RUM model it is assumed that, while an individual knows her preferences with certainty and does not consider them stochastic or otherwise behave in a random manner, nevertheless her preferences contain some components that are unobservable to the econometric investigator and are treated by the investigator as random [McFadden (1974), Manski (1977)]. The unobservables could be characteristics of the individual and/or attributes of the items considered for choice and/or they can signify both variation in preferences among members of a population and measurement error or missing data. For now, we represent the stochastic component of preferences by ε without yet specifying whether it is a scalar or a vector, and we write the indirect utility function as $v(p, q, y; \varepsilon)$. Substituting $v(p, q, y; \varepsilon)$ into (1) yields $C(q^0, q^1 p, y; \varepsilon)$, which itself is a random variable. In a RUM model, while the individual's WTP for the change in q is something that she herself knows with certainty, it is something that the investigator does not know with certainty; and therefore, models as a random variable.

---

[44] Early examples of the regression analysis of open-ended CV response data can be found in Hammack and Brown (1974), Brookshire, Ives and Schulze (1976), and McConnell (1977). In closed-ended CV, the approach based on the specification of a WTP distribution was emphasized by Cameron (1988) and Cameron and James (1987) and is sometimes referred to as the Cameron approach; Duffield and Patterson (1991a) refer to it as the tolerance approach because of the close analogy between the WTP distribution and the tolerance distribution in bioassay.

The RUM approach proceeds by specifying a particular indirect utility function $v(p, q, y; \varepsilon)$ and a particular distribution for ε.[45] An example of a RUM version of the restricted Box–Cox model is

$$u_q = \alpha_q + \beta\left(\frac{y^\lambda - 1}{\lambda}\right) + \varepsilon_q, \quad q = 0, 1, \tag{14a}$$

where ε_0 and ε_1 are random variables with a mean of zero. Consequently,

$$C = y - \left(y^\lambda - \frac{\alpha}{b} - \frac{\eta}{b}\right)^{1/\lambda}, \tag{14b}$$

where $\alpha \equiv \alpha_1 - \alpha_0$, $b \equiv \beta/\lambda$ and $\eta \equiv \varepsilon_1 - \varepsilon_0$. The comparison of (14b) with (13) illustrates the difference between the two approaches to the formulation of a WTP distribution. Inserting an additive random term in the utility function (14a), leads to a random term that enters the formulas for C in a *nonadditive* manner. Thus, even if these disturbances were normal random variables, the distribution of C would *not* in general be normal.[46] For example, when $\lambda = 0$ one has the logarithmic model from Hanemann (1984b)

$$u_q = \alpha_q + \beta \ln y + \varepsilon_q, \tag{15a}$$

which yields

$$C = y\left(1 - \exp\left[-(\alpha + \eta)\right]/\beta\right). \tag{15b}$$

In this case, if ε_0 and ε_1 are normal, C has a lognormal distribution. Alternatively, the linear model ($\lambda = 1$) is written as

$$u_q = \alpha_q + \beta y + \varepsilon_q, \tag{16a}$$

which yields[47]

$$C = \frac{\alpha + \eta}{\beta}. \tag{16b}$$

This is a special case of the Box–Cox model in which C has the same form of distribution as ε; if ε_0 and ε_1 are normal random variables then C is normal as well. Moreover, if the term α/β depends on covariates through a linear regression of the form $\alpha/\beta = Z\gamma$

---

[45] This is sometimes called the Hanemann, or utility difference approach after Hanemann (1984b). As McConnell (1990) notes, the distinction between the Hanemann and Cameron approaches lies where the random term is appended.

[46] Note that one can also introduce a random term into a RUM model in a nonadditive manner by making a coefficient such as β in (7) random. It should also be noted that not all the parameters of the random utility function are necessarily identifiable from the WTP function. In the case of (14a,b), α_0 and α_1 are not separately identifiable, only their difference. Similarly, the CDFs of the additive random terms in the utility function ε_0 and ε_1, are not separately identifiable, only the CDF of η.

[47] It turns out in this case that $C = E$.

and letting $\varepsilon \equiv \eta/\beta$, one recovers the linear regression formulation in (10). In this case, the two approaches for specifying a WTP distribution lead to an identical result.[48]

Besides the Box–Cox model, another RUM which has featured prominently in the CV literature is the Bishop–Heberlein utility model.[49,50]

$$v(p, q^0, y; \varepsilon_0) = y + \xi,$$

$$v(p, q^1, y; \varepsilon_1) = y + \xi + \exp\left[\frac{\alpha + \eta}{\beta}\right]$$

(17a)

which yields[51]

$$C = \exp\left[\frac{\alpha + \eta}{\beta}\right].$$

(17b)

3.3. Statistical model of CV responses

The statistical model of the CV survey responses depends on the specific form of the question used in the survey. Here we focus on the closed-ended, single-bounded question format where the respondent is asked "Would you vote to support the change from q^0 to q^1 if it would cost you $\$A$?" As noted above, the probability that she answers "yes" can be represented in terms of the WTP distribution by[52]

$$\Pr(\text{Response is 'yes'}) = \Pr\{C(q^0, q^1, p, y; \varepsilon) \geqslant A\} \equiv 1 - G_C(A).$$

(9)

An equivalent representation of the response probability in terms of the RUM utility function is

$$\Pr\{\text{response is 'yes'}\} = \Pr\{v(q^1, p, y - A; \varepsilon) \geqslant v(q^0, p, y; \varepsilon)\}.$$

(18)

Given that $\mu_C = E[C(q^0, q^1, p, y; \varepsilon)]$, let $\sigma_C^2 = \text{Var}[C(q^0, q^1, p, y; \varepsilon)]$, and let $G(\cdot)$ be the cumulative distribution function of the standardized variate $\omega = (C - \mu_C)/\sigma_C$.

---

[48] In general, for any given regression formulation of a WTP distribution, one can always find a RUM formulation which generates this distribution. In this sense, any given WTP distribution can be derived using either approach. However, except for (16a, b), for a given WTP distribution, the random term to be added in the regression approach and the random term to be inserted into the RUM model are different.

[49] The model was presented by Bishop and Heberlein at the AAEA summer meetings but was not actually described in the short published version of the proceedings [Bishop and Heberlein (1979)]. It is described in a subsequent working paper by Bishop and Heberlein (1980), and it first appeared in print in Bishop, Heberlein and Kealy (1983).

[50] While it was first thought [Hanemann (1984b)] that there exists no explicit RUM which could generate the Bishop–Heberlein WTP distribution (17b), Hanemann and Kanninen (1999) later showed that it is generated by (17a).

[51] In this case, too, it turns out that $C = E$.

[52] For now, we assume that the only other possible response is "no"; hence, $\Pr\{\text{response is "no"}\} = 1 - \Pr\{\text{response is "yes"}\}$. The treatment of "Don't know" responses is discussed in Section 6.

Switching from $G_C(\cdot)$ to $G(\cdot)$, we can re-write (9) as

$$\Pr\{\text{response is 'yes'}\} = 1 - G\left(\frac{A - \mu_C}{\sigma_C}\right)$$

$$\equiv 1 - G(-\gamma + \delta A) \tag{9'}$$

$$\equiv H(A), \tag{9''}$$

where $\gamma \equiv \mu_C/\sigma_C$ and $\delta \equiv 1/\sigma_C$. This expresses the response probability in the form of a statistical model for a binary dependent variable as a function of a covariate, A, where δ is the coefficient on A.[53] In effect, (9) or (9') constitute the integrability condition for single-bounded CV: a binary response statistical model representing the "yes" and "no" responses to a closed-ended CV survey as a function of the dollar amount in the survey is consistent with an economic model of maximizing behavior *if and only if it can be interpreted as the survivor function of an economic WTP distribution.*[54] The response probability model can be parametric or nonparametric depending on whether the WTP distribution whose survivor function is represented by the right-hand side of (9) has a parametric or nonparametric representation. The only requirement is that, since this is a survivor function, the graph relating a dollar amount A to the probability that the respondent would say "yes," to paying this amount, should be nonincreasing.[55] The graph of the response probability distribution can be viewed as a demand curve for the change in q, and the restriction is that this demand curve should not slope upward.

As an illustration of a parametric response model, the response probability distribution for the version of the Box–Cox model in (13) takes the form

$$\Pr\{\text{response is 'yes'}\} = 1 - \Pr\left\{y - \left(y^\lambda - \frac{\alpha}{b}\right)^{1/\lambda} + \varepsilon \leqslant A\right\}, \tag{19}$$

whereas the response probability formula for the RUM version of the Box–Cox model (14) is

$$\Pr\{\text{response is 'yes'}\} = 1 - \Pr\left\{y - \left(y^\lambda - \frac{\alpha}{b} - \frac{\eta}{b}\right)^{1/\lambda} \leqslant A\right\}. \tag{20}$$

In the linear model, where $\lambda = 1$, this simplifies to

$$\Pr\{\text{response is 'yes'}\} = 1 - \Pr\left\{\frac{\alpha + \eta}{\beta} \leqslant A\right\}. \tag{21}$$

---

[53] A binary response model is a statistical model for a binary dependent variable which represents the probabilities that it takes each possible value as functions of covariates, of the form $\Pr(\text{response} = j) = H_j(A)$; these functions must return values in the interval $[0, 1]$, and they must sum to unity, conditions satisfied by (9'').

[54] The survivor function of a random variable $\widetilde{X}$ with the CDF $F_X(x)$ is $S_X(x) \equiv \Pr\{\widetilde{X} \geqslant x\} = 1 - F_X(x)$.

[55] This is because from (9'), $\partial \Pr\{\text{"yes"}\}/\partial A = -g_C(A) \leqslant 0$.

To be more specific, if η in (21) is a standard normal random variable, the response formula becomes a probit model[56]

$$\text{Pr\{response is 'yes'\}} = \Phi(\alpha - \beta A). \tag{22}$$

If η is a standard logistic random variable, the response formula becomes a logit model[57]

$$\text{Pr\{response is 'yes'\}} = \frac{1}{1 + \exp(-\alpha + \beta A)}. \tag{23}$$

With the Bishop–Heberlein RUM model, (17), the response probability distribution takes the form

$$\text{Pr\{response is 'yes'\}} = 1 - \text{Pr}\left\{\frac{\alpha + \eta}{\beta} \leqslant \ln A\right\}, \tag{24}$$

that resembles the Box–Cox RUM response model (21) except that $\ln A$ appears in place of A. If η in (24) is a standard normal random variable, the response distribution becomes a lognormal distribution

$$\text{Pr\{response is 'yes'\}} = \Phi(\alpha - \beta \ln A), \tag{25}$$

while if η is a standard logistic random variable, the response distribution becomes log-logistic

$$\text{Pr\{response is 'yes'\}} = \frac{1}{1 + \exp(-\alpha + \beta \ln A)}, \tag{26}$$

which is the form actually used by Bishop and Heberlein (1979) when they introduced the closed-ended single-bounded response format. If $(-\eta)$ has the standard extreme value distribution, the response distribution is a two-parameter Weibull distribution[58]

$$\text{Pr\{response is 'yes'\}} = \exp\left[-\exp(-\alpha + \beta \ln A)\right]. \tag{27}$$

Figure 2 shows the graphs of the logit response model (23) and the log-logistic model (26); their shapes differ because, as $A \to 0$, the probability of a "yes" response converges on unity in Figure 2(b) but not in Figure 2(a).

---

[56] The distribution of η is standard normal if one assumes that ε_0 and ε_1 in (16a) are i.i.d. normal with mean zero and variance 0.5. We use $\Phi(\ )$ to denote the standard normal CDF.

[57] The CDF of a logistic with scale parameter $\tau > 0$ and location parameter μ is $F(x) = [1 + \exp(-(x - \mu)/\tau)]^{-1}$; this has a mean and median of μ, and a variance of $\tau^2\pi^2/3$. In the standard logistic, $\mu = 0$ and $\tau = 1$. This logit model arises if the ε_q in (14a) are extreme value variates. The CDF of an extreme value variate with location parameter ς and scale parameter $\tau > 0$ is $F(\varepsilon) = \exp[-\exp(-\varepsilon - \varsigma)/\tau]$; the mean is $\varsigma + 0.5772\tau$ and the variance is $\tau^2\pi^2/6$. In the standard extreme value, $\varsigma = 0$ and $\tau = 1$. If ε_1 and ε_0 are independent extreme value variates with separate location parameters ς_1 and ς_0 and a common scale parameter τ, $\eta \equiv \varepsilon_1 - \varepsilon_0$ has a logistic distribution with location parameter $\mu = \varsigma_1 - \varsigma_0$ and scale parameter τ. The standard logistic arises when $\varsigma_1 = \varsigma_0$ and $\tau = 1$.

[58] The two-parameter Weibull distribution with scale parameter $\theta > 0$ and shape parameter $\gamma > 0$ has a survivor function $S(x) = \exp[-(x/\theta)^\gamma]$. Setting $\gamma = 1$ produces the exponential distribution; setting $\gamma = 2$ produces the Rayleigh distribution. When $(-\eta)$ in (17a) is a standard extreme value variate, C in (17b) is Weibull with parameters $\theta = e^{\alpha/\beta}$ and $\gamma = \beta$.

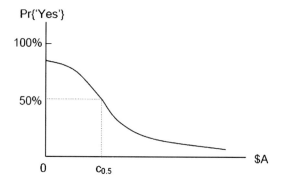

(a) Logit response model

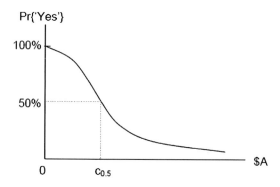

(b) Log-logistic response model

Figure 2. Logit and log-logistic response models.

Whatever the specific formula, these parametric response probabilities provide the link to statistical estimation of the CV survey responses. Index respondents by i and bid values by k. Let N denote the total number of respondents and K the total number of separate bid values, and let N_k denote the number of respondents randomly assigned a bid value of $\$A_k$.[59] We use $\mathbb{1}_{i,\text{response}}$ as an indicator variable equal to one, if respondent i gives a specific response, and zero, otherwise – in this case, where the eligible responses are "yes" and "no;" this reduces to $\mathbb{1}_{i,Y}$ and $\mathbb{1}_{i,N}$. The most common approach

---

[59] The choice of the bid levels A_k and the determination of how many respondents are allocated to each bid N_k are discussed in Section 6.

to estimation in the CV literature is maximum likelihood.[60] Given that respondent i receives bid A_k, the probability that she responds "yes" is denoted $\pi_i^Y(A_k)$, where this might be given by one of the formulas listed above, and the probability that she responds "no" is denoted $\pi_i^N(A_k)$.[61] Assuming that the N respondents are allocated at random to one of the K bid levels, given the sample of respondents, the set of bid values, and the observed yes or no responses from each respondent, the likelihood of observing this pattern of responses is given by

$$L = \prod_{k=1}^{K} \prod_{i=1}^{N_k} \left[\pi_i^Y(A_k)\right]^{1_{i,Y}} \left[\pi_i^N(A_k)\right]^{1_{i,N}}. \tag{28a}$$

The corresponding log-likelihood function is

$$\ln L = \sum_{k=1}^{K} \sum_{i=1}^{N_k} \left[1_{i,Y} \ln\left(\pi_i^Y(A_k)\right) + 1_{i,N} \ln\left(\pi_i^N(A_k)\right)\right]. \tag{28b}$$

By contrast, the nonparametric approach to the specification of a response probability model views this as an *unknown* function of the bid amount $H(A)$, whose value is observed only at a discrete set of points, namely $A_k, k = 1, \ldots, K$.[62] The function can be estimated only at those points, not at other points which are unobserved. The fully nonparametric response model, therefore, takes the form of a step function representing K constants $\pi_k^Y = H(A_k)$, corresponding to the K points at which $H(A)$ is observed; this graph is illustrated in Figure 3(a). The resulting nonparametric likelihood function is

$$L = \prod_{k=1}^{K} \prod_{i=1}^{N_{A_k}} \left[\pi_k^Y\right]^{1_{i,Y}} \left[1 - \pi_k^Y\right]^{1_{i,N}}, \tag{29}$$

where the parameters to be estimated are now the K constants $\pi_k^Y, k = 1, \ldots, K$.

Two points about the nonparametric approach should be noted. First, this approach treats each bid level as a separate experiment; it does not impose any structure across the bids. Second, by design the nonparametric estimator provides an estimate of the response probability distribution only at a set of points. It is necessary for some purposes, including the calculation of welfare measures (discussed below), to have an estimate of the response probability distribution at *other* points; this requires some form of extrapolation to "connect the dots" in Figure 3(a). Several different approaches have been used in the literature, including: (i) piecewise linear interpolation between each pair of

---

[60] Alternatives to maximum likelihood will be considered in Section 6. An excellent overview of likelihood based statistical procedures can be found in Pawitan (2001).

[61] Since these are the only two eligible responses, it follows that $\pi_i^Y(A_k) + \pi_i^N(A_k) = 1$.

[62] We adopt the convention that the bid values are indexed in ascending order, so that A_1 is the lowest bid, and A_K the highest.

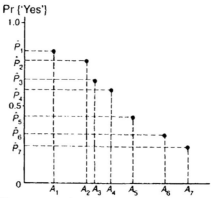

(a) Non-parametric estimate of response distribution

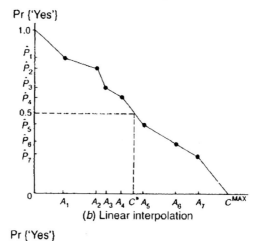

(b) Linear interpolation

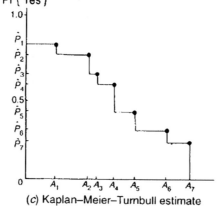

(c) Kaplan–Meier–Turnbull estimate

Figure 3. Nonparametric estimation of response model.

nonparametrically estimated response probabilities $[\hat{\pi}_k^Y, \hat{\pi}_{k+1}^Y]$ [Kriström (1990)]. This is illustrated in Figure 3(b). (ii) A more conservative extrapolation assumes that over the interval $[A_k, A_{k+1}]$, $\pi^Y(A) = \hat{\pi}_{k+1}^Y$, $k = 1, \ldots, K - 1$, as illustrated in Figure 3(c) [Carson et al. (1992)]. This is a conservative assumption since, with $\pi^Y(A)$ monotone nonincreasing, we know that $\pi^Y(A) \geqslant \hat{\pi}_{k+1}^Y$ over the interval. (iii) Alternatively, a nonparametric smoothing estimator can be applied to the $\hat{\pi}_k^Y$'s; such as, the kernel estimator suggested by Copas (1983) if one is prepared to assume that the underlying WTP distribution is smooth.[63]

3.4. Summary measures of welfare

Having fitted a response model to the CV survey responses, what does one do next? The goal of the study was presumably to develop some summary measure of people's WTP for the change in q. How is this obtained from the fitted response model? The key to the interpretation of the fitted response model is the fact, noted in Section 3.2, that this is derived from an underlying WTP distribution, $G_C(x)$. By exploiting this relationship, one recovers the underlying WTP distribution from the fitted response model.

With the closed-ended, single-bounded format, as noted in (9), $\pi^Y(A) = 1 - G_C(A)$.[64] This makes it possible to derive welfare measures directly from the graph of the response probability distribution. For example, *percentiles* of the estimated WTP distribution can be read directly from the graph of the fitted response model. The θ-percentile of the WTP distribution C_θ satisfies

$$\theta = G_C(C_\theta) = 1 - \pi^Y(C_\theta), \tag{30}$$

i.e., there is a $100(1 - \theta)\%$ probability that the individual would be willing to pay at least C_θ for the change in q.[65] In particular, the median estimated WTP is the quantity $C_{0.5}$, such that

$$0.5 = G_C(C_{0.5}) = 1 - \pi^Y(C_{0.5}), \tag{31}$$

i.e., there is a 50–50 chance that the individual would be willing to pay at least $C_{0.5}$. This was illustrated graphically in Figure 2 for the logit and log-logistic response models.

---

[63] The smoothing estimator could be applied to either the raw response probabilities or the PAV estimates; in the former case, one would choose the bandwidth parameter so as to ensure that the estimated response probability is nonincreasing.

[64] With other response formats, there still exists a relationship between the response model and the WTP, but it takes a different form.

[65] The analogs of C_θ in the biometrics literature are the effective dose $ED_{100\theta}$ and the lethal dose $LD_{100\theta}$. These are the dose levels or concentrations at which, on average, $100\theta\%$ of subjects respond (or succumb). The distribution of which they are the quantiles is usually called the tolerance distribution, analogous to the WTP distribution in the CV context. Much of the attention in the biometrics literature focuses on the medians ED_{50} and LD_{50}.

The analytic formulas for $C_{0.5}$ in these models are as follows. In the linear response model (21), if η has a symmetric distribution with a median (and mean) of zero, such as the standard normal or the standard logistic which generate the probit and logit response models (22) and (23), then

$$C_{0.5} = \frac{\alpha}{\beta}. \tag{32}$$

In the case of the Bishop–Heberlein model (17), if η has a symmetric distribution with a median (and mean) of zero, such as the standard normal or the standard logistic which generate the log-normal and log-logistic response models (25) and (26), then

$$C_{0.5} = \exp\left[\frac{\alpha}{\beta}\right]. \tag{33}$$

In the case of the nonparametric response model illustrated in Figure 3(a), while the definitions in (30) and (31) still apply, unless one of the estimated $\hat{\pi}_k^Y$ just happens to coincide with the quantile of interest, some form of interpolation is required; for example, in Figure 3(a), the point estimate of $C_{0.5}$ lies somewhere in the interval $[A_4, A_5]$. Any of the three approaches to interpolation mentioned above can be used. For example, Figure 3(b) shows the estimate of $C_{0.5}$ when one uses piecewise linear interpolation.

The alternative way to summarize the estimated WTP distribution is through the mean,

$$C^+ \equiv E\{C(q^0, q^1, p, y; \varepsilon)\} = \int_{C^{\min}}^{C^{\max}} c g_C(c)\, dc, \tag{34}$$

where $C^{\min}$ and $C^{\max}$ are the lower and upper support of the estimated WTP distribution, and $g_C(\cdot)$ is the pdf corresponding to the estimated WTP distribution. With a parametric WTP distribution, the formula for C^+ varies according to the specific distribution selected. In the linear response model (21), for example, if η has a mean of zero, as with the standard normal or standard logistic, which generate the probit and logit response models (22) and (23),[66]

$$C^+ = \frac{\alpha}{\beta} = C_{0.5}. \tag{35}$$

In this case, mean WTP coincides with median WTP. However, in the case of the Bishop–Heberlein model (17), if η is standard normal or standard logistic which generate the log-normal and log-logistic response models (25) and (26), mean and median WTP are *different*. With the lognormal response model (25)

$$C^+ = \exp\left[\frac{\alpha}{\beta}\right] \exp\left[\frac{1}{2\beta^2}\right] = C_{0.5} \exp\left[\frac{1}{2\beta^2}\right] \tag{36}$$

---

[66] The reader should be warned that the formulas for C^+ given in (35), (36) and (37) violate the utility-theoretic bound on the WTP distribution even though these formulas are commonly used in the literature. See Section 6 for further discussion.

while with the log-logistic response model (26),

$$
C^+ = \begin{cases} \exp\left[\dfrac{\alpha}{\beta}\right]\Gamma\left[1+\dfrac{1}{\beta}\right]\Gamma\left[1-\dfrac{1}{\beta}\right] & \text{if } \beta > 1, \\ \infty & \text{if } \beta \leqslant 1. \end{cases} \tag{37}
$$

In both cases $C^+ \geqslant C_{0.5}$, which reflects the fact that these WTP distributions are skewed to the right.

In addition to analytic formulas for C^+, there is also a graphical representation which depends on the support of the WTP distribution. Suppose for now that $C(q^0, q^1, p, y; \varepsilon)$ has a lower support of $C^{\min} = 0$.[67] The graphical representation of C^+ comes from a standard result about the relation between the mean of a positive random variable and the integral of its CDF [Parzen (1960)]:

$$
\begin{aligned}
C^+ &= \int_0^{C^{\max}} \left[1 - G_C(A)\right] dA \\
&= \int_0^{C^{\max}} \pi^Y(A)\, dA
\end{aligned} \tag{38}
$$

that corresponds to the shaded area under the graph of the response function in Figure 4.

The graphical representation of mean WTP in (38) sheds some light on the reason why this can differ from median WTP. Whereas $C_{0.5}$ depends on the location of the response probability graph at a particular point, namely the 50% probability level, C^+ depends on the location of the response probability graph *throughout its entire range*. When comparing any two response probability distributions, small differences in the right tail have essentially no effect on the median but they can effect the mean greatly.[68] This explains why the relation between mean and median WTP can vary with the

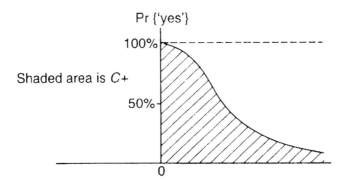

Figure 4. Mean WTP with nonnegative preferences.

---

[67] Whether or not this is an appropriate lower support is discussed further in Section 6.

[68] Boyle, Welsh and Bishop (1988) and Ready and Hu (1995) refer to this as the 'fat tails' problem.

specification of the WTP distribution. It illustrates the fact that in a RUM model, the specification of the stochastic component can have important economic implications.

In the case of the nonparametric response model illustrated in Figure 3(a), the calculation of C^+ is complicated by the fact that the nonparametric approach provides estimates of only a limited set of points within the support of the WTP distribution. This creates two problems. First, we need to "connect the dots" and flesh out the distribution at all *other* points within the range of observed bid values $[A_1, A_K]$. Second, we do not know what the response probability function looks like for amounts *lower* than A_1 or *greater* than A_K. For the first problem, three approaches to interpolation were noted above and two of these will lead to analytical expressions for C^+. In order to solve the second problem, one has to make some assumption about the unobserved portion of the response probability graph to the left of A_1 and to the right of A_K. A common approach is to fix the lower support of the WTP distribution by setting $\pi^Y(0) = 1$ (this will be revisited in Section 6), and to fix the upper support by assuming that there is some known amount $C^{\max}$, such that $\pi^Y(C^{\max}) = 0$. Combining these assumptions about the supports with the linear interpolation procedure (A), yields the graph depicted in Figure 3(b). Then, the nonparametric estimate of C^+ is obtained by applying (42) to this graph – i.e., by integrating the area under it. The resulting estimator of mean WTP corresponds to what is known in biometrics as the Spearman–Karber estimator $\hat{\mu}_{SK}$.[69] Setting $A_0 \equiv 0$ and $A_K \equiv C^{\max}$, the formula for $\hat{\mu}_{SK}$ can be written compactly as[70]

$$\hat{\mu}_{SK} = \sum_{k=1}^{K+1} (\hat{\pi}_k^Y - \hat{\pi}_{k-1}^Y)(A_k + A_{k-1}). \tag{39}$$

An alternative and far more conservative approach to dealing with the upper and lower supports of the WTP distribution assumes that $\pi^Y(A) = \hat{\pi}_1^Y$ for $0 < A \leqslant A_1$ and $\pi^Y(A) = 0$ for all $A \geqslant A_K$. Combining these assumptions with the conservative interpolation (B) mentioned above, and integrating the area under the graph in Figure 3(c), yields an estimate of mean WTP [Carson et al. (1992)] that corresponds to what is known in biometrics as the Kaplan–Meier–Turnbull estimator, $\hat{\mu}_{KM}$. This is given by[71]

$$\hat{\mu}_{KM} = \sum_{k=1}^{K} (\hat{\pi}_k^Y - \hat{\pi}_{k+1}^Y) A_k. \tag{40}$$

Because of the conservative assumptions on which it is based, $\hat{\mu}_{KM}$ should be viewed as a lower bound on the mean of the WTP distribution.[72] An alternative estimator is

---

[69] In the CV literature, this estimator was used by Kriström (1990).

[70] We are assuming here that the fitted response probability graph is nonincreasing.

[71] The nonparametric estimate of mean WTP proposed by Duffield and Patterson (1991a) is a slight variant of this.

[72] A potential drawback of the Kaplan–Meier–Turnbull lower bound on the mean WTP is that it is sensitive to the particular design points used in the following sense. The estimator is consistent in that as the possible

obtained by placing all of the density at the *upper* end of the intervals in Figure 3(c); this yields an upper bound on the estimate of mean WTP. This estimator bound the range from above and from below in which any estimate of mean WTP that is consistent with the observed data can fall.[73] The estimate of the Kaplan–Meier–Turnbull lower bound on mean WTP, in particular, is often very precisely defined if the sample size at each design point is fairly large.[74]

Given the difference between the mean C^+ and median $C_{0.5}$ as welfare measures, deciding which to use involves considerations of both statistics and economics. Suppose that the survey data came from repeated questioning of a single individual – while this is fairly impractical, one could imagine it happening. In that case, even though we were estimating a single individual's WTP, it still would be a random variable for us as outside observers because of the RUM hypothesis. The issue would then be just one of representation – what is the best way to summarize the probability distribution? The answer depends on the statistical loss function: with a sum-of-squared-errors loss function, the mean is the optimal measure of central tendency; with a sum-absolute errors loss function, the median is optimal. For this reason, the mean is more sensitive to skewness or kurtosis in the WTP distribution [Stavig and Gibbons (1977)]. This could be important because most RUM models with nonnegative preferences imply a skewed distribution of WTP. In that case, it can happen that the point estimate of the median is more robust, or has a much smaller sampling error than the estimate of the mean.

Now consider the more realistic situation where the survey data come from questioning different individuals in a population. In that case, the summary measure of the WTP distribution would be multiplied by the number of people in the population to produce an estimate of aggregate value. Thus, the choice of a summary statistic implies a particular approach to the aggregation of welfare across the population. The mean is equivalent to adopting the Kaldor–Hicks potential compensation principle. While the Kaldor–Hicks criterion is often invoked by economists, it can lead to logical inconsistencies and it has been severely criticized on ethical grounds [Little (1957)].[75] As a way to aggregate values, the median is equivalent to applying the principle of majority voting

---

support for the WTP distribution is filled in by using more and more design points, the Kaplan–Meier–Turnbull estimator increases toward the sample's WTP from below. An easy way to see the nature of the sensitivity to the design points chosen is to note that if the only design points used are small (relative to where most of the WTP distribution) lies, the Kaplan–Meier–Turnbull estimator cannot exceed the largest design point used.

[73] The upper bound on mean WTP is infinity as long as there is any fraction of the subsample receiving the highest design point is WTP that amount and no further restriction (discussed below) such as income is imposed as an upper bound on WTP.

[74] The formula for standard error of the Kaplan–Meier estimator is simply a linear combination of differences in the percent in favor at different design points and the magnitude of those design points.

[75] Critics of CV from outside of economics [e.g., Sagoff (1994)] are often in reality critics of benefit–cost analysis rather CV *per se*. It is CV's claim to encompass all "economic" value that makes the use of CV more troublesome to such critics.

(i.e., the change is desirable if a majority of the population would vote for it).[76] Using a lower quantile of the WTP distribution would correspond to super-majority voting; for example, it would correspond to requiring a two-thirds majority vote. It is known that majority voting rules do not satisfy Pareto efficiency; but they still may be considered ethically superior. In view of these welfare-theoretic implications, choosing a measure of central tendency is essentially a value judgment. Moreover, different circumstances may call for different welfare measure. Politicians tend to favor measures like the maximum amount a majority of the voters would approve, while in a natural resource damage assessment mean WTA is the natural measure because of the implied property right and legal requirement to restore all those who were injured to their original position. These are judgments that the researcher and policymakers must make.

4. Types of value/motives for valuation

So far we have made no assumption about the individual's motive for valuing q, or the nature of this value; whatever the reason why she cares for q, if she does care, this is reflected in her direct and indirect utility functions $u(x, q)$ and $v(p, q, y)$. In fact, the literature has developed an extensive set of potential motives and potential types of value [Mitchell and Carson (1989), Carson, Flores and Mitchell (1999)]. The standard typology distinguishes between existence value, bequest value, option value, and quasi-option value. Each of these can be explained in terms of a specific formulation of the individual's preference structure and a specific conceptualization of what is being valued by the individual. These conceptualizations are summarized below.

4.1. Existence value

The notion of existence value, also called passive use value, was first proposed by Krutilla (1967) who observed that people might be willing to pay for an environmental resource – say a national park – even if they knew that neither they nor their children would ever visit it because, as he famously put it, they "obtain satisfaction from mere knowledge that part of the wilderness in North America remains, even though they would be appalled by the prospect of being exposed to it." The underlying notion here is that these people value the park for motives unconnected with the possible use of the

---

[76] Calculation of the aggregate WTP estimate using majority approval is straightforward with a flax tax. This is no longer the case if the tax price can vary with agent characteristics like income. Werner and Groves (1993) look at this case by partitioning the population into groups and uses the average of the medians for each group. Suppose there are H groups; each group has a WTP distribution that has a mean C_h^+ and a median $C_{0.5,h}$. Werner and Groves' statistic, the average of the group medians, is $C^W \equiv (1/H) \sum C_{0.5,h}$. They establish that C^W generally lies between the overall population median $C_{0.5}$ and mean C^+, and that for a given sample size, while estimates of C^W do not have quite as low a variance as $C_{0.5}$, they have a considerably lower variance than C^+.

park. Hence, this value has also been called nonuse value, to distinguish it from an (active) use value that would be motivated by considerations of the enjoyment from using the resource in some fashion (e.g., visiting it). As we show below, although use and nonuse value are conceptually distinct, they are not mutually exclusive; they can both co-exist within the same individual.

Although several formalisms have been proposed in the literature for representing the concept of existence value, the one now most commonly used takes the following form. Suppose the direct utility function takes the specific form

$$u = u(x, q) = T\big[\bar{\phi}(x), q\big], \tag{41a}$$

where $T[\cdot, \cdot]$ is a bivariate function,[77] and $\bar{\phi}(\cdot)$ is a subfunction that aggregates the x's. Note that (41) involves a weak separability between the x's and q since the marginal rate of substitution between the consumption of any pair of market commodities, x_i and x_j, is entirely independent of the level of q. A consequence of the formulation in (41a) is that the ordinary demand functions for the x's are each independent of q; they take the form

$$x_i = h^i(p, q, y) = \bar{h}^i(p, y), \quad i = 1, \ldots, N, \tag{41b}$$

where the functions $\bar{h}^i(\cdot)$ are in fact the ordinary demand functions associated with the maximization of the subutility function $\bar{\phi}(\cdot)$ alone: maximizing $u(x, q)$ and $\bar{\phi}(x)$ subject to a budget constraint on the x's leads to exactly the same solution. The corresponding indirect utility function takes the form

$$u = v(p, q, y) = T\big[\bar{\psi}(p, y), q\big], \tag{41c}$$

where $\bar{\psi}(p, y)$ is the indirect utility function that corresponds to maximization of the subutility function $\bar{\phi}(\cdot)$ alone. While the person cares for q – it enters her direct and indirect utility functions via the $T[\cdot, \cdot]$ function – the presence of q in her utility function has *no* effect on her utility maximizing choice of the x's. It is in this sense that one could say that this individual values q for reasons *unconnected* with her valuation of the market goods x. In this case, q would be said to have a pure nonuse (existence, passive use) value.

Now consider a modified version of the above utility function

$$u = u(x, q) = T\big[\bar{\phi}(x, q), q\big], \tag{42a}$$

where, as before, $T[\cdot, \cdot]$ is a bivariate function and $\bar{\phi}(\cdot)$ is a subfunction. In this case, q enters the utility twice, once through its appearance in $\bar{\phi}(\cdot)$ and the other time as the second argument in $T[\cdot, \cdot]$. Here, the individual values q for two reasons: one reason is connected with her consumption of the x's and is represented by the interaction of x and q in $\bar{\phi}(x, q)$; the other reason is unconnected with her consumption of the x's and

---

[77] This is assuming that q is a scalar.

is represented by the appearance of q as the second argument of $T[\cdot,\cdot]$. In this case, the ordinary demand functions *do* depend on q: they take the form

$$x_i = h^i(p,q,y) = \bar{h}^i(p,q,y), \quad i = 1,\dots,N, \tag{42b}$$

where the functions $\bar{h}^i(p,q,y)$ are in fact the ordinary demand functions associated with the maximization of the subutility function $\bar{\phi}(x,q)$ alone. The crucial implication of this fact is that revealed preferences based purely on estimation of the demand functions for market goods $\bar{h}^i(p,q,y)$, $i = 1,\dots,N$, will recover only the subutility function $\bar{\phi}(x,q)$, but *not* the function $T[\cdot,\cdot]$. The indirect utility function associated with (42a,b) is

$$u = v(p,q,y) = T\big[\bar{\psi}(p,q,y),q\big], \tag{42c}$$

where $\bar{\psi}(p,q,y)$ is the indirect utility function that corresponds to maximization of the subutility function $\bar{\phi}(x,q)$ alone. Applying (1) to (42a), the total value that the individual places on a change in q, denoted C^{TOT}, is given by

$$T\big[\bar{\psi}\big(p,q^1,y - C^{\text{TOT}}\big),q^1\big] = T\big[\bar{\psi}\big(p,q^0,y\big),q^0\big]. \tag{42d}$$

This has both a use value component, associated with $\bar{\psi}(p,q,y)$, and a nonuse value component, associated with $T[\cdot,q]$; the use component, C^{U}, satisfies

$$\bar{\psi}\big(p,q^1,y - C^{\text{U}}\big) = \bar{\psi}\big(p,q^0,y\big), \tag{42e}$$

while the nonuse component C^{NU} would be defined as the difference

$$C^{\text{NU}} \equiv C^{\text{TOT}} - C^{\text{NU}}. \tag{42f}$$

From a CV modeling perspective, the distinction between use and nonuse components of the individual's total value for a change in q could in principle be captured by formulating a CV response probability model based on a specification of a utility function that conforms to the structure of (42a,c), where the $\bar{\psi}(p,q,y)$ and $T[\cdot,\cdot]$ functions could be separately identified. The crucial feature of this structure is that prices and income interact in a manner that is partially separable from q.[78] However, the very simple specifications of the indirect utility function employed in the literature to date, in which commodity prices are not generally explicit variables, makes it unlikely that this can be done; and therefore, unlikely that the use and nonuse components of C^{TOT} can effectively be disentangled in the econometric estimation of CV responses if the *only* information elicited in the survey relates to C^{TOT}.

Several CV researchers have approached the problem by first asking respondents for their total value and then requesting that they allocate this total among several specific motives. When this has been done, it has been in the context of an open-ended CV elicitation format.[79] Suppose for the moment that the only motives are use and nonuse

---

[78] Entirely separable in the case of (41a,c).

[79] For an example see Walsh, Loomis and Gillman (1984).

value (the other components will be considered below). It seems unlikely that total value plus the elicited allocation between the two components could be used effectively to recover the specific underlying utility function – i.e., the separate components $\bar{\phi}(x, q)$ and $T[\cdot, \cdot]$. Aside from this theoretical consideration, there are several empirical objections to this type of decomposition approach. In terms of survey practice, it seems unwise to employ a top–down approach of first asking for a total, without identifying the specific individual items to be included in this total, and only afterwards specifying the individual components that the researcher has in mind and asking about them. On cognitive grounds, if people think holistically about an item, it may be difficult for them to produce a meaningful and reliable decomposition of this whole *ex post*. For both these reasons, a bottom–up approach seems preferable in which respondents are introduced to the separate components and asked about each of them, with the adding up occurring subsequently. In addition to the cognitive difficulty, Mitchell and Carson (1989), Carson and Mitchell (1991) and Cummings and Harrison (1995) point out that these decompositions are generally not unique since the portion of value allocated to a particular motivation may differ depending on the other elicited motivations and the sequence in which they are elicited. Moreover, given all of the potential motivations, no list could ever be exhaustive for *all* individuals.

4.2. Combining CV and RP data to measure use versus nonuse value

Given the structure of (42a–f) which generates the decomposition of the total value for the change in q into a use value component based on $\bar{\psi}(p, q, y)$, and a nonuse value component based on $T[\cdot, q]$; a more fruitful approach to identifying the two separate components of value is to collect two sets of information, one being total value from a CV survey and the other being revealed preference (RP) data on the demand functions for one or more of the x's. Suppose, for simplicity, there is sufficient revealed preference data to estimate a complete demand system for the x's. This would be combined with CV data on total value, using an assumed specification of the indirect utility function along the lines of (42a) to estimate a system consisting of

$$x_1 = h^1(p, q, y) = -\frac{\partial \bar{\psi}(p, q, y)/\partial p_1}{\partial \bar{\psi}(p, q, y)/\partial y},$$

$$\vdots \tag{43}$$

$$x_N = h^N(p, q, y) = -\frac{\partial \bar{\psi}(p, q, y)/\partial p_N}{\partial \bar{\psi}(p, q, y)/\partial y},$$

$$T[\bar{\psi}(p, q^1, y - C^{\text{TOT}}), q^1] = T[\bar{\psi}(p, q^0, y), q^0].$$

The advantage of this approach is that the revealed preference data enrich the CV data, the two sets of data are analyzed in a mutually consistent manner, and they permit the estimation of the separate components of total value; at least in this particular case, where there are only use and nonuse components in total value. Pioneering studies following this approach include Cameron (1992) and Adamowicz, Louviere and Williams (1994).[80]

4.3. Contingent behavior

Before going on to consider other possible types of value, it is useful to take note of an approach that parallels the type of data combination in (43) but is restricted only to the estimation of use value in a pure revealed preference context. The goal of this approach is solely to estimate a demand function or system of demand functions; but the conventional data on prices and quantities consumed is supplemented by responses to a survey question with a discrete-response format question that is analogous to a CV question. The survey question focuses on demand behavior rather than willingness to pay *per se*; hence, this approach has been called contingent behavior by Chapman, Hanemann and Kanninen (1993).

The setting is typically that the researcher envisages a two-good demand system where one good is the particular commodity of interest (e.g., sport fishing at lakes and rivers in Wisconsin) and the second good is a Hicksian composite commodity of all other consumption.[81] The researcher has individual-level data on the price of the first good and the number of fishing trips taken by each angler and has used a survey to supplement this data. The survey question asks about circumstances under which the angler would stop fishing altogether (i.e., make his consumption of x_1 equal to zero). There are two alternative versions of the survey question. One version focuses on the price of the commodity p_1, and asks something like "If you had to pay an extra price per trip of Δ_p as an increment to the cost of fishing in Wisconsin, would you still keep fishing in Wisconsin, albeit perhaps at a reduced level, or would you stop fishing altogether?" The other version introduces the notion of annual permit, which entails an income reduction as opposed to a price increase; with this version, the question is something like "If you had to buy an annual permit costing Δ_y to be allowed to go fishing in Wisconsin would you buy this permit or would you give up fishing in Wisconsin altogether?" In either case, the response to the survey question is combined with data on the current number of fishing trips in Wisconsin taken by the angler, x_1, and the current cost of fishing there, p_1. Suppose the angler says that he *would* keep fishing despite the

---

[80] For recent review of the issues involved in combining the two sources of data see Azevedo, Herriges and Kling (2003). There exist a parallel literature in the transportation and marketing literatures [e.g., Ben-Akiva and Morikawa (1990)]. Swait and Louviere (1993) point out that there is no reason to expect the underlying variance parameters to be the same in the revealed and stated preference data sources; and, that this must be allowed for statistically when combining the two sources of data. Statistical issues related to this topic are further pursued in Hensher, Louviere and Swait (1999).

[81] There is a particular justification for focusing on this two-good model because it is only in this case that the Kuhn–Tucker conditions for a corner solution for the commodity of interest ($x_1 = 0$) can be represented fully in terms of the simple inequality on the demand function presented in (44); see Lee and Pitt (1986) and Hanemann (1985) for an elaboration of these conditions.

increment Δ_p or Δ_y. With the first version of the survey question, by combining the survey response with the travel cost data, the researcher knows the following about the individual's demand function for fishing

$$x_1 = h^1(p_1, p_2, y),$$
$$h^1(p_1 + \Delta_p, p_2, y) > 0. \tag{44a}$$

With the second version of the survey question, if the angler says he would still keep fishing in Wisconsin, the researcher knows that[82]

$$x_1 = h^1(p_1, p_2, y),$$
$$h^1(p_1, p_2, y - \Delta_y) > 0. \tag{44b}$$

The system of equations in (44a) and (44b) is the basis for estimation – for example, to formulate a likelihood function for maximum likelihood estimation – in a manner similar to that employed with (43).

4.4. Bequest value

In addition to existence value, Krutilla (1967) also introduced the concept of "bequest value" – some people would be willing to pay to protect a national park because they want to preserve it for their children and grandchildren. This motivation can be incorporated in the utility model used above in the following manner. As far as these people are concerned, the future generations' consumption is something that they care for but it is not something that they see themselves as controlling. Thus it enters their utility function in a manner analogous to q – something that affects their welfare but is exogenous to them. We can think now of q as being a vector with two separate components, $q = (q_1, q_2)$, where q_1 is the existence of the national park, which affects them either as visitors to the park (a use value) and/or for nonuse reasons associated with the significance of its existence value to them and where q_2 is the well-being of their children and grandchildren. Because of the bequest motive, the protection of the park now involves a shift in *both* elements of q. With this, the formalism in (1) and (2) carries over as the definition of the individual's WTP and WTA to protect the park. Thus, the bequest motive leads to a potential re-specification of the underlying utility function but does not otherwise change the formal theory of the CV response probability function.

4.5. Option value

In addition to the work of Krutilla (1967), the other foundational paper on extensions of use value was Weisbrod (1964) who, like Krutilla, adopted the premise that the natural

---

[82] The first version of the survey question leading to (44a) was proposed by Hanemann (1985) and applied by Chapman, Hanemann and Kanninen (1993). The second version of the survey question leading to (44b) was employed by Cameron (1992).

environment is not a conventional type of economic commodity and that some people's motives for valuing it differ from those for valuing private market goods. Weisbrod focused on uncertainty and what became known as "option value": some people who do not now visit a national park, say, may still be willing to pay money to protect it from destruction or irreversible damage because they want to preserve their option of visiting it in the future. Following the publication of Weisbrod's paper, there was extensive literature discussing the precise formulation of a formal utility-theoretic definition of the value that Weisbrod alluded to. Obviously, this involves a model of choice under uncertainty, unlike the model of certain choice employed thus far. A full and final resolution of the discussion on formalizing Weisbrod's concept was provided by Graham (1981, 1984). Cameron and Englin (1997) applied Graham's formalism for analyzing responses to a CV question on option value, and we follow their development here, using the context of protecting a national park from environmental damage as an example.

Two core features of Graham's model are state-dependent preferences and uncertainty about the state of world. The utility model of Section 3 is now adapted to incorporate these features.[83] There are two possible future states of the world; in one state, the individual is an active user (visitor) of the national park, while in the other state, the individual is not an active user but may or may not derive existence (or bequest) value from it. Conditional on the first state occurring, the individual's indirect utility function is $v_a(q, y)$; conditional on the second state occurring, the individual's utility is $v_n(q, y)$. As far as the park is concerned, that can either be environmentally damaged or undamaged; let $q = 0$ denote the situation where the park is damaged, and $q = 1$ is the situation where, presumably as the result of some policy intervention, the park is undamaged. Finally, π denotes the individual's subjective probability that he will in future be a user of the park, while $1 - \pi$ is the probability of not being a user. Cameron and Englin allow for the possibility that this probability itself depends on the state of the park, so that $\pi = \pi(q)$; if the park is environmentally damaged, the probability of visiting it is lowered, $\pi(0) < \pi(1)$. In addition, there may be uncertainty that the environmental damage will occur: $P(1)$ is the individual's subjective probability that $q = 1$, while $P(0) = 1 - P(1)$ is the subjective probability that $q = 0$.

Following Graham (1981) and others in the theoretical literature on this topic, there is a distinction between option price and expected surplus. The expected surplus is derived as follows. If the individual knew for sure that he would be an active user of the park, his WTP to protect it from environmental damage would be S_a, where this satisfies

$$v_a(1, y - S_a) = v_a(0, y);$$ \hfill (45a)

conversely, if he knew for sure that he would *not* be an active user, his WTP would be S_n, where

$$v_n(1, y - S_n) = v_n(0, y).$$ \hfill (45b)

---

[83] For simplicity, we suppress the commodity prices p.

These are both *ex post* measures of WTP for $q = 1$ versus $q = 0$. *Ex ante*, the expected value of this WTP, known as the *expected surplus*, is

$$E\{S\} = \left[\pi(1)P(1) + \pi(0)P(0)\right]S_a + \left[\left(1 - \pi(1)\right)P(1) + \left(1 - \pi(0)\right)P(0)\right]S_n. \tag{45c}$$

Using Hirschleifer's (1965, 1966) extension of the von Neumann–Morgenstern expected utility theorem, the individual's baseline expected utility when no policy intervention is undertaken is

$$E\{V\}^* = \pi(0)P(0)v_a(0, y) + \left(1 - \pi(0)\right)P(0)v_n(0, y). \tag{46}$$

The option price is the sure payment that, regardless of uncertain user status, the individual is willing to pay to ensure that the park is protected from environmental damage. It is the quantity OP, which satisfies the following equality:

$$E\{V\}^* = \pi(1)P(1)v_a(1, y - OP) + \left(1 - \pi(1)\right)P(1)v_n(1, y - OP). \tag{47}$$

An empirical implementation of these measures requires explicit models for (i) $\pi = \pi(q)$, the subjective conditional probability of participation given the environmental status of the national park; (ii) $P(q)$, the subjective probability of the status of the park; and (iii) $v_a(q, y)$ and $v_n(q, y)$, the state-dependent utilities, which could be any of the utility models given in Section 3.

Cameron and Englin (1997) provide an empirical implementation of this framework to responses from surveys of the general population in four New England states in 1989 which had asked a discrete-response CV question "If acid rain damaged fishing in one fifth of all currently fishable high-altitude lakes in the Northeast, would you be willing to pay $\$X$ per year to prevent this?" They point out that because the survey question was not sufficiently explicit, there are two possible interpretations of the respondents' answers. One possibility is that respondents harbored *no* uncertainty regarding their future use condition – for example, they assumed that their condition now will carry over into the future, so that if they are a user now, they assume they will be a user in the future; while if they are not a user now, they assume they will not be a user in the future. In that case, their survey response is based on the surplus S_a or S_n – they answered "yes" if $S_j > X$, $j =$ a or n, and "no" otherwise. This would then be a standard discrete-response CV of the type discussed in Section 3. However, another possibility is that respondents were unsure of their future use status (and, perhaps also, the extent of future damage to the park) when they answered the survey question. In that case, their response would correspond to OP in (47), and they would have answered "yes" if $OP > X$, and "no" otherwise.

5. Elicitation formats for stated preference information

Originally, economists tended to take one of two positions with regard to surveys (see Section 2): either survey respondents tell the truth, in which case useful information can could be obtained from surveys, or they strategically misrepresent their preferences, in which case no useful information can be obtained. This all-or-nothing stance led to a paralysis among economists seeking to measure preferences using surveys until the empirical breakthrough by Davis (1963a) which produced "reasonable" and convincing survey results. This was followed up by a close comparison of the CV welfare estimate with one from a travel cost model by Knetsch and Davis (1966) which showed the two results were broadly similar. Further support was provided by Bohm's classic market experiment comparing "hypothetical" and "actual" payments, which suggested that the problems with a hypothetical survey were far less than economists had feared. As a result, the use of CV rapidly expanded and, as it did, a new issue presented itself. It became evident that different ways of asking preference questions yielded different estimates of willingness to pay.

The first CV surveys, starting with Davis (1963a), used what was called the "bidding game" format. In this format, respondents were asked a series of questions, along the lines of: "Would you continue to use this recreational area if the cost was to increase by $A?" or "Would you be willing to pay $A for this item?" If the respondent said "yes" the question was then repeated with a larger value for A; if "no," it was repeated with a lower value for A. This continued until the response switched from "yes" to "no," or from "no" to "yes," thereby isolating a specific amount that was the most that the respondent was willing to pay. It was this final amount that was recorded by the researcher as the respondent's WTP. Researchers eventually began to focus attention on the starting bid utilized in the question sequence. Rowe, d'Arge and Brookshire (1980) found that the starting point had a sizeable influence on the final estimate of willingness to pay. However, Thayer (1981) found no such effect.

The lingering concern about the possible influence of the starting bid then led researchers to employ a simpler approach in which respondents were asked a single, open-ended question along the lines of "What is the most that you would be willing to pay for this item?" It was found that this sometimes produced a large number of "don't know" responses. To deal with this, Mitchell and Carson (1981) proposed the payment card approach, whereby respondents were given a card containing an array of numbers and asked to choose a number on the card (or any number in between) which best represented their maximum willingness to pay. Desvousges, Smith and Fisher (1987) tested these alternative approaches in the context of valuing water quality improvements and found that they produced different results: the lowest estimate of WTP was produced by a bidding game with a $25 starting point, followed by the direct (open-ended) question and the payment card, with the bidding game using a $125 starting point resulting in the highest estimate. In some comparisons, the $25 and $125 starting point bidding games differed statistically but in others they did not. In effect, these results fell somewhere between Rowe, d'Arge and Brookshire (1980) and Thayer (1981). The Desvousges, Smith and Fisher study was noteworthy for the care given to the investigation of how the different payment approaches affected the distribution of responses, something that had not been considered in the earlier literature.

Implicit in the elicitation formats considered so far was an effort to "isolate" the individual's exact maximum willingness to pay. Bishop and Heberlein (1979, 1980) took a different approach and sought to bound it rather than measure it exactly. They asked a single, closed-ended question along the lines of "If the cost to you was A, would you buy (vote for) this item?" Only one question was asked of each respondent, but the valuation amount A was varied across respondents, using random assignment with a set number of alternative values for A. In effect, this was analogous to a dose-response experiment in biometrics where A corresponded to the stimulus in the experiment and yes/no was the response; as illustrated in Figure 3, the plot of the percent of yes responses against the bid amount provided a useful response surface. This approach subsequently became known as the referendum, single-bounded, or binary discrete-response format.

The drawback with this approach was that it provided limited information about the respondent's willingness to pay, only that it was greater or less than A. Compared to the open-ended question format, one needed a large number of respondents to obtain an estimate of WTP with the same given precision. Carson (1985) showed that one could use a double sampling framework to ask a second binary discrete choice question conditional on the response to the first. If the respondent said "yes" to the first valuation question, the question was repeated with a higher value for A; if "no," it was repeated with a lower value for A. Hanemann (1985), Carson and Steinberg (1990) and Hanemann, Loomis and Kanninen (1991) were to further develop this notion into what is now known as the double-bounded approach because it has the potential to generate both an upper and a lower bound on the respondent's WTP.[84]

Many of the early CV studies asked respondents questions about several different changes in air quality [e.g., Randall, Ives and Eastman (1974)], outdoor recreation [Cicchetti and Smith (1973)], or water quality [Mitchell and Carson (1981)].[85] This was relatively straightforward to do, although concerns about impact of question order clearly existed [Mitchell and Carson (1986)]. The most natural way to extend this framework was to ask a series of paired comparisons, along the lines of "Which do you prefer – program 1, which involves paying A_1 and obtaining outcome q_1, or program 2, which involves paying A_2 and obtaining outcome q_2?"[86] The standard single-bounded question format can be viewed as a special case of a paired comparison with one alternative being the *status quo* – pay nothing and obtain nothing – and the other being the specific program in question. The paired comparison approach extends this by

---

[84] If two binary discrete choice questions could be asked, then a third could also be asked as proposed by Bateman et al. (2001).

[85] The usual intention here was to estimate a valuation function that gave WTP as a function of the level of the environmental amenity being valued and respondent characteristics. Perhaps the best know example is the national water quality valuation function in Carson and Mitchell (1993) that has been heavily used by the U.S. Environmental Protection Agency for a variety of policy purposes including valuing the benefits of the U.S. Clean Water Act. Carson, Mitchell and Ruud (1990) provide an example using health and visibility effects from air quality improvement programs. They fit a response surface design to the continuous WTP data elicited to allow interactions between the two program attributes.

[86] For a review of the approach see Brown and Peterson (2003).

permitting a sequence of paired comparisons involving multiple programs compared sequentially to a common *status quo* or to each other. In implementing this approach, one needs to choose the payment amounts A_j in such a way that they do not appear mutually inconsistent – i.e., a more extensive program should cost more than a less extensive program.

An alternative to a sequence of pairwise comparisons is a single, multinomial comparison, along the following lines: "The government is considering three possible programs: program 1, which involves paying A_1 and obtaining outcome q_1; program 2, which involves paying A_2 and obtaining outcome q_2; and program 3, which involves paying A_3 and obtaining outcome q_3. Alternatively, the government could take no action, which will cost you nothing but will lead to no change in the present situation. Which of these options do you prefer?" The responses can be analyzed in keeping with the random utility model proposed by McFadden (1974).[87] In the first environmental application [Carson et al. (1987), Carson, Hanemann and Steinberg (1990)] of what is now known as the choice experiment format, respondents were offered the possibility of purchasing varying numbers of fishing stamps that each allowed the right to catch and keep one Alaskan Kenai King salmon. The cost of the different options was randomly assigned and a no purchase option was offered. The major advantage of this approach, in addition to its improved statistical efficiency, is that it permits the researcher to estimate how changes in the individual attributes across the choice alternatives alter the respondents' choices and, hence, to value changes in individual attributes.[88]

An alternative to having the respondent select the best out of a set of multinomial choice alternatives is to have her rank the complete set of alternatives. This approach had been popular in the marketing and psychology literatures and was first implemented in the environmental valuation literature by Rae (1982) for air quality improvements in Cincinnati. However, the approach proved to be difficult and time consuming to implement as the number of choices and attributes grew. The method was shown by Ruud (1986) to produce results that seem to violate economic theory in the sense that respondents either had lexicographic preferences or ignored some attributes in ranking the alternatives.[89] In later years, it was not often implemented. Mackenzie (1993) revived

---

[87] For a review of this literature see Chapter 15 by Phaneuf and Smith in this Handbook or Herriges and Kling (1999).

[88] It is possible to ask multiple multinomial choice questions to gain even greater statistical efficiency. As explained below, a drawback of the approach, not recognized at first, is that for public goods (as opposed to private or quasi-private goods) only one configuration of the public good can actually be provided. This creates the possibility that truthful preference revelation is not a dominate strategy in the multinomial choice setting.

[89] This issue was explored in more depth in Hausman and Ruud (1987). If the set of alternatives is completely ranked and the usual i.i.d. error assumption made in a multinomial logit model holds, then it should be possible to explode the ranked ordered data into the set of choices implied [Chapman and Staelin (1982)]. Hausman and Ruud's analysis suggest that people pay less attention to alternatives ranked in the middle so that the i.i.d. assumption is violated. If it is necessary to model the "scale" factor associated with each level of ranking then much of the gain from the complete ranking exercise disappears.

the format to some degree by tying it to binary discrete choice CV and moving in the direction of using rating data.

Although it is hard for respondents to completely rank a large set of alternatives, it is not difficult for them to pick their most preferred and least preferred alternatives in what is called "best–worst" approach [Marley and Louviere (in press)]. Another approach asks respondents to give a "rating" which describes the intensity with which they prefer one alternative to another [Johnson and Desvousges (1997)]. Both these approaches are now seeing considerable application in the marketing literature. The best–worst approach maintains the tight link to random utility; however, the rated pairs approach veers off towards cardinal utility because it treats the rating as a measure of preference intensity.

5.1. Response probability models for alternative elicitation formats

As noted earlier, the statistical model of the CV survey responses depends on the specific form of the question used in the survey. The response probability models presented in Section 3.3 correspond to the single-bounded referendum format. For the open-ended question formats, whether the bidding game version, the payment card version, or the direct open-ended questions, the response probability model is a regression equation along the lines of (10) or (11).

In the case of the double-bounded format, the response probability model is given by a natural extension of (9) or (18). In this case, with two valuation questions, there are four possible response outcomes: (yes, yes); (yes, no); (no, yes) and (no, no). Let the dollar amount in the initial valuation question be denoted by A. If the response to that question is yes, this is followed with a second valuation question using a higher amount A_U; if no, it is followed up using a lower amount A_L.[90] Accordingly, the general formula for the various response probabilities is:[91]

$$
\begin{aligned}
&\Pr(\text{Response is yes/no}) = \Pr(A_U \geqslant C \geqslant A) \equiv G_C(A_U) - G_C(A), \\
&\Pr(\text{Response is no/yes}) = \Pr(A \geqslant C \geqslant A_L) \equiv G_C(A) - G_C(A_L), \\
&\Pr(\text{Response is yes/yes}) = \Pr(C \geqslant A_U) \equiv 1 - G_C(A_U), \\
&\Pr(\text{Response is no/no}) = \Pr(A_L \geqslant C) \equiv G_C(A_L).
\end{aligned}
\tag{45}
$$

[90] It is worth commenting on how this differs from the bidding game format. The key difference is that, in the bidding game, the final response is conceptualized as being exactly equal to the respondent's maximum WTP, while in the double-bounded format the response is seen as yielding bounds on the WTP rather being than a direct estimate of WTP itself. Similarly, the payment card format can be conceptualized as yielding either an exact expression of WTP – as in Mitchell and Carson (1981) – or upper and lower bounds on WTP, which is the interpretation applied by Cameron and Huppert (1989).

[91] Another possibility is to ask a *third* valuation question, using a higher or lower bid amount that used in the second question, depending on the response; this "triple bound" format was considered by Bateman et al. (2001). As long as one views the final response as providing bounds rather than an exact measure of WTP, the response probability model takes the same form as (45).

With choice experiments, it is necessary to represent the response in terms of the random utility function rather than the willingness to pay function. Suppose there are K alternatives, each involving a cost of A_k and an outcome q_k; in a paired comparison, $K = 2$, while in a multinomial choice experiment $K > 2$. Suppose the individual selects alternative number 1; the probability of this response is given by

Pr{alternative 1 selected}

$$= \Pr\{v(q_1, p, y - A_1; \varepsilon) \geqslant v(q_k, p, y - A_k; \varepsilon), \ k = 1, \ldots, K\}. \tag{46}$$

With ranking, suppose for simplicity that there are 3 alternatives in addition to the status quo (q_0, $A_0 = 0$), and suppose the respondent prefers all of the alternatives to doing nothing and ranks them in the order 1, then 2, and then 3. The probability of this response is given by

Pr{1 preferred to 2 preferred to 3 preferred to status quo}

$$= \Pr\{v(q_1, p, y - A_1; \varepsilon) \geqslant v(q_2, p, y - A_2; \varepsilon)$$

$$\geqslant v(q_3, p, y - A_3; \varepsilon) \geqslant v(q_0, p, y; \varepsilon)\}. \tag{47}$$

Analogous formulas apply for "best–worst" ranking format.

So far in this section, the focus has been a parametric representation of the response probability function. Just as with the single-bounded approach, the double-bounded format also lends itself well to nonparametric estimation of the response probabilities, in a manner parallel to that associated with (29) and Figure 3. It is now convenient to work with the probability of saying no rather than yes; let $\pi^N(A)$ denote the probability of saying no in a single-bounded survey. Considered nonparametrically, this can be represented by viewed as an unknown function of the bid amount that is observed only at a discrete set of points, namely A_k, $k = 1, \ldots, K$. We supplement them with two "artificial" bid amounts, A_0 and A_{K+1}. These are to be defined such that $\pi^N(A_0) = 0$ and $\pi^N(A_{K+1}) = 1$; a natural choice for the first is $A_0 = 0$ while for the second one chooses some amount that the researcher considers an upper bound on the likely WTP, $A_{K+1} = C^{\max}$, such that $\pi^N(C^{\max}) = 1$. Define the $K + 1$ constants $\omega_k = G(A_k) - G(A_{k-1})$, $k = 1, \ldots, K + 1$, corresponding to the increase in the probability of a "no" response over the $K + 1$ intervals at which $G(A)$ is observed, including the two artificial bids. Observe that, for each $k = 1, \ldots, K + 1$,

$$G(A_k) = \sum_1^k \omega_j, \tag{48a}$$

while the ω_k satisfy the restrictions that

$$\omega_k \geqslant 0, \quad k = 1, \ldots, K + 1, \tag{48b}$$

which ensures that the $G(A_k)$ are monotone nondecreasing, and

$$\sum_1^{K+1} \omega_k = 1. \tag{48c}$$

The likelihood function analogous to (29) for the double-bounded response probabilities in (45) is given by

$$L = \prod_{k=1}^{K+1} [\omega_k]^{N_k}, \tag{49}$$

where the parameters ω_k, $k = 1, \ldots, K + 1$, are to be estimated subject to the constraints in (48b,c). Turnbull (1976) developed the maximum likelihood estimator for (49) analogous to the Ayer et al. (1955) nonparametric estimator for (29). He shows that the first-order conditions for the likelihood maximization imply the pool-adjacent violators principle so that, if the observed sample $S(A_k)$ are decreasing in some region, one combines adjacent bids until the sequence is nondecreasing.[92] Given the Turnbull estimates of ω_k, the corresponding estimates of $S(A_k)$ are obtained recursively by repeated application of (48a).

Whichever response format is adopted, once the parameters of the WTP distribution and/or the random utility functions have been estimated, the welfare measures are calculated in the same way as described above in Section 3.4 in connection with the single-bounded format. The percentiles of WTP distribution are given by (3) and (31); the mean is given by (34) and (38); and, with the nonparametric Turnbull estimates of double-bounded data, the nonparametric Spearman–Karber and Kaplan–Meier estimates of the mean are given by (39) and (40).[93]

5.2. The issue of incentive compatibility

If all of these elicitation approaches produced statistically similar estimates of willingness to pay, the debate over the choice of format to use might have stayed focused on issues of statistical efficiency. Even that debate, though was being pulled in a different direction from the pragmatic perspective of survey administration. Conceptually, the simple direct question yielded the most information about an individual respondent's WTP for the good. This was perhaps the hardest elicitation format, however, to actually get respondents to answer in a survey and tended to result in large nonresponse rates and a much larger than expected number of zero responses. In any event, however, the estimates from different elicitation formats were not generally statistically equivalent and the differences between them were sometimes quite large.

One interpretation of this phenomenon is that respondents did not have well-formed/well-developed preferences for the environmental goods they were being asked

---

[92] This nonparametric approach was first applied to double-bounded CV data by Carson and Steinberg (1990).

[93] The Kaplan–Meier estimate is now popularly called the Turnbull lower bound on mean WTP [Carson et al. (1994), Haab and McConnell (1997)] after Turnbull (1976) who generalized the estimator to cover a wide range of possible data types.

about in CV surveys. The foundation for this viewpoint was the psychological literature which contended that preferences were "labile" and impacted by how questions
were framed [Lichtenstein and Slovic (1971), Fischhoff, Slovic and Lichtenstein (1980),
Tversky and Kahneman (1986)].[94] Preferences, in the sense thought of by economists
as something, not necessarily fixed, but temporally quite stable [e.g., Stigler and Becker
(1977)], were not seen as a valid concept by these psychologists.[95] Ironically, while
framing effects can be shown to exist, preferences, at least at from the perspective of
aggregate level valuation in a CV study, have been found to be quite constant over time
periods of several years.[96]

An alternative explanation often advanced by economists, was that the environmental
goods being valued were something new to respondents and the context in which they
were being valued was novel, and as such respondent's lacked "market experience." The
sensitivity to the way in which the elicitation question was asked and to other aspects of
the scenario; such as, the payment vehicle, the order in which goods were valued, and
the amount of information being provided, was seen as a specific issue for environmental valuation, rather than something that was problematic for economics as a whole.[97]
As time went on, however, it became clear that the critique raised by psychologists and
the burgeoning new field of behavioral economics had little to do with environmental
valuation *per se* but was rather a critique of neoclassical consumer demand theory. In
retrospect, this should not have been surprising. Many of the framing issues discovered by psychologists had long been exploited in marketing; and hence, were readily
demonstrable with goods and choice contexts that were very familiar to consumers.

5.3. Some general results on incentives

Economists working on CV had occasionally paid attention to strategic incentives facing
respondents. The first key insight was by Brookshire, Ives and Schulze (1976) who
noted that strategic behavior would lead to a flatter WTP distribution, in the sense that
there would be more low WTP amounts and more high WTP amounts if such behavior

---

[94] There have been occasional attempts [e.g., Fischhoff and Furby (1988)] to draw upon this literature to
provide guidance on how to design reliable CV questions.

[95] Part of the debate here is semantic in nature. Economists don't really think that people walk around with
a vector of willingness to pay for all possible goods in all possible contexts imprinted in their minds; even if
formal theoretical models appear to implicitly make this assumption. Empirical models allow for the possibility of optimization errors and rational choice theory simply assumes that the errors made by agents are not
systematic and predictable in advances. The heuristics and bias view of the world adapted by these psychologists has played a large role in influencing what is now termed behavioral economics [Camerer, Loewenstein
and Rabin (2003)]. McFadden (1999a) provides an insightful discussion from the perspective of modeling
choice data. Ironically, preferences, at least at from the perspective of aggregate level valuation in a CV study,
have proven to be quite reliable over time periods of several years.

[96] For an example, see Carson et al. (1997).

[97] The best known attack on CV from the psychology perspective was Kahneman and Knetsch (1992) known
widely for its "embedding" test. This issue is discussed at more length in Section 9.

existed, than in the true WTP distribution. The difficulty with this insight was that it required knowing the true WTP distribution. Brookshire, Ives and Schulze looked at this issue by providing respondents with information about the WTP distribution of the other respondents but this did not seem to have a large impact on subsequent responses.

Interest in exploring the implications of strategic behavior seemed to flounder until Hoehn and Randall (1987) and Mitchell and Carson (1989). Hoehn and Randall, who looked at binary discrete choice questions, made the pivotal jump to seeing strategic behavior as critically linked to the properties of the elicitation format used. Mitchell and Carson took the possibility of strategic behavior seriously in a variety of contexts and showed that some widely held views simply did not pan out. They explored the implications of the growing literature on incentive compatibility.

The implications of Hoehn and Randall's insight was far ranging. If the incentives for strategic behavior were tied to the elicitation format used, then different elicitation formats might well produce different results. Indeed, as Carson, Groves and Machina (2000) [hereafter CGM] were to argue in a comprehensive analysis of different elicitation formats, if different response formats did not yield different answers, then respondents were not acting as the standard maximizing economic agents they were assumed to be. This has turned on its head the criticism of CV that different elicitation formats result in different answers.

The CGM framework took, as its central core, maximizing agents and an n-person game theory approach. Survey questions can be divided into two types: inconsequential and consequential. In inconsequential questions, either agents do not care about the outcomes of the choices they are asked about or their responses have no influence on those outcomes. Economic theory has nothing to say about inconsequential survey questions and nothing can be learned from such a question about preferences in an economic sense. From this perspective, any effort to avoid strategic behavior by making a preference question "purely hypothetical" is destined to be ill-fated. Some respondents will not believe language to the effect that the survey is inconsequential as they observe a substantial effort being put into the administration of the survey and ask the reasonable question – to what purpose are the survey results likely to be used. If they do believe the language, then survey responses are uninterpretable from an economic perspective.

The starting point in the CGM framework is to note that the well-known theorem of Gibbard (1973) and Satterthwaite (1975) says that no mechanism with larger than a binary message space can be incentive compatible without restricting the space of allowable preference functions. The Gibbard–Satterthwaite theorem does not, however, say that all binary discrete choice questions are incentive compatible. For this to be true, further conditions must be imposed. Some of these are well known from the voting literature [Farquharson (1969)]. For the standard ballot proposition requiring binding plurality approval (e.g., majority or two-thirds in favor), the conditions for incentive compatibility are: (a) that a take-it-or-leave-it offer be made where the vote doesn't influence any other offer that may be made to agents and (b) that the payment mechanism be coercive in the sense that agents can be required to pay independent of their own vote if the requisite plurality is in favor. It should be noted that the requirement for a coercive payment mechanism rules out voluntary contributions for public goods and voluntary purchases of private goods. The other provisions rule out the case where an agent may vote against a measure that is preferred to the *status quo* because a "no" vote might encourage an even better offer.

CMG show that the binding plurality approval vote provision of the typical ballot measure is a special case of a more general condition, that the probability that a specific alternative is provided is weakly monotonically increasing in terms of the percent of voters that favor it. This general condition, not the binding nature of the vote, is what is needed for incentive compatibility. CMG then show that the results of the vote can be considered probabilistically by policymakers, as long as that probability is greater than zero without altering the incentive properties of the mechanism. The resulting class of incentive compatible mechanisms includes binding referenda as well as advisory referenda. Finally, CMG rely on a result by Green and Laffont (1978) to show that an exogenously chosen sample of the population of interest can be substituted for an actual vote by all members of the population without altering the incentive properties of the mechanism. These conditions combined to show that an "advisory survey" has the same incentive properties as a binding referendum vote.

There are two main ways that incentive compatibility can be violated. The first keeps the binary discrete choice format but relaxes the take-it-or-leave-it nature of the question, or does not use a coercive payment mechanism. Many binary discrete choice CV questions fall into this category. Sometimes this is done by design, for example, when a voluntary contribution payment vehicle is used. Often, however, the problem stems from difficulty in posing a clear, credible take-it-or-leave-it choice.[98] Further, it is difficult to find a payment vehicle that is appropriate to the policy and coercive for all members of the population of interest. The second is to use some format other than a binary discrete choice.

Other preference elicitation formats generally fall into two categories: those that attempt to elicit a continuous WTP response, and those that ask more complicated discrete questions. Formats that directly elicit WTP (i.e., open-ended formats) are sometimes referred to as an equivalency or matching question because the respondent is asked to identify the maximum amount he would be willing to pay, which would render him indifferent whether or not the good is provided. The optimal response to this question depends upon the expected cost to the agent if the project is undertaken. The optimal response of an agent whose WTP is less than his expected cost is to give the lowest possible amount, typically zero.[99] This is true for almost any plausible belief about how

---

[98] In particular, it may be difficult to convince respondents that if the proposed alternative to the status quo is not approved that a different alternative will not be offered or that there may be the possibility of some third party paying all or part of the cost. See Richer (1995) for a CV example involving the Desert Protection Act which had been debated over many years in different forms.

[99] Popular variants of the direct WTP question include the bidding game and the payment card. Both of these elicitation formats back off of asking for actual WTP in favor of isolating WTP to a reasonably small interval. To some degree, these formats can also be seen as a series (potentially) long of repeated binary discrete

the government will aggregate/use the WTP response from the survey. The empirical evidence suggests that there is almost always a large group of zero responses. While it is possible that agents who give a zero response are truly indifferent, the most telling aspect of the empirical evidence is that there are typically few, if any, very small positive WTP responses. Conversely, for an agent whose WTP is greater than the expected cost, the optimal strategy depends upon his beliefs about the decision rule being used by the government and about the responses of the other agents. If the agent believes a strict benefit–cost decision rule is being followed and his true WTP is considerably above what he believes is the average of the other agents' WTP, then he may have an incentive to give the highest plausible WTP amount. However, extremely large amounts are not often observed, and when they are, they at most constitute a small fraction of the sample. While this may reflect the absence of nontruthful strategic behavior or a belief that very large WTP responses are not plausible, it likely reflects a belief that the government decision rule is not a strict benefit–cost one. Many other plausible rules, and in particular, those that have the government trying to reallocate costs toward or taking surplus from an agents (or types of agents) indicating WTP amounts higher than cost. The reported amounts from these agents should increase toward their true WTP from below as uncertainty over the expected cost increases.[100]

The simplest variant of asking a more complex discrete choice question is the double-bounded dichotomous choice format. In this case, the respondent is asked two closed-ended questions with the bid amount in the second question dependent on the response to the first question. The usual approach to analyzing this question [Hanemann, Loomis and Kanninen (1991)], as reflected in (45), assumes that the two responses are based on comparing the amounts asked about to true WTP. The empirical evidence suggests that respondents tend not answer the two questions in this way, although their two responses are clearly highly correlated [Cameron and Quiggin (1994), Herriges and Shogren (1996), Alberini, Kanninen and Carson (1997), León and Vazquez-Polo (1998)]. Nor should they answer in this way, because one of two things needs to be true for the second question to make sense. Either the cost is uncertain (which for a pure pubic good with a coercive payment vehicle will depress WTP relative to the single binary discrete choice question with a certain cost) or something about the good has to have changed between the first and second question – otherwise there would have been no

choice questions. This allows these formats to overcome to some degree some of the response problems associated with a straightforward question that directly elicits WTP. The payment card format further introduces uncertainty over what the cost of providing the good will be. This uncertainty can encourage more truthful preference revelation.

[100] One of the reasons that the payment card format seems to work is that it seems to induce the "right" amount of cost uncertainty. Unless extreme ranges of amounts are used on the payment card or there is a large gap between zero and the first positive amount, the payment card estimates seem reasonably robust to the particular amounts used. See Rowe, Schulze and Breffle (1996) for an experiment looking at the properties of the payment card.

need to ask the second question.[101] These considerations change the respondent's perception of what the second question means, and therefore affect her response. If there is uncertainty, the respondent may answer the second question on the basis of some type of weighted average between the first amount and the second. Alternatively, the respondent may conclude that the quality of the good or its probability of provision have changed commensurate with the change in cost; or that the government wants more information about WTP in order to extract surplus from high WTP-type agents and reallocate the cost toward them. CGM investigate the theoretical implications of such different beliefs. Most of these lead to "too many" no–no responses, but there is more ambiguity about other response patterns. Burton et al. (2003a, 2003b) provide an empirical investigation but it is unclear how generalizable results will be due to the dependence on particular beliefs about costs, good quality, and government use of the responses.

As one might expect, similar issues arise when one moves to even more complex choice formats. Consider a sequence of paired comparisons where respondents are asked whether they favored or opposed two alternative programs to provided specified levels of local air quality at specified costs amounts. While each of the questions could be answered independently, some respondents will ask how the government is going to pick a single level of air quality to provide for all local residents. This naturally causes the questions to be linked with almost any plausible belief about how the government might use the numbers. To see this, let the respondent assume a very simple rule, that the program getting the largest fraction in favor, in any paired comparison, will be the air quality level chosen. The respondent may now have an incentive to misrepresent responses to one or more of the paired comparisons; and indeed, may find it optimal to be in favor of a program that actually lowers utility in order to help prevent a program that would impose an even larger loss from being adopted.

A variant of the same issue occurs with the popular multinomial choice experiment format. Assume for a moment that there are three (or more) possible alternatives and the respondent assumes that the one receiving the largest plurality will be enacted. This can be seen as akin to a three candidate race with a plurality winner.[102] Only the two alternatives that the respondent believes will get the highest fractions in favor (independent of

---

[101] The one-and-a-half bound format introduced by Cooper, Hanemann and Signorello (2002) attempts to avoid the problem of changing the price unexpectedly when asking two valuation questions by framing the situation a little differently. The respondent is told up front that the cost is not known for certain, and can range from A_L to A_U. One of these amounts is selected at random, and he is asked if he would be willing to pay that amount. If this initial amount is A_L and the response is no, there is no follow up question; if the response is yes, the respondent is then asked about A_U. Conversely, if the initial amount is A_U and the response is yes, there is no follow-up question while, if the answer is no, there is a follow-up question about A_L. This generates a likelihood function similar to (45). Cooper, Hanemann and Signorello find that this retains most of the gain in statistical efficiency relative to the single-bounded approach, and it greatly reduced the discrepancy between the responses to the first and second valuation questions.

[102] In a three candidate race with a simple plurality winner, the candidate perceived to be in third place will always try to convince voters that there is no difference (in utility) between the two front runners and that there is a chance the candidate will win. In the more general formulation of this voting problem, these two factors are traded-off in utility terms against the possibility of casting a "wasted" vote.

the respondent's answer) are viable choices, so a respondent may pick other than his or her most preferred alternative. It is important to note here the respondent should not pick randomly but rather should pick between the two most viable alternatives. The common practice of asking a sequence of multinomial choice questions raises the same issue as does a sequence of paired comparisons about how preference information across the choices sets would be aggregated by the government.

The multinomial choice question may not face the same problem when the good is a quasi-public or private one where different agents can, for example, go to different recreational sites or buy different computers.[103] But the larger issue of how the information from the question will be used still remains. Agents tend to see such questions as either a provision or pricing exercise. Response strategies tend to follow from that belief coupled with some notion of how the information will be used. More generally, agents should try to induce the supply of the good configured in their most desired manner at the lowest cost. There are some fairly simple strategies to signal an unhappiness with "price gouging" that imply not picking the most preferred alternative when its cost is seen as higher than it should be, in favor of picking something close to it which is available at a low price. Nontruthful preference revelation of this sort should cause violations of the independence of irrelevant alternatives condition.[104]

Asking respondents to completely rank the alternative simply allows the ranked alternatives to be "exploded" [Beggs and Hausman (1981), Chapman and Staelin (1982)] into a complete set of choice data. This amplifies the opportunities and incentives for misrepresenting preference information. The best–worst format of Marley and Louviere (in press) achieves a substantial part of the efficiency gain from a complete ranking while minimizing any additional incentives for misrepresentation. Another popular response format using "rated" pairs is difficult to analyze from a mechanism design perspective. In addition to inheriting all of the issues associated with a sequence of paired comparisons, respondents also need to make an assumption about how the ratings will be translated in any preference revelation exercise.

5.4. A typology of the incentive structure of elicitation formats

Figure 5 provides a typology of the structure of preference elicitation format incentives. At the top is a single binary discrete choice question that we have labeled "one

---

[103] CGM show that if respondents are offered K private/quasi-public goods as the choice alternatives and they believe that $K - 1$ will be provided, then the choice question is incentive compatible. That is because the worst off an agent can be is to get their second most preferred alternative made available. Effectively then, the choice question reduces to a binary one, where the agent's most preferred alternative is put up against an unknown alternative in a competition for which of the two goods will not be supplied. As such, the agent should always pick the most preferred alternative from the set.

[104] Standard tests of whether SP and RP data are consistent with each other [e.g., Swait and Louviere (1993)] are effectively tests of whether one of the data sources is either random or systematically different on multiple parameters, not tests of whether there is a systematic distortion in one of the parameters, typically the coefficient on price.

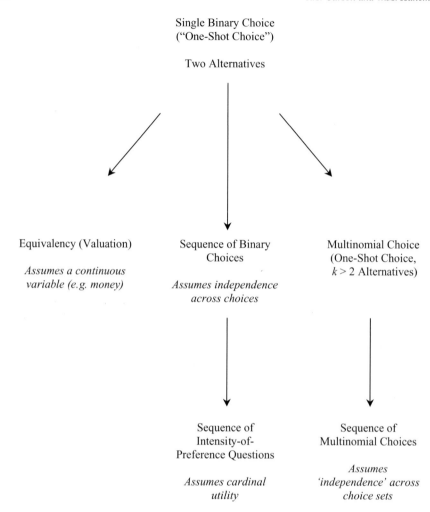

Figure 5. Typology of the structure of preference elicitation format incentives.

shot" since only one question is asked. Without the other conditions, such as a coercive payment mechanism discussed in the previous section, this elicitation format is not incentive compatible, in that truthfully revealing preferences may not be optimal for all agents depending upon their expectations. However, this typology illustrates the additional assumptions that need to be made for the subsequent elicitation format to maintain the same incentive properties of the original one-shot binary discrete choice question, whatever these may be. For example, the sequence of paired comparison format must assume independence across the pairs for this to hold. The continuous (direct WTP) response question must assume that there is a continuous underlying quantity (typically money) that sets the change in utility from the program to zero and that the incentives for revealing a continuous response are the same as revealing a binary discrete choice response. The multinomial choice format must assume that moving from $K = 2$ to $K > 2$ choice alternatives does not alter the incentive structure. Moving to a sequence of such questions further requires the same assumption as for a sequence of paired comparisons: independent responses across choice sets. The rated pairs format requires cardinal utility; and for it to be equivalent to the sequence of paired comparisons, the revelation of the ratings (or other intensity) measure cannot alter the incentive structure.

5.5. Promoting incentive compatibility

To summarize, there are three views of the world: (a) people try to truthfully reveal their preferences irrespective of the incentives they face, (b) people tell the truth if there are no consequences associated with their answer, and (c) people only try to tell the truth when it is in their economic interest to do so. The empirical results in Carson et al. (2004b) and many other studies suggest that (a) and (b) are false.[105] That leaves (c) which is the perspective that one would if CV survey responses represented consequential economic actions by standard economic agents. The difficulty with (c) is that it makes the design of CV survey questions and their analysis much more challenging.

The additional assumptions required for the various elicitation formats in Figure 5 to be incentive compatible are often not likely to hold. However, the use of these other elicitation formats is motivated by the desire to obtain additional preference information in the form of tighter confidence intervals, or information about more possible configurations of a good, at a lower survey cost. The binary discrete choice format is potentially incentive compatible because it does not reveal much information. As such, there is an inherent conflict between the cost of obtaining preference information and the need to assess the performance of different formats (in light of the fact that they should produce different results).

One relevant question is what features promote incentive compatibility? Here one major factor appears to be cost, or more specifically, beliefs about cost. It has often been thought that survey respondents may state as their WTP amount what they perceive to be the cost of the item. In instances where there is a well-established price, a large faction of respondents simply give that number as their WTP amount. That sort of behavioral anomaly was once seen as an indication that people did not have well defined preference. The anomaly disappears once one realizes that the optimal response strategies generally pivot on the perceived cost of the good. Open-ended, direct questions are particularly problematic because many respondents simply said something akin to "tell me the cost" and "I will tell you whether I favor or oppose the project." Further, many

---

[105] It is important to note that this statement that some people don't always truthfully reveal their preferences, only that some will have an incentive not to and will not.

respondents believed that if the government has seriously worked out the details of how to implement the project then the cost had to be known. Promoting incentive compatibility will typically require that some sort of cost information be provided and that the statistical procedures, used correctly, are conditional on that information.[106]

Care needs to be taken in matching elicitation formats with the nature of the good being valued. The multinomial choice experiment is a natural one for quasi-public goods like recreation sites where the agent has the ability to choose a different good than another agent. It is often possible to use survey language to justify why different levels of a pure public good are being inquired about that may be natural in a sequence of paired comparisons but which makes no sense in a multinomial choice question.

More generally, there are three factors that contribute to incentive compatibility in a CV survey that are independent of the elicitation format used. The first of these is ensuring that all respondents see the survey as consequential. To accomplish this one needs to emphasize that policymakers want to know whether the public supports the project, given its cost. The second is to ensure that the good(s) being valued, including the different attribute levels and cost, are seen as plausible. The last and, perhaps, most important is to find the appropriate payment vehicle that can impose costs on all agents if the government undertakes the project. Voluntary contribution schemes, in particular, do not provide any way of asking respondents to make a real commitment with their survey response.

6. Econometric issues

6.1. Structure of WTP distributions

The key output of a CV study is an estimate of the WTP distribution for the good of interest.[107] From Section 3, two approaches are possible. One can adopt a parametric approach using some parametric functional form for the WTP distribution, relying on economic theory to guide the specification of the model, or one can adopt a completely nonparametric approach, letting the data speak for itself without imposing any assumptions about the nature of the data generating process. In either case, several issues of model specification arise.[108]

---

[106] In this sense, a variation on a payment card might be used to convey some sense of the range of possible costs. It is also possible to draw a connection between using a payment card in this way and the one and half bound discrete choice format proposed by Cooper, Hanemann and Signorello (2002).

[107] The discussion in this section is couched in terms of the WTP distribution for the good of interest. It could have been written more generally with some modifications to encompass a broader range of issues; such as the estimation of WTA distributions or the WTP distribution for changes in the level(s) of one or more attributes of a good.

[108] For information on the estimation of the chosen model, the reader may consult a standard graduate econometrics text such as Greene (2002) or a specialized text on the econometrics of nonmarket valuation such as Hanemann and Kanninen (1999) or Haab and McConnell (2002).

A useful way to characterize the issues is to think about the underlying shape of the WTP distribution, using the survival function representation of the WTP distribution and assuming some type of discrete choice elicitation format such as a binary discrete response, as in (9). As illustrated in Figure 2, the responses to the WTP question trace out the survival function for the WTP distribution. This representation illustrates some of the key decisions that the researcher has to make. The first decision is whether one should allow for *negative* WTP amounts. The second is whether there may be some number of respondents who have a *zero* WTP for the good. The third is how to ensure that the WTP distribution exhibits weak monotonicity as the monetary amount increases. The fourth is to determine how smooth the WTP distribution has to be away from zero. The fifth is how to deal with the right-hand tail of the response probability distribution – whether to impose some restriction on the WTP distribution as the monetary amount grows large and approaches income or wealth.

If one wishes to allow for negative WTP amounts, this implies that, for some negative amounts $\tilde{A} < 0$, $\pi^Y(\tilde{A}) < 1$; that is, the respondent would not necessarily accept the item even if he was paid to take it. This seems implausible for a wide range of environmental amenities. While it is easy to see the case where someone might not care one way or the other about say an improvement in air quality, say, it is hard to believe that someone would require compensation for an improvement in air quality in order to maintain their current level of utility.[109]

Assume for now that negative WTP is ruled out, which means that for all $\tilde{A} < 0$, $\pi^Y(\tilde{A}) = 1$. Next, there is the question of what happens at $A = 0$. Here there are two possibilities. One possibility is that $\pi^Y(0) = 1$; the other possibility is that $\pi^Y(0) < 1$, which implies that, even if the item costs them nothing, some people do not care one way or the other whether it is provided. In the latter case, the probability is $\theta \equiv 1 - \pi^Y(0)$ that people are indifferent to the item. Such a model is also said to have a "spike" at zero, the magnitude of the spike being given by θ. Given the treatment of the left tail, the next issue for the researcher is to ensure that the body of the response probability function exhibits weak monotonicity as the monetary amount increases.[110] If one uses a parametric response model, this will be satisfied automatically because weak monotonicity is a natural property of the survivor function. If one adopts a nonparametric approach resulting in the likelihood function (29), in the single-bounded case, or (49), in the double-bounded case, as noted earlier the maximum likelihood estimator automatically

---

[109] There are, of course, situations where some respondents may have negative WTP while others have a zero or positive WTP. Kriström (1997), looking at a change in traffic at an airport in Stockholm, shows that all three groups exist because of how the reduction in noise is traded-off against the reduction in convenience. An important case where one may see negative WTP values is in studies involving preservation versus development. Here it is not unusual to see the agents living far away from the site being considered for preservation having only zero or positive WTP values for preservation, while the WTP of some of those living close to the site may be quite negative because of the perceived connection between local jobs and development of the site.

[110] This restriction was noted earlier in footnote 9.

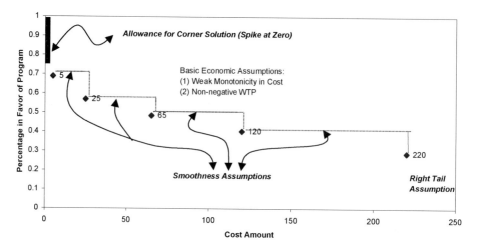

Figure 6. WTP distribution (survival representation).

imposes weak monotonicity through the pool – adjacent-violators algorithm of Ayer et al. (1955) and Turnbull (1976).

Figure 6 depicts these issues using data from a study valuing the prevention of oil spills along California's Central Coast [Carson et al. (2004a)], where respondents were randomly assigned to one of five monetary amounts ($5, $25, $65, $120, $220) in a single-bounded format. Here, the assumption has been made that no respondent *prefers* oil spills (i.e., has a negative WTP to prevent them), but the possibility of a "spike" at zero is allowed for.[111] For these data, the estimate of the Kaplan–Meier–Turnbull lower bound on mean WTP is $85.39. The standard error of this estimate is $3.90.

The final decision to be made is how to treat the right tail of the response probability distribution. This is highly influential with regard to the estimate of mean WTP which, as indicated in (38), depends crucially on the specification of $C^{\max}$, the upper support of the WTP distribution. It is natural to think of the researcher as imposing an estimate of this upper support before proceeding to calculate mean WTP. The most straightforward way to do this might seem to be simply asking some subsample of respondents about an extremely large amount. The difficulty here is that it is not credible to ask respondents about extremely high monetary amounts. Faced with an implausible cost amount, they will answer the question without reference to that amount and use what they think might be a reasonable amount.[112] One can fall back on economic theory which suggests WTP

---

[111] The percent in favor at the five design points in increasing order are 68.9% (219) at $5, 56.9% (216) at $25, 45.8% (241) at $65, 40.3% (181) at $120, and 28.9% (228) at $220 where the number in parentheses is the sample size at that design point.

[112] This problem is not unique to CV. Extremely high prices that come close to choking off demand are rarely, if ever, observed in data from actual markets. CV can help extend the range of prices available for the

has to be limited by wealth. Further, it might be reasonable to think that income, disposable income or some fraction of disposable income, are appropriate limits on the upper bound of an individual agent's WTP. Haab and McConnell (1998) and Carson and Jeon (2000) show that imposing such restrictions can rule out some otherwise plausible WTP distributions and dramatically reduces the sensitivity of the estimate of mean WTP to distributional assumptions which are consistent with the restriction imposed on the right tail of the WTP distribution.

6.2. Issues in fitting binary discrete choice models

The previous section has largely discussed the structure of the WTP distributions largely in terms of the nonparametric approach. There are a number of reasons why one might want to move away from this approach and fit a parametric or semi-parametric model. These include: (a) the desire to fit a particular utility function (see Section 3) to obtain a more precise estimate of mean WTP, (b) to reduce dependence of the estimate on the particular design points used, (c) to include continuous covariates, or (d) to incorporate information from more than one binary choice question, leading one to use parametric or semi-parametric estimators. In this section, we discuss several issues in the context of binary discrete choice models that can play a large role in the estimates obtained.

The first of these is the inclusion of a spike parameter (or other more complex way) of handling the possibility of a nontrivial fraction of the sample with a zero or close to zero WTP. Failure to include such a parameter often lies at the heart of many CV estimates that appear to be "too large" to be plausible. There is a simple intuition behind this result. Most of the parametric distributions fit to discrete choice CV data are proper survival distributions, such as the log-normal or Weibull. The location and scale parameters in these distributions are tightly linked. Fitting the fraction of the sample at or near zero can only be done by blowing up the scale parameter. Since mean WTP is a function of both the location parameter (the median in a log-normal and the 62nd quantile in a Weibull) and the scale parameter, the estimate of mean WTP can become greatly inflated. Ironically, an estimate suggesting a "fat right tail" problem is often blamed on the presence of so-called "yea-sayers" who answer "yes" without considering the specific amount they are asked about. However, fitting a spike parameter (which will include the nay-sayers) will often dramatically reduce the estimate of mean WTP by "dropping" the right tail. After doing so, a separate parameter of the possibility of yea-sayers is often no longer statistically significant.[113]

---

analysis but it cannot push that price range out beyond what most consumers would find to be plausible. The extreme sensitivity of consumer surplus measures to functional form/distributional assumption made about the far right tail is an intrinsic problem with any approach to economic valuation that looks at nonmarginal changes.

[113] There is much confusion in the literature about "yea-sayers." There is usually only a small fraction of "yes" responses to CV questions at reasonably high prices with effective payment vehicles. The strong tendency of double bounded questions to draw relatively few "yes–yes" responses if the highest design point is

The second is the choice of distributional assumptions. There are some choices that are reasonable and some that usually cause problems. The normal distribution generally implies some agents have negative WTP and as such should be generally be avoided unless negative values are thought possible. The log-logistic has very thick tails and a very wide range of plausible parameter values implies an infinite WTP. The Weibull generally has a shorter right tail than the log-normal and, in its "spike" configuration [Kriström (1997)], usually performs well. This specification should probably be the workhorse of applied CV analysis. More flexibility, as noted in Section 3, usually requires using some variant of a Box–Cox model or making a smoothness assumption and moving to a semi-parametric approach [e.g., Chen and Randall (1997), Creel and Loomis (1997), Cooper (2002)].

One of the main motivations of using parametric or semi-parametric models is the ease with which covariates can be used in the modeling exercise. This is particularly useful for assessing the validity of the CV exercise.[114] Specification of how the covariates should enter into the model can be difficult though particularly when there is a spike at zero. Werner (1999) provides an empirical example whereby income is negatively related to the probability that one has a positive WTP for preserving an area, but, conditional on having a positive willingness to pay, income is positively related to the magnitude of WTP. Simply entering income as a regressor in the standard way obscures the two offsetting effects. Haab (1999) provides a related analysis focusing on the issue of nonparticipants.

As one moves away from a single binary discrete choice question to either a double-bounded dichotomous choice format or a sequence of paired comparisons, there are two issues that should be taken into account. The first is that asking one respondent will generally result in less information from a statistical vantage point than asking the same questions to different respondents. This can be dealt with either by using an appropriate weighting scheme or by constructing one measure (such as the interval from a double bounded dichotomous choice question) from the set of questions asked. The second concerns the fact that each question asked may alter the incentive structure for subsequent questions. It is possible to test for these effects [e.g., Alberini, Kanninen and Carson (1997)] but correcting for them requires making assumptions about how the incentive/informational structure was altered.

---

both reasonably high and plausible runs counter to a suggestion that true yea-sayers represent a large fraction of the sample in most good CV studies. This is not to say though that problems do not exist in some individual CV studies. A large fraction of yes (or yes–yes) responses at the highest design point generally indicates a problem with the original choice of the design points or an incentive problem associated with payment vehicle. In the latter situation, it is not that the respondents are answering yes without paying attention to the amount, but that they answer yes because they want the good but will not have to pay for it. An approach such as the Turnbull lower-bound on the mean is quite robust against the sort of deviation in the right tail that a small fraction of yea-sayers might cause.

[114] For the simple purpose of describing the WTP distribution, an unconditional approach may work fine and avoids a number of modeling issues related to correctly specifying the conditional WTP distribution. However, policymakers generally want to see the conditional estimates as they care who the gains and losses accrue to.

6.3. Bid design

Collection of discrete choice data requires the use of a set of design points that represent the cost to agents, who are then randomly assigned to those design points. The choice of those design points can greatly influence how many observations are required for a given level of statistical efficiency.[115]

A good starting point is to think about the linear regression model with a single co-variate and ask the question: if you had n observations and could run the experiment at two values of the covariate, what values would you chose and how many observations should you allocate to each in order to minimize the confidence interval on the covariate's parameter estimate? The answer is to pick the two values of the covariate as far apart as feasible and to allocate half the sample to each of the two values of the covariate. Some of this basic intuition carries over to binary discrete choice models which are effectively dose-response experiments where the "cost" is the "poison" and the percent of the population alive (those still in "favor") falls as the cost increases. This dose response model is nonlinear so that optimal design now depends upon having an estimate of the unknown model parameters. The optimal design, if the model's parameters were known, is generally to have the same number of design points as model parameters. The design points are not, however, placed at the far extremes of the (cost) stimulus variable because in contrast to the linear model there is too little density far out in the tails. Rather the design points are placed in the cost space in order to minimize some criteria. The most popular criterion is d-optimality which maximizes the determinant of the information matrix. This is a natural criterion when using maximum likelihood estimation and is the easiest to calculate [Cooper (1993)]. The d-optimal design, however, does not result in the smallest confidence interval for mean WTP as the estimator for that statistic is generally the ratio of two parameters and the statistical design that minimizes this quantity is known as the c-optimal design. Alberini and Carson (1990) and Alberini (1995) show that the c-optimal (fiducial) design can be substantially more efficient (on the order of 50%) than the d-optimal design under conditions relevant to CV studies. All three designs result in two design points being utilized if the underlying distribution is assumed to be fully characterized by two parameters and the design is not constrained to have more design points.[116] The designs differ in where the points are places with the d-optimal design generally resulting in placement further out in the tails. Kanninen (1993a) and Alberini (1995) provide comparisons of different design criteria for double-bounded estimators.

---

[115] Like survey design, experimental design is a topic not generally taught in economic departments. A classic text is Box, Hunter and Hunter (1978). For a more modern, comprehensive reference, see Atkinson and Donev (1992) or Wu and Hamada (2000).

[116] The design can be constrained to have more design points but note that forcing a design to have four design points will result in the second two design points being replicates of the original two design points, or arbitrarily close to them if they are forced to be distinct. If the distribution is assumed to be symmetric, an equal number of observations are generally assigned to corresponding design points on either side of the median. Asymmetric distributions can result in an asymmetric assignment of observations being optimal.

In practice, the main difficulty is that the model parameters are unknown when the design for the CV survey has to be derived. The natural thing to do is to use data from earlier development work such as pre-test and pilot studies. Kanninen (1993b) discusses the issues involved in sequential design which is the correct way to think about the issue. In general, the more uncertainty about the nature of the underlying WTP distribution, the more design points should be used; and it is possible to give a formal Bayesian interpretation to the design problem. The key issue though is that there is a clear tradeoff between the precision at which the distribution is pinned down at the design points and the number of design points. Alberini and Carson's (1990) work suggests that it is hard to justify more than eight design points and they show that the use of four to six design points which span the expected quartiles of the expected WTP distributions is usually preferable. This design produces estimates that are both reasonably efficient and robust to fairly large deviations between the expected and observed WTP distributions.[117]

6.4. Treatment of don't knows and protest zeros

All surveys generate "don't know" responses to some questions. Some of these don't know responses indicate a genuine "don't know" while other represent a desire not to put forth the effort needed to answer the question. Offering respondents an explicit "don't know" response tends to pick out the genuine don't knows while encouraging those who want to get through the survey quickly to effectively skip the question. The long standing wisdom in the survey research literature [Converse (1974), Schuman and Presser (1981)] was that attempting to obtain attitude/preference/knowledge information from people who do not actually possess it results in low quality answers from these respondents.[118] This view is embodied in the NOAA Blue Ribbon Panel on Contingent Valuation report [Arrow et al. (1993)] in the form of a recommendation that respondents be offered a "don't know" categorical response in addition to the usual favor/oppose options in a binary discrete choice question. There has long been a dissenting view [e.g., Bradburn and Sudman (1988)] which holds that, with some probing, many don't know responses can reliably be converted into clear opinions. Krosnick et al. (2002) review both the theoretical and existing empirical evidence and then look at nine experiments. They show in general that not offering an explicit "don't know" category does not harm the quality of survey responses and that offering an explicit "don't know" response reduces, often substantially, the amount of useful information that is collected.

Even without an explicit "don't know" response being offered, there will be some volunteered don't know responses and it will be necessary econometrically to decide how

---

[117] McFadden (1999b) shows that a much different design must be used involving spacing of a large number of design points over the support of WTP if one wants to be able to consistently estimate mean WTP without making parametric assumptions about the nature of the distribution.

[118] CV surveys differ from the classic public opinion survey where a respondent may be asked whether they favor a very briefly described policy that the respondent may not be familiar with. A good CV survey provides respondents with a considerable amount of information about a program being considered and then asks the respondent whether they favor the program.

to deal with them. There are three standard options available: (a) drop them, (b) treat them as "not favor" responses or (c) impute them using some type of model. Dropping them is equivalent to allocating them proportionate to the favor/nonfavor response pattern. This might be justified if one did not have any prior information about how "don't know" responses usually translate into favor/not-favor votes. In voting on ballot measures, it is clear that don't know responses in surveys taken prior to the election tend to disproportionately split with most becoming "not favor" responses. Carson et al. (1998) look at the issue specifically within the context of replicating the Exxon Valdez survey questionnaire [Carson et al. (1992)] and find that "don't know" responses (in the case where a don't know option is explicitly offered and in the case where it is not) tend to look like "not favor" responses.[119] A conservative approach, that will always tend to underestimate WTP, is to treat all don't know responses as "not favor" responses.[120]

A "protest zero" can be seen as a variant of a "don't know" response, in the sense that the respondent effectively said "no" but has given some type of response which suggests that it might not be a true zero.[121] Protest zeros were once routinely dropped from the analysis of CV data. This practice is being gradually abandoned because of growing evidence that most protest zeros tend to resemble "no" responses in discrete choice formats or "low" amounts in continuous responses formats. Further, an examination of the reasons for the protest often reveals that some aspect of the scenario is not fair, such as taxing a particular group of consumers in a particular way. Such reasoning does not really suggest a desire for the good but rather a desire not to pay for it. It is exactly the sort of additional behavior in a survey that someone who wanted to discourage the government from supplying the good should engage in. What seems clear is that these respondents would not "vote" in favor if given the opportunity. These agents may be willing to pay for the good under some quite different set of circumstances, but one cannot divorce the CV estimate from the scenario to get some "context" free value for the good.[122] Such a value in economic terms does not and cannot exist.

6.5. Treatment of respondent uncertainty

Belief that some respondents did not have well-defined preferences has led to a number of papers that propose some way to introduce an "extra" source of uncertainty

---

[119] Groothuis and Whitehead (2002) find a similar result for willingness to pay but not willingness to accept.

[120] This is also the cultural norm in some places where an affirmative response is required to indicate agreement with the proposition and formal disagreement with a proposition rarely voiced.

[121] For a serious attempt to statistically model don't know and protest responses see Strazzera et al. (2003). Some of these approaches rely on auxiliary questions. The key thing to remember here is that responses to such questions, while informative, can never been taken as definitive because of incentive issues and the difficulty of getting respondents to answer a question with an implausible cost.

[122] Seeing a large number of protest zeros being generated by particular aspects of a CV scenario can be important information for policymakers because it says something about one or more elements of the program that many respondents dislike. Protest responses are likely to be particularly sharp when a clearly coercive payment vehicle is used and as such protest responses *per se* do not represent a problem with a particular CV scenario.

into statistical models of CV responses and a large literature has grown up around this topic [e.g., Hanemann and Kriström (1995), Li and Mattsson (1995), Ready, Whitehead and Blomquist (1995), Champ et al. (1997), Dubourg, Jones-Lee and Loomes (1997), Ready, Navrud and Dubourg (2001)]. There can be several potential problems encountered with this approach. First, in the standard RUM model with a single observed choice, it is impossible to statistically distinguish Thurston's (1927) conceptualization of the error component in a choice model as representing a truly random element rather than the Manski–McFadden view that there is no true random component but rather aspects of the choice context that are not observed by the econometrician. As such, there is no room for an extra source of uncertainty without adding more structure to the model.

Second, identification of the extra source of uncertainty depends upon either assuming some particular specification for the utility function (and defining the deviation from that model as related to the extra uncertainty) or in having some extra piece of information that effectively reveals something about the nature of this extra source of uncertainty. The difficulty with assigning the deviation from an assumed model as the extra preference uncertainty is that there will almost always be such a deviation in any parsimoniously parameterized model. Use of an extra piece of information would be acceptable if there is a strong theoretical or practical basis for this or if empirically its introduction in a model resulted in small changes in the estimate of mean WTP and moderate increases in its confidence interval. However, models using an extra source of information tend to be *ad hoc* and the results tend to be very sensitive to specific assumptions employed.

This sensitivity has lead to increased reliance on the use of an extra source of information to identify the preference uncertainty. Typically this is obtained by asking a follow-up survey question that asks the respondent how certain they are of their answer or trying to calibrate the discrete choice answer to the estimate obtained from some other CV elicitation format. If a separate question is asked it is often posed on say a 7 (or 10) point scale with 1 labeled "completely certain" and 7 labeled "completely uncertain." There are a several potential difficulties. First, different respondents may use the same scale in different ways so that a "3" to one respondent may mean a "5" to another respondent. Second, asking for an assessment of certainty of the answer to a previous question may be taken as challenging the respondent as to whether he made the "correct" choice; there can be considerable heterogeneity in the response to such a challenge that has little to do with preference uncertainty. Third, there is inevitably some endogenity in the "certainty scale" response in that an agent's whose WTP is close to the particular bid amount is more likely to be uncertain than one whose WTP is far away from that amount. Fourth, it is not necessarily clear how one translates different levels of certainty into different purchase propensities.[123] A related issue arises when trying

---

[123] There may be some empirical regularity that allows the use of this certainty level in some type of calibration exercise. These exercises are popular in the marketing literature, where one can often observe repeated comparisons of survey results and actual market behavior. The difficulty here is keeping the marketing effort constant across the different comparisons or systematically accounting for differences in it.

to calibrate the discrete choice response obtained using a different elicitation format. If theoretically there should be differences between the two formats then there is no reason to make the two responses conform.

Another way to approach these phenomena is through the scale parameter in a RUM setting. Some agents may have more uncertainty about their future economic status, a possibility under the Manski–McFadden view of RUM models, or, some agents may have a larger random element to their purchase behavior, a possibility under the Thurston view of choice models. Survey design can also be seen as having an influence on errors of optimization that is not uniform across respondents. Any of these possibilities induces heterogeneity in the error component. Two main ways to deal with this are to use a nonparametric estimator like the Kaplan–Meier–Turnbull that does not require an estimate of the scale parameter to obtain an estimate of mean or median WTP, or to formally model the error component as a function of variables reflecting the respondents and the circumstances of the preference elicitation.[124]

6.6. Continuous response CV data

The statistical analysis of data from CV formats eliciting continuous (open-ended) responses is in principle straightforward except for two main sets of problems. First, the incentive structure of the format tends to produce substantial distortions in the response obtained, as discussed in Section 5. Second, respondents tend not to give answers with tremendous precision like $11.14, but rather, tend to give more general and less specific responses like $10.

The incentive structure of open-ended CV surveys gives rise to a substantial number of "zero" WTP responses and few positive, yet very small, responses. There have been many attempts to sort the zero WTP responses into two types: true zero WTP responses and "protest" zero responses. While such efforts may be of some help in understanding the zero responses, they may never perform this classification task really well. This is because it is in the strategic interest of respondents who have already misrepresented their WTP to continue to do so.[125]

As Brookshire, Ives and Schulze (1976) first pointed out, strategic behavior in a CV question that obtains a continuous, or close to continuous response can flatten out the observed WTP distribution relative to the true WTP distribution.[126] This observation

---

[124] Louviere et al. (2002) consider a wide-range of issues associated with efforts to model differences in the scale component across agents and their implications for commonly used statistics such as WTP.

[125] This is also true of efforts preceding a WTP question (discrete choice or continuous response) to try to sort out those with a positive WTP from those with a zero WTP. It is in the interest of respondents who think that their WTP is less than what they expected the cost of the program to be to indicate a zero WTP initially and such a question may be answered with expected cost in mind rather than the "zero" or "trivial" cost that the researcher intended.

[126] In Brookshire, Ives and Schulze's original formulation higher bids increased the probability of provision without shifting the cost burden. This flattening may not occur on the upper end of the distribution if the respondent believes the government willing to shift the cost burden toward those types that indicate a high WTP for the good.

naturally leads to the proposal in Mitchell and Carson (1989) to use an α-trimmed mean where an α in the statistics is often set to 0.05 or 0.10 so that 5% or 10% of the observations are "trimmed" off before calculating the mean on the remaining observations. Because measurement error is common and generally not normal as often assumed, a 10% α-trimmed mean has even been shown to perform better [Stigler (1977)] than the ordinary sample mean even in estimating physical constants from experiments. However, one problem with the family of α-trimmed means is that they involve symmetric trimming, which can substantially alter the estimate of mean WTP if the true underlying distribution is asymmetric, as can often be the case with WTP data. There are two approaches to dealing with this problem. The first is to use a variant of an α-trimmed mean known as a windsorized mean; here, instead of dropping the trimmed observations before calculating the mean, the α-smallest observations are set equal to the smallest nonwinsorized observation and the α-largest observations are set equal to the largest nonwinsorized observation.[127] This will preserve much of the asymmetry in the WTP distribution as long as most of the value is not concentrated in far right tail. The second is to trim observations conditional on the observed covariates based on their likelihood of being an outlier using the approach proposed by Belsley, Kuh and Welsch (1980) and pioneered in a CV context by Smith and Desvousges (1986).[128]

6.7. Choice experiments

Choice experiments have become a very popular elicitation format in recent years. They generalize the binary discrete choice CV format by allowing for the valuation of changes in one or more of the attributes of the good of interest. The standard binary discrete choice CV question generally asks for a choice between a bundle of attributes, which could be labeled as the status quo good, and another bundle of attributes which could be labeled as the "alternative." One of the attributes of the alternative (usually cost) is randomly assigned to respondents and this allows the researcher to trace out WTP for the alternative relative to the status quo. The choice experiment format expands upon this by varying more than the cost attribute.

The simplest way to do this is to create two variants of survey instrument that differ only by changing one of the noncost attributes of the alternative, and administer each to statistically equivalent samples. Now two WTP distributions will be available that differ

---

[127] The Kaplan–Meier–Turnbull lower bound on mean WTP can be seen as a variant of a windsorized estimator for the highest design point, as it assumes the fraction estimated to be WTP the highest design point are willing to pay only that amount and no more.

[128] Because the incentive properties of the payment card are reasonably well known and generally conservative in the sense of being biased downward, if some light trimming of the right tail is done if a few large outliers are present, it may be a good format to use in studies where there is one program to be valued and it is not possible to use the large sample size required to obtain reasonable precision from a binary discrete choice question.

only by the difference in the attribute levels between the scenarios in the two different surveys. This variant of a choice experiment is sometimes referred to as a scope test [Arrow et al. (1993), Carson (1997a, 1997b)]. All of the parametric and nonparametric approaches [Carson et al. (1994)] can be used to test whether there is a difference in the WTP distributions corresponding to the difference in scope. Poe, Giraud and Loomis (2005) also show how the convolutions and bootstrap approaches can be applied to this case.

More than one level of an attribute can be valued simply by expanding the number of variants of the survey with one binary discrete choice question in each survey and the same clearly defined status quo in each one. Different attributes can also be valued in the same way either alone or in combinations. The difficulty with this approach is that it may become very expensive in terms of survey costs, as fairly large sample sizes are needed for each variant of the survey. The typical choice experiment gets around this problem by asking respondents a sequence of choice questions, each with a different alternative, or by asking a multinomial choice question featuring two or more alternatives to the status quo or both.[129]

In these models, the utility for a particular alternative using the standard RUM formulation is: $U_{ij} = V_{ij} + \varepsilon_{ij}$, where U_{ij} is the utility of the jth alternative to the ith agent, V_{ij} is the systematic part of the utility function, potentially observable to the econometrician subject to some sort of parameterization and ε_{ij} is an unobservable component. V_{ij} without loss of generality can be written as $f_i(X_j)$, where X_j is a vector of k attributes for the jth alternative. If one is prepared to assume that ε_{ij} are i.i.d. error terms that have a generalized extreme value distribution and that $V_{ij} = X_j\beta$, then the estimation task is straightforward, fit a linear in the parameters conditional logit model to the data.

However, these assumptions may be questionable in practice [Hensher, Rose and Greene (2005)]. Relaxing the independence part of the i.i.d. assumption on the error term leads to nested logit models or multinomial probit models which allow some type of correlation structure between the error terms from different alternatives. Relaxing the identical part of the model allows for different respondents to have different scale effects, which can play an important role in estimating the distribution of WTP for a change in an attribute.[130] When a respondent answers multiple choice questions, one

---

[129] Louviere, Hensher and Swait (2000) provide a comprehensive overview of choice experiments from multiple perspectives including environmental valuation, marketing and transportation. They provide a wealth of advice on experimental design and fitting statistical models. Reviews in the environmental valuation literature include Hanley, Wright and Adamowicz (1998), Adamowicz et al. (1999), Hanley, Mourato and Wright (2001), Bateman et al. (2002) and Holmes and Adamowicz (2003).

[130] The key thing to keep in mind here is that the parameters estimated in these models are actually β_k/σ where σ is the scale term. Obtaining an estimate for β_k requires an estimate for σ, which is usually parameterized as $-1/\beta_p$, where β_p is the coefficient on the cost term. Allowing σ to differ across either individuals or alternatives raises interesting issues with respect to determining the WTP distribution for a marginal change in the kth attribute. There is growing evidence that σ varies with demographic variables like age and education and some alternatives involve more uncertainty than others in a way that is not reflected in the measured X_j. DeShazo and Fermo (2002) show how the complexity of the choice task can influence the error component.

might also reasonably expect that the error component is correlated in some fashion across choice questions for the same respondent. Relaxing the $V_{ij} = X_j\beta$ assumption can take several forms. The first is to allow different agents to have different preference parameters. This can take the form of a random coefficients model [Layton (2000)] if one believes there is some reasonably continuous distribution of preferences, or a latent class model [Morey, Thatcher and Breffle (in press)] if one believes that there are a small number of consumer types. The second is to relax the linearity assumption. This can be done in two ways. The first is by allowing nonlinear transformation of the individual attributes comprising X_j. The second is by allowing interactions between the different attributes comprising X_j. Both of these raise the issue of whether the nonlinear transformation and/or interaction terms are statistically identified. What features of the attribute space are identified is a function of the experimental design used.[131]

What should be clear from this discussion is that it is far removed from the nonparametric Turnbull framework, where one could impose the very minimal assumptions of economic theory on the data and rely on a fairly simple random assignment of cost across respondents. The choice experiment framework with a nontrivial number of attributes and multiple questions asked of each respondent requires a large number of modeling assumptions in order to recover the parameters of interest. Results are often sensitive to those modeling assumptions, although statistical tests of fit can often be used to rule out some alternative specifications.

From Section 5 we know that moving away from the binary discrete choice framework, either by adding additional alternatives or asking about additional choice sets, can introduce incentives for nontruthful preference revelation. Because respondents do not pick randomly but, rather, want their most preferred bundle of attributes supplied at the lowest possible cost, these deviations from truthful preference revelation are likely to be reflected in picking an alternative in utility space close to the most preferred one. As such, one would expect the incentive structure of choice experiments to generate IIA violations.[132] Because nontruthful preference revelation relies on information about other alternatives and beliefs about how the responses will be used, the estimated parameters of the model may change as the respondent goes through a sequence of choice questions. This phenomenon has often been labeled as "learning" [about preferences]. From an incentive perspective, there may be learning but about incentive structure of the mechanism being used to elicit preference information rather than preferences themselves. It will generally be impossible to sort out which type of learning is going on.

An attraction of the choice experiment format to some is that it allows tradeoffs between different goods and between different configurations of the same good. There is a

---

[131] Statistical identification and statistical efficiency are two distinct concepts with the former being a necessary condition for the latter.

[132] Unfortunately, there are a multitude of other reasons for observing such violations so that their presence cannot be used as a test for nontruthful preference revelation, although the absence of IIA violations would imply that there were not incentive problems.

temptation to take this property of choice experiments and go a step forward and eliminate cost as an attribute. Particular in natural resource damage assessments, there is an interest in doing "resource to resource" scaling in the sense of replacing the damaged resource with some type of substitute. As Flores and Thatcher (2002) show, however, just because one is substituting other resources for the damaged ones, the lack of need for "money" in the model is largely an illusion. In order to be able to consistently aggregate welfare measures over heterogeneous consumers one needs at least one attribute that has a common metric. Money is the obvious attribute and there is not generally a good substitute.

6.8. Models with covariates

For many purposes, all that is needed is an estimate of the unconditional WTP distribution or statistics derived from that distribution. However, policy makers will often want to know various aspects of the conditional distribution; such as, whether there are WTP differences between different income groups and between residents of different geographic areas. In addition, one of the standard ways to look at the reliability of a CV survey is to construct a regression model to predict differences in WTP as a function of other variables in the survey; such as income, past recreational use, and various attitude and knowledge questions concerning the good. An equation with reasonable explanatory power and coefficients with the expected signs provides evidence in support of the proposition that the survey has measured the intended construct. If this is not the case, either the research team has failed to collect the relevant covariates in the survey, suggesting inadequate development work, or the WTP responses are random and completely useless. From an econometric perspective there are no special issues involved in estimating the WTP equation beyond those normally experienced with survey data.[133]

7. Survey design

The valuation scenario presented in the survey instrument lies at the heart of any CV study. The scenario must convey the change in the good to be valued, how that change would come about, how it would be paid for, and the larger context that is relevant for considering the change. It must do this in a way that is consistent with the underlying scientific/engineering reality and yet still be comprehensible to respondents who may

---

[133] Some of the typical issues that will arise are that while theory might suggest that a particular covariate is positively related to WTP, it rarely gives any guidance on the functional form. Many variables from survey data are categorical or ordinal in nature. Different respondents may use questionnaire scales in different ways. Endogeneity issues can arise with respect to the incorporation of covariates derived from debriefing questions. Measurement error is likely to attenuate the coefficients for many variables, and income in particular. Missing values will be present on some covariates and the pattern is not likely to be missing at random, so that dropping observations with missing regressors can create problems.

know little or nothing about the good in question. The respondent needs to be given enough information to be able to make an informed decision, but without being overwhelmed by the information. In general, this is not an easy task because few economists are trained in survey design. The best of the CV surveys represent the current state-of-the-art in survey design.

The development of the survey scenario is a key aspect of a CV study.[134] This is because it forces the sponsor of the survey to decide what the environmental good offered actually will provide to the public in terms that the public cares. In this regard, it is often surprising to find out that the policymakers seeking to evaluate policies do not know what the regulations they are contemplating will actually accomplish in terms of changes in environmental quality.[135] The effort by the survey team to get the interested parties to endorse the depiction of the good described in the CV scenario often exposes deep conflicts about what the proposed policy will actually do and, perhaps just as importantly, what the current baseline *status quo* is.

A CV survey should have what is known as "face validity." The environmental good and the circumstances under which it would be provided should be described clearly and accurately, and the tradeoff that the respondent is asked to make should be a plausible one. The information provided should be adequate for the decision the respondent is asked to perform but should not overwhelm the respondent with unimportant technical details. It is sometimes the case that a high level decision maker who has not been substantially involved earlier in the process of evaluating the policy at hand can learn more about the actual decision by reading the CV survey instrument than the various technical reports on the proposed project.

While it is generally impossible to provide concrete advice that is universally applicable, most good CV surveys contain the following: (a) an introductory section that helps set the general context for the decision to be made; (b) a detailed description of the good to be offered to the respondent; (c) the institutional setting in which the good will be provided; (d) the manner in which the good will be paid for; (e) a method by which the survey elicits the respondent's preferences with respect to the good; (f) debriefing questions about why respondents answered certain questions the way that they did; and (g) a set of questions regarding respondent characteristics including attitudes and demographic information.

A substantial amount of development work is usually required to produce a high quality CV survey instrument. Sometimes there is a substantial amount of prior work to draw on that resolves the major conceptual issues concerning the good and its provision.

---

[134] Further, with good development work through the pilot study phase, the survey team should have a reasonable idea of the results that are likely to be obtained from fielding the survey instrument to a large random sample of the population of interest.

[135] In some instances, there will be substantial scientific uncertainty about what the risks associated with a particular policy are. If there are a small number of distinct outcomes, then it is possible to value each outcome separately to see how sensitive the results are. Carson, Wilks and Imber (1994) provide an example involving proposed mining in the Kakadu Conservation Zone in Australia.

In such cases, there may still need to be local adaptation and careful modification for the inevitable difference between the good being valued in the earlier survey and the current one. In other cases, the type of good to be valued and/or the context in which the valuation is to take place will have been little studied. In this situation, conducting a successful CV study will require considerably more development work.

Development work typically includes focus groups and in-depth interviews to help determine the plausibility and understandability of the description of good to be provided and the context in which it is being provided. The task of translating technical material into a form understood by the general public is often a difficult one. Developing a useful CV survey instrument requires the research team to clearly define what the proposed project will produce in terms of outputs that people care about and in language they understand. Pretests and pilot studies will usually need to be conducted to assess how well the survey works as a whole. Some elements of the survey will usually be needed redesign to improve respondent understanding and the overall flow of the survey.

There are five key issues that will almost always need to be addressed during the development phase of a CV survey. The first is how much information to provide to respondents. Respondents need to be given enough information to make an informed decision but without being overwhelmed with information that they don't think they need. What information to give respondents will depend in large part on what information they already possess. The most difficult cases are where respondents are misinformed about key elements of the scenario and hold their views strongly.[136] Another difficult situation is where the information set held varies considerably across respondents with a substantial fraction of the population being very well informed and a substantial fraction of the population having little prior knowledge.

The second issue, one that always has to be addressed, concerns payment for the good. Here the payment vehicle has to be plausible and, as noted in Section 5, it has to be coercive in nature if incentive compatibility is desired. It is often hard to meet both criteria for every respondent. Another aspect of payment is whether it is a one time lump sum or recurrent payment. As a general rule, something which looks like a capital investment, such as setting aside a wilderness area, should use a lump sum payment mechanism while something like a water quality improvement that would disappear if there were not continued payments should use a recurring payment.[137]

---

[136] Likewise, prior experience with the good can be useful or detrimental when designing a CV scenario. It is useful when it reduces the amount of information that must be given to respondents and it is harmful when there are substantial differences between the current state of the good and its condition at the respondent's time of prior use. While some critics of CV claim that prior experience with a good is a necessary condition for CV to work, such a condition neither follows from economic theory nor accords with people acting as rational agents purchasing unfamiliar goods or voting on new political candidates. By contrast, when respondents are largely uniformed about the good to be valued, this is fairly straightforward for a good survey designer.

[137] If payment is on less than an annual time scale (e.g., a monthly utility) bill it may be helpful to also provide the cost to the respondent on an annual basis so there is no confusion and the recurring nature of the payment made obvious.

The third issue is the formulation of questions to help explain respondent WTP for the good. While it is certainly possible to design a good CV scenario without attention to this part of the survey instrument, it is always desirable to being able to explain differences in the WTP responses; and doing so, enhances faith in their reliability. In some instances, economic theory directly provides guidance and in others there are obvious relationships that should hold between attitudinal or resource use variables. A different set of relationships are likely to exist with indicators related to beliefs about the underlying scenario. Focus groups are a good source of information on what motivates different types of responses. In large samples substantial differences in WTP may be found across different demographic groups, although these relationships may not be linear ones.

As one might expect, respondents who do not believe that the good promised can be delivered with certainty are likely to discount how much they are willing to pay for the program to deliver the good. While it is a desirable goal to minimize divergence between the stated survey scenario and what respondents believe, there will always be some divergences. Debriefing questions can help the researcher in determining the implications of any such divergences.

The fourth issue that needs to be addressed in the design of the CV survey is making respondents feel comfortable with making either a "favor" or "oppose" decision.[138] In particular, respondents need to feel that while the technical details of the proposed program have been well-worked out, the implementation of the program is not at all a foregone conclusion and the public's input via the survey will play an important role in that decision.[139] This consideration needs to run throughout the CV survey. Before the response to the main valuation question is elicited, it is useful to briefly summarize why someone might be for or against the project. After obtaining the response to the valuation question and asking the standard set of debriefing questions and demographics including income, it may be useful to give respondents who favor the program an opportunity to change their answer.

The fifth issue that often must be confronted in the development work for a survey are the choice of stimulus, such as cost amounts and the range of other attribute levels. There are several considerations here. First, the levels of the attributes have to be plausible. This can be explored in focus groups but more subtle problems sometimes manifest

---

[138] The advice in this paragraph bears some resemblance to the use of "cheap talk" language in experiments advocated by Cummings and Taylor (1999) that tells agents to act as if the experiment was real and that people in hypothetical situations tend to over-estimate. While experiments can prove a fruitful venue for testing the efficacy of such interventions, there tend to be two main issues in evaluating their relevancy to CV surveys. The first of these is that good CV surveys should not be posed as "inconsequential," purely hypothetical questions because there are no theoretical predictions about what the response to such questions should be. As such results from experiments with a purely hypothetical (inconsequential) payment may be of very limited use. The second is that the "actual" monetary or behavior transaction in experiments held up as the benchmark often has incentive issues of its own.

[139] The danger in providing a very sketchy idea of a plan to provide a good is that the respondent may take the question posed as asking about whether the government should develop a concrete proposal on this topic or not. As such the respondent may not pay much attention to the cost stated in the survey because that amount is not thought to represent a firm estimate for the program.

themselves in pretest and pilots studies of the survey instrument administered under field conditions. Second, the choices of attribute levels need to provide for reasonable efficiency in statistical modeling. Generally, optimal design for attribute levels depend upon unknown parameters but reasonable inference about these parameter values can often be drawn from pretest and pilot study data. Third, there will often be experiments of one sort or another that will be performed in the course of the main study. Determination of the sample sizes to provide adequate power to test the hypotheses of interest will also require statistical information that can be taken from pretest and pilot studies.[140]

It is beyond the scope of this chapter to get into further details of how to conduct the survey research needed to design a good CV survey. CV surveys are among the most challenging surveys to design. They can be thought of as a structured conversation with a respondent; whereby, a large amount of information is conveyed and where the respondent is engaged in the task of providing preference information about a proposed policy change. Fortunately, there are a number of good books on designing and testing survey instruments [e.g., Bradburn et al. (2004), Presser et al. (2004), Tourangeau et al. (2000)].[141] There is also specific advice for designing CV studies in several books [Mitchell and Carson (1989), Louviere, Hensher and Swait (2000), Bateman et al. (2002), Champ, Boyle and Brown (2003), Alberini, Bjornstad and Kahn (in press)] and a pair of recent journal articles [Mitchell (2002), Whittington (2002)]. The latter article specifically focused on conducting CV studies in developing countries, which can pose some unique challenges.

8. Survey administration

8.1. Defining the population of interest

In much of economic analysis, the issue of defining the relevant population is routinely ignored because it is assumed to be obvious; in other words, those in the marketplace who buy the good of interest. The question of the relevant population becomes difficult, however, once it is asked: who are potential buyers of a good in a market or users of a

---

[140] It is all too common to see CV studies with sample sizes that are much too small to answer the question(s) being asked. Underlying WTP distributions are generally characterized by fairly large variances so that even studies using elicitation formats that obtain continuous responses need large sample sizes. Sample size requirements are further increased when discrete responses are collected. Collecting multiple responses from a single respondent can sometimes reduce sample size requirements but because of the correlated nature of such responses much less information is collected than often assumed. A basic reference on statistical power in experimental design is Bausell and Li (2002).

[141] Stanley Payne's (1951) book, *The Art of Asking Questions* is still invaluable reading for anyone thinking about how to structure a survey interview. Perhaps the best advice to readers is that they "will be disappointed if [they] expect to find here a set of definite rules or explicit directions. The art of asking questions is not likely ever to be reduced to some easy formulas (p. xi)."

government service under a different set of circumstances?[142] CV studies almost always have to face this issue. For example, an improvement in water quality may induce more households to fish.

There are two different perspectives on defining the population of interest in a CV survey. The first perspective is a legal/political one. The agency sponsoring the survey may only care about the welfare of particular subgroups such as taxpayers in their jurisdiction. The second perspective is based on a rough consideration of the cost and benefits of sampling from different groups. For instance, while there may be some value of a change in a local public good to an agent living far away, such agents may be few and far between. To concentrate the interviewing effort on such agents would neglect the agents near the resource who would experience the largest change in utility from the change in the resource.

8.2. Survey mode

There are a number of different ways in which a survey can be administered, including mail, telephone, and in-person.[143] There are four main considerations in choosing the mode of survey administration. The first of these has to do with how the characteristics of the sample of the population of interest are influenced by the survey administration mode. The second has to do with the nature of the stimuli that can be presented to the respondent. The third is the degree of control that the survey mode gives to the researcher over the order and consistency in which stimuli are presented to respondents. The fourth is the cost in term of money and time to obtain a sample of the desired size.

Some of these considerations may be more important for CV surveys valuing particular types of goods. For example, a survey trying to value visibility improvements in a national park will likely require a visual depiction of those changes; and hence, would be unsuitable for administration over the telephone. In-person interviews that take place at a recreation site may be the only feasible way to obtain a reliable set of survey responses from visitors to that site. Further, the prevalence of technology, such as the fraction of households possessing telephones or connected to the internet, or cultural norms that may differ across countries in ways that should be taken into account when deciding what mode of survey administration should be chosen for the CV survey.

---

[142] Defining the population of users is a contentious issue in litigation involving issues of potential harm from unfair trade practices. In marketing there are many examples (e.g., low cost airlines) where moving away from the usual surveying of current users to considering potential users who might be "in the market" if one or more attributes of the good were changed resulted in dramatically expanded sales.

[143] There is a very large literature on how to sample from the population of interest and undertake the physical administration of surveys. On sampling, the interested reader should consult a standard statistical text such as Cochran (1977) or Levy and Lemeshow (1999). On the administration of surveys, the interested reader should consult one or more of the following standard texts: Dillman (in press), Fowler and Mangione (1989), Groves et al. (2004), Lavrakas (1993), and Presser et al. (2004).

There are three classic survey administration modes: in-person with an interviewer, telephone and self-administered. These can be seen at some level as representing the survey questions being (a) read face-to-face by the interviewer to the respondent, (b) having the survey questions read to the respondent but not face-to-face, and (c) having no direct interaction with an interviewer when responding to the questions. The most common variant of a self-administered survey is a mail survey. Other variants include "intercept" surveys where a potential respondent is found at some location (other than their home or place of work) and given a survey to fill-out at that location[144] and more recently internet based surveys.

Hybrid variants of the three classic modes are also sometimes implemented. One can, for instance, do a telephone–mail–telephone survey [Smith and Mansfield (1998)] where respondents are recruited to take the survey (as well as providing responses to some questions), information (often visual) is mailed to them often with some self-administered questions and a follow-up telephone interview used to collect the answers to those questions and to ask additional questions. The use of this hybrid survey points to a key issue in the calculation of response rates. The standard way of calculating response rates will multiply the response rates at each stage together to obtain the final response rate.[145] As such, even if the response rate at each stage is considered to be quite reasonable by survey standards, final response rate will look fairly low. For the same response rate, the sample selection bias in this type of multistage survey is likely to be much lower than the equivalent selection bias in a single stage survey with the same response rate.

8.3. Sampling approaches

The key to drawing appropriate inference from any sample is that each member of the population of interest must have a known positive probability of being included in the sample. This implies either the existence of a list of the population or some way of generating that list. An example of the former is a database of fishing licenses if the population of interest consists of those that fished during a particular year. An example of the latter is using random digit dialing in a telephone survey. In the absence of a list or means of accurately generating a list, it may be necessary to do some type of enumeration before sampling from it. A different issue arises when the choices made by a respondent influence their probability of being included in a sample. An example here includes any type of on-site recreation survey [Moeltner and Shonkwiler (2005)]. The frequent characteristic of a choice-based sample is that it excludes people who are not currently undertaking an activity, which can be important when a main focus of the

---

[144] The intercept approach can also be used in conjunction with giving respondents a survey to fill out later and return by mail.

[145] Any type of internet panel with an initial stage of randomly recruited participants will have similar sampling properties.

policy change of interest is on the margin between some use and no use rather than solely focused on changing the amount of use by users.

Stratification of a sample increases its efficiency in that a small sample size is needed relative to simple random sampling for the same level of statistical precision. It does this by pre-determining the size of the subsamples from different strata. For example, in a national survey, states/provinces are natural strata, and drawing the correct proportion from each stratum eliminates the possibility of having a sample that comes disproportionately from one state.

The other common survey design feature is clustering, whereby multiple individuals are interviewed in fairly close proximity. Clustering in a sample reduces the efficiency of a sample relative to simple random sampling. It is often done in conjunction with in-person surveys to reduce interviewer travel time and costs. A variant of clustering is when one chooses (randomly) a relatively small number of locations at which to conduct an on-site survey. Clustering effects with preference data are not generally large if the number of clusters is reasonably large because of the degree of heterogeneity generally observed. However, measurements of other phenomena such as income or ethnicity can be highly correlated within a cluster which can give rise to large cluster effects.

In most instances, sampling is done "proportionately" so that each selected agent has the same weight. There are cases, however, where this is intentionally not the case. The usual example is where it is desirable to report estimates for some specific subgroup of the population of interest and a level of statistical precision beyond what their proportionate representation in the overall sample is desired. In such an instance, members of the subgroup can be over-sampled. The more common case occurs when the response rate to the survey differs systematically across identifiable subgroups of the population of interest. Here, the usual solution is to create sample weights so after weighting the data obtained that each subgroup is represented in the correct proportion in the weighted sample. Professional survey companies which administer the questionnaire usually supply the appropriate weights.

The departures from simple random sampling discussed in this section are generally corrected by some type of weighting scheme. For large samples with proportionate sampling and high response rates, the influence of stratification and clustering on response data from CV preference elicitation questions is typically small. This is not the case once one is dealing with small samples, nonproportionate sampling and/or choice-based samples. Standard sampling texts such as Cochran (1977) and Kish (1967) lay out the relevant details.

8.4. Nonresponse

With any survey, one gets nonresponse [Madow, Olkin and Rubin (1983), Groves et al. (2001)]. Nonresponse is of two types: failure to respond to the survey as a whole, and failure to respond to a particular question. The latter is often referred to as item nonresponse. The simplest case is where the response is considered "missing at random" [Little and Rubin (2002)]. A complete interview or response to a particular survey question is missing at random if dropping it does not alter either the unconditional or conditional distribution of interest. If this is the case, then for the purpose of simple tabulation of responses on a particular question, then the missing interview or missing answer on a particular question can be ignored with the effective sample size simply being smaller.

The situation is more difficult when the response is not missing at random. There are two relevant cases here. The first one is where the missing at random assumption holds after conditioning on a set of observable covariates. An important instance of this condition occurs when different identifiable subgroups in a population respond to the survey as a whole or to a particular survey question at different rates. As noted in the previous section, one way to deal with this issue is to weight the data using the information on how the response rate is related to the covariates. A different (but to a large degree similar) way to deal with this issue is to impute the missing values using a nonparametric [Mitchell and Carson (1989)] or parametric framework [Little and Rubin (2002)]. The second is where the response is not missing at random after conditioning on the available covariates. This leads one to use some type of sample selection model along the lines pioneered by Heckman (1979). Sample selection bias is most likely to occur when potential respondents can decide, as is typically the case in a mail survey, whether to answer the survey questions after learning the main focus of the questionnaire. The nature of the selection bias in such cases may be very bimodal, with those with the highest and lowest values for the good most likely to respond.

8.5. Sample size

The issue of sample size should be considered in the context of issues related to survey mode and the likely divergences from simple random sampling including stratification, clustering, and nonresponse issues.[146] The level of precision needed for the policy decision at hand and testing the hypotheses of interest should drive the sample size decision. The degree of precision necessary for the CV results to provide a useful input to the decision making process can vary substantially. In some instances, only a rough order of magnitude comparison between benefits and costs may be required, while in other instances, relatively small changes in an estimate may influence the preferred outcome.[147] This consideration should be reflected in the sample size chosen.

---

[146] Care should be taken in assessing all these issues due to the use of different conventions. In particular, how response rates in surveys are calculated varies considerably. For example, it is often the case in mail surveys that surveys returned due to "moved/bad addresses" are taken out of both the numerator and denominator before calculating the response rate. This would not be the case in a door-to-door survey as the new resident of the dwelling unit is eligible to be interviewed. Thus, there is some interaction between how the response rate to a survey is defined and the nature of any sample selection problem related to a deviation between the effective sample frame used and the population of interest.

[147] Further, where the cost estimate for the project is known before the CV survey is conducted, it may not be necessary to trace out the entire WTP distribution, only the part relevant to the decision at hand. This has implications for the design points used in the survey and the sample size required.

There are too many CV surveys that are carried out with a sample size that is inadequate to meet a study's objectives. There are areas where there are legitimate tradeoffs that can be made involving sample size. For instance, while it may be desirable to do in-person surveys, an internet-based survey with careful attention to matching the demographics of the population of interest may be able to obtain reasonable results at substantially lower cost. For the same cost, a mail survey with a high response rate may well be preferable to an in-person survey with a low response rate. Further, while it may be desirable to ask only a single binary discrete choice question, substantially more information can be obtained from either shifting to a different elicitation format such as a payment card or by asking multiple questions. While this may introduce some bias from an incentive perspective, Cameron and Huppert (1991) show that the use of a binary discrete choice without a large sample size and careful attention to the design points can produce estimates that have very high variances.

The standard warning that nonsampling errors may be important in any survey should be taken seriously. Groves et al. (2004) provides a good overview of thinking about surveys from a total error perspective.

9. Consistency of CV results with theoretical prediction

There are a number of interesting issues that CV results have raised about neoclassical economic theory which have prompted extensions or clarifications of that theory. CV surveys have sometimes revealed violations of neoclassical economic theory; however, similar violations can also be found in consumer behavior in actual markets. CV raises issues of incentive structures that are largely ignored in the conventional analysis of consumer demand but which dominate much of contemporary game theory. CV also raises some issues about the structure of markets and the aggregation of preferences which were of relatively little practical import until it was possible to use CV as an empirical measuring tool. The flexibility of CV takes the economist away from the role of using data passively and into the realm of survey and experimental design. Surveys and experimental design interact in interesting ways because of the possibility of doing random assignment, the key aspect of experiments, in the context of different variants of a survey instrument. Finally, CV raises issues related to consumer knowledge and understanding that are little discussed in the conventional context of consumer demand analysis.

9.1. Neoclassical theory and contingent valuation

One of the more interesting aspects of the history of CV is its role in motivating a much deeper understanding of the implications of neoclassical economic theory in the case of pure public goods. Careful examination of neoclassical economic theory helps to explain phenomena that at various times have been pointed to as anomalies, suggesting that CV surveys do not measure economic value [Hausman (1993)]. These include the

(a) magnitude of the divergence between WTP and WTA, (b) the magnitude of the income elasticity often estimated in CV studies, (c) the large effect the order in which goods are valued can play, and (d) the failure of the Diamond (1996) adding-up test to hold in many situations.

The key to understanding these issues was the unraveling of structure of demand for imposed quantity changes that was set in motion by Hanemann (1991). In that paper, the possibility of sharp difference between price changes and quantity changes emerged so that WTA could be infinity while WTP was a small finite number. Hicks himself seems to be aware that the structure of neoclassical theory was quite different. This is clearly reflected in the title of his classic article "The Four Consumer Surpluses" which today rather than equivalence and compensating variations and surpluses could have could have been characterized as WTP versus WTA crossed with small price changes versus imposed quantity changes. The inherited wisdom though was largely driven by Willig's seminal paper (1976) that argued that the difference between WTP and WTA was sufficiently small to be ignorable (for small price changes) where the qualification in parentheses was almost always dropped. Willig was careful not to include quantity changes in his analysis and it took quite some time for the full ramifications of the difference between the price change and imposed quantity changes cases to emerge.[148] Eventually, Cornes and Sandler (1996) was to show that pure public goods was simply a special case of rationed (i.e., imposed quantity change) goods.

9.2. WTP versus WTA

If total value, in an economic sense, can always be expressed in terms of WTP and WTA and the two measures differ substantially, either theoretically or empirically, the appropriate measure for a benefit–cost analysis depends upon the *property right*. The difference between the Willig and Hanemann theoretical results is that for a price change, an income effect alone governs the difference between WTP and WTA; and for a quantity change, both an income effect and a substitution effect together govern the difference. One of the earliest findings from CV studies was that WTP and WTA measures differed substantially [e.g., Hammack and Brown (1974)]. Based upon Willig's work, it was thought either one or both of the CV estimates were wrong, rather than understanding of the relevant theory being wrong. Work proceeded in several directions. One was to

---

[148] Randall and Stoll (1980) were the first to expand Willig's framework to consider the imposed quantity changes but the full import of the differences between the two cases was not clear until Hanemann (1991). The discovery of these differences first found in the context of CV studies, coupled with the initial belief that Willig's results were more widely applicable, caused some researchers to claim the observed CV results violated economic theory. Hanemann (1991), in a standard neo-classical theoretical framework, shows that for imposed quantity changes, WTP and WTA can be infinitely far apart due to interactions between income and substitution effects. Kahneman and Tversky (1979) had earlier put forth an alternative they called "prospect theory" where losses are valued more highly than gains. In the situation usually considered by economists, a single imposed quantity change, Kahneman and Tversky and Hanemann's models yield the same results.

show that large differences between WTP and WTA estimates were not an artifact of the survey context, but rather, consistently large differences were found in a variety of settings using actual transactions [e.g., Knetsch, Thaler and Kahneman (1990)].[149] Even financial assets such as junk bonds and over-the-counter stocks, when thinly traded, often show much larger bid (WTP)-ask (WTA) spreads than would be predicted by Willig's work. Another direction was to show that the WTA question format had a number of shortcomings, both from the perspective of its strategic incentives and of getting respondents to accept it as a legitimate framework for a policy choice. Still another direction was to suggest new theories outside the neoclassical framework [Kahneman and Tversky (1979)] and to show that within that framework [Hanemann (1991)] that the theory being applied failed to capture key aspects of the situation.[150] Much of the problem with the current framework may stem from its inherent static nature. Recent models that incorporate bargaining, information effects, transactions cost/experience, dynamic considerations and uncertainty, show considerable promise in being able to explain the magnitude of the divergence between WTP and WTA amounts [e.g., Kolstad and Guzman (1999), Kling, List and Zhao (2003), Zhao and Kling (2004), List (2000)]. The key implication of this divergence for applied policy work is that property rights can have a substantial influence on the magnitude of the welfare measure. This is true particularly when considering a reduction in an environmental service, where the common practice of substituting a WTP estimate for the desired WTA measure can result in a substantial underestimate, which, in turn, can have substantial policy implications [Knetsch (1990)].

9.3. Income elasticity of WTP

Drawing inferences about economic values from intuition regarding the demand for private goods, one expects to see a positive relationship between income and WTP, if the good being valued is a "normal" good. A frequent made claim, for which there is surprisingly little empirical support, is that most environmental goods are "luxury" goods.

---

[149] A striking feature is the standard empirical finding that WTA estimates based on actual transactions are usually much larger than CV WTP estimates for the same good. In particular, Horowitz and McConnell's (2002) review of the literature suggests that the ratio of WTA to WTP estimates is roughly the same for surveys and actual transactions. For a deep critique of the WTP–WTA divergence that is prepared to abandon substantial parts of neoclassical theory in the direction of some of the main tenets of behavioral economics and that recognizes that the issues involved are "not specific to CV surveys" see Sugden (1999).

[150] That a price change where the consumer is free to adjust is different from an imposed quantity change where the consumer cannot adjust seems obvious in retrospect. Indeed, it was clear to Hicks (1943) who first clearly developed the concept of utility constant welfare measures. Willig was also careful to specify that he was looking at price changes. This acknowledgement was largely left behind in the rapid incorporation of Willig's work in benefit–cost texts. Willig's work showing that WTP and WTA were close in most situations involving price changes and that the Marshallian consumer surplus measure lay between WTP and WTA. This justified the common applied practice of using the Marshallian consumer surplus as adequate approximation to the desired Hicksian measure.

If this were the case, one would expect the income elasticity to be greater than one. The usual empirical result from CV studies is to find a positive income elasticity of WTP substantially less than one for environmental commodities. This empirical result has been cited as evidence that contingent values are theoretically deficient. For instance, McFadden (1994) reporting on one of Exxon's studies notes:

> An economic interpretation of the results on the relationship of income to WTP in these experiments is that preservation of Selway-Bitterroot wilderness is a "necessary" good, with a low-income elasticity. However, it seems economically plausible that preservation would be a "luxury" good that for poor households is displaced by needs for food and shelter.

The problem is that the terms *necessary* (e.g., normal but not luxury) and *luxury* are defined in terms of the income elasticity of *demand*, not in terms of the income elasticity of WTP. Flores and Carson (1997) show that the two types of income elasticities are fundamentally different. The two income elasticities can be shown to be functionally related using the concept of a shadow or virtual price that responds to changes in the levels of rationed goods. WTP is found by simply integrating (summing) the virtual prices for infinitesimal quantity changes over the discrete quantity change in the rationed good of interest. The relationship between the ordinary income elasticity of demand and the income elasticity of WTP for two goods is given by:

$$
\begin{bmatrix} \eta_1^{v} \\ \eta_2^{v} \end{bmatrix} = - \begin{bmatrix} \sigma_{11}^{d} & \sigma_{12}^{d} \\ \sigma_{21}^{d} & \sigma_{22}^{d} \end{bmatrix}^{-1} \begin{bmatrix} \eta_1^{d} \\ \eta_2^{d} \end{bmatrix} \frac{y}{e^{v}},
$$

where η_i^{v} are the (virtual) income elasticities of WTP, the σ^{d} are the cross price elasticities of demand, η_i^{d} are the ordinary income elasticities, and y/e^{v} is income divided by e^{v} which is equal to income plus the value of *all* public goods consumed expressed in monetary terms, which may well be quite large.

Flores and Carson's results show that for any fixed value of the income elasticity of demand, the income elasticity of WTP can differ significantly in magnitude and even sign. Thus, a good which is a luxury good in a demand sense may have a WTP income elasticity which is less than zero, between zero and one, or greater than one. If the matrix of cross-price elasticities is an identity matrix, the virtual price income elasticity is equal to the ordinary income elasticity of demand multiplied by a scale factor (the ratio of income to income *plus* the monetized value of all public goods), which must be less than one and probably substantially less. Thus, the income elasticity[151] of WTP is likely to be less than the corresponding income elasticity of demand.

---

[151] In empirical estimates of the income elasticity of WTP there also may be measurement issues associated with income that tend to bias the estimate toward zero. It is well-known that income is often poorly measured in surveys without a great deal of time and effort in the survey devoted to structuring this task. Further, disposable income after taxes and other fixed expenses such as housing and car payments is likely to be the relevant income measure. It is also likely that agents have mental accounts [Thaler (1985)] they consider when making decisions about environmental goods that may greatly reduce the relevant income available.

9.4. Sequencing, nesting, scope insensitivity and the adding-up test

We now turn to the relationship between CV estimates for multiple, possibly unrelated goods. Here, the context in which the CV exercise takes place is crucial. Two issues have received the most attention. The first involves the implications of adding together CV WTP estimates for different goods. The second involves the influence exerted on the estimated value of the good by the order in which it is valued as part of a sequence of goods. The two typical empirical findings turn on the same underlying theoretical issue: substitution and income effects.

The first empirical finding suggests that adding up what people say they are willing to pay for specific goods, each valued independently as the only change to the *status quo* (or equivalently valued first in a sequence), might easily exceed the income of some people. This strikes many nontechnically oriented CV critics as conclusive proof that CV estimates, if not complete nonsense, are gross over-estimates. However, Hoehn and Randall (1989) show theoretically why adding together independently derived WTP estimates for goods is likely to overstate the value of the set of goods taken as a package, and often grossly so. At an intuitive level, the reason is simple: each new public good the agent obtains reduces the agent's available income to spend on private goods. Further, if the public goods are substitutes for each other, then each one added to the package looks less desirable than when valued as if it were the only new addition to the stock of public goods. The problem should not be seen as residing with the original CV estimates, but with the analyst's incorrectly aggregating them without taking into account income and substitution effects.[152] The second standard empirical finding is that the value of a good falls, often precipitously, the later it is valued in a sequence of goods. Consider a stylized example reminiscent of some of the early work on air pollution valuation [Randall, Hoehn and Tolley (1981)]. A subsample of respondents in Chicago are willing to pay $100 for a specified air quality change in Chicago; and when offered an additional specified air quality improvement in the Grand Canyon, they are willing to pay $30 more. A different subsample of respondents for whom the sequence is reversed are willing to pay $60 for the Grand Canyon improvement and $70 for the Chicago improvement. Such a result may be disturbing to the policy maker who expects a good to have only one "true" value.

The standard economic explanation for this phenomenon is substitution and income effects. Carson, Flores and Hanemann (1998) show that if one assumes that the goods being valued are normal goods and (Hicksian) substitutes for each other, the value of a particular public good should be progressively smaller the later in a WTP sequence it is valued. An implication of this result is that the package of goods should be valued less than the sum of its independently valued constituents. The opposite effect occurs

---

[152] The problem of taking account of multiple changes has long been known to be troublesome in the benefit–cost literature [Just, Hueth and Schmitz (1982)] and is in no way specific to the use of CV estimates. The problem is often ignored in many benefit–cost applications due to the time and expense associated with determining the interactions between the different goods and the belief or hope that such effects are small.

in a WTA sequence; the later in a sequence the good is valued, the more highly it is valued.[153] Furthermore, the usual weak assumptions made concerning the curvature properties of utility functions effectively rule out the existence of a single context independent value for a particular public good.

CV critics counter that the sequence effects observed are too large because they contend the income effects should be small and goods such as those in the air quality example above are not close substitutes.[154] However, the CV critics' arguments about the likely magnitude of income and substitution effects are faulty because they are based on intuition derived from looking at price changes for private goods. Public goods are a special case of quantity rationed goods and, as a result, the focus should be on quantity space with an inverse demand system rather than price space with an ordinary demand system where consumers are free to choose their optimal consumption levels. Flores (1995) shows that the set of virtual price substitution elasticities that should lie behind the magnitude of any sequence effects is the inverse of the set of cross-price elasticities of demand upon which the CV critics' intuition appears to be based.

Consider the following set of compensated, cross-price elasticities of demand (σ_{ij}^{d}) taken from Deaton's (1974) well-known analysis of consumer demand in the United Kingdom. Good one is food and good two is clothing:

$$\begin{bmatrix} \sigma_{11}^{d} & \sigma_{12}^{d} \\ \sigma_{21}^{d} & \sigma_{22}^{d} \end{bmatrix} = \begin{bmatrix} -0.28 & 0.08 \\ 0.21 & -0.17 \end{bmatrix}.$$

Note that own-price (-0.28 for food and -0.17 for clothing) and cross-price elasticities (0.08 for the effect on food demand of a price increase in clothing and 0.21 for the effect on clothing demand of a price increase in food) in this example are all quite small. Thus, with respect to either good, the percentage change in demand will be small relative to the percentage change in either own price or the other good's price. Hence, particularly large context effects for price changes would not be expected. However, if one restricts choices, as is the case with environmental goods where the levels are usually collectively decided, a regime of partial rationing is in effect.

Rationing requires consideration of the inverse relationship – how the shadow or virtual prices for the rationed goods (food and clothing) respond to changes in the rationed levels of both of these goods. These measures of responsiveness, the virtual price substitution elasticities (σ_{ij}^{v}), are related inversely, as a system, to the compensated price

---

[153] The reason for this is that one is destroying existing public goods in a WTA sequence. As one goes farther and farther out in the sequence, fewer substitute public goods remain, and since the agent is compensated with money at each step in the sequence, income is increasing. Carson, Flores and Hanemann (1998) further show WTP for a good valued first in a WTP sequence is less than WTA for the good valued in any order in a WTA sequence.

[154] A typical example is Kahneman and Knetsch (1992). McFadden (1994) makes the argument in a somewhat different way as a conclusion based upon his empirical analysis of a CV data set from a wilderness area study: "These results indicate that either there are extraordinarily strong diminishing returns to preserving additional wilderness areas, or that there is a context effect that makes responses inconsistent with classical economic preferences."

elasticities [Madden (1991), Flores (1995)]. For the food and clothing example, the virtual price matrix of substitution terms is:

$$\begin{bmatrix} \sigma_{11}^v & \sigma_{12}^v \\ \sigma_{21}^v & \sigma_{22}^v \end{bmatrix} = \begin{bmatrix} \sigma_{11}^d & \sigma_{12}^d \\ \sigma_{21}^d & \sigma_{22}^d \end{bmatrix}^{-1} = \begin{bmatrix} -5.60 & -2.55 \\ -7.19 & -9.33 \end{bmatrix}.$$

The same demand system cross-price elasticities which implied fairly small increases in demand of one good when the price of the other good increases (an 8% increase in food demand accompanying a 100% price increase in clothing and a 21% increase in clothing demand accompanying a 100% price increase in food), now implies very large reductions (255% and 719%, respectively) in WTP if a unit of the other good has already been provided first in the WTP sequence. This example with private goods shows that one need not resort to explanations of inconsistent preferences or goods with peculiar characteristics to predict quite large context effects with respect to public good values.

Substitution effects are sufficient to drive the sequence effects observed in CV studies. Income effects, however, are likely to play a role as well. CV critics argue that since respondent WTP is usually just a small fraction of income, income effects should be small. Much of a household's income is already committed so that available discretionary income is much smaller, particularly if payment is required over a short time period. Further, income is known to be poorly measured in general population surveys [Sudman and Bradburn (1982)]. These sources of measurement error probably bias estimated income effects downward.

CV critics such as Kahneman and Knetsch (1992) respond that if sequence effects are indeed large, then CV estimates are arbitrary because they can be manipulated by the choice of the sequence order. Kahneman and Knetsch's statement is applicable to economic analysis in general which, if done correctly, is context specific,[155] as value in an economic sense is always a relative rather than absolute concept [Debreu (1959)]. Even more to the point is Flores's (1999) demonstration of a formal equivalence between the agenda control problem and WTP sequences for a set of public goods. As agenda control is a central issue in public choice [Mueller (1989)], it would have been surprising to see the use of CV somehow avoided it.[156]

Closely related to the issue of sequencing and often confused with it are the issues of nesting and scope [Carson and Mitchell (1995)].[157] Nesting occurs when one good can be considered a proper subset of another. This can occur in two distinct ways. One

---

[155] For specific examples of context effects on consumer surplus measures for price changes for private goods, see Lave (1984) or Randall and Hoehn (1996). The economic intuition behind such effects is the loss in consumer surplus for a specified increase in the price of chicken that is likely to be much larger if there are also large concurrent increases in prices of beef, pork, and fish.

[156] At least partially for reasons of agenda control, benefit–cost analysts are almost always told by policy makers to focus on whether a proposed program potentially improves social welfare rather than being asked how to globally maximize societal well-being.

[157] The term "embedding" was originally used by Kahneman and Knetsch (1992) in their well-known paper to refer two distinct phenomena. One involved sequencing of goods where neoclassical economic theory, as discussed above, predicts the same good should have different values depending upon the order in which it

situation is where different items are being valued and these can be considered in different combinations; the other is where different numbers of units of the *same* item are considered. An example of the first case is where one values some specified quantity of forests, fish and birds. This good nests the same quantities of forests and fish, which in turn nests the same quantity of forests. In the second case, the large quantity nests the smaller one. The key to sequence effects involving nested goods is the degree of substitution or complementarity between the separate items; as noted above, large sequencing effects here are consistent with neoclassical theory.

When two goods, one of which nests the other, are valued in the same order, there is a clear theoretical prediction that the larger good should be valued the same or higher than the smaller good, if both the nested good and its complement are seen as desirable. The test of this proposition has become known as the scope insensitivity hypothesis. Again, the key here is the nature of individual preferences. If scope insensitivity cannot be rejected, there could be two possible economic explanations. One possibility is the inability to perceive an *effective* difference in quantity; just as an individual might not notice the difference between 50 grams of sugar and 51 grams, so too she might not consider the difference between a 250 page novel and a 300 page novel to be a meaningful difference. Another explanation is satiation: additional units of the item have zero marginal utility. A less extreme and probably common variant of this is that the environmental amenity is subject to sharply declining marginal utility [Rollins and Lyke (1998)]. If so, fairly large sample sizes will be needed to adequately test the scope insensitivity hypothesis; and more generally, power is often a concern in empirical tests of this hypothesis since it is meaningless to fail to reject differences of plausible magnitude.

The empirical evidence is that there is some sensitivity to scope for a wide range of goods. Carson (1997a, 1997b) reviews a fairly large number of studies where two nested goods were valued separately (typically for policy purposes and a desire not to contaminate the response to different scenarios) and finds that the hypothesis of scope insensitivity is usually rejected. There are, however, clear examples where it is not. These examples seem to fall into a few key areas. First, the use of voluntary payments seems to be associated with scope insensitivity, which should not be surprising given the incentive structure associated with this type of mechanism. Second, instances where there is an attempt to value a good such as preserving a particular species but where it is clear that any effective protection plan has to involve preserving a larger set of species. The issue here appears to be plausibility of the provision mechanism. A different variant of this issue sometimes occurs when respondents believe that a "small" good is much more likely to be successfully provided than a "larger" variant of the good that nests the smaller one.[158] The third is where there are multiple metrics on which the good can be

---

is valued. The other involved the relationship between the value of two goods where one of the goods in the language of Carson and Mitchell (1995) nests another other. Carson and Mitchell (1995) recommend that the term "embedding" not be used because of ambiguity in its meaning and relationship to theoretical predictions.

[158] Ironically, this problem is often caused by trying to keep the survey language for the two goods as close as possible, whereas it often takes more effort in terms of survey design to get the perceived probability of provision for the larger good equal to that of the smaller good.

measured. The best known example here is the Desvousges et al. (1993b) chapter of the Hausman (1993) volume which finds respondents having roughly the same WTP to save the lives of 2,000 birds, described as much less than 1% of the population; 20,000 birds, described as less than 1% of the population; and 200,000 birds, described as about 2% of the population. If respondents were concerned about the percentage impact, rather than the absolute impact, these difference would seem trivial.[159] Finally, the valuation of changes in low level risk seems to always present substantial difficulties. This should not be surprising, though, given the difficulty people have in actual markets dealing with these issues.

Another context-related consistency test, termed an adding-up test, has been proposed by Diamond (1996). At an abstract level, the test follows from satisfying duality properties that are commonly assumed [and commonly violated, e.g., Bateman et al. (1997)] in other areas of applied microeconomics. The test requires that a sequence of specified changes add-up to the set of changes taken as a package. There are two practical difficulties with the test that come to light in trying to operationalize it using multiple subsamples of respondents. The usual approach to structuring the CV survey questions involves asking at least one of the subsamples to "pretend" that they had already received a specified good and paid a specified amount for it. It may be difficult, however, to get respondents to take such an exercise seriously. The other involves making the substitution assumption implicit in Diamond's illustrative example that respondents are indifferent between a program which prevents some number of existing birds from being killed and a hatchery program which produces the same number of new birds [Smith and Osborne (1996), Kopp and Smith (1997)]. Substitute children for birds and the implication of this assumption becomes striking.[160]

10. Consistency of CV results with actual behavior

Distrust of survey results often leads economists down the path of asking "How do CV results correspond with actual behavior?" A little reflection here, however, suggests that the question is ill-posed, at least to the extent that asking this question usually implies that a divergence would indicate a problem with CV. Ideally, one would like to see CV

---

[159] A recent replication of the bird survey from Desvousges et al. (1993b) using just 1% versus 10% of the population finds significant scope sensitivity; Hanemann and Felipe Vasquez (2005).

[160] The difficulty with the test can also be illustrated with a simple example involving hotel rooms where the substitution issue becomes sharply focused. Consider three scenarios. In scenario 1, your maximum WTP for a shabby hotel room (the only one available) in a city you are interested in traveling to is $50. In scenario 2, you have already made a nonrefundable payment for the shabby hotel room and your employer for some reason offers to reimburse you for the $50 you paid for this room so your income is back to the same level as in scenario 1. Now a room becomes available at a 5-star luxury hotel and your maximum WTP for it is $200. In scenario 3, you have the opportunity to make a reservations that includes both the shabby hotel and the luxury hotel. For Diamond's adding up test to work, you need to be willing to pay $250 for this opportunity in scenario 3.

estimates consistent with actual behavior when theory suggest they should be consistent and divergent when theory suggest that they should be divergent.

It may be useful to get the two main divergent cases out of the way first as they seem to be the examples CV critics often focus on. The first is the case of comparing actual voluntary contributions to survey derived estimates of likely contributions.[161] The second is the case of comparing willingness to pay or purchase rates for private goods to estimate of the same quantity based on surveys.[162] Sometimes the "revealed" behavior is taken from actual markets and sometimes from economic experiments.[163]

Comparing actual contributions to survey-based estimated suggests that that the survey estimate is higher than the actual contributions and often by a very considerable factor. This is what one should expect. The actual contributions should grossly underestimate actual willingness to pay because of the free-rider problem that has long been at the core of issues surrounding the provision of public goods. Less obvious is that the estimate from the survey should over-estimate true WTP. That is because if the survey is consequential as noted in Section 5, the main effect that indicating a willingness to contribute can have is to encourage an actual (voluntary) fundraising drive to be mounted. That effort must be taken in order for the agent to have the opportunity to get the good for free by having others pay for it through their voluntary contributions. Thus, all that can be said is that actual contributions should over-estimate true WTP and the survey responses should underestimate it.[164]

Private goods do not suffer the free-riding problem that is seen with public goods. As such, many CV proponents and critics have thought private goods represented the "best case" situation for comparing market and survey-based estimates. What this perspective failed to take into account is the incentive structure that respondents face in the CV survey. A "yes" response indicates a willingness to purchase the new good, and as such encourages the firm to produce the good and offer it to consumers. If the good is produced, the consumer can decide whether to purchase the good. The agent's response to the survey might still be informative in the sense that a "no" response to a particular amount might be interpretable as an actual no, but a "yes" response only translates to a "maybe" under the right future conditions. As such, a survey for a new private good traces out "potential" demand not "actual" demand. While this is useful information from a marketing perspective, the expected result is again the observed result: surveys tend to over-estimate, often by a substantial fraction, the percent who

---

[161] For examples, see Duffield and Patterson (1991b), Seip and Strand (1992), and Champ et al. (1997).

[162] For examples, see Infosino (1986), Neill et al. (1994), and Cummings, Harrison and Rutström (1995).

[163] In the economic experiments, agents are said to have "home-grown" preferences/values rather than having those assigned by the experiments. See [Harrison and List (2004)] for a review of this issue.

[164] Chilton and Hutchinson (1999) correctly point out that this bound doesn't necessarily hold if one switches the provider of the good (from say a respected nonprofit organization to the government) and agents who provide the good. This issue is potentially important if agents care about the type of provider even if the coercive nature of the payment mechanism is unchanged.

actually purchase the good. Contrary to popular wisdom, the private goods case should be seen as a worst-case rather than best-case situation for comparing actual behavior to survey-based estimates.

There are a couple of important caveats to this statement that surveys should over-estimate purchase behavior with respect to new goods. The first is that this over-estimation finding is typical with respect to those that purchase over some fairly short time horizon. Again, this is what one would expect. Over time, the fraction of purchases is likely to converge toward the survey estimate as the "right circumstances" happen for more and more agents.[165] The diffusion of information about the good, as well as the marketing effort, can influence this horizon. The second is that the expected result from a marketing survey that is interpreted as a "pricing" exercise rather than a "new goods provision" exercise will be the opposite. Respondents will be more price sensitive, that is they indicate they are less willing to purchase at a given price, than agents actual do in the marketplace [Brownstone and Small (2005)]. Again, this is a common finding in the marketing and transportation literature when dealing with an existing rather than a new product.[166]

One can turn to two situations where CV is heavily used where it is possible to make comparisons of survey-based estimates with revealed behavior. The first of these is with quasi-public goods, such as outdoor recreation, where there are other techniques such as the averting behavior, hedonic pricing, and travel cost analysis that can be used with different types of revealed behavior. Carson et al. (1996) perform a meta-analysis of 616 comparisons of CV estimates to revealed preference (RP) estimates from 83 separate studies and find that the mean ratio of CV to RP estimates is 0.89 with a 95% confidence interval of [0.81–0.96], suggesting that CV estimates in the case of quasi-public goods are on average a bit lower than RP estimates and fairly highly correlated (0.78).[167] What is perhaps just as interesting is that there is a clear publication bias, in that, two types of studies are most likely to get published: those with a CV/RP ratio close to 1 and those with very large CV/RP ratios.

Mechanism design theory suggests that a consequential binary discrete choice question with a coercive payment mechanism and a take-it-or-leave-it offer should be incentive compatible. Long-standing evidence in the polling literature suggests that surveys

---

[165] This is consistent with the results of a major World Bank review [Water Demand Research Team (1993)] of CV estimates of water system hook-ups in developing countries where CV estimates initially over-estimated the percent of households subscribing to water services. However, the CV estimates were reasonably accurate and not systematically biased forecasts of behavior over long time horizons.

[166] It is interesting that without a coherent theory of how people respond to surveys, the two marketing survey literature results, over-estimate for new goods and "too" price sensitive for existing goods, have coexisted in the form of simply "forecast" problems using surveys.

[167] There are more estimates than studies because some studies valued multiple goods or used a different statistical approach to value the same good. Giving equal weight to each study rather than each comparison, results in an average CV/RP ratio of 0.92, where the confidence interval [0.81–1.03] does not reject the ratio, is 1 at the 5% level. Meta-analysis of particular types of goods, such as outdoor recreation [e.g., Rosenberger and Loomis (2000)] suggests a similar conclusion.

done right before the election do well in predicting two candidate races and ballot initiatives, providing some support for this proposition.[168] Carson, Hanemann and Mitchell (1987) did a CV survey modeled on proposed California ballot measure on a water quality bond issue as part of a Field Institute California Poll and found a close correspondence between their survey estimate and the percent in favor in the actual vote.[169] More recently Champ and Brown (1997) found a similar result on a road related referendum in Colorado and Vossler et al. (2003) found a similar result looking at an open-space bond issue in Oregon.[170]

The other approach to looking at whether the theoretical prediction holds in practice is with some type of economic experiment. Here, the evidence is mixed and much more controversial. List and Gallet (2001) survey the experimental literature and find that experiments with "real" economic commitments tend to result in lower estimates than comparable "hypothetical" treatments. As Little and Berrens (2004) note, most of the studies List and Gallet (2001) review are not directly relevant to assessing the performance of binary discrete choice questions cast in a referendum context. Cummings et al. (1997) perform such an experiment that was later extended by Cummings and Taylor (1998). These two papers show that the "hypothetical" treatment had a higher fraction in favor than the treatment where agents were required to pay if their group voted in favor; and that the percent in favor monotonically declined as the probability that the group's vote was binding. The Carson, Groves and Machina (2000) framework shows neoclassical economic theory provides no prediction about how agents faced with a "purely hypothetical," that is an inconsequential survey question should behave. That framework does, however, provide a strong prediction that as long as the probability of influencing the decision is positive, then the vote/survey response should be invariant to the actual probably. Carson et al. (2004b) conduct an experiment looking at this prediction. In the experiment, groups vote (privately) on whether to supply a public good where the probability that the vote would be binding was randomly assigned before the

---

[168] There are two important caveats here. The first is that the "survey" is taken close to the election. Elections are to a large degree information campaigns where the two sides disseminate their version of the "truth" and the information set held by voters often changes considerably over the course of an election. The second is that the "don't know" responses to a ballot measure question appear to get largely translated into a "not in favor" vote in the election. This is not surprising, since voting for the "not in favor" alternative almost always maintains the *status quo*.

[169] The measure was put on the ballot by the state legislature and did not have any organized group who spent substantial amounts supporting or opposing the measure. Surveys of support for a ballot measure are incentive compatible if respondents believe that there is any type of bandwagon effect such that other voters are more likely to favor a measure the higher the percent in favor when the survey results are released to the public.

[170] In both of these studies, as in the Carson, Hanemann and Mitchell (1987) study it is necessary to disproportionately allocate the don't know respondents to be "not favor" responses. This is consistent with the survey literature on ballot measures. Vossler and Kerkvliet (2003) working with more detailed data from the Oregon land use measure find disproportionate allocation of the don't knows to "not favor" is not needed to get a close correspondence between the actual vote and the survey results, suggesting that the issue may be related to a divergence between the survey population and those who vote.

vote, and find this to be the case.[171] They do find that the inconsequential case does behave differently in terms of providing a higher percent in favor.[172]

As a final note in this section, there is a literature [e.g., Blackburn, Harrison and Rutström (1994)] that attempts to find a calibration factor that would scale CV estimates so they would equal an unbiased measure of "true" willingness to pay. However, it is unlikely that there can exist a single scaling factor that applies to all circumstances. The Carson, Groves and Machina (2000) theoretical framework suggests that in some contexts there should be a divergence and in other cases there should not – a result consistent with the empirical evidence. Further, the inconsequential case which should play no role in CV appears to play a large role in such calibration schemes. Calibration schemes are potentially of more use in circumstances such as marketing where an incentive compatible format is not usually available. In a marketing context, factors such as advertising/informational campaigns can be varied, and there are repeated opportunities to first observe the survey response and then the actual purchase decision over a specific time frame. In such cases, there may be useful empirical regularity that can be exploited for forecasting purposes. Even then, it is important to carefully consider what is being observed and what the researcher would like to observe. For instance, there may well be an empirical regularity between survey indications of likely contributions to a voluntary fund to provide a good and actual contributions toward it, but neither is the correct measure of the benefits of providing the good.

11. Concluding remarks

After over twenty-five years of working on CV from both a theoretical and empirical perspective, we are struck by one key insight – there is nothing particularly unique about CV. Once one realizes that responses to consequential surveys represent economic behavior in the standard sense that economist think about, then much of the previously troubling differences between different ways of eliciting preference information and the differences observed across different types of goods and contexts makes sense. Once one realizes that the predictions of neoclassical economic theory are quite different for the small price changes that characterize most discussions of welfare economics and the imposed quantity changes that typify much of environmental valuation using CV, then

---

[171] The experimental setup involved participants at a sports memorabilia show who were randomly assigned to treatment groups. Each group voted on whether to provide one ticket stub to a famous baseball game. In the base treatment if a majority voted in favor, all members had to pay the stated price and got one ticket each. Otherwise, all members of the group paid nothing and did not get a ticket stub.

[172] Carson et al. (2004b) develop a treatment in which the vote can influence a second outcome. In this case, the theoretical prediction is that the vote in favor should be monotonically decreasing with the probability that the vote is binding. They further argue that this is the problem in the Cummings and Taylor (1998) experimental setup because a vote in favor might encourage a fundraising effort that could provide the good at no cost.

results that were once characterized as aberrant become consistent with standard theory if not expected.

CV does pose challenges, however. Few economists are experienced at crafting survey instruments. They typically make do with whatever data is available and try to acknowledge its limitations. Economists have little experience in thinking through the nuances of collecting data in an ideal form. Even with ideal data, questions of functional form do not disappear and addressing questions of consistency with theoretical predictions requires auxiliary assumptions.

In part because there is a substantial degree of control of what data is collected, it is easy to demonstrate that respondents violate some of the tenets of the standard narrowly self-interested rational optimizing model that is commonly assumed in modern economics. Often these tenets do not follow directly from neoclassical economic theory, but rather, are assumed because they make the usual analyses much easier to conduct. CV respondents seem to care about many aspects of how programs are implemented and their impacts on other people. This should not be surprising, since this is what actually happens in the real world. Policymakers would like to believe that economic values are independent of details like whether a sales tax or utility bill is used to pay for the good. They would also like to have the value of the public good as if it were provided without any complications. Unfortunately, the willingness to pay estimates must of necessity be for the program to provide the good and not the good itself.[173] CV estimates, like all economic estimates, are context specific. It behooves the analyst and the policymaker to understand the context in which the valuation estimate was obtained.

Where CV has had its largest effect in environmental economics is in opening up the operational possibility of measuring the benefits of a wide range of changes in environmental goods. Obtaining preference about these goods was always technically possible, through having the public directly vote on the issue, but for all practical purposes, infeasible when extended very far. Until the widespread use of CV, economists were often left examining only the cost side of a benefit–cost analysis which gave rise to many of the stereotypical views of economists on environmental issues. Being able to measure the public's willingness to pay for environmental goods is, though, a double edge sword that invites controversy. The value will inevitably be too high or too low for one of the parties with a vested interest. Because the tool involves expensive and time consuming original data collection, CV will tend to be used when there is conflict that needs to be resolved.

While it is always wise to scrutinize specific CV studies and the specific uses that they are put to, the danger of not using CV seems to us much larger. David Starrett (1988, p. 293) makes the same point well with reference to welfare economics in general:

---

[173] This statement is indeed true of all consumer goods in the marketplace even though it is routinely ignored by economists but not marketers. Reputation matters in the form of brand effects as do measures such as warranties and "money back guarantees." Akerlof's (1970) now classic lemons papers underlines how pervasive perception of quality and likelihood of future service flows are in determining consumer willingness to pay.

It is very important to reject the view that since welfare measurement is still quite imprecise we may as well leave pubic decision making to the politicians. To do so invites mistakes that are costly on a scale that dwarfs any possible measurement error.[174]

CV can help decision makers to identify the public's interest. It is particularly useful in two cases. One is where the benefits of providing an environmental good are large but diffuse and its provision is opposed by a powerful special interest group. In this case a countervailing interest group pushing for the good's provision is unlikely to spring up. The other is where there is a strong lobby in favor of providing an environmental good, with the public as a whole footing the bill and their aggregate willingness to pay for it being much smaller than its cost. The nature of the political process will often be to supply the good to the determinant of the public's welfare as long as there is not a strong group opposing it. In both cases, an estimate of the public's WTP for the good can help illuminate the nature of the decision at hand.

References

Abala, D.O. (1987). "A theoretical and empirical investigation of the willingness to pay for recreational services: a case study of Nairobi National Park". Eastern Africa Economic Review 3, 111–119.

Acton, J.P. (1973). "Evaluating public progress to save lives: the case of heart attacks". Rand Research Report R-73-02. RAND Corporation, Santa Monica, CA.

Adamowicz, W.L., Louviere, J.J., Williams, M. (1994). "Combining revealed and stated preference methods for valuing environmental amenities". Journal of Environmental Economics and Management 26, 271–292.

Adamowicz, W.L., Boxall, P.C., Louviere, J.J., Swait, J. (1999). "Stated preference methods for valuing environmental amenities". In: Bateman, I.J., Willis, K.G. (Eds.), Valuing Environmental Preferences: Theory and Practice of the Contingent Valuation Method in the USA, EC, and Developing Countries. Oxford University Press, New York.

Akerlof, G. (1970). "The market for lemons: quality uncertainty and the market mechanism". Quarterly Journal of Economics 84, 488–500.

Alberini, A. (1995). "Optimal designs for discrete choice contingent valuation surveys: single-bound, double-bound, and bivariate models". Journal of Environmental Economics and Management 28, 287–306.

Alberini, A., Bjornstad, D., Kahn, J.R. (Eds.) (in press). Handbook of Contingent Valuation. Edward Elgar, Northampton, MA.

Alberini, A., Carson, R.T. (1990). "Choice of thresholds for efficient binary discrete choice estimation". Discussion Paper 90-34. Department of Economics, University of California, San Diego.

Alberini, A., Kanninen, B.J., Carson, R.T. (1997). "Modeling response incentives in dichotomous choice contingent valuation data". Land Economics 73, 309–324.

Arrow, K. (1958). "Utilities, attitudes, choices: a review note". Econometrica 26, 1–23.

Arrow, K., Fisher, A.C. (1974). "Environmental preservation, uncertainty, and irreversibility". Quarterly Journal of Economics 88, 313–319.

---

[174] It is possible to make a similar statement with respect to "experts" by asking the natural questions "whose experts" and whether there is any reason to believe that their preferences (given the same technical information) correspond to the public's?

Arrow, K., Solow, R., Portney, P.R., Leamer, E.E., Radner, R., Schuman, H. (1993). "Report of the NOAA panel on contingent valuation". Federal Register 58, 4601–4614.

Atkinson, A.C., Donev, A.N. (1992). Optimum Experimental Designs. Oxford University Press, New York.

Audience Research, Inc. (1958). "A study of outdoor recreational activities and preferences of the population living in the region of the Delaware river basin". Report prepared for the U.S. National Park Service.

Ayer, M., Brunk, H.D., Ewing, G.M., Silverman, E. (1955). "An empirical distribution function for sampling with incomplete information". Annals of Mathematical Statistics 26, 641–647.

Azevedo, C.D., Herriges, J.A., Kling, C.L. (2003). "Combining revealed and stated preferences: consistency tests and their interpretations". American Journal of Agricultural Economics 85, 525–537.

Barrett, L.B., Waddell, T.E. (1973). "Costs of air pollution damage: a status report". Report No. AP-85 to the U.S. Environmental Protection Agency. Center for Economics Research, Research Triangle Institute, Research Triangle Park, NC.

Bateman, I.J., Munro, A., Rhodes, B., Starmer, C., Sugden, R. (1997). "Does part-whole bias exist?: an experimental investigation". Economic Journal 107, 322–332.

Bateman, I.J., Langford, I.H., Jones, A.P., Kerr, G.N. (2001). "Bound and path effects in double and triple bounded dichotomous choice contingent valuation". Resource and Energy Economics 23, 191–214.

Bateman, I.J., Carson, R.T., Day, B., Hanemann, W.M., Hanley, N.D., Hett, T., Jones-Lee, M.W., Loomes, G., Mourato, S., Özdemiroglu, E., Pearce, D.W., Sugden, R., Swanson, J. (2002). Economic Valuation with Stated Preference Techniques. Edward Elgar, Northampton, MA.

Bausell, R.B., Li, Y.-F. (2002). Power Analysis for Experimental Research: A Practical Guide for the Biological, Medical and Social Sciences. Cambridge University Press, New York.

Beardsley, P.L., Kovenock, D.M., Reynolds, W.C. (1974). Measuring Public Opinion on National Priorities: A Report on a Pilot Study. Sage Publications, Beverly Hills.

Beardsley, W.G. (1971). "Economic value of recreation benefits determined by three methods". U.S. Forest Service Research Notes, RM-176, Rocky Mountain Experiment Station, Colorado Springs.

Beggs, S.C., Hausman, J.A. (1981). "Assessing the potential for electric cars". Journal of Econometrics 16, 1–19.

Belsley, D.A., Kuh, E., Welsch, R.E. (1980). Regression Diagnostics: Identifying Influential Data and Sources of Collinearity. Wiley, New York.

Ben-Akiva, M., Morikawa, T. (1990). "Estimation of mode switching models from revealed preferences and stated intentions". Transportation Research A 24, 485–495.

Berger, M.C., Blomquist, G.C., Kenkel, D., Tolley, G.S. (1987). "Valuing changes in health risks: a comparison of alternative measures". Southern Economic Journal 53, 967–984.

Bergstrom, J.C., Dillman, B.L., Stoll, J.R. (1985). "Public environmental amenity benefits of private land: the case of prime agricultural land". Southern Journal of Agricultural Economics 17, 139–149.

Berry, D. (1974). "Open space values: a household survey of two Philadelphia parks". RSRI Discussion Paper Series No. 76. Regional Science Research Institute, Philadelphia.

Binkley, C.S., Hanemann, W.M. (1978). "The recreation benefits of water quality improvement: analysis of day trips in an urban setting". Report No. EPA-600/5-78-010. U.S. Environmental Protection Agency, Washington, DC.

Bishop, R.C., Heberlein, T.A. (1979). "Measuring values of extra market goods". American Journal of Agricultural Economics 61, 926–930.

Bishop, R.C., Heberlein, T.A. (1980). "Simulated markets, hypothetical markets, and travel cost analysis: alternative methods of estimating outdoor recreation demand". Staff Paper Series No. 187. Department of Agricultural Economics, University of Wisconsin, Madison, WI.

Bishop, R.C., Heberlein, T.A., Kealy, M.J. (1983). "Contingent valuation of environmental assets: comparisons with a simulated market". Natural Resources Journal 23, 619–633.

Blackburn, M., Harrison, G.W., Rutström, E.E. (1994). "Statistical bias functions and informative hypothetical surveys". American Journal of Agricultural Economics 76, 1084–1088.

Blank, F., Brookshire, D.S., Crocker, T.D., d'Arge, R.C., Horst, R., Jr., Rowe, R.D. (1978). "Valuation of aesthetic preferences: a case study of the economic value of visibility". Research Report to EPRI (Electric

Power Research Institute). Resource and Environmental Economics Laboratory, University of Wyoming, Laramie, WY.

Blinder, A.S. (1991). "Why are prices sticky: preliminary results from an interview study". American Economic Review 81, 89–100.

Bohm, P. (1972). "Estimating demand for public goods: an experiment". European Economic Review 3, 111–130.

Bohm, P. (1984). "Revealing demand for an actual public good". Journal of Public Economics 24, 135–151.

Boulier, B.L., Goldfarb, R.S. (1998). "On the use and nonuse of surveys in economics". Journal of Economic Methodology 5, 1–21.

Bowen, H.R. (1943). "The interpretation of voting in the allocation of economic resources". Quarterly Journal of Economics 58, 27–48.

Box, G.E.P., Hunter, W.G., Hunter, J.S. (1978). Statistics for Experimenters: An Introduction to Design, Data Analysis, and Model Building. Wiley, New York.

Boyle, K.J., Welsh, M.P., Bishop, R.C. (1988). "Validation of empirical measures of welfare change: comment and extension". Land Economics 64, 94–98.

Bradburn, N., Sudman, S. (1988). Polls and Surveys: Understanding What They Are Telling Us. Jossey-Bass, San Francisco.

Bradburn, N.M., Sudman, S., Wansink, B. (2004). Asking Questions: The Definitive Guide to Questionnaire Design – For Market Research, Political Polls, and Social and Health Questionnaires. Jossey-Bass, San Francisco.

Brookshire, D.S., Ives, B.C., Schulze, W.D. (1976). "The valuation of aesthetic preferences". Journal of Environmental Economics and Management 3, 325–346.

Brookshire, D.S., Randall, A., Stoll, J.R. (1980). "Valuing increments and decrements in natural resource service flows". American Journal of Agricultural Economics 62, 478–488.

Brown, G.M., Jr., Charbonneau, J.J., Hay, M.J. (1978). "Estimating values of wildlife: analysis of the 1975 hunting and fishing survey". Working Paper No. 7. Division of Program Plans, U.S. Fish and Wildlife Service, Washington, DC.

Brown, G.M. Jr., Hammack, J. (1972). "A preliminary investigation of the economics of migratory waterfowl". In: Krutilla, J.V. (Ed.), Natural Environments: Studies in Theoretical and Applied Analysis. Johns Hopkins University Press, Baltimore, MD, pp. 171–204.

Brown, T.C., Peterson, G.L. (2003). "Multiple good valuation with focus on the method of paired comparison". In: Champ, P.A., Boyle, K.J., Brown, T.C. (Eds.), A Primer on Nonmarket Valuation. Kluwer Academic, Norwell, MA.

Brownstone, D., Bunch, D.S., Train, K. (2000). "Joint mixed logit models of stated and revealed references for alternative-fuel vehicles". Transportation Research B 34, 315–338.

Brownstone, D., Small, K. (2005). "Valuing time and reliability: assessing the evidence from road pricing demonstrations". Transportation Research A 39, 279–293.

Burton, A.C., Carson, K.S., Chilton, S.M., Hutchinson, W.G. (2003a). "An experimental investigation of explanations for inconsistencies in responses to second offers in double referenda". Journal of Environmental Economics and Management 46, 472–489.

Burton, A.C., Carson, K.S., Chilton, S.M., Hutchinson, W.G. (2003b). "An analysis of response strategies in double-bounded dichotomous choice contingent valuation". Paper presented at the American Agricultural Economics Association Meeting, Montreal.

Camerer, C.F., Loewenstein, G., Rabin, M. (Eds.) (2003). Advances in Behavioral Economics. Princeton University Press, Princeton, NJ.

Cameron, T.A. (1988). "A new paradigm for valuing nonmarket goods using referendum data: maximum likelihood estimation by censored logistic regression". Journal of Environmental Economics and Management 15, 355–379.

Cameron, T.A. (1992). "Combining contingent valuation and travel cost data for the valuation of nonmarket goods". Land Economics 68, 302–317.

Cameron, T.A., Englin, J. (1997). "Welfare effects of changes in environmental quality under individual uncertainty about use". RAND Journal of Economics 28 (Supplement), 45–70.

Cameron, T.A., Huppert, D.D. (1989). "OLS versus ML estimation of nonmarket resource values with payment card interval data". Journal of Environmental Economics and Management 17, 230–246.

Cameron, T.A., Huppert, D.D. (1991). "Referendum contingent valuation estimates: sensitivity to the assignment of offered values". Journal of the American Statistical Association 86 (416), 910–918.

Cameron, T.A., James, M.D. (1987). "Efficient estimation methods for 'closed-ended' contingent valuation surveys". Review of Economics and Statistics 69, 269–276.

Cameron, T.A., Quiggin, J. (1994). "Estimation using contingent valuation data from a 'dichotomous choice with follow-up' questionnaire". Journal of Environmental Economics and Management 27, 218–234.

Carson, R.T. (1985). Three essays on contingent valuation. Dissertation, University of California, Berkeley.

Carson, R.T. (1991). "Constructed markets". In: Braden, J.B., Kolstad, C.D. (Eds.), Measuring the Demand for Environmental Commodities. North-Holland, Amsterdam, pp. 121–162.

Carson, R.T. (1997a). "Contingent valuation: theoretical advances since the NOAA panel". American Journal of Agricultural Economics 79, 1501–1507.

Carson, R.T. (1997b). "Contingent valuation and tests of insensitivity to scope". In: Kopp, R.J., Pommerhene, W., Schwartz, N. (Eds.), Determining the Value of Non-Marketed Goods: Economic, Psychological, and Policy Relevant Aspects of Contingent Valuation Methods. Kluwer Academic, Boston.

Carson, R.T. (2000). "Contingent valuation: a user's guide". Environmental Science and Technology 34, 1413–1418.

Carson, R.T. (in press). Contingent Valuation: A Comprehensive Bibliography and History, Edward Elgar, Northampton, MA.

Carson, R.T., Flores, N.E., Hanemann, W.M. (1998). "Sequencing and valuing public goods". Journal of Environmental Economics and Management 36, 314–323.

Carson, R.T., Flores, N.E., Meade, N.F. (2001). "Contingent valuation: controversies and evidence". Environmental and Resource Economics 19, 173–210.

Carson, R.T., Flores, N.E., Mitchell, R.C. (1999). "The theory and measurement of passive use value". In: Bateman, I.J., Willis, K.G. (Eds.), Valuing Environmental Preferences: Theory and Practice of the Contingent Valuation Method in the US, EC, and Developing Countries. Oxford University Press, Oxford.

Carson, R.T., Groves, T., Machina, M.J. (2000). "Incentive and informational properties preference questions". Paper presented at the Kobe Conference on Theory and Application of Environmental Valuation, Kobe University, Kobe.

Carson, R.T., Hanemann, W.M., Mitchell, R.C. (1987). "The use of simulated political markets to value public goods". Discussion Paper 87-7. Department of Economics, University of California, San Diego.

Carson, R.T., Hanemann, W.M., Steinberg, D. (1990). "A discrete choice contingent valuation estimate of the value of kenai king salmon". Journal of Behavioral Economics 19, 53–68.

Carson, R.T., Jeon, Y. (2000). "On overcoming information deficiencies in estimating willingness to pay distributions". Paper presented at the European Association of Environmental and Resource Economists Annual Conference, University of Crete, Rethymnon.

Carson, R.T., Meade, N.F., Smith, V.K. (1993). "Passive use values and contingent valuation: introducing the issues". Choices 8 (2), 4–8.

Carson, R.T. Mitchell, R.C. (1991). "The value of diamonds and water". Paper presented at the European Association of Environmental and Resource Economists Annual Conference, Stockholm.

Carson, R.T., Mitchell, R.C. (1993). "The value of clean water: the public's willingness to pay for boatable, fishable, and swimmable quality water". Water Resources Research 29, 2445–2454.

Carson, R.T., Mitchell, R.C. (1995). "Sequencing and nesting in contingent valuation surveys". Journal of Environmental Economics and Management 28, 155–173.

Carson, R.T., Mitchell, R.C., Ruud, P.A. (1990). "Valuing air quality improvements: simulating a hedonic equation in the context of a contingent valuation scenario". In: Mathai, C.V. (Ed.), Visibility and Fine Particles. Air & Waste Management Association, Pittsburgh, pp. 639–646.

Carson, R.T., Steinberg, D. (1990). "Experimental design for discrete choice voter preference surveys". In: 1989 Proceeding of the Survey Methodology Section of the American Statistical Association. American Statistical Association, Washington, DC.

Carson, R.T., Wilks, L., Imber, D. (1994). "Valuing the preservation of Australia's kakadu conservation zone". Oxford Economic Papers 46, 727–749.

Carson, R.T., Costanzo, M., Hanemann, W.M., Wegge, T. (1987). "South Central Alaska area sport fishing economic study". Final Report to the Alaska Department of Fish and Game by Jones and Stokes Associates.

Carson, R.T., Mitchell, R.C., Hanemann, W.M., Kopp, R.J., Presser, S., Ruud, P.A. (1992). A Contingent Valuation Study of Lost Passive Use Values Resulting from the Exxon Valdez Oil Spill. Anchorage, AK.

Carson, R.T., Hanemann, W.M., Kopp, R.J., Krosnick, J.A., Mitchell, R.C., Presser, S., Ruud, P.A., Smith, V.K. (1994). Prospective Interim Lost Use Value Due to DDT and PCB Contamination in the Southern California Bight, vols. 1 & 2. Report to the National Oceanic and Atmospheric Administration.

Carson, R.T., Flores, N.E., Martin, K.M., Wright, J.L. (1996). "Contingent valuation and revealed preference methodologies: comparing the estimates for quasi-public goods". Land Economics 72, 80–99.

Carson, R.T., Hanemann, W.M., Kopp, R.J., Krosnick, J.A., Mitchell, R.C., Presser, S., Ruud, P.A., Smith, V.K. (1997). "Temporal reliability of estimates from contingent valuation". Land Economics 73, 151–163.

Carson, R.T., Hanemann, W.M., Kopp, R.J., Krosnick, J.A., Mitchell, R.C., Presser, S., Ruud, P.A., Smith, V.K. (1998). "Referendum design and contingent valuation: the NOAA panel's no-vote recommendation". Review of Economics and Statistics 80, 484–487.

Carson, R.T., Mitchell, R.C., Hanemann, W.M., Kopp, R.J., Presser, S., Ruud, P.A. (2003). "Contingent valuation and lost passive use: damages from the Exxon Valdez oil spill". Environmental and Resource Economics 25, 257–286.

Carson, R.T., Conaway, M.B., Hanemann, W.M., Krosnick, J.A., Mitchell, R.C., Presser, S. (2004a). Valuing Oil Spill Prevention: A Case Study of California's Central Coast. Kluwer Academic, Boston.

Carson, R.T., Groves, T., List, J., Machina, M. (2004b). "Probabilistic influence and supplemental benefits: a field test of the two key assumptions underlying stated preferences". Paper present at NBER Public Economics Workshop, Palo Alto.

Champ, P.A., Boyle, K.J., Brown, T.C. (Eds.) (2003). A Primer on Non-Market Valuation. Kluwer Academic Press, Boston.

Champ, P.A., Brown, T.C. (1997). "A comparison of contingent and actual voting behavior". Proceedings from W-133 Benefits and Cost Transfer in Natural Resource Planning, 10th Interim Report.

Champ, P.A., Bishop, R.C., Brown, T.C., McCollum, D.W. (1997). "Using donation mechanisms to value nonuse benefits from public goods". Journal of Environmental Economics and Management 33, 151–162.

Chapman, D.J., Hanemann, W.M., Kanninen, B.J. (1993). "Nonmarket valuation using contingent behavior: model specification and consistency tests". Working Paper, Department of Agricultural and Resource Economics, UC Berkeley.

Chapman, R.G., Staelin, R. (1982). "Exploiting rank ordered choice set data within the stochastic utility model". Journal of Marketing Research 19, 281–299.

Chen, H.Z., Randall, A. (1997). "Semi-nonparametric estimation of binary response models with an application to natural resource valuation". Journal of Econometrics 76, 323–340.

Chilton, S.M., Hutchinson, W.G. (1999). "Some further implications of incorporating the warm glow of giving into welfare measures: a comment on the use of donation mechanisms by Champ et al.". Journal of Environmental Economics and Management 37, 202–209.

Cicchetti, C.J., Smith, V.K. (1973). "Congestion, quality deterioration, and optimal use: wilderness recreation in the Spanish peaks primitive area". Social Science Research 2, 15–30.

Cicchetti, C.J., Smith, V.K. (1976a). The Cost of Congestion. Ballinger, Cambridge, MA.

Cicchetti, C.J., Smith, V.K. (1976b). "The measurement of individual congestion costs: an economic application to a wilderness area". In: Lin, S.A. (Ed.), Theory and Measurement of Externalities. Academic Press, New York.

Ciriacy-Wantrup, S.V. (1947). "Capital returns from soil-conservation practices". Journal of Farm Economics 29, 1181–1196.

Ciriacy-Wantrup, S.V. (1952). Resource Conservation: Economics and Policies. University of California Press, Berkeley.

Clawson, M., Knetsch, J. (1966). Economics of Outdoor Recreation. Johns Hopkins University Press, Baltimore.

Clark, J.M. (1915). "The concept of value: a rejoinder". Quarterly Journal of Economics 29, 709–723.

Cocheba, D.J., Langford, W.A. (1978). "Wildlife valuation: the collective good aspect of hunting". Land Economics 54, 490–504.

Cochran, W.G. (1977). Sampling Techniques, 3rd ed. Wiley, New York.

Conrad, J.M., LeBlanc, D. (1979). "The supply of development rights: results from a survey in Hadley, Massachusetts". Land Economics 55, 269–276.

Converse, P.E. (1974). "Comment: the status of nonattitudes". American Political Science Review 68, 650–660.

Cooper, J.C. (1993). "Optimal bid selection for dichotomous choice contingent valuation surveys". Journal of Environmental Economics and Management 24, 25–40.

Cooper, J.C. (2002). "Flexible functional form estimation of willingness to pay using dichotomous choice data". Journal of Environmental Economics and Management 43, 267–279.

Cooper, J.C., Hanemann, W.M., Signorello, G. (2002). "One-and-one-half-bound dichotomous choice contingent valuation". Review of Economics and Statistics 84, 742–750.

Copas, J.B. (1983). "Plotting p against x". Applied Statistics 32, 25–31.

Cornes, R., Sandler, T. (1996). The Theory of Externalities, Public Goods, and Club Goods. Cambridge University Press, New York.

Corso, P.S., Hammitt, J.K., Graham, J.D. (2001). "Valuing mortality-risk reduction: using visual aids to improve the validity of contingent valuation". Journal of Risk and Uncertainty 23, 165–184.

Creel, M.D., Loomis, J.B. (1997). "Semi-nonparametric distribution-free dichotomous choice contingent valuation". Journal of Environmental Economics and Management 32, 341–358.

Cummings, R.G., Brookshire, D.S., Schulze, W.D. (1986). Valuing Environmental Goods: An Assessment of the Contingent Valuation Method. Rowman and Allanheld, Totowa, NJ.

Cummings, R.G., Harrison, G.W. (1992). "Identifying and measuring nonuse values for natural and environmental resources: a critical review of the state of the art". Report to American Petroleum Institute.

Cummings, R.G., Harrison, G.W. (1995). "The measurement and decomposition of nonuse values: a critical review". Environmental and Resource Economics 5, 225–247.

Cummings, R.G., Harrison, G.W., Rutström, E.E. (1995). "Homegrown values and hypothetical surveys: is the dichotomous choice approach incentive-compatible?". American Economic Review 85, 260–266.

Cummings, R.G., Taylor, L.O. (1998). "Does realism matter in contingent valuation surveys". Land Economics 74, 203–215.

Cummings, R., Taylor, L.O. (1999). "Unbiased value estimates for environmental goods: a cheap talk design for the contingent valuation method". American Economic Review 89, 649–665.

Cummings, R.G., Elliot, S., Harrison, G.W., Murphy, J. (1997). "Are hypothetical referenda incentive compatible?". Journal of Political Economy 105, 609–621.

Currie, J.M., Murphy, J.A., Schmitz, A. (1971). "The concept of economic surplus". Economic Journal 81, 741–799.

Darling, A.H. (1973). "Measuring benefits generated by urban water parks". Land Economics 49, 22–34.

Davidson, J.D. (1973). "Forecasting traffic on STOL". Operations Research Quarterly 24, 561–569.

Davis, R.K. (1963a). The value of outdoor recreation: an economic study of the maine woods. Dissertation, Harvard University.

Davis, R.K. (1963b). "Recreation planning as an economic problem". Natural Resources Journal 3, 239–249.

Deaton, A.S. (1974). "The analysis of consumer demand in the United Kingdom". Econometrica 42, 341–367.

Debreu, G. (1959). Theory of Value. Wiley, New York.

DeShazo, J.R., Fermo, G. (2002). "Designing choice sets for stated preference methods: the effects of complexity on choice consistency". Journal of Environmental Economics and Management 43, 360–385.

Devine, D.G., Marion, B.W. (1979). "The influence of consumer price information on retail pricing and consumer behavior". American Journal of Agricultural Economics 61, 228–237.

Desvousges, W.H., Smith, V.K., Fisher, A. (1987). "Option price estimates for water quality improvements: a contingent valuation study for the monongahela river". Journal of Environmental Economics and Management 14, 248–267.

Desvousges, W.H., Gable, A.R., Dunford, R.W., Hudson, S.P. (1993a). "Contingent valuation: the wrong tool for damage assessment". Choices 8 (2), 9–11.

Desvousges, W.H., Johnson, F.R., Dunford, R.W., Boyle, K.J., Hudson, S.P., Wilson, K.N. (1993b). "Measuring natural resource damages with contingent valuation: tests of validity and reliability". In: Hausman, J.A. (Ed.), Contingent Valuation: A Critical Assessment. North-Holland, Amsterdam, pp. 91–164.

Diamond, P.A. (1996). "Testing the internal consistency of contingent valuation surveys". Journal of Environmental Economics and Management 30, 337–347.

Diamond, P.A., Hausman, J.A. (1994). "Contingent valuation: is some number better than no number?". Journal of Economic Perspectives 8 (4), 45–64.

Dillman, D.A. (in press). Mail and Internet Surveys, 3rd ed. Wiley, New York.

Dubourg, W.R., Jones-Lee, M.W., Loomes, G. (1997). "Imprecise preferences and survey design in contingent valuation". Economica 64, 681–702.

Ducci, J. (1988). "Metodolodia de cuantificacion de beneficios: Uruguay, sanemiento ambiental de Montevideo". Unpublished Background Paper. Technical Annex, Inter-American Development Bank, Washington, DC.

Duffield, J.W., Patterson, D.A. (1991a). "Inference and optimal design for a welfare measure in dichotomous choice contingent valuation". Land Economics 67, 225–239.

Duffield, J.W., Patterson, D.A. (1991b). "Field testing existence values: an instream flow trust fund for Montana rivers". Paper presented at the American Economic Association Annual Conference.

Eastaugh, S.R. (1991). "Valuation of the benefits of risk-free blood: willingness to pay for hemoglobin solutions". International Journal of Technology Assessment in Health Care 7, 51–57.

Eastman, C., Randall, A., Hoffer, P.L. (1974). "How much to abate pollution?". Public Opinion Quarterly 38, 574–584.

Eckstein, O. (1958). Water Resource Development. Harvard University Press, Cambridge.

Farquharson, R. (1969). Theory of Voting. Yale University Press, New Haven.

Fiedler, J.A. (1972). "Condominium design and pricing: a case study in consumer trade-off analysis". In: Venkatesan, M. (Ed.), Proceedings of the Third Annual Conference of the Association for Consumer Research, pp. 279–293.

Fischhoff, B., Furby, L. (1988). "Measuring values: a conceptual framework for interpreting transactions with special reference to contingent valuation of visibility". Journal of Risk and Uncertainty 1, 147–184.

Fischhoff, B., Slovic, P., Lichtenstein, S. (1980). "Knowing what you want: measuring labile values". In: Wallsten, T.S. (Ed.), Cognitive Processes in Choice and Decision Behavior. Lawrence Erlbaum Associates, Hillsdale, NJ.

Flores, N.E. (1995). "The effects of rationing and virtual price elasticities". Discussion Paper 95-20. Department of Economics, University of California, San Diego.

Flores, N.E. (1999). "The importance of agenda and willingness to pay". Working Paper No. 99-30. Department of Economics, University of Colorado.

Flores, N.E., Carson, R.T. (1997). "The relationship between the income elasticities of demand and willingness to pay". Journal of Environmental Economics and Management 33, 287–295.

Flores, N.E., Thatcher, J. (2002). "Money, who needs it? Natural resource Damage Assessment". Contemporary Economic Policy 20, 171–178.

Fowler, F.J., Mangione, T.W. (1989). Standardized Survey Interviewing: Minimizing Interviewer-Related Error. Sage, Beverly Hills, CA.

Freeman III, A.M. (1979). The Benefits of Environmental Improvement: In Theory and Practice. Johns Hopkins University Press, Baltimore MD.

Freeman, A.M. (1993). The Measurement of Environmental and Resource Values: Theory and Methods. Resources for the Future, Washington.

Ganiats, T.G., Carson, R.T., Hamm, R.M., Cantor, S.B. (2000). "Population-based time preferences for future health outcomes". Medical Decision Making 20, 263–270.

Garbacz, C., Thayer, M.A. (1983). "An experiment in valuing senior companion program services". Journal of Human Resources 18, 147–152.

Georgiou, S., Whittington, D., Pearce, D.W., Moran, D. (1997). Economic Values and the Environment in the Developing World. Edward Elgar, Northampton, MA.

Gerking, S., de Haan, M., Schulze, W.D. (1988). "The marginal value of job safety: a contingent valuation study". Journal of Risk and Uncertainty 1, 185–199.

Gibbard, A. (1973). "Manipulation of voting schemes: a general result". Econometrica 41, 587–601.

Gluck, R.J. (1974). An economic evaluation of the rakai fishery as a recreational resource. Master's Thesis, University of Canterbury.

Graham, D.A. (1981). "Cost benefit analysis under uncertainty". American Economic Review 71, 715–725.

Graham, D.A. (1984). "Cost benefit analysis under uncertainty: reply". American Economic Review 74, 1100–1102.

Gramlich, F.W. (1977). "The demand for clean water: the case of the Charles river". National Tax Journal 30, 183–194.

Grandstaff, S., Dixon, J.A. (1986). "Evaluation of Lumpinee park in Bangkok, Thailand". In: Dixon, J.A., Hufschmidt, M.M. (Eds.), Economic Valuation Techniques for the Environment: A Case Study Workbook. Johns Hopkins University Press, Baltimore.

Green, J.R., Laffont, J.J. (1978). "A sampling approach to the free rider problem". In: Sandmo, A. (Ed.), Essays in Public Economics. Lexington Books, Lexington, MA.

Greene, W.H. (2002). Econometric Analysis, 5th ed. Prentice-Hall, Englewood Cliffs, NJ.

Greenley, D.A., Walsh, R.G., Young, R.A. (1981). "Option value: empirical evidence from a case study of recreation and water quality". Quarterly Journal of Economics 96, 657–672.

Groothuis, P.A., Whitehead, J.C. (2002). "Does don't know mean no? Analysis of 'don't know' responses in dichotomous choice contingent valuation questions". Applied Economics 34, 1935–1940.

Groves, R.M., Dillman, D.A., Eltinge, J.L., Little, R.J.A. (2001). Survey Nonresponse. Wiley, New York.

Groves, R.M., Fowler, F.J., Couper, M.P., Lepkowski, J.M., Singer, E., Tourangeau, R. (2004). Survey Methodology. Wiley, New York.

Groves, T. (1973). "Incentives in teams". Econometrica 41, 617–631.

Haab, T.C. (1999). "Nonparticipation or misspecification? The impacts of nonparticipation on dichotomous choice contingent valuation". Environmental and Resource Economics 14, 443–461.

Haab, T.C., McConnell, K.E. (1997). "Referendum models and negative willingness to pay: alternative solutions". Journal of Environmental Economics and Management 32, 251–270.

Haab, T.C., McConnell, K.E. (1998). "Referendum models and economic values: theoretical, intuitive, and practical bounds on willingness to pay". Land Economics 74, 216–229.

Haab, T.C., McConnell, K.E. (2002). Valuing Environmental and Natural Resources. Edward Elgar, Northampton.

Hammack, J., Brown, G.M. Jr. (1974). Waterfowl and Wetlands: Toward Bioeconomic Analysis. Johns Hopkins University Press, Baltimore, MD.

Hanemann, W.M. (1978). A methodological and empirical study of the recreation benefits from water quality improvement. Dissertation, Harvard University.

Hanemann, W.M. (1984a). "Discrete/continuous models of consumer demand". Econometrica 52, 541–561.

Hanemann, W.M. (1984b). "Welfare evaluations in contingent valuation experiments with discrete responses". American Journal of Agricultural Economics 66, 332–341.

Hanemann, W.M. (1985). "Some issues in continuous- and discrete-response contingent valuation studies". Northeastern Journal of Agricultural Economics 14, 5–13.

Hanemann, W.M. (1991). "Willingness to pay and willingness to accept: how much can they differ?". American Economic Review 81, 635–647.

Hanemann, W.M. (1992). "Preface". In: Navrud, S. (Ed.), Pricing the European Environment. Oxford University Press, New York, pp. 9–35.

Hanemann, W.M. (1994). "Valuing the environment through contingent valuation". Journal of Economic Perspectives 8 (4), 19–43.

Hanemann, W.M. (1995). "Contingent valuation and economics". In: Willis, K.G., Corkindale, J.T. (Eds.), Environmental Valuation: New Perspectives. CAB International, Wallingford, UK, pp. 79–117.

Hanemann, W.M. (1999). "Neo-classical economic theory and contingent valuation". In: Bateman, I.J., Willis, K.G. (Eds.), Valuing Environmental Preferences: Theory and Practice of the Contingent Valuation Method in the US, EU and Developing Countries. Oxford University Press, New York, pp. 42–96.

Hanemann, W.M., Felipe Vasquez, F. (2005). "Strictly for the birds: A scope test revisited". Working Paper, UC Berkeley Department of Agricultural & Resource Economics, October.

Hanemann, W.M., Kanninen, B.J. (1999). "The statistical analysis of discrete-response CV data". In: Bateman, I.J., Willis, K.G. (Eds.), Valuing Environmental Preferences: Theory and Practice of the Contingent Valuation Method in the US, EU and Developing Countries. Oxford University Press, Oxford, UK, pp. 302–441.

Hanemann, W.M., Kriström, B. (1995). "Preference uncertainty, optimal designs and spikes". In: Johansson, P.-O., Kriström, B., Mäler, K.-G. (Eds.), Current Issues in Environmental Economics. Manchester University Press, New York, pp. 58–77.

Hanemann, W.M., Loomis, J.B., Kanninen, B.J. (1991). "Statistical efficiency of double-bounded dichotomous choice contingent valuation". American Journal of Agricultural Economics 73, 1255–1263.

Hanley, N.D., Mourato, S., Wright, R.E. (2001). "Choice modelling approaches: a superior alternative for environmental valuation?". Journal of Economic Surveys 15, 435–462.

Hanley, N.D., Wright, R.E., Adamowicz, W.L. (1998). "Using choice experiments to value the environment-design issues, current experience and future prospects". Environmental and Resource Economics 11, 413–428.

Hardie, I., Strand, I.E. (1979). "Measurement of economic benefits for potential public goods". American Journal of Agricultural Economics 61, 311–317.

Harrison, G., List, J.A. (2004). "Field experiments". Journal of Economic Literature 42, 1009–1055.

Hausman, J.A. (Ed.) (1993). Contingent Valuation: A Critical Assessment. North-Holland, Amsterdam.

Hausman, J.A., Ruud, P.A. (1987). "Specifying and testing econometric models for rank-ordered data". Journal of Econometrics 34, 83–104.

Heckman, J. (1979). "Sample selection bias as a specification error". Econometrica 47, 153–161.

Hensher, D.A. (1994). "Stated preference analysis of travel choices: the state of practice". Transportation 21, 107–133.

Hensher, D.A., Louviere, J.J., Swait, J. (1999). "Combining sources of preference data". Journal of Econometrics 89, 197–221.

Hensher, D.A., Rose, J.M., Greene, W.H. (2005). Applied Choice Analysis: A Primer. Cambridge University Press, New York.

Hensher, D.A., Truong, P. (1985). "Valuation of travel time savings: a direct experimental approach". Journal of Transport Economics and Policy 19, 237–261.

Herriges, J.A., Kling, C.L. (Eds.) (1999). Valuing Recreation and the Environment: Revealed Preference Methods in Theory and Practice. Edward Elgar, Northampton, MA.

Herriges, J.A., Shogren, J.F. (1996). "Starting point bias in dichotomous choice valuation with follow-up questioning". Journal of Environmental Economics and Management 30, 112–131.

Hicks, J.R. (1943). "The four consumer surpluses". Review of Economic Studies 11, 31–41.

Hirschleifer, J. (1965). "Investment decision under uncertainty: choice theoretic approaches". Quarterly Journal of Economics 79, 509–536.

Hirschleifer, J. (1966). "Investment decision under uncertainty: applications of the stated preference approach". Quarterly Journal of Economics 80, 252–277.

Hines, L.G. (1951). "Wilderness areas: an extra-market problem in resource allocation". Land Economics 27, 306–313.

Hoehn, J.P., Randall, A. (1987). "A satisfactory benefit cost indicator from contingent valuation". Journal of Environmental Economics and Management 14, 226–247.

Hoehn, J.P., Randall, A. (1989). "Too many proposals past the benefit cost test". American Economics Review 79, 544–551.

Hoinville, G., Berthoud, R. (1970). Identifying and Evaluating Trade-Off Preferences: An Analysis of Environmental Accessibility Priorities. Social and Planning Research, London. Publication P-117.

Holmes, T.P., Adamowicz, W.L. (2003). "Attribute base method". In: Champ, P.A., Boyle, K.J., Brown, T.C. (Eds.), A Primer on Nonmarket Valuation. Kluwer Academic, Norwell, MA, pp. 171–219.

Horowitz, J.K., McConnell, K.E. (2002). "A review of WTA/WTP studies". Journal of Environmental Economics and Management 44, 426–447.

Infosino, W.J. (1986). "Forecasting new product sales for likelihood of purchase ratings". Marketing Science 5, 372–390.

Jansen, H.M.A., Opschoor, J.B. (1973). "Waardering van de invloed van het vliegtuiglawaai op woongebied rond de potentiele locaties van de Tweede nationale luchthaven (Valuation of the effects of aircraft noise on residential areas around the potential locations of the second Dutch national airport)". Working Paper Series A, Nos. 4 and 5. Institute for Environmental Studies, Vrije University, Amsterdam.

Johannesson, M., Fagerberg, B. (1992). "A health economic comparison of diet and drug treatment in obese men with mild hypertension". Journal of Hypertension 10, 1063–1070.

Johansson, P.-O. (1995). Evaluating Health Risks: An Economic Approach. Cambridge University Press, New York.

Johnson, F.R., Desvousges, W.H. (1997). "Estimating stated preferences with rated-pair data: environmental, health, and employment effects of energy programs". Journal of Environmental Economics and Management 34, 79–99.

Johnson, R.M. (1974). "Trade-off analysis of consumer values". Journal of Marketing Research 11, 121–127.

Jones-Lee, M.W. (1974). "The value of changes in the probability of death or injury". Journal of Political Economy 82, 835–849.

Jones-Lee, M.W. (1976). The Value of Life: An Economic Analysis. University of Chicago Press, Chicago.

Jones-Lee, M.W., Hammerton, M., Philips, P.R. (1985). "The value of safety: results of a national sample survey". Economic Journal 95, 49–72.

Just, R.E., Hueth, D.L., Schmitz, A. (1982). Applied Welfare Economics and Public Policy. Prentice-Hall, Englewood Cliffs, NJ.

Kahneman, D., Knetsch, J.L. (1992). "Valuing public goods: the purchase of moral satisfaction". Journal of Environmental Economics and Management 22, 57–70.

Kahneman, D., Tversky, A. (1979). "Prospect theory: an analysis of decision under risk". Econometrica 47, 263–291.

Kanninen, B.J. (1993a). "Optimal experimental design for double-bounded dichotomous choice contingent valuation". Land Economics 69, 138–146.

Kanninen, B.J. (1993b). "Design of sequential experiments for contingent valuation studies". Journal of Environmental Economics and Management 25, S1–S11.

Keeney, R., Raiffa, H. (1976). Decisions with Multiple Objectives. Wiley, New York.

Kish, L.F. (1967). Survey Sampling. Wiley, New York.

Kling, C.L., List, J.A., Zhao, J. (2003). "WTP/WTA disparity: have we been observing dynamic values but interpreting them as static?". CARD Working Paper #03-WP 333, Iowa State University.

Knetsch, J.L. (1990). "Environmental policy implications of disparities between willingness to pay and compensation demanded measures of values". Journal of Environmental Economics and Management 18, 227–238.

Knetsch, J.L., Davis, R.K. (1966). "Comparisons of methods for resource evaluation". In: Kneese, A.V., Smith, S.C. (Eds.), Water Research. Johns Hopkins University Press, Baltimore, MD, pp. 125–142.

Knetsch, J.L., Thaler, R.H., Kahneman, D. (1990). "Experimental tests of the endowment effect and the coase theorem". Journal of Political Economy 98, 1325–1349.

Kolstad, C.D., Guzman, R.M. (1999). "Information and the divergence between willingness to accept and willingness to pay". Journal of Environmental Economics and Management 38, 66–80.

Kopp, R.J., Smith, V.K. (1997). "Constructing measures of economic value". In: Kopp, R.J., Pommerehne, W.W., Schwarz, N. (Eds.), Determining the Value of Non-Marketed Goods: Economic, Psychological, and Policy Relevant Aspects of Contingent Valuation Methods. Kluwer Academic, Boston.

Kriström, B. (1990). "A nonparametric approach to the estimation of welfare measures in discrete response valuation studies". Land Economics 66, 135–139.

Kriström, B. (1997). "Spike models in contingent valuation". American Journal of Agricultural Economics 79, 1013–1023.

Krosnick, J.A., Holbrook, A., Berent, M.K., Hanemann, W.M., Kopp, R.J., Mitchell, R.C., Ruud, P.A., Smith, V.K., Moody, W.K., Green, M.C., Conaway, M.B. (2002). "The impact of 'no opinion' response options on data quality: non-attitude reduction or an invitation to satisfy?". Public Opinion Quarterly 66, 371–403.

Krutilla, J.V. (1967). "Conservation reconsidered". American Economic Review 57, 777–786.

Krutilla, J.V., Eckstein, O. (1958). Multiple Purpose River Development. Johns Hopkins University Press, Baltimore, MD.

Lansing, J.B., Morgan, J.N. (1971). Economic Survey Methods. Survey Research Center of the Institute for Social Research, University of Michigan, Ann Arbor.

LaPage, W.F. (1968). "The role of fees in camper's decisions". USDA Forest Service Research Paper No. 188. Northeastern Forest Experiment Station, Upper Darby, PA.

Lavrakas, P.J. (1993). Telephone Survey Methods: Sampling, Selection, and Supervision. Sage, Beverly Hills, CA.

Lave, L.B. (1984). "Controlling contradictions among regulations". American Economic Review 74, 471–476.

Layton, D.F. (2000). "Random coefficient models for stated preference surveys". Journal of Environmental Economics and Management 40, 21–36.

Lee, L.F., Pitt, M. (1986). "Microeconomic demand systems with binding nonnegativity constraints: the dual approach". Econometrica 54, 1237–1242.

León, C.J., Vazquez-Polo, F.J. (1998). "A Bayesian approach to double bounded contingent valuation". Environmental and Resource Economics 11, 197–215.

Lester, R.A. (1946). "Shortcomings of marginal analysis for wage-unemployment problems". American Economic Review 36, 63–82.

Levy, P., Lemeshow, S. (1999). Sampling of Populations: Methods and Applications. Wiley, New York.

Li, C.-Z., Mattsson, L. (1995). "Discrete choice under preference uncertainty: an improved structural model for contingent valuation". Journal of Environmental Economics and Management 28, 256–269.

Lichtenstein, S., Slovic, P. (1971). "Reversals of preferences between bids and choices in gambling decisions". Journal of Experimental Psychology 89, 46–55.

List, J. (2000). "The incredible disappearing act: the effect of market experience on the WTP/WTA disparity". Paper presented at the European Association of Environmental and Resource Economists Meeting, Rythymnon, Greece.

List, J., Gallet, C. (2001). "What experimental protocol influence disparities between actual and hypothetical stated values? Evidence from a meta-analysis". Environmental and Resource Economics 20, 241–254.

Little, I.M.D. (1957). A Critique of Welfare Economics. Oxford University Press, Oxford, UK.

Little, J., Berrens, R. (2004). "Explaining disparities between actual and hypothetical stated values: further investigation using meta-analysis". Economic Bulletin 3 (6), 1–13.

Little, R.J.A., Rubin, D.B. (2002). Statistical Analysis with Missing Data, 2nd ed. Wiley, New York.

Loehman, E.T., De, V.H. (1982). "Application of stochastic choice modeling to policy analysis of public goods: a case study of air quality improvements". Review of Economics and Statistics 64, 474–480.

Louviere, J.J. (1974). "Predicting the evaluation of real stimulus objects from an abstract evaluation of their attributes: the case of trout streams". Journal of Applied Psychology 59, 572–577.

Louviere, J.J. (1994). "Conjoint analysis". In: Bagozzi, R. (Ed.), Advanced Methods in Marketing Research. Blackwell, Oxford, UK.

Louviere, J.J., Hensher, D.A. (1983). "Using discrete choice models with experimental design data to forecast consumer demand for a unique cultural event". Journal of Consumer Research 10, 348–361.

Louviere, J.J., Hensher, D.A., Swait, J.D. (2000). Stated Choice Methods: Analysis and Application. Cambridge University Press, New York.

Louviere, J.J., Woodworth, G. (1983). "Design and analysis of stimulated consumer choice experiments or allocation experiments: an approach based on aggregate data". Journal of Marketing Research 20, 350–367.

Louviere, J., Ainslie, J.A., Cameron, T., Carson, R.T., DeShazo, J.R., Hensher, D., Kohn, R., Marley, T., Street, D. (2002). "Dissecting the random component". Marketing Letters 13, 177–193.

Machlup, F. (1946). "Marginal analysis and empirical research". American Economic Review 36, 519–554.

Mackenzie, J. (1993). "A comparison of contingent preference models". American Journal of Agricultural Economics 75, 593–603.

Madden, P. (1991). "A generalization of Hicksian substitutes and complements with application to demand rationing". Econometrica 59, 1497–1508.

Madow, W.G., Olkin, I., Rubin, D.B. (Eds.) (1983). Incomplete Data in Sample Surveys. Academic Press, San Diego.

Magat, W.A., Viscusi, W.K., Huber, J. (1988). "Paired comparison and contingent valuation approaches to morbidity risk valuation". Journal of Environmental Economics and Management 15, 395–411.

Mäler, K.-G. (1974). Environmental Economics: A Theoretical Inquiry. Johns Hopkins University Press, Baltimore, MD.

Manski, C. (1977). "The structure of random utility models". Theory and Decision 8, 229–254.

Manski, C.F., Straub, J.D. (2000). "Worker perceptions of job insecurity in the mid-1990s: evidence from the survey of economic expectations". Journal of Human Resources 35, 447–479.

Marley, A.A.J., Louviere, J.J. (in press). "Some probabilistic models of best, worse, and best–worst choices". Journal of Mathematical Psychology.

Mathews, S.B., Brown, G.M. (1970). "Economic evaluation of the 1967 sport salmon fisheries of Washington". Technical Report No. 2. Department of Fisheries, Olympia, Washington, DC.

Melinek, S.J. (1974). "A method of evaluating human life for economic purposes". Accident Analysis and Prevention 6, 103–114.

McConnell, K.E. (1977). "Congestion and willingness to pay: a study of beach use". Land Economics 53, 186–195.

McConnell, K.E. (1990). "Models for referendum data: the structure of discrete choice models for contingent valuation". Journal of Environmental Economics and Management 18, 19–34.

McConnell, K.E., Ducci, J.H. (1989). "Valuing environmental quality in developing countries: two case studies". Paper presented at the Association of Environmental and Resource Economists Annual Conference.

McFadden, D.L. (1974). "Conditional logit analysis of qualitative choice behavior". In: Zarembka, P. (Ed.), Frontiers in Econometrics. Academic Press, New York, pp. 105–142.

McFadden, D.L. (1986). "The choice theory approach to market research". Marketing Science 5, 275–297.

McFadden, D.L. (1994). "Contingent valuation and social choice". American Journal of Agricultural Economics 76, 689–708.

McFadden, D.L. (1999a). "Rationality for Economists?". Journal of Risk and Uncertainty 19, 73–105.

McFadden, D.L. (1999b). "Computing willingness-to-pay in random utility models". In: Moore, J., Riezman, R., Melvin, J. (Eds.), Trade, Theory, and Econometrics: Essays in Honor of John S. Chipman. Routledge, London.

McFadden, D.L., Leonard, G.K. (1993). "Issues in the contingent valuation of environmental goods: methodologies for data collection and analysis". In: Hausman, J.A. (Ed.), Contingent Valuation: A Critical Assessment. North-Holland, Amsterdam, pp. 165–216.

Meyer, P.A. (1974). "Recreation and preservation values associated with salmon of the Fraser river". Information Report Series No. PAC/IN-74-1. Environmental Canada Fisheries and Marine Service, Southern Operations Branch, Vancouver.

Meyer, R.J., Levin, I.P., Louviere, J.J. (1978). "Functional analysis of mode choice". In: Transportation Forecasting and Travel Behavior. Transportation Research Records Report #673. Transportation Research Board, Washington, DC, 1–7.

Mierheim, H. (1974). Nutzen–Kosten Analysen Öffentlicher Grunanlagen im Innerstädtischen Bereich. Eine Untersuchung über die Anwendbarkeit am Beispiel Berlin-West (Benefit–cost analysis of public parks in inner city areas: an evaluation of its applicability concerning the example of Berlin-West). Dissertation, Technical University of Berlin.

Miles, G.A. (1967). "Water based recreation in Nevada". Report B-14. College of Agriculture, University of Nevada, Reno.

Mishan, E.J. (1971). "Evaluation of life and limb: a theoretical approach". Journal of Political Economy 90, 827–853.

Mishan, E.J. (1976). Cost–Benefit Analysis, 2nd ed. Praeger, New York.

Mitchell, R.C. (1982). "On the use of the contingent valuation approach to value public services in developing nations". Report prepared for the Country Policy Department, World Bank, Washington, DC.

Mitchell, R.C. (2002). "On designing constructed markets in valuation surveys". Environmental and Resource Economics 22, 297–321.

Mitchell, R.C., Carson, R.T. (1981). "An experiment in determining willingness to pay for national water quality improvements". Report to the Environmental Protection Agency, Resources for the Future, Washington, DC.

Mitchell, R.C., Carson, R.T. (1986). "The use of contingent valuation data for benefit–cost analysis in water pollution control". Final Report to the Environmental Protection Agency, Resources for the Future, Washington, DC.

Mitchell, R.C., Carson, R.T. (1989). Using Surveys to Value Public Goods: The Contingent Valuation Method. Johns Hopkins University Press, Baltimore, MD.

Moeltner, K., Shonkwiler, J.S. (2005). "Correcting for on-site sampling in random utility models". American Journal of Agricultural Economics 87, 327–339.

Morey, E.R., Thatcher, J., Breffle, W.S. (in press). "Using angler characteristics and attitudinal data to identify environmental preferences classes: a latent class model". Environmental and Resource Economics.

Moser, D.A., Dunning, C.M. (1986.) A Guide for Using the Contingent Valuation Method in Recreation Studies, National Economic Development Procedures Manual – Recreation, vol. 2. IWR Report 86-R-T. Institute for Water Resources, U.S. Army Corp of Engineers, Fort Belvoir, VA.

Mueller, D.C. (1989). Public Choice II. Cambridge University Press, Cambridge.

Mulligan, P.J. (1978). "Willingness to pay for decreased risk from nuclear plant accidents". Working Paper No. 43. Center for the Study of Environmental Policy, Pennsylvania State University.

Navrud, S. (1992). "Willingness to pay for preservation of species: an experiment with actual payments". In: Navrud, S. (Ed.), Pricing the European Environment. Oxford University Press, New York, pp. 231–246.

Neill, H.R., Cummings, R.G., Ganderton, P.T., Harrison, G.W., McGuckin, T. (1994). "Hypothetical surveys and real economic commitments". Land Economics 70, 145–154.

O'Hanlon, P.W., Sinden, J.A. (1978). "Scope for valuation of environmental goods: comment". Land Economics 54, 381–387.

Oster, S. (1977). "Survey results on the benefits of water pollution abatement in the Merrimack river basin". Water Resources Research 13, 882–884.

Parzen, E. (1960). Modern Probability Theory and its Applications. Wiley, New York.

Palmatier, M. (1969). "Willingness to pay for health services: a sampling of consumer preferences". Unpublished Paper. Department of Economics, University of Southern California, Los Angeles.

Pattison, W.S. (1970). Economics of moose hunting activities. Master's Thesis, Department of Rural Economy, University of Alberta.

Pawitan, Y. (2001). In All Likelihood: Modeling and Inference Using the Likelihood. Oxford University Press, New York.

Payne, S. (1951). The Art of Asking Questions. Princeton University Press, Princeton, NJ.

Pearce, D.W., Markandy, A. (1989). Environmental Policy Benefits: Monetary Evaluation. Organization for Economic Cooperation and Development (OECD), Paris.

Pendse, D., Wyckoff, J.B. (1972). "Determining preference for environmental goods". Paper presented at the Meeting of the Pacific Division of the American Academy for the Advancement of Science, Eugene, OR.

Peterson, G.L., Worrall, R.D. (1970). "An analysis of individual preferences for accessibility to selected neighborhood services". In: Highway Research Record, vol. 305. Highway Research Board, Washington, DC.

Plowden, S.P.C. (1970). The Cost of Noise. Metra Consulting Group Ltd., London.

Plowden, S.P.C., Sinnott, P.R.J. (1977). "Evaluation of noise nuisance: a study of willingness to receive payment for noise introduced into the home". Supplementary Report 261. Transport and Road Research Laboratory, Crowthorne, UK.

Poe, G.L., Giraud, K.L., Loomis, J.B. (2005). "Computational methods for measuring the difference of empirical distributions". American Journal of Agricultural Economics 87, 353–365.

Portney, P.R. (1994). "The contingent valuation debate: why economists should care". Journal of Economic Perspectives 8 (4), 3–18.

Propper, C. (1990). "Contingent valuation of time spent on NHS lists". Economic Journal 100, 193–199.

Presser, S., Rothgeb, J.M., Couper, M.P., Lessler, J.T., Martin, E., Martin, J., Singer, E. (2004). Methods for Testing and Evaluating Survey Questionnaires. Wiley, New York.

Rae, D.A. (1982). "Benefits of visual air quality in Cincinnati". Report to the Electric Power Research Institute, Charles River Associates, Boston.

Randall, A. (1973). "Frontiers of nonmarket valuation". In: Stoll, J.R., Shulstad, R.N., Smathers, W.M., Jr. (Eds.), Nonmarket Valuation: Current Status and Future Directions, Proceedings of a Regional Workshop. SNREC Publication No. 18. Southern Rural Development Center/Farm Foundation.

Randall, A. (1993). "Passive-use values and contingent valuation: valid for damage assessment". Choices 8 (2), 12–15.

Randall, A. (1998). "Beyond the crucial experiment: mapping the performance characteristics of contingent valuation". Resource and Energy Economics 20, 197–206.

Randall, A., Grunewald, O., Pagoulatos, A., Ausness, R., Johnson, S. (1978). "Reclaiming coal surface mines in central Appalachia: a case study of the benefits and costs". Land Economics 54, 427–489.

Randall, A., Hoehn, J.P. (1996). "Embedding in market demand systems". Journal of Environmental Economics and Management 30, 369–380.

Randall, A., Hoehn, J.P., Tolley, G.S. (1981). "The structure of contingent markets: some experimental results". Paper presented at American Economic Association Meeting, Washington, DC.

Randall, A., Ives, B.C., Eastman, C. (1974). "Bidding games for the valuation of aesthetic environmental improvements". Journal of Environmental Economics and Management 1, 132–149.

Randall, A., Stoll, J.R. (1980). "Consumer's surplus in commodity space". American Economic Review 70, 449–455.

Ready, R.C., Hu, D. (1995). "Statistical approaches to the fat tail problem for dichotomous choice contingent valuation". Land Economics 71, 491–499.

Ready, R.C., Navrud, S., Dubourg, W.R. (2001). "How do respondents with uncertain willingness to pay answer contingent valuation questions?". Land Economics 77, 315–326.

Ready, R.C., Whitehead, J.C., Blomquist, G.C. (1995). "Contingent valuation when respondents are ambivalent". Journal of Environmental Economics and Management 29, 181–196.

Reardon, G., Pathak, D.S. (1988). "Monetary valuation of benefits of pharmacy services". Topics in Hospital Pharmacy Management 8 (2), 66–75.

Reizenstein, R.C., Hills, G.E., Philpot, J.W. (1974). "Willingness to pay for control of air pollution: a demographic analysis". In: Curhan, R.C. (Ed.), New Marketing for Social and Economic Progress and Marketing's Contributions to the Firm and to Society. American Marketing Association, Chicago.

Richer, J.R. (1995). "Willingness to pay for desert protection". Contemporary Economic Policy 13, 93–104.

Ridker, R.G. (1967). Economic Cost of Air Pollution. Praeger, New York.

Ridker, R.G., Henning, J.A. (1967). "The determinants of residential property values with special reference to air pollution". Review of Economics and Statistics 49, 246–257.

Roberts, K., Thompson, M.E., Pawlyk, P.W. (1985). "Contingent valuation of recreational diving at petroleum rigs, gulf of Mexico". Transactions of the American Fisheries Society 114, 214–219.

Rollins, K., Lyke, A. (1998). "The case for diminishing marginal existence values". Journal of Environmental Economics and Management 36, 324–344.

Rosenberger, R.S., Loomis, J.B. (2000). "Using meta-analysis for benefit transfer: in-sample convergent validity tests of an outdoor recreation database". Water Resources Research 36, 1097–1107.

Roskill, The Honorable Mr. Justice Chairman (1970). Commission on the Third London Airport: Papers and Proceedings. HMSO, London.

Rowe, R.D., d'Arge, R.C., Brookshire, D.S. (1980). "An experiment on the economic value of visibility". Journal of Environmental Economics and Management 7, 1–19.

Rowe, R.D., Schulze, W.D., Breffle, W.S. (1996). "A test for payment card biases". Journal of Environmental Economics and Management 31, 178–185.

Rushton, G. (1969). "Analysis of spatial behavior by revealed space preference". Annals of the Association of American Geographers 59, 391–400.

Ruud, P.A. (1986). "Contingent ranking surveys: their application and design in estimating the value of visibility". In: Bhardwaja, P.S. (Ed.), Visibility Protection: Research and Policy Aspects. Air Pollution Control Association, Pittsburgh, pp. 206–217.

Sagoff, M. (1994). "Should preferences count". Land Economics 70, 127–144.

Samples, K.C., Dixon, J.A., Gower, M.M. (1985). "Information disclosure and endangered species valuation". Paper presented at the Annual Meeting of the American Agricultural Economics Association, Ames, IA.

Samuelson, P. (1954). "The pure theory of public expenditures". Review of Economics and Statistics 36, 387–389.

Sarja, M. (1969). Lappajärven ja Venetjoen tekojärven virkistyskäyttötutkimus ja virkistsarvon määrittäminen (A study on recreation use and recreation value of lake Lappjärvi and artificial lake in Venetjoki). Master's Thesis. Department of Geography, Helsinki University.

Satterthwaite, M. (1975). "Strategy-proofness and arrow conditions: existence and correspondence theorems for voting procedures and welfare functions". Journal of Economic Theory 10, 187–217.

Schelling, T. (1968). "The life you save may be your own". In: Chase, S. (Ed.), Problems in Public Expenditure Analysis. Brookings Institute, Washington, DC.

Schuman, H., Presser, S. (1981). Questions and Answers in Attitude Surveys: Experiments on Question Form, Wording, and Context. Academic Press, New York.

Seip, K., Strand, J. (1992). "Willingness to pay for environmental goods in Norway: a CV study with real payment". Environmental and Resource Economics 2, 91–106.

Shechter, M., Enis, R., Baron, M. (1974). "Mt. Carmel National Park: the demand for outdoor recreation". Unpublished Paper. Center for Urban & Regional Studies. Technion (Israel Institute of Technology), Haifa.

Sinden, J.A. (1974). "A utility approach to the valuation of recreational and aesthetic experiences". American Journal of Agricultural Economics 56, 61–72.

Sinden, J.A., Worrell, A.C. (1979). Unpriced Values: Decisions without Market Prices. Wiley, New York.

Smith, V.K. (1976). "The treatment of intangibles in benefit–cost analysis". Environmental Control Newsletters 4 (5).

Smith, V.K. (1984). Environmental Policy Under Reagan's Executive Order: The Role of Benefit–Cost Analysis. University of North Carolina Press, Chapel Hill, NC.

Smith, V.K., Desvousges, W.H. (1986). Measuring Water Quality Benefits. Kluwer Academic, Boston.

Smith, V.K., Desvousges, W.H., Freeman, A.M. III (1985). Valuing Changes in Hazardous Waste Risks: A Contingent Valuation Analysis, vol. I. Draft Report to the Environmental Protection Agency no. RTI Project No. 41U-2699. Research Triangle Institute, Research Triangle Park, NC.

Smith, V.K., Mansfield, C. (1998). "Buying time: real and hypothetical offers". Journal of Environmental Economics and Management 36, 209–224.

Smith, V.K., Osborne, L. (1996). "Do contingent valuation estimates pass a scope test? A meta analysis". Journal of Environmental Economics and Management 31, 287–301.

Starrett, D.A. (1988). Foundations of Public Economics. Cambridge University Press, New York.

Stavig, G.R., Gibbons, J.D. (1977). "Comparing the mean and median as measures of centrality". International Statistical Review 45, 63–70.

Stewart, B.E. (1961). Recreational use of private land in a portion of Eastern Maine. Master's Thesis, Department of Agricultural and Resource Economics, University of Maine.

Stigler, G.J., Becker, G.S. (1977). "De gustibus non est disputandum". American Economic Review 67, 76–90.

Stigler, S.M. (1977). "Do robust estimators work with real data?". Annals of Statistics 5, 1055–1098.

Strauss, R.P., Hughes, G.D. (1976). "A new approach to the demand for public goods". Journal of Public Economics 6, 191–204.

Strazzera, E., Scarpa, R., Calia, P., Garrod, G.D., Willis, K.G. (2003). "Modelling zero values and protest responses in contingent valuation surveys". Applied Economics 35, 133–138.

Sudman, S., Bradburn, N.M. (1982). Asking Questions: A Practical Guide to Questionnaire Design. Jossey-Bass, San Francisco.

Sugden, R. (1999). "Alternatives to the neo-classical theory of choice". In: Bateman, I.J., Willis, K.G. (Eds.), Valuing Environmental Preferences: Theory and Practice of the Contingent Valuation Method in the USA, EC, and Developing Countries. Oxford University Press, New York.

Swait, J., Louviere, J.J. (1993). "The role of the scale parameter in the estimation and use of multinomial logit models". Journal of Marketing Research 30, 305–314.

Thaler, R.H. (1985). "Mental accounts and consumer choice". Marketing Science 4, 199–214.

Thaler, R.H., Rosen, S. (1976). "The value of saving a life". In: Terleckyj, N.E. (Ed.), Household Production and Consumption. National Bureau of Economic Research, New York.

Thayer, M.A. (1981). "Contingent valuation techniques for assessing environmental impacts: further evidence". Journal of Environmental Economics and Management 8, 27–44.

Throsby, C.D. (1984). "The measurement of willingness to pay for mixed goods". Oxford Bulletin of Economics and Statistics 46, 279–289.

Thurstone, L. (1927). "A law of comparative judgment". Psychological Review 34, 273–286.

Tolley, G.S., Randall, A., Blomquist, G.C., Fabian, R.G., Fishelson, G., Frankel, A., Hoehn, J.P., Krumm, R., Mensah, E. (1986). Establishing and valuing the effects of improved visibility in the Eastern United States. Report to the Environmental Protection Agency No. Cooperative Agreement 807768-01-0, University of Chicago, Chicago.

Tourangeau, R., Rips, L.J., Rasinski, K. (2000). The Psychology of Survey Response. Cambridge University Press, New York.

Turnbull, B. (1976). "The empirical distribution function with arbitrarily grouped, censored and truncated data". Journal of the Royal Statistical Society B 38, 290–295.

Tversky, A., Kahneman, D. (1986). "Rational choice and the framing of decisions". Journal of Business 59, S251–S278.

Ullman, E.L., Volk, D.J. (1961). "An operational model for predicting reservoir attendance and benefits: implications of a location approach to water recreation". Washington University, St. Louis, MO.

U.S. Department of the Interior. United States (1986). "Final rule for natural resources damage assessments under the comprehensive environmental response compensation and liability act of (CERCLA)". Federal Register 51, No. 1148, 27674–27753.

U.S. Senate Committee on Public Works (1957). "Evaluation of recreation benefits". 85th Congress 1st Session, Washington, DC.

U.S. Water Resources Council (1979). "Procedures for evaluation of national economic development (NED) benefits and costs in water resources planning (level C), final rule." Federal Register 44, No. 242, 72892–72976.

Viscusi, W.K. (1993). "The value of risks to life and health". Journal of Economics Literature 31, 1912–1946.

Vossler, C.A., Kerkvliet, J. (2003). "A criterion validity test of the contingent valuation method: comparing hypothetical and actual voting behavior for a public referendum". Journal of Environmental Economics and Management 45, 631–649.

Vossler, C.A., Kerkvliet, J., Polasky, S., Gainutdinova, O. (2003). "Externally validating contingent valuation: an open-space survey and referendum in Corvallis, Oregon". Journal of Economic Behavior and Organization 51, 261–277.

Walsh, R.G., Loomis, J.B., Gillman, R.A. (1984). "Valuing option, existence and bequest demands for wilderness". Land Economics 60, 14–29.

Walsh, R.G., Miller, N.P., Gilliam, L.O. (1983). "Congestion and willingness to pay for expansion of skiing capacity". Land Economics 59, 195–210.

Walsh, R.G., Sander, L.D., Loomis, J.B. (1985). Wild and scenic river economics: recreation use and preservation values. Report to the American Wilderness Alliance, Department of Agriculture and Natural Resource Economics, Colorado State University.

Water Demand Research Team. World Bank (1993). "The demand for water in rural areas: determinants and policy implications". World Bank Research Observer 8, 47–70.

Weisbrod, B.A. (1964). "Collective consumption services of individual consumption goods". Quarterly Journal of Economics 78, 471–477.

Werner, M.J. (1999). "Allowing for zeros in dichotomous-choice contingent-valuation models". Journal of Business and Economic Statistics 17, 479–486.

Werner, M.J., Groves, T. (1993). "A practical procedure for public policy decisions: or 'contingent valuation and demand revelation – without apology'." Discussion Paper 93-51. Department of Economics. University of California, San Diego.

Whittington, D. (1988). Guidelines for conducting willingness to pay studies for improved water services in developing countries. USAID Water and Sanitation for Health Project No. Washington Field Report No. 306. U.S. Agency for International Development, Washington, DC.

Whittington, D. (1998). "Administering contingent valuation surveys in developing countries". World Development 26, 21–30.

Whittington, D. (2002). "Improving the performance of contingent valuation studies in developing countries". Environmental and Resource Economics 22, 323–367.

Whittington, D., Mujwahuzi, M., McMahon, G., Choe, K.-A. (1988). Willingness to pay for water in Newala district, Tanzania: strategies for cost recovery. USAID Water and Sanitation for Health Project Field Report No. 246. U.S. Agency for International Development, Washington, DC.

Willig, R. (1976). "Consumer's surplus without apology". American Economic Review 66, 589–597.

World Bank (1987). "Willingness to pay for water in rural areas". Research Proposal. Water and Urban Development Department, World Bank, Washington, DC.

Wu, C.F.J., Hamada, M. (2000). Experiments: Planning, Analysis, and Parameter Design Optimization. Wiley, New York.

Zeckhauser, R., Shepard, D. (1976). "Where now for saving lives?". Law and Contemporary Problems 40, 5–45.

Zhao, J., Kling, C.L. (2004). "Willingness to pay, compensating variation, and the cost of commitment". Economic Inquiry 42, 503–517.

Chapter 18

COGNITIVE PROCESSES IN STATED PREFERENCE METHODS

BARUCH FISCHHOFF

*Department of Social and Decision Sciences, Department of Engineering and Public Policy,
Carnegie Mellon University, Pittsburgh, PA 15213-3890, USA*

Contents

Q51

Handbook of Environmental Economics, Volume 2. Edited by K.-G. Mäler and J.R. Vincent
DOI: 10.1016/S1574-0099(05)02018-8

Abstract

Cognitive psychology is best known, to many environmental economists, through the filter of acrimonious debates over the validity of contingent valuation methods (CVM). Psychologists' views on CVM reflect concerns that are deeply rooted in their profession's history and theories. Although psychologists have participated in some CVM studies, their roles have rarely allowed them to present a comprehensive design philosophy, illustrated in actual studies. This chapter sets psychologists' critiques and alternatives within a general cognitive perspective on value elicitation, including stated preferences for environmental goods. It begins with a historical review, organized around two converging streams of psychological research. One stream leads from psychophysics to attitude research. The second leads from decision theory to decision analysis and behavioral decision research. The next section reports some environmental valuation studies arising from each tradition. These studies do not directly monetize environmental goods. However, they can still directly inform policies that do not require monetization and indirectly inform policies that do, by shaping studies with that ambition. The following section considers the role of cognitive studies in helping investigators to know what issues matter to people and present them comprehensibly. The concluding section of the chapter presents a cognitive approach to stated preference methods for environmental values – one that could be developed most fully in collaboration with economists. It is built around a cognitive task analysis of the four main elements in any evaluation process: (a) specifying the valuation question, (b) understanding its terms, (c) articulating a value for that specific question (from more general basic values), and (d) expressing that value in a public form.

Keywords

environment, preferences, elicitation, values, uncertainty

JEL classification: Q51, C9

1. Overview

Cognitive psychology is best known, to many environmental economists, through the filter of acrimonious debates over the validity of contingent valuation methods (CVM) [Arrow et al. (1993), Cummings, Brookshire and Schulze (1986), Mitchell and Carson (1989, Chapter 11)]. Psychologists' views on CVM reflect concerns that are deeply rooted in their profession's history and theories. However, expressing these views through the filter of controversy precludes systematic exposition of the research motivating them. It also makes psychologists seem like unrelenting critics, unconcerned with the critical environmental policy issues that CVM research directly addresses, whatever its strengths and weaknesses.

Although psychologists have participated in some CVM studies, their roles have rarely allowed them to present a comprehensive design philosophy, illustrated in actual studies. Psychologists' own CVM-related studies often seem like destructive exercises, attempting to undermine CVM, without concern for the vital need that it addresses. For example, many experiments [Kahneman, Diener and Schwarz (1999)] are presented as demonstrating respondents' insensitivity to the "scope" of the environmental good being evaluated (e.g., the number of birds, or lakes, protected). That would represent a fundamental failure of measurement [which should show sensitivity to relevant features of the good being evaluated, and insensitivity to irrelevant features; Fischhoff (1988b)]. Demonstrating problems does not, however, provide alternative, putatively better methods for producing the quantitative valuations needed for cost–benefit analyses and compensatory damage assessments. It does not even clarify what policy makers should do if they accept these claims. In the absence of an alternative, rejecting CVM leaves a vacuum. Decisions still need to be made. Without accepted valuations, environmental goods may be neglected. As a result, psychologists might be seen as showing a radical skepticism toward CVM that embodies radical indifference toward the environment.

This chapter sets psychologists' critiques and alternatives within a general cognitive perspective on value elicitation, including stated preferences for environmental goods. It begins with a historical review, organized around two converging streams of psychological research. One stream leads from psychophysics to attitude research. The second leads from decision theory to decision analysis and behavioral decision research. The next section reports some environmental valuation studies arising from each tradition. These studies do not directly monetize environmental goods. However, they can still directly inform policies that do not require monetization and indirectly inform policies that do, by shaping studies with that ambition. The following section considers the role of cognitive studies in helping investigators to know what issues matter to people and present them comprehensibly. The concluding section of the chapter presents a cognitive approach to stated preference methods for environmental values – one that could be developed most fully in collaboration with economists. It is built around a cognitive task analysis of the four main elements in any evaluation process: (a) specifying the valuation question, (b) understanding its terms, (c) articulating a value for that specific question (from more general basic values), and (d) expressing that value in a public form.

2. Origins

Cognitive psychology's approach to stated preference methods draws on several research traditions. To a first approximation, these can be described as arising from psychophysics and decision theory. Each stream characterizes responses by comparing them with a normative standard, then looking for the psychological processes shaping (and limiting) performance.

2.1. Psychophysics stream

2.1.1. History

Evaluation has been a central topic in experimental psychology, since its inception in the mid-to-late 1800s. Emerging from the natural sciences, early psychologists focused on *psychophysics*, determining the sensory equivalent of physical stimuli. According to the simple model underlying these studies, various physiological and psychological mechanisms translate external stimuli into states of arousal. If asked, individuals can report those states, with a word, number, or action (e.g., squeezing a handgrip or adjusting an illumination level to equal the experience of a tone). Those reports could reflect a subjective magnitude (e.g., loudness) or valuation (e.g., pleasantness).

Over the intervening century-plus, researchers have discovered the complexity of these ostensibly simple processes. One family of complications arises from people's sensitivity to seemingly irrelevant procedural features. For example, a detection threshold might depend on whether successive stimuli (e.g., tones, weight differences, figures on a background) are presented in ascending or descending order [e.g., Woodworth and Schlosberg (1954)]. Table 1 collects some of these effects. Their discovery has often led to full-fledged research programs, examining their detailed operation. McGuire (1969) characterized this process as converting an *artifact* into a *main effect*. A classic example is tracing inconsistent celestial observations to differences in the reaction time of astronomers' assistants. Subsequent research identified underlying processes that are important in their own right (e.g., nerve conductance, concurrent distractions, speed-accuracy tradeoffs). Another family of productive artifacts involves the subtle ways that interviewers communicate their expectations. The methodological challenges of controlling these (often unwitting) cues has informed basic research into nonverbal communication.

Some of these effects primarily interest specialists in the relevant psychological or sensory systems. For example, an important auditory ability is accommodating to low ambient sound levels, making it easier to detect weak signals. (Indeed, under extremely quiet conditions, most people eventually pick up nonexistent sounds, even experiencing tinnitus in sound-proof rooms.) These effects should matter to stated preference researchers who must present auditory stimuli (e.g., in studies evaluating noise pollution levels). Similarly, the nuances of color and form discrimination are central to eliciting valuations for atmospheric visibility levels [e.g., Tolley et al. (1986)]. Those studies

Table 1
From artifact to main effect

Lability in judgment due to	Led to
Organism	
Inattention, laziness, fatigue, habituation, learning, maturation, physiological limitations, natural rhythms, experience with related tasks	Repeated measures Professional subjects Stochastic response models Psychophysiology Proactive and retroactive inhibition research
Stimulus presentation	
Homogeneity of alternatives, similarity of successive alternatives (especially first and second), speed of presentation, amount of information, range of alternatives, place in range of first alternative, distance from threshold, order of presentation, areal extent, ascending or descending series	Classic psychophysical methods The new psychophysics Attention research Range-frequency theory Order-effects research Regression effects Anticipation
Response mode	
Stimulus–response compatibility, naturalness of response, set, number of categories, halo effects, anchoring, very small numbers, response category labeling, use of end points	Ergonomics research Set research Attitude measurement Assessment techniques Contrasts of between- and within-subject design Response-bias research Use of blank trials
"Irrelevant" context effects	
Perceptual defenses, experimenter cues, social pressures, presuppositions, implicit payoffs, social desirability, confusing instructions, response norms, response priming, stereotypic responses, second-guessing	New look in perception Verbal conditioning Experimenter demand Signal-detection theory Social pressure, comparison, and facilitation research

Source: Fischhoff, Slovic and Lichtenstein (1980).

need visual displays that accurately represent the degree of light extinction associated with alternative policies (e.g., emission standards). The basic science of psychophysics can guide such designs (and determine the validity of previously conducted studies).

2.1.2. Design framework

In addition to effects that are specific to sensory modalities, psychophysics research has identified general effects, found in many studies. One large set pertains to the use of

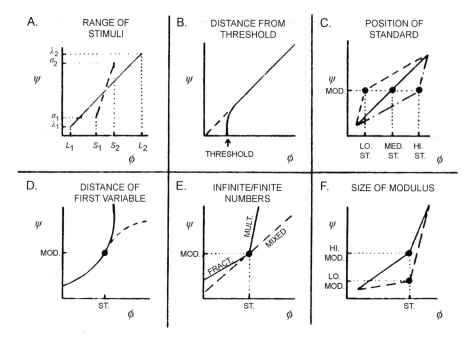

Figure 1. Six "laws of the new psychophysics," depicting the influence of experimental design on the numerical response used to describe the psychological state (ψ) equivalent to a physical stimulus (ϕ). Figure A shows that a narrower stimulus range (S_1, S_2) will use a proportionately larger portion of the response range than would the same stimuli, when embedded in a larger response range (L_1, L_2). Figure B considers the effects of assumptions regarding the treatment of stimuli below the threshold of perception or evaluation. Figure C considers the effects of where a standard stimulus falls in the response range, after it has been assigned a numerical valuation (or modulus). Figure F shows the reverse effects where a modulus value, for a given standard stimulus, falls within the response range. Figure D shows the effects of where the first judged stimulus is relative to the standard. Figure E shows the effects of using fractional or integer response values, for stimuli smaller than the standard. Fuller details are found in Poulton (1968), from which this exhibit was taken; they are elaborated and extended in Poulton (1989, 1994).

numbers – both ones that people produce by themselves and ones proposed by others ("Is that a 10?"). Figure 1 shows a summary, derived by Poulton (1968) from secondary analyses of research in the paradigm of Stevens (1975), perhaps the central figure in mid-20th century psychophysics. Stevens and colleagues attempted to estimate the rate of decreasing marginal sensitivity ("the shape of the Weber–Fechner law," to psychologists), for many sensory modalities. Based on the shapes of the curves, investigators proposed theories about the physiology of these modalities. Poulton argued, however, that these curves were strongly influenced by the methodological conventions of researchers studying each modality. These conventions induced consistent results among studies on a single modality, while limiting comparisons across modalities.

The figures summarize these artifacts, showing how responses are shaped by design features that investigators must somehow set, when creating tasks. For example, Figure 1A shows how a narrower stimulus range $[S_1, S_2]$ elicits a proportionately larger portion of the response range than do the same stimuli, embedded in a larger response range $[L_1, L_2]$. Figure 1C shows how values assigned to larger stimuli are cramped if the initial (or standard) stimulus is relatively large (and spread out if it is relatively small).

Such effects occur because, however well respondents understand their feeling regarding a stimulus, they must translate it into the investigators' terms. Where those terms differ from their natural mode of expression (or where there is none, because the task is so novel), respondents rely on general heuristics for using response scales. Because these *response preferences* are often widely shared [Tune (1964)], they lend an artifactual consistency to results. For example, other things being equal, people try to use the entire response scale; they look for patterns in randomly ordered stimuli; they deduce an expected level of precision, such as the tradeoff to make between speed and accuracy. Thus, their responses are shaped by a task's form as well as by its substance, when they are unsure what to say – and must seek clues in task details.

The importance of these effects depends on how responses are used. For example, the patterns in Figure 1 all maintain response order. Investigators requiring just ordinal information can ignore these design issues. When investigators require stronger metric properties, they must match study conditions to those in the analogous real-world context. For example, they should avoid fractional responses, if people rarely use them. They should show the full stimulus range, so that respondents need not infer it from the initial stimuli. If there is no (single) natural context, then investigators can use relationships like those in Figure 1 to extrapolate from a context that has been studied to other ones. For example, if a study used a restricted stimulus range, then one can assume that its largest members would receive lower values, if embedded in a larger range. Conversely, if a study uses a narrow range, one should expect respondents to make finer distinctions and spread out their responses, relative to a real-world situation with a narrower focus.

Psychophysical considerations complicate research design, by adding features that require explicit attention. However, they also simplify it, by providing an orderly, empirically based foundation for focusing on the (perhaps few) features that really matter when designing and interpreting studies. If people are, indeed, sensitive to these features, then (in the words of an American auto repair commercial) it is "pay now" (by explicitly addressing the features) or "pay later" (by having to disentangle their effects).

2.1.3. Evaluative extensions

As attitude research developed, especially during the second quarter of the past century, the psychophysical paradigm held great appeal, for attitude researchers. It had a distinguished pedigree, with some of psychology's most distinguished researchers having contributed theories, procedures, results, and analytical methods. It had been applied to diverse domains (e.g., the intensity of smell, cold, weight). Its method seemed relatively straightforward: pose a clear question; offer clear response options; report the responses. Moreover, attitude questions seem to avoid the response-mode ambiguity arising with physical stimuli having unfamiliar measures (e.g., lumens, decibels). Attitude scales can use terms that seem objective and consensually interpreted (e.g., anchors like "strongly agree" and "strongly disagree," or "very happy" and "very unhappy").

Unfortunately, such scales have often proven less objective and consensual than was hoped. It turns out that "there's 'very happy' and then there's 'very happy' " [Turner and Krauss (1978)]. Here, too, respondents seek contextual cues for interpreting their task. These cues might be found in a question's wording, the topics preceding it, the study's sponsor, or the consent form, among other places. Conversely, relatively clear response scales may be used to disambiguate unclear questions. As a result, respondents may attach different meanings to both the question and the answer of an apparently standard task [Budescu and Wallsten (1995), Fischhoff (1994), Tanur (1992)].

Schwarz (1999) offers an example with an 11-point scale, anchored at "not at all successful" and "extremely successful." Respondents' evaluations of their lives differ when these anchors were assigned the numbers [0, 10] or [−5, +5]. Apparently, negative numbers suggest the possibility of abject failure – whereas 0 suggests lack of success, as the worst possible outcome. Other contextual cues can signal whether to evaluate success relative to a comparison group (and, if so, which one) or relative to one's own dreams (or to one's realistic expectations). People can shift perspectives in the research context, just as they do in everyday life, as they try to determine (in the words of a former New York mayor), "How'm I doing?"

Such artifacts have long been known in the survey research literature. Their prevalence depends on the inferential task imposed on respondents [Fischhoff (1991), National Research Council (1982), Schwarz (1996), Turner and Martin (1984)]. Unambiguous questions and answers reduce the need for contextual cues. So does posing tasks for which respondents already have *articulated* values, in the sense of knowing what they want and how to express themselves. With a novel question, respondents must derive their preferences from the relevant *basic* values – just as they would when facing unfamiliar choices in everyday life. Table 2 offers conditions favorable to having articulated values – and, therefore, to stated preferences that are resistant to meaningless procedural and wording changes (and sensitive to meaningful ones).

According to Poulton (1968), Figure 1 captures the six key sources of interpretative cues for quantitative judgment tasks. No such summary is available, or perhaps even possible, for the myriad of verbal cues that people might use, when they read between the lines of verbal questions and answers – in surveys or everyday life. Creating a manageable science of task construal requires treating surveys as conversations. An increasingly influential approach assumes that respondents interpret survey questions as though the investigator has adhered to the conversational norms of their common culture, and that they will respond in kind (expecting their answers to be similarly interpreted). Those norms provide a structured way for investigators to analyze respondents' construal of questions and answers [Schwarz (1996, 1999)].

Table 2
Conditions favorable to respondents having articulated values

Aspects of the topic	Aspects of the consequences	Aspects of the respondent
Familiar issues	Few – providing simplicity	Able to play a single role –
Familiar formulation	Similar – providing	avoiding agency issues
Publicly discussed – providing	commensurability	Able to generate alternative
opportunities to hear and share	Previously experienced – allowing	perspectives
views	the formation of tastes	Motivated to consider issues
Stable – allowing the formation	Certain – reducing complexity	Able to consider topic in isolation
of tastes		

Source: Fischhoff (1991).

A prominent summary of conversational norms is Grice's (1975) four maxims, which require speakers to be *relevant, concise, complete,* and *honest.* An investigator following these norms would ask whether a question–answer pair contains irrelevant details, says things that could go without saying (thereby lacking conciseness), omits things that respondents could not confidently infer, or misleads respondents (or even gives the appearance of dishonesty). The more familiar the topic and the respondents, the more confidently investigators can make these evaluations. If they need evidence to support their claims, it could come from dedicated studies (e.g., think-aloud protocols) or general studies – both considered below [Fischhoff, Welch and Frederick (1999)]. The return on that investment is reduced uncertainty about whether tasks were interpreted as intended.

2.2. Decision theory stream

Von Neumann and Morgenstern's (1947) landmark work prompted two lines of psychological research (often with collaborators from other disciplines) [Edwards (1954, 1961), Yates (1990)]. One line, *behavioral decision research,* studies the descriptive validity of the decision theoretic axioms [Dawes (1988), Fischhoff (1988a), Kahneman and Tversky (1984), McFadden (1999)]. These studies may directly test people's adherence to the axioms, characterize the cognitive skills that facilitate (and constrain) rationality, or identify behaviorally realistic approaches to decision making (e.g., reliance on heuristics). One general (and perhaps unsurprising) result is that people do best when they have conditions conducive to acquiring decision-making abilities as learned skills. These conditions include prompt, unambiguous feedback that rewards rationality (rather than, say, bravado or evasiveness). People also need enough feedforward to make the desired behaviors part of their repertoire. It is hard to master unheard-of or counterintuitive principles.

The second line of research, *decision analysis,* seeks to increase the descriptive validity of the axioms, by helping people to make more rational choices [Clemen (1996),

Raiffa (1968), von Winterfeldt and Edwards (1986)]. It uses behavioral decision research to identify where people need help in achieving the performance standard set by the normative axioms. Decision analysts elicit individuals' probabilities and utilities for possible consequences of their action options. They hope to overcome their clients' known judgmental limitations in three ways: (a) Structuring the elicitation process, so that people make systematic use of what they know about themselves and their world; (b) Focusing people's limited attention on the most critical issues, as identified by procedures such as sensitivity analysis and value-of-information analysis; (c) Computing the expected utility of options, thereby avoiding the vagaries and omissions of mental arithmetic.

The success of this enterprise hinges on participants' ability to express their beliefs and values in the required form, probabilities and utilities. The conceptually clear structure of decision analytic questions should reduce the ambiguity endemic to attitude measurement. So should its reliance on explicit probability and utility scales, avoiding the well-documented vagueness of verbal quantifiers (e.g., rare, likely, possible), terms that can mean different things to different people in a single context and to a single person in different contexts [Lichtenstein and Newman (1967), Budescu and Wallsten (1995)]. The interaction between client and decision analyst constitutes an actual conversation (albeit a somewhat stilted one). That provides opportunities to identify and resolve residual miscommunications, beyond what is possible with the generic conversations of standardized surveys. In order to exploit these opportunities, decision analysts "look for trouble," presenting tasks from multiple perspectives, in order to ensure mutual understanding [Fischhoff (1980), Keeney (1996), von Winterfeldt and Edwards (1986)].

As a result, in decision analysis, elicitation is a *reactive* measurement procedure: It can change participants, as they reflect on their beliefs and values. That process should deepen their thinking, without imposing the elicitors' perspectives. That is, it should reduce random error, without adding systematic error. The process assumes that people sometimes need help, in order to understand what they believe and want. That help may include presenting a balanced selection of opinions, lest clients miss a critical perspective just because it did not occur to them at the time.

Such concern for completeness and reflection contrasts radically with the nonreactivity of psychophysical research. Investigators there seek immediate, "natural" responses to task stimuli. The procedure is seen as a neutral conduit for those responses. As a result, psychophysical studies have impassive interviewers, standardized questions, no clarification (beyond perhaps scripted paraphrasing), and limited time to think.

These two elicitation philosophies place different weights on sins of commission (inappropriately influencing respondents) and sins of omission (leaving respondents to misunderstand the issue or their position on it). Fearing the former discourages interaction with respondents; fearing the latter may require it. The degree of interaction should depend on the risk of respondents saying, subsequently, "I wish I had thought of that perspective," "I wish I had been able to keep it all in my head," or "How could I have forgotten that?" That risk should be small with tasks fulfilling the conditions of Table 2.

For example, people may know just what they want, after a vigorous political campaign thoroughly airs the issues. With complex, novel questions, though, people may need a chance to think and hear others' thinking, before they can formulate stable, independent views.

Behavioral decision research also provides alternative perspectives, for helping respondents triangulate on their values. For example, the framing effects of prospect theory [Kahneman and Tversky (1979, 1984)] suggest views that might not otherwise occur to them (e.g., "be sure to think about both the number of salmon that will be left and the number that will be lost"). Contrasting perspectives can be derived from any context effect from psychophysics research (Table 1, Figure 1). For example, making a number salient will bring responses toward it – even when that *anchor* is clearly chosen arbitrarily [e.g., Tversky and Kahneman (1974)]. Such anchoring (which partially underlies Figure 1's effects) can work in two (nonexclusive) ways: (a) directly "priming" that specific response, making it more available when people look for what to say, and (b) prompting respondents to evaluate that number's appropriateness, a search that disproportionately primes reasons justifying it. Investigators fearing these effects can provide multiple anchors (as a way to provide multiple perspectives) or try to avoid suggesting any number.

Eliciting consistent responses with a single procedure is necessary but not sufficient for demonstrating articulated values. Such consistency may just mean that respondents devised an efficient ad hoc strategy in order to get through their task (e.g., "I see that they are varying the price of the fictitious student apartments 'offered' in this study. I'll focus on that feature, since it's so easy to do."). Even if such strategies reflect real concerns (e.g., price does matter), the resulting consistency could fragment in more realistic contexts. Part of psychology's lore is how easily people find some way to answer any question that researchers pose, as seen in the low nonresponse rates to questions about fictitious issues [Plous (1993)]. Successful elicitation should capture the residual uncertainty and incoherence in respondents' preferences.

Behavioral decision research has also shaped value elicitation by identifying the limits to judgment under conditions of uncertainty [Dawes (1988), Gilovich, Griffin and Kahneman (2002), Kahneman, Slovic and Tversky (1982)]. With uncertain environmental choices, those limits require a special effort to ensure that respondents understand the facts of their choices [Fischhoff (1998, 1999), Slovic (1987)]. Assessing that understanding means eliciting respondents' uncertain beliefs. Generally speaking, that is straightforward: just use clear probability scales and well-defined events [Slovic and Lichtenstein (1971), Wallsten and Budescu (1983), Yates (1990)]. However, there are still anomalies that complicate interpreting expressed beliefs. One is that people sometimes use "50" to express *epistemic* uncertainty (not knowing what to say), rather than a numeric probability. As a result, they seem to overestimate small probabilities, when they are not actually giving a number. Such scale misuse is less common with structured response scales, controllable events, and children (until they learn the phrase "fifty–fifty") [Fischhoff and Bruine de Bruin (1999)]. A second anomaly arises from people not appreciating how small risks (or benefits) mount up through repeated exposure (or even that a long-term perspective is warranted). As a result, one cannot infer beliefs about single and multiple events from one another.

Less is known about communicating the events that the probabilities amplify [Fischhoff (1994), Fischhoff, Welch and Frederick (1999)]. As mentioned, events have many more possible cues for events than do probabilities, hence require much messier scientific accounts: Grice's maxims, rather than Poulton's laws. Furthermore, there is rather less research on substantive aspects of task descriptions, compared to quantitative ones. That imbalance reflects both personal predilections and the limited success of attempts to determine broadly relevant values [e.g., Rokeach (1973)].

2.3. Confluence

Two points of confluence might clarify the interrelationship of these research streams, as well as the balance sought by those eliciting values within each.

(a) Psychophysicists historically have sought immediate responses to stimuli, for comparison with the corresponding physical measurements. However, some complex stimuli are not easily summarized. Researchers needing a standard for comparison have sometimes trained people to be *human meters*, synthesizing sounds, lights, smells, pressures, or tastes. The training attempts to accelerate them along the path that others will take, as they experience a new auditorium (or chocolate or wine). A similar logic guides citizen juries, which try to determine public values where none exists, by simulating the learning process of a well-conducted public inquiry [Guston (1999)]. These procedures focus on participants' summary judgments, taking accompanying explanations with a grain of salt. Cognitive psychology has long been wary of introspective accounts, fearing that they reflect people's intuitive theories about cognitive processes, rather than their actual processes. Concurrent verbal reports, or think-aloud protocols, have greater credibility, as ways to catch thinking in the raw [Ericsson and Simon (1994), Nisbett and Wilson (1977)].

(b) Decision theory provided psychophysicists with a systematic approach to an old question: how do uncertain respondents decide what to say? (Did I really hear something? Is it really sweeter? Am I actually 'very happy'? Am I 70% or 80% sure?) The *theory of signal detection* (TSD) distinguishes between how well individuals discriminate among different states and how willing they are to risk different errors when expressing those feelings [Green and Swets (1966)]. The former reflects their evaluative (or diagnostic) ability, the latter their incentives. TSD produced new experimental designs, and disentangled seemingly inconsistent results. It revealed better ways to train "human meters" (e.g., as interpreters of complex medical images [Swets (1992)]). It increased psychologists' sensitivity to incentives, while revealing the difficulties of conveying them. For example, response time often varies greatly with small differences in error rate. Yet, it is hard to tell someone how hard to work in order to achieve a 1% vs. a 2% error rate, or to demonstrate the difference without providing feedback on a very large sample of behavior [Wickelgren (1977)].

3. Evaluating environmental changes

3.1. Psychophysics stream

Contemporary attitude research generally assumes a dual-process model of evaluation [Eagly and Chaiken (1993), Fiske (1998)]. One process involves more global, superficial, affective, connotative evaluations, as people ask themselves, "How do I feel about this, in general?" The second process involves more specific, detailed, cognitive, denotative evaluations, asking, "How much is it worth to me?" The processes are linked, so that evaluations at one level still activate the other. For example, an ostensibly simple request like, "Give me your first impression" may evoke more detailed questions like "What do they want from me?" and "What will they think about me, if I say … ?" Conversely, detailed questions can evoke powerful emotions, confounding the desire (or request) to be "rational." Research on dual-process models examines such topics as: What conditions evoke each mode of processing? How do the processes interact? What do people extract from stimuli, when directed to one level or the other?, and How do individuals differ in their general propensity to seek details (sometimes called their "need for cognition")?

Psychophysical studies of environmental values can address either level. Affect-level studies ask people how they feel about some environment: facing them, depicted, or just imagined. Cognitive-level studies ask for more explicit evaluations (e.g., how natural, attractive, rich … is it?) [e.g., Daniel and Meitner (2001)]. Contingent valuation falls in the latter category. As mentioned, the two processes can intrude on one another. For example, cognitive tasks can make people mad (as seen in the "protest responses" of some stated preference studies), whereas anger can engage their thinking. Environments judged more "natural" can make people feel better [Frumkin (2001)], heal faster during hospitalization [Ulrich (1984)], and require less healthcare [Moore (1981)]. The fact that researchers had to discover these effects shows a limit to introspection as a guide to environmental valuation [Nisbett and Wilson (1977)]: Individuals may not appreciate these "environmental services," just as they may not realize the negative impacts of seasonal affective disorder. Without such understanding, environmental valuations are incompletely informed.

A research strategy that addresses both attitude levels considers the features that people notice in environmental stimuli. For example, respondents might be asked to sort, by similarity or preference, pictures of scenes that vary in the roles of natural and built objects [Cantor (1977), Kelly (1955)]. Using pictures frees respondents from having to verbalize what they see and like. As a result, the process may capture attitudes for which people lack the right words or hesitate to use them (e.g., because of social unacceptability or uncertainty about terminology). One set of recurrent properties, identified in such studies, is *coherence, complexity, legibility*, and *mystery* [Kaplan and Kaplan (1989)].

Although this research strategy frees respondents from verbalization, it increases investigators' interpretative burden – and freedom. That is, investigators can – and must – decide: Just what were respondents looking at? Was their attention drawn to a feature that happened to vary a lot in the picture set, exaggerating its importance? How do respondents derive uncertainty from a concrete scene? Analogous interpretative concerns arise with other psychophysical procedures, such as direct ratings [e.g., the Scenic Beauty Estimation procedure; Daniel and Vining (1983)] or similarity judgments, subjected to multi-dimensional scaling [Berlyne (1971), Gärling (1976)]. These are the attitude-research equivalent of the specification problems facing revealed preference studies. Researchers must determine which of the (often correlated) features of complex situations best account for behavioral regularities [Dawes and Corrigan (1974), Leamer (1983)]. The many degrees of interpretative freedom mean that each study must be viewed in the context of related ones, using varied methods and stimuli – with only recurrent patterns being trusted.

Whatever their limits, these studies place important constraints on ones using other procedures. Features that play a robust role in attitude studies should be represented in stimuli used with other methods. Otherwise, respondents must infer the missing features from available ones. Even when respondents guess correctly, fragmenting their experience may prevent them from articulating values that integrate cognitive and affective responses. Environments have emergent properties, only partially captured by pictures, much less by verbal or vector-like descriptions of their characteristics [Brunswick (1947), Gibson (1979), Larkin and Simon (1987)]. Respondents naturally seek guidance in the investigators' choice of features ("If they think that it's important, so should I"), and overlook neglected ones.

The preferences observed in attitude studies should also be seen in research using other stated preference methods. If not, then one must question the robustness of either the studies or the preferences. As with revealed preferences, interpreting individual stated preference studies should consider the entire literature. For example, some studies have found an aversion to scenes that are hard to understand. That aversion could reduce the value assigned to environments depicted in cluttered pictures, relative to the value of the actual settings, where people could get their bearings (and understand them). If that "clutter" is necessary for ecosystem health, then using pictures will undervalue healthy ecosystems and overvalue manicured ones. Similarly, unless respondents understand what they are seeing, they may assign equal value to water cleared by reducing algae blooms and by introduced zebra mussels (or they may love pollution-induced red sunsets). Without background information, respondents may not realize the complexity of healthy environments.

The research literature on environmental attitudes is large and complex, reflecting the great variety of possible environments, representations, and respondents. As such, it frustrates the desire for simple summary statements of environmental attitudes. On the other hand, the diversity of studies increases the chances of finding ones relevant to the focal environment in any stated preference study. Their stimuli might be reused, taking advantage of previous development work; their results pose a consistency test for subsequent ones. Without a comprehensive perspective, anything goes – in the sense of taking results in isolation, without context or constraint. Points of entry to the environmental attitudes literature include Cassidy (1997), Dunlap et al. (2000), Fischhoff (2001), Gardner and Stern (1996), Kempton, Boster and Hartley (1995), and Nasar (1992).

Attitude researchers are often challenged to demonstrate "attitude–behavior consistency." It might be prompted by observing people who espouse positive attitudes toward other ethnic groups, but still associate primarily with their own kind – or by observing sloth among people who express positive attitudes toward exercise (not to mention "environmentalists" driving SUVs). In decision-making terms, of course, even deeply held, well-measured values may have little necessary relationship to many potentially related behaviors. Choices should depend on attitudes towards the other expected outcomes of possible actions. Thus, people who like exercise may not act on that attitude because of the implications of their attitudes towards time, health, family, career, etc. (The strength of their attitude toward exercise might still be captured in how badly they feel about not doing – even when that remorse cannot be observed directly.)

Studies in areas as diverse as health, race, and the environment find that "attitudes are more predictive of behavior when both are measured at the same level of specificity and when the behaviors are easier to perform" [Cassidy (1997, p. 209), summarizing Ajzen and Fishbein (1980), among others]. The same applies when the behaviors are personal actions (e.g., recycling) or public ones (e.g., voting for deposit laws). Stern (1992) summarizes predictors of environmental behavior, including personal norms (a generalized attitude), public commitment, perceived barriers, and perceived efficacy.

Thus, the desire for behavioral realism has drawn some attitude researchers to pay increased attention to situational details. That can lead to task specifications as detailed as those pursued by economists who design stated preference studies motivated by particular policy concerns. Incorporating these factors transforms attitudes into something like the values (or utilities) of decision-making models. (Progress in the other direction occurs when economists elaborate their notion of the individuals making choices.)

A critical departure from the decision-making perspective is that attitude research focuses on a single option, and not a choice among options. In principle, attitudes toward one option could incorporate the alternatives, in terms of the opportunity costs of forgoing them. For example, the strength of one's attitude toward a personal norm could incorporate the cost of violating it. If so, then evaluation would reflect the action's expected net benefits. Cognitively, though, the alternatives will be less clear than the focal option. With a large option set, the alternatives may not even be fully enumerated. With two complementary options (e.g., go/don't go), raising one should immediately call the other to mind. Nonetheless, thinking about one option may evoke different consequences than thinking about the other [Beyth-Marom et al. (1993)], not to mention different valuations.

Kahneman, Ritov and Schkade (1999) offer a general account of the costs and benefits of treating attitudes as values, presented as a critique of "dollar responses to public issues." They point to a robustness of attitudes that is both boon and bane to stated preference studies. On the one hand, attitudes are so strong and easily evoked that individuals can draw upon them, whatever question they face. On the other hand, that general view can be hard to overcome when a specific evaluation is required (e.g., how much one is willing to pay for a particular good in a particular policy context). Attitudes have an affective component, central to dual-process theories. Those feelings can draw respondents into a task, at the price of distracting them from its details.

When stated preference tasks evoke attitudes, that should reduce the chance of responses showing the *scope sensitivity* sought by contingent valuation researchers [Arrow et al. (1993), Mitchell and Carson (1989), Frederick and Fischhoff (1998), Kahneman and Knetsch (1992)]. Envisioning the death of wildfowl makes many people sad, affecting some more than others. Envisioning the death of many wildfowl should create more sadness than the death of a few. However, that number should have a weaker representation, both cognitively and affectively, than the associated event (birds dying). Dual-process theories show the challenge of evoking full evaluations. On the one hand, one must engage respondents in ways that challenge their intellect, so that they absorb the details essential to policy-related decisions (e.g., the scope of the damages). On the other hand, one must preserve the affective component of valuation, lest the process "anaesthetiz[e] moral feeling" [Tribe (1972)], and evoke preferences that respondents do not fully understand or endorse.

3.2. Decision theory stream

Behavioral decision research entered environment valuation through a back door. The early modern environmental movement confronted many technology managers with opposition that they could not, or would not, understand. One natural response was to view their opponents as irrational. Whatever truth they might hold, such claims could also reflect biased observations. Technologists may not realize that they see their opponents in unrepresentative circumstances (e.g., primarily in the heat of battle); they may want to believe the worst about them. The ensuing research revealed a more complicated picture. Nonetheless, strong claims regarding public competence persist [Okrent and Pidgeon (1998)].

Initial studies used psychophysical methods. They found patterns that have borne up fairly well over time. (a) Lay and statistical estimates of annual fatalities from different sources tend to be strongly correlated. (b) The best-fit curve, relating lay and statistical estimates tends to be flat, with lay estimates spanning a smaller range than statistical ones. (c) There are systematic deviations from that curve, partially attributable to the relative *availability* of different causes of death (because people hear more about some causes than others of equal frequency). (d) There is considerable ordinal (and even ratio scale) consistency among estimates elicited with different methods (e.g., estimates of fatalities or of relative death rates). (e) There is considerable inconsistency in absolute estimates, across response modes (reflecting anchoring, among other things). Thus, respondents reveal a fairly robust feeling for relative risk levels, emerging however these unusual questions are asked. Nonetheless, the task is sufficiently unfamiliar that contextual cues strongly affect responses (consistent with general psychophysical principles) [Lichtenstein et al. (1978)]. [As an aside, the flat curve (point (b)) is often cited as showing that people overestimate small risks and underestimate large ones. However, its slope and intercept are procedure dependent, precluding inferences about absolute judgments from any one study.]

Later studies presented similar stimuli, but elicited judgments of "risk," rather than of "fatalities in an average year" – and found rather different estimates. These differences were traced to the multi-attribute character of "risk," so that technologies' "riskiness" depends on more than just average-year fatalities [Slovic, Fischhoff and Lichtenstein (1979, 1980)]. Catastrophic potential was quickly identified as one potentially important additional attribute. That is, other things being equal, people may be more averse to technologies that can claim many lives at once. This hypothesis emerged from anecdotal observation of preferences apparently stated or revealed in public actions, such as concern over plane crashes or nuclear power (given citizens' recognition that, in an average year, few people die from commercial flight or nuclear power). Catastrophic potential was taken seriously enough to be mooted in the US Nuclear Regulatory Commission's attempt to set explicit safety goals for nuclear power plants [Bier (1988), Fischhoff (1984)]. One proposal was to apply an exponent to the number of deaths from an accident sequence in risk analyses. Some critics objected to that proposal as an immoral preference for how deaths are "packaged." Others objected to how the value of the exponent could dominate regulatory proceedings.

Subsequent research suggested, however, that catastrophic potential per se did not drive lay risk concerns [Slovic, Lichtenstein and Fischhoff (1984)]. Rather, people are averse to the uncertainty often surrounding technologies that can produce catastrophic accidents. That represents a different ethical principle, with different public policy implications. For example, regulating catastrophic potential would mean encouraging small, remotely located technologies. Regulating uncertainty would mean promoting research that sharpens risk estimates and discouraging innovative technologies (which can't be known that well).

The role of catastrophic potential continued to be pursued, as one of many possible attributes of risk. The impetus to this research program was Starr's (1969) claim that, for a given level of benefit, the public tolerates higher risk levels for voluntary activities (e.g., skiing) than for involuntary ones. He backed this claim with a sort of revealed preference analysis, plotting estimates of societal risks and economic benefits from eight activities. He sketched two parallel "acceptable risk" lines, an order of magnitude apart, for voluntary and involuntary risks. Although the paper's integration of concepts was seminal, its technical treatment was but a first approximation [Fischhoff et al. (1981)]. The estimates reflected statistical estimates, rather than the lay judgments that, presumably, drove society's risk–benefit tradeoffs. Lowrance (1976) noted that voluntariness is only one feature of risk that might affect preferences. A straightforward research response to these two concerns asks citizens to evaluate technologies in terms of risk, benefits, and other attributes (such as catastrophic potential, dread, controllability, known to science, known to the public – and voluntariness). A first study [Fischhoff et al. (1978), Slovic, Fischhoff and Lichtenstein (1979)] found

(a) substantial discrepancies between lay and statistical risk and benefit estimates;

(b) a weak correlation between lay estimates of current risks and current benefits (so that society is not seen as having exacted greater benefit from riskier technologies);

(c) no greater correlation between current risk and benefit judgments, after partialing out judgments of voluntariness – or any other attribute (so that society is not seen as having set a double standard);

(d) a belief that most (but not all) technologies had unacceptable current risk levels (contrary to the hypothesis of societal revealed preferences);

(e) a significant correlation between judgments of current benefits and of acceptable risks (indicating willingness to incur greater risk in return for greater benefit);

(f) an increased correlation between perceived benefits and acceptable risks after partialing out voluntariness, and many other attributes (indicating a willingness to have double standards for qualitatively different risks).

These stated preferences indicate a willingness to accept risk–benefit tradeoffs – which might surprise some critics of public rationality. They suggest the risk attributes to consider when designing technologies or regulatory mechanisms. They imply that stated preference studies need to characterize risks in multi-attribute terms [Keeney and Raiffa (1976), von Winterfeldt and Edwards (1986)]. Fischhoff, Watson and Hope (1984) showed how the relative riskiness of energy technologies could depend on how one weighted these attributes, as well as more conventional morbidity and mortality measures. Subsequent studies have found a desire to regulate more strongly technologies with disliked attributes [McDaniels, Kamlet and Fischer (1992), Slovic (1987)].

Dealing with many attributes is unwieldy, cognitively and analytically. As a result, Fischhoff et al. (1978) looked for redundancy in ratings of its 9 attributes. Simple factor analysis found that two factors accounted for much of the variance in the ratings. In one factor, the central concept was something like how well risks are known; in the second, something like how much the risks are dreaded. Uncertainty and catastrophic potential load heavily on the former, as does voluntariness. Catastrophic potential and dread load on the second. The details of these correlations have been explored in dozens of studies, examining many attributes, elicitation procedures, data reduction methods, respondent populations, and target technologies [reviewed by Jenni (1997)]. By and large, the same two factors emerged. A third factor, when found, seems to center on present and future catastrophic potential (pulling that attribute out of the other factors).

Most subsequent studies compared attribute ratings with overall risk evaluations. As such, they fall in the psychophysical, attitude research stream – assigning numbers to objects. Given the robustness of these results, stated preference studies would be missing something if they failed to characterize risks in multi-attribute terms. The key dimensions should be clear in the stimuli, and considered when analyzing preferences. Investigators who assume that risk is just about fatalities have only part of the story. A multi-attribute representation is natural to studies using conjoint measurement and related techniques. In some cases, just mentioning a technology evokes attribute knowledge (e.g., how uncertain or dreadful it is). If can be established that an attribute goes without saying, then precious bandwidth can be saved for describing other task features.

When a multi-attribute representation is used, investigators must decide how to represent each factor. Although empirically correlated, voluntariness and uncertainty may suggest different ethical principles and evoke different preferences. For example, opposition to nuclear power sounds different when attributed to how casualties are aggregated (catastrophic potential) or to how well it is understood (uncertainty). Voluntariness sounds more egocentric than the closely correlated equity.

Morgan et al. (1996) proposed a procedure for representing attributes without drowning respondents in detail. They attempted to formalize the process used by the US Environmental Protection Agency (1990a, 1990b) in its 50 or so state and regional efforts to set risk priorities [Davies (1996)]. These exercises assembled groups of diverse citizens, for extended periods, and produced (more or less) consensual reports, ranking heterogeneous risks. These stated preferences had enough internal credibility for EPA's Scientific Advisory Board to undertake its own ranking, as a guide to agency policies. Nonetheless, it was unclear how any panel had weighted any attribute. Without transparency, it is hard to justify their rankings to nonparticipants or to aggregate rankings across exercises.

Although some standardization is needed, the panels' ability to structure their own work seemed critical to their success. Morgan et al.'s (1996) procedure uses the risk factor research to create a flexible form of standardization. It offers a fixed set of attributes, representing each risk factor, from which respondents could choose the one(s) closest to their concerns. A standard display (like Table 3) characterizes each hazard in these terms. The displays draw on risk communication research and were extensively pretested, to ensure comprehensibility and reduce sensitivity to formally irrelevant differences in display designs. Values are elicited with multiple procedures in order to help respondents absorb information and derive the implications of their basic values for these specific risks [following Gregory, Lichtenstein and Slovic (1993), Keeney (1996), McDaniels, Kamlet and Fischer (1992), National Research Council (1996), Payne, Bettman and Schkade (1999)]. Because it is an overtly reactive process, the methodology includes guidance on providing balanced, accurate materials.

The process uses two pairs of triangulating operations. One pair has respondents both perform holistic rankings and provide attribute weights from which implicit priorities are computed. They can then reconcile any inconsistencies as they see fit. The second pair alternates self-study and group discussion, with procedures designed to ensure respect for both perspectives: views are recorded in private and summarized for the group; instructions note that personal views may differ from ones expressed when seeking consensus; moderators are trained to restrain dominating personalities. Studies have found that the process increases participants' satisfaction, the agreement of holistic judgments and ones derived from attribute weights, and the agreement of public and private preferences.

Table 3
A general framework for characterizing environmental risks

Number of people affected	Degree of environmental impact	Knowledge	Dread
Annual expected number of fatalities:	Area affected by ecosystem stress or change:	Degree to which impacts are delayed:	Catastrophic potential:
0–**450**–600 (10% chance of zero)	**50 km^2**	**1–10** years	**1000** times expected annual fatalities
Annual expected number of person-years lost:	Magnitude of environmental impact:	Quality of scientific understanding:	Outcome equity:
0–**9000**–18000 (10% chance of zero)	**modest** (15% chance of large)	**medium**	**medium** (ratio = 6)

Each column includes two markers for a dimension of risk, found to affect overall judgments of riskiness, desire for regulation, and other evaluative judgments [Slovic (1987, 2001)]. For example, catastrophic potential and outcome equity are two attributes that tend to be correlated with one another, with judgments of the dread that a hazard evokes, and with other attributes often described representing a dimension called "dread." Source: Morgan et al. (1996).

Studies have also found increasing agreement among participants. However, a valid procedure could also reveal and clarify disagreements [Florig et al. (2001), Morgan et al. (2001a, 2001b)]. This convergence would be a sign of success, if one had reason to believe that participants shared underlying preferences, a sign of failure if one had reason to believe that they did not (suggesting that the process somehow manipulated them to agree). The British government has recommended a variant on this procedure for structuring deliberations over risk [HM Treasury (2005)].

4. A cognitive approach to eliciting stated preferences for environmental outcomes

Thus, cognitive approaches to preference elicitation draw on two of psychology's major streams, as developed over the past century-plus. The psychophysical stream envisions stimuli as evoking evaluative feelings, which then must be translated into policy-relevant terms, through an intellectual process. The decision theory stream envisions specific values as being derived intellectually from basic values. However, these inferences must connect with the feelings and trial-and-error learning of everyday life, lest they be but transient artifacts. Thus, researchers in each stream have struggled to overcome its limits. Attitude research has become more cognitively complex, while decision theory has elaborated the roles of effect, experience, and reflection in choice processes [Kahneman, Diener and Schwarz (1999), Lerner and Keltner (2000), Slovic (2001), Loewenstein (1996)].

Despite their different emphases, both streams recognize common steps toward formulating meaningful values:

(1) Encode the task – in order to understand the choices;
(2) Access relevant personal values – in order to structure the evaluation process;
(3) Interpret those values in the specific context – in order to construct a preference;
(4) Translate that preference into suitable terms – in order to state a preference.

Of course, everyday life itself may not provide these conditions, witness individuals' occasional confusion regarding what they want from various (central and peripheral) decisions in their lives. However, investigators owe it to their respondents and their readers to create such conditions and to evaluate their success – in order to demonstrate that they have elicited stated preferences worth taking seriously.

Researchers' aspirations can be arrayed along a continuum, ranging from *gist* to *contractual* studies. *Gist* studies claim to elicit general answers to general questions, such as how much people support the environment, worry about pollution, trust industry, or dislike regulation. *Contract* studies claim to elicit valuations for specific transactions, such as "willingness to pay 7% for 'green' products" (with "green" suitably defined) or "to incur a 0.2% rise in unemployment in order to meet Kyoto obligations."

Researchers have an obligation to provide respondents with the conditions needed to produce the valuations they seek [Fischhoff (2000)]. Otherwise, they (and those who use their work) may misrepresent respondents. Gist responses should provide only vague direction. Respondents haven't said very much; no one should read very much into their responses. Doing more is akin to politicians basing strong, specific mandates on diffuse electoral indicators. Gist researchers should oppose misuse of their work, in terms such as, "All they (the public) said was that they wanted cleaner cars; they didn't say that they wanted to mandate that particular fuel system," or "Respondents' general support for 'free trade' does not imply knowledge and advocacy of all WTO environmental provisions." Contractual claims bear a much greater burden of proof, for demonstrating that respondents have completed the four tasks – hence really understand the agreement they are endorsing. With a fixed budget, meeting these demands will mean smaller samples. That means achieving statistical power through more precise measurement, rather than through increased sample size (whose effects are more easily estimated).

The remainder of this section considers how cognitive psychologists approach the challenge posed by contractual studies – which have greater interest for policy makers (and environmental economists). With gist studies, the primary risk is asking respondents to reflect too hard on their values, taking them beyond their initial gut reactions, perhaps even throwing them into question [Fischhoff (1991, 2000), Wilson et al. (1993)].

In many ways, eliciting environmental values is no different than eliciting any other values. For example, it is generally true that: (a) Multiple methods are needed when eliciting preferences, in order to demonstrate method invariance. (b) Constructive elicitation is needed – unless respondents have articulated values that they can "read off" for the specific question. (c) Communication studies are needed when respondents lack an understanding of the issues that they are evaluating. Eliciting stated preferences for environmental changes is unique in the substance of its problems and the frequent severity of these design challenges. When policy questions define contractual evaluations, respondents often must master details that are unfamiliar in that specific combination, even when familiar in general. They may also face deceptively simple questions, as when researchers demand a contractual response to a nuanced general principle (e.g., discount rate, equity) [Frederick, Loewenstein and O'Donoghue (2002)]. Omitting features does not keep respondents from reading them between the lines of a task description [Fischhoff, Welch and Frederick (1999)].

The first step to ensuring shared understanding is creating a full task specification, addressing each feature important to the investigators or respondents. Table 4 shows a framework for eliciting contractual stated preferences for environmental changes. It holds that the respondent and the investigator must agree about the meaning of the *good*, the *payment*, and the *social context* of the proposed *transaction*. If not, then respondents are answering a different question than the one being asked. Fischhoff and Furby (1988) describe how each feature might matter when evaluating changes in atmospheric visibility.

Table 4

A framework for defining transactions (features that may require specification, if an evaluation task is to be understood similarly by respondents, investigators, and policymakers)

The good (e.g., visibility)

  Substantive definition (aspects of proposed change in good that may matter to evaluators)

    Focal attribute(s)
      (e.g., haze intensity, visual range, plume color, light extinction)
    Context (giving particular value to attribute)
      (e.g., natural or built, judged uniqueness, associated activities (such as hiking,
      viewing, playing), significance (such as religious, cultural, historical))
    Source of change (in focal attribute)
      predominantly natural (e.g., vegetation, forest fires, dust storms, humidity) or
      human (e.g., power plant, other factory, field burning, slash burning, motor vehicles)

  Formal definition (specifying extent of change in valued focal attributes)

    Reference and target levels (of good, before and after change)
      magnitude and direction of change, statistical summary, form of
      representation (mode, richness, organization)
    Extent of change
      geographical, temporal
    Timing of change (when will it happen?)
    Certainty of provision (will it really happen?)

(*continued on next page*)

Table 4
(*Continued*)

The value measure (e.g., money, time, discomfort, effort)

Substantive definition (aspects of proposed change in payment that may matter to evaluators)

Focal attribute(s)
dollars (for money)
foregone leisure or work (for time)
physical or emotional toll (for discomfort or effort)
Context
electric bill, sales tax, income tax, park entry fee, environmental fund (for money)
when convenient, when demanded (for time)
when rested, when exhausted (for effort)
Constituency

Formal definition (specifying extent of change in valued focal attributes)

Reference and target levels
magnitude and direction of change, statistical summary, elicitation procedure
(response mode, response format, cues, feedback)
Extent of payment
frequency, duration
Timing of payment (when will it happen?)
Certainty of payment (will it really happen?)
The social context

Other people involved

Provider of the good
Others present

Resolution mechanism (determining whether transaction will actually occur)

Determining parties
Iterations, constraints

Other stakes involved

Externalities
Precedents
Legitimacy of process

Source: Fischhoff and Furby (1988).

Table 5 presents a second framework, for specifying tasks involving time preferences. It shows the various things that might differ when a good could be provided at two times – in addition to the utility of receiving it. For example, respondents could believe that they are less likely to receive a good at a latter time, investigators' reassurances notwithstanding. If so, then they should value the future prospect less, even if the good itself would have equal utility at either time. These concurrent changes in task features confound interpreting choices over time as expressing pure time preferences.

Table 5
Reasons for evaluating goods differently at different times

Model	Corresponding description in words
DU (time preference only)	Future utility should be discounted because we should care less about the later parts of our life (for some unexplained reason)
DU + probability	Future utility should be weighted by the probability that the consequence that gives rise to the utility will actually occur
DU + changes in objective consequence	The objective properties of some coarsely defined consequence may depend on the time at which it occurs
DU + changes in utility function	The subjective utility associated with a particular objective consequence may change over time
DU + utility from anticipation	The utility at a given moment may be influenced by the anticipation of future utility
DU + utility from memory	The utility at a given moment may be influenced by the recollection of past utility
DU + opportunity cost	Utility depends on the current consumption level, and the potential consumption level depends on current income and past investment

Source: Frederick, Loewenstein and O'Donoghue (2002).

There is, of course, some circularity in needing to know how much features matter in a context before evaluating environmental changes with those features in that context. That circle is broken by the cumulative empirical record of how much those features have typically been found to matter for that class of changes. Formal properties such as the scope and probability of the change (see Table 4) always need to be specified.

The effort needed to convey a task definition depends on how familiar respondents are with it. As mentioned, when voting on a widely debated referendum, many citizens know what contractual commitment it implies – and could respond reliably to an opinion poll. Similarly, many citizens know the verdict that they want from one of our periodic show trials (Clinton, Simpson), and how that would vary with changed evidence or charges. In such situations, many details "go without saying." Omitting them maintains conversational norms and leaves time for communicating less obvious features.

Investigators can approach their communication challenge in a piecemeal or holistic way. That is, they can try either to convey the few most important individual features or to create a meaningful whole that facilitates recalling and inferring features [Fischhoff (1999, 2000)]. The piecemeal strategy creates a supply curve for features, focusing on those that respondents most need to learn [Merz, Small and Fischbeck (1992), Riley, Small and Fischhoff (2000)]. That perspective frames communications adequacy in terms of how much has been conveyed. Sometimes, only a few things really matter. Sometimes, many do. One might expand the envelope of comprehension through more intensive, interactive procedures [e.g., Gregory, Lichtenstein and Slovic (1993), Whittington (1998)]. Or, one might settle for a gist study, getting across just the rough idea.

People absorb information more quickly, when they can organize it into *chunks*, processed cognitively as units [Miller (1956)]. Mnemonists take this skill to high art [Luria (1968)], creating chunks from diverse elements, by integrating them into highly flexible templates. Ordinary people organize information into less coherent, domain-specific *mental models*. Activating a mental model allows some task features to go without saying, while making others easier to absorb. Mental models can also prompt unintended inferences and hinder the processing of unexpected features. For example, "referendum" is a widely used metaphor in CVM studies, asking respondents to imagine voting on a proposed transaction [McDaniels (1996)]. Respondents might naturally infer a government sanctioned, legally binding, take-it-or-leave-it choice, decided by majority rule and open to all citizens. If so, then the single term predictably evokes multiple features. That is good, if they are legitimate inferences; bad, if they are not (e.g., if they lead respondents to exaggerate the probability of the promised good or payment being delivered).

Psychology has studied mental models in many domains [Bartlett (1932), Gentner and Stevens (1983), Rouse and Morris (1986)]. These studies take advantage of the coherence of natural systems to create holistic pictures, allowing respondents to integrate fragmentary beliefs, absorb new features and infer unspoken ones. These results, and the methods that produced them, provide a resource for communicating evaluation tasks [Fischhoff (1999), Morgan et al. (2001a, 2001b)].

Once investigators have finished communicating, they must assess their success. One standard assessment method is the *think-aloud protocol* [Ericsson and Simon (1994), Schkade and Payne (1994), Schriver (1989)]; whereby respondents describe whatever comes into their minds, as they read their task. The interviewer requests enough elaboration to be sure that respondents' meaning is understood. In addition to cases of obvious ambiguity, prompts are needed when people are known to use a term in different ways – for example, "safe sex" [McIntyre and West (1992)], "climate" [Read et al. (1994)], "employed," or "room" [Turner and Martin (1984)].

Placed at the end of a task, *manipulation checks* ask respondents to report their understanding of critical features. Table 6 shows results of three manipulation checks, administered after a short stated preference task. A plurality of respondents reported the actual value for the first check. They did less well on the two other checks. Despite the task's brevity, most respondents did not hear, believe, or remember these features. They were, in effect, answering a different question than the one that was asked.

When performed in pretests, think-aloud protocols and manipulation checks allow predicting how well the task will be mastered by participants in the actual study, who work equally hard. When performed on actual respondents, these assessments show where respondents fall relative to the acceptable level of misunderstanding, hence what conclusions the study can support.

Table 6

Manipulation checks (percent of respondents choosing each offered value of the stimulus feature; bold indicates the value actually in the stimulus)

Condition	Offered values of each stimulus feature			
	Miles of river in proposed cleanup			
	0–100 miles	101–1000 miles	1001–10000 miles	Don't know
30 miles	**62**	9	1	29
1000 miles	4	**34**	32	31
	Feasibility of proposed cleanup			
	Eliminated completely	Good headway	Not much progress	Did not think
30 miles	**35**	46	4	13
1000 miles	**18**	52	10	18
	Payment vehicle for proposed cleanup			
	Taxes	Higher prices	Donations	Other
30 miles	63	**25**	22	19
1000 miles	65	**31**	28	16

The task

In a phone interview, Pittsburgh-area respondents were asked about their willingness to pay (in higher prices for goods and services) to complete cleaning up an environment problem. For the 1000-mile condition they were told "Presently, a large number of the rivers in Pennsylvania are seriously polluted. These rivers include the Delaware, Susquehanna, Monongahela, Allegheny, Ohio, Clarion, Schuylkill and Lehigh. All together, there are more than 3,000 miles of rivers, of which more than 1,000 miles are polluted. Authorities caution against swimming in or eating fish caught from these polluted portions of the rivers." The 30-mile condition mentioned only the Susquehanna River. The first manipulation check asked which of the three ranges contained the value that had been read to them in the 30-mile condition, 62% of respondents reported a value in the correct (0–100 mile) range. The rest reported incorrect values or did not know [source: Fischhoff et al. (1993)].

Even a clear specification and a diligent presentation will leave some gaps between the question being asked and the one being answered. There are three ways to deal with the residual imperfections: (a) *Disqualify* respondents whose task construal strays too far from the intended one; (b) *Adjust* stated preferences to undo the effects of the misconstrual (e.g., double the value assigned to a good that the task promised but a respondent saw but a 50% chance of actually receiving); (c) *Accommodate* misconstruals, when reporting study results (e.g., separate the preferences stated by respondents demonstrating different degrees of task mastery; note common forms of disbelief). Participants in Table 6's study showed greater scope sensitivity when their responses were analyzed in terms of the question that they reported answering, rather than the one actually presented.

5. Conclusions

In the short run, the costs of all this design work can be reduced by exploiting solutions already in the cognate literatures (e.g., proven ways to describe an ecosystem). The analytical frameworks of Tables 4 and 5 represent two ways to hasten the accumulation of such knowledge. Each identifies essential features of tasks, for which regularities can be sought. Over the long run, design costs should decline as a cumulative empirical record is created, on issues central to eliciting environmental values (e.g., how to convey the time period for a payment or the magnitude of a change, how to convince respondents that a change will really happen). As mentioned, such research can simplify otherwise complex tasks, by showing which features can go without saying or need no explanation. However, design research may also reveal investigators to be victims of a *curse of cleverness*. We prize novel tasks, whose formulation captures nuances that eluded our colleagues or address emerging policy concerns. Such tasks are necessarily even more novel for respondents. The greater the novelty, the greater the need for explanatory exposition and constructive elicitation – if respondents are to understand the choice being posed and their own preferences. The reward for such efforts is improving the signal from stated preference studies, by reducing respondents' uncertainty about the investigator's question and their answer. The research literature of cognitive psychology both demonstrates the reality of these challenges and offers resources for addressing them.

6. Contingent valuation: a postscript

As mentioned, cognitive psychology is best known to many environmental economists through controversies over contingent valuation. The potential constructive contributions of the other literatures cited here are rarely mentioned, while the controversies have a polemic character, ill suited to fostering collaboration and understanding [Driver, Peterson and Gregory (1988), Fischhoff and Furby (1986), Furby and Fischhoff (1988), Kahneman and Knetsch (1992), Kopp, Pommerehne and Schwarz (1997), Schkade and Payne (1994)]. From the tenor of these interactions, one might infer that cognitive psychologists are fundamentally opposed to eliciting stated preferences for environmental goods. However, their opposition is to the methods used to ask questions, not to pursuit of the answers. As long as contingent valuation adopts the psychophysics paradigm, most cognitive psychologists will remain skeptical of its claims – believing that attitude-research methods cannot elicit values supporting the contractual claims sought by CV researchers [e.g., Fischhoff (1991, 2000), Gregory, Lichtenstein and Slovic (1993), Kahneman, Knetsch and Thaler (1991), Kahneman, Diener and Schwarz (1999), Payne, Bettman and Johnson (1993), Payne, Bettman and Schkade (1999)]. Eliciting more than just the gist of environmental preferences will require constructive procedures, rooted in the decision theory stream. Creating them will require accepting reactive measurement, and the philosophy of science that supports it. It will demand better-specified tasks and more extensive manipulation checks than has been common – in order to ensure that respondents answer the specific question that interests policy makers. It will afford and require opportunities for collaboration among psychologists, economists, and others.

References

Ajzen, I., Fishbein, M. (1980). Understanding Attitudes and Predicting Social Behavior. Prentice-Hall, Englewood Cliffs, NJ.

Arrow, K., Solow, R., Portney, P., Leamer, E., Radner, R., Schuman, H. (1993). "Report of the NOAA panel on contingent valuation". Federal Register 58, 4601–4614.

Bartlett, R.C. (1932). Remembering. Cambridge University Press, Cambridge.

Berlyne, D.E. (1971). Aesthetics and Psychobiology. Appleton-Century-Crofts, New York, NY.

Beyth-Marom, R., Austin, L., Fischhoff, B., Palmgren, C., Quadrel, M.J. (1993). "Perceived consequences of risky behaviors". Developmental Psychology 29, 549–563.

Bier, V.M. (1988). "The US Nuclear Regulatory Commission's safety goal policy: A critical review". Risk Analysis 8, 563–568.

Brunswick, E. (1947). Systematic and Representative Design of Psychological Experiments. University of California Press, Los Angeles, CA.

Budescu, D.F., Wallsten, T.S. (1995). "Processing linguistic probabilities: General principles and empirical evidence". In: Busemeyer, J.R., Hastie, R., Medin, D.L. (Eds.), Decision Making from a Cognitive Perspective. Academic Press, New York, pp. 275–318.

Cantor, D. (1977). The Psychology of Place. Architectural Press, London, UK.

Cassidy, T. (1997). Environmental Psychology. Taylor and Frances, London, UK.

Clemen, R.T. (1996). Making Hard Decisions: An Introduction to Decision Analysis. Duxbury, Belmont, CA.

Cummings, R.G., Brookshire, D.S., Schulze, W.D. (Eds.) (1986). Valuing Environmental Goods: An Assessment of the Contingent Valuation Method. Rowman & Allanheld, Totowa, NJ.

Daniel, T.C., Meitner, M.M. (2001). "Representational validity of landscape visualizations: the effects of graphical realism on perceived scenic beauty of forest landscapes". Journal of Environmental Psychology 21, 61–72.

Daniel, T.C., Vining, J. (1983). "Methodological issues in the assessment of landscape quality". In: Altman, I., Wohlwill, J.F. (Eds.), Human Behavior and Environment, vol. 16. Plenum Press, New York, NY, pp. 39–84.

Davies, C. (Ed.) (1996). Comparing Environmental Risks. Resources for the Future, Washington, DC.

Dawes, R.M. (1988). Rational Choice in an Uncertain World. Harcourt, Brace Jovanovich, San Diego, CA.

Dawes, R.M., Corrigan, B. (1974). "Linear models in decision making". Psychological Bulletin 81, 95–106.

Driver, B., Peterson, G., Gregory, R. (Eds.) (1988). Evaluating Amenity Resources. Venture, New York.

Dunlap, R.E., Van Liere, K.D., Mertig, A.G., Jones, R.E. (2000). "Measuring endorsement of the new ecological paradigm: A revised NEP scale". Journal of Social Issues 56, 425–442.

Eagly, A.H., Chaiken, S. (1993). The Psychology of Attitudes. Harcourt, Brace & Jovanovic, Orlando.

Edwards, W. (1954). "A theory of decision making". Psychological Bulletin 54, 380–397.

Edwards, W. (1961). "Behavioral decision theory". Annual Review of Psychology 12, 473–498.

Ericsson, A., Simon, H. (1994). Verbal Reports as Data, 2nd ed. MIT Press, Cambridge, MA.

Fischhoff, B. (1980). "Clinical decision analysis". Operations Research 28, 28–43.

Fischhoff, B. (1984). "Setting standards: A systematic approach to managing public health and safety risks". Management Science 30, 823–843.

Fischhoff, B. (1988a). "Judgment and decision making". In: Sternberg, R.J., Smith, E.E. (Eds.), The Psychology of Human Thought. Cambridge University Press, New York, pp. 153–187.

Fischhoff, B. (1988b). "Specifying value measurements". In: Driver, B., Peterson, G., Gregory, R. (Eds.), Evaluating Amenity Resources. Venture, New York, pp. 107–116.

Fischhoff, B. (1991). "Value elicitation: Is there anything in there?". American Psychologist 46, 835–847.

Fischhoff, B. (1994). "What forecasts (seem to) mean". International Journal of Forecasting 10, 387–403.

Fischhoff, B. (1998). "Communicate unto others . . .". Reliability Engineering and System Safety 59, 63–72.

Fischhoff, B. (1999). "Why (cancer) risk communication can be hard". Journal of the National Cancer Institute Monographs 25, 7–13.

Fischhoff, B. (2000). "Informed consent in eliciting environmental values". Environmental Science and Technology 38, 1439–1444.

Fischhoff, B. (2001). "Environmental cognition, perception, and attitudes". In: Baltes, P.B., Smelser, N.J. (Eds.), International Encyclopedia of the Social and Behavioral Sciences, vol. 7. Pergamon, Kidlington, UK, pp. 4596–4602.

Fischhoff, B., Bruine de Bruin, W. (1999). "Fifty/fifty = 50?". Journal of Behavioral Decision Making 12, 149–163.

Fischhoff, B., Furby, L. (1986). A review and critique of Tolley, Randall et al. "Establishing and valuing the effects of improved visibility in the Eastern United States". ERI Technical Report 86-8. Eugene, OR, Eugene Research Institute.

Fischhoff, B., Furby, L. (1988). "Measuring values: A conceptual framework for interpreting transactions". Journal of Risk and Uncertainty 1, 147–184.

Fischhoff, B., Slovic, P., Lichtenstein, S. (1980). "Knowing what you want: Measuring labile values". In: Wallsten, T. (Ed.), Cognitive Processes in Choice and Decision Behavior. Erlbaum, Hillsdale, NJ, pp. 117–141.

Fischhoff, B., Watson, S., Hope, C. (1984). "Defining risk". Policy Sciences 17, 123–139.

Fischhoff, B., Welch, N., Frederick, S. (1999). "Construal processes in preference elicitation". Journal of Risk and Uncertainty 19, 139–164.

Fischhoff, B., Lichtenstein, S., Slovic, P., Derby, S.L., Keeney, R.L. (1981). Acceptable Risk. Cambridge University Press, New York.

Fischhoff, B., Slovic, P., Lichtenstein, S., Read, S., Combs, B. (1978). "How safe is safe enough? A psychometric study of attitudes towards technological risks and benefits". Policy Sciences 8, 127–152.

Fischhoff, B., Quadrel, M.J., Kamlet, M., Loewenstein, G., Dawes, R., Fischbeck, P., Klepper, S., Leland, J., Stroh, P. (1993). "Embedding effects: Stimulus representation and response modes". Journal of Risk and Uncertainty 6, 211–234.

Fiske, S. (1998). Social Psychology. Wiley, New York.

Florig, H.K., Morgan, M.G., Morgan, K.M., Jenni, K.E., Fischhoff, B., Fischbeck, P.S., DeKay, M. (2001). "A test bed for studies of risk ranking". Risk Analysis 21, 913–922.

Frederick, S., Fischhoff, B. (1998). "Scope insensitivity in elicited values". Risk Decision and Policy 3, 109–124.

Frederick, S., Loewenstein, G., O'Donoghue, T. (2002). "Time discounting and time preference: A critical review". Journal of Economic Literature 40, 351–401.

Frumkin, H. (2001). "Beyond toxicity: The greening of environmental health". American Journal of Preventive Medicine 20, 47–53.

Furby, L., Fischhoff, B. (1988). "Specifying subjective evaluations. A critique of Dickie et al.'s interpretation of their contingent valuation results for reduced minor health symptoms". USEPA Cooperative Agreement No. CR814655-01-0. Eugene Research Institute, Eugene, OR.

Gardner, G.T., Stern, P.C. (1996). Environmental problems and human behavior. Allyn & Bacon, Boston, MA.

Gärling, T. (1976). "The structural analysis of environmental perception and cognition". Environment and Behavior 8, 258–263.

Gentner, D., Stevens, A.L. (Eds.) (1983). Mental Models. Erlbaum, Hillsdale, NJ.

Gibson, J.J. (1979). The Ecological Approach to Visual Perception. Houghton Mifflin, Boston, MA.

Gilovich, T., Griffin, D., Kahneman, D. (Eds.) (2002). The Psychology of Judgment: Heuristics and Biases. Cambridge University Press, New York.

Green, D.M., Swets, J.A. (1966). Signal Detection Theory and Psychophysics. Wiley, New York.

Gregory, R., Lichtenstein, S., Slovic, P. (1993). "Valuing environmental resources: A constructive approach". Journal of Risk and Uncertainty 7, 177–197.

Grice, H.P. (1975). "Logic and conversation". In: Davidson, D., Harman, G. (Eds.), The Logic of Grammar. Dickenson, Encino.

Guston, D. (1999). "Evaluating the first US consensus conference: The impact of the citizens' panel on telecommunications and the future of democracy". Science, Technology and Human Values 24, 451–482.

HM Treasury (2005). Managing Risks to the Public. HM Treasury, London.

Jenni, K. (1997). Attributes for Risk Evaluation. Unpublished doctoral dissertation. Department of Engineering and Public Policy, Carnegie Mellon University.

Kahneman, D., Knetsch, J.L. (1992). "Valuing public goods: The purchase of moral satisfaction". Journal of Environmental Economics and Management 22, 57–70.

Kahneman, D., Tversky, A. (1979). "Prospect theory: An analysis of decision under risk". Econometrica 47, 263–281.

Kahneman, D., Tversky, A. (1984). "Choices, values, and frames". American Psychologist 39, 341–350.

Kahneman, D., Diener, E., Schwarz, N. (Eds.) (1999). Well-being: The Foundations of Hedonic Psychology. Russell Sage Foundation Press, New York.

Kahneman, D., Knetsch, J.L., Thaler, R.H. (1991). "The endowment effect, loss aversion, and status quo bias". Journal of Economic Perspectives 5, 193–206.

Kahneman, D., Ritov, I., Schkade, D. (1999). "Economic preferences or attitude expression?". Journal of Risk and Uncertainty 19, 203–242.

Kahneman, D., Slovic, P., Tversky, A. (Eds.) (1982). Judgment under Uncertainty: Heuristics and Biases. Cambridge University Press, New York.

Kaplan, R., Kaplan, S. (1989). The Experience of Nature: A Psychological Perspective. Cambridge University Press, Cambridge, UK.

Keeney, R. (1996). Value-focused Thinking. MIT Press, Cambridge, MA.

Keeney, R., Raiffa, H. (1976). Decisions with Multiple Objectives: Preferences and Value Trade-offs. Wiley, New York.

Kelly, G.A. (1955). The Psychology of Personal Constructs. Norton, New York, NY.

Kempton, W., Boster, J.S., Hartley, J.A. (1995). Environmental Values in American Culture. MIT Press, Cambridge, MA.

Kopp, R., Pommerehne, W.W., Schwarz, N. (Eds.) (1997). Determining the Value of Nonmarketed Goods. Kluwer, New York.

Larkin, J.H., Simon, H.A. (1987). "Why a diagram is (sometimes) worth 10,000 words". Cognitive Science 11, 65–100.

Leamer, E. (1983). "Let's take the con out of econometrics". American Economic Review 72 (1), 31–43.

Lerner, J.S., Keltner, D. (2000). "Beyond valence: Toward a model of emotion-specific influences on judgment and choice". Cognition and Emotion.

Lichtenstein, S., Newman, J.R. (1967). "Empirical scaling of common verbal phrases associated with numerical probabilities". Psychonomic Science 9, 563–564.

Lichtenstein, S., Slovic, P., Fischhoff, B., Layman, M., Combs, B. (1978). "Judged frequency of lethal events". Journal of Experimental Psychology: Human Learning and Memory 4, 551–578.

Loewenstein, G. (1996). "Out of control: Visceral influences on behavior". Organizational Behavior and Human Decision Processes 65, 272–292.

Lowrance, W.W. (1976). Of Acceptable Risk: Science and the Determination of Safety. William Kaufman, Los Altos, CA.

Luria, A.R. (1968). The Mind of a Mnemonist. Basic Books, New York.

McDaniels, T. (1996). "The structured value referendum: Eliciting preferences for environmental policy alternatives". Journal of Policy Analysis and Management 15, 227–251.

McDaniels, T., Kamlet, M.S., Fischer, G.W. (1992). "Risk perception and the value of safety". Risk Analysis 12, 495–503.

McFadden, D. (1999). "Rationality for economists?". Journal of Risk and Uncertainty 19, 73–110.

McGuire, W. (1969). "Suspiciousness of experimenter's intent". In: Rosenthal, R., Rosnow, R.L. (Eds.), Artifact in Behavioral Research. Academic Press, New York.

McIntyre, S., West, P. (1992). "What does the phrase "safer sex" mean to you? Understanding among Glaswegian 18-year olds in 1990". AIDS 7, 121–126.

Merz, J.F., Small, M., Fischbeck, P. (1992). "Measuring decision sensitivity: A combined Monte Carlo – logistic regression approach". Medical Decision Making 12, 189.

Miller, G.A. (1956). "The magical number seven, plus or minus two: Some limits on our capacity for processing information". Psychological Review 63, 81–97.

Mitchell, R.C., Carson, R.T. (1989). Using Surveys to Value Public Goods: The Contingent Valuation Method. Resources for the Future, Washington, DC.

Moore, E.O. (1981). "A prison environment's effect on health care service demands". Journal of Environmental Systems 11, 17–34.

Morgan, K.M., DeKay, M.L., Fischbeck, P.S., Morgan, M.G., Fischhoff, B., Florig, H.K. (2001a). "A deliberative method for ranking risks: Evaluating validity and usefulness". Risk Analysis 21, 923–938.

Morgan, M.G., Fischhoff, B., Bostrom, A., Atman, C. (2001b). Risk Communication: The Mental Models Approach. Cambridge University Press, New York.

Morgan, M.G., Fischhoff, B., Lave, L., Fischbeck, P. (1996). "A proposal for ranking risks within federal agencies". In: Davies, C. (Ed.), Comparing environmental risks. Resources for the Future, Washington, DC, pp. 111–147.

Nasar, J.L. (Ed.) (1992). Environmental Aesthetics: Theory Research and Applications. Cambridge University Press, New York, NY.

National Research Council (1982). Survey Measure of Subjective Phenomena. National Academy Press, Washington, DC.

National Research Council (1996). Understanding Risk. The Council, Washington, DC.

Nisbett, R.E., Wilson, T.D. (1977). "Telling more than we know: Verbal reports on mental processes". Psychological Review 84, 231–259.

Okrent, D., Pidgeon, N. (Eds.) (1998). Actual versus Perceived Risk. Reliability Engineering and System Safety 59 (1998). Special issue.

Payne, J.W., Bettman, J.R., Johnson, E. (1993). The Adaptive Decision Maker. Cambridge University Press, Cambridge.

Payne, J.W., Bettman, J.R., Schkade, D. (1999). "Measuring constructed preferences: Toward a building code". Journal of Risk and Uncertainty 19, 243–270.

Plous, S. (1993). The Psychology of Judgment and Decision Making. McGraw–Hill, New York.

Poulton, E.C. (1968). "The new psychophysics: Six models for magnitude estimation". Psychological Bulletin 69, 1–19.

Poulton, E.C. (1989). Bias in Quantifying Judgment. Lawrence Erlbaum, Hillsdale, NJ.

Poulton, E.C. (1994). Behavioral Decision Making. Lawrence Erlbaum, Hillsdale, NJ.

Raiffa, H. (1968). Decision Analysis: Introductory Lectures on Choices under Uncertainty. Addison-Wesley, Reading, MA.

Read, D., Bostrom, A., Morgan, M.G., Fischhoff, B., Smuts, T. (1994). "What do people know about global climate change? Part 2. Survey studies of educated laypeople". Risk Analysis 14, 971–982.

Riley, D.M., Small, M.J., Fischhoff, B. (2000). "Modeling methylene chloride exposure–reduction options for home paint-stripper users". Journal of Exposure Analysis and Environmental Epidemiology 10 (3), 240–250.

Rokeach, M. (1973). The Nature of Human Values. The Free Press, New York.

Rouse, W.B., Morris, N.M. (1986). "On looking into the black box: Prospects and limits in the search for mental models". Psychological Bulletin 100, 349–363.

Schkade, D., Payne, J.W. (1994). "How people respond to contingent valuation questions: A verbal protocol analysis of willingness to pay for an environmental regulation". Journal of Environmental Economics and Management 26, 88–109.

Schriver, K.A. (1989). Plain Language for Expert or Lay Audiences: Designing Text Using Protocol Aided Revision. Communications Design Center, Carnegie Mellon University.

Schwarz, N. (1996). Cognition and Communication: Judgmental Biases, Research Methods and the Logic of Conversation. Erlbaum, Hillsdale, NJ.

Schwarz, N. (1999). "Self-reports: How the questions shape the answers". American Psychologist 54, 93–105.

Slovic, P. (1987). "Perceptions of risk". Science 236, 280–285.

Slovic, P. (Ed.) (2001). The Perception of Risk. Earthscan, London.

Slovic, P., Lichtenstein, S. (1971). "Comparison of Bayesian and regression approaches to the study of information processing in judgment". Organizational Behavior and Human Performance 6, 649–744.

Slovic, P., Fischhoff, B., Lichtenstein, S. (1979). "Rating the risks". Environment 21 (4), 14–20, 36–39.

Slovic, P., Fischhoff, B., Lichtenstein, S. (1980). "Facts and fears: Understanding perceived risk". In: Schwing, R., Albers, W.A. Jr. (Eds.), Societal Risk Assessment: How Safe Is Safe enough?. Plenum Press, New York, pp. 181–214.

Slovic, P., Lichtenstein, S., Fischhoff, B. (1984). "Modeling the societal impact of fatal accidents". Management Science 30, 464–474.

Starr, C. (1969). "Social benefit versus technological risk". Science 165, 1232–1238.

Stern, P.C. (1992). "Psychological dimensions of global environmental change". Annual Review of Psychology 43, 269–302.

Stevens, S.S. (1975). Psychophysics: Introduction to Its Perceptual, Neural and Social Prospects. Wiley, New York, NY.

Swets, J.A. (1992). "The science of choosing the right decision threshold in high-stakes diagnostics". American Psychologist 47, 522–532.

Tanur, J.M. (Ed.) (1992). Questions about Questions. Russell Sage Foundation, New York.

Tribe, L.H. (1972). "Policy science: Analysis or ideology?". Philosophy and Public Affairs 2, 66–110.

Tolley G. et al. (1986). "Establishing and valuing the effects of improved visibility in the Eastern United States". Report to the Environmental Protection Agency.

Tune, G.S. (1964). "Response preferences: A review of some relevant literature". Psychological Bulletin 61, 286–302.

Turner, C.F., Krauss, E. (1978). "Fallible indicators of the subjective state of the nation". American Psychologist 33, 456–470.

Turner, C.F., Martin, E. (Eds.) (1984). Surveying Subjective Phenomena. Russell Sage Foundation, New York.

Tversky, A., Kahneman, D. (1974). "Judgment under uncertainty: Heuristics and biases". Science 185, 1124–1131.

Ulrich, R.S. (1984). "View through a window may influence recovery from surgery". Science 224, 420–421.

US Environmental Protection Agency (1990a). Reducing Risk: Setting Priorities and Strategies. US Environmental Protection Agency, Washington, DC.

US Environmental Protection Agency (1990b). Comparative Risk. US Environmental Protection Agency, Washington, DC.

von Neumann, J., Morgenstern, O. (1947). Theory of Games and Economic Behavior, 2nd ed. Princeton University Press, Princeton.

von Winterfeldt, D., Edwards, W. (1986). Decision Analysis and Behavioral Research. Cambridge University Press, New York.

Wallsten, T., Budescu, D. (1983). "Encoding subjective probabilities: A psychological and psychometric review". Management Science 29, 135–140.

Whittington, D. (1998). "Administering contingent valuation surveys in developing countries". World Development 26, 21–30.

Wickelgren, W. (1977). "Speed–accuracy trade-off and information processing dynamics". Acta Psychologica 41 (1), 67–85.

Wilson, T.D., Lisle, D.J., Schooler, J.W., Hodges, S.D., Klaaren, K.J., LaFleur, S.J. (1993). "Introspecting about reasons can reduce post-choice satisfaction". Personality Social Psychology Bulletin 19, 331–339.

Woodworth, R.S., Schlosberg, H. (1954). Experimental Psychology. Holt, New York.

Yates, J.F. (1990). Judgment and Decision Making. Wiley, New York.

Chapter 19

EXPERIMENTAL METHODS AND VALUATION

JASON F. SHOGREN

University of Wyoming

QS1

D61

Contents

Handbook of Environmental Economics, Volume 2. Edited by K.-G. Mäler and J.R. Vincent
© 2005 Elsevier B.V.   All rights reserved
DOI: 10.1016/S1574-0099(05)02019-X

Abstract

This chapter explores how economists use experimental methods to understand better the behavioral underpinnings of environmental valuation. Economic experiments, in the lab or field, are an attractive tool to address intricate incentive and contextual questions that arise in assessing values through direct statements of preferences. By combining empirical observation with theoretical insight, researchers use the experimental method and mindset to help explain how economic and social contexts matter to valuation. Herein we consider three themes in applying the experimental method to valuation – rational choice theory and stated values, direct value elicitation in the field and lab, and "testbedding" survey designs prior to field application. First, experimental tests of rational valuation are discussed. This lab work examines whether respondents make choices and state values in a manner consistent with standard rational choice theory. The circumstances of rational valuation are illustrated by the malleability of two classic anomalies – the WTP–WTA divergence and the preference reversal phenomenon. Second, direct experimental methods to measure actual values for public and private goods are examined. These experiments ask people to buy and sell actual goods to elicit real values, in which researchers test how alternative exchange institutions affect these values. Third, we survey testbed experiments designed to identify potential incentive problems caused by hypothetical valuation questions. Four topics are discussed: testing for hypothetical bias, calibrating real and hypothetical values, examining surrogate values (or scoping) for specific environmental preferences, and evaluating the incentive (in)compatibility of alternative elicitation mechanisms.

Keywords

valuation, experiments, auctions, mechanism design, calibration

JEL classification: B4, C9, H4, Q2

1. Introduction

How do people value environmental protection? This question has captivated econo-mists for decades. Driven by academic curiosity, Presidential Executive Orders, and court cases over natural resource damage assessment, the United States has witnessed a push to produce absolute numbers so that society can add nonmarket considerations onto the benefit–cost balance sheets that help shape government policymaking and legal decisions. The same is also true of many other nations, e.g., Sweden, United Kingdom. It might not be an overstatement to say that probably as much collective energy has been spent on defining, estimating, and debating nonmarket valuation as any other topic in environmental economics. And in particular, people have pondered the challenge of control and accuracy in nonmarket valuation through public opinion surveys, i.e., con-tingent valuation and other stated preference methods.

The desire for more control and accuracy in revealing nonmarket values through di-rect questions about actual goods led researchers like Peter Bohm, Richard Bishop, and Thomas Heberlein in the 1970s toward the methods of experimental economics and the insights gained from the experimental mindset that emerged in the 1960s.[1] While Bohm, Bishop and Heberlein were primarily interested in field valuation work, a typi-cal economics experiment is run in a laboratory just like in chemistry or physics. Here test tubes and particle accelerators are replaced with experimental instructions and net-worked computers programmed to create interactive markets, auctions, and strategic games. Monitors then observe the actual behavior of people within these institutions given initial endowments of rules, resources, technology, and preferences. Over 100 experimental economics labs now exist around the world, to which experimentalists re-cruit both students and non-students to participate to test theory, look for patterns, and to explore new phenomenon that arise in choices made within and outside of exchange institutions.

The push to make the experimental method a part of nonmarket valuation began in earnest with the state of the art assessment of contingent valuation summarized in Cummings, Brookshire and Schulze (1986), and the early work of Knetsch and Sin-den (1984), Coursey and Schulze (1986), and Bennett (1983).[2] Today, more researchers draw on the experimental mindset, in both the lab and the field, to understand better how people learn about incentive systems and what this might imply for valuing envi-ronmental protection.

This chapter explores how economists use the experimental method to better un-derstand the behavioral underpinnings of environmental valuation. We consider three intertwined areas of the experimental method in valuation:

---

[1] Useful introductions to experimental economics include Smith (1982), Plott (1987, 1989), Davis and Holt (1993), Friedman and Sunder (1994), and Kagel and Roth (1995).

[2] Early experiments looking at individual choice, utility and preference emerged in the published literature in the 1940s and 1950s. The work of Mosteller and Nogee (1951) was an early attempt to measure the nature of preferences with the experimental method. They were interested in using a laboratory experiment to measure "the value to individuals of additional money income" (p. 371).

(i) methods to test rational choice theory, the principles that define the economic surplus measures upon which nonmarket valuation rests;

(ii) direct methods to measure actual values for public and private goods, in the field and the lab; and

(iii) methods to use the lab as a "testbed" for defining incentive systems prior to the field application of hypothetical surveys.

As with any survey, the chapter focuses its attention on a few themes. Other reviews and opinions on experimental methods in environmental economics include Cummings, McKee and Taylor (2000), Cummings and Taylor (2001), Harrison (1996), Shogren and Nowell (1992), Shogren and Hurley (1999), and Shogren (1993, 2002).

2. The experimental method and mindset

With all the available theoretical and empirical tools in economics, why bother do an experiment? Three reasons come to mind – to test theory, for pattern recognition, and for testbedding. First, one can use experiments to test *a priori* expectations about behavior, rational or otherwise. Researchers use experiments to test the predictive power of a theory, to test the robustness of the axioms underlying the theory, to test the specific boundaries of a general theory, and to measure the gradient of behavioral change (i.e., comparative statics). Experiments provide a sterile environment to test theory by controlling for noise and other confounding factors. Given this control, a researcher can assess the ability of a theory and its alternatives to organize observed behavior. For valuation work, the lab is used to test whether stated values are consistent with economic theory (e.g., the divergence between willingness to pay and willingness to accept measures of value).

Second, people use the lab to look for patterns of behavior. This more pragmatic use of the lab allows people to explore how people construct preferences and beliefs, identify and measure breakdowns from rationality, examine how contextual frames affect behavior, determine reactions to new information, and consider how people coordinate actions voluntarily and under duress. Pattern recognition can provide the motivation for people to develop alternative theories (i.e., prospect theory) based on ex post explanations of observed behavior. Howard Raiffa's (1982) work on negotiation is a good example of pattern recognition. Raiffa created a classroom "quasi-laboratory" in which students negotiated over alternative controlled scenarios. They then interpreted their observed behavior, so as to design modified experiments and re-sample new subjects. They then collectively discussed whether the heuristic insight gained from observing actual behavior in the lab could translate into real world applications. For valuation work, pattern recognition involves the direct elicitation of values for goods or services in a lab auction or field exchange given alternative incentive mechanisms, endowments, information sets, and with and without the signals set through repeated market experience.

Third, laboratory experiments are used as a testbed for *economic design* – the construction of new institutions and mechanisms designed for efficient resource allocation.

The most prominent example is the use of the lab to test pilot the efficiency of the proposed FCC spectrum auctions [see, for example, Plott (1994)], to compare alternative policy options, to explore how friction affects efficiency and the distribution of wealth, and to consider how institutional power can transform patterns of behavior. An example of valuation testbedding is examination of the potential incentive compatibility of alternative value elicitation mechanisms (e.g., discrete choice or referenda questions). The ultimate success of testbedding different mechanisms rests in the open question of external validity – is the behavior in the lab a reliable guide to behavior in the real world? Experimental economists believe so, albeit within reasonable limits. Lab results represent real evidence about how certain people will behave in a given economic environment. Additional real-world complexity can then be added into the lab environment in a controlled fashion to identify likely conditions that might cause a mechanism to fail in the wilds.

The wide-ranging idea that experimental research provides the *definitive* evidence prompted worldly philosophers like Bishop George Berkeley and John Stuart Mill to take the extreme position that "... nothing beyond experimental knowledge is either possible or necessary" [Kline (1985, p. 19)]. This predilection toward experiments as science led ecologist Heath (1976, p. 3) to claim: "Science consists essentially in an attempt to understand *relations* of selected aspects of things and events in the real world, an attempt which should have both intuitive and logical components, and which must be based on observation and tested by further observation. This definition of course excludes mathematics, which does not have to be based on observation (data) but only on postulates which need not have any relevance to the real world."

While more inclined to blend the empiricist and rationalist traditions, John Herschel's (1997 [1830]) 19th-century discourse on the philosophy of science still elevated experiment as method: "By putting in action cases and agents over which we have control, and purposely varying their combinations, and noticing what effects take place; this is *experiment* .... We cross-examine our witness, and by comparing one part of his evidence with the other, while he is yet before us, and reasoning upon it in his presence, are enabled to put pointed and searching questions, the answers to which may at once enable use to make up our mind. Accordingly it has been found invariably, that in those departments of physics where the phenomena are beyond our control, or into which experimental enquiry, from other causes, has not been carried, the progress of knowledge has been slow, uncertain, and irregular; while in such as admit of experiment, and in which mankind have agreed to its adoption, it has been rapid, sure, and steady" (pp. 76, 77).

Obviously others question such passionate beliefs on experimentation. Theory and nonexperimental empirics have long dominated the economist's toolbox, causing some to ask whether economists who use the small-scale experimental method and mindset have anything to say about large-scale environmental risks in the wild. Many economists who run experiments, including myself, believe the answer is *yes* – the experimental method matters for environmental economics. Experiments backup with data the idea that economic incentives matter, and that by addressing such behavior explicitly in the lab we can better understand the ultimate success and failure of a policy. While no general panacea, experiments have many uses in the policy arena: to support or counter some specific policy initiative; to increase the costs to policy makers who choose to ignore economic behavior; to shift the burden of proof in a policy debate; to demonstrate how friction (or the lack of it) affects a policy; to reveal how (in)sensitive benefits and costs are to context and frames; to reveal how people tend to react to absolute and relative levels of risk; and to support the notion of why and when flexibility can lead to more environmental protection at lower cost. The challenge is to not oversell the lab results.

The defense of the experimental method, in general, and applied to environmental issues in particular, rests on the foundations laid down by Vernon Smith, Charles Plott, and Peter Bohm. Their path-breaking work and the ensuing literature has moved economics further toward being considered an experimental science, with its own set of protocols and rules for the lab and field [see the chapters in Kagel and Roth (1995)].[3] Today economists who use experiments to address environmental policy have a lot in common with natural scientists. Although economics has traditionally devoted its energy toward theory and empirical work based on field data, environmental economists now use controlled experimentation like their colleagues in the life sciences (e.g., biology and ecology), the people upon whom environmentalists usually rely on to make the case for more environmental protection [Shogren and Nowell (1992), Shogren (2002)].

Figure 1 illustrates a basic triad that illustrates the experimental method and mindset.[4] The triad reflects the three components that underlie an experiment: the initial endow-

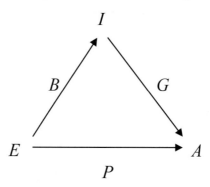

Figure 1. Experimental economic triad [Mount and Reiter (1974), Smith (1982)].

---

[3] The experimental method as applied to economics continues to have its open-minded critics. A good example is Ariel Rubinstein (2001), who accepts the idea that experiments can help theorists protect themselves from misguided intuition. Rubinstein, however, points out that "we rely on our own integrity to such extent that economics (so I am told) is one of the only major academic professions that lacks a code of ethics .... It is hard to avoid the thought that the lack of clear standards in experimental economics and the burdens placed on experimental research procedures actually serve as barriers to entry into the field" (pp. 625, 627).

[4] The triad is a simplified version of that found in Mount and Reiter (1974) and Smith (1982).

ment that defines the human and natural environment (E); the institution or mechanism of exchange (I); and the actual behavior of the subjects (A). The environment includes basic economic endowments like preferences, technology, physical constraints, property rights, and information structure. The institution specifies the rules that aggregate and generate information and coordinate actions, and it outlines the rules of exchange and its consequences. Repeated exposure to the institution is common practice in the lab so that people have the opportunity to gain experience with the institution, new information, and their own mind to better understand their endowed or personal preferences. Given the environment, people send a message (B), which could be an auction bid or stated value to the institution. Based on the set of messages received, the institution then allocates resources and costs G given the known rules of exchange. Researchers then observe how people actually make choices in the lab or field, and how this behavior matches up with a specific performance criterion like Pareto efficiency (P).

Based on this triad, we categorize environmental economic experiments into two groups – *institutional and valuation*. Institutional experiments control the environment (E) to explore how alternative market and nonmarket mechanisms (I) affect the allocation of scarce resources. Evolving from informal games and role-playing, these experiments are now used to address the question of economic design, i.e., the efficient institutional design given administrative failure, public goods, externalities, asymmetric information, and incomplete markets. By far, institutional experiments dominate the experimental economic literature. In a different volume of this Handbook, Peter Bohm considers institutional experiments examining control issues in environmental policy.

In contrast, valuation experiments stand the experimental triad on its head [Coursey (1987)]. Now the researcher wants to control the *institution and actual behavior* through a design that generates predictable patterns of behavior. If a researcher wants people to sincerely reveal their preferences about a good or service, they can employ an exchange mechanism that is demand-revealing in theory, e.g., the uniform-price auction. If the goal is to create an upper and lower bound on potential values, one can design the lab environment to create incentives for people to either overstate their values or understate their preferences for the good.

The key is that the lab is flexible, the design is under the researcher's control, and the decisions are real. Real choices, albeit stylized, are another key to using the experimental method in valuation work. The common belief is that performance-based payoff systems produce behavior that more closely parallels real life or market behavior than flat-rate payoff systems or no payoff at all. Most economists are suspicious of hypothetical choices because by definition these decisions are not salient – people do not have an unqualified right to the corresponding rewards or punishment because they are hypothetical. Saliency is one of Smith's (1982) five sufficient conditions for a controlled economics experiment.[5] Bergstrom and Stoll (1989) make the case that hypothetical

---

[5] The other four conditions include nonsatiation, dominance (net benefits of participation are positive), privacy, and parallelism (behavior in one choice transfers to another similar choice, holding conditions constant).

choices are indeed salient if people get benefits from simply making a hypothetical choice; if they are altruists; or if they expect some reward based on their choice to come to them at some date in the future. While creative, it stretches things to argue that people always believe their answers will be translated in full to social policy, either today or in the future. It is also a stretch to presume that goodwill and altruism are one-to-one proxies for the rational choices people are presumed to be making about a hypothetical good.

The issue of saliency reveals that at its core, the experimental method is about *control* – the researcher wants to control institutions, endowments, incentives, and sometimes preferences, and then observe motivated economic behavior. This holds in general, not just for valuation work [see Harrison (1992)]. An experimenter should try to control for all the confounding factors in the design by holding $n - 1$ factors constant; and he should make the rewards significant enough so subjects are motivated to make rational decisions. The goal is to design experiments to avoid the classic problem of under-identification, in which two or more variables change at once, either in the lab's external environment or in the person's internal environment (e.g., preferences for more wealth versus preferences to be viewed as generous) so as to confound one's understanding of cause-and-effect. The loss of control implies that a researcher does not know whether unpredicted behavior is due to a weak theory or a poor experimental design, or both.[6]

But one researcher's gain of control can be another's loss of context. These researchers argue that it is these *confounding factors* (e.g., uncontrolled body language sent in face-to-face bargaining) that provide the rich economic context that motivates

---

If you relate this to the involuntary unemployment and credit rationing literatures, adverse selection says that one should not use a subject willing to work for such low wages because he is most likely going to shirk anyway. But defining the elements that *must* exist in an experimental design to satisfy each of these conditions is arguably a judgment call. Appeals to "common sense" and decrees of "sloppy designs" rest in many cases on the ability to measure whether subjects are making motivated choices or not, which can differ across people and context, in often subtle ways. A good example is the Kachelmeier and Shehata (1992) experiment that examined risk preferences over high stakes lotteries (three times their monthly wages) in China. They conclude that monetary incentives seem to induce a measurable response only under extremely high rewards; otherwise the level of reward seemed to make little difference.

And while spirited, these debates have yet to rise to the rank reported in the February 27th 1918 edition of the Cloquet *Pine Knot* [as quoted in Fahlstrom (1997, pp. 85, 86)]: "A couple of Finns who had evidently been pouring out (or rather pouring in) copious libations in honor of St. Patrick, got into a theological discussion in Osborne's saloon on Saturday afternoon last. One of them attempted to emphasize his remarks with a 10 pound cuspidor, the true inwardness of which, running down the face of his adversary, added nothing to his comeliness. Whereupon five of his countrymen joined in a fight and for a time the battle raged with great vigor .... Then Policeman Olin appeared, and selecting the cuspidor conversationalist ... he marched him off to the calaboose, where he passed the night. Sunday morning he awoke sober and penitent, and considering that he had been sufficiently punished, he was released with an admonition to be less emphatic in his discussions in the future."

[6] Some have argued that hypothetical surveys are *experiments* because they satisfy the sufficient conditions of a controlled microeconomic experiment [Bergstrom and Stoll (1989), Smith (1989)]. The term *choice experiment* has been used to describe work that uses hypothetical pairwise choices to estimate marginal values for a good.

real-world behavior. They point out that striving for complete control is self-defeating because it creates an economic environment that is too sterile, too abstract, too unreal, with no parallel in the real-world, and therefore generates subjects who are motivated by salient payoffs, but unmotivated by the context in which these payoffs are earned. The inspiration is that economic theory should be robust enough to explain actions in real-world social interactions that have copious contextual cues that occur simultaneously. In response, advocates of more control point out that too much context makes the experiment too much like an open-ended case study or descriptive naturalist observations. Experiments based on too many confounding factors and misidentified motivation yields no universal patterns based on first principles, which creates little ability to generalize beyond the specific case. One might even argue this approach is nonexperimental. The recommendation is that when examining such contextual studies one should note whether the method permits the conclusions that the author has made. A causal inference may have been made when the design does not allow such inference.

But this debate is not new. Fifty years ago, Harvard chemist James Conant (1951, p. 56) defined this deep-rooted conflict of control and context within a scientific discipline as *the degree of empiricism* – "the extent to which our knowledge can be expressed in terms of broad conceptual schemes." His notion characterized a discipline as falling along a continuum determined by the fraction of work in controlled hypothesis testing and contextual pattern recognition. Conant expands on the confluence of scientific experimentation and the "sooty empiric:"

> "About three centuries ago the trial-and-error experimentation of the artisan was wedded to the deductive method of reasoning of the mathematician; the progeny of this union have returned after many generations to assist the 'sooty empiric' in his labors. In so doing the applied scientist finds himself face to face with one of his distant ancestors, so to speak .... In those practical arts where the degree of empiricism is still high, men with the most advanced scientific training and using the latest equipment will often have to resort to wholly empirical procedures. On the one hand they will labor to reduce the degree of empiricism as best they can; on the other they must improve the art by using the knowledge and methods then at hand. In short, advances in science and progress in the practical arts today go hand in hand" (pp. 59–60).

Conant's remarks hold today for stated preference methods in valuation. Here the degree of empiricism is high. Nothing comparable to the theory of market efficiency exists in stated preference work that provides a mathematical basis for how a person's hypothetical intentions toward the environment translate into his actual actions (see Section 5.2). Hoehn and Randall's (1987) theory of value formation is the rare attempt to develop a theory that relates stated preference answers to valuation questions. They maintain that respondents are still rational and motivated but have imperfect information and incomplete optimization about the good in question. But the economics of hypothetical or unmotivated behavior has not been formulated into broad theoretical terms of general acceptance. That is why observing behavior under controlled conditions in the lab still matters. But we are dealing with people not protons, so there are degrees of control and the relevant decision is rarely either–or, but how much. We also need to understand why and how people react in the real-world environmental entanglement of markets, missing markets, and no markets.

The lab is the natural milieu to help reduce the degree of empiricism in this search. And the debate over control and context will continue on. What is *unique* to one researcher can be *bizarre* to another. The challenge is to find the "correct" balance of control and context to create an experimental design for an economic situation in which the experimenter is confident that people are motivated to do what they do for the reason she thinks they are doing it.[7] Searching for this correct balance arises because environmental economic experiments, especially valuation studies, lie at the intersection of three general areas of experimental research – traditional experimental economics that explicitly considers markets, standard experimental psychology that presume no markets, and environmental economics that acknowledges that markets are missing (see Figure 2).

Consider each area. Experimental economics usually examines the behavior of people within the context of an active exchange institution like the market. The market allows a rational person to exploit nonrational choices, which then helps to reinforce rational decision-making throughout the population. Psychological experiments usually focus on isolated individual behavior, and decisions made outside an exchange institution. Isolated choices are then compared to a benchmark model of rational choice (e.g., expected utility theory). Valuation experiments must confront the issue that people make decisions in both market and nonmarket settings, and that this interaction of exchange institutions could well affect the values that are elicited. This intersection of methods requires the researcher to explore all three literatures because they are intertwined in valuation work. The lab can be very helpful in pulling together and sorting out isolated and socialized choices and statements of value. The goal is to better understand how people make choices and form values given they make decisions both inside and outside of markets.

This recognition that valuation methods need input from many sources has forced many people interested in valuation to be quite pragmatic in their research style. They look for patterns, either deviations from standard rational choice theory or new, unexpected behavior that emerges, similar to experimentation in the life sciences [see, for example, Heath (1976), Hölldobler (1985)]. Pragmatism implies that methods and choices result from the workability of common sense rather than formal, predetermined rules of evidence.[8] Questions of method are answered by experience about what works

---

[7] Read the exchanges between Cummings, Brookshire and Schulze (1986) and the outside reviewers (e.g., Ken Arrow, Daniel Kahneman, Sherwin Rosen, Rick Freeman, Rich Bishop, Kerry Smith) during the state of the art assessment of the contingent valuation method. Design features Cummings, Brookshire and Schulze presented as a tool for control, others argued were simplistic and artificial [see Bishop and Heberlein (1986)].

[8] Economists who run experiments today can identify with linear programmers and econometricians from the past. Fifty years ago, an economist might need a day to run a regression or linear program given the limited capacity and computing power, especially if the run was done by hand in an auditorium packed with

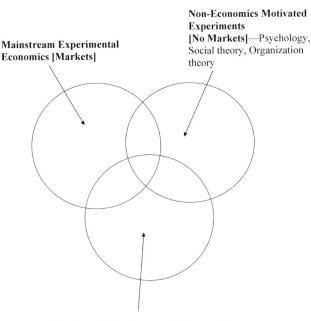

Mainstream Experimental Economics [Markets]

Non-Economics Motivated Experiments [No Markets]—Psychology, Social theory, Organization theory

Experimental Environmental Economics [Missing markets]: Risk, Conflict, Cooperation, Control, Valuation, and Prosperity

Figure 2. An intersection of experimental methods.

rather than on preconceived notions of methodological principles. And those economists who use the lab to study environmental economic phenomena learn to appreciate our ancestors who lived when pragmatism ruled. Limited capacity, time, and money imposed a discipline on those forerunners to identify and test the critical valuation questions.

Experimental economics demands the same discipline today. One identifies a phenomenon, designs an experiment, runs the treatments, and explores the restrictions that best organize observed behavior. Working along with theory and prior empirical information, experiments become habitual; another productive approach to discipline one's thinking about economics and valuation.[9] This chapter focuses on these valuation experiments. We consider how the experimental method has been used in valuation research

---

people using adding machines and passing slips of paper. Once the runs were complete, one either lived with the results or went through the process of collecting more funds for more time-consuming runs.

[9] Experimenters should be wary of the classic Hawthorne effect: the presence of monitors affects subjects' behavior, which then confounds results and makes interpretations untrustworthy. The effect is named for the episode at the Hawthorne plant of the Western Electric Company in Chicago when monitors were asked to track how job performance affected productivity. With the monitors watching over their workers' shoulder, they improved their job performance and productivity [Benson (1994)]. By explicitly looking for more productivity the monitors induced the productivity they were looking for. This concern over the self-fulfilling

over the past three decades, starting with methods to establish whether statements of economic value are rational as defined by traditional welfare economics.

3. Methods to establish rational valuation

Rational choice theory and welfare economics provide the traditional analytical foundation upon which conventional environmental valuation methods rest [see Mäler (1985), Freeman (1993)]. The presumption of rational choices made within active exchange institutions underpins the economic definition of value [Samuelson (1938)]. People are assumed to have core preferences that reflect what they want, which then they can articulate into monetary values. If a person's preferences satisfy well-defined axioms, his behavior can be modeled as if he is maximizing his well-being. One's stated preferences for changes in the level of environmental goods and services have purpose and meaning because they are grounded by a core set of preferences and a binding budget constraint.

But researchers have used laboratory experiments to challenge rational choice theory, and hence economic approaches to value the environment. Psychologists and economists have evidence of systematic deviations in behavior from the predictions of rational choice. Their experiments have revealed that behavioral anomalies abound when people confront risks similar to those emerging in environmental issues, like climate change. Classic examples include inconsistent preferences when choosing between risky and safer gambles [Allais (1953)]; extra aversion to risks that have ambiguous probabilities [Ellsberg (1961)]; and a systematic discrepancy between choosing and valuing alternative gambles, i.e., the preference reversal phenomenon [Lichtenstein and Slovic (1971)]. These anomalies, and many others, matter for the rational valuation of environmental protection because they undercut the internal validity of the cost–benefit estimates economists use to evaluate alternate protection strategies [see Machina (1987), Thaler (1992), Camerer (1995), Rabin (1998)].

Challenges to rational choice theory are threats to rational nonmarket valuation. If people do not follow rational choice theory, and instead make irrational or inconsistent choices or if values are momentary declarations, one becomes concerned that preferences and stated values are transient artifacts of context [see Tversky and Simonson (1993)]. And if uncontrolled or unmeasured contextual cues affect stated values, the challenge is to judge whether stated values represent some notion of "true" preferences. If stated values do not reflect preferences, economic behavior is unlikely to have the welfare-economic implications normally ascribed to choices and valuations. This threatens the validity of the cost–benefit estimates economists use to evaluate alternate

---

prophecy has also been called the "Pygmalion effect," named after the sculptor Pygmalion of Cyprus who fell in love with his own creation – an ivory statue of the ideal woman named Galatea. The goddess Venus eventually granted Pygmalion's prayers to bring Galatea to life, and the couple lived happily ever after. See, however, Jones (1992) who found little evidence of the Hawthorne effect in the original study.

policies, regardless of whether one is using experimental methods, market prices, or hypothetical surveys.

This section uses two examples to illustrate how the experimental method can be used to assess whether valuation is rational – the disparity between the willingness to pay (WTP) and the willingness to accept (WTA) compensation measures of economic value, and the case of preference reversals. These two examples illustrate the challenge in establishing whether valuation is based on rational choice theory.

3.1. The divergence between WTP and WTA

The experimental method has played a prominent role in addressing one of the most intriguing questions of rational valuation – the gap between WTP and WTA measures of value. Rational choice theory suggests that with small income effects and many available substitutes, the willingness to pay for a commodity and the willingness to accept compensation to sell the same commodity should be about equal [see Hanemann (1991)]. But evidence has accumulated over the past two decades that suggests that a significant gap exists between WTP and WTA. WTA exceeds WTP by up to tenfold.[10]

Since these value measures are used to help guide public policy decisions, the divergence raises questions about which measure to use in actual practice. If the decision is to conserve some environmental amenity, using a WTA measure could likely generate a significantly greater economic value for conservation than would a WTP measure – perhaps enough of a difference to tip the balance towards conservation. But if WTA is based on irrational or inconsistent behavior, its usefulness for policy can be questioned.

The first lab experiment to examine the WTP–WTA divergence was Knetsch and Sinden (1984). They asked subjects to value lottery tickets, in which the prize and price levels were selected to avoid wealth effects. The subjects were split into two groups – half were given a lottery ticket and then offered cash to sell the ticket. The other half was offered the chance to buy a ticket and play the lottery. Using identical money amounts, the percentage of people willing to pay differed significantly from the percentage of people willing to accept. This was taken as evidence that a gap existed between WTP and WTA. When participants were quizzed on how they would advise another person who faced the same situation, no significant difference was observed.

Coursey, Hovis and Schulze (1987) reconsidered the WTP–WTA question. They asked whether experience with an incentive compatible auction might remove the gap. While far from the acme of perfection, their experiment deserves attention because it was the first test of the WTP–WTA gap within an active lab exchange institution. Their challenge was to assess whether rational valuation should be defined as an individual or a social construct. Psychologists usually view rationality as an individual construct, whereas most economists view it as a social construct, in which active exchange institutions work to reinforce rational decisions.[11] The advantage of laboratory

---

[10] See the surveys by Cummings, Brookshire and Schulze (1986), and Horowitz and McConnell (2002).
[11] See Becker (1962), Nau and McCardle (1991), and Smith (1991).

experimentation over survey measures of WTP and WTA is that with repeated trials the subjects can learn about the market and the market-clearing price.

Students at the University of Wyoming were told about the "very bitter-tasting and unpleasant substance," sucrose octa-acetate (SOA), and the asked hypothetical questions about WTP and WTA values. Students then tasted a drop of the SOA and were asked to bid again. Monitors then tried to lower or raise the stated bids to determine what they called a semi-hypothetical iterative bid. Finally, the design used a modified version of the uniform price Vickrey (1961) auction to elicit the WTP and WTA values: a fifth-price auction with a veto rule. Here the four highest-bidders each bought one unit of a good and paid the fifth highest bid, provided none of the four winners vetoed the exchange.

In general, the Vickrey auction is incentive compatible, provided there is no veto rule. The auction is designed to induce people to sincerely reveal their private preferences for new goods and services. People have an incentive to tell the truth because the auction separates what they say from what they pay. Sincere bidding is the weakly dominant strategy. Underbidding risks foregoing a profitable purchase, whereas overbidding risks making an unprofitable purchase. Evidence from induced value experiments suggests the auction can produce efficient outcomes in the aggregate, although the average person tends to overbid [see Kagel (1995)]. The appeal of the auction for valuation work is that it is demand revealing in theory, relatively simple to explain, and it has an endogenous market-clearing price.

The veto rule changes the incentives of the auction, however, because no bidders are connected through the veto. Coursey, Hovis and Schulze's auction, therefore, is no longer incentive compatible, so the following results must be assessed with this knowledge. Their results suggest that while hypothetical bids displayed a large disparity, mean WTP and WTA bids converged with repeated exposure to the Vickrey auction environment. The convergence of the bids with market experience was argued to support received theory of rational choice – preferences were independent of initial endowments. This rational value convergence story, however, was weakened significantly by the observation that one outlier had a substantial effect on the average values [see Gregory and Furby (1987)].

Knetsch and Sinden's reply to Coursey, Hovis and Schulze revealed little deference for the iterative market explanation, and in fact hinted at the potential flaw with Vickrey with veto auction [see Harrison (1992)]. Knetsch then came back with a series of new experiments aimed at revealing why the divergence is a reality and not some transient artifact. First, Knetsch (1989) attributes the willingness to pay and willingness to accept to the *endowment effect* – people are less willing to surrender something they own compared to their eagerness to acquire something new. One of several experiments conducted by Knetsch consisted of giving half of the participants a candy bar and the other half of the subjects a coffee mug of approximately the same value. Subjects were then offered the opportunity to trade for the other commodity. Preferences for the mug over the candy bar varied from ten to eighty-nine percent depending purely on which commodity the person was given first. Other experiments by Knetsch offered similar results [see, for example, Borges and Knetsch (1998)].

The next influential paper was Kahneman, Knetsch and Thaler (1990), who report experimental evidence to support their idea of the *endowment effect* as why WTP diverges from WTA. The effect exists if people offer to sell a commonly available good in their possession at a substantially higher rate than they will pay for the identical good not in their possession (e.g., pens and coffee mugs). To illustrate the robustness of the effect, they used a Becker, DeGroot and Marschak (1964) mechanism to elicit preferences in the fifth treatment. Like the Vickrey auction, the BDM mechanism separates what people say from what they pay. A person's weakly dominant strategy is to state her true WTP or WTA. Unlike Vickrey, the BDM market-clearing price is exogenous. In addition, the BDM is with a single individual, not with a group as in the Vickrey auction. After collecting all bidding sheets from buyers and sellers, a market-clearing price was randomly selected from some distribution known by the subjects. A buyer willing to pay at least this market price bought the commodity; a seller willing to accept less than or equal to the price sold the commodity. The market price and buyers and sellers were then determined [also see Grether and Plott (1979)].

The results from the Kahneman et al. treatments make a case for the existence of a fundamental endowment effect – WTA exceeded WTP in all treatments over all iterations. People's preferences seemed to depend on initial endowments of resources, a violation of rational choice theory. The idea behind this psychological argument for the endowment effect is that people treat gains and losses asymmetrically – the fear of a loss weighs more heavily than the benefit from an equal gain. People who like the status quo demand relatively more to accept a change for the worse. Additional support for this view is found in MacDonald and Bowker (1994), who support the existence of an endowment effect based on the significance of perceived property rights on WTP for improved air quality versus WTA to forgo better air quality [also see Morrison (1998)].

In contrast, the lab valuation experiments of Shogren et al. (1994) observed no significant divergence between WTP and WTA for similar goods. They designed an experiment to test the proposition that given positive income elasticity and repeated market participation, WTP and WTA will converge for a market good with close substitutes (e.g., the candy bar and mugs) but will not converge for the nonmarket health risk with imperfect substitutes (risky sandwich). They also tested for whether transaction costs could explain the WTP–WTA gap by having a large supply of the market goods right outside the lab door that could be purchased by the subjects once the experiment was over. The results showed that WTP and WTA values did converge with repeated trials for candy bars and mugs – goods with many available substitutes; but that the values continued to diverge for the reduced health risks from safer food – one's health has little substitutes.

A key difference between the two experiments is that Shogren et al. used a Vickrey second-price auction with endogenous market-clearing price feedback. These results raise the question of whether the endowment effect is a fundamental part of choice or simply an artifact of a weak exchange environment. The weaker the exchange institution, the weaker the socialization of rational behavior and the stronger the potential hold of asocial anomalies on choice. If the objective is to elicit values for commodities in market-like settings that punish mistakes and reward good decisions, an exchange institution such as the Vickrey auction with repeated trials is appropriate.

The question is why the different results in the Kahneman, Knetsch and Thaler and Shogren et al. experimental designs? Was the difference is auction enough to cause a difference in values? Earlier lab work on alternative market institutions suggests that the answer might be "yes." But too many differences existed across the two experimental designs, however, to confirm or reject this suspicion by just looking at the existing data. In response, Shogren et al. (2001a) address this issue by designing an experiment to specifically address this mechanism-dependence question, in which the auction was the treatment. The thesis was that if it is the endowment effect that accounts for observed behavior, the effect should be observable and persistent for any mechanism used to elicit WTP and WTA, provided the mechanism is incentive compatible. They test this thesis by evaluating the impact of three auction mechanisms in the measurement of WTP and WTA measures of value for goods with close substitutes – the Becker–DeGroot–Marschak mechanism with random, exogenous price feedback, Vickrey's second-price auction with endogenous market-clearing price feedback, and a random nth-price auction with endogenous market-clearing price feedback [see Fox et al. (1998)].

The random nth-price auction combines elements of the Vickrey auction and the BDM mechanism, such that the market-clearing price is random but endogenously determined. Randomness is used to engage all bidders, and to reduce the incentive to fixate on any given price. A random nth-price auction works as follows: each bidder submits a bid (offer); each bid (offer) is rank-ordered from lowest to highest; the monitor selects a random number – the n in the nth-price auction, uniformly-distributed between 2 and n (n bidders); and in the WTP case, the monitor sells one unit of the good to each of the $n - 1$ highest bidders at the nth-price; in the WTA case, the monitor buys one unit each from the $n - 1$ lowest bidders and pays the nth-lowest bid.

Table 1 summarizes the design parameters in Kahneman, Knetsch and Thaler (1990), Shogren et al. (1994), and the new treatment. The experimental parameters are auctioned goods: a brand-name candy bar in stage 1 and an University coffee mug in stage 2; initial monetary endowment: $15 paid up-front; number of trials: ten trials per experiment, in which wealth effects were controlled by randomly selecting one trial to be binding; retail price information: none was provided; subject participation: voluntary students participants; number of subjects per session: 8–10 subjects in the second-price auctions and 20 for the BDM mechanism; and the three auction mechanisms.

The results from these new experiments show that initial bidding behavior in each auction did not contradict the idea of an endowment effect. Figure 3, for example, shows the ratio of mean WTA and WTP bids across trials and auctions for the university mug. We see that if it is an endowment effect that originally governs bidding, these results show that the effect can be eliminated with repetitions of a second-price or random nth-price auction. If the thesis is correct that an endowment effect should persist across auction mechanisms and across trials, these experimental results show that the case for

Table 1
Summary of experimental design parameters

	Original experimental designs		Shogren et al. (2001b)	
Design parameter	Original Kahneman, Knetsch and Thaler (1990)	Original Shogren et al. (1994)	New experiments	Random nth-price auction
Auctioned goods	Tokens, pens, and mugs	Candy bar, sandwich, and mugs	Candy bar and mugs	Candy bar and mugs
Initial monetary endowment	None	$3: candy bar $15: sandwich or mug	$15	$15
Number of trials	Varied between 3–7	5: candy bar 20: sandwich 10: mugs	10: candy bar 10: mugs	10: candy bar 10: mugs
Retail price information	Provided for some treatments	None provided	None provided	None provided
Subject participation	In-class	Voluntary	Voluntary	Voluntary
Number of subjects per session	Varied between 30 and 44	12 to 15	8–10: SPA 20: BDM	10: random nth-price auction
Auction institution	Simon Fraser U. Becker–DeGroot–Marschak mechanism (BDM)	Iowa State U. Second-price auction (SPA)	Iowa State U. Both the BDM and the SPA	U. Central FL Random nth-price auction

such a fundamental effect is open to challenge. Rutström (1998) also observed behavioral differences across incentive-compatible auctions. She detected WTP differences elicited in the BDM and Vickrey auctions.

3.2. Preference reversals

Expected utility theory is the cornerstone of modern decision making under risk, and consequently the cost–benefit analysis of environmental protection. The theory presumes that people are fairly sophisticated such that they can evaluate both old and new gambles consistently. Laboratory evidence emerged, however, which showed that many people *reverse their preferences*. A preference reversal is said to occur when a person's choices – a direct reflection of his preferences – between two options is inconsistent with the ranking of his buying/selling prices – an indirect reflection of his preferences. The preference reversal phenomenon contradicts the presumption that elicited preferences should be invariant to the elicitation method.[12]

---

[12] See, for example, Camerer's (1995) overview on procedural invariance and preference reversals.

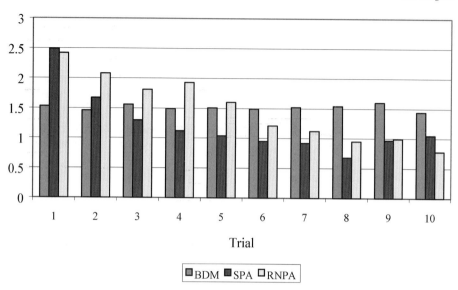

Figure 3. Ratio of mean WTA and WTP by auction (Mugs).

The preference reversal phenomenon is one of the best-documented violations of rationality.[13] Grether and Plott (1979), doubtful of the robustness of psychology experiments, ran their own economic experiments to explore whether economic incentives would stop this inconsistency. Their lab evidence, however, revealed a robust pattern of preference reversals, despite inducements like greater rewards, different presentations, training, and record keeping. The phenomenon has caused some observers to conclude that traditional valuation exercises and choice-based surveys are unreliable, and that economists need to channel resources to "develop new methods for valuing environmental resources" [Irwin et al. (1993)]. This is a serious charge because it implies that preferences for environmental protection are ephemeral, affected by poorly understood psychological contextual cues, and therefore of limited use in traditional cost–benefit analysis. If researchers who want to estimate the benefits of protection ask people their willingness to pay for lower risk, and people state values for this risk reduction that are inconsistent with their underlying preferences, researchers obtain no useful information with which to judge the benefits of alternate policies.

Consider a common example used to induces preference reversals. A monitor presents a person with some variation of the following pair of bets and asks him to choose one bet out of the pair:

Pbet: p chance of $\$X$ \$bet: q chance of $\$Y$
        $1 - p$ chance of $\$x$ $1 - q$ chance of $\$y$

---

[13] See, for example, Slovic and Lichtenstein (1983) and Tversky, Slovic and Kahneman (1990).

where $X > x$, $Y > y$, $p > q$, and $Y > X$. The subjects were then asked to value each bet by stating the maximum (minimum) they were willing to pay (accept) to buy (sell) the bet. A specific gamble commonly used is:

    Pbet: 35/36 chances to win \$4   and   1/36 chance to lose \$1,

    \$bet: 11/36 chances to win \$16   and   25/36 chances to lose \$1.50.

The two gambles have the same approximate expected value, \$3.86. Expected utility theory requires that the bet selected would also be the bet that was valued the highest. Usually around half the subjects from any given population violated this prediction by choosing the Pbet and assigning a higher value to the \$bet.

While preference reversals have caused some theorists to develop alternative models with nontransitive preferences over bets,[14] others have questioned its robustness for choices in market settings with nontrivial lotteries and arbitrage. Knez and Smith (1987), for example, challenged the robustness of the phenomenon with market trading and repeated responses. They found that in double auction asset trading, market values followed expected utility theory even if individual responses did not. Individual responses even approached rational behavior with repeated trials. In addition, Cox and Epstein (1989) found consistent preference reversals, but observed that by paying subjects for each gamble instead of randomly choosing one, subjects reversed symmetrically. Chu and Chu (1990) showed how arbitrage eliminates preference reversals quickly; Cox and Grether (1996) observed that the phenomenon tended to disappear with monetary incentives, immediate feedback, and repetition.

Consider three market tests in detail. Bohm (1994a, 1994b) and Bohm and Lind (1993) designed three field experiments to determine whether the robust laboratory results hold up in the field with (i) choice objects of nontrivial values, (ii) elicited bids or asks for real auctions, and (iii) engaged subjects who were engaged with the lottery. Bohm (1994a) used nontrivial real choice objects which the test subjects had revealed an interest in buying, and in which uncertainty was characterized by subjective probabilities and more than two outcomes [Bohm (1994a)]. Used cars (a Volvo and an Opel) were selected as an example of "nonlottery" objects whose performance (outcome) is uncertain. Two cars were bought – both priced at SEK (Swedish kronor) 8,000 or \$1,200 1990 U.S. dollars – to be sold at an auction, offered to some 2,000 students at Stockholm University. Twenty-six showed up, test drove the cars, checked inspection reports, and participated in a hypothetical second-price auction (of two bicycles) to make them more familiar with this type of auction. Given the reputations of the two cars, the Volvo bore some resemblance to a Pbet and the Opel to a \$bet. No preference reversals were observed – bids on the preferred car never fell short of bids on the other car.

Bohm and Lind (1993) challenge preference reversals by constructing an experiment that used real-world lotteries with more than two (7–12) levels of prizes and separated the subjects interested in buying lottery tickets from those who were not interested.

---

[14] See, for example, Karni and Safra (1987) and Fishburn (1988).

Student subjects choose between three options: (i) SEK 40 ($7 US dollars in 1991) in cash, (ii) an SEK 40 share of a package of $bet-type Swedish state lottery tickets, with the highest prize being SEK 1,000,000; and (iii) an SEK 40 share of a package of Pbet-type Swedish state lottery tickets, which had a highest prize of SEK 100,000. Both lottery options have expected payoffs of SEK 20 and at least seven prize levels. As a comparative benchmark to mimic earlier work, subjects were also asked to choose between lotteries that had similar expected values with smaller variance. Relative to the benchmark, subjects reversed preferences significantly less with real-world lotteries – 23 percent versus 73 percent.

Bohm (1994b) revisited the question of whether people reverse their preference when confronted with temporal choice, as suggested by Tversky, Slovic and Kahneman (1990). In hypothetical cases, some people are inconsistent in their choice of and values for claims redeemed at different future dates. For instance, a person's choices and values were inconsistent for a short-term claim of $1,600 received in 1.5 years versus a long-term claim of $2,500 received in 5 years. Short-term claims and long-term claims play a role similar to that of Pbets and $bets. Bohm tested the robustness of this hypothetical finding using real claims and subjects expected to be confronted with decisions of this type, here mid-level bank employees and third-year students in Finance. He observed that real claims reduced preference reversal rates to 15 percent from 62 percent in a benchmark hypothetical case.

But while "significant" incentive levels and real-world lotteries with more than two outcomes eliminate preference reversals, these institutions usually do not exist for most environmental goods. This leaves the debate about rational valuation far from over. Many environmental assets, for instance, lack well-defined exchange institutions. As a consequence, when people are asked to value improvements in the environment, researchers are uncertain as to whether they might continue to reverse preferences because the lotteries are less concrete and no arbitrage exist to discipline bad behavior.

But the distinction between market and nonmarket behavior is not binary. Most people make choices in both thick and nonexistent institutions in their daily decisions. The key question therefore is whether the rationality induced from arbitrage in a thick market could spill over to behavior in nonmarket choice. If markets make people reverse preferences less, could this induced rationality spill over to their choices in nonmarket settings?

Cherry, Crocker and Shogren (2003) address this question of whether the induced rationality from an arbitraged market could spill over to a second nonmarket choice that would otherwise promote preference reversals. They design a set of experimental treatments to test whether the rationality that markets induce can spill over to nonmarket settings involving isolated individuals, and whether any spillovers that occur are due to preference mutations or to a relaxation of constraints internal to the individual agent.

The experimental design simulates two simultaneous but independent settings – a market and nonmarket setting. The market setting arbitraged preference reversals, whereas the nonmarket setting did not. Treatments were combinations of three variations: (1) real versus hypothetical, (2) arbitrage versus no-arbitrage, and (3) money versus environmental. With *real* choices, subjects were endowed with money and participated in market transactions that affected their money balances and take-home earnings. *Hypothetical* choices did not involve money endowments or market transactions. *Arbitrage* choices identified preference reversals and extracted the potential rent from the irrational behavior. *No-arbitrage* choices left preference reversals uncontested. *Money* choices involved lotteries that had winnings and losses in monetary terms. *Environmental* choices have lotteries comprised of environmental states of the world, e.g., odds of seeing a grizzly bear in Yellowstone, the odds of viewing an eagle or osprey.

With arbitrage, rents from subjects who reversed their preferences were extracted in three steps. The market sold the least preferred/most valued lottery to the subject; next it traded the most preferred lottery for the least preferred lottery; and finally, it bought the most preferred/least valued lottery from the subject. The subject now owned neither lottery, and was left with only a hole is his pocketbook equaling the difference between the stated values for the two lotteries. Arbitrage began in round 6. They also ran a comparative benchmark treatment in which reversals were never arbitraged.

Figure 4 shows the fraction of preference reversals for the market-like gambles. We see the benchmark no-arbitrage treatment hovering around 25 to 30 percent preference reversals. Once arbitrage is introduced in round 6, we see the rate of preference reversals declines significantly in all three arbitrage-treatments. Rates fall until the reversals were nearly eliminated by round 15. This decline in irrationality is expected given previous work that showed how direct arbitrage eliminates reversals: when irrational choices cost money, people learn to be rational. The question is whether this learned rationality could spill over to the choices in the nonmarket setting.

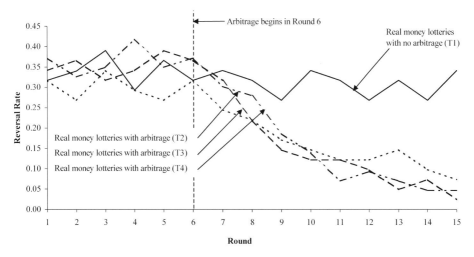

Figure 4. Preference reversal rates in the market setting.

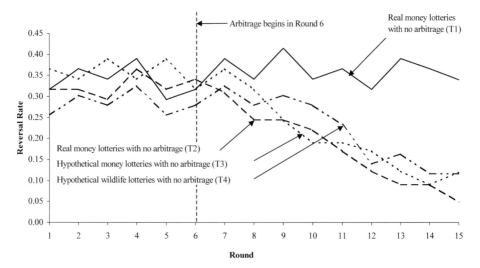

Figure 5. Preference reversal rates in the nonmarket setting.

Figure 5 shows that in fact it does – a rationality spillover exist. Figure 5 depicts behavior in the nonmarket setting, which were choices over lotteries made simultaneously
with the market setting. There was no arbitrage in the nonmarket setting. Nevertheless,
after arbitrage was introduced in the *other*, marketlike setting in round 6, preference
reversals also declined in the nonmarket setting. Figure 5 shows that the percentage of
reversals in the nonmarket setting declines over the rounds, even though no direct arbitrage took place, the nonmarket choices were hypothetical, and the lotteries became
wildlife experiences in Yellowstone National Park. Subjects were apparently taking
what they leaned in the market setting, which included arbitrage, and applying it in
the nonmarket setting, which did not include arbitrage. People learned that preference
reversals can come at cost, and they transferred this lesson to the nonmarket context,
even though it did not matter to their pocketbook. Arbitrage is a powerful factor on
choices and values.

The next question they asked is whether the people who stop reversing preferences do
so by altering their preference ordering, or by changing their stated values for the gambles. The evidence suggests that preference reversals decrease not because the person's
preferences changed for risky lotteries, but rather because his stated values decreased.
Preferences seemed to hold in tact, people just revised downward their stated value for
the riskier lotteries. One could argue that this is good news for valuation work in that
preferences are not on some unstable pinwheel fluttering wildly in any new context, but
rather people simply overestimated the price the market would pay for a risky lottery.[15]
People make these adjustments all the time when they try to buy low and sell high.

[15] Cherry and Shogren (2005) explored whether the rationality impact of arbitrage extended to a set of diverse
decision-making tasks over preferences for gambles. Their results suggest that arbitrage in one setting can

This rationality spillover result raises a question about future research in nonmarket choice and rational valuation: how much effort should we allocate between trying to explain biases in behavior versus developing active exchange institutions that induce rationality spillovers which tempers these biases? Currently many economists proceed as if the rational choice paradigm unequivocally holds for nonmarket choices (e.g., the random utility model) despite considerable evidence that many people make biased and inconsistent decisions in these settings. Accordingly, the rationality spillover results suggest that additional effort spent on developing parallel market and nonmarket exchange institutions that generate the rationality spillovers that keep *homo economicus* intact might be worth the cost. If such lab methods cannot be developed, we might need to develop further a theory of value unaffected by institutional discipline that is more applicable to "irrational" behaviors.

3.3. Synopsis on rational valuation

Standard models of nonmarket valuation presume people make rational choices and reveal consistent values for environmental protection (e.g., household production theory, Hicksian surplus measures). But enough evidence of behavioral anomalies now exists to undercut this presumption of rational choice for people isolated from the repeated give and take with others in an exchange institution [see, for example, Hey and Orme (1994)]. And since exchange institutions do not exist for environmental assets, a person can act as if his value expressions will go uncontested; he is asocial, and need not be accountable to others. Unless one presumes he is a perfect image of an anonymous competitive market that is broad in scope, he may lack the incentives to act in accordance with the utility maximization paradigm and provide the rational valuation one would expect. Without an exchange institution to arbitrage his irrational choices, the unsocialized person can engage in behaviors inconsistent with the paradigm. Unsocialized people fail to exploit existing gains from trade *and* engage in behaviors that allow others to exploit these gains [see Akerlof (1997), Crocker, Shogren and Turner (1998)].

The lab work on WTP–WTA and the preference reversals illustrates that it is difficult to dismiss as irrelevant the wide range of observed behavioral anomalies. The work also reveals a fundamental difference in conviction about what rational economic valuation means. This difference in conviction underlies the under-debated inconsistency in the valuation literature. At issue is whether one chooses to believe that rational choice is a property of the individual alone or within the social and economic context within which it is embedded. This is a key difference between the debate between the psychology and economic worldview toward rational choice, and the ongoing discussion about which view should dominate how we do research on valuing the environment.

---

crossover to affect choices over unrelated tasks: stated values for safer food dropped by 20 to 50 percent, and the frequency of the Allais paradox falls by half. But as expected, the frequency of the more distinct Ellsberg paradox remained the same. They also found that the type of arbitrage, real market-like experience or a simple oral description, did not affect the results.

Some researchers with a foot in the psychological camp suggest that we should be interested in "what is in people's minds, pure and simple." If one believes that researchers should measure what is in a person's mind, one could argue that it is acceptable to test economic rationality of people isolated from interactive experience in social exchange institutions. This view might argue that auctions, which are relatively free from any information that would make a person aware of a broader social view, are the most useful demand-revealing tool. For instance, a market-clearing price selected at random does not provide information to the bidder; it is an uninformative number that separates those who pays from those who do not. Advocates of rationality as conscious cognition could then argue that anomalies like the endowment effect matter for valuation.

This viewpoint suggests that much more attention should be devoted to understanding the cognitive processes at work in choice and valuation (see Chapter 18 in this Handbook by Baruch Fischhoff). The danger here is that the economists who venture into this cognitive minefield alone will end up fifty years behind the psychologist's times.[16] In fact, most economic models that attempt to generalize the classic expected utility model do so by adding a needed degree of freedom to explain otherwise unexplainable behavior. The process is to insert an "emotional adder" into the theoretical preference, such as envy, regret, disappointment, malice, and anticipatory feelings, which can then extend the reach of the model [see, for example, Brennan (1973), Sugden (1993), Caplin and Leahy (2001), Grant, Kajii and Polak (2001)]. But this gradualist approach to emotional degrees of freedom begs the question as to why add just one emotion – why not several at once if the goal is to more accurately capture the cognitive process at work? One reason might be that few economists probably feel equipped to try and explain restriction on the cross-partial derivative of multiple emotions, say envy and disappointment, or malice and anticipation.

As an alternative, one could choose to work from idea that choices placed in the social context of an active exchange institution are the most informative for economic valuation. This view would argue that tests of economic rationality should not be separated from the interactive experience provided by an exchange institution. Institutions matter because experience can make rational choice transparent to a person – probably the key rediscovery made over three decades of experimental economics research [see, for example, the theory and examples in Plott (1996)]. Asking that choices be made within a social exchange institution, such as second-price and random nth-price

---

[16] Harrison (1992, p. 1441) makes the point with more aplomb: "the analysis of financially unmotivated behavior can be left to those most equipped intellectually to handle it: psychologists .... We arguably have no useful business fussing around in an attempt to make sense out of unmotivated behavior." But Harrison's message can be pushed too far for some aspects of environmental protection. Most environmental goods exist outside the market but along side others goods bought and sold in a market. It is an empirical question whether the emotive preferences for the environment affect or are affected by the rational preferences for wealth and durables. Environmental economists need to confront the mix of transaction modes that people actually operating in when asked to value environmental protection. It is unclear exactly how "motivated" or "unmotivated" people really are within this mix. It is an empirical question that must be tested in environmental that have markets, missing markets, and no markets (recall Figure 2).

auction, in which market prices signal the broader social context is what separates an economics experiment from a psychology experiment. One who supports rationality as a social construct can argue that a result like the endowment effect is not robust when confronted by the social context of an active exchange institution.[17]

Both the psychological and economic perspectives can have an important place in understanding how people make choices and state values, depending on the degree market pressure. One can argue that contact with people making similar decisions helps put in context the economic maxim that choices have consequences. Before one rejects economic rationality as too thin to explain the WTA and WTP gap or preference reversals, one should give the theory the best chance to succeed by testing it within the context that it was motivated – choice within a social exchange institution. The open question is how to make this economic interaction operational for real public goods. The rationality spillover results in Cherry, Crocker and Shogren (2003) suggest that a dynamic environment may be a necessary condition. Repeated exposure to competition and discipline was needed to achieve rationality. In becoming rational, people refined their statements of value to better match their preferences. This suggests that efforts to harness the rationality spillover phenomenon could be worth more attention in nonmarket valuation research, especially when trying to value changes in risky events that defines environmental protection (e.g., climate change, biodiversity loss). A design that uses interactive Web-based surveys that exploit the power of rationality spillovers could impose more discipline on rational behavior than the typical one-shot questionnaire. How exactly to move the active exchange institutions in the lab into the field in a meaningful way remains an open question worthy of more research.

4. Methods to measure values

We start by examining how the experimental method has been used to directly measure the value of public and private goods, both in the lab and the field. These experiments create unique exchange institutions to elicit values for real goods and services, some with the intention of improving the nature of hypothetical surveys. Lab valuation offers an alternative to hypothetical surveys to elicit values for new products. These experimental markets are actual markets selling goods to people, usually within a stylized setting. The experimental method works to understand, isolate and control how different auctions and market settings affect values, in a setting of replication and repetition. Experiments with repeated market experience provide an environment that allows a person to learn whether sincere revelation of his or her true preferences should be his or her best strategy given the institutional setting.

---

[17] Some observers argue a person's interaction with a market will affect the preferences the researcher is trying to measure. The notion is that markets do more than just allocate resources, they also affect the "evolution of values, tastes, and personalities" [Bowles (1998, p. 75)]. This viewpoint suggests that if the idea is to use social interaction through markets to keep consistent preferences reigned in, the researcher might instead be changing the nature of these preferences by exposure to the market.

4.1. Experiments valuing public goods

Since many environmental services are public goods – goods that are nonrival and nonexcludable in consumption – it is not surprising that the first use of the experimental methods to elicit values focused on real-world public goods. The early work was in direct response to the claims by some economists that the best approach available was to ask well-structured hypothetical questions about the willingness to pay (WTP) for the public good. Early experiments challenged the claim that these hypothetical valuation statements were good enough approximations even in the face of incentives to distort, or not carefully consider, responses to hypothetical questions.

Bohm's (1972, 1984) real-world valuation studies of deliverable, nontrivial public goods are the seminal experiments. These two studies addressed whether incentives to misrepresent WTP produce strong free-rider behavior when WTP for public goods is elicited in the field, and whether combinations of simple, non-truth-revealing mechanisms could attain verifiable approximations useful for actual demand estimation. Consumers knew that the provision of the public good depended on whether their aggregate WTP exceeded production costs, and if the goods were produced, they would pay according to the predetermined payment rules.

In addition, the monitor told participants about the various arguments likely to appear in a public elicitation process. The goal was to mimic a public decision making process in which people had time to discuss the issues with others and would be likely to have heard the media examine the issues and possibly argue in favor of a particular kind of "voting" behavior. Given this objective, attempts were made in the tests to reveal the principal arguments likely to be exposed in such a process and their implications for information about the incentives confronting the respondents.[18]

In Bohm (1972), a random sample of the inhabitants in Stockholm was asked to participate in a new type of TV rating. Bohm initiated and designed the experiment, which was then run as the Swedish public TV company. Subjects were asked to assign a money value to a new program they could watch if their aggregate WTP were high enough to cover costs. This was in 1969 – TV was still exciting in Sweden; the new program was expected to attract wide interest.

Subjects summoned to the premier of a TV program with well-known features and quality were divided into six groups. Subjects in the first five groups were told that if their aggregate stated WTP exceeded a certain cost of showing them the program, they would be given the opportunity to watch the program, prior to which each person would have to pay:

---

[18] Although it is difficult to speculate on the nature of an equilibrium state of such information, it was presumed that certain incentives to misrepresent WTP would be widely known and talked about, and that the organizers of the "referendum" would try to counter these incentives by referring to the "duties" of citizens participating in this kind of public process or the meaninglessness of conducting "referenda" of this type if voters gave in to such incentives. Bohm's dialogue with his subjects can be interpreted as an early attempt at what is now called "cheap talk," which is discussed in Section 5.2.

Group I: The WTP stated.
Group II: A percentage (as explained) of the WTP stated.
Group III: The WTP stated or a percentage (as explained) of the amount stated or 5 kronor or nothing, all four with equal probability.
Group IV: 5 kronor, the current average price of a cinema ticket.
Group V: Nothing; taxpayers would foot the bill.

Groups I and II, and those in group IV whose WTP fell short of 5 kronor, were exposed to incentives to understate WTP; group V, and those in group IV whose WTP exceeded 5 kronor, were exposed to incentives to overstate WTP. With a dominating number of WTP statements above 5 kronor in group IV (as turned out to be the case), this group can be taken to offer an overstated mean WTP. There were no clear misrepresentation incentives for group III.

Two key results emerged. First, Bohm observed no significant differences between mean WTP in these five groups. This suggests that there were no signs of strong free-rider behavior; the same order of magnitude of true aggregate WTP could have been elicited using any of the five approaches. Second, subjects in the sixth group (VI[h], h for hypothetical) were asked to "estimate in money how much you think watching this program would be worth to you" without indicating whether the program would be shown or whether their responses could have an effect on such a decision. Comparing mean WTP responses to this hypothetical question with the pool of the responses to the five nonhypothetical questions [Bohm (1994a, 1994b)], a Kolmogoroff–Smirnov test showed a difference at the five percent level of significance, i.e., the hypothetical version tended to give an overstatement of the WTP. We return to the question of hypothetical bias in Section 4.1.

In Bohm (1984), the public good was an information package that could only be made available by the government, while the decision to produce the package was to be determined by the actual consumers. In 1982, a Swedish government committee investigating potential operational demand criteria for deciding whether or not to produce costly statistics allowed one particular statistical investment project (providing access to information about certain attributes of housing in Sweden) to be determined by the *interval method*. If the interval containing the true aggregate or average WTP is small enough, it effectively replaces a true WTP; if large, the output decision is referred back to the politicians.

Potential consumers were identified as the 279 local governments in Sweden. The governments were then randomly split roughly into two groups, A and B. If the good were to be provided, people in group A would pay a percentage of the WTP stated such that the mean payment equaled per capita costs of the project. In contrast, members of group B who stated a WTP of at least SEK 500 would pay a fixed fee of SEK 500 (in 1982, about $100), while those stating a WTP below SEK 500 would be excluded from access to the service. The mean responses from these two groups estimated a lower and an upper bound to the true mean WTP, since group A had incentive to under-report, whereas group B had incentive to over-report.

The results indicate that regardless of the two alternative designs of the WTP interval, the natural decision was to have the public good produced. Of the 279 local governments, 274 responded and all of the 130 respondents who qualified for consumption of the good paid the charges. The results reveal a small direct WTP interval – about 7% of the interval midpoint, and a "95% confidence interval" of 38%, 8/9 of which exceeded the cost figure.

The next prominent use of the experimental method to value a public good was Brookshire and Coursey (1987). The nonmarket good in this case was the density of trees in a city park in Fort Collins, Colorado. The objective was to compare and contrast values obtained from hypothetical elicitation methods with values obtained in a market setting. The study consisted of three parts: a hypothetical contingent valuation (CV) study, a field study using the Smith auction (defined shortly), and a lab experiment with the Smith auction.

An artist created a series of pictures depicting different tree densities in the park. A door-to-door CV survey was conducted in which interviewers asked citizens of the community how much they would be willing to pay (or accept in compensation) for an increase (decrease) in the number trees in the park. Each interviewer carried the artist's renditions of what the park would look like under various different tree densities, either an increase from 200 to 225 or 250 trees or a decrease from 200 to 175 or 150 trees. Citizens did not pay anything.

Brookshire and Coursey (1987) then blended elements of a Smith auction process into their field experiment. The Smith auction has been tested in the lab [Smith (1980)]. The results suggest people on average reveal their true induced preferences for public goods – this "on average" is weak if individual incentive compatibility is the goal, but could arguable be tolerable if efficient provision is the target. The auction collects bids from people. If aggregate bids do not exceed costs to produce the public good, the good is not provided. But if aggregate bids are not less than the cost, each respondent is asked to pay a proportionally scaled-back amount of their bid. People then vote on whether they agree to the price and quantity of the good to be provided. Unanimity is required – one "no" vote kills the process.[19] Brookshire and Coursey did not use the unanimity rule in their field test.[20]

Brookshire and Coursey then examined valuation in the lab with a repeated market-like structure and nonhypothetical transactions. Five trials of the Smith auction were conducted, in which people privately submitted WTP bids or WTA offers. If the subjects' bids cover the actual cost of providing additional trees, they paid their adjusted bid. The payments were contributed to the Fort Collins recreation department. The divergence between WTA and WTP declined to five-to-one in the lab experiments,

---

[19] Note that Banks, Plott and Porter (1988), however, showed that unanimity actually decreases the efficiency of the Smith auction because the rule cause people to lose money.
[20] During the same time period, Bennett (1983) emulated Bohm's work, using a variant of the Smith auction both for a real public good, the communal viewing of a film.

considerably smaller than the 75-1 difference in the contingent valuation study. Unfortunately, these WTP–WTA comparisons are easily challenged since the two value measures were inconsistently defined.

4.2. Experiments valuing private risks

Few attempts have been made to use the lab to value directly some private good associated with environment protection. The reason is the difficulty to deliver the private good in the lab, due to the costs. Lab valuation of private goods has primary focused on new food products or processes [see the pioneering work in Menkhaus et al. (1992) and Hoffman et al. (1993)]. The private-good lab work most closely relates to environmental protection is the experiments to value health risk reductions, as created by foodborne pathogens [see Hayes et al. (1995)]. While one might ask what foodborne illness has to do with endangered species or climate protection, the lessons learned about how people value reductions in low probability/high severity risks have implications for environmental protection. Like environmental hazards, pathogens pose risks to people. Understanding how people value reductions in risks to life and limb remain a critical part of the valuation question.[21] Lab experiments can address basic questions about how context of exchange affect people's values for risk reduction in controlled settings. The goal is to understand how actual people react to the consequences of deliverable real risks, and valuing reduced pathogen risks provides a useful case study.

Consider the Hayes et al. (1995) experimental auction market for reduced risk from foodborne pathogens. Hayes et al. construct an experimental auction market to elicit the value of risk reduction. The experimental markets elicit the option price measures of value for five food-borne pathogens – *Campylobacter, Salmonella, Staphylococcus aureus, Trichinella spiralis,* and *Clostridium perfringens.* They also ran six treatments to explore how people responded to changes in the risk of illness holding the illness constant. All experiments use money, real food, repeated opportunities to participate in the auction market, and full information on the probability and severity of the food borne pathogen. Subjects ate the food before leaving the lab.

Performed at a meat-testing lab at Iowa State University, the experimental design followed a two stage procedure – first, a pre-auction with candy bars introduced people to Vickrey's second-price auction. Second, two types of food were introduced, a regular good with the typical odds of being contaminated with a foodborne pathogen, and the same good stringently screened for pathogens with a low probability (1 in 100 million) of illness. Over twenty trials, the second-price auction elicited bids to upgrade to the stringently controlled food from the regular good. After trial 10, information was revealed about the objective odds and severity.

Figure 6 summarizes the average bidding behavior. Three results emerged. First, subjects underestimate the annual probability of becoming ill from a food-borne pathogen,

---

[21] See the Handbook Chapter 20 by W. Kip Viscusi and Ted Gayner on risk assessment and management.

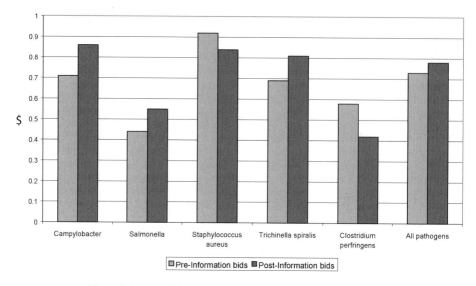

Figure 6. Average bid to exchange risky sandwich for riskless sandwich.

a result inconsistent with earlier observations on other health risks. Second, the stated values were not robust to changes in the relative risk levels of the five pathogens. Values are fairly constant across pathogens, even given a wide range of risks. Third, examining how people respond to increases in the probability of illness, holding the severity of the illness constant, showed that the marginal option price decreases as risk increases. This observation is consistent with the hypothesis that people will pay more to eliminate the last bit of a risk than they will pay for an equal decrease that still leaves them facing a substantial risk.

The use of the lab to elicit values for reduce risk raises several questions of experimental method. Consider five.

4.2.1. Does the unique lab environment inflate values?

The observed premium paid in the Hayes et al. experiments exceeded the expectations of some experts about what people would pay in a real retail market. One explanation might be the novelty of the experimental experience. These auctions are a novel, one-time experience. The concern is that people might be experimenting with their bids by overbidding because the costs of doing so are low.

Theory suggests an alternative explanation for the observed high price premia in the lab – the novelty of the good. Many bidders have never experienced the goods up for auction, e.g., reduction in risks due to some specified or unspecified technology. Here theory says that a bid should reflect two elements of value – the consumption value of the good and the information value of learning how the good fits into his or her preference set [Crocker and Shogren (1991)]. Preference learning would exist if people bid large amounts for a good because they wanted to learn about an unfamiliar good they had not previously consumed, because it was unique, or because it was unavailable in local stores.

Shogren, List and Hayes (2000) tested these two competing explanations by auctioning off three goods that vary in familiarity – candy bars, mangos, and irradiated pork, in four consecutive experimental auctions over two-weeks. The experimental design followed other private good valuation experiments – second-price auction, repeated trials, posted market-clearing prices. The only difference was that the subjects came back to the lab after several days to let the novelty of the lab experience wear off. The results strongly support the hypothesis that preference learning can explain the high price premia. No statistical change in bids was measured for candy bars and mangos, whereas the price premia for irradiated pork dropped by 50 percent over the four sessions. These findings suggest that people benefit from the information they gain about how an unfamiliar good fits into their preference ordering.

4.2.2. How do posted prices affect bidding behavior?

Lab valuation exercises use multiple trials with posted market prices to provide experience to bidders who walk into these auctions cold. The information sent by a posted market price can help bidders learn about the market mechanism and the upper support of the valuation distribution. But concerns have been raised that market experience "contaminates" bids as posted prices turn independent private values into affiliated private values, especially if people are unfamiliar with the good up for sale [Harrison, Harstad and Rutström (1995)].[22] List and Shogren (1999) explore this possibility by examining panel data from over forty second-price auctions with repeated trials.

Three results emerged. The market price affects bidding behavior for unfamiliar products, as implied by affiliated private values; the price effect dissipates when bidders receive nonprice information about the good or are familiar with the product before entering the lab; and evidence of strategic behavior independent of any price signal still exists. Buyers start bidding low and sellers start offers high, and then bids quickly stabilize after 1 or 2 trials. These results suggest posted prices can influence bidding behavior for unfamiliar products, but the effect dissipates when people have nonprice information about the good or are familiar with the good. The results have two implications for lab valuation research: the affiliation of private values can be reduced, if not removed, by providing product information prior to bidding, and a few trials help people learn about the market mechanism.

4.2.3. How does external information affect bidding behavior?

In many environmental controversies (e.g., climate change), the public has had to decide between assertions about levels of risks made by environmental and industry advocacy

---

[22] Affiliation exists when one bidder who values the good highly increases the chance that other bidders will also put a high value on the good.

groups, government officials and scientific experts. The assertions seem at odds to the general public. The experimental method is well-suited to explore how contradictory information affects valuation. One example is the study by Fox, Hayes and Shogren (2002) on the demand for reducing health risk from food through irradiation. They explore how favorable and unfavorable information on irradiation affects WTP to control the food-borne pathogen *Trichinella* in irradiated pork. Using literature currently available to the public, the favorable description emphasizes the safety and benefits of the process; the unfavorable description stresses the potential risks.

Using a random sample of 200 households obtained from a commercial survey company, eighty-seven primary food shoppers were recruited to participate in what was described only as a "consumer economics experiment" in return for a payment of $40.00. Following the experimental design used in earlier work, Fox et al. elicit WTP values in a repeated-trial, second price auction in which the binding trial is chosen at random. They used this feature to examine the adjustment in WTP values that follows the introduction of new information when all participants start from a common informational baseline.

The surprising result is that when Fox et al. presented both positive and negative information at the same time, people were alarmists – the negative information clearly dominated the demand for risk reduction (see Figure 7). This was true even though the source of the negative information was identified as being a consumer advocacy group and the information itself was written in a nonscientific manner. They re-ran this particular experiment four times to ensure that the result was robust, and it was. Negative reports concerning irradiation had a larger impact on participant preference and values than positive reports – even when the negative reports were unscientific [also see Viscusi (1997)]. This asymmetric response to pro and con information can be explained by several theories, including loss aversion, status quo bias, aversion to

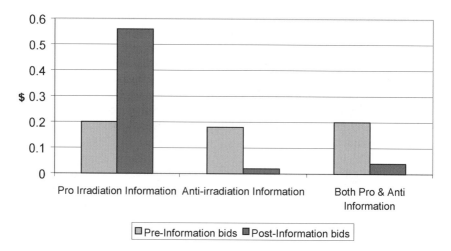

Figure 7. Average bid to exchange meat for irradiated meat before and after information.

ambiguity, and Bayesian updating. Which theory best organizes alarmist reactions to new information is an open question.

4.2.4. How do lab choices compare to retail market behavior?

Lab experiments are designed to introduce new price and nonprice information and then observe the subsequent changes in bidding behavior. But people still know that they are being monitored in a stylized setting, and the range of alternative purchases is more limited than in a retail setting. Shogren et al. (1999) compare the similarity of lab valuation choices to retail store choices for risk reduction. They also compare choices made in hypothetical surveys. All subjects came from the same small college town and made choices between typical chicken breasts versus chicken breasts irradiated to reduce the risk of food-borne pathogens.

Figure 8 shows that the results from both the survey and experimental market suggested significantly higher levels of acceptability of irradiated chicken than in the retail trial at an equal or discounted price for irradiation. Consumer choices were more similar across market settings at a price premium for irradiation. They observed that in a mail survey and a lab experiment, both of which included information about irradiation, 80 percent of participants preferred irradiated to nonirradiated chicken breasts when they were offered at the same price. When the irradiated product was offered at a higher price, the survey and experimental results predicted market share in a subsequent retail trial remarkably well. About thirty percent of survey respondents, experimental market participants, and shoppers were willing to pay a 10 percent premium for the irradiated chicken, and fifteen to twenty percent were willing to pay a 20 percent premium [also see the in-store experimental method used in Lusk et al. (2001)].

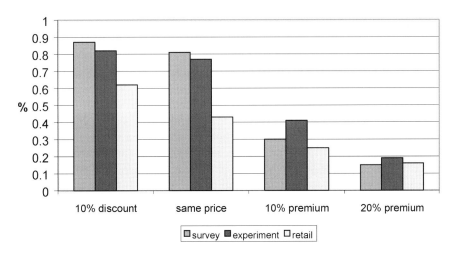

Figure 8. "Yes" to stated price for irradiated chicken (percent).

While differences in choices across institutions were observed in Shogren et al. (1999), each of the three decision settings involved unique features and incentives that were absent from the other two settings. Retail purchases involved payment of real money for real products within an environment where thousands of products competed for the consumer's dollar. Any attempt to collect consumer information in a retail setting was liable to interfere with the realism of the market itself. The goal of the retail setting was to establish the most realistic baseline possible against which one could judge the lab or survey. In contrast, while the experiments also required exchange of real money for real goods, the participants knew they are being monitored and the range of alternative purchases was limited. The survey involved hypothetical decisions, information about irradiation, and people knew that they would not be held accountable for choices they made. Perfectly simulating a retail experience in the lab or a survey so as to control every nuance is unattainable. Rather the goal should be to compare lab and survey choices relative to a real world baseline. The research program that emerges for future work is to explore how comprehensive the lab or survey environments must be to come closer to replicate an actual market outcome.

4.2.5. Does the risk reduction mechanism matter?

People protect themselves from environmental risk through self-protection and self-insurance. They self-protect by curtailing pollution to lower the likelihood that bad states of nature occur; they self-insure by changing production and consumption decisions to reduce the severity of a bad state if it does occur [Ehrlich and Becker (1972)]. Risk is endogenous. Self-protection and self-insurance jointly determine risks and the costs to reduce them. And since private citizens have the liberty to adapt on their own accord, a policy maker must consider these adaptive responses when choosing the optimal degree of public mitigation of risk [Shogren and Crocker (1991)]. Otherwise, policy actions are more expensive than need be with no additional reduction in risk.

The question is whether risk reduction mechanisms, alone or in combination, affect the value of reduced risk. Shogren and Crocker (1994) designed a set of experimental auctions of sequential substitution between private and collective self-protection or self-insurance. The goal was to reveal implicit preferences for alternative risk reduction mechanisms. The first hypothesis they examined was whether valuation was independent of the sequencing of the private and collective mechanisms. In an early experiment, people preferred private reduction to collective in the single mechanism markets [Shogren (1990)]. This preference could remain in the multiple mechanism markets regardless of the sequence of the private or collective auction. The second hypothesis was whether people preferred self-protection to self-insurance. Theory suggests that self-protection that guarantees no risk should be preferred to self-insurance.

The experiment constructed private and collective risk reduction mechanisms by combining two auctions for self-protection and self-insurance. The private auction is a Vickrey sealed bid, second price auction where the highest bidder secures the 100% risk reduction and pays the highest losing bid. The Vickrey auction has been promoted as a possible elicitation device for contingent valuation because of its well-known preference-revealing properties. The collective auction was a modified Smith (1980) sealed bid auction, in which the cost to reduce risk equaled the sum of the subjects' expected consumer surplus. Costs were not public information. If the sum of collective bids exceed the costs of provision, the mean collective bid was posted as the reigning price. Unanimity was required such that any one subject could veto collective risk reduction, which in retrospect probably reduced efficiency [see Banks, Plott and Porter (1988)]. Collective reduction was also rejected if the summed bids were less than costs.

Shogren and Crocker's results suggest the combined risk reduction mechanism matters to valuation, but not as much as when the mechanisms are separated. When private reduction was available prior to collective action, people place a greater value of the private action. But if private action was accessed after collective action, values were independent of the action. They also rejected the hypothesis that self-protection was valued more highly than self-insurance. Di Mauro and Maffioletti (1996) confirmed this result, finding no evidence that the mechanisms constitute a "frame."

In contrast, Shogren (1990) found that the mechanism used to reduce risk mattered; reducing risk by altering the probability or severity of an undesired event through a private or a collective mechanism generated significantly different values.[23] Generally, the upper bound on value was the private reduction of the probability of an undesired event; the lower bound was the collective reduction of severity. The preference for a mechanism occurred for several reasons including the sense of personal control, the marginal productivity, and whether the odds or severity are altered.

Finally, Kask et al. (2002) found evidence in a contingent valuation survey on valuing reduced risks from dioxin that people had a clear preference for the reduction mechanisms. Nearly everyone avoided the collective insurance approach. About 40 percent of the subjects preferred the collective protection approach to all others. But in the mortality sample, private approaches were slightly more preferred to collective approaches. Overall, the results say that people do prefer both the level of risk reduction and how the risk is reduced, but the results are sensitive the economic context.

4.3. Synopsis on direct valuation

As a complement to traditional tools like econometrics, hedonics, and contingent valuation, experimental methods directly applied to questions of valuation in the field and the lab continue to develop into useful tools for eliciting consumer values for real decisions in a controlled environment. They entail real payments and binding budget constraints: experiments use auctions to sell goods for money, albeit within a stylized setting. More importantly, experimental designs can isolate and control the market setting to address

---

[23] Shogren (1990) also observed that with repeated market trials, the initial bid was a significant predictor of the final experienced bid; the implication is that an initial bid, adjusted for learning, could reflect the value of reduced risk in an experienced market.

specific questions. After decades of work, the experimental procedures have passed at least one critical test: they have enabled researchers to learn things about behavior that would have been impossible to discover from any of the alternative procedures. For example, when faced with both positive and negative information about new food technologies, consumers react as if they had received only negative information.

The contextual design of laboratory auctions also matters. First among these is having a subject make actual decisions such that they exchange money for real goods. Real exchanges of money and goods are aimed at inducing sincere behavior and punishing irrational behavior. Lab research has also found seemingly trivial aspects of the protocol to be important. Paying participants of an experimental auction prior to the auction rather than afterwards reinforces the monetary incentive. Further, reminding the participants that bidding zero is acceptable mitigates any assumption that positive bidding is expected. Auction multiple goods at once also can be done, but designing demand-revealing auctions becomes more complicated.

We also know that repeated trials in laboratory auctions can affect bidding behavior. The repetition allows bidders to bid again after observing the market-clearing price for a new product that has just entered into their opportunity set, a nontrivial event for a distinctive commodity like irradiated meat. Some bidders react to the posted market price by changing their bids in the next round; others do not. Repetition has both plus and minus for value elicitation. If the goal is to elicit each bidder's value independent of signals from the market, repetition is not recommended [see Harrison (1996)]. Evidence suggests that posted prices can influence bidders who are inexperienced or unfamiliar with the good in question. A one-shot auction provides these raw values "uncontaminated" by market information. But if the goal is to understand how a person's valuation of a good reacts to market experience and new information – provided by either a market price or a written description, repeated trials provide the flexibility for a researcher interested in informed bidding behavior. Repeated second-price auctions, for example, eliminated the divergence between WTP and WTA in the case of market goods with close substitutes. The impact of information can also be estimated by observing bidding behavior before and after the release of information. Similarly, the impact of marketing and taste tests can be estimated with repeated auctions.

We have also learned that there are limitations to what can be achieved with experiments. Collecting refined information about the value of risk reductions can be difficult – people have general preferences for clusters of goods rather than specific goods. But if this is the case in a sterile laboratory it is likely to hold for survey valuation research too. Subtle changes in the experimental procedure such as whether participants were paid ahead of time, whether the reported WTP or WTA, or whether they knew the market-clearing price can significantly impact the results. Bids for new, unfamiliar goods can be unrealistically high when participants viewed them as a novelty. And over time as designs are refined, improved reality-based valuation experiments seem likely to develop into a useful method for applied economists.

5. Methods to testbed surveys

The idea to use public opinion surveys to assign values the natural environment took flight with Davis's (1963) groundwork on hypothetical iterative bidding games. The path-breaking idea seems simple enough now – just ask people how much they would be willing to pay for a hypothetical change in environmental protection. A researcher could construct a hypothetical "contingent" market containing features that parallel real-world markets and institutions. This pseudo-market could be manipulated to conform to the problem at hand. Quantity and quality dimensions such as temporal context, spatial dimensions, property right entitlements, and uncertainty could be varied to reflect specific policy questions. Ideally, a well-structured contingent valuation survey would let each person solve his own trade-off problems and reveal his *ex ante* valuation for the hypothetical change. And as discussed in the chapter on stated-preference methods in this Handbook, researchers around the world now use surveys to elicit stated preferences for all categories of environmental issues [also see Hanemann (1994)].

But it is no secret that using surveys to elicit values has drawbacks and detractors.[24] Using the lab to overcome these drawbacks was why some environmental economists were drawn to the experimental method in the first place. In the 1980s, Cummings, Brookshire and Schulze (1986) promoted the lab as just the tool to strengthen surveys before they are implemented in the field. Their idea was to use the lab as a *testbed* for hypothetical surveys. The lab could be used to help researchers understand how people learn about incentive systems before these designs were used in the field. Lab testbeds have more control and can be repeated. The lessons learned from isolating and controlling potential biases prior to field implementation could improve the accuracy of the final survey. Ideally, as Coursey and Schulze (1986, p. 48) note, survey practitioners would "walk away from the laboratory with a 'best set' of questionnaires," accurately revealing preferences for the environmental asset.

We now consider two broad areas in which the experimental method is being used to explore behavior, with the ultimate goal being to improve hypothetical survey work – hypothetical bias and framing effects.

5.1. Hypothetical bias I: does it exist?

The classic jab at valuation surveys remains: "ask a hypothetical question, get a hypothetical answer" [A. Scott, as quoted in Bishop and Heberlein (1986)]. Despite numerous attempts to dismiss it, survey work has never shaken this troublesome gibe from four decades ago.[25] McCloskey (1985, p. 181) notes that "one can get an audience of econo-

---

[24] See Cummings, Brookshire and Schulze (1986) and Carson, Flores and Meade (2001) for discussions of the various potential biases and the likely impact on the validity and reliability of contingent valuation.

[25] The concern with hypothetical survey questions can be traced at least as far back as Wallis and Friedman's (1942) critical review of Thurstone's (1931) seminal experimental measurement of an indifference curve. They argue that "[f]or a satisfactory experiment it is essential that the subject give actual reactions to actual stimuli .... The response are valueless because the subject cannot know how he would react" (p. 180).

mists to laugh out loud" by suggesting to send out a questionnaire. Economists prefer observations from actual market behavior to public opinion surveys, which in some eyes, has tarnished contingent valuation results. They hold up results like the Forsythe et al. (1992) experiment on the Iowa Political Stock Market. The IPSM allows traders to buy and sell portfolios of shares in political candidates in a double auction market. Their results show that the IPSM outperformed opinion polls on the 1988 presidential election, despite the judgment bias of individual traders.

Plus, the trial and error approach that dominated earlier valuation research left some observers concerned; they worry that no rational economic theory exists to help explain hypothetical choices based on intended behavior. The lack of replication to verify survey results has also troubled some observers. We now consider studies that have explored the question of hypothetical bias. We begin with Bohm's (1972) classic experimental lab study, which compared bids in hypothetical and actual experimental markets that elicited subjects' stated value to preview a Swedish television show. His results suggest people moderately overstate their actual values when asked a hypothetical question.

The tendency to overstate actual cash commitments was supported in the seminal field experiments by Bishop and Heberlein (1979, 1986) on the value of goose and deer hunting permit experiments in Wisconsin. In the goose experiment, they found that average and median actual cash values to hunters were significantly less than those suggested in the hypothetical question. The deer hunting experiment generated the same result – overvaluation in the survey relative to actual cash outlays.

Subsequent research has generally supported the observation that hypothetical values exceed actual WTP [e.g., Seip and Strand (1992), Neill et al. (1994), Frykblom (1997), Balistreri et al. (1998), Spencer, Swallow and Miller (1998)]. Exceptions exist – some experiments have found no significant difference in real and hypothetical behavior [e.g., Dickie, Fisher and Gerking (1987), Loomis et al. (1996), Sinden (1988), Smith and Mansfield (1998)]. And a few other studies found mixed results. Battalio, Kagel and Jiranyakul (1990), for instance, tested for differences in responses for hypothetical verses real payoffs. They found systematic and significant quantitative differences over real and hypothetical choice questions. Subjects were more risk averse with real payoffs than with hypothetical payoffs. But even though there were significant quantitative differences between hypothetical and real payoffs, the qualitative findings with respect to real verses hypothetical payoffs were similar.

The mass of the evidence, however, suggests that the average person exaggerates his or her actual willingness to pay across a broad spectrum of goods with vastly different experimental parameters [see Harrison and Rutström's review (1999)]. For instance, the ratio of hypothetical-to-actual overbidding, which ranged from 2.2 to 3.5 for baseball cards, falls between the ratios observed for irradiated pork, watercolor paintings, maps, and other goods that ranged from, 1.0 to 10.0 [see Diamond and Hausman (1994)]. They reinforce the argument that people tend to overstate their actual WTP when confronted with hypothetical questions.

Researchers have spent less energy on understanding the relationship between the real and hypothetical WTA measure of value. The lab evidence from this relatively small lot of studies is mixed. Bishop et al. found that Wisconsin goose hunters overstated their actual WTA to sell goose-licenses; deer hunters in a sealed-bid auction understated their actual WTA to sell deer-permits, while hunters in a dichotomous choice institution overstated their real WTA. Coursey, Hovis and Schulze (1987) found that people overstated their actual WTA to experience a drop of the sucrose octa-acetate (SOA); Smith and Mansfield's (1998) field survey suggests that real and hypothetical WTA statements for the opportunity to spend time in a second set of interviews on an undisclosed topic are statistically equivalent. Again these results suggest that the real-hypothetical WTA gap might be case-specific, conditional on the good and the context. List and Shogren (2002) calibrate real and hypothetical WTA estimates elicited for consumer goods in a multi-unit, random nth-price auction. Their results suggest that people understated their real WTA in the hypothetical regimes, framed both as demand and nondemand revealing exchanges.

5.2. *Hypothetical bias II: calibration*

Another relevant question suited for the lab is whether values elicited from hypothetical surveys can be *calibrated* to reflect the amounts individuals would pay for proposed programs. The National Oceanic and Atmospheric Administration's (NOAA) blue-ribbon panel recommended that hypothetical bids from surveys be calibrated using a "divide by 2" rule, unless these bids can be adjusted using actual market data [NOAA (1994)]. The NOAA rule has served as an ad hoc placeholder to motivate more research into the nature of calibrating hypothetical and actual values.[26]

To illustrate, consider List and Shogren's (1998) field experiment that compares bidding behavior in a hypothetical and actual second-price auction for baseball cards – a good with many characteristics favorable for a calibration exercise including familiarity, the ability to deliver, and an intangible quality. Three samples were run – 1 card, 1 card among 10, and 1 card bid on by sportscard dealers presumed more experienced with the market than the general population. While the results support the view that people overstate actual bids, the calibration function estimated to correct for this exaggeration is both good- and context-specific, i.e., other goods and market experience affect the calibration function.

Calibration research is continuing to develop in the lab. One alternative method is the CVM-X method [Fox et al. (1998)]. CVM-X works in four steps.

Step 1: use a survey to elicit hypothetical values for the good in question.
Step 2: bring subsamples of the survey respondents into the laboratory and elicit real bids for the actual good in an incentive-compatible auction that employs real goods, real money, and repeated market experience.

---

[26] Others offer an alternative vision. Randall (1997, p. 200), for example, states that: "[t]he calibration issue, it seems to me, is an audacious attempt to promote a Kuhnian paradigm shift . . . . I would argue vigorously that the essential premise is unproven and the question is therefore premature and presumptuous. The proposed new calibration paradigm is at this moment merely a rambunctious challenger to the dominant external validation paradigm."

Step 3: estimate a calibration function relating the auction market bids of the sub-sample to the hypothetical survey bids.

Step 4: use the estimated calibration function to adjust the values of the survey respondents who did not participate in the laboratory auction.

CVM-X could be a cost-effective tool that combines the advantages of the stated preference, contingent valuation method (CVM) and experimental auction markets (X). The method could be used to increase the validity and accuracy of surveys while broadening the scope of nonmarket valuation in the lab.

The CVM-X application studied by Fox et al. (1998) is the reduction in health risk from the parasite *Trichinella* achieved with food irradiation. Irradiated foods are not yet widely available in the U.S., and most people are unfamiliar with the process – which gives it a feature common to many nonmarket environmental goods like biodiversity. Nearly two hundred randomly selected households participated in the survey. They were asked the maximum they would be willing to pay to upgrade from their less-preferred sandwich to their sandwich of choice in an open-ended elicitation question. At the end of the interview, participants who were pork eaters were asked if they would be interested in participating in a consumer economics experiment.

In the lab experiment, participants were assigned to one of two treatments – the irradiated or the nonirradiated treatment. The experimental auction procedures followed those in Hayes et al. (1995) – stage I was the candy bar auction (second-price); stage II was the food auction. Figures 9 and 10 show individual bids between the survey and trial 2 in both treatments. The results suggest that an upward bias in hypothetical bids exists, and that the lab can be used to correct for this bias, but the calibration function might be commodity-specific.

Researchers are usually more interested in public goods and programs, items that lack the deliverability of reduced health risk. Future research should explore whether a

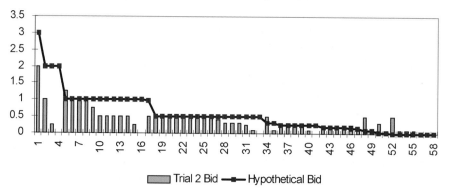

Figure 9. Comparison of hypothetical and auction bids for irradiated pork.

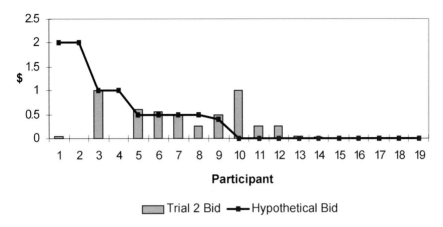

Figure 10. Comparison of hypothetical and auction bids for nonirradiated pork.

private good is a reasonable proxy for a public good, and whether a systematic method exists to cluster goods into classes of calibration functions. Consider two other attempts to calibrate hypothetical and real values across goods. The cross-commodity "bias function" approach of Blackburn, Harrison and Rutström (1994) rests on the presumption that bias for a good in one context is measurable and transferable to another good in another context. Blackburn, Harrison and Rutström use discrete choice data on subjects who participated first in a hypothetical and then in a real valuation setting for one private good. A multinomial logit model is used to explain the pattern of responses (yes–yes, yes–no, no–no) and to determine whether the bias in hypothetical responses is systematically related to socio-economic characteristics. The evidence to support transferability of the bias function to a second private good is inconclusive given the relatively large standard errors of the estimated coefficients [also see the discussion on calibration method in Swallow (1994)].

Harrison et al. (1997) calibrate open-ended values for wetlands protection using two bias functions: one to account for the downward bias due to free riding and the other to account for hypothetical bias. The free riding bias function is measured in a comparison of two real valuation situations for a nature calendar, one of which features public provision of the calendar. This bias function is used to calibrate both real and hypothetical bids for the preservation of local wetlands with the corrected bids used to estimate the hypothetical bias function. Both calibration functions, free riding followed by hypothetical, are then applied to bids elicited for national wetlands preservation. While intuitively appealing, the approach rests on little tested assumptions about transferability of bias functions between different contexts: real versus hypothetical values, private versus public goods. The approach also makes an implicit and untested presumption that these biases are additive.[27]

Cummings and Taylor (1999) propose a different path to remove the hypothetical bias – a so-called *cheap talk* survey design. Their idea is that one might be able reduce hypothetical bias before it starts by the choice of wording in the survey. They propose that simply telling a respondent, before he answers the valuation question, about the hypothetical bias issue might remove the bias. If people are told that they usually exaggerate their reported values, the hypothesis is that this frank revelation will cause him to reflect and revise his hypothetical bid downward toward the value he might pay. Cummings and Taylor run sixteen different treatments that compare stated values with and without cheap talk to a benchmark treatment that elicited actual contributions to four different public goods (e.g., contributions to the Nature Conservancy in Georgia). Their results suggest that the cheap talk design worked to make responses to hypothetical questions indistinguishable to responses involving actual cash payments, and that this effect was robust across changes in script and public good, with one exception.

While promising, neither the calibration nor the cheap talk research provide a substantive explanation as to why people react the way they do when making hypothetical choices.[28] An open question is why respondents reduce hypothetical values when told that people have a tendency to inflate hypothetical values. Perhaps there is some deep cognitive reason or maybe it is just the Hawthorne effect at work – subjects want to meet the expectations of the experimenter. It is unanswered questions like this that keep fears over hypothetical behavior alive in nonmarket valuation debates. One cannot argue with Mansfield's (1998, p. 680) point that "the power of the calibration model could be improved by a better understanding of how individuals answer valuation questions, including the traits or attitudes that inspire individuals to give more or less accurate answers." No camp has thus far provided a convincing axiomatic explanation as to what creates or removes the wedge between intentions and actions. The lack of an analytical framework increases the odds that this discussion will stagnate into "did not, did too." The debate will continue until a robust and parsimonious theory emerges as to why the wedge occurs and whether it can be predicted and controlled systematically.

5.3. Framing effects I: surrogate bidding (scope/embedding)

Most researchers involved in valuation surveys know that how a question is asked is as important as what is asked. These so-called framing effects show up in many forms in

---

[27] Another classic contingent valuation bias arises with some types of calibration procedures – strategic bias. If respondents know that their hypothetical values will be calibrated with actual values later, they might have incentive to act strategically and inflate their initial values.

[28] Early on, Bishop and Heberlein's (1986) called for more attention to the social psychology literature. But rather than digging into to an unfamiliar discipline, some observers have a more pragmatic view toward cheap talk. If cheap talk works to lower values, does it really matter why it works? While nice to know, we do not need to know the theory of physics to ride a bike.

valuation questions: the description of the good, the payment mechanism, the description of available outside options and substitutes, and reminders of budget constraints. Whatever the reason, the main concern is that a hypothetical survey on the environment does not measure what it is supposed to measure, or it measures values left uncontrolled by the experimental design. Consider two areas of experimental work that can be used to better understand how framing affects values – surrogate bidding (this section) and incentive compatibility (the next section).

In the state of the art review of valuation surveys, Kahneman (1986) pointed out that hypothetical questions might produce surrogate bidding, also called embedding or insensitivity to scope. Surrogate bidding exists when hypothetical (or nonhypothetical) values for a specific good reflect preferences for environmental phenomena in general; or when values are insensitive to changes in the quantity or quality of the good. A person asked to state his WTP to protect one endangered Wyoming Toad might be revealing his value to protect all toads, or to protect every endangered species. For example, McClelland et al. (1992) found that up to one-half of the reported values for a specific environmental charge can be attributed to surrogate values. The basic instinct behind surrogate bidding is reflected in the language used to describe this behavior: warm glow, the purchase of moral satisfaction, insensitivity to scope (quantity or quality), part-whole bias, and embedding.[29] These terms suggest that people might be insufficiently sensitive to the continuum of goods or services they are valuing; a person's stated value captures his general feeling toward this class of goods. Surrogate bidding means that values for specific goods cannot be relied on as accurate indicators of preference because it is unclear what values are being elicited.

Most tests of surrogate bidding have been performed using data from contingent valuation surveys [see, for example, Hammitt and Graham (1999)]. A few surrogate bidding experiments examining nonhypothetical choices have been run in the lab to gain more control through real economic commitments. Kealy, Montgomery and Dovidio (1990) is the first classroom experiment. They designed an experiment to test the reliability of survey methods given the general concern about surrogate bidding, focusing on the effect of familiarity with the good. The experiment used students from an undergraduate psychology class at Colgate University. The students were asked their WTP to contribute to the New York Department of Environment Conservation for decreasing acid rain in the Adirondacks. The objective was to compare behavior for a private good with which the students had experience to behavior for a public good with which they had little experience. Some subjects were warned that they would be asked to actually make the contributions that they claimed they were willing to pay; others were not warned.

Of the warned students, nearly 95 percent paid an average WTP of about $18. Of those not warned, 27 percent refused to pay, and those that did pay had an average WTP of about $5. This result suggests that people were valuing something other than what the study purported to measure. Many people who found a legitimate reason to back out

---

[29] See the exchange between Kahneman and Knetsch (1992) and Smith (1992).

of the contribution did so, which suggests the questionnaire might have been eliciting surrogate preferences toward the Adirondacks, not just contributions for a specific (but vague) program to decrease acid rain.

Three ensuing lab experiments also point toward surrogate bidding. Boyce et al. (1992) designed a lab experiment to elicit nonuse values for environmental protection. Their experimental design asked people to value a houseplant (a Norfolk pine) that would be destroyed unless they protected it by buying the plant. People paid more when they were explicitly told that the plant would be killed if they did not buy it. But it is unclear however what value this design was capturing – the nonuse value for the houseplant or a statement of rejection to a situation in which someone would take a morally objectionable action.

Hayes et al. (1995) also explore whether surrogate bidding existed in the value of risk reduction. They compared the bidding behavior from each foodborne pathogen treatment to the bids from a treatment that combines the risks of all the pathogens – a 1 in about 46,000 chance of illness per meal from at least one of the five pathogens. Their hypothesis was that similar bidding behavior across treatments would not contradict the idea of surrogate bidding. The results suggest that surrogate bidding existed for reduced health risk: bids for a cluster of pathogens were indistinguishable from bids for specific pathogens. Using a contingent valuation survey, Hammitt and Graham (1999) reproduced the Hayes et al. study, and found the same insensitivity to probability.

Bateman et al. (1997) found similar results for restaurant meals. They considered the existence of surrogate bidding, or part-whole bias, in the lab. They used an incentive compatible mechanism to auction off vouchers for parts of a restaurant meal. They elicited values for the parts and the whole were elicited. They observed that the sum of the parts exceeded the whole, again supporting the idea that values seem to reflect general preferences for a good.

Some observers, however, remain unconvinced that surrogate bidding, or insensitivity to scope, is a major problem for valuation. Citing evidence from the hypothetical survey literature, Carson, Flores and Meade (2001, p. 183) say that "[p]oorly executed survey design and administration procedures appear to be a primary cause of problems in studies not exhibiting sensitivity to scope." If the poor design tag is also aimed at lab results, the proposition can be tested. Researchers can replicate these experiments under new economics conditions to test the robustness of the results, which at the present time suggests some level of surrogate bidding. This is the beauty of the experimental method – if you do not agree with the findings or you doubt certain design features, you are free to run your own experiments to refute or replicate earlier work.

A new lab experiments could also be construct to test whether arbitrage could remove the tendency for surrogate bidding. A clever design could be created in which the monitor buys and sells different bundles of these goods such that the person is left with less for more. He then might have the needed economic incentive to think through his stated valuations for changes in both quantity and quality.

5.4. Framing II: incentive compatibility

Now consider framing and incentive compatibility. Can one defining an exchange institution as incentive compatible, or demand-revealing, even though the exchange is hypothetical? Experimental economics has long explored the nature of incentive design in the provision of public goods like environmental protection. These experiments explore how behavior differs from the received theory which predicts that rational, self-interested people free-ride off the contributions of others, and thus markets will fail to provide the optimal level of the public good making alternative organizations necessary. While several variants exist on the public good experiment, the basic design captures the idea that the efficient outcome is to cooperate but the dominant strategy is to free-ride.[30]

For valuation surveys, however, it is unclear whether people will (1) tell the truth, (2) free ride if they think they might pay for the good, or (3) overstate their bids if this increases the chance of getting the good at a low cost. While some survey supporters have interpreted the lab results as saying that free riding is not a problem [e.g., Mitchell and Carson (1989)], the evidence is mixed: some people free ride, while others coordinate actions [see Ledyard (1995)]. The findings suggest that incentive compatible mechanisms can be used to increase efficiency, but truth telling is not the predominant observed behavior [see Taylor (1998)].

The early public good experiments prompted valuation researchers to compare these mechanisms to the standard survey method of asking a direct WTP question. Bennett (1987), for instance, examined how a modified Smith auction eliminated strategic behavior in the provision of a hypothetical public good relative to a direct question approach (recall the Smith auction was also used in Brookshire and Coursey (1987). He found that direct statements of hypothetical values lead to over-bidding of induced value, whereas the Smith auction lead to under-bidding. He suggested that the most promising avenue to estimate values in real-world cases is to combine the direct statements of value with the lab experiments to tease out truthful bidding.

Prince et al. (1992) used the lab to consider the properties of another public good provision mechanism – a contribution game mechanism. They wanted to know whether this mechanism could be used to increase the accuracy of surveys. The contribution game pulls together a group of people and asks them to contribute to a public good. Subjects know the group size, cost of the good, and the payoff to each individual. Individuals choose how much to contribute. If contributions fall below costs, the good is withheld and contributions returned. If contributions exceed costs, the good is provided, with surplus funds going to the supplier. The Prince et al. results suggest that surveys that use the contribution game mechanism can be incentive compatible and might overcome several observed cognitive problems, at least for an identifiable subset of the population.

---

[30] Suppose four people are each endowed with $5. Each person is asked to make either a private contribution of either $0 or $5 to a collective program. Every $1 contribution returns $2 to the group – $0.50 to the contributor and $1.50 to the other three subjects. The efficient outcome is for everyone to contribute $5, but the dominant strategy is to contribute $0 since the private net return is negative.

Rondeau, Schulze and Poe (1999) explored the properties of a *provision point mechanism* for public good provision. Their design used induced values and an environment designed to mimic field conditions. The one-shot provision point mechanism works as follows: A relatively large group (50+) is pulled together, and each participant is endowed with an initial balance of, say $6. Each person then enters a bid indicating how much of the $6 he or she will contribute to a group investment fund. The sum of the bids contributed to the investment fund must equal or exceed an "investment cost" for the investment to be made on behalf of the group. This investment cost is predetermined but unknown to the bidders.[31] If the sum of group bids equals or exceeds the investment cost, each member of the group receives a randomly assigned private payoff that may differ from other group members' payoffs. Each person's earnings depend on his or her bid and on whether the investment cost for the group was reached.

Two possible outcomes were considered: (1) if the investment cost was not met by the group, the full amount of a person's bid was refunded; or (2) if the investment cost was exactly met or exceeded, each person received his or her payoff from the group investment. And if the bids exceeded the cost, all of the excess was rebated to the group. The rebate was directly proportional to the amount of one's bid relative to the total amount of the group's bids. Thus, if someone's bid was 30 percent of the sum of bids for the group, his rebate would be 30 percent of the excess bids.

The results suggest that the provision point mechanism is demand revealing "in aggregate" for a large group with heterogeneous preferences. Rondeau et al. argue that these results suggests a relatively simple mechanism could be used in the field to elicit preferences leading to the efficient provision of a public good.

But here is the rub with this provision point mechanism. The mechanism is argued to be incentive compatible *at the group level*. Unfortunately, the economic theory of incentive compatibility is defined at *the individual level* – each person should have incentive to bid sincerely. Incentive compatibility is an individual concept, not a group concept. If the group reaches the provision point because low value bidders overstate WTP and high value bidders understate WTP just means that the mechanism might be lead to an efficient outcome on average; it does not mean it is incentive compatible. The idea of using this mechanism in field surveys begs the skeptic's question of whether a mechanism that is "just right" on average is close enough for valuation work.

Another incentive compatible issue is the claim that the dichotomous choice (DC) method used in survey work is demand revealing. The DC method asks a person to say *yes* or *no* to paying a fixed dollar amount for a hypothetical change in some good or service. If the DC method is incentive compatible in a survey, it implies that a person would answer the same way when faced with a real cash commitment. Cummings, Harrison and Rutström (1995) use the lab to test this proposition. They construct treatments to

---

[31] It is unclear why one would want to create an environment in which the subjects were uncertain about the investment costs if the mechanism is intended for real-world collective decisions. A significant fraction of the people in the real world would probably want to know the likely costs of the project up front before they commit resources to this public sector plan.

compare behavior between- and within-subjects. The between-subject treatments draw two samples from the same population. Each person in the first group was asked whether he or she would pay actual cash for the good at a given price; people in the other group were asked the same question, but it was hypothetical and no binding exchanges were made. The within-subject treatments asked a person if hypothetically he or she would buy the good at a give price, and then the good was provided and the question was repeated, except now the commitment was real. The result that hypothetical responses overstated the actual value paid by the subjects caused Cummings, Harrison and Rutström to reject the thesis that the hypothetical DC method was incentive compatible.

Additional experimental work has followed up on the demand revealing nature of the DC question. For example, Brown et al. (1996) explored valuation for an environmental good under four conditions: real cash payments to direct and DC questions, and hypothetical payments to direct and DC requests. Based on the results, they concluded that the DC mechanism seems to be more of an issue than hypothetical behavior. The DC question causes people to say *yes* too often, irrespective of whether the choice is hypothetical or real. Frykblom and Shogren (2000) sold people a volume of the Swedish National Atlas called *Environment* using either a DC choice or within Vickrey auction. All sales were real, nothing hypothetical. Their results suggest that while the DC format induced greater mean WTP than the Vickrey auction (e.g., 81.41SEK vs. 71.02SEK), the difference was not statistically significant. Following the quasi-experimental method used in the Bishop–Heberlein goose studies, Champ et al. (1997) compared how a sample of Wisconsin residents react to hypothetical referenda versus actual DC contributions to a road-removal program at the North Rim of Grand Canyon National Park. Their results again show that the hypothetical donations were poor predictors of actual contributions.

Johannesson et al. (1999) considered the idea that sometimes a *yes* does not mean *yes*. They compared a DC question with real cash commitment, but this time only an "absolutely sure yes" is counted as a *yes*. Their results suggest while a standard hypothetical "yes" overestimates the real "yes," an *absolutely sure hypothetical yes* did not [also see the similar results in Blumenschein et al. (1998)]. The question mark with this line of research is that while one might wonder what a *yes* means, no theory exists to suggest a systematic reason why one *yes* means something different than another *yes*. Such "what is 'is' " debates on the semantics of what a choice really meant seems has to require more attention to the details in the cognitive psychology literature on language and imagery, a new area for most economists.

Along the lines of the DC experiments, Cummings et al. (1997) examined whether a hypothetical referenda over the provision of a public good is incentive compatible. The valuation literature has advanced the thesis that a reference should be demand revealing because if people prefer the public good at the hypothetical posted price, they should vote "yea;" otherwise, they vote "nay." There should be no reason to misrepresent their preferences, or inferred willingness to pay. Cummings et al.'s experiment was an attempt to empirically test the thesis of whether behavior under real and hypothetical referenda differed or not.

The experiment worked as follows. Thirteen distinct groups were pull together, and told the following: if at least half of the group voted for the public good for a $10 donation per person, the good would be provided and everyone in the group would make the donation; otherwise, no donations would be made. The treatment across was whether the vote was for real or hypothetical. The real-voting groups were told the money would be collected immediately after the vote if the "yea's" have it; the hypothetical-voting groups were told that no money would be exchange, but they should make their decisions as if their vote and donation were real. The public good was $2N$ (N – people in a voting group) bilingual "citizens guide" booklets that described areas in Albuquerque that overlie contaminated groundwater, how to test for contamination, and what self-protection actions are available if a well is contaminated.

Based on their analysis of the data, Cummings et al. rejected their thesis that voting behavior was independent of the use of a real or hypothetical referendum. They then conclude with a reprimand for anyone who would presume incentive compatibility for hypothetical referenda without testing empirically for it first. In response, Haab, Huang and Whitehead (1999) take up the empirical gauntlet by reevaluating the Cummings et al. data. They relax the presumption of homoskedasticity across treatments because real votes (with real opportunity costs) are expected to have less variability than hypothetical votes. They show that once the error scales are correctly identified, they rejected Cumming et al. original null hypothesis – no significant difference was observed between real and hypothetical referenda, and that both voting rules are quite noisy signals of WTP. Haab et al.'s constructive re-evaluation clearly tosses the question of (in)sincere voting in hypothetical referenda back to the lab for more examination.

5.5. Synopsis on testbedding

This brief review illustrates the movement made over the last two decades toward achieving Coursey and Schulze's (1986) aim of using the lab to testbed field surveys. More researchers, but not many, now use the lab to better understand how people react to incentives provided by valuation questions prior to field application. The one sign that the lab valuation work has impacted valuation research is that the approach now has its own formal critics. They stress that a laboratory testbed has its own problems that restrict the applicability of findings for survey work. And as usual for experiments, the debate is usually over the lack or loss of experimental control. If concerns over uncontrolled incentives in the lab make sense, lab results can be challenged as openly as the hypothetical surveys the lab research was designed to address.

Bishop and Heberlein (1986), for example, considered the lab work on the Vickrey auction as a "red herring." They pointed out that while a second-price auction might be demand-revealing in theory for a private good, most environmental problems are public goods. Moreover, complicated incentive-compatible auctions for private or public goods might simply increase costs, increase confusion, and decrease response rates for a survey.

Another criticism of lab work involves uncontrolled outside options, and this affects real and hypothetical bidding. Suppose a researcher thinks that the lab is producing untainted values for a real private good, whereas bidding behavior is conditioned by the market price of the same or similar goods sold outside the lab.[32] The existence of such unmeasured prices for outside options has been argued to explain differences in laboratory behavior when hypothetical payments exceed real payments for the same good [Harrison (1992), Smith (1994)]. Hypothetical bids, so the argument goes are not too high. Rather, real bids are too low because they are truncated at an actual market price set outside the lab. If this is the case, insights about valuation that arise from lab results might be less instructive than previously believed.

Smith and Mansfield (1998) advance this dissent to form the most cogent set of criticisms to date. They first challenge the negative concerns raised about contingent valuation work because they were "based on diverse experimental evidence drawn from small, specialized samples involving purchase of private goods and contributions for goods with public attributes." They go on to rebuke the experimental literature for providing "little systematic treatment of how the circumstances of choice influence the analyst's ability to describe preference relations from choice functions." They conclude by noting that no objective benchmark exists to determine a value's "realness" or the "degree of 'hypotheticality' " elicited in any experiment that does not explicitly control private preferences.

These are reasonable concerns that deserve answers. Consider each point in turn. First, the diversity of experiments and sample populations should not be seen as a weakness of the lab, but rather as a strength. The weight of the evidence from both student and lay subject pools in numerous settings involving many different goods, elicitation methods, and contexts run by many different analysts point in one direction – hypothetical values usually exceed actual values. It is difficult to dismiss the experimental evidence as "hazy" in light of Harrison and Rutström's (1999) review that shows 34 of 39 tests revealing hypothetical bias, ranging from 2 to 2600 percent.

Second, while more research into behavior will always be desirable, it is amiss to argue that little systematic treatment exists on how context affects choice and values in the lab. The literature reveals the patterns that have emerged for valuation: frames matter [e.g., Kahneman, Knetsch and Thaler (1990)], the nature of the good matters [e.g., Hayes et al. (1995)], information matters [e.g., Cummings and Taylor (1999), Fox, Hayes and Shogren (2002)], exchange institutions matter [e.g., Bohm (1972), Rutström (1998)], market experience matters [Shogren et al. (1994)], information on the market-clearing price can matter [Fox et al. (1998)], and substitutes and complements can matter [List and Shogren (1998)]. Rather than dismissing experimental valuation research as a hodgepodge of unrelated and ad hoc treatments, it is more constructive to note that one experiment begets another experiments. The lab valuation literature continues to follow the classic experimental strategy: start simple, and add complexity

---

[32] See Harrison, Harstad and Rutström (1995).

slowly to understand what factors matter, and why. As peer-reviewed evidence continues to accumulate, a clearer and more definitive picture will emerge about the context of choice and valuation.

Finally, Smith and Mansfield are correct in that no one will ever know with absolute certainty whether someone is bidding sincerely in the lab given private and wild preferences. Two strategies exist: surrender the search and follow Bohm's (1984) idea of the interval method, in which a "value interval" is created by splitting the sample into those with an incentive to free ride and those with an incentive to overstate values; or keep on the trail by testing and retesting the reliability of incentive compatible mechanisms given preferences controlled or induced by the monitor [see Forsythe and Isaac (1982)]. For instance, the second-price auction has been a popular mechanism because it is demand-revealing in theory, relatively simple to explain, and has an endogenous market-clearing price. But the auction has its problems, even with induced values. People bid insincerely, especially bidders who are off the margin (bidders whose value is far below or above the market-clearing price). The auction seems not to engage low-value bidders who think they will never win, which suggests the auction is unreliable if one is trying to measure the entire demand curve for a real-world good.

But rather than debating about criteria for "realness," such problems point the way toward potential solutions. For instance, Shogren et al. (2001b) examine the potential for the random nth-price auction to attempt to engage these otherwise disengaged off-the-margin bidders. The auction now has a random and endogenously determined market-clearing price. Like the Becker–DeGroot–Marschak (BDM), randomness is used to engage all bidders because everyone has a chance to buy a unit of the good, and the endogenous price guarantees that the market-clearing price retains some relation to bidders' private values. The lab evidence suggests that the auction can induce sincere bidding behavior in theory and practice. Does this mean the success of the auction translates automatically for private preferences? No, but it does suggest that one can use the lab to help increase the confidence in the tools we use. While advocates of the lab, including myself, may have overstated the case, it is clear that using the experimental method can help improve field valuation through repetition and the accumulation of evidence both for and against alternative auctions and contexts. What has emerged thus far is that the relationship between real and hypothetical values seems to be both good- and context-specific, and that attempts to bridge the gap statistically might be difficult since the gap appears to be nontransferable across commodities.

6. Concluding remarks

Thirty-five years ago, Kneese (1966, p. 87) wrote: "optimal rules, standards, or other techniques for controlling environmental quality must result from analysis of values, contrary to the usual approach which is still narrowly focused on physical effects and objectives. Research in the economic values associated with environmental management has made significant progress along some lines, but has barely begun to shed light on many difficult problems." Today the valuation literature has nearly four decades of enlightenment under its belt. And each step forward has uncovered even deeper questions about the behavioral underpinnings of valuation. Within each new insight dwells another doubt, a progression that plays to the strength of the experimental method and mindset. The beauty of the experimental method is that questions of increasing difficulty and complexity can be addressed step by step in the lab or the field. By combining observations with first principles the 'sooty empiric' using the experimental method in valuation work has shown that economic context does matter to valuation. A review of the experimental method applied to valuation helps pinpoint what seems to matter the most: the nature of the good, information sets, exchange institutions, market experience, price information, and outside options. The experimental method applied to valuation can highlight what matters and why by creating a controlled setting in which treatments are replicated under similar conditions. Systematic work of replication and validation will help to increase the acceptance of valuation research. The lab or the field can be used to test how well general theories hold in specific cases, or how additional complications affect both hypothetical and real stated values.

Debates will continue over control and context, realism and simplicity, role-playing and anonymous economic agents, and instinctual reactions and experienced behavior within and along side markets. Walking the fence line between realism and control generates lively exchanges because both are concepts that can be achieved within broad limits defined by human subjects – realism to one researcher is a lack of control to another; control to one represents an artificial edifice to another. Regardless the goal should be to create a valuation environment in which people make motivated choices with economic consequences.

And even if the appropriate mix of control and realism can be agreed on, even motivated respondents who are answering valuation questions can have preferences, beliefs, and skill that differ from those of the traditional *homo economicus* [see, for example, Mazzotta and Opaluch (1995)]. Some exchange institutions are robust in an efficiency measure to these behavioral differences (e.g., the double-oral auction); others are not. The challenge is to understand what makes an institution robust, how much reality can be added to the lab without losing perceptible control, and whether the person's choices are motivated by economic considerations or not – tasks especially relevant to valuation research which for the most part presumes rational decision makers.

The pitch for the experimental mindset in valuation is two fold: the method imposes a discipline on researchers to test and explore the key behavioral elements that underlie a valuation problem; and once identified, the method gives researchers a pliable tool to sample and resample institutional rules to help find systematic behavioral patterns in both motivated and unmotivated statements of value. The experimental mindset for environmental valuation holds regardless on whether one chooses to believe that rational choice is a property of the individual alone or is embedded within the social context of the decision. The choice, however, sets on a distinctive path. If one believes that researchers should measure the value that exists in a person's mind at the time the question was asked, one could make the case that valuation should be isolated from interactive experience in real social exchange institutions. Here isolated value statements of value reveal preferences free from any information that would make a person aware of a broader social view towards the good on the auction block. Less economic context and weaker exchange institutions to punish irrational behavior creates an environment in which the wide range of psychological contextual cues can take over choices and values. When psychological context is all that matters, economists do not have a comparative advantage in understanding why and how; it becomes the psychologist's job to understand the range of contextual stimuli and responses.

In contrast, if one believes that choices and values emerge in the social context of an active exchange institution [e.g., Arrow (1987), Becker (1962)], estimates of value should not be separated from the interactive experience provided by an exchange institution, either directly or indirectly. Institutions matter because experience can make rational choice transparent to a person [see Smith (1991)]. Asking that choices be made within a real social exchange institution is what separates an economics valuation experiment from a psychology valuation experiment. The institutional context matters for economic choices and values. Environmental economists can advance this research direction further by addressing the reality that most people make allocation decisions in many institutional settings each day – markets, missing markets, and nonmarkets. The question to take to the lab then is: how do the rational choices and preferences formed within active exchange institutions affect nonmarket behavior and stated values for environmental protection? This inquiry matters because it is the contact with others who are making similar decisions that puts in context the economic maxim that choices have consequences, and values have meaning. Valuing environmental protection should not be the exception.

Acknowledgements

Thanks to the USDA/ERS, NSF, and USEPA for helping support this work. Thanks to Bjorn Carlén, Todd Cherry, Tom Crocker, Ron Cummings, Sean Fox, Shane Frederick, Peter Frykblom, Dermot Hayes, Terry Hurley, Jayson Lusk, Greg Parkhurst, Charlie Plott, Laura Taylor, and Jeff Vincent for their helpful comments. This paper is dedicated to Peter Bohm for all his comments, encouragement, and support over two decades of friendship. Thanks to Peter Bohm for his comments, encouragement, and support. All views remain my own.

References

Akerlof, G. (1997). "Social distance and social decisions". Econometrica 65, 1005–1028.
Allais, M. (1953). "Le comportement de l'homme rationnel devant le risque: Critique des postulats et axiomes de l'école Americaine". Econometrica 21, 503–546.

Arrow, K. (1987). "Rationality of self and others in an economic system". In: Hogarth, R., Reder, M. (Eds.), Rational Choice: The Contrast between Economics and Psychology. University of Chicago Press, Chicago, IL.

Balistreri, E., McClelland, G., Poe, G., Schulze, W. (1998). "Can hypothetical questions reveal true values? A laboratory comparison of dichotomous choice and open-ended contingent values with auction values". WP 97-15, Cornell University.

Banks, J., Plott, C., Porter, D. (1988). "An experimental analysis of unanimity in public goods provision mechanisms". Review of Economic Studies 55, 301–322.

Bateman, I., Munro, A., Rhodes, B., Starmer, C., Sugden, R. (1997). "Does part-whole bias exist? An experimental investigation". Economic Journal 107, 322–332.

Battalio, R., Kagel, J., Jiranyakul, K. (1990). "Testing between alternative models of choice under uncertainty: some initial results". Journal of Risk and Uncertainty 3, 25–50.

Becker, G. (1962). "Irrational behavior and economic theory". Journal of Political Economy 70, 1–13.

Becker, G., DeGroot, M., Marschak, J. (1964). "Measuring utility by a single response sequential method". Behavioral Science 9, 226–236.

Bennett, J. (1983). "Validating revealed preferences". Economic Analysis and Policy 13, 2–17.

Bennett, J. (1987). "Strategic behaviour: some experimental evidence". Journal of Public Economics 32, 355–368.

Benson, P. (1994). "Hawthorne effect". In: Corsini, R. (Ed.), Encyclopedia of Psychology, vol. 2. 2nd ed. Wiley, New York, pp. 108–109.

Bergstrom, J.C., Stoll, J.R. (1989). "Application of experimental economics concepts and precepts to CVM field survey procedures". Western Journal of Agricultural Economics 14, 98–109.

Bishop, R., Heberlein, T. (1979). "Measuring values of extramarket goods: are indirect measures biased?". American Journal of Agricultural Economics 61, 926–930.

Bishop, R., Heberlein, T. (1986). "Does contingent valuation work?". In: Cummings, R., Brookshire, D., Schulze, W. (Eds.), Valuing Environmental Goods: An Assessment of the Contingent Valuation Method. Rowman and Allenheld, Totowa, NJ, pp. 123–147.

Blackburn, M., Harrison, G., Rutström, E.E. (1994). "Statistical bias functions and informative hypothetical surveys". American Journal of Agricultural Economics 76, 1084–1088.

Blumenschein, K., Johannesson, M., Blomquist, G., Liljas, B., O'Conor, R. (1998). "Experimental results on expressed certainty and hypothetical bias in contingent valuation". Southern Economic Journal 65, 169–177.

Bohm, P. (1972). "Estimating demand for public goods: an experiment". European Economic Review 3, 111–130.

Bohm, P. (1984). "Revealing demand for an actual public good". Journal of Public Economics 24, 135–151.

Bohm, P. (1994a). "Behavior under uncertainty without preference reversal: a field experiment". Empirical Economics (Special issue, J. Hey (Ed.)) 19, 185–200.

Bohm, P. (1994b). "Time preference and preference reversal among experienced subjects: the effect of real payments". Economic Journal 104, 1370–1378.

Bohm, P., Lind, H. (1993). "Preference reversal, real-world lotteries, and lottery-interested subjects". Journal of Economic Behavior and Organization 22, 327–348.

Borges, B., Knetsch, J. (1998). "Tests of market outcomes with asymmetric valuations of gains and losses: smaller gains, fewer trades, and less value". Journal of Economic Behavior and Organization 33, 185–193.

Bowles, S. (1998). "Endogenous preferences: the cultural consequences of markets and other economic institutions". Journal of Economic Literature 36, 75–111.

Boyce, R., McClelland, G., Brown, T., Peterson, G., Schulze, W. (1992). "An experimental examination of intrinsic values as a source of the WTA–WTP disparity". American Economic Review 82, 1366–1373.

Brennan, G. (1973). "Pareto desirable redistribution: the case of malice and envy". Journal of Public Economics 2, 173–183.

Brookshire, D., Coursey, D. (1987). "Measuring the value of a public good: an empirical comparison of elicitation procedures". American Economic Review 77, 554–566.

Brown, T., Champ, P., Bishop, R., McCollum, D. (1996). "Which response format reveals the truth about donations to a public good?". Land Economics 72, 152–166.

Camerer, C. (1995). "Individual decision making". In: Kagel, J., Roth, A. (Eds.), Handbook of Experimental Economics. Princeton University Press, Princeton, NJ, pp. 587–703.

Caplin, A., Leahy, J. (2001). "Psychological expected utility theory and anticipatory feelings". Quarterly Journal of Economics 116, 55–79.

Carson, R., Flores, N., Meade, N. (2001). "Contingent valuation: controversies and evidence". Environmental and Resource Economics 19, 173–210.

Champ, P., Bishop, R., Brown, T., McCollum, D. (1997). "Using donation mechanisms to value nonuse benefits from public goods". Journal of Environmental Economics and Management 33, 151–163.

Cherry, T., Crocker, T., Shogren, J. (2003). "Rationality spillovers". Journal of Environmental Economics and Management 45, 63–84.

Cherry, T., Shogren, J. (2005). "Rationality crossovers". Working Paper, University of Wyoming.

Chu, Y.-P., Chu, R.-L. (1990). "The subsidence of preference reversals in simplified and marketlike experimental settings: a note". American Economic Review 80, 902–911.

Conant, J. (1951). Science and Common Sense. Yale University Press, New Haven, CT.

Coursey, D. (1987). "Markets and the measurement of value". Public Choice 55, 291–297.

Coursey, D., Hovis, J., Schulze, W. (1987). "The disparity between willingness to accept and willingness to pay measures of value". Quarterly Journal of Economics 102, 679–690.

Coursey, D., Schulze, W. (1986). "The application of laboratory experimental economics to the contingent valuation of public goods". Public Choice 49, 47–68.

Cox, J., Epstein, S. (1989). "Preference reversals without the independence axiom". American Economic Review 79, 408–426.

Cox, J., Grether, D. (1996). "The preference reversal phenomena: response mode, markets, and incentives". Economic Theory 7, 381–405.

Crocker, T., Shogren, J. (1991). "Preference learning and contingent valuation methods". In: Dietz, F., Van der Ploeg, R., van der Straaten, J. (Eds.), Environmental Policy and the Economy. North-Holland, Amsterdam, pp. 77–93.

Crocker, T., Shogren, J., Turner, P. (1998). "Incomplete beliefs and nonmarket valuation". Resources and Energy Economics 20, 139–162.

Cummings, R., Brookshire, D., Schulze, W. (1986). Valuing Environmental Goods: An Assessment of the Contingent Valuation Method. Rowman and Allanheld, Totowa, NJ.

Cummings, R., Harrison, G., Rutström, E. (1995). "Homegrown values and hypothetical surveys: is the dichotomous choice approach incentive compatible?". American Economic Review 85, 260–266.

Cummings, R., McKee, M., Taylor, L. (2000). "To whisper in the ears of princes: laboratory experiments and public policy". In: Folmer, H., Rose, A., Gerking, S., Gabel, H. (Eds.), Frontiers of Environmental Economics. Edward Elgar, Cheltenham, UK, pp. 121–147.

Cummings, R., Taylor, L. (1999). "Unbiased value estimates for environmental goods: a cheap talk design for the contingent valuation method". American Economic Review 83, 649–665.

Cummings, R., Taylor, L. (2001). "Experimental economics in environmental and natural resource management". In: Folmer, H., Tietenberg, T. (Eds.), International Yearbook of Environmental and Resource Economics. Edward Elgar, Cheltenham, UK, pp. 123–149.

Cummings, R., Elliot, S., Harrison, G., Murphy, J. (1997). "Are hypothetical referenda incentive compatible?". Journal of Political Economy 105, 609–621.

Davis, R. (1963). "Recreation planning as an economic problem". Natural Resource Journal 3, 239–249.

Davis, D., Holt, C. (1993). Experimental Economics. Princeton University Press, Princeton, NJ.

Diamond, P., Hausman, J. (1994). "Contingent valuation: is some number better than no number?". Journal of Economic Perspectives 8, 45–64.

Dickie, M., Fisher, A., Gerking, S. (1987). "Market transactions and hypothetical demand data: a comparative study". Journal of the American Statistical Association 82, 69–75.

Di Mauro, C., Maffioletti, A. (1996). "An experimental investigation of the impact of ambiguity on the valuation of self-insurance and self-protection". Journal of Risk and Uncertainty 13, 53–71.

Ehrlich, I., Becker, G. (1972). "Market insurance, self-insurance and self-protection". Journal of Political Economy 80, 623–648.

Ellsberg, D. (1961). "Risk, ambiguity, and the Savage axioms". Quarterly Journal of Economics 75, 643–669.

Fahlstrom, P. (1997). Old Cloquet, Minnesota: White Pine Capital of the World. Gateway Press, Baltimore, MD.

Fishburn, P. (1988). Nonlinear Preference and Utility Theory. Johns Hopkins University Press, Baltimore, MD.

Forsythe, R., Isaac, M. (1982). "Demand-revealing mechanisms for private good auctions". In: Smith, V. (Ed.), Research in Experimental Economics, vol. 2. JAI Press, Greenwich, CT, pp. 45–61.

Forsythe, R., Nelson, F., Neuman, G., Wright, J. (1992). "Anatomy of an experimental political stock market". American Economic Review 82, 1142–1161.

Fox, J., Hayes, D., Shogren, J. (2002). "Consumer preferences for food irradiation: how favorable and unfavorable descriptions affect preferences for irradiated pork in experimental auctions". Journal of Risk and Uncertainty 24, 75–95.

Fox, J., Shogren, J., Hayes, D., Kliebenstein, J. (1998). "CVM-X: calibrating contingent values with experimental auction markets". American Journal of Agricultural Economics 80, 455–465.

Freeman, A.M. (1993). The Measurement of Environmental and Resource Values: Theory and Methods. Resources for the Future, Washington, DC.

Friedman, D., Sunder, S. (1994). Experimental Methods: A Primer for Economists. Cambridge University Press, New York.

Frykblom, P. (1997). "Hypothetical question modes and real willingness to pay". Journal of Environmental Economics and Management 34, 275–287.

Frykblom, P., Shogren, J. (2000). "An experimental testing of anchoring effects in discrete choice questions". Environmental and Resource Economics 16, 329–341.

Grant, S., Kajii, A., Polak, B. (2001). "Different notions of disappointment aversion". Economics Letters 70, 203–208.

Gregory, R., Furby, L. (1987). "Auctions, experiments, and contingent valuation". Public Choice 55, 273–289.

Grether, D., Plott, C. (1979). "Economic theory of choice and the preference reversal phenomenon". American Economic Review 69, 623–638.

Haab, T., Huang, J.-C., Whitehead, J. (1999). "Are hypothetical referenda incentive compatible? Comment". Journal of Political Economy 107, 186–196.

Hammitt, J., Graham, J. (1999). "Willingness to pay for health protection: inadequate sensitivity to probability?". Journal of Risk and Uncertainty 18, 33–62.

Hanemann, W.M. (1991). "Willingness to pay and willingness to accept: how much can they differ?". American Economic Review 81, 635–647.

Hanemann, W.M. (1994). "Valuing the environment through contingent valuation". Journal of Economic Perspectives 8, 19–43.

Harrison, G. (1992). "Theory and misbehavior of first-price auctions: reply". American Economic Review 82, 1426–1443.

Harrison, G. (1996). Experimental economics and contingent valuation. Economics Working Paper 96-10, Division of Research, College of Business Administration, University of South Carolina.

Harrison, G., Harstad, R., Rutström, E. (1995). "Experimental methods and the elicitation of values". Working Paper, University of South Carolina.

Harrison, G., Rutström, E. (1999). "Experimental evidence of hypothetical bias in value elicitation methods". Working Paper, University of South Carolina.

Harrison, G., Beekman, R., Brown, L., Clements, L., McDaniel, T., Odom, S., Williams, M. (1997). "Environmental damage assessment with hypothetical surveys: the calibration approach". In: Bowman, M., Brannlund, R., Kriström, B. (Eds.), Topics in Environmental Economics. Kluwer Academic Publishers, Amsterdam.

Hayes, D., Shogren, J., Shin, S., Kliebenstein, J. (1995). "Valuing food safety in experimental auction markets". American Journal of Agricultural Economics 77, 40–53.

Heath, O.V.S. (1976). "In praise of experiments". In: Sunderland, N. (Ed.), Perspectives in Experimental Biology, vol. 2: Botany. Pergamon Press, Oxford, pp. 1–8.

Herschel, J. (1997 [1830]). A Preliminary Discourse on the Study of Natural Philosophy. University of Chicago Press, Chicago, IL.

Hey, J., Orme, C. (1994). "Investigating generalizations of expected utility theory using experimental data". Econometrica 62, 1291–1326.

Hoehn, J., Randall, A. (1987). "A satisfactory benefit cost indicator from contingent valuation". Journal of Environmental Economics and Management 14, 226–247.

Hoffman, E., Menkhaus, D., Chakravarti, D., Field, R., Whipple, G. (1993). "Using laboratory experimental auctions in marketing research: a case study of new packaging for fresh beef". Marketing Science 12, 318–338.

Hölldobler, B. (1985). "Karl von Frisch and the beginning of experimental behavioral ecology". In: Hölldobler, B., Lindauer, M. (Eds.), Experimental Behavioral Ecology and Sociobiology. Teubner Verlag, Stuttgart, pp. 1–3.

Horowitz, J., McConnell, K. (2002). "A review of WTA/WTP studies". Journal of Environmental Economics and Management 44, 426–447.

Irwin, J., Slovic, P., Lichtenstein, S., McClelland, G. (1993). "Preference reversals and the measurement of environmental values". Journal of Risk and Uncertainty 6, 5–18.

Johannesson, M., Bloomquist, G., Blumenschein, K., Johansson, P.-O., Liljas, B., O'Conor, R. (1999). "Calibrating hypothetical willingness to pay responses". Journal of Risk and Uncertainty 18, 21–32.

Jones, S. (1992). "Was there a Hawthorne effect?". American Journal of Sociology 3, 451–468.

Kachelmeier, S., Shehata, M. (1992). "Examining risk preferences under high monetary incentives: experimental evidence from the People's Republic of China". American Economic Review 82, 1120–1142.

Kagel, J. (1995). "Auctions: a survey of experimental research". In: Kagel, J., Roth, A. (Eds.), Handbook of Experimental Economics. Princeton University Press, Princeton, NJ, pp. 501–585.

Kagel, J., Roth, A. (Eds.) (1995). Handbook of Experimental Economics. Princeton University Press, Princeton, NJ.

Kahneman, D. (1986). "Comments". In: Cummings, R., Brookshire, D., Schulze, W. (Eds.), Valuing Environmental Goods: An Assessment of the Contingent Valuation Method. Rowman and Allenheld, Totowa, NJ, pp. 185–194.

Kahneman, D., Knetsch, J. (1992). "Valuing public goods: the purchase of moral satisfaction". Journal of Environmental Economics and Management 22, 57–70.

Kahneman, D., Knetsch, J., Thaler, R. (1990). "Experimental tests of the endowment effect and the Coase theorem". Journal of Political Economy 98, 1325–1348.

Karni, E., Safra, Z. (1987). "Preference reversals and the observability of preferences by experimental methods". Econometrica 55, 675–685.

Kask, S., Cherry, T., Shogren, J., Frykblom, P. (2002). "Using flexible scenarios in benefits estimation: an application to the cluster rule and the pulp and paper industry". In: List, J., deZeeuw, A. (Eds.), Recent Advances in Environmental Economics. Edward Elgar, Cheltenham, pp. 232–256.

Kealy, M., Montgomery, J., Dovidio, J. (1990). "Reliability and predictive validity of contingent values: does the nature of the good matter?". Journal of Environmental Economics and Management 19, 244–263.

Kline, M. (1985). Mathematics and the Search for Knowledge. Oxford University Press, Oxford.

Kneese, A. (1966). "Research goals and progress toward them". In: Jarrett, H. (Ed.), Environmental Quality in a Growing Economy. Johns Hopkins University Press, Baltimore, MD, pp. 69–87.

Knetsch, J. (1989). "The endowment effect and evidence of nonreversible indifference curves". American Economic Review 79, 1277–1284.

Knetsch, J., Sinden, J.A. (1984). "Willingness to pay and compensation demanded: experimental evidence of an unexpected disparity in measures of values". Quarterly Journal of Economics 99, 507–521.

Knez, M., Smith, V.L. (1987). "Hypothetical valuations and preference reversals in the context of asset trading". In: Roth, A. (Ed.), Laboratory Experimentation in Economics: Six Points of View. Cambridge University Press, New York, pp. 131–154.

Ledyard, J. (1995). "Public goods: a survey of experimental research". In: Kagel, J., Roth, A. (Eds.), Handbook of Experimental Economics. Princeton University Press, Princeton, NJ, pp. 111–194.

Lichtenstein, S., Slovic, P. (1971). "Reversals of preference between bids and choices in gambling decisions". Journal of Experimental Psychology 89, 46–55.

List, J., Shogren, J. (1998). "Calibration of the difference between actual and hypothetical valuations in a field experiment". Journal of Economic Behavior and Organization 37, 193–205.

List, J., Shogren, J. (1999). "Price information and bidding behavior in repeated second-price auctions". American Journal of Agricultural Economics 81, 942–949.

List, J., Shogren, J. (2002). "The calibration of willingness to accept". Journal of Environmental Economics and Management 43, 219–233.

Loomis, J., Brown, T., Lucero, T., Peterson, G. (1996). "Improving validity experiments of contingent valuation methods: results of efforts to reduce the disparity of hypothetical and actual willingness to pay". Land Economics 72, 450–461.

Lusk, J., Fox, J., Schroeder, T., Mintert, J., Koohmaraie, M. (2001). "In-store valuation of steak tenderness". American Journal of Agricultural Economics 83, 539–550.

MacDonald, H., Bowker, J. (1994). "The endowment effect and WTA: a quasi-experimental test". Journal of Agricultural and Applied Economics 26, 545–551.

Machina, M. (1987). "Choice under uncertainty: problems solved and unsolved". Journal of Economic Perspectives 1, 121–154.

Mäler, K.-G. (1985). "Welfare economics and the environment". In: Kneese, A., Sweeney, J. (Eds.), Handbook of Natural Resource and Energy Economics, vol. 1. North-Holland, Amsterdam, pp. 3–60.

Mansfield, C. (1998). "A consistent method for calibrating contingent value survey data". Southern Economic Journal 64, 665–681.

Mazzotta, M., Opaluch, J. (1995). "Decision making when choices are complex: a test of Heiner's hypothesis". Land Economics 71, 500–515.

McClelland, W., Schulze, W., Lazo, J., Walurang, D., Doyle, J., Eliot, S., Irwin, J. (1992). Methods for measuring non-use values: a contingent valuation study of groundwater cleanup. Center for Economic Analysis, Boulder, CO.

McCloskey, D. (1985). The Rhetoric of Economics. University of Wisconsin Press, Madison.

Menkhaus, D., Borden, G., Whipple, G., Hoffman, E., Field, R. (1992). "An empirical application of laboratory experimental auctions in marketing research". Journal of Agricultural and Resource Economics 17, 44–55.

Mitchell, R., Carson, R. (1989). Using Surveys to Value Public Goods: The Contingent Valuation Method. Resources for the Future, Washington, DC.

Morrison, G. (1998). "Understanding the disparity between WTP and WTA: endowment effect, substitutability, or imprecise preferences?". Economics Letters 59, 189–194.

Mosteller, F., Nogee, P. (1951). "An experimental measurement of utility". Journal of Political Economy 59, 371–404.

Mount, K., Reiter, S. (1974). "The informational size of message spaces". Journal of Economic Theory 8, 161–192.

National Oceanic and Atmospheric Administration (1994). "Natural resource damage assessments proposed rules". Federal Register 59, 1062.

Nau, R., McCardle, K. (1991). "Arbitrage, rationality, and equilibrium". Theory and Decision 31, 199–240.

Neill, H., Cummings, R., Ganderton, P., Harrison, G., McGuckin, T. (1994). "Hypothetical surveys and real economic commitments". Land Economics 70, 145–154.

Plott, C. (1987). "Dimensions of parallelism: some policy applications of experimental methods". In: Roth, A. (Ed.), Laboratory Experimentation in Economics: Six Points of View. Cambridge University Press, New York, pp. 193–219.

Plott, C. (1989). "An updated review of industrial organization: applications of experimental methods". In: Schmalensee, R., Willig, R. (Eds.), Handbook of Industrial Organization, vol. 2. North-Holland, Amsterdam, pp. 1111–1176.

Plott, C. (1994). "Market architectures, institutional landscapes and testbed experiments". Economic Theory 4, 3–10.

Plott, C. (1996). "Rational individual behavior in markets and social choice processes". In: Arrow, K., Colombatto, E., Perlman, M., Schmidt, C. (Eds.), The Rational Foundations of Economic Behavior. Macmillan/St. Martin Press, London/New York, pp. 225–250.

Prince, R., McKee, M., Ben-David, S., Bagnoli, M. (1992). "Improving the contingent valuation method: implementing the contribution game". Journal of Environmental Economics and Management 23, 78–90.

Rabin, M. (1998). "Psychology and economics". Journal of Economic Literature 36, 11–46.

Raiffa, H. (1982). The Art and Science of Negotiation. Belknap Press of Harvard University Press, Cambridge, MA.

Randall, A. (1997). "Calibration of CV responses: discussion". In: Bjornstad, D., Kahn, J. (Eds.), The Contingent Valuation of Environmental Resources. Edgar Elgar, London, pp. 198–207.

Rondeau, D., Schulze, W., Poe, G. (1999). "Voluntary revelation of the demand for public goods using a provision point mechanism". Journal of Public Economics 72, 455–470.

Rubinstein, A. (2001). "A theorist's view of experiments". European Economic Review 45, 615–628.

Rutström, E. (1998). "Home-grown values and the design of incentive compatible auctions". International Journal of Game Theory 27, 427–441.

Samuelson, P. (1938). "A note on the pure theory of consumers' behavior". Economica 5, 61–71.

Seip, K., Strand, J. (1992). "Willingness to pay for environmental goods in Norway: a contingent valuation study with real payment". Environmental and Resource Economics 2, 91–106.

Shogren, J. (1990). "The impact of self-protection and self-insurance on individual response to risk". Journal of Risk and Uncertainty 3, 191–204.

Shogren, J. (1993). "Experimental markets and environmental policy". Agricultural and Resource Economic Review 3, 117–129.

Shogren, J. (2002). "Micromotives in global environmental policy". Interfaces, 47–61.

Shogren, J., Crocker, T. (1991). "Risk, self-protection, and ex ante economic value". Journal of Environmental Economics and Management 21, 1–15.

Shogren, J., Crocker, T. (1994). "Rational risk valuation with sequential reduction opportunities". Economics Letters 44, 241–248.

Shogren, J., Hurley, T. (1999). "Experiments in environmental economics". In: van den Bergh, J. (Ed.), Handbook of Environmental and Resource Economics. Edgar Elgar, Cheltenham, UK, pp. 1180–1190.

Shogren, J., List, J., Hayes, D. (2000). "Preference learning in consecutive experimental auctions". American Journal of Agricultural Economics 82, 1016–1021.

Shogren, J., Nowell, C. (1992). "Economics and ecology: a comparison of experimental methodologies and philosophies". Ecological Economics 3, 1–21.

Shogren, J., Shin, S., Hayes, D., Kliebenstein, J. (1994). "Resolving differences in willingness to pay and willingness to accept". American Economic Review 84, 255–270.

Shogren, J., Fox, J., Hayes, D., Roosen, J. (1999). "Observed choices for food safety in retail, survey, and auction markets". American Journal of Agricultural Economics 81, 1192–1199.

Shogren, J., Cho, S., Koo, C., List, J., Park, C., Polo, P., Wilhelmi, R. (2001a). "Auction mechanisms and the measurement of WTP and WTA". Resource and Energy Economics 23, 97–109.

Shogren, J., Margolis, M., Koo, C., List, J. (2001b). "A random nth-price auction". Journal of Economic Behavior and Organization 46, 409–421.

Sinden, J.A. (1988). "Empirical tests of hypothetical biases in consumers' surplus surveys". Australian Journal of Agricultural Economics 32, 98–112.

Slovic, P., Lichtenstein, S. (1983). "Preference reversals: a broader perspective". American Economic Review 73, 596–605.

Smith, V.K. (1992). "Arbitrary values, good causes, and premature verdicts". Journal of Environmental Economics and Management 22, 71–89.

Smith, V.K. (1994). "Lightning rods, dart boards, and contingent valuation". Natural Resources Journal 34, 121–152.

Smith, V.K., Mansfield, C. (1998). "Buying time: real and hypothetical offers". Journal of Environmental Economics and Management 36, 209–224.

Smith, V.L. (1980). "Experiments with a decentralized mechanism for public good decisions". American Economic Review 70, 548–590.

Smith, V.L. (1982). "Microeconomic systems as an experimental science". American Economic Review 72, 589–597.

Smith, V.L. (1989). "Theory, experiment and economics". Journal of Economic Perspectives 3, 151–169.

Smith, V.L. (1991). "Rational choice: the contrast between economics and psychology". Journal of Political Economy 99, 877–897.

Spencer, M., Swallow, S., Miller, C. (1998). "Valuing water quality monitoring: a contingent valuation experiment involving hypothetical and real payments". Agricultural and Resource Economics Review 27, 28–42.

Sugden, R. (1993). "An axiomatic foundation for regret theory". Journal of Economic Theory 60, 159–180.

Swallow, S. (1994). "Value elicitation in laboratory markets: discussion and applicability to contingent valuation". American Journal of Agricultural Economics 76, 1096–1100.

Taylor, L. (1998). "Incentive compatible referenda and the valuation of environmental goods". Agricultural and Resource Economics Review 27, 132–139.

Thaler, R. (1992). The Winner's Curse: Paradoxes and Anomalies of Economic Life. Free Press, New York.

Thurstone, L. (1931). "The indifference function". Journal of Social Psychology 2, 139–167.

Tversky, A., Simonson, I. (1993). "Context-dependent preferences". Management Science 39, 1179–1189.

Tversky, A., Slovic, P., Kahneman, D. (1990). "The causes of preference reversal". American Economic Review 80, 204–217.

Vickrey, W. (1961). "Counterspeculation, auctions, and competitive sealed tenders". Journal of Finance 16, 8–37.

Viscusi, W.K. (1997). "Alarmist decisions with divergent risk information". Economic Journal 107, 1657–1670.

Wallis, W.A., Friedman, M. (1942). "The empirical derivation of indifference functions". In: Lange, O., McIntyre, F., Yntema, T. (Eds.), Studies in Mathematical Economics and Economics in Memory of Henry Schultz. Chicago University Press, Chicago, pp. 175–189.

Chapter 20

QUANTIFYING AND VALUING ENVIRONMENTAL HEALTH RISKS

W. KIP VISCUSI

Harvard University, USA

TED GAYER

Georgetown University, USA

Q51
D61
J17
(US)

Contents

Handbook of Environmental Economics, Volume 2. Edited by K.-G. Mäler and J.R. Vincent
© 2005 Elsevier B.V.   *All rights reserved*
DOI: 10.1016/S1574-0099(05)02020-6

Abstract

This chapter provides an overview of the current methodology for assessing environmental health risks. Our primary focus is on the practices that U.S. regulatory agencies use for assessing cancer risk, although we also provide a brief comparison to the methodology used in Western Europe. We then discuss the potential biases that may be inherent in the various components of the assessment methodology, and we discuss the implications of these biases towards regulatory policy. This chapter also provides an overview of the current methodology for valuing risks of both mortality and morbidity, placing particular emphasis on *ex ante* measurements of individuals' willingness to pay for risk reductions. We present the underlying theory, the estimation concerns, and the policy implications of labor market, housing market, and survey studies of estimating the value of risk reductions. Once we have established the economic framework of efficient regulatory policies, we then provide an overview of the extent to which U.S. regulatory performance meets these efficiency goals and offer suggestions for better achieving these goals.

Keywords

cost–benefit analysis, risk assessment, value of statistical life, hedonic models, risk–risk analysis

JEL classification: Q2, J3, K2

1. Introduction

Environmental policies provide diverse benefits including cleaner water, cleaner air, and ecosystems that are more supportive of wildlife. A necessary condition for these efforts to pass a test of economic efficiency is that the costs do not exceed the benefits. In such an assessment the benefits must be properly assessed and discounted to take into account the time when they accrue. The improvement to human health resulting from better environmental quality is a key component of benefits that provides the justification for many environmental policies. The health benefits of environmental policies may include, for example, reductions in the incidence of cancer, respiratory ailments, or pesticide poisonings.

The evaluation of the benefits of reducing health risks is a straightforward extension of public finance principles of valuation, in which the appropriate estimation is society's willingness to pay for the benefits. In this context, the benefit is the reduction in the health risks, or the improvement in the health risk lottery structure. There are two principal components involved in assessing society's willingness to pay for environmental health benefits. The first component is the estimation of the physical effects of the environmental health risk under consideration. More specifically, for a given environmental policy, one must estimate the decrease in the probability of the adverse health effects for the affected population. It is also important to assess the number of people affected by the risk reduction policy. Protecting a large population from a health hazard provides greater total health benefits than a comparable health risk reduction for a smaller population or, in the more extreme case, for a hypothetical individual. This broad component of quantitative risk analysis is a key building block for assessing environmental health benefits.

The second component of the benefit assessment task is to attach a societal willingness-to-pay value to the estimated risk reductions for the populations. These values are derived from a variety of sources of evidence. Market data are available for transactions implicitly involving many hazards, such as job risks, auto safety risks, and housing price responses to hazardous waste site risks. Moreover, as in natural resource damages contexts, it is often possible to use survey and contingent valuation techniques to elicit individual benefit valuation amounts. If no monetary values are available, the policy maker must make the subjective judgment that the health benefits exceed the net monetized costs for the other components. Knowing what these health effects are, their severity, and the extent of the population affected can assist in this policy-choice task.

This chapter is broadly concerned with the health benefit assessment process. Section 2 explores the methodology of risk assessment, focusing particularly on the practices in the U.S. government. Section 3 examines some of the implications and potential problems with current risk assessment practices. Section 4 examines the techniques for estimating willingness to pay for reductions in health risks, and Section 5 looks at the regulatory performance of U.S. regulatory policies for health risks. Section 6 concludes with a review of open policy issues.

2. Risk assessment methodology

The policy reference point that we will adopt is that the objective should be to maximize the expected benefits, less expected costs, of risk and environmental policies. The task of risk assessment is consequently to develop accurate and unbiased estimates of the probabilities of different hazards and measures of how the probabilities respond to different policy interventions. By focusing on expected benefits to society, we assume that in its policy-making role, the government is risk neutral. This assumption does not, however, assume risk neutrality on the part of those affected by the policy. The benefit values that enter the policy benefit calculations are based on the personal willingness to pay of those affected by the policy for the risk reduction, where these values can reflect aversion to risk.

2.1. Historical background and current regulatory guidelines in the U.S.

In 1983, under the directive of Congress, the National Research Council (NRC) published *Risk Assessment in the Federal Government: Managing the Process*. The goal of this report was to "strengthen the reliability and objectivity of scientific assessment that forms the basis for federal regulatory policies applicable to carcinogens and other public health hazards" [NRC (1983, opening letter)], and to ensure that "government regulation rests on the best available scientific knowledge" [NRC (1983, p. 1)]. The report presented the first systematic governmental formulation of the definitions and concepts involved in assessing health risks, and as a result, it had a major influence on the practice of risk assessment within the government's regulatory agencies.

Before the NRC's report, federal agencies faced the task of meeting recent regulatory laws that addressed issues of public health, while still relying on the outdated practice (derived in the 1950s) of using short-term, acute animal studies to establish no-observed-effect levels (NOELs) for chemicals. Analysts based this practice on the threshold hypothesis, which holds that human health is not affected below a certain exposure level. The NOEL is the level at which animals are not affected by the chemical, and in order to assure that there is a "reasonable certainty of no harm," this level is then divided by 100. This seemingly arbitrary factor was based on the assumption that the average person was up to 10 times more sensitive to chemicals than animals and that some people were up to 10 times more sensitive than the average person. These assumptions were not based on any supporting evidence.

Between the 1950s and the early 1980s, there was growing concern about exposure to environmental carcinogens. The NOEL assessment standards seemed inadequate since there was no clear evidence that carcinogens act through threshold mechanisms, or if a threshold did exist, that it could be reliably identified. Nevertheless, the U.S. Environmental Protection Agency (EPA) still used the NOEL criterion and the no-observed-adverse-effect level (NOAEL) criterion for assessing many health risks. In this atmosphere of limited understanding, regulators either resorted to banning carcinogens (for example, in the "Delaney Clause" for food additives), or where this was infeasible, choosing (somewhat arbitrarily) a maximal permissible exposure level for the carcinogens. Typically, agencies set these limits based on some concept of technical feasibility, instead of using criteria based directly on health risks or cost–risk tradeoffs.

In the 1960s and 1970s, the U.S. Food and Drug Administration (FDA) and the EPA began adopting new methods to assess potential cancer risks. A further impetus towards using risk assessment methodology occurred in a 1980 Supreme Court ruling in which the Court struck down the U.S. Occupational Safety and Health Administration (OSHA) policy of reducing concentrations of carcinogens as far as technically possible, without due consideration of whether the concentrations posed a significant health risk.[1] The implication of this ruling was that OSHA (and other regulatory agencies) could regulate hazards only if they first found a significant risk of harm. This decision increased the need for quantitative risk assessments. To have a scientific basis for this risk assessment effort, Congress asked the NRC, with support from the FDA, to examine and establish a set of risk assessment practices for federal regulatory agencies. This led to the 1983 NRC report mentioned previously.

In 1985 the Office of Science and Technology Policy [OSTP (1985)] issued guidelines similar to the NRC recommendations. Alone among the regulatory agencies, the EPA shortly thereafter responded to these studies and released *The Risk Assessment Guidelines of 1986* [EPA (1987)]. The five sections of this report included *Guidelines for Carcinogen Risk Assessment*, *Guidelines for Mutagenicity Risk Assessment*, *Guidelines for the Health Risk Assessment of Chemical Mixtures*, *Guidelines for the Health Assessment of Suspect Developmental Toxicants*, and *Guidelines for Estimating Exposures*.

For our examination of risk assessment methodology, we will focus on these EPA guidelines, specifically the guidelines for carcinogen risk assessment.[2] Our focus in this section is on risk assessment, not risk management. The former deals with the methods of estimating the adverse health consequences of exposure to chemicals, while the latter combines the risk assessment with legislative, economic, technical, and political concerns to arrive at a specific strategy for controlling exposure to these toxic agents.

The EPA's guidelines adopted the NRC's definitions of the components of risk assessment. These components are hazard identification, dose–response assessment, exposure assessment, and risk characterization. Hazard identification is the process of determining whether exposure to an agent can cause an increase in the incidence of cancer. Dose–response assessment defines the relationship between the dose of an agent and the

---

[1] See Industrial Union Department, AFL-CIO v. American Petroleum Institute, 448 U.S. 607 (1980).

[2] After 1986 the EPA published proposed guidelines for assessing female reproductive risk, male reproductive risk, and exposure-related measurements, and it published final guidelines on developmental toxicity in 1991. As a response to the NRC's 1994 publication of *Science and Judgment in Risk Assessment*, the EPA (1996) released *Proposed Guidelines for Carcinogen Risk Assessment* in order to address some of the recent concerns with risk assessment methodology. Since these guidelines have yet to be formally accepted, we will focus our discussion on the existing 1986 guidelines. We will, however, discuss the updated *Guidelines for Exposure Assessment* in Section 2.1.3.

incidence of a carcinogenic effect. The exposure assessment is the method of estimating the intensity, frequency, and duration of human exposure to an agent. The risk characterization combines the results of the dose–response assessment with the exposure assessment in order to arrive at an estimate for the carcinogenic risk. The risk characterization also includes a description of the uncertainties involved within each component. Figure 1 depicts the relationships among the four components of risk assessment and between risk assessment and risk management. Within this section we will discuss each of these components, highlighting some of the concerns entailed by each. In Section 3 we will discuss some broader concerns with current risk assessment practices.

2.1.1. Hazard identification

Epidemiological studies of human populations and animal bioassay studies are the main sources of information on whether a chemical agent has the potential of increasing the incidence of cancer. The EPA's criteria for assessing the accuracy of an epidemiological study include "the proper selection and characterization of exposed and control groups, the adequacy of duration and quality of follow-up, the proper identification and characterization of confounding factors and bias, the appropriate consideration of latency effects, the valid ascertainment of the cause of morbidity and death, and the ability to detect specific effects" [EPA (1987, p. 1.6)]. Not surprisingly, such epidemiological studies are difficult to conduct, and are thus not in abundance. The primary difficulty with epidemiological studies that use non-experimental data is that the chemical agent is likely to be correlated with unobservable characteristics, thus resulting in biased estimates of the health effect.[3] In the case of carcinogens, estimating a causal link is further complicated by the long latency period of cancer.

Most epidemiological studies establish correlation, at best, rather than a causal relationship. Given this, and given the difficulty for epidemiological studies to assess small changes in risk, the EPA advises against using negative results from such studies to establish the absence of carcinogenic risks. However, the EPA allows studies that do not indicate a statistically significant risk as evidence that the magnitude of the risk is small or difficult to disentangle from the other causal agents.

The limitations of the epidemiological studies often lead to a reliance on animal bioassay studies for identifying potential carcinogenic risks, since data for such animal studies are more commonly available. Such studies are based on the premise that one can make inferences on the effects of chemical agents on humans by conducting experiments on the effects of these agents on animals. (We will revisit this issue in Sec-

---

[3] In their study of the effect of air pollution on infant mortality, Chay and Greenstone (2003) attempt to address this bias inherent in nonexperimental studies. They use sharp, differential air quality changes across regions (attributable to geographic variation in the effects of a recession) to estimate the relationship between infant mortality and air pollution. Since the differential pollution reductions appear to be orthogonal to other characteristics related to infant mortality, their results provide credible, unbiased estimates of the dose–response relationship.

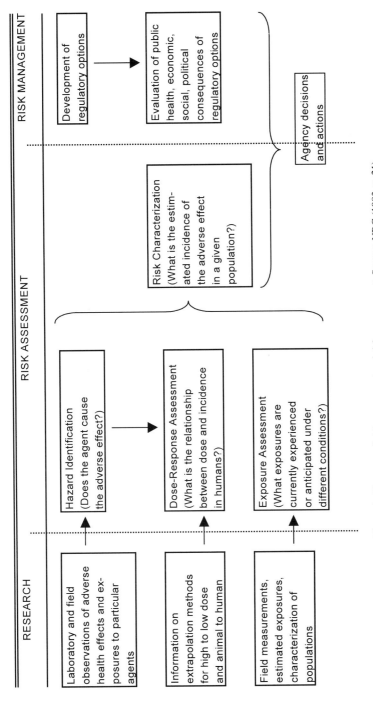

Figure 1. Elements of risk assessment and risk management. Source: NRC (1983, p. 21).

tion 2.1.2.) These studies assess carcinogenicity by comparing the tumor response in dosed animals (the doses are typically at or near the "maximum tolerated dose level") with the tumor response in control animals.[4] The EPA advises that "evidence of carcinogenic effects should be based on the observation of statistically significant tumor responses in specific organs or tissues," yet the appropriate level of statistical significance is "a matter of overall scientific judgment" [EPA (1987, p. 1.6)].

For both epidemiological and animal bioassay studies, the EPA gives general guidance for assessing the weight of evidence of studies with different results and different procedures. For example, the weight of evidence of a carcinogenic agent found in animal studies increases "with the increase in number of tissue sites affected by the agent; with the increase in number of animal species, strains, sexes, and number of experiments and doses showing a carcinogenic response; with the occurrence of clear-cut dose–response relationships as well as a high level of statistical significance of the increased tumor incidence in treated compared to control groups; when there is a dose-related shortening of the time-to-tumor occurrence or time to death with tumor; and when there is a dose-related increase in the proportion of tumors that are malignant" [EPA (1987, p. 1.5)].

The means by which the EPA pools risk evidence fails to adhere to sound statistical principles. Suppose that there are differing experimental results of equal credibility and that there is no other information at hand to inform one's judgments about the efforts. Then presumably these studies should receive equal weight in forming a risk assessment value. One's concern with policy objectives should not be permitted to contaminate the underlying statistical analysis. Once the risk assessment has been completed in an objective scientific manner, one can then bring to bear whatever risk management concerns are pertinent. However, the EPA's guidelines place a greater burden of proof on studies that do not find a carcinogenic effect than on studies that do. Such studies do not necessarily negate studies that do find a carcinogenic effect. Multiple negative studies that are essentially identical in all other respects "may indicate that the positive results are spurious" [EPA (1987, p. 1.6)]. For epidemiological studies, the weight of evidence "increases with the number of adequate studies that show comparable results on populations exposed to the same agent under different conditions" [EPA (1987, p. 1.6)].

Table 1 shows the EPA's categorization of the epidemiological and animal evidence. Chemical agents in Groups A and B are designated human carcinogens and possible human carcinogens. Such hazards are regarded as suitable for quantitative risk assessments. Agents that are not classifiable as human carcinogens or for which there is no evidence of carcinogenicity are in Groups D and E. In EPA's view, neither of these categories is suitable for quantitative risk assessment. Agents in Group C are possible human carcinogens and are generally considered suitable for a quantitative risk assessment. EPA permits judgment on a case-by-case basis for these agents. While the EPA provides guidelines for considering the weight of evidence, such guidelines are inherently

---

[4] The EPA's guidelines consider both malignant and benign tumors in the evaluation of the hazard identification since it is believed that chemicals that induce benign tumors frequently also induce malignant tumors, and that benign tumors often progress to malignant tumors [EPA (1987, pp. 1.4, 1.5)].

Table 1
Categorization of evidence of carcinogenicity

	Group	Criteria for classification
A	Human carcinogen	Sufficient evidence from epidemiologic studies
B	Probable human carcinogen (two subgroups)	Limited evidence from epidemiologic studies and sufficient evidence from animal studies (B1); or inadequate evidence from epidemiologic studies (or no data) and sufficient evidence from animal studies (B2)
C	Possible human carcinogen	Limited evidence from animal studies and no human data
D	Not classifiable as to human carcinogenicity	Inadequate human and animal data or no data
E	Evidence of noncarcinogenicity in humans	No evidence of carcinogenicity from adequate human and animal studies

Source: NRC (1994, p. 60).

judgmental and cannot be applied rigidly. As such, the EPA advises that the hazard identification include a narrative summary of the strengths and weaknesses of the evidence.

2.1.2. Dose–response assessment

Once the hazard identification provides evidence of a carcinogenic effect, the next step is to estimate the relationship between the dose of the agent and the incidence of cancer in the range of human exposure. As with hazard identification, evidence based on suitable epidemiological studies is preferable since such studies directly analyze the effects on humans. However, since the limitations of these studies described above still apply, animal studies (most often studies of rats and mice) more frequently form the basis for evaluating the dose–response assessment. There are two main difficulties with dose–response assessments: (1) extrapolating to low doses from the high doses administered to the animals; and (2) extrapolating the risks to humans from experiments on animals.

Regulatory agencies are typically concerned about very low risks to humans from chemical agents. Given the high costs of conducting animal studies and the difficulty inherent in directly testing low-dose responses, most studies have been designed for hazard identification, in which the treatment group is exposed to high levels of the dose (typically, the "maximum tolerated dose"). Researchers then fit a curve to the animal data in order to extrapolate the risks at low doses. However, there is no definitive evidence on the true shape of this curve, and a number of the extrapolation methods fit the data reasonably well. As shown in Figure 2, the choice of dose–response curve leads to dramatically different estimates of risk at low doses. The supralinear models imply that low doses are risky, the threshold models imply zero risk from low doses, with the linear and sublinear cases being intermediate in riskiness. The NRC suggests that the supralinear model is biologically implausible, and that the threshold model, while plausible, cannot be confirmed and should therefore be avoided. The EPA's guidelines

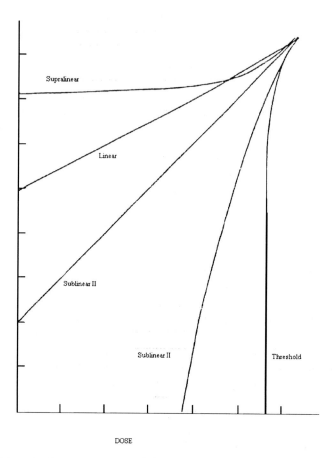

Figure 2. Results of alternative dose–response extrapolation models for the same experimental data. Source: NRC (1983, p. 26).

suggest using a linearized multistage procedure in the absence of adequate information to the contrary, since this model results in "a plausible upper limit to the risk that is consistent with some proposed mechanisms of carcinogenesis" [EPA (1987, p. 1.9)]. The linearized multistage model involves estimating a polynomial relationship between dose and the probability of effect, but then retaining only the linear term once the relationship is estimated. A feature of this model is that it is linear at low doses, and thus results in similar dose–response estimates as the linear model. The EPA also suggests using various models for comparison with the linearized multistage procedure.[5]

_____

[5] Assuming a nonthreshold model, such as the linearized multistage model, is equivalent to assuming that one molecule of an agent can cause cancer. We will discuss criticisms of the dose–response assumptions in Section 3.

Biological and empirical evidence generally supports the hypothesis that responses to chemical agents can be extrapolated across species. Nonetheless, the evidence is not rigorous enough to support definitive statements about interspecies effects. Most notably, the metabolic differences among species can significantly affect the validity of extrapolating from animals to humans. Other complications cited by the EPA include differences between humans and animals "with respect to life span, body size, genetic variability, population homogeneity, [and] existence of concurrent disease" [EPA (1987, p. 1.9)]. In order to extrapolate from animals to humans, the doses are typically standardized to account for differences between the species. The standardized factors include "mg per kg body weight per day, ppm in the diet or water, mg per m^2 body surface area per day, and mg per kg body weight per lifetime" [EPA (1987, p. 1.9)]. The EPA suggests using a standardized factor based on surface area.[6]

2.1.3. Exposure assessment

The EPA's *Risk Assessment Guidelines of 1986* contained a section of *Guidelines for Estimating Exposures*. In 1988, the EPA published the *Proposed Guidelines for Exposure-Related Measurements*. After a period of receiving comments from the EPA's Science Advisory Board and from the public, the EPA combined and updated these guidelines and, in 1992, released *Guidelines for Exposure Assessment*, which replaced the former guidelines. These new guidelines more explicitly considered the need to estimate the distribution of exposures of individuals and populations, as well as the need to incorporate uncertainty analysis into exposure assessment. As these guidelines give very extensive instructions in performing exposure assessments, we will focus only on the general concepts.

The goal of an exposure assessment is to estimate the intensity, duration, and frequency of exposure to a chemical agent. This exposure can occur through ingestion, inhalation, or dermal penetration.[7] Depending on the instances, some or all of these mechanisms of exposure may be pertinent. Consider the case of hazardous chemical wastes. It is possible to ingest these chemicals due to groundwater contamination, contaminated food (e.g., fish), or ingesting contaminated dirt (e.g., airborne dust or pica children who eat dirt). Inhalation can occur from airborne chemical vapors from the site, and dermal contact can arise through direct contact with the chemicals at the site.

Combining this exposure estimate of the potential dose with the toxicity information yields a quantitative risk estimate.[8] A scenario evaluation is the least expensive, and thus most commonly used, means of estimating exposure. In a scenario evaluation, the

---

[6] We will discuss what this assumption implies in Section 3.

[7] The EPA defines exposure as contact with "the visible exterior of the person (skin and openings into the body such as mouth and nostrils)" [EPA (1992, p. 16)].

[8] The potential dose is the amount of a chemical contained in material ingested, air breathed, or bulk material applied to the skin. Since dose–response assessments are typically based on potential dose, these estimates are readily comparable for the purposes of arriving at a quantitative risk assessment.

researcher estimates the concentrations of each chemical for different media, and then links this information with estimates of the frequency and duration of contact that individuals or populations have with the chemical. The chemical concentration and the time of contact are characterized separately. The potential dose for each pathway is found by multiplying the estimate of chemical concentration for each pathway by the ingestion rate and exposure duration for each pathway. This potential dose is for a given time period. The average daily doses are calculated by dividing the estimate by the body weight and averaging time (i.e., a parameter reflecting the period over which the dose is averaged). Thus, the general equation for the average daily dose (ADD) for a given chemical in a given pathway is as follows:

$$\text{ADD} = \frac{C \times IR \times ED}{BW \times AT}, \tag{1}$$

where C is the chemical concentration, IR is the ingestion rate, ED is the exposure duration, BW is the body weight, and AT is the averaging time. The estimated risk level is the product of ADD and the potency of the chemical as reflected in the estimated dose–response relationship.

The exposure assessment can be categorized either for a population or for a specified individual. The common goal of individual risk assessments is to find the risk to a hypothetically exposed individual who is often assumed to be at a high exposure level. Before the 1992 guidelines, the EPA used the standard of a maximum exposed individual (MEI) to determine individual risk.[9] The MEI is estimated as the plausible upper bound of the distribution of individual exposures. This estimate involves many conservative assumptions. For example, it assumes that the MEI lived for 70 years at the location receiving the heaviest dose of concentration, that the MEI stayed there 25 hours per day, and that there was no difference between outdoor and indoor concentrations. In the 1992 guidelines, the EPA advised the use of a high-end exposure estimate (HEEE) as a "plausible estimate of the individual exposure for those persons at the upper end of an exposure distribution" [EPA (1992, p. 45)]. Conceptually, the high end of the distribution "means above the 90th percentile of the population distribution, but not higher than the individual in the population who has the highest exposure" [EPA (1992, p. 45)]. The guidelines do not give specific instructions on determining this measure, only that the objective is to arrive at an estimate that "will fall within the actual distribution, rather than above it" [EPA (1992, p. 45)].

Population risks can be calculated by summing the individual risks for all individuals within a population. Typically this is accomplished by applying the estimated dose to the population instead of computing the doses to each individual. Given that individual risk estimates are usually upper bound measures, applying these estimates to the population will also result in conservative population estimates of risk. The EPA takes a

---

[9] In the case of Superfund, the Office of Solid Waste and Emergency Response uses individual risk assessments based on "reasonable maximum exposure" in the remediation decision-making.

precautionary tone with respect to population cancer risks, stating that "these estimates are not meant to be accurate predictions of real (or actuarial) cases of disease" [EPA (1992, p. 48)].

2.1.4. Risk characterization

The carcinogenic risk estimate results from linking the dose–response assessment with the exposure assessment. These numerical results are presented in the risk characterization, along with a description of the strengths and weaknesses of the assessment process. The EPA's guidelines list a number of ways to present the risk estimates. The cancer risk can be expressed as the "excess lifetime risk due to a continuous constant lifetime exposure of one unit of carcinogen concentration" [EPA (1987, p. 1.10)]. The risk can be presented as the dose corresponding to a given level of risk. Risks may also be presented "either in terms of the excess individual lifetime risks, the excess number of cancers produced per year in the exposed population, or both" [EPA (1987, p. 1.10)]. When computing the risk from multiple chemicals, the EPA advises that the risks be added, thus ruling out synergistic and antagonistic effects.

The risk estimates should be presented with the qualitative weights as described in Table 1. Within the risk characterization, the risk estimates should also be accompanied by a summary of all the components of the risk assessment, as well as a description of the reliability of the estimates. This description of the reliability of the estimates should include all the "major assumptions, scientific judgments, and, to the extent possible, estimates of the uncertainties embodied in the assessment" [EPA (1987, pp. 1.10, 1.11)]. Table 2 contains a list of the uncertainty issues that must be addressed at each of the four stages of the risk assessment: the hazard identification, the assessment of the dose–response relationship, the exposure assessment, and the overall characterization of the risk for policy. Table 3 contains the EPA's uncertainty checklist for risk assessments done for hazardous waste cleanups for what is called the Superfund program. This checklist pertains to each narrowly defined component of the risk assessment process, where at each stage of uncertainty there is the potential for biasing the risk assessment through conservatism factors, as will be discussed below in Section 3. Instead of letting the numbers stand alone, the EPA desires the risk characterization to serve as a means of informing the risk managers of the likelihood that the estimates reflect the true risk.

2.2. Risk assessment in other countries

While the focus of this chapter is on the United States, it is useful to briefly compare U.S. risk assessment practices to those of Western European.[10] As described in Section 2.1, there are standardized risk assessment guidelines for U.S. regulatory agencies.

---

[10] Our comparison countries are the United Kingdom, Germany, and the Netherlands, as well as the harmonization of risk assessment in the European Union. For a more detailed discussion of European risk assessment practices, see Mazurek (1996) and Pugh and Tarazona (1998).

Table 2
Uncertainty issues to be addressed in each risk assessment step

A. *Hazard identification.* What do we know about the capacity of an environmental agent for causing cancer (or other adverse effects) in laboratory animals and in humans?
  1. the nature, reliability, and consistency of the particular studies in humans and in laboratory animals;
  2. the available information on the mechanistic basis for activity; and
  3. experimental animal responses and their relevance to human outcomes.

B. *Dose–response assessment.* What do we know about the biological mechanisms and dose–response relationships underlying any effects observed in the laboratory or epidemiology studies providing data for the assessment?
  1. relationship between extrapolation models selected and available information on biological mechanisms;
  2. how appropriate data sets were selected from those that show the range of possible potencies both in laboratory animals and humans;
  3. basis for selecting interspecies dose scaling factors to account for scaling dose from experimental animals to humans; and
  4. correspondence between the expected route(s) of exposure and the exposure route(s) utilized in the hazard studies, as well as the interrelationships of potential effects from different exposure routes.

C. *Exposure assessment.* What do we know about the paths, patterns, and magnitudes of human exposure and number of persons likely to be exposed?
  1. The basis for the values and input parameters used in each exposure scenario. If based on data, information on the quality, purpose, and representatives of the database is needed. If based in assumptions, the source and general logic used to develop the assumption (e.g., monitoring, modeling, analogy, professional judgment) should be described.
  2. The major factor or factors (e.g., concentration, body uptake, duration/frequency of exposure) thought to account for the greatest uncertainty in the exposure estimate, due either to sensitivity or lack of data.
  3. The link of the exposure information to the risk descriptors. These risk descriptors should include: (1) individual risk including the central tendency and high end portions of the risk distribution, (2) important subgroups of the population such as highly exposed or highly susceptible groups or individuals (if known), and (3) population risk. This issue includes the conservatism or non-conservatism of the scenarios, as indicated by the choice of descriptors. In addition, information that addresses the impact of possible low probability but possible high consequence events should be addressed.

       For individual risk, information such as the people at highest risk, the risk levels these individuals are subject to, the activities putting them at higher risk, and the average risk for individuals in the population of interest should be addressed. For population risk, information as to the number of cases of a particular health effect that might be probabilistically estimated in this population for a specific time period, the portion of the population that are within a specified range of some benchmark level for non-carcinogens; and, for carcinogens, the number of persons above a certain risk level should be included. For subgroups, information as to how exposure and risk impact the various subgroups and the population risk of a particular subgroup should be provided.

(continued on next page)

These guidelines include default parameter assumptions for each step of the risk assessment process. This approach contrasts with the approach in Western European countries, where expert advisory committees (not regulatory agencies) handle risk assessment on a case-by-case basis, and thus have more flexibility in assigning values for different parameter assumptions.

Table 2

(*Continued*)

D. Risk characterization. What do other assessors, decision-makers, and the public need to know about the primary conclusions and assumptions, and about the balance between confidence and uncertainty in the assessment? What are the strengths and limitations of the assessment?

 1. Numerical estimates should never be separated from the descriptive information that is integral to the risk assessment. For decisionmakers, a complete characterization (key descriptive elements along with numerical estimates) should be retained in all discussions and papers relating to an assessment used in decision-making. Differences in assumptions and uncertainties, coupled with non-scientific considerations called for in various environmental statutes, can clearly lead to different risk management decisions in cases with ostensibly identical quantitative risks; i.e., the "number" alone does not determine the decisions.

 2. Consideration of alternative approaches involves examining selected plausible options for addressing a given uncertainty. The strengths and weaknesses of each alternative approach and as appropriate, estimates of central tendency and variability (e.g., mean, percentiles, range, variance). The description of the option chosen should include the rationale for the choice, the effect of option selected on the assessment, a comparison with other plausible options, and the potential impacts of new research.

Source: NRC (1994, pp. 71–72).

The European countries currently base their risk assessment practices on the four stages used by the U.S.: hazard identification, dose–response assessment, exposure assessment, and risk characterization. Traditionally, the Europeans have tended to place greater reliance on a "weight of evidence" approach to assess the uncertainties involved in the risk assessment stages. The case-by-case and weight of evidence approaches used by the Europeans lead to assumptions based on the available evidence and the appropriate framework, which is different from the conservatively-defined standardized assumptions used by the U.S. [Mazurek (1996)]. Thus, European risk assessments are likely to be less conservative than U.S. risk assessments, which as we discuss below, is a desirable feature. To take just one example, European risk assessments tend to place equal weight on studies of negative findings, whereas U.S. risk assessments discount such studies.

Except for the Netherlands, the European countries do not rely on the quantitative dose–response model used by the U.S. [Mazurek (1996)]. Instead, they base their models on biological data and are more reluctant to rely on the mathematical assumptions of the dose–response model. Much like the U.S. before the 1983 NRC Report, the European countries are more concerned with the hazard identification stage, and thus seek to estimate the threshold below which there are no adverse health effects.

Recently, the European Union has attempted to harmonize the risk assessment practices of the Member States. Commission Directive 93/67/EEC of July 1993 and Commission Regulation No. 1488/94 of June 1994 describe the principles for assessing the risks to humans and the environment for existing and new substances.[11]

---

[11] European Commission (1996) contains the detailed procedures for conducting risk assessments.

Table 3
EPA guidance for uncertainty analysis in superfund risk assessments

List physical setting definition uncertainties
For chemicals not included in the quantitative risk assessment, describe briefly:
  – reason for exclusion (e.g., quality control), and
  – possible consequences of exclusion on risk assessment (e.g., because of widespread contamination, underestimate of risk).
For the current land uses describe:
  – sources and quality of information, and
  – qualitative confidence level.
For the future land uses describe:
  – sources and quality of information, and
  – information related to the likelihood of occurrence.
For each exposure pathway, describe why pathway was selected or not selected for evaluation.
For each combination of pathways, describe any qualifications regarding the selection of exposure pathways considered to contribute to exposure of the same individual or group of individuals over the same period of time.

Characterize model uncertainties
List/summarize the key model assumptions.
Indicate the potential impact of each on risk:
  – direction (i.e., may over- or underestimate risk); and
  – magnitude (i.e., order of magnitude).

Characterize toxicity assessment uncertainties
For each substance carried through the quantitative risk assessment, list uncertainties related to:
  Qualitative hazard findings (i.e., potential for human toxicity);
  Derivation of toxicity values, e.g.,
  – human or animal data,
  – duration of study (e.g., chronic study used to set subchronic RfD), and
  – any special considerations.
  The potential for synergistic or antagonistic interactions with other substances affecting the same individuals; and
  Calculation of lifetime cancer risks on the basis of less-than-lifetime exposures.

For each substance not included in the quantitative risk assessment because of inadequate toxicity information, list:
  Possible health effects; and
  Possible consequences of exclusion on final risk estimates.

(continued on next page)

Reflecting the Europeans' relative skepticism of the linear dose response model, the E.U. guidelines seek to establish the No Observable Effect Level (NOEL) or a No Observable Adverse Effect (NOAEL) for the chemical substance [Pugh (1998), Pearce (1998)]. Their goal is to identify toxic chemicals and to determine the exposure level at which there is no threat to human health, regardless of cost.

While we address the efficiency of U.S. regulatory performance in a later section, it is worth noting to what extent the E.U. relies on cost–benefit analysis. Historically, European countries have not used cost–benefit analysis in establishing environmental regulations, since they have tended to view benefit estimation techniques as flawed.

Table 3
(*Continued*)

Risk characterization

Confidence that the key site-related contaminants were identified and discussion of contaminant concentrations relative to background concentration ranges;

A description of the various types of cancer and other health risks present at the site (e.g., liver toxicity, neurotoxicity), distinguishing between known effects in humans and those that are predicted to occur based on animal experiments;

Level of confidence in the quantitative toxicity information used to estimate risks and presentation of qualitative information on the toxicity of substances not included in the quantitative assessment;

Level of confidence in the exposure estimates for key exposure pathways and related exposure parameters assumptions;

The magnitude of the cancer risks and noncancer hazard indices relative to the Superfund site remediation goals in the NCP (e.g., the cancer risk range of 10^{-4} to 10^{-7} and noncancer index of 1.0).

The major factors driving the site risks (e.g., substances, pathways, and pathway combinations);

The major factors reducing the certainty in the results and the significance of these uncertainties (e.g., adding risks over several substances and pathways);

Exposed population characteristics; and

Comparison with site-specific health studies, when available.

Source: NRC (1994, p. 73).

However, in the United Kingdom there has been a recent trend towards taking into account the costs and benefits of a policy, although cost–benefit analysis is still not explicitly required in formulating policy [Pearce (2000)].[12] The United Kingdom was also successful in influencing the European Commission to adopt Article 130R(3) of the Single European Act (the Masstricht Treaty), which requires that regulatory decisions be based on several factors, including "the potential benefits and costs of action or lack of action." As a result, cost-effectiveness and cost–benefit analyses are currently more common within the E.U. However, it is still not clear what role such analyses will play in formulating policy.[13]

3. Issues in risk assessment

3.1. Conservative risk assessment practices

In Section 2 we indicated some instances in which the EPA opts for conservative assumptions in its risk analyses. When faced with uncertain parameter or model assumptions, the EPA tends to choose default options that lead to higher assessments of the risk. This bias is greater than that reflected in the approach of European countries.

---

[12] Article 37 of the British Environment Act of 1995 codified the need to take into account costs in formulating policies that protect the environment.

[13] See Pearce (1998) for an overview of risk assessment and benefit–cost procedures in the E.U.

By relying on conservative assumptions, the EPA has chosen to represent the upper region of the range of risks suggested by current scientific knowledge. These are risks that conceivably might happen but are not expected to happen based on mean risk values. One possible explanation for the EPA's use of conservatism is that the agency has institutionalized the ambiguity aversion bias generally found among individuals. The ambiguity aversion bias is reflected in the Ellsberg paradox [Ellsberg (1961)], in which people prefer to choose a black or white ball from an urn where the proportion of balls is known to be half and half, rather than choosing from an urn where the proportion is unknown. The rational default assumption for the latter choice is 50 : 50, yet people generally prefer the former choice since it is based on a "hard" probability. In the case of losses, subjects are generally averse to risk ambiguity when facing low probability events. For very high probabilities of losses, there is a reversal as risk ambiguity is desirable.[14] In the case of health risks, this evidence suggests that people would be averse to ambiguous chances of harm. In this section we will briefly review some of these conservative assumptions and then discuss the implications of conservatism in risk assessments.

Since there is no theoretical support for any particular dose–response function, the EPA relies on the linearized multistage model. Since this model implies low-dose linearity, it produces upper-bound estimates of low-dose risks. Such a model assumes that there is no threshold below which a chemical has no carcinogenic effect (i.e., even one molecule of the chemical can produce cancer).[15] Nonlinear models in which risk falls more than proportionately as the dose declines would lead to substantially smaller estimates of risk. The EPA also opts for conservatism in considering both benign and malignant tumors in the hazard identification stage.

In using the animal studies to extrapolate the risks to humans, the EPA suggests adjusting the doses by the surface area of the corresponding species. Because surface area increases by much less than weight as one moves from rodents to humans, this scaling leads to much higher risk estimates than scaling by weight would.[16] Additionally, in selecting data from animal studies the EPA places greater emphasis on data from "long-term animal studies showing the greatest sensitivity" [EPA (1987, p. 1.8)]. Underlying this recommendation is the conservative assumption that "human sensitivity is as high as the most sensitive responding animal species" [EPA (1987, p. 1.8)]. One assumption that is not conservative is the recommendation to combine the risks from several chemicals additively. To the extent that there are synergistic effects, this leads to an underestimation of the actual risk [Finkel (1989)].[17]

---

[14] See Viscusi and Chesson (1999).

[15] The EPA does allow the use of another model, given that there is "adequate evidence" that the mechanism through which the substance is carcinogenic is more consistent with a different model.

[16] Using the surface area conversion instead of the weight conversion leads to a difference in risk of a factor of thirteen for mouse data and six for rat data [Nichols and Zeckhauser (1986)].

[17] Of course, to the extent that there are antagonistic effects, this leads to an overestimation of the actual risk.

As discussed in Section 2.1.3, the goal of EPA's exposure assessments is to find the risk to a highly exposed person. Traditionally, the EPA used the standard of a maximum exposed individual (MEI) or a reasonable maximum exposure (RME) to estimate individual risk. In 1992 the EPA changed the standard to a high-end exposure estimate (HEEE), which is defined as the 90th percentile of the population distribution. However, the EPA does not give specific instructions on how to arrive at this level of confidence, instead relying on default assumptions that are assumed to arrive at the HEEE. Table 4 lists some of the EPA's default assumptions for exposure parameters used at Superfund sites, and compares these to the mean values and values at different confidence levels. The degree of conservatism varies for the different parameters. Except for the child soil ingestion rate, the other parameters are all well above the mean value. The default option for exposure duration is 30 years, which is almost at the 90th percentile, and the default option for adult soil ingestion rate is between the mean and the 90th percentile.

Using upper bound estimates for the exposure parameters and conservative assumptions of the toxicity model leads to a cumulative effect known as "cascading conservatism" [Burmaster and Harris (1993)]. The multiplicative effect of each conservative assumption can lead to overwhelming overestimation of health risks. For example, studies by the Michigan Manufacturers Association (1993) and the Chemical Manufacturers Association (1991) found that exposure values using EPA risk assessment are significantly greater than the 95th percentile of a distribution generated by Monte Carlo simulation. Cullen (1994) found that conservative parameter estimates lead to risk estimates greater than the 99th percentile of a simulated distribution. Finley and

Table 4
Parameter values used for risk sensitivity analysis

	Adult soil ingestion rate (mg/day)	Child soil ingestion rate (mg/day)	Adult water ingestion rate (L/day)	Child water ingestion rate (L/day)	Exposure duration (years)	Contaminant concentration (mg/kg or ug/1)
EPA default	100	200	2.0[a]	1	30[a]	RME[b]
EPA mean	50	200	1.4	1	9	Site documents
Alternative mean	46.6	75	1.3	0.7 (ages 0–10) 0.9 (ages 11–18)	11	–
Alternative 90th percent.	176	1190	2.1	1.2 (ages 0–10) 1.6 (ages 11–18)	26	–
Alternative 95th percent.	196	1751	2.5	1.4 (ages 0–10) 1.9 (ages 11–18)	33	–
Alternative 99th percent.	211	–	3.5	2.0 (ages 0–10) 2.7 (ages 11–18)	47	–

Source: Viscusi, Hamilton and Dockins (1997, p. 193).
[a]Value is approximately the 90th percentile.

[b]Reasonable maximum exposure is the maximum detected or 95th upper confidence limit on the mean, whichever is lower.

Paustenbach (1994) found that risk estimates are in the 99th percentile for the case of groundwater contamination and in the 99.99th percentile for risks arising from dioxin emission in the food chain. Smith (1994) found risk estimates between the 90th and 95th percentile.

In their analysis of 141 Superfund sites, Viscusi, Hamilton and Dockins (1997) found that over 40 percent of sites requiring remediation would shift into the discretionary cleanup range if the default assumptions for chemical concentration, exposure duration, and ingestion rates were changed to their mean values. Table 5 reproduces the results from Viscusi, Hamilton and Dockins (1997). The table compares the mean and median risk assessments using the default assumptions with the mean and median risk assessments when one or all of the assumptions are changed to their mean values. According to EPA guidance for Superfund sites, sites with risks less than 1×10^{-6} require no remedial action, sites with risks between 1×10^{-6} and 1×10^{-4} are within a discretionary range, and sites with risks greater than 1×10^{-4} require remedial action. By changing the parameter estimates to the mean values, the distribution of sites within these three categories changes dramatically. For example, for the soil and groundwater ingestion pathways, a change to the mean values for ingestion rate, exposure duration, and concentration leads to a 21 percent increase in the number of sites in which no remedial action is required. Thus, the use of mean parameter estimates greatly affects the cleanup policy decisions.

The large overestimation of risks due to cascading conservatism affects policy in two important ways. First, the extreme upper-bound estimates of risk distort the relative risk levels of the environmental risks facing society. There will be an over-emphasis of regulatory control of the hazards for which the distribution of the possible risk is imprecise. Given limited resources, the efficient way to address health risks would be to target resources where the expected health benefits most outweigh the expected costs. The high-risk estimates generated by conservative risk assessment practices distort the benefits of risk reduction of environmental hazards.[18]

While an exaggerated view of the magnitude of risks may lead to an inefficient use of resources, the bigger concern is that conservative risk assessments may alter our risk reduction priorities. For example, since estimates are always based on the most sensitive species tested, the degree of bias will rise with the number species tested [Nichols and Zeckhauser (1986)]. Thus, it is plausible that a less harmful chemical will have a higher assessment of risk if it is tested on more species than another more harmful chemical. In general, given that the conservatism is compounded with each parameter assumption, a chemical's risk assessment will increase given the number of parameter assumptions. Nichols and Zeckhauser (1986) demonstrate this point with the following example. Suppose there are two chemicals, A and B, and that the true carcinogenic risk of A is twice that of B. Because of differing degrees of conservatism, however, the risk

---

[18] For example, Ames and Gold (1996) argue that the major causes of cancer are smoking and poor diet and that pollution accounts for less than 1 percent of human cancer. The implication is that too much regulatory effort is placed on environmental health problems since their risks are over-represented in the risk assessment process.

Table 5
Risk estimates with parameter values replaced with EPA means

Pathway type	Permutation (parameter varied)	Percentage no action[a]	Percentage discretionary	Percentage take action	Mean	Median[b]	t statistic for means	Count
Soil ingestion	Site documents	1.5	81.3	17.2	1.4×10^{-3}	1.5×10^{-5}	2.5	268
	IR only	5.2	79.9	14.9	1.2×10^{-3}	1.1×10^{-5}		
	Site documents	1.2	85.9	12.9	9.2×10^{-4}	1.3×10^{-5}	2.3	162
	ED only	11.7	83.3	5.0	2.8×10^{-4}	3.9×10^{-6}		
	Site documents	0.7	78.9	20.4	2.5×10^{-3}	1.6×10^{-5}	2.7	147
	CC only	8.8	83.0	8.2	1.5×10^{-3}	7.5×10^{-6}		
	Site documents	1.5	83.8	14.7	2.1×10^{-3}	1.1×10^{-5}	2.2	68
	All (IR, ED, CC)	57.4	41.2	1.4	1.8×10^{-4}	7.2×10^{-7}		
Groundwater ingestion	Site documents	0.9	35.9	63.2	1.7×10^{-2}	3.1×10^{-4}	3.9	451
	IR only	2.4	36.6	61.0	1.3×10^{-2}	2.3×10^{-4}		
	Site documents	1.2	30.4	68.4	2.1×10^{-2}	5.3×10^{-4}	3.7	332
	ED only	7.8	39.5	52.7	4.6×10^{-3}	1.2×10^{-4}		
	Site documents	0.7	39.1	60.2	1.3×10^{-2}	3.3×10^{-4}	2.7	294
	CC only	2.0	48.3	49.7	3.6×10^{-3}	1.0×10^{-4}		
	Site documents	0.9	33.2	65.9	1.7×10^{-2}	6.0×10^{-4}	2.9	214
	All (IR, ED, CC)	10.7	56.1	33.9	5.6×10^{-4}	2.9×10^{-5}		
Soil and groundwater ingestion	Site documents	1.1	52.9	46.0	1.1×10^{-2}	7.1×10^{-5}	3.9	719
	IR only	3.5	52.7	43.8	8.6×10^{-3}	5.2×10^{-5}		
	Site documents	1.2	48.6	50.2	1.5×10^{-2}	1.0×10^{-4}	3.8	494
	ED only	9.1	53.8	37.1	3.2×10^{-3}	3.0×10^{-5}		
	Site documents	0.6	52.4	47.0	9.7×10^{-3}	8.4×10^{-5}	2.8	441
	CC only	4.3	59.9	35.8	2.9×10^{-3}	3.4×10^{-5}		
	Site documents	1.1	45.3	53.6	1.3×10^{-2}	2.0×10^{-4}	3.0	282
	All (IR, ED, CC)	22.0	52.5	25.5	4.7×10^{-4}	1.1×10^{-5}		

Note: In this table IR denotes ingestion rate, ED denotes exposure duration, and CC denotes contaminant concentration.

Source: Viscusi, Hamilton and Dockins (1997, p. 196).

[a] According to EPA guidance, risks less than 1×10^{-6} require no remedial action in the Superfund program. Risks from 1×10^{-6} to 1×10^{-4} allow the site manager to use discretion with an explanation given if remedial action is taken. Risks greater than 1×10^{-4} are deemed unacceptable and require remedial action.

[b] All median pairs are significantly different according to the sign test for equality of medians.

from A is overestimated by a factor of two while the risk from B is overestimated by a factor of 10. Policy makers are likely to conclude that B is substantially more dangerous and deserves more stringent control than A, when in fact the reverse is true. Such distortions result in some low-level risks being regulated too much with respect to other high-level risks. Critics of these conservative risk assessment practices therefore claim that a movement towards expected value assessments will lead to a more rational use of regulatory dollars. More expected lives will be saved for any given expenditure if one relies on mean risk values.

3.2. Synthetic v. natural chemicals

As was discussed in Section 2.1.2, there is no precise way to extrapolate the risk from low doses of chemicals using the animal studies of maximum tolerated doses. Some critics argue that extrapolating from the maximum tolerated dose leads to misinterpretations of low-dose effects. They claim that a plausible explanation for the high frequency of positive results in animal bioassays is that testing at the maximum tolerated dose frequently can cause chronic cell killing and consequent cell replacement – a factor for cancer that can be limited to high doses [Ames and Gold (1990, 1996)]. Therefore, it is "the dose that makes the poison," and almost any chemical exposure at extremely high doses will lead to carcinogenic effects.[19] The EPA acknowledges that the linearized multistage dose–response model does not necessarily lead to a realistic estimate, and they state that the true risk may conceivably be zero.

If the carcinogenic effects found in risk assessments are due to the size of the dose, then one would expect to find a similar carcinogenic effect between synthetic and natural chemicals. The findings of Ames and Gold (1990), Gold et al. (1992, 1993) support this claim. They found that approximately half of all natural chemicals and half of all synthetic chemicals are rodent carcinogens. For example, of the more than one thousand natural chemicals found in roasted coffee, nineteen of the twenty-six that were tested were found to be rodent carcinogens. Table 6 lists the carcinogenic and noncarcinogenic chemicals that exist in roasted coffee. Using a measure of human exposure/rodent potency (HERP), Gold et al. (1992) ranked the possible carcinogenic hazards from natural and synthetic chemicals. This ranking is reproduced in Table 7, with the natural chemicals appearing in boldface.

While high doses of natural chemicals (for example, those found in fruits and vegetables) have carcinogenic effects in rats, humans (as well as rats) can eat small doses of these natural chemicals without deleterious effects since we are extremely well protected by many general defense enzymes [Ames, Profet and Gold (1990a)].[20] Since our enzymes are equally effective against synthetic chemicals, the critics of current risk assessment practices believe that the evidence does not support the claim that low doses of these synthetic chemicals are harmful.[21]

Relying on the risk assessments of synthetic chemicals while ignoring the risks from the natural background chemicals leads to a distorted view of risks and thus an inefficient allocation of resources devoted to protecting public health. Indeed, Viscusi (1995) found that, controlling for the level of risk, there was a consistent regulatory

---

[19] More specifically, they believe that the carcinogenic effects of the high doses are due to induced cell divisions, and that these secondary effects would not exist at lower doses.

[20] Ames, Profet and Gold (1990b) estimate that 99.99% (by weight) of the pesticides in the American diet are natural chemicals, produced by plants in order to defend themselves against fungi, insects, and animal predators.

[21] Ames, Profet and Gold (1990a) cite numerous studies that find that general defenses against natural synthetics also protect against synthetic chemicals. See, for example, Jakoby (1980).

Table 6
Carcinogenicity status of natural chemicals in roasted coffee

Positive	Not positive	Yet to test
Acetaldehyde	Acrolein	~1,000 chemicals
Benzaldehyde	Biphenyl	
Benzene	Eugenol	
Benzofuran	Nicotinic acid	
Benzo(a)pyrene	Phenol	
Caffeic acid	Piperidine	
Catechol	[Uncertain: caffeine]	
1,2,5,6-dibenzanthracene		
Ethanol		
Ethylbenzene		
Formaldehyde		
Furan		
Furfural		
Hydrogen peroxide		
Hydroquinone		
Limonene		
MeIQ		
Styrene		
Toluene		

Source: Ames and Gold (1996, p. 28).

bias towards synthetic chemicals. In 1996, a report by the NRC states that "unlike most naturally occurring dietary constituents, synthetic ones such as direct and indirect food additives and pesticide residues are highly regulated, with stringent limits placed on their allowable levels of synthetic chemicals in foods" [NRC (1996, p. 303)]. Viscusi and Hakes (1998) used a comprehensive sample of 350 chemicals that were tested for cancer potency. They found that, controlling for the cancer risk, the FDA (though not the EPA or OSHA) is more likely to regulate chemicals if they are synthetic.[22] These results suggest that regulatory efforts to address health risks are not efficient.

3.3. Actual v. perceived risk

What is the appropriate role of government policy in terms of focusing on actual and perceived risks? Perceived risks often generate the political pressure for intervention. The public is guided by its own risk beliefs and fears, and will exert political pressures on environmental policy makers. Similarly, government officials may also be subject to cognitive biases and heuristics and may often be subject to, political pressures. For

---

[22] Interestingly, this study also found that the FDA's regulatory efforts are higher for chemicals with lower level of risks.

Table 7
Ranking possible carcinogenic hazards from natural and synthetic chemicals

Possible hazard: HERP (%)	Daily human exposure	Human dose of rodent carcinogen
140	EDB: workers' daily intake (high exposure)	EDB, 150 mg (before 1977)
17	Clofibrate (average daily dose)	Clofibrate, 2 g
16	Phenobarbital, 1 sleeping pill	Phenobarbital, 60 mg
[14]	Isoniazid pill (prophylactic dose)	Isoniazid, 300 mg
6.2	Comfrey–pepsin tablets, 9 daily	*Comfrey root, 2.7 g*
[5.6]	Metronidazole (therapeutic dose)	Metronidazole, 2 g
4.7	*Wine (250 ml)*	*Ethyl alcohol, 30 ml*
4	Formaldehyde: workers' average daily intake	Formaldehyde, 6.1 mg
2.8	*Beer (12 oz; 354 ml)*	*Ethyl alcohol, 18 ml*
1.4	Mobile home air (14 hr/day)	Formaldehyde, 2.2 mg
1.3	Comfrey–pepsin tablets, 9 daily	*Symphytine, 1.8*
0.4	Conventional home air (14 hr/day)	Formaldehyde, 598 ug
[0.3]	Phenacetin pill (average dose)	Phenacetin, 300 mg
0.3	*Lettuce, 1/8 head (125 g)*	*Caffeic acid, 66.3 mg*
0.2	*Natural root beer (12 oz; 354 ml)*	*Safrole, 6.6 mg (banned)*
0.1	*Apple, 1 whole (230 g)*	*Caffeic acid, 24.4 mg*
0.1	*Mushroom, 1 (15 g)*	*Mix of hydrazines, etc.*
0.1	*Basil (1 g of dried leaf)*	*Estragole, 3.8 mg*
0.07	*Mango, 1 whole (245 g; pitted)*	*d-limestone, 9.8 mg*
0.07	*Pear, 1 whole (200 g)*	*Caffeic acid, 14.6*
0.07	*Brown mustard (5 g)*	*Allyl isothiocyanate, 4.6 mg*
0.06	Diet cola (12 oz; 354 ml)	Saccharin, 95 mg
0.06	*Parsnip, 1/4 (40 g)*	*8-methoxypsoralen, 1.28 mg*
0.04	*Orange juice (6 oz; 177 ml)*	*d-limestone, 5,49 mg*
0.04	*Coffee, 1 cup (from 4 g)*	*Caffeic acid, 7.2 mg*
0.03	*Plum, 1 whole (50 g)*	*Caffeic acid, 6.9 mg*
0.03	*Safrole: U.S. average from spices*	*Safrole, 1.2 mg*
0.03	*Peanut butter (32 g; 1 sandwich*	*Aflatoxin, 64 ng*
0.03	*Comfrey herb tea (1.5 g)*	*Symphytine, 38 ug*
0.03	*Celery, 1 stalk (50 g)*	*Caffeic acid, 5.4 mg*
0.03	*Carrot, 1 whole (100 g)*	*Caffeic acid, 5.16 mg*
0.03	*Pepper, black: U.S. average (446 mg)*	*d-limonene, 3.57 mg*
0.02	*Potato, 1 (225 g; peeled)*	*Caffeic acid, 3.56 mg*
0.008	Swimming pool, 1 hour (for child)	Chloroform, 250 ug
0.008	*Beer, before 1979 (12 oz; 354 ml)*	Dimethylnitrosamine, 1 ug
0.006	Bacon, cooked (100 g)	Diethylnitrosamine, 0.1 ug
0.006	Well water, 1 liter contaminated (worst in Silicon Valley, Calif.)	Trichloroethylene, 2.8 mg
0.005	*Coffee, 1 cup (from 4 g)*	Furfural, 630 ug
0.004	*Bacon, pan fried (100 g)*	N-nitrosopyrrolidine, 1.7 ug
0.003	*Nutmeg: U.S. average (27.4 mg)*	d-limonene, 466 g
0.003	*Mushroom, 1 (15 g)*	Glutamyl p-hydrazino-benzoate, 630 ug

(*continued on next page*)

Table 7

(*Continued*)

Possible hazard: HERP (%)	Daily human exposure	Human dose of rodent carcinogen
0.003	Conventional home air (14 hr/day)	Benzene, 155 ug
0.003	*Sake (250 ml)*	Urethane, 43 ug
0.003	*Bacon, cooked (100 g)*	Dimethylnitrosamine, 300 ng
0.002	*White bread, 2 slices (45 g)*	Furfural, 333 ug
0.002	Apple juice (6 oz; 177 ml)	UDMH, 5.89 (from Alar)
0.002	*Coffee, 1 cup (from 4 g)*	Hydroquinone, 100 ug
0.002	*Coffee, 1 cup (from 4 g)*	Catechol, 400 ug
0.002	DDT: daily dietary average	DDT, 13.8 ug (before 1972 ban)
0.001	*Celery, 1 stalk (50 g)*	8-methoxypsoralen, 30.5 ug
0.001	Tap water, 1 liter	Chloroform, 83 ug (U.S. average, 1976)
0.001	*Heated sesame oil (15 g)*	Sesamol, 1.13 mg
0.0008	DDE: daily dietary average	DDE, 6.91 ug (before 1972 ban)
0.0006	Well water, 1 liter contaminated (Woburn, MA)	Trichloroethylene, 267 ug
0.0005	*Mushroom, 1 (15 g)*	p-hydrazinobenzoate, 165 ug
0.0005	*Jasmine tea, 1 cup (2 g)*	Benzyl acetate, 460 ug
0.0004	EDB: daily dietary average	EDB, 420 ng (from grain; before 1984 ban)
0.0004	*Beer (12 oz, 354 ml)*	Furfural, 54.9 ug
0.0004	Tap water, 1 liter	Chloroform, 25 ug (U.S. average, 1987–1992)
0.0003	Well water, 1 liter contaminated (Woburn, MA)	Tetrachloroethylene, 21 ug
0.0003	Carbaryl: daily dietary average	Carbaryl, 2.6 ug (1990)[a]
0.0002	Apple, 1 whole (230 g)	UDMH, 598 ng (from Alar)
0.0002	*Parsley, fresh (1 g)*	*8-methoxypsoralen, 3.6 ug*
0.0002	Toxaphene: daily dietary average	Toxaphene, 595 ng (1990)[a]
0.0001	*Salmon steak, baked (3 oz; 85 g)*	*PhIP, 176 ng*
0.00008	*Salmon steak, baked (3 oz; 85 g)*	*MeIQx, 111 ng*
0.00008	DDE/DDT: daily dietary average	DDE, 659 ng (1990)[a]
0.00006	*Hamburger, pan fried (3 oz; 85 g)*	*PhIP, 176 ng*
0.00003	*Whole wheat toast, 2 slices (45 g)*	*Urethane, 540 ng*
0.00003	*Hamburger, pan fried (3 oz; 85 g)*	*MeIQx, 38.1*
0.00002	Dicofol: daily dietary average	Dicofol, 544 ng (1990)[a]
0.00002	*Cocoa (4 g)*	*a-methylbenzyl alcohol 5.2 ug*

(*continued on next page*)

example, the cleanup of hazardous chemical waste sites heads the list of concerns of the public, but risk experts view these hazards as less severe.

The viewpoint we propose here is that the government should maximize the spread between expected benefits and costs, where this expectation is based on the best expert risk judgments rather than public risk beliefs. Thus, in the health area our concern should be with the expected number of lives actually at risk rather than with what peo-

Table 7
(*Continued*)

Possible hazard: HERP (%)	Daily human exposure	Human dose of rodent carcinogen
0.00001	*Larger beer (12 oz; 354 ml)*	*Urethane, 159 ug*
0.000005	*Hamburger, pan fried (3 oz; 85 g)*	*I.Q. 638 ng*
0.000001	Lindane: daily dietary average	Lindane, 32 ng (1990)[a]
0.0000004	PCNB: daily dietary average	PCNB (quintozene), 19.2 ng (1990)[a]
0.0000001	Chlorobenzilate: daily dietary average	Chlorobenzilate, 6.4 ng (1989)[a]
<0.00000001	Chlorothalonil: daily dietary average	Chlorothalonil, <6.4 ng (1990)[a]
8E-09	Folpet: daily dietary average	Folpet, 12.8 ng (1990)[a]
6E-09	Captan: daily dietary average	Captan, 11.5 ng (1990)[a]

Notes. Natural chemicals are in italics.

Daily human exposure. Reasonable daily intakes are used to facilitate comparisons.

The calculations assume a daily dose for a lifetime. Where drugs are normally taken for only a short period, we have bracketed the human exposure/rodent potency (HERP) index.

Possible hazard. The human dose of rodent carcinogen is divided by 70 kg to give an mg/kg of human exposure, and this dose is given as the percentage of the daily life-time dose rate estimated to halve the proportion of tumor-free animals by the end of a standard lifetime. Those values in our Carcinogenic Potency Database span a ten-millionfold range. In the HERP calculation those values are averages calculated by taking the harmonic mean of the positive tests in that species from the Carcinogenic Potency Database. Average values have been calculated separately for rats and mice, and the more sensitive species is used for calculating possible hazard.

Source: Ames and Gold (1996, p. 29).

[a]Estimate is based on average daily dietary intake for 60–65-year-old females, the only adult group reported for 1990. Because of the agricultural usage of those chemicals and the prominence of fruits and vegetables in the diet of older Americans, the residues are generally slightly higher than for other adult age groups.

ple may perceive these risks to be. Suppose, for example, there were two equally costly policy options, where policy option *A* saves 10 expected lives based on both expert and private risk judgements. In contrast, policy option *B* saves 1 expected life according to the experts, but an alarmed public believes that 100 lives will be saved. Popular support will give a preference to option *B*, which has less real effect on risk reduction. Our preference is for policy option *A* because misinformed personal decisions should not be permitted to override objective risk reductions.

Government agencies conduct risk assessments in order to foster rational decision-making concerning the regulations to control health risks. Another aim of regulatory agencies is to provide the public with accurate information on health risks.[23] Before examining some specific issues concerning risk assessment methodology, it is important to look at how people perceive health risks and how perceptions are affected by the

---

[23] For example, the Emergency Planning and Community Right-To-Know Act of 1986, the Pollution Prevention Act of 1990, and the Food and Drug Administration Modernization Act of 1997 all have the aim of providing information on risks to the public.

information provided by the risk assessments. An understanding of how people perceive health risks is critical to creating effective policies of informing people about these health risks.

One model of the risk perception process is Viscusi's (1998) prospective reference theory. In this model the nature of utility functions is the same as in standard expected utility theory. What changes is the character of risk beliefs. Using the beta distribution for probabilistic beliefs, the perceived risk p^* associated with any actual risk p is given by

$$p^* = \frac{\gamma q + \xi p}{\gamma + \xi},$$ (2)

where q is the individual's prior belief, and the individual acts as if he or she has observed γ trials in forming his or her prior belief of q and ξ trials when receiving information about the true risk p. In effect, q and p are weighted by the fraction of the informational content associated with each. This formulation is potentially consistent with rational Bayesian learning and Bayesian expected utility theory.

One strength of the model is that it predicts many of the anomalies in the literature on the rationality of individual choice as being unambiguous consequences of the model. In contrast, Kahneman and Tversky's (1979) prospect theory model is not consistent with expected utility theory and does not predict these anomalies. Rather, prospective reference theory has sufficient flexibility that one can find functional forms consistent with the anomalies. As a practical matter, what the prospective reference theory model predicts is that risk beliefs may be quite different from actual risk levels. This discrepancy may occur even within the context of controlled experiments because people do not take the probabilistic information at face value.

If people do not have accurate risk beliefs, the government can inform them through a hazard-warnings policy. Such efforts may be costly and not fully effective, especially in situations where the γ value is high. The position we propose here is that the government should base policies on the actual risk levels.

A frequently cited result in the risk perception literature is that people tend to overestimate low probability events and underestimate high probability events. Figure 3 shows the results from Viscusi (2000b) that parallel those in Lichtenstein et al. (1978), which was the seminal work that demonstrated this perceptional bias. Unlike earlier results based on student samples and other selected groups, these estimates are based on perceptions for a sample of almost 500 adults. A number of patterns are noteworthy. First, small risks of the size that are typically addressed by government policies tend to be overestimated. The perceived risk curve lies above the 45-degree line for small risks. To the extent that environmental hazards are known and involve relatively small probabilities, people will tend to overreact to the risks. Second, the overestimation of small risks implies that the gains to eliminating risks to zero will be overvalued. There will consequently be a certainty premium that arises because people overassess the extent of the risk reduction when a small risk is completely eliminated. Third, large risks tend to be underestimated. People will consequently place far too little weight on the fundamental

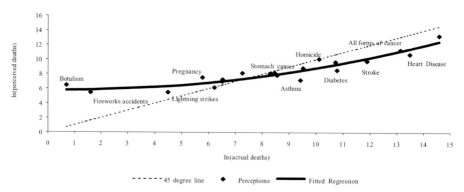

Figure 3. Comparison of perceived and actual mortality risks. Source: Viscusi (2000a).

risks to their lives, such as heart disease, and instead will exert political pressures to avert minor environmental risks.

These phenomena are not unexpected. They are predictions of the prospective reference theory equation given above. According to that equation, perceived risk is a linear function of the true risk level. The intercept $\gamma q/(\gamma + \xi)$ depends on the level of prior beliefs and the weight placed on the prior. People overestimate small risk categories because they are not fully cognizant of the risks. The result also is that a decrease from a small stated risk to a risk level that is truly zero will be perceived by people as greater a decline than it actually is. Perhaps for that reason environmental risk policies purport to make people "safe" or even to provide a "margin of safety" rather than to simply reduce the risks we face. The undervaluation of large risks is also a prediction of the model, as $\xi/(\gamma + \xi)$ will be below 1, except in cases of full information.

Psychological studies have identified a number of judgmental rules, known as heuristics, that people use in order to simplify the task of assessing probabilistic events.[24] While these heuristics often lead to valid inferences about the level of risk, at times they can lead to biases. For example, one explanation of the bias demonstrated in Figure 3 is that individuals rely on the availability heuristic. This heuristic describes the tendency of people to judge the likelihood of an event if instances of it are easy to recall. Therefore, if one's experiences are biased, then one's perceptions will also tend to be biased. Combs and Slovic (1979) provide evidence that the overestimation of low probability events and the underestimation of high probability events may be due to biases in the reporting of fatalities in newspapers. Since people base their perceptions on the ease with which they can call up an event in their mind, biased newspaper coverage leads to biased perceptions of health risks.

This phenomenon also has an interpretation from the standpoint of prospective reference theory. Media coverage of risks informs people that there have been a certain

---

[24] See Kahneman, Slovic and Tversky (1982) for an in-depth discussion of these heuristics.

number of adverse outcomes without giving them the denominator needed to do the risk calculation (i.e., the number of trials). Thus, for example, one learns that scooter injuries soared in the summer of 2000, but one does not receive information on the huge increase in scooter usage at that time. The result is that when people map the injury, death, and illness statistics into probabilities, the risk levels are overassessed.

Another heuristic that may lead to biased perceptions is the representativeness heuristic, in which the probability of an event is evaluated by the degree to which that event resembles another event. For example, Kahneman and Tversky (1973) found that people assess the likelihood that someone is in a given occupation almost exclusively on the description of the personality of the individual, without considering the base-rate frequency of each profession. With respect to health risks, this heuristic can lead to biases if a hazard does not have the characteristics of what is commonly believed to be risky characteristics. For example, since radon is both odorless and colorless, people may be inclined to underestimate its risks. Again, Bayesian learning could produce a similar phenomenon.

People also demonstrate the tendency to estimate probabilities by first starting from an initial value and then adjusting to yield a final assessment. This heuristic, known as anchoring, can lead to biased perceptions if the adjusting is not sufficient. The influence of anchors may reflect a form of irrationality, but, depending on the context, may also reflect rational Bayesian learning. People use a variety of sources of information in making risk judgements, which is what we would want from the standpoint of rational learning. Anchoring on information creates problems only to the extent that it is the result of focusing on question framing or extraneous information rather than data that legitimately should influence risk beliefs.

Anchoring can be particularly problematic in attempts to inform people of risks. Different formats for presenting the information may lead to different anchors, and thus different final assessments. For example, Fischhoff and MacGregor (1980) asked people to judge the lethality of various potential causes of death. They used four different, yet formally equivalent, formats in asking for assessments: (1) For each 100,000 people afflicted, how many die? (2) X people were afflicted, how many died? (3) For each person who died, how many were afflicted but survived? (4) Y people died, how many were afflicted but did not die? The judgments of lethality varied greatly depending on the format of the question. For example, people who were asked the first question judged the lethality rate of influenza as 393 deaths per 100,000 cases. When told that 80,000,000 people catch influenza in a normal year and asked to estimate the number who die, respondents' mean response was 4,800, representing a death rate of 6 per 100,000 cases.

While these psychological studies suggest that people assess risks using heuristics that can lead to biases, other research indicates that people do learn and adjust their perceptions when presented with new information. Viscusi and O'Connor (1984) found that workers act as Bayesian decision-makers when they process risk information about job hazards. Viscusi, Magat and Huber (1987) found that consumers adjust their perceptions of risk from household items when presented with detailed information about the risks. Smith et al. (1988) found that households learn from information about Radon risks, and they found, as did Viscusi, Magat and Huber (1987), that the learning process is influenced by the format of the risk information. Gayer, Hamilton and Viscusi (2000a, 2000b) found that residents adjust their perceptions of Superfund toxic waste risks after the EPA releases its detailed risk information.

4. Valuing environmental health risks

4.1. The value of a statistical life v. the human capital approach

Quantifying the magnitude of health risks is only the first step towards formulating reasonable government regulations. Economic efficiency entails weighing the costs of such risk regulations against the benefits to society from the reductions in health risks. Though non-economists may view it as impossible to place a dollar value on risks to health, such tradeoffs are made each day. A key distinction is that what is being valued is the reduction in a small probability of an adverse health effect, not the certainty of death or illness. For example, the decision to purchase a fuel-efficient small car instead of a safer gas-guzzling car implies a tradeoff between risk to one's health and money. Given the myriad health risks facing society and our limited resources for addressing these risks, the efficient use of regulatory dollars is to reduce risks where the net benefits of such reductions are greatest for each dollar expended.

A recurring question for environmental policy is how should society measure the value of risk reductions. The mainstream economic approach is to base these benefit values on individual preferences rather than imposing the preferences of policy makers. The appropriate means of assessing these risk–money tradeoffs is by estimating the value individuals bearing the risk are willing to pay for improved safety.[25] The basis for this approach is the broader maxim in the public finance literature that the value of the benefits of a public policy consists of the willingness to pay for these benefits by the affected population.[26] In this instance, the good being valued is the reduction in the probability of adverse health effects rather than the certainty of such consequences. This formulation uses the revealed preferences of the citizenry to value the risk reduction, and is often based on market data. For these preferences to be meaningful, however, they must be based on accurate assessments of the risk. Alarmist responses to hazards will generate excessive tradeoff amounts, while ignorance of the risks will lead to inadequate tradeoff levels. In the situation of random measurement error, we encounter the usual errors-in-variables problem, and estimated money–risk tradeoffs will be biased downward.

To capture the meaning of the statistical value-of-life approach it is useful to consider a simple illustrative example. Suppose that there are 10,000 people at risk, each of whom

---

[25] See Schelling (1968) for an early discussion of the value of a statistical life.

[26] See Stokey and Zeckhauser (1978) for a review of these public finance principles.

faces a 1/10,000 risk of death. Thus, on average one statistical life will be lost. Suppose that each member of this group is willing to pay $600 to eliminate the risk, so the total amount contributed would be $6 million. This $6 million figure to prevent one statistical death is referred to as the value of a statistical life. The task for economists is to estimate the level of these tradeoff values. A variety of approaches have been used, some of which are explicitly linked to the willingness to pay for risk reduction methodology, and others which are not.[27]

At one time, the federal government relied on the present value of lost earnings as the value of the loss of life. The genesis of this human capital approach is that it provides the basis for assessing the value of compensation in personal injury cases arising in tort liability. However, this court measure focuses on the objective of insurance after the injury rather than deterrence, or the value of reducing risks of death. The human capital measure does not provide an accurate estimate of society's willingness to pay for risk reduction, since one may be willing to pay a proportion of one's potential earnings that is greater than the proportion of risk reduction for small changes in risk. As in the example above, it is entirely consistent for someone to be willing to pay $600 for a reduction of risk by 1/10,000, even if $600 is more than 1/10,000th of this person's lifetime earnings. The budget constraint of the person's income is not binding for small risks. Relying on the accounting measure of human capital results in benefit estimates that are approximately an order of magnitude lower than the value of a statistical life. This undervaluation of the benefits of risk reduction could lead to regulations not being adopted since they fail a cost–benefit test, while using the appropriate measure of the value of a statistical life will lead to adoption of the regulation.[28]

Over the past three decades, there has been a substantial literature devoted to estimating the tradeoffs between health risks and dollars. Many of these studies use the hedonic model to examine the actual market choices made by individuals in order to infer the value they place on risk reductions. Thus, rather than asking people directly what is their willingness to pay, most studies have used the tradeoff rates implicit in the actual risky choices people make in labor markets, housing markets, and product markets. Since measures of objective and perceived risks are more readily available for occupational hazards, the majority of these studies have focused on the labor market. Some of these labor market studies have also included a measure of nonfatal risk in order to estimate the value of a statistical injury. Other studies, however, have examined the tradeoff between housing prices and environmental risk, and still others have examined the tradeoff between the opportunity cost of time and risk reductions from seatbelt use or automobile safety.[29] In situations where no market data are available, or where researchers were interested in corroborating other valuation measures for a related context, some studies

---

[27] Note that the pertinent issue is the value of a *statistical* life (or the risk–dollar tradeoff involving a small mortality risk), not the amount an individual is willing to pay to prevent a certain death.

[28] See Viscusi (1992) for an analysis of the effect of using the two standards on OSHA's regulations.

[29] There have also been some studies that use the hedonic property model to estimate willingness to pay for reductions in the risk of natural disasters such as earthquakes and floods. For example, Brookshire et al.

have used survey data in order to estimate risk–dollar tradeoffs. Within this section, we will examine the hedonic wage model and discuss empirical evidence from labor market and non-labor market studies, as well as survey studies. While our primary focus will be on assessing the valuation of reductions in occupational risks, one should keep in mind that both the methodology and the estimates could frequently be used to assess other environmental health risks. For example, the product market analysis is analogous.

Two principal distinctions arise when presenting the evidence from the labor market, housing market, and other contexts pertaining to the value of a statistical life. First, the fatalities involved may differ. Being killed on the job through a job accident is likely to be quite similar to the loss experienced when killed in an auto crash. The character of the death is similar in that it involves some extreme traumatic injuries. Indeed, these valuations prove to be similar empirically. However, fatal cases of cancer may be quite different in terms of the level of pain and suffering as well as people's overall willingness to pay to prevent the risk. The possibility of having different values based on the character of the death is quite rational.

Second, the mix of people affected by different risks may also differ. Male workers in their twenties and thirties who face most job fatality risks may have quite different preferences than the rest of the population. Indeed, their willingness to bear risk may have led them to self-select into these risky pursuits. Moreover, the length of life at risk, quality of life, income level, and other factors driving risk valuation may differ as well.

Ascertaining how these classes of concerns affect the use of such estimates for environmental benefit assessment comes under the general heading of "benefits transfer" problems. Extrapolating across risky contexts and different populations often entails strong assumptions of comparability. These comparability conditions are most in doubt with respect to extremes of the population, such as infants at risk and those with advanced respiratory disease who would have a short life expectancy even in the absence of air pollution. Unfortunately, there are currently no reliable means of directly estimating the benefits of risk reduction to such groups, and policy analysts must therefore rely on estimates obtained from other settings. A related benefits-transfer issue exists with respect to valuing morbidity and mortality risks outside of the United States, especially in developing countries. We discuss this issue in a later subsection.

4.2. Valuing morbidity risks

Although Section 4 focuses on the value of reduced mortality risks, this subsection briefly outlines the theoretical model for valuing reductions in morbidity risks. As is the case with valuing mortality risks, the appropriate value measure for reduced morbidity risk is the affected population's willingness to pay for the reduction in risks. Frequently,

---

(1985) find that residents in Los Angeles and San Francisco were willing to pay for houses located in areas where the expected earthquake damage was relatively low. Their estimates were consistent with the expected utility framework of consumer maximization. See also Beron et al. (1997), Murdoch, Harinder and Thayer (1993), and Shilling, Sirmans and Benjamin (1989).

analysts have relied on the "cost of illness" approach instead of the willingness to pay approach to valuing morbidity risks.[30] This approach estimates the benefits of reducing morbidity risks as the savings from medical expenditures plus the forgone opportunity costs of being sick. This cost of illness approach underestimates the willingness to pay for reduction of morbidity risks, since it does not account for the disutility of being sick or the savings in averting behavior expenditures. Moreover, it values the certain event such as the spell of illness, rather than the probability of illness. We will formally demonstrate this difference later in this subsection.

The formal health capital model for valuing morbidity risks stems from Grossman (1972). This seminal paper introduced the health production function, in which health is viewed as a capital stock that yields an output of "healthy days." Cropper (1977, 1981) applied this model to focus on the value of a reduction in morbidity due to a reduction in pollution. Our goal in this section is to examine the relationship between the cost of illness approach and the willingness to pay approach. This comparison was first done by Harrington and Portney (1987) and then expanded upon by Freeman (1993). We base our discussion on their work.

The health production function postulates the number of days an individual is sick, s, as a function of the exogenous variable for pollution (γ). The number of sick days is also a function of the averting behavior the individual takes (a) as well as the mitigating behavior the individual takes (m). For example, in the case of air pollution an individual can avert exposure by staying indoors more often and by purchasing an air filtration unit. An individual could mitigate the affects of the pollution by visiting the doctor more often when afflicted by respiratory illness. Thus, the health production function is as follows:

$$s = s(a, m; \gamma), \tag{3}$$

where $\partial s / \partial a < 0$, $\partial s / \partial m < 0$, and $\partial s / \partial \gamma > 0$.

An individual derives utility from a numeraire good (X) and leisure time (T_L), and derives disutility from sick days. The total time available is denoted as T. An individual receives Y dollars in nonlabor income, a wage rate of w, and pays p_a and p_m per unit of averting behavior and mitigating behavior, respectively. Thus, the Lagrangian expression for the individual's optimization problem is as follows:

$$L(X, T_L, a, m) = u[X, T_L, s(a, m; \gamma)] + \lambda[Y + w(T - T_L - s(a, m; \gamma)) - X - p_a a - p_m m].$$

Note that the model is in terms of a certain stream of sick days rather than a lottery with respect to health status. The first-order conditions are as follows:

$$X: \quad \frac{\partial u}{\partial X} = \lambda,$$

---

[30] For some early examples of this method, see Lave and Seskin (1973, 1977).

$$T_{\mathrm{L}}: \quad \frac{\partial u}{\partial T_{\mathrm{L}}} = \lambda w,$$

$$a: \quad \frac{\partial u}{\partial s} - \lambda w = \lambda \frac{p_a}{\partial s/\partial a},$$ (4)

$$m: \quad \frac{\partial u}{\partial s} - \lambda w = \lambda \frac{p_m}{\partial s/\partial m}.$$

The goal is to estimate the individual's willingness to pay for a reduction in pollution γ. We employ the indirect utility function V which is the maximum utility obtainable for a given set of parameter values. The willingness to pay for a morbidity risk reduction is the reduction in nonlabor income (Y) that leaves V constant. Denote this willingness to pay function as $Y(\gamma)$. Taking the total derivative of $V = V[Y(\gamma), \gamma]$ and setting it equal to zero yields the marginal willingness to pay for a change in morbidity risk, which is as follows:

$$\frac{\partial Y}{\partial \gamma} = -\frac{\partial V/\partial \gamma}{\partial V/\partial Y}.$$ (5)

Since $\partial V/\partial \gamma = [(\partial u/\partial s) - \lambda w](\partial s/\partial \gamma)$, and since $\partial V/\partial Y = \lambda$, then the marginal willingness to pay function can be re-written (by substituting in the last two first-order conditions) as follows:

$$\frac{\partial Y}{\partial \gamma} = -\frac{\partial s}{\partial \gamma} \frac{p_a}{\partial s/\partial a} = -\frac{\partial s}{\partial \gamma} \frac{p_m}{\partial s/\partial m}.$$ (6)

Thus, the marginal willingness to pay for a reduction in mortality risk is the reduction in sick days given the change in pollution multiplied by the marginal cost of reducing sick days (either through averting or mitigating behavior). This value is greater than the observable cost of illness.

To see this, note that both the demand for averting behavior (a^*) and the demand for mitigating behavior (m^*) are functions of the level of pollution. By totally differentiating the health production function one obtains the following equation:

$$\frac{ds}{d\gamma} = \frac{\partial s}{\partial a} \frac{\partial a^*}{\partial \gamma} + \frac{\partial s}{\partial m} \frac{\partial m^*}{\partial \gamma} + \frac{\partial s}{\partial \gamma},$$ (7)

which can be rearranged as follows:

$$\frac{\partial s}{\partial \gamma} = \frac{ds}{d\gamma} - \frac{\partial s}{\partial a} \frac{\partial a^*}{\partial \gamma} - \frac{\partial s}{\partial m} \frac{\partial m^*}{\partial \gamma}.$$ (8)

Multiplying this equation by the first-order condition (with respect to a) of the Lagrangian

$$\frac{p_a}{\partial s/\partial a} = \frac{\partial u/\partial s}{\lambda} - w,$$ (9)

yields the following equation:

$$-\frac{\partial s}{\partial \gamma}\frac{p_a}{\partial s/\partial a} = \left(w - \frac{\partial u/\partial s}{\lambda}\right)\frac{ds}{d\gamma} - \left(w - \frac{\partial u/\partial s}{\lambda}\right)\frac{\partial s}{\partial a}\frac{\partial a^*}{\partial \gamma}$$
$$- \left(w - \frac{\partial u/\partial s}{\lambda}\right)\frac{\partial s}{\partial m}\frac{\partial m^*}{\partial \gamma}. \tag{10}$$

Substituting and rearranging terms yields the following equation:

$$\frac{\partial Y}{\partial \gamma} = w\frac{\partial s}{\partial \gamma} - \frac{\partial u/\partial s}{\lambda}\frac{ds}{d\gamma} + p_a\frac{\partial a^*}{\partial \gamma} + p_m\frac{\partial m^*}{\partial \gamma}. \tag{11}$$

As mentioned earlier, the cost of illness approach measures the opportunity costs incurred by being sick (the first term in the above equation) and the expenditures on mitigating behavior (the last term in the above equation). This serves as a lower bound of the marginal willingness to pay since it neglects the disutility of being sick (the second term in the above equation) and the expenditures on averting behavior (the third term in the above equation).

4.3. Using labor market data to estimate the value of a statistical life

4.3.1. The hedonic wage model

The hedonic wage model examines the interaction of labor supply and labor demand in order to estimate the compensating differential that workers receive for risk. Figure 4 illustrates the partial relationship between wages and risk in the labor market.[31] The curves FF and GG are the isoprofit curves for two different firms. They indicate the wage that each firm will offer for different risk levels. These curves indicate that as risk is reduced, the firms' profits remain constant by decreasing the level of wages. Therefore, the wage offer curves are an increasing function of job risk. From the standpoint of the workers, all that is relevant is the highest wage available for a given level of risk.

The curves EU_1 and EU_2 represent the indifference curves for two different workers, reflecting the different preferences between the two people. That is, they represent the set of points that yield equal levels of expected utility. These curves are generated through considering a formulation of the von Neumann–Morgenstern expected utility model with state-dependent utilities. Suppose that utility in each state depends on one's wages, and that $U(w)$ denotes the utility of being healthy and $V(w)$ denotes the utility of being unhealthy (e.g., death, cancer, injury). We assume that individuals prefer being healthy to being unhealthy $[U(w) > V(w)]$ and that the marginal utility of income is positive $[U'(w) > 0, \; V'(w) > 0]$. We also assume that individuals are either risk-averse or risk-neutral, $[U''(w) \leqslant 0, \; V''(w) \leqslant 0]$. Note that financial risk aversion

---

[31] Thaler and Rosen (1976), Smith (1979), and Viscusi (1979) also provide overviews of the hedonic wage model.

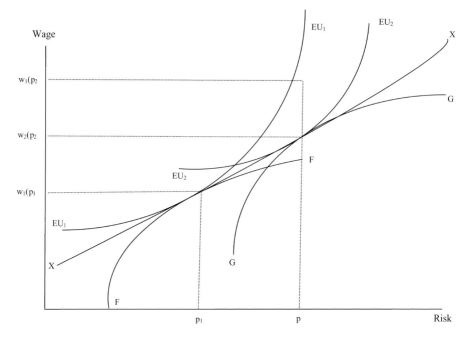

Figure 4. The market process of determining compensating differentials.

is not the same as finding risky jobs unattractive. All people who prefer being healthy to being injured will require some additional compensation to bear extra health risks, irrespective of their attitude toward financial gambles.

Suppose that there is some fixed level of expected utility Z that we will vary to trace out workers' constant expected utility loci, which are the analogs of indifference curves. Then the set of combinations of job risks p and wages w that provides this fixed utility level Z is the set of points that satisfy $Z = (1 - p)U(w) + pV(w)$.

Each worker will select the risk–wage bundle that maximizes expected utility, or that puts the worker on the highest constant expected utility locus. This optimum occurs where the constant expected utility curve is tangent to a firm's offer curve. In Figure 4 the optimal point for the first worker is the point where the expected utility locus for this worker is tangent to FF, and the optimal point for the second worker is the point where the expected utility locus for this worker is tangent to GG. By implicitly differentiating the expected utility function described in the previous paragraph, one obtains the following wage–risk tradeoff:

$$\frac{\partial w}{\partial p} = \frac{U(w) - V(w)}{(1 - p)U'(w) + pV'(w)}. \tag{12}$$

The above equation is positive; i.e., workers will demand compensation for the risk of being unhealthy.[32]

The hedonic wage curve XX consists of the envelope of the points of tangency between workers' expected utility curves and firms' isoprofit curves. In essence, the hedonic wage function reflects the joint influence of both the demand and supply side of the labor market equilibrium. Thus, the slope of the hedonic wage function is the marginal willingness to pay of the worker for risk reduction and the marginal cost to the firm of reducing risk. Since each point on the hedonic wage function represents the slope of the expected utility curve, the function can be used to estimate the welfare effects of a marginal change in job risk.

Extrapolating to more substantial risk changes is not appropriate. The hedonic wage function will understate the willingness-to-accept amounts for large increases in risk and overstate the willingness-to-pay amount for large risk decreases. For example, for an increase in risk from p_1 to p_2, the hedonic wage equation suggests that wages would increase from $w_1(p_1)$ to $w_2(p_2)$. However, the appropriate measure of the first worker's willingness to accept this risk increase is the change from $w_1(p_1)$ to $w_1(p_2)$.

If all workers had homogeneous preferences, then there would be only one expected utility curve in Figure 4, and the observable points on the hedonic wage equation would represent the constant expected utility locus. In such a case, the hedonic wage equation could be used to estimate the benefits of both marginal and infra-marginal reductions in risk. Similarly, if the firms were homogeneous, the hedonic wage equation would approximate the firm's offer curve, and it could thus be used to estimate the costs of both marginal and infra-marginal reductions in risk. Nonetheless, the usual assumption is to recognize that the labor market consists of both heterogeneous workers and heterogeneous firms. In such a case, one would ideally want to estimate the constant expected utility curves in order to estimate the willingness to pay for risk reductions (or the willingness to accept risk increases).[33] However, since it is the locus of tangencies that is observable in the labor market data, most studies rely on estimating this hedonic wage function. Some studies have used other econometric techniques in order to estimate the structural willingness-to-pay equation.[34]

An alternative to attempting to estimate the locus of tangencies that make up the hedonic wage curve is to use information on two or more points on the constant expected utility locus in order to extrapolate the shapes of the utility curve in the healthy state $U(\cdot)$

---

[32] This result holds whether individuals are risk averse or risk-neutral. However, if people are risk-lovers, the second-order conditions may not hold.

[33] On theoretical grounds, the willingness to pay for a marginal reduction of risk should equal the willingness to accept for a marginal increase in risk. However, the empirical work of Viscusi, Magat and Huber (1987) found substantial differences in these two values. Using a survey on consumer risks, they found that willingness to accept is much larger than willingness to pay for a risk reduction.

[34] Brown (1983) and Kahn and Kevin (1988) discuss the theory behind estimating the structural hedonic equations. Biddle and Zarkin (1988) provide an empirical estimation of the structural hedonic equations. Viscusi and Moore (1989) and Moore and Viscusi (1990a, 1990b) obtain structural estimates by modeling the functional form of workers' preferences.

and the utility curve in the unhealthy state $V(\cdot)$. Market data do not enable one to do this, as it is necessary to use surveys in order to estimate individuals' compensatory demands for a change in risk and then fit these points to a flexible functional form of the utility curves. Viscusi and Evans (1990) used data based on Viscusi and O'Connor's (1984) survey of workers from four chemical firms in order to obtain two data points on the expected utility curve. They obtained one point on the expected utility curve by first asking each worker to assess his current job risk and to report his current wage. The worker then received information on a chemical's risk and was told that the chemical would replace the chemicals that the worker was currently using. The second point on the expected utility locus was obtained by eliciting the worker's assessment of the new job risk and the wage rate necessary to compensate for this risk. Thus, the survey obtained all the necessary components of the following equality:

$$(1 - p_1)U(w_1) + p_1 V(y_1) = (1 - p_2)U(w_2) + p_2 V(y_2), \tag{13}$$

where p_1 is the worker's initial assessment of risk, w_1 is the worker's initial wage rate, p_2 is the worker's assessment of risk of the new chemical, w_2 is the wage rate demanded by the worker for the new chemical risk, and y_1 and y_2 are the benefit levels paid out upon death. Viscusi and Evans (1990) solved this equation by assuming a logarithmic functional form for the utility functions, and then by using a Taylor series approximation of the general utility function. This yielded an estimate of the workers' willingness to pay for risk reductions.

By estimating the structure of individual utility functions, Viscusi and Evans (1990) were able to obtain a more precise understanding of a variety of aspects of worker preferences. First, accidents reduce both the utility level and the marginal utility of income. This result has practical consequences for the optimal level of insurance after an accident. In particular, it implies that full income replacement is not optimal. Indeed, for job accidents the optimal replacement rate is 85 percent. Second, the results imply that the required rate of compensation for job risks increases with the extent of the risk increase. Thus, the willingness-to-accept amount per unit risk, which is the implicit value of a statistical life or the implicit value of a statistical injury, is not constant but increases with the extent of the risk increase. Similarly, if one is focusing on decreases in risk, the willingness to pay per unit risk reduction decreases with the extent of the decline in risk that is being purchased. The practical implication of this result for environmental policy is that societal willingness to pay for risk reductions will have a lower unit benefit value if large reductions in environmental risk are involved.

4.3.2. The empirical specification of the hedonic wage equation

For most hedonic wage studies, the goal is to estimate the equation for XX in Figure 4, and the basic specification is given as

$$w_i = \alpha + \sum_{j=1}^{n} \beta_j x_{ij} + \gamma_1 p_i + \gamma_2 r_i + \gamma_3 r_i WC_i + u_i, \tag{14}$$

where w_i is worker i's wage rate (or the log of the wage rate), x_{ij} are the individual and job characteristics for worker i, p_i is the occupational fatality risk to worker i, r_i is the occupational nonfatality risk to worker i, WC_i is the workers' compensation benefits that are payable to worker i in the event of an injury, and u_i is the error term. Some studies include in the specification interaction variables of individual characteristics with the job risk in order to test whether willingness to pay for risk reduction varies by personal characteristics. For example, Hersch and Viscusi (1990), Hersch and Pickton (1995), and Viscusi and Hersch (2000) found that people who value good health relatively less (e.g., smokers and non-seatbelt wearers) have a lower willingness to pay for reduction in job risks. The interaction of education and risk reflects the joint influence of differences in worker preferences as well as differences in firms' offer curves for workers with different educational levels.

Early efforts to estimate the hedonic wage equation were restricted by the lack of available, detailed, individual-level data. Without such data, the studies relied on aggregate job characteristics across each industry. This aggregation averages out the effects of heterogeneous workers' preferences and heterogeneous firms' offer curves, making it difficult to reliably estimate the risk–dollar tradeoff. The more recent studies that use micro-level data can more reliably estimate the tradeoff and can examine how differences in worker characteristics lead to sorting along the hedonic wage curve. For example, using worker-level data on wealth, one can examine whether wealthier workers have a higher preference for risk reduction.[35] Wealthier workers are likely to sort themselves on the low-risk part of the hedonic curve, since the wage that a worker requires to accept any given level of risk will increase with wealth, and the risk–dollar tradeoff ($\partial w / \partial p$) will also increase with wealth.

The dependent variable in the hedonic wage equation is each worker's hourly wage rate. Researchers often must infer this measure using annual income or weekly earnings. The relevant measure is after-tax wages, but since tax rates frequently do not vary substantially among workers, this is easily computed by scaling wages by a factor of proportionality. However, when one includes a variable for workers' compensation, it is necessary to express the benefits and wages in comparable after-tax terms.

The occupational risk variable is the key variable of interest in the hedonic wage equation. As mentioned in Section 3.3, psychological studies find that individual perceptions of risk tend to systematically differ from the actual risk. Specifically, individuals tend to overestimate low-probability events and underestimate high-probability events. Thus, for a given decrease in risk, the perceived decrease will be smaller than the actual change, and the required compensation to a worker will thus be lower. Therefore, the compensating differential to a worker will be smaller due to the systematic bias of perceptions.

In order to assess accurately the welfare effects of a change in risk, one ideally should use a measure of each worker's perception of the occupational risk. The available data,

---

[35] Job safety is commonly considered to be a normal good [Thaler and Rosen (1976), Jones-Lee (1976), Viscusi (1979), Viscusi and Evans (1990)].

however, are less than ideal. The University of Michigan Survey of Working Conditions and Quality of Employment Survey includes a measure of whether each worker
believes that he or she faces a job hazard. Estimates using this variable are comparable
to those obtained using objective measures of industry risk. Before 1971, the Bureau
of Labor Statistics (BLS) published industry-based death risk data for three-digit SIC
codes; however, these data did not include information on government employees. After
1971, the BLS published death risk data for one-digit SIC codes, which made the data
more aggregate. The National Institute of Occupational Safety and Health (NIOSH)
publishes death risk data for one-digit SIC codes for each state, and the Society of Actuaries publishes death risk data based on occupational risks for 37 occupations, rather
than industry risks. More recently, data have come to be available on a more refined
basis.

Ideally, what is needed is a measure of workers' own subjective risk beliefs and a
corroboration of the relationship of these beliefs to objective risk levels. This comparison was the focus of Viscusi and O'Connor (1984), who elicited job risk assessments for
nonfatal injury risks to chemical workers. These estimates were very similar to those obtained based on objective risk measures. Many psychology studies [such as Lichtenstein
et al. (1978)] suggest that people underestimate low mortality risks and overestimate
high mortality risks. These biases were not apparent with respect to workers' perceptions of the risks posed by their jobs. Viscusi and O'Connor (1984) found that chemical
workers were very well informed of the risks they faced.

4.3.3. Accounting for the duration and quality of life

The effect of job risk on wages is a function of the worker's age, since the pertinent
issue is the amount of life potentially lost or affected by the job risk. A younger worker
exposed to risk faces a greater potential loss than an older worker exposed to the same
level of risk. However, an offsetting influence may be that younger people have a different preference for risk than older people do. They have fewer family obligations and
may have a lower personal investment in their earnings-related human capital. Some
studies interact the worker's age with the job risk in order to capture this influence of
the duration of life [Thaler and Rosen (1976), Viscusi (1979)]. This interaction measure
is imperfect since it neglects the changes in life expectancy as people age. In order to
capture changes in life expectancy, as well as the preference for deferring risks, a more
refined measure used by Moore and Viscusi (1988b) is the interaction of risk with the
discounted loss of life expectancy. In this study, the job risk variable is $p(1 - e^{-rT})/r$,
where p is the job risk, T is the remaining period of life, and r is the rate of discount.
Using this measure, the study estimated the value of a statistical life, the value per discounted expected life year lost, and the rate of time preference that the workers use in
discounting life years. [36]

---

[36] The estimated rate of time preference in this study was 10 to 12 percent with respect to expected life years.

In addition to adjusting for the quantity of life years, one should also take into account the quality of life at risk. [37] Recognizing that the quality of life matters is much simpler than trying to value quality differences. Labor market studies of fatalities have not incorporated explicit measures of life quality except for general controls for health status and exploration of the role of nonfatal injuries and associated disability. Moreover, many of the practical attempts to deal with quality issues are not grounded in the willingness to pay methodology but instead involve ad hoc ratings or preferences elicited without the reliance on an expected utility framework.

The difficulty of measuring the quality of life is highlighted in *The Global Burden of Disease* [Murray and Lopez (1996)]. This extensive study published by the World Health Organization devised a standardized quality measure, known as the Disability-Adjusted Life Year (DALY), to express years of life lost to premature death and years lived with a disability of specified severity and duration. This measure only considers differences in age and sex when calculating the burden of a given health outcome to an individual. Thus, a DALY does not vary by income, nor does it vary by nationality, even though expected life years can vary tremendously for people living in different countries. The DALY measure assumes that the life expectancy at birth for women is 82.5, and the life expectancy at birth for men is 80 years. It also assumes that the value of a year of life varies nonlinearly with age. Figure 5 shows how DALYs incorporate

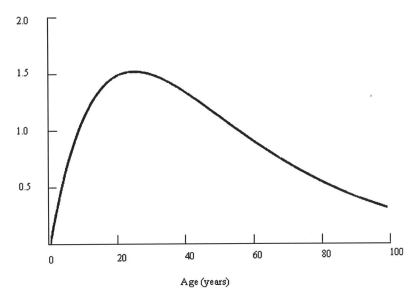

Figure 5. The relative value of a year of life lived at different ages, as incorporated into DALYs. Source: Murray and Lopez (1996, p. 9).

[37] Zeckhauser and Shepard (1976) develop a quality-adjusted measure in order to recognize the distinction between quantity and quality of life.

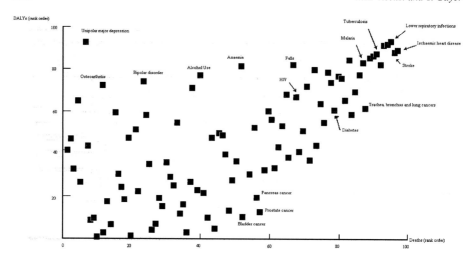

Figure 6. The relationship between the rank order of causes of global ill–health when measured using deaths alone or total disease burden, 1990. Source: Murray and Lopez (1996, p. 25).

differences in the relative value of a year of life for different age groups, with the greatest weight placed on people in their early 20s. The DALY measure also assumes a three-percent discount rate.

Measuring the burden of health risks in DALYs, as opposed to fatality risks, significantly changes the rank order of the leading health risks. Figure 6 shows the relationship between the rank order of fatalities and DALYs. While the formulation of DALYs has shed light on the assessment of fatal and nonfatal health risks throughout the world, there are no studies that incorporate this measure in a hedonic evaluation of the value of a statistical life.

Valuing the effects of quality of life changes also raises fundamental economic issues regarding the valuation reference point. The appropriate economic measure for valuing risk reduction is the person's willingness to pay for a decrease in risk of the adverse health effect. But matters become more complicated if people incorrectly assess the adverse health consequences of the ailment for their welfare. For example, Sloan et al. (1998) find that people faced with the prospect of multiple sclerosis view the disease as having more catastrophic implications for their welfare than patients with multiple sclerosis actually believe to be the case. Valuations of risk should be *ex ante*, but *ex ante* understanding of the consequences may be in error.

4.3.4. Labor market evidence of risk tradeoffs

Here we will report selected representative studies pertaining to the value of a statistical life. The entire literature on the value of a statistical life is much more extensive than indicated here.[38] Moreover, there is a comparable literature on the implicit value of job-related injuries, but these injuries tend to differ from the kinds of health outcomes that are typically valued in environmental contexts.[39]

Table 8 summarizes a series of representative estimates from the larger literature on the value of a statistical life, mainly in the U.S. Overall, the estimates tend to cluster

Table 8

Summary of selected labor market studies of the value of a statistical life in the U.S. (unless otherwise noted)

Author (year)	Sample	Risk variable	Mean risk	Implicit value of a statistical life ($ millions)[a]
Smith (1974)	Industry data	Bureau of Labor Statistics (BLS)	NA	8.6
Smith (1976)	Current Population Survey (CPS)	BLS	0.0001	5.5
Thaler and Rosen (1976)	Survey of economic opportunity	Society of actuaries	0.001	1.0
Viscusi (1978, 1979)	Survey of working conditions	BLS	0.0001	4.9
Brown (1980)	National longitudinal survey of young men	Society of actuaries	0.002	1.8
Viscusi (1981)	Panel Study of Income Dynamics (PSID)	BLS	0.0001	7.7
Olson (1981)	CPS	BLS	0.0001	6.2
Arnould and Nichols (1983)	U.S. Census	Society of actuaries	0.001	1.1
Moore and Viscusi (1988a)	PSID	BLS	0.00005	3.0
Moore and Viscusi (1988a)	PSID	National traumatic occupational fatality survey	0.00008	8.7
Kniesner and Leeth (1991)	Industry data for Japan		0.00003	13.8
Kniesner and Leeth (1991)	Industry data for Australia		0.0001	3.9
Kniesner and Leeth (1991)	CPS data for U.S.		0.0004	0.7

Source: Viscusi (2000a).
[a]Dollar values expressed in 1998 dollars.

[38] See Viscusi (1998) for a more extensive review of such studies.
[39] Viscusi (1993) reports a summary of estimates for the implicit value of job injuries.

in the $3 million–$8 million range, with a midpoint value of about $5 million. The estimates in Table 8 mostly fall in this range as well. This table lists each study, the sample used, the risk variable and the mean level, and the estimated value of a statistical life.

The value of a statistical life is not a universal constant. It will differ according to the sample mix in each study and the individuals' attitudes toward risk. Thus, the fact that the estimates differ is not a signal that the methodology is flawed but could reflect the underlying heterogeneity in the value of a statistical life.

Many of the studies in Table 8 focus on limited samples that exclude females or white-collar workers. These limitations stem from the fact that these estimates involve the matching of industry or occupational risk measures to the workers based on their re-ported job. Such average risk estimates are often not pertinent to white-collar and female employees, who have jobs with different characteristics than blue-collar male employ-ees. Hersch (1998) used gender-specific nonfatal injury risk measures and found that not only were women at risk, but that their wage–risk tradeoff rates were comparable to those of men.

Although the first study in Table 8 by Smith (1974) and the estimates for Japan and Australia by Kniesner and Leeth (1991) used aggregate data by industry, the remaining studies used individual employment information. There are three studies using Society of Actuaries data for the total mortality risks for people in different occupations – Thaler and Rosen (1976), Brown (1980), and Arnould and Nichols (1983). These estimates tend to be somewhat low because the sample consists of disproportionately high-risk workers in jobs with an annual fatality risk of 0.001–0.002, which is roughly an order of magnitude greater than the economywide average. The risk measures also include all mortality risks for people in different occupations, including risks off the job. As a result, the lower estimates of life reflect the different risk tradeoffs that one would expect from those who gravitate toward the high-risk jobs for which such data are available.

These studies also differ in terms of the other variables included in the analysis. Job fatality risks tend to be correlated with other unpleasant job characteristics, including nonfatal job injuries. Ideally, one should control for the set of pertinent job attributes so as to disentangle the premium for job risks from the premium for other negatively valued job characteristics. The estimates in Viscusi (1978, 1979, 1981) include detailed controls of this type, yielding estimates that are not too dissimilar from those in other studies.

Both the occupational mix and the job risk level arise with respect to self-selection effects that may affect benefits transfer of these estimates. Market-based risks by their very nature may reflect a voluntary decision. While some environmental risks emerge from voluntary choices, many environmental hazards are broadly based and are not the reflection of a low personal money–risk tradeoff. The estimates in Viscusi (1981) apply to a broad sample of white-collar and blue-collar workers and tend to be somewhat higher than the estimates for the higher-risk groups.

4.3.5. Survey evidence of risk tradeoffs

A number of studies have also used survey evidence to estimate the value of a statistical life. While not the result of market choices in which people actually incur risks, such revealed tradeoffs can be elicited for broader population groups. Moreover, one can alter the source of death (e.g., auto accident) and the nature of the health consequences that led to the fatality, making it possible to distinguish illnesses from accidents.

Table 9 summarizes a series of such willingness-to-pay studies in which individuals confronted a series of hypothetical tradeoffs involving risks to life and some monetary component, such as higher cost of living or taxes. Although the first two studies involve very small samples, the other studies in Table 9 pertain to larger groups who valued job safety and auto safety in the U.S., the UK, and New Zealand. These estimates are roughly the same magnitude of the estimates derived from labor market studies.

Table 9
Summary of estimates of the value of a statistical life based on survey evidence in OECD countries

Author (year)	Nature of risk	Survey methodology	Implicit value of life ($ millions)
Acton (1973)	Improved ambulance service, post-heart attack lives	Willingness to pay question, door-to-door small (36) Boston sample	0.1
Jones-Lee (1976)	Airline safety and locational life expectancy risks	Mail survey willingness to accept increased risk, small (30) UK sample, 1975	15.6
Gerking, De Haan and Schulze (1988)	Job fatality risk	Willingness to pay, willingness to accept change in job risk in mail survey, 1984	3.4 willingness to pay, 8.8 willingness to accept
Jones-Lee (1989)	Motor vehicle accidents	Willingness to pay for risk reduction, UK survey, 1982	3.8
Viscusi, Magat and Huber (1991)	Automobile accident risks	Interactive computer program with pairwise auto risk–living cost tradeoffs until indifference achieved, 1987	2.7 (median) 9.7 (mean)
Miller and Guria (1991)	Traffic safety	Series of contingent valuation questions, New Zealand survey, 1989/1990	1.2

Note. All values in December 1990 U.S. dollars.
Source: Viscusi (1993, p. 1940).

These estimates all pertain to money–risk tradeoffs. Another potentially instructive metric is to ascertain the probability of some standardized health outcome that is equivalent to the health risk in question. If the reference point can be linked to money–risk tradeoff values, then it is possible to establish a risk–risk metric for the value of health risks. Viscusi, Magat and Huber (1991), which will be discussed below, introduced this approach in an analysis of chronic bronchitis.

Let us first consider how this approach can be used to value different kinds of death. Let there be some standardized lottery in which there is a probability q of being killed in an automobile accident. The other choice involves some risk s of death from cancer. The respondent's task is to determine the probability q of auto accident death that provides the same expected utility level as from a probability s of dying from cancer, or

$$(1 - q)U(\text{life}) + q V(\text{auto accident death})$$
$$= (1 - s)U(\text{life}) + s V(\text{cancer death}). \tag{15}$$

One can obtain the cancer risk–dollar tradeoff by either combining the risk–risk tradeoff estimate with an estimate of the tradeoff between auto accident death and dollars, or by combining the risk–risk estimate with the mean values of a statistical life derived from other wage hedonic studies. The results in Magat, Viscusi and Huber (1996) indicate that fatal lymphoma has a value of \$4.1 million, which is comparable to the estimates of the value of a statistical life. This comparability is crucial for those seeking to transfer the benefit values from acute accidental deaths to outcomes such as cancer.

Similarly, one can also use this approach when what is at risk is a certain health outcome, as compared to a lottery on life and death. In particular, for chronic bronchitis from air pollution, the task posed in the survey by Viscusi, Magat and Huber (1991) was to establish the value of s that equilibrated

$$U(\text{chronic bronchitis}) = (1 - s)U(\text{life}) + s V(\text{auto accident death}). \tag{16}$$

A potential advantage of this risk–risk metric is that subjects can consider tradeoffs within a single dimension of health rather than being forced to consider tradeoffs of money against health risks. In addition, the presence of a tradeoff involving two worthy health causes should avoid some of the problems that might arise with the trading off of hypothetical contingent valuation money against health risks, as such money may be undervalued by respondents.

The findings in Table 10 present willingness-to-pay values for a variety of health outcomes, some of which involve payments to avoid certain events such as the common cold, and others of which involve lotteries. More values arising from consideration of health risks reflect the pertinent willingness-to-pay value but do not always provide an appropriate guide to policy. For example, the bleach poisoning and gassing outcomes in Viscusi and Magat (1987) involved very small probabilities. People are not able to process information about small risks reliably and tend to have exaggerated responses to low probability risks. The resulting valuation numbers reflect this bias in the processing of small probability hazards, as, for example, chloramine gassings due to combining

Table 10
Summary of valuations of nonfatal health risks in the U.S.

Author (year)	Survey methodology	Nature of risk	Value of health outcome
Berger et al. (1987)	Contingent valuation interviews with 119 respondents, 1984/1985	Certain outcome of one day of various illnesses	$98 (coughing spells), $35 (stuffed-up sinuses), $57 (throat congestion), $63 (itching eyes), $183 (heavy drowsiness), $140 (headaches), $62 (nausea)
Viscusi and Magat (1987)	Paired comparison and contingent valuations interactive computer survey at mall, hardware store, 1984	Bleach: chloramine gassings, child poisonings; drain opener: hand burns, child poisonings	$1.78 million (bleach gassing), $0.65 million (bleach poisoning), $1.60 million (drain opener hand burns), $1.06 million (drain opener and child poisoning)
Viscusi, Magat and Huber (1987)	Contingent valuation computer survey at mall, hardware stores, 1986	Morbidity risks of pesticide and toilet bowl cleaner, valuations for 15/10,000 risk decrease to zero	Insecticide $1,504 (skin poisoning), $1,742 (inhalation), $3,489 (child poisoning), toilet bowl cleaner $1,113 (gassing), $744 (eye burn), $1,232 (child poisoning)
Viscusi, Magat and Forrest (1988)	Contingent valuation computer survey at mall, hardware stores, 1986	Insecticide inhalation–skin poisoning, inhalation-child poisoning	Inhalation-skin poisoning $2,538 (private), $9,662 (NC altruism), $3,745 (U.S. altruism); inhalation-child poisoning $4,709 (private), $17,592 (NC altruism), $5,197 (U.S. altruism)
Evans and Viscusi (1991)	Contingent valuation computer survey at mall, hardware stores, 1986	Morbidity risks of pesticides and toilet bowl cleaner; utility function estimates of risk values. T values pertain to marginal risk–dollar tradeoffs, and L values pertain to monetary loss equivalents	Insecticide: $761 ($T$), $755 ($L$) (skin poisoning); $1,047 ($T$), $1,036 ($L$) (inhalation-no kids); $2,575 ($T$) (inhalation-children) $1,748; $3,207 ($T$), $2,877 ($L$) (child poisoning); toilet bowl cleaner $633 ($T$), $628 ($L$) eye burn; $598 ($T$), $593 ($L$) gassing (no kids); $717 ($T$), $709 ($L$) gassing (children); $1,146 ($T$), $1,126 ($L$) child poisoning

(continued on next page)

bleach with ammonia-based cleaners have a value of $1.78 million. Increasing the magnitude of the risk by several orders of magnitude (as was done in Viscusi, Magat and Huber (1987) reduces the comparable chloramine gassing value to $1,113, which is more in line with the injury severity.

The study by Viscusi, Magat and Huber (1987) also identified two potential biases in individual responses to risk. First, there is a strong influence of the starting point, or what

Table 10
(*Continued*)

Author (year)	Survey methodology	Nature of risk	Value of health outcome
Magat, Viscusi and Huber (1996)	Risk–risk computer survey at mall, 1990	Environmental risk of nonfatal nerve disease, fatal lymphoma, nonfatal lymphoma	$1.6 million (nerve disease), $2,6 million (nonfatal lymphoma), $4.1 million (fatal lymphoma)
Viscusi, Magat and Huber (1991)	Risk–risk and risk–dollar computer survey at mall, 1988	Environmental risk of sever chronic bronchitis morbidity risk	0.32 fatality risk or $904,000 risk–risk; $516,000 risk–dollar
Krupnick and Cropper (1992)	Viscusi, Magat and Huber (1991) survey for sample with chronic lung disease, 1989	Environmental risk of sever chronic bronchitis morbidity risk	$496,800–$691,200 (median)

Source: Viscusi (1993, p. 1941, 1942).

the authors term a "reference risk effect." Whereas the earlier literature had identified starting point and status quo effects with respect to income levels, this result pertained to probabilities. Second, respondents exhibited substantial certainty premiums. They were willing to pay much more to reduce the risk from 5/10,000 to 0 than to reduce it from 15/10,000 to 5/10,000. This difference arises from the premium people place on complete elimination of the risk, which arises at least in part from the overestimation of the risks from low probability events (as was discussed in Section 3.3).

Environmental policies protect the citizenry at large, not just those with a disease. Nevertheless, it is instructive to ask whether people with a particular ailment place a different value on it than those who do not. In the case of severe chronic bronchitis, the population at large surveyed in Viscusi, Magat and Huber (1991) valued it at $516,000 based on risk–dollar tradeoffs and $904,000 based on risk–risk tradeoffs. Using a sample of respondents who had chronic lung disease, Krupnick and Cropper (1992) estimated a median value of $496,800–$691,200, which brackets the risk–dollar estimates for the general population.

4.3.6. Risk tradeoffs in other countries

Tables 8–10 list estimates of willingness to pay for mortality and morbidity risk reductions based on data from industrialized nations (primarily the U.S). Yet there is also a need to obtain estimates of risk reduction benefits in developing countries. To efficiently allocate resources, agencies such as the World Bank and the U.S. Agency for International Development, as well as regulatory agencies within the developing countries, must have reliable estimates of the benefits of proposed programs that reduce environmental health risks. Since the relevant data is more accessible in the U.S., many researchers have resorted to transferring willingness-to-pay estimates obtained in U.S. studies to the country under consideration, often with adjustments to the income differentials between the two countries. This approach is clearly less desirable than developing country-specific data. Attitudes toward risk vary with factors other than income levels, but it is difficult to measure many cultural factors that differ across countries.

The first step in conducting a benefits transfer for developing countries is to obtain estimates of the health effects of the environmental policy within the country under consideration. For example, a program to reduce total particulates may have different effects on a population in a developing country than it would in one in the U.S. These differences may arise from differences in the age, socioeconomic conditions, general health status, health habits, and averting behavior of the populations. Also, due to non-linearities in the dose–response function, it is difficult to extrapolate the effects from low levels of pollution in the industrialized world to the effects from higher levels of pollution in the developing world.

The analyst's job, therefore, is to estimate the population dose–response relationship between the environmental hazard (e.g., air pollution) and mortality within the country under consideration. As discussed previously in this chapter, obtaining nonexperimental epidemiological dose–response estimates is not an easy task. It is highly likely that air pollution is correlated with unobservable characteristics that affect mortality, thus leading to biased estimates. The studies cited in this section rely on dose–response estimates obtained by regressing the health outcome against levels of pollution (such as particulate matter) and other covariates. While the studies conduct tests for robustness, by their own admission, they are rough estimates of the population dose–response relationship.

Ostro et al. (1998, 2000) find that the dose–response relationship for air pollution in Santiago, Chile is remarkably similar to the relationship that exists in industrialized countries. In their study of air pollution health risks in Volgograd, Russia, Larson et al. (1999) couple air pollution data with a dose–response relationship from the literature and find that 12–28% of cardiovascular deaths each year in Volgograd (and 7–20% of total Volgograd mortality) might be attributable to particulate emissions.[40] Taking into account the significantly higher levels of air pollution in Russia compared to the U.S., these findings are consistent with dose–response relationships found in U.S. studies. In their study of air pollution health effects in Bangkok, Chestnut, Ostro and Vichit-Vadakan (1997) also find that their estimates of the effects of particulates on mortality are reasonably comparable to estimates based on U.S. studies.

Not all studies show that health effects are comparable between the industrial world and the developing world. Cropper et al. (1997), for example, find that a given reduction in particulates reduces deaths in Delhi by a smaller percentage than predicted by U.S.

---

[40] Earlier epidemiological studies on air pollution and health risks in China include Xu et al. (1994) and Xu, Li and Huang (1995).

studies. The percentage decrease in deaths corresponding to a 100-microgram reduction in particulates is about one-third of the effect found in the U.S. They also find that the largest impact of particulates on daily deaths in the U.S. occurs among people 65 years old and older, whereas in Delhi the largest impact occurs for people 15 to 44 years old.

Given an estimate of the health effects of an environmental policy, one can obtain benefit estimates by multiplying the estimated number of lives saved by value-of-life estimates obtained from U.S. studies, and then adjusting by the relative income between the country of interest and the U.S. (since risk reduction is assumed to be a normal good). The choice of the income elasticity for the value of a statistical life is, however, a key parameter in such calculations. This method was done by Vincent et al. (1997) in order to estimate the benefits of air pollution reduction in Malaysia. Using a $5 million estimate of the value of a statistical life (obtained from U.S. studies), they adjusted for Malaysian income to arrive at a $600,000 estimate for the value of a statistical life in Malaysia. Using the same method, Larson et al. (1999) estimate the value of a statistical life for Russians as approximately $120,000.[41]

There are a number of reasons to believe that the willingness-to-pay function would be parametrically different in developing countries, thus suggesting that the benefits transfer method would yield misleading results.[42] For example, one would expect that the various institutional and cultural differences among countries would result in different preferences for risk reduction, and that these differences would not be captured by simply adjusting U.S. parameters with the relevant country's income levels.

Recently, some studies have addressed this issue by directly estimating willingness to pay for risk reductions using data from the country under consideration. Many of these studies then compare their results with those obtained by the benefits transfer method of adjusting U.S. estimates with income data. For example, using labor market data from Taiwan, Liu, Hammitt and Liu (1997) estimate a value of statistical life of approximately $450,000 (1990 dollars). They then estimate a meta-hedonic that regresses estimates of the value of a statistical life against income for various U.S. studies. By substituting Taiwanese mean income into this regression equation, they obtain an estimate of the value of a statistical life of $1.4 million, which is approximately three times the estimate they obtain using Taiwanese data. Chestnut, Ostro and Vichit-Vadakan (1997) use survey data of Thai residents in order to obtain willingness to pay estimates for avoiding one day of respiratory illness. They find that the mean willingness to pay for one less day of symptoms or one less day of reduced activity is very similar to mean willingness to pay estimates found by adjusting estimates from U.S. studies.

Alberini et al. (1997) survey Taiwanese residents to obtain an estimate of their willingness to pay to avoid a recurrence of an acute respiratory illness. They then compare these estimates with estimates derived from three benefits transfer methods: (1) income adjustments to U.S. estimates based on the assumption that the elasticity of willingness

---

[41] An earlier example of this benefits transfer approach is Ostro (1994).

[42] See Krupnick (1993) for a short summary of the issues surrounding benefits transfer.

to pay with respect to income is 1.0; (2) income adjustments to U.S. estimates based on the assumption that the elasticity of willingness to pay with respect to income is 0.4; and (3) substituting mean values of the characteristics of one country into an estimated willingness-to-pay function from another country. They conclude that none of the three benefits transfer methods outperforms the others, yet their results about the reliability of benefits transfer are ambiguous. Some of the benefits transfer estimates fall within the confidence interval of their Taiwanese estimates, while others are outside the confidence interval, depending on the U.S. studies used.

These studies suggest that the best way to obtain benefits estimates of environmental health policies is to estimate the preferences for risk reduction within the pertinent country.[43] Nonetheless, while benefits transfer methods frequently do not arrive at precise willingness-to-pay estimates, the general perception is that they are better than making policy decisions based on no attempt to quantify the benefits.

4.4. Using housing market data to estimate the value of a statistical cancer case

Most hedonic property studies examine the tradeoff between housing prices and distance to an environmental disamenity. Chapter 16 by Raymond Palmquist in this *Handbook* presents detailed analyses of these studies, so in this section we will examine only those few studies that explicitly examine the tradeoff between housing prices and risks.[44] Much like the hedonic wage model, the hedonic property model examines the interaction between consumer demand and producer supply of housing characteristics, with the hedonic price curve representing the locus of tangencies between the offer and bid curves. The consumer's bid curve is derived by assuming that individuals maximize expected utility over two states of the world, with V representing utility in the cancer state and U representing utility in the noncancer state. Utility in each state is a function of a vector of characteristics of the house z, and a composite good x. The consumer purchases one house at price h, which is a function of housing characteristics and cancer risk p. Each consumer's expected utility locus consists of those points that satisfy

$$Z = pV(x, z) + (1 - p)U(x, z), \tag{17}$$

subject to the constraint $y = x + h(z, p)$.

Each consumer selects the price–risk bundle that maximizes expected utility, which occurs where the expected utility locus is tangent to a producer's offer curve. The offer curve consists of the points that represent constant profits for risk–price tradeoffs. The first-order condition for this equilibrium is as follows:

$$\frac{\partial h}{\partial p} = \frac{V(x, z) - U(x, z)}{p \partial V / \partial x + (1 - p) \partial U / \partial x}. \tag{18}$$

[43] Some other recent studies that estimate willingness to pay in developing countries include Shanmugam (1997), Liu and Hammitt (1999), and Simon et al. (1999).

[44] We also defer to Chapter 16 by Raymond Palmquist in this Handbook concerning the empirical specification of the hedonic price function.

Given the assumption that individuals prefer to be healthy ($U(x, z) > V(x, z)$), and that the marginal utility of income is positive in both states ($\partial V/\partial x > 0$, $\partial U/\partial x > 0$), then the above equation is negative, suggesting that the slope of the hedonic price equation with respect to cancer risk is negative (i.e., the marginal willingness to pay for risk reduction is positive).

As we discussed in the section on the hedonic wage model, one would ideally want to estimate the structural willingness-to-pay function for consumers. This would allow for welfare estimates of nonmarginal changes in the risk. However, as shown by Bartik (1987) and Epple (1987), the endogeneity of marginal prices and housing characteristics makes it difficult to identify the structural equations. Instead, most studies focus on estimating the hedonic price function, which allows welfare estimates of marginal changes in risk.[45]

The above model assumes that consumers are aware of the risks associated with the housing choice. If, instead, individual perceptions of risk π were a function of the actual risk p, as in the prospective reference theory model discussed above, then the first-order equilibrium condition would be given as follows:

$$\frac{\partial h}{\partial p} = \frac{[V(x, z) - U(x, z)]\partial \pi/\partial p}{p\partial V/\partial x + (1 - p)\partial U/\partial x}. \tag{19}$$

Thus, estimation of the hedonic price gradient conflates individuals' preferences for risk tradeoffs with individuals' perceptional bias of the risks.[46]

Many hedonic property studies estimate the tradeoff between housing prices and the distance to the environmental disamenity. Such studies typically assume that cleaning up a disamenity is equivalent to moving a house to a distance at which the gradient levels off.[47] One difficulty associated with the distance gradient is that it does not offer an accessible means of aggregating the risks from multiple disamenities in the vicinity of a house. It is also difficult to use the distance gradient to estimate the benefits given a partial reduction in risk, which is often the EPA's goal. Some studies have attempted to directly estimate a risk gradient (instead of a distance gradient) in order to get around these difficulties, as well as to estimate the value of a statistical life associated with environmental risks.

---

[45] Palmquist (1992) showed that price changes given by the hedonic price equation (adjusting for moving costs) offer accurate welfare measurements for nonmarginal changes, given that the disamenities are local. Bartik (1988) showed that under certain conditions the hedonic price function might provide an approximation of the welfare effects of nonmarginal changes, even in the case of a nonlocal disamenity.

[46] As mentioned in Section 3.3, Lichtenstein et al. (1978) presented evidence that the slope of perceptions with respect to the actual risk is less than one; i.e., individuals tend to overestimate low probability events and underestimate high probability events. In an analysis of the two-way effect of risk and housing prices, Gayer (2000) examined only housing sales that took place after information was provided by the EPA and assumes that people informed of the risks do not have perceptional biases.

[47] Hedonic property studies that use the distance gradient include Kohlhase (1991) and Kiel and McClain (1995).

Portney (1981) was the first housing market study that estimated the value of a statistical life. This was achieved by coupling the estimate of the price gradient with respect to total dustfall with a separate EPA study that related total particulate concentration to mortality rates. By linking the study on dustfall with the study on particulate concentration, Portney (1981) demonstrated that the ratio of these two estimates is a measure of the value of a statistical life, which was estimated to be $0.3 million (1996 dollars).

Using a data set that includes detailed information of the risks from six Superfund hazardous waste sites in the Greater Grand Rapids housing market, Gayer, Hamilton and Viscusi (2000a) found that housing prices reflect a willingness to pay for risk reduction. This study also found that the willingness to pay decreased after the EPA released its risk information, suggesting that informed people lower their perceptions of the risk. Using the estimate for the marginal willingness to pay for risk reduction, Gayer, Hamilton and Viscusi (2000a) found that the value of avoiding a statistical cancer case is between $3.9 million and $4.6 million (1996 dollars). This range of estimates makes intuitive sense since it is similar to estimates of the value of a statistical life found in labor market studies (see Table 8). Nevertheless, the housing estimates are slightly lower, though the confidence interval for these estimates includes the midpoint of the estimated value of a statistical life from the labor market.

5. Regulatory performance

The methods described in Section 4 provide a means of estimating the benefits of regulatory efforts to reduce environmental health risks. Efficient regulation of environmental risks consists of targeting regulatory dollars to risk reduction efforts that result in a maximization of net health and environmental benefits, where we assume that these are valued appropriately. Currently, government regulations often aim to eliminate lifetime fatality risks that are one in a million or greater. Yet Wilson (1979) found that fatality risks of one in a million are incurred for risky events that occur several times or more in people's lifetimes. There is a one in a million fatality risk every time one has a chest x-ray, lives two days in New York or Boston (air pollution), travels 10 miles by bicycle, or eats 40 tablespoons of peanut butter (which contains the carcinogen aflatoxin B). Devoting regulatory dollars to address such small health risks, without regard to costs, very likely leads to a use of resources that can better be used elsewhere (perhaps, on education, housing, or medical care).

Yet suppose that due to legislative constraints or other factors, policy makers are not permitted to impose a benefit–cost test. A second-best option would still be to target risk reduction efforts cost-effectively. That is, if society aims to reduce health risks by a certain level (regardless of the dollar benefits), the goal should be to achieve this reduction level at least cost. Or similarly, if society decides upon a fixed amount of money to spend on risk reduction, the goal should be to achieve the maximum possible reduction of risk. If reducing risks to life is our sole objective, the practical implication is that we should equalize the cost per life saved within an agency's programs and across agencies. Currently, there is no such cost-effectiveness requirement in the U.S., leading to widespread gaps in regulatory performance. This shortfall implies that lives are being sacrificed by failing to exploit the opportunity presented by more cost-effective policies.

Table 11 lists a series of cost-effective risk regulations that pass a benefit–cost test. The last column in the table lists the cost per life saved for each regulation. An efficient risk-reduction policy would reallocate resources so that the marginal benefit of risk reduction equals the marginal cost over each risk. In some cases the scale of the cost-effective regulations cannot be expanded. Once floor emergency lighting is installed in an aircraft, the benefits have been reaped. More lighting may not be worthwhile. Given a reasonable estimate of $5 million dollars for the value of a statistical life, each of these regulations passes a cost–benefit test. The regulations listed in Table 12 are less effective in saving lives, as they each fail a cost–benefit test. The most egregious violation listed in the table is the $72 billion cost per life saved for OSHA's regulation of formaldehyde (both tables are reproduced from Viscusi (1996)). These tables indicate that a cost-effective regulatory strategy that shifts resources from regulations in Table 12 to regulations in Table 11 can achieve considerable increases in lives saved for the same level of expenditure.

Many of these reallocations involve shifts across agencies rather than within agency programs. A principal source of the differences is the character of the legislative mandates of different agencies. OSHA and EPA tend to have legislative mandates that either prohibit basing policies on benefit–cost tests or place undue emphasis on risk reduction rather than appropriate balancing of benefits and costs. In contrast, the U.S. Department of Transportation is not hindered by similar legislative constraints. The result is that Department of Transportation's agencies (i.e., the Federal Aviation Administration and the National Highway Traffic Safety Administration) appear in Table 11's listing of cost-effective lifesaving efforts, whereas OSHA and EPA regulations dominate the list of inefficient policies in Table 12.

This difference across agencies is reflected in the guidelines within agencies for the promulgation of policies. Traditionally, EPA does not formally use benefit–cost analysis to select its policies, though it does provide such an analysis as part of the executive oversight process. In contrast, the U.S. Department of Transportation uses a cost–benefit analysis in its regulatory decision-making, in which it caps the value of a statistical life at $3 million. As a consequence, the regulations of the FAA and the NHTSA pass a cost–benefit test.

The policies in Tables 11 and 12 pertain only to policies for which regulations must be promulgated before the policy is enacted. Many policy efforts by EPA and other agencies do not require new regulations, but nevertheless involve risk reductions and potential inefficiencies. A prominent example is the Superfund program for the cleanup of hazardous waste. This effort enables EPA to mandate stringent cleanup of existing hazardous waste sites for which the costs are paid by the potentially responsible parties, chiefly by private industry. The agency does not issue regulations to guide each new cleanup, and indeed the guidelines for agency policy are internal guidance documents resulting from agency decisions but not a formal rulemaking process. The resulting

Table 11
The cost of risk-reducing U.S. regulations that pass a benefit–cost test

Regulation	Agency, year and status	Initial annual risk	Annual lives saved	Cost per life saved (millions of 1984 $)
Unvented space heaters	CPSC 1980 F	2.7 in 10^5	63	$0.10
Oil and gas well service	OSHA 1983 P	1.1 in 10^3	50	$0.10
Cabin fire protection	FAA 1985 F	6.5 in 10^8	15	$0.20
Passive restraints/belts	NHTSA 1984 F	9.1 in 10^5	1,850	$0.30
Underground construction	OSHA 1989 F	1.6 in 10^3	8.1	$0.30
Alcohol and drug control	FRA 1985 F	1.8 in 10^6	4.2	$0.50
Servicing wheel rims	OSHA 1984 F	1.4 in 10^5	2.3	$0.50
Seat cushion flammability	FAA 1984 F	1.6 in 10^7	37	$0.60
Floor emergency lighting	FAA 1984 F	2.2 in 10^8	5	$0.70
Crane suspended personnel platform	OSHA 1988 F	1.8 in 10^3	5	$1.20
Concrete and masonry construction	OSHA 1988 F	1.4 in 10^5	6.5	$1.40
Hazard communication	OSHA 1983 F	4.0 in 10^5	200	$1.80
Benzene/fugitive emissions	EPA 1984 F	2.1 in 10^5	0.31	$2.80

Note. "Initial annual risk" indicates annual deaths per exposed population; an exposed population of 10^3 is 1,000, 10^4 is 10,000, etc. In "Agency, year and status" column, P, R, and F represent proposed, rejected and final rule, respectively. CPSC stands for the Consumer Product Safety Commission, OHSA stands for the Occupational Health and Safety Administration, EPA stands for the Environmental Protection Agency, FAA stands for the Federal Aviation Administration, NHTSA stands for the National Highway Traffic Safety Administration.
Sources: Viscusi (1992) and Morrall (1986). These statistics were updated by John F. Morrall, III, via unpublished communication with Viscusi, July 10, 1990.

cost-effectiveness of this effort is quite bleak, with a median cost per case of cancer prevented estimated by Viscusi and Hamilton (1999) to be $6 billion.

This inefficiency can be traced not only to the failure to apply a benefit–cost test but also to the character of the risk analysis. As the earlier discussions indicated, overly

Table 12
The cost of risk-reducing U.S. regulations that fail a benefit–cost test

Regulation	Agency year and status	Initial annual risk	Annual lives saved	Cost per life saved (millions of 1984 $)
Grain dust	OSHA 1987 F	2.1 in 10^4	4	5.3
Radionuclides/ uranium mines	EPA 1984 F	1.4 in 10^4	1.1	6.9
Benzene	OSHA 1987 F	8.8 in 10^4	3.8	17.1
Arsenic/glass plant	EPA 1986 F	8.0 in 10^4	0.11	19.2
Ethylene oxide	OSHA 1984 F	4.4 in 10^4	2.8	25.6
Arsenic/copper smelter	EPA 1986 F	9.0 in 10^4	0.06	26.5
Uranium mill tailings, inactive	EPA 1983 F	4.3 in 10^4	2.1	27.6
Uranium mill tailings, active	EPA 1983 F	4.3 in 10^4	2.1	53
Asbestos	OSHA 1986 F	6.7 in 10^5	74.7	89.3
Asbestos	EPA 1989 F	2.9 in 10^5	10	104.2
Arsenic/glass manufacturing	EPA 1986 R	3.8 in 10^5	0.25	142
Benzene/storage	EPA 1984 R	6.0 in 10^7	0.043	202
Radionuclides/ DOE facilities	EPA 1984 R	4.3 in 10^6	0.001	210
Radionuclides/ elem. phosphorous	EPA 1984 R	1.4 in 10^5	0.046	270
Benzene/ethyl- benzenol styrene	EPA 1984 R	2.0 in 10^6	0.006	483
Arsenic/low-arsenic copper	EPA 1986 R	2.6 in 10^4	0.09	764
Benzene/maleic anhydride	EPA 1984 R	1.1 in 10^6	0.029	820

(*continued on next page*)

conservative risk assessments can distort allocations. In the case of Superfund, not only do the calculated risks incorporate upper-bound assumptions, but the cleanup priorities are also distorted because of the focus on hypothetically exposed individuals rather than on assessing the size of the existing populations exposed to the risk.

While the information in Tables 11 and 12 is telling, the estimates treat all lives saved as being homogeneous, placing equal weight on lives with very short and very long

Table 12
(*Continued*)

Regulation	Agency year and status	Initial annual risk	Annual lives saved	Cost per life saved (millions of 1984 $)
Land disposal	EPA 1988 F	2.3 in 10^8	2.52	3,500
EDB	OSHA 1989 R	2.5 in 10^4	0.002	15,600
Formaldehyde	OSHA 1987 F	6.8 in 10^7	0.01	72,000

Note. "Initial annual risk" indicates annual deaths per exposed population; an exposed population of 10^3 is 1,000, 10^4 is 10,000, etc. In "Agency year and status" column, P, R, and F represent proposed, rejected and final rule, respectively. OSHA stands for the Occupational Health and Safety Administration, and EPA stands for the Environmental Protection Agency.
Sources: Viscusi (1992) and Morrall (1986). These statistics were updated by John F. Morrall, III, via unpublished communication with Viscusi, July 10, 1990.

expected duration. Recall from Section 4.3.3 that the measure of lives lost is not completely appropriate from an economic standpoint since it ignores the role of the duration of life lost and the discounting of future risks. For example, while one regulation may have a higher cost per life saved, if it is targeted at younger individuals, it will tend to save lives of longer length compared to other regulations. However, agency practices typically do not recognize quantity of life issues. Doing so has a differential effect on the assessed efficacy of regulatory policies. Viscusi, Hakes and Carlin (1997) devised a measure of discounted lost life expectancy (LLE) that accounts for both life expectancy and discounting of future risks based on the type of health risk targeted by the regulation. Table 13 presents the cost per life saved for various regulations and the cost per life saved normalized by LLE. Regulatory policies that focus on illnesses such as cancer, which have long latency periods and tend to affect older members of the population, will decrease in attractiveness compared to policies that avert accidents. The findings in Table 13 suggest that the variance between the least and most cost-effective regulations increases after taking into account the lost life expectancy. Thus, the regulations that were previously seen as the best uses of regulatory dollars are even better than first thought, and the worst uses of regulatory dollars are even poorer than was first thought. This differential effect arises because adjusting for the quantity of life at risk diminishes the cost-effectiveness of cancer prevention efforts, which already were relatively poor performers on a cost per life saved basis.

This discrepancy lends more impetus to the efforts to reform current regulatory efforts. In the next subsection we will examine the legislative mandates of the various regulatory agencies and the role of regulatory oversight by the executive branch in order to provide a better understanding of what generated the observed regulatory inefficien-

Table 13
U.S. estimates of regulatory costs and cost-effectiveness in saving lives

Regulation	Year	Agency	Cost per death averted, millions 1990 $	Cost per life saved, millions of 1990 $	Cost per normalized life saved, 1995 $	Cost per year of life saved, 1995 $
Unvented space heater ban	1980	CPSC	0.1	0.1	0.1	0.0
Aircraft cabin fire protection standard	1985	FAA	0.1	0.1	0.1	0.0
Seat belt/air bag	1984	NHTSA	0.1	0.1	0.1	0.0
Steering column protection standard	1967	NHTSA	0.1	0.1	0.1	0.0
Underground construction standards	1989	OSHA	0.1	0.1	0.1	0.0
Trihalomethane in drinking water	1979	EPA	0.2	0.2	0.6	0.0
Aircraft seat cushion flammability	1984	FAA	0.4	0.5	0.6	0.0
Alcohol and drug controls	1985	FRA	0.4	0.5	0.6	0.0
Auto fuel-system integrity	1975	NHTSA	0.4	0.5	0.5	0.0
Auto wheel rim servicing	1984	OSHA	0.4	0.5	0.6	0.0
Aircraft floor emergency lighting	1984	FAA	0.6	0.7	0.9	0.0
Concrete and masonry construction	1988	OSHA	0.6	0.7	0.9	0.0
Crane suspended personnel platform	1988	OSHA	0.7	0.8	1.0	0.1
Passive restraints for trucks and buses	1989	NHTSA	0.7	0.8	0.8	0.0
Auto side-impact standards	1990	NHTSA	0.8	1.0	1.0	0.1
Children's sleepwear flammability ban	1973	CPSC	0.8	1.0	1.2	0.1
Auto side door supports	1970	NHTSA	0.8	1.0	1.0	0.1
Low-altitude windshear equipment and training	1988	FAA	1.3	1.6	1.9	0.1
Metal mine electrical equipment standards	1970	MSHA	1.4	1.7	2.0	0.1
Trenching and excavation standards	1989	OSHA	1.5	1.8	2.2	0.1
Traffic alert and collision avoidance systems	1988	FAA	1.5	1.8	2.2	0.1
Hazard communication standard	1983	OSHA	1.6	1.9	4.8	0.2
Trucks, buses and MPV side-impact	1989	NHTSA	2.2	2.6	2.6	0.1
Grain dust explosion prevention standards	1987	OSHA	2.8	3.3	4.0	0.2

(*continued on next page*)

Table 13
(*Continued*)

Regulation	Year	Agency	Cost per death averted, millions 1990 $	Cost per life saved, millions of 1990 $	Cost per normalized life saved, 1995 $	Cost per year of life saved, 1995 $
Rear lap/shoulder belts for autos	1989	NHTSA	3.2	3.8	3.8	0.2
Stds for radionuclides in uranium mines	1984	EPA	3.4	4.1	10.1	0.5
Benzene NESHAP (original: fugitive emissions)	1984	EPA	3.4	4.1	10.1	0.5
Ethylene dibromide in drinking water	1991	EPA	5.7	6.8	17.0	0.8
Benzene NESHAP (revised: coke by-products)	1988	EPA	6.1	7.3	18.1	0.9
Asbestos occupational exposure limit	1986	OSHA	74	88.1	220.1	10.6
Asbestos occupational exposure limit	1972	OSHA	8.3	9.9	24.7	1.2
Benzene occupational exposure limit	1987	OSHA	8.9	10.6	26.5	1.3
Electrical equipment in coal mines	1970	OSHA	9.2	11.0	13.3	0.6
Arsenic emission standards for glass plants	1986	MSHA	13.5	16.1	40.2	1.9
Ethylene oxide occupational exposure limit	1984	EPA	20.5	24.4	61.0	2.9
Arsenic/copper NESHAP	1986	EPA	23	27.4	68.4	3.3
Haz. waste listing of petroleum refining sludge	1990	EPA	27.6	32.9	82.1	3.9
Cover/move uranium mill tailings (inactive)	1983	EPA	31.7	37.7	94.3	4.5
Benzene NESHAP (revised: transfer operations)	1990	EPA	32.9	39.2	97.9	4.7
Cover/move uranium mill tailings (active sites)	1983	EPA	45	53.6	133.8	6.4
Acrylonitrile occupational exposure limit	1978	OSHA	51.5	61.3	153.2	7.3
Coke ovens occupational exposure limit	1976	OSHA	63.5	75.6	188.9	9.1
Lockout/tagout	1989	OSHA	70.9	84.4	102.4	4.9
Arsenic occupational exposure limit	1978	OSHA	106.9	127.3	317.9	15.2

(*continued on next page*)

Table 13
(*Continued*)

Regulation	Year	Agency	Cost per death averted, millions 1990 $	Cost per life saved, millions of 1990 $	Cost per normalized life saved, 1995 $	Cost per year of life saved, 1995 $
Asbestos ban	1989	EPA	110.7	131.8	329.2	15.8
Diethylstilbestrol (DES) cattlefeed ban	1979	FDA	124.8	148.6	371.2	17.8
Benzene NESHAP (revised: waste operations)	1990	EPA	168.2	200.2	500.2	24.0
1,2-dichloropropane in drinking water	1991	EPA	653.0	777.4	1,942.1	93.1
Hazardous waste land disposal ban	1988	EPA	4,190.40	4,988.70	12,462.7	597.4
Municipal solid waste landfills	1988	EPA	19107.0	22,746.80	56,826.1	2,724.2
Formaldehyde occupational exposure limit	1987	OSHA	86,201.80	102,622.80	256,372.7	12,290.0
Atrazine/alachlor in drinking water	1991	EPA	92,069.70	109,608.50	273,824.4	13,126.8
Hazardous waste listing for wood-preserving chemicals	1990	EPA	570000.0	6,785,822.0	16,952,364.9	812,673.3

Note: The Regulations are all for U.S. agencies. EPA stands for the Environmental Protection Agency, OSHA stands for Occupational Safety and Health Administration, FDA stands for the Food and Drug Administration, FAA stands for the Federal Aviation Administration, NHTSA stands for the National Highway Traffic Safety Administration, CPSC stands for the Consumer Product Safety Commission, and MSHA stands for Mine Safety Health Administration.
Source: Viscusi, Hakes and Carlin (1997, p. 229).

cies. We will then examine the role that risk–risk analysis can play in improving the cost-effectiveness of health regulations.

5.1. Legislative mandates, judicial review, and executive oversight in the U.S.

The 1970s witnessed the emergence of a variety of new agencies and programs to regulate the environment and other risks. The Clean Air Act amendments of 1970 and 1977, the Occupational Safety and Health Act of 1970, the Federal Water Pollution Control Act Amendments of 1972, the Clean Water Act of 1977, the Resource Conservation and Recovery Act of 1976, the Toxic Substances and Control Act of 1976, and the Comprehensive Environmental Response Compensation, and Liability Act of 1980 bear witness to the growing concern of health risks during this time. With each piece of legislation, Congress set out broad goals to be promoted by the regulatory agencies within the executive branch. The regulatory agencies were then required to establish regulations to achieve these goals. Under current practices, these regulations first undergo a review by the U.S. Office of Management and Budget, as well as a public comment period.

Judicial review can overturn existing health regulations if the original legislation is found to be unconstitutional, or more likely, if the regulations are found to be inconsistent with the legislation. Given the hybrid of practices stipulated in the legislation, the current framework often leads to inconsistent regulatory practices within and between agencies. For example, the Clean Air Act and Clean Water Act prohibit the consideration of costs when assessing the merits of a regulation, while the Toxic Substances Control Act mandates the consideration of costs.

In some instances the judicial branch has also had to address whether the regulatory agencies are falling short of the legislative aims, and in other instances whether it has exceeded its powers as constituted in the legislation. This stems in large part from the sometimes ambiguously worded goals of the legislation. For example, the Clean Air Act directs that ambient standards for common air pollutants be set at levels that provide an "adequate margin of safety," while standards for hazardous air pollutants be set at levels that provide an "ample margin of safety." The Federal Water Pollution Control Act of 1972 set as its goal the elimination of all discharge of pollutants into navigable waters, and that all of the nation's water bodies be "fishable and swimmable." The goal of the Occupational Safety and Health Act of 1970 is "to assure so far as possible every man and woman in the Nation safe and healthful working conditions."

The ambiguous regulatory goals have led to many court rulings. For example, as was mentioned in Section 2.1, the Supreme Court ruled in 1980 that OSHA was first required to demonstrate that their standard for benzene regulation would generate significant risk reductions and that the standard would be "reasonably necessary or appropriate to provide safe and healthful employment." [48] The court also deemed that promoting safety was not the same as eliminating all occupational risks, no matter how small. In 1981, the Supreme Court ruled that the legislative requirement that OSHA regulations be "feasible" does not warrant a broad economic interpretation of feasibility (i.e., one that passes a cost–benefit test). Rather, the court interpreted the legislative mandate in terms of whether a regulatory goal is "capable of being done." [49] For the most part, however, judicial rulings have deferred to the agency's discretion in interpreting its legislative mandate. In 1984, the Supreme Court ruled that the EPA could use a "bubble" policy to control emissions, since this was a reasonable interpretation by the EPA of its legislative mandate. [50] Recent rulings, however, potentially open the door to the use of economic analysis in formulating health standards. In 1991, the D.C. Court of Appeals ruled that

---

[48] See the Supreme Court's decision in *Industrial Union Department, AFL-CIO v. American Petroleum Institute*, 448 U.S. 607 (1980).

[49] See the Supreme Court's decision in *American Textile Manufacturer's Institute v. Donovan*, 452 U.S. 490 (1981).

[50] See the Supreme Court's decision in *Chevron USA Inc. v. NRDC*, U.S. 837 (1984).

OSHA was allowed to use benefit–cost analysis in promulgating its regulations.[51] And in May 1999, the D.C. Court of Appeals ruled that the EPA had arbitrarily set standards for permissible levels of fine soot, and that it must first justify its setting of standards in terms of its legislative mandate. More important, the Court also ruled that in setting national ambient air quality standards (NAAQS) the EPA had exceeded its powers, and that the "construction of the Clean Air Act on which EPA relied in promulgating the NAAQS at issue here effects an unconstitutional delegation of legislative power." However, the Court still held that "the EPA is not permitted to consider the cost of implementing [NAAQS] standards."[52]

While environmental laws provide the legal context for agencies, the executive branch also maintains the power of regulatory oversight through its use of executive orders. Executive order number 12044 during the Carter administration required that regulations be cost-effective and that the agency quantify the benefits and costs of the regulation. However, this cost-effectiveness test did little to screen out inefficient regulations since truly dominant regulatory alternatives that were not selected could be identified in only a few cases. Executive order number 12291 during the Reagan administration required that agencies show that the benefits of a regulation exceed the costs, except when the agency's legislative mandate prohibits a benefit–cost test. Executive order number 12866 during the Clinton administration requires that benefits of regulations "justify" the costs. This order created the peculiar scenario in which the EPA, by executive order, was required to conduct a cost–benefit analysis for a regulation, yet by legislative mandate, was not allowed to consider the costs of a regulation that falls under the Clean Air Act.

5.2. Risk–risk analysis

Though economists espousing economic efficiency would prefer a comparison of all the health and nonhealth benefits and costs in order to assess the desirability of a regulation, many health-related regulatory laws prohibit such an analysis. Even where cost–benefit analysis is permitted it might not be used, since many government officials distrust the practice of placing monetary values on health risks. There is also controversy over benefit–cost tests in circumstances in which the gainers do not compensate the losers. However, most reluctance to using benefit–cost analysis is generic in nature and does not pertain to any particular policy circumstances. In this subsection, we explore the use of risk–risk analysis as an imperfect, yet second-best, substitute for cost–benefit analysis. A risk–risk analysis imposes a much looser criterion for regulatory assessment. Instead of requiring that a regulation's benefits outweigh its costs, risk–risk analysis

---

[51] See the D.C. Court of Appeals decision in *UAW v. Occupational Safety and Health Administration*, 938 F.2d 1310 (1991).

[52] See the D.C. Court of Appeals decision in *American Trucking Associates, Inc. et al. v. U.S. Environmental Protection Agency* 97-1440 (1999).

only requires that a regulatory policy result in a net reduction of human health risks, which would seem to be a test that would be a minimal requirement for policy efficacy.

How might a regulatory policy that aims to protect public health result in an increase in health risks? A regulatory policy could lead to an increase in risk if it leads to a change in behavior that carries with it risks of its own. The production and maintenance of control technologies put in place due to the regulation may lead to an increase in occupational hazards. In the extreme case, if policies are no more beneficial than digging ditches and filling them back up again then some people will be injured in the process. Risk could also increase if the product being regulated has some health benefits that must be forgone with the enactment of the regulation. And finally, regulations entail a real opportunity cost as these resources could have been allocated by consumers to achieve the health benefits of a consumption bundle including medical care, nutrition, and housing. We will examine each of these regulatory health effects in detail below.

5.2.1. Moral hazard and forgone health benefits

Regulatory agencies frequently fail to consider the possibility that people will change their behavior due to a regulation. This omission causes particular problems when the averting behavior has inherent risks of its own. For example, Peltzman (1975) examined the influence of seatbelt use on driver behavior. All things being equal, introducing safety mechanisms such as seatbelts would lead to a decrease in accident fatalities. However, precautionary behavior is not likely to remain unchanged. Since seatbelts increase the safety of drivers for any given speed, there will be a greater incentive to drive faster in order to reduce travel time. The result is that the risk reduction that accompanies the introduction of seatbelts will be at least somewhat offset by the increase of risks due to faster driving, most notably the increase of risks to motorcyclists and pedestrians. Whether the net effect of improved car safety results in an increase or a decrease in risk is a matter of considerable debate.[53]

Viscusi (1984) examined the influence of child safety caps on potentially poisonous consumer products. The introduction of such safety caps could lead parents to take fewer safety precautions, such as keeping the products out of reach of children, particularly to the extent that parents now perceive the products to be completely safe. Also, the difficulty of opening such safety caps may lead some people to leave off the caps altogether, resulting in more child poisonings. The net result, according to Viscusi (1984), is that the introduction of safety caps led to an increase in poisoning from aspirin and analgesics. Moreover, no product with safety caps exhibited a statistically significant decrease in poisonings. In a similar analysis of safety mechanisms on cigarette lighters, Viscusi and Covallo (1994) found that the net effect of the safety regulation was a decrease in risk since the efficacy of the safety mechanism outweighed the decrease in parental care.

---

[53] See Blomquist (1988, 1991), Crandall et al. (1986), and Adams (1995) for a review of this evidence and for additional perspectives.

A regulation could also lead to more direct increases in risk. For example, consider the case of the artificial sweetener saccharin, which was found to be a rodent carcinogen. There is an explicit tradeoff between the risk of cancer due to saccharin consumption and the risks associated with obesity due to use of sugar in lieu of saccharin. While the FDA first wanted to ban saccharin, the public reaction led Congress to allow its use, provided that a warning label accompanied it. Other regulatory policies face similar risk tradeoffs. Nitrates are carcinogenic, yet their use as preservatives in cured meats reduces the risk of botulism. Chlorination of water is beneficial since it reduces the spread of many diseases, but chlorinated water is also a carcinogen. A recent example is the case of bisphenol-A, a substance that can leach out from clear plastic baby bottles. There is some evidence of harmful effects to the reproductive systems of male mice born from pregnant mice who were fed the substance. This has led to calls for parents to throw out plastic baby bottles. Yet the alternative is to use glass bottles, which leads to an increase in the risk of cuts and gouges.

5.2.2. Occupational risks associated with risk-reduction regulations

A regulation frequently leads to increases in the production of certain products, and this increase in production could cause an increase in health risks to workers. For example, the production and installation of pollution-control equipment may involve thousands of person-hours of work with heavy equipment, as well as worker exposure to the chemicals being remediated. These risks must be counted against the risk reductions of the regulation in order to obtain a net measure of the effect on health risks. Viscusi and Zeckhauser (1994) use an input-output analysis to isolate the final product risks and the intermediate output risks and to determine the total direct and indirect risks of expenditures. They find that the occupational risks generally account for 3–4% of total costs, and that many particularly cost-ineffective regulatory activities thus result in net increases in health risks.

While their estimates distinguish these costs by industry, a simple example based on the 4 percent health cost figure illustrates the nature of the effect. Suppose that $5 million is the reference point for the value of a statistical life. Then a regulation that costs $125 million or more per life saved (i.e., $5 million/4 percent) will produce as many health losses as benefits. In particular, for each life saved it will generate at least $5 million in health losses (i.e., 4 percent × $125 million). Such regulations do not advance society's risk reduction efforts since they generate health hazards at least as large as the environmental health benefits they generate.

5.2.3. The opportunity costs of risk-reduction regulations

Another way that a health-related regulation can increase risk is through the opportunity cost of regulatory policies. The work by Viscusi (1978) and Wildavsky (1980, 1988) found that there is a link between the wealth and the health of an individual. That is, risk reduction is a normal good and will therefore be consumed in greater quantities by more affluent individuals and societies. As one's wealth increases, one's health will improve because the increase will be spent in part on healthful practices such as better nutrition and preventive health care. To the extent that resources are diverted from these health-related goods, there will be an adverse effect on health. Wildavsky referred to this idea as the "richer is safer" theory, and contended that economic growth, not government regulation, is the primary cause of this century's increase in life expectancy and health status. Government regulations aimed at improving public health must therefore consider the indirect negative health effects due to decreases in economic growth and, more generally, reducing the public's disposable income for personal consumption expenditures.[54]

Table 14 provides a summary of some studies that estimate the implicit income gains necessary to avoid one statistical death. Keeney (1990) was the first to develop empirical estimates of the negative effects of regulations on fatality risks. He found that a $12.3 million loss of income (1992 dollars) results in one statistical death. Duleep (1986, 1989, 1991) controlled for physical disability and education and found that an income loss between $2.6 million and $6.5 million will result in one statistical fatality. Lutter and Morrall (1994) used international data on GDP and mortality to estimate the effect of wealth on mortality. These results, presented in Table 15, demonstrate a significant relationship between GDP and mortality rates. These results imply that a loss of income between $8.0 million and $9.6 million will result in an additional statistical death.

In a 1991 ruling by the D.C. Court of Appeals, Judge Stephen F. Williams cited the estimates by Keeney (1990) to support the decision that OSHA's safety standards for accidental start-ups of hazardous machinery could conceivably result in an increase in fatalities.[55] The Wildavsky and Keeney studies, as well as the ruling by the D.C. Court of Appeals, were cited in a letter from OMB to the Department of Labor on March 10, 1992.[56] In this letter, OMB suspended its review of an OSHA proposed regulation on workplace air contaminants, claiming that OSHA must first perform a risk–risk analysis before it would resume the review.

As a consequence of this letter, the Committee on Government Affairs, chaired by Senator John Glenn, called for hearings on OMB's demand for such an analysis. Senator Glenn also asked the General Accounting Office (GAO) to review the OMB's analysis.

---

[54] The analysis of the increase in health risks due to the wealth–health linkage is frequently referred to as health–health analysis to distinguish it from risk–risk analysis, which focuses on the risks posed by averting behavior, direct substitutes of the product, and the production and maintenance of the regulatory control technologies. Since we are interested in the net change in risk due to a regulation, we use risk–risk analysis to refer to all the possible dampening effects that a regulation might have on health.

[55] See the D.C. Court of Appeals decision in *UAW v. Occupational Safety and Health Administration*, 938 F.2d 1310 (1991). Also, see Williams (1993) for a discussion of the legal implications of risk–risk analysis.

[56] The letter was from James B. MacRae, Jr., Acting Administrator, Office of Information and Regulatory Affairs, U.S. Office of Management and Budget, to Nancy Risque-Rohrbach, Assistant Secretary for Policy, U.S. Department of Labor.

Table 14
Summary of selected studies on income and health

Study	Data	Implicit income gains necessary to avert one death (millions)	Comments
Keeney (1990)	Used income and mortality correlation from Kitagawa and Hauser (1973) data, and others	$12.3	Cited in UAW v. OSHA, as $7.25 1980 dollars. Represents an upper-bound
U.S. Congress, Joint Economic Committee (1984)	Aggregate U.S. income, employment, mortality, and morbidity; 1950–1980	$1.8 to $2.7	Reflects income loss from recession of 1974/1975
Anderson and Burkhauser (1985)	4,878 male workers over 10 years, 1969–1979	$1.9 (wages) $4.3 (other income)	Older workers aged 58–63. Measured effects of wages and of value of one's home on mortality
Duleep (1986)	9,618 white married male workers aged 35–64 over 6 years, 1973–1978	$2.6	Controls for prior disability, and educational attainment
Duleep (1989)	13,954 white married male workers aged 25–64 over 6 years, 1973–1978	$6.5	Finds income effects at all income levels
Duleep (1991)	9,618 white married male workers aged 35–64 over 6 years, 1973–1978	$3.9	Controls for prior disability, educational attainment, and exposure to occupational hazards
Wolfson et al. (1992)	500,000 Canadian workers, over 10–20 years	$6	Investigates longevity rather than mortality. Finds income effects at highest quintiles of income
U.S. National Institutes of Health (1992)	1,300,000 Americans, all ages, 1979–1985	$12.4	Estimate reflects effect of income changes on family mortality. Study does not use multiple regression, does not control for prior health status or education
Chirikos and Nestel (1991)	5,020 men, aged 50–64 studied during 1971–1983	$3.3	Uses two measures of health endowments
Chapman and Hariharan (1994)	5,836 older men over 10 years	$12.2	Uses four distinct controls for prior health conditions
Graham, Hung-Chang and Evans (1992)	38 years of age-adjusted mortality and income data for the U.S.	$4.0	Distinguishes effects of permanent income from those of transitional income

Source: Lutter and Morrall (1994, p. 49).

Table 15
Summary of regressions of mortality and income

Estimation method	OLS/White's	Fixed effects	Random effects
Dependent variable	Ln(mortality)	Ln(mortality)	Ln(mortality)
Intercept	4.613[a]		4.63
	(0.130)		(0.175)
Ln(GDP)	−0.269[a]	−0.321[a]	−0.288
	(0.0178)	(0.0688)	(0.0237)
Year dummy	−0.241[a]		
	(0.0413)		
R^2	0.55	0.83	0.48
Observations	202	202	202
WTS	$\dfrac{GDP}{0.269 \times mortality}$	$\dfrac{GDP}{0.321 \times mortality}$	$\dfrac{GDP}{0.288 \times mortality}$
WTS for the U.S. (in millions)	$9.6	$8.0	$9.0

Note: The superscript [a] denotes significance at the 1-percent level.
Source: Lutter and Morrall (1994, p. 55).

This 1992 GAO report concluded that a "risk–risk analysis is a narrowly focused examination of the risks derived from an intervention compared with those that result from no
intervention" [GAO (1992, p. 10)]. GAO's claim was that Keeney's methodology examines the economic effects of the regulation on society, and thus constitutes a cost–benefit
analysis, which is not permissible by law. This conclusion reflects a misunderstanding
of risk–risk analysis, which has nothing whatsoever to do with risk–cost tradeoffs. The
sole focus is on whether agency programs reduce risk. The report also stated that, even
if it were acceptable to use such an analysis, the current evidence only supports a correlation between wealth and health, not a causal link. The report pointed out that empirical
studies of this link are made difficult by the multitude of confounding effects (e.g., education, social class, and opportunity), and that wealth could also be endogenous (i.e.,
increases in health cause increases in wealth).[57]

Smith, Epp and Schwabe (1994) followed up on this claim by examining some of
the difficulties involved with empirically establishing a causal link between wealth and
health. They replicated cross-country data from Lutter and Morrall (1994), updating it
for the current year and including independent variables that control for other socioeconomic effects on health, such as literacy rates. They also re-estimated the mortality-GDP
equation using subsamples of rich and poor countries. Their findings suggest that the
effect of wealth on health in international data is not robust to these changes in specification. They concluded, along with Portney and Stavins (1994), that the conventional

---

[57] Chapman and Hariharan (1994) addressed the issue of reverse causality by using measures of initial health
in order to focus on the effect from greater wealth to greater health. Using a duration model, they found that
regulations that cost more than $12.2 million per life saved are likely to result in a net increase in fatalities.

benefit–cost analysis ought to remain the principal tool of economic assessments of a regulation, since such an analysis correctly takes into account the nonrisk attributes of the regulation.

The proponents of risk–risk analysis likewise recognize that benefit–cost analysis is a more comprehensive and superior efficiency test. However, because of the practical role of legislative constraints, agencies such as EPA often promulgate regulations with very high costs per life saved, well beyond what might be consistent with a benefit–cost norm. The practical task is to determine what level of regulatory expenditure leads to the opportunity cost of one statistical life lost.

To avoid the causality problems associated with linking income and mortality risks and to establish consistency with benefit–cost tests using the value of a statistical life approach, Viscusi (1994) developed a theoretical linkage between the two approaches. If the only personal health related expenditures are mortality-reducing health expenditures, then the loss in income that leads to the loss of one statistical life is given by

$$\frac{\text{value of a statistical life}}{\text{marginal propensity to spend on health}}.$$

With a value of a statistical life figure of $5 million and with the marginal propensity to spend on health assumed to be 0.1, this approach yields an estimate of $50 million as the income loss that leads to the loss of a statistical life.

Not all increases in income produce health-enhancing expenditures. Lutter, Morrall and Viscusi (1999) generalized the Viscusi (1994) model to include income-related harmful behavior, such as smoking and drinking. Doing so suggests that regulations become counterproductive once cost per life saved levels hit a figure of $20 million or somewhat less.

There is as yet no consensus regarding the cost per life saved cutoff above which regulations become counterproductive by causing more adverse health effects than beneficial effects. However, the basic economic concept is correct. Profligate regulatory efforts will eventually become counterproductive, resulting in costs both in terms of money and personal health.

6. Conclusion

Environmental benefits include more than effects on natural resources. Indeed, many of the key concerns driving environmental benefits pertain to human health effects, chiefly cancer. Establishing dollar values on fatalities and other health outcomes is feasible, particularly once the focus is on statistical risks to health rather than certain events.

The methodology for establishing empirical estimates for the value of a statistical life and health is well established and has a large literature. Market estimates obtained using hedonic wage and price studies are often instructive in reflecting the tradeoffs people are actually willing to make. As in other environmental benefit contexts, survey and contingent valuation techniques often prove useful for health outcomes for which market evidence is not fully informative.

Many of the most salient remaining issues pertain to heterogeneity in the value of a statistical life and health estimates. The problem is twofold. First, is it empirically possible to distinguish effects pertaining to the quantity and quality of life? Second, even if reliable estimates exist, will policy makers be willing to implement these values in the policy evaluation and choice process? Currently, concern with efficient economic tradeoffs is not the central focus of environmental policy, at least not in the U.S.

Acknowledgements

For their helpful comments, we thank Anna Alberini, Tony Fisher, Ray Palmquist, David Pearce, and Jeff Vincent. Kip Viscusi's research is supported by the Harvard Olin Center for Law, Business, and Economics, and the Sheldon Seevak Research Fund. Ted Gayer's research was supported by the Robert Wood Johnson Foundation.

References

Acton, J.P. (1973). Evaluating Public Programs to Save Lives: The Case of Heart Attacks. The Rand Corporation, Santa Monica.

Adams, J. (1995). Risk. University College of London Press, London.

Alberini, A., Cropper, M.L., Fu, T., Krupnick, A., Liu, J.-T., Shaw, D., Harrington, W. (1997). "Valuing health effects of air pollution in developing countries: the case of Taiwan". Journal of Environmental Economics and Management 34, 107–126.

Ames, B.N., Gold, L.S. (1990). "Chemical carcinogenesis: too many rodent carcinogens". Proceedings of the National Academy of Sciences 87, 7772–7776.

Ames, B.N., Gold, L.S. (1996). "The causes and prevention of cancer". In: Hahn, R.W. (Ed.), Risks, Costs, and Lives Saved: Getting Better Results from Regulation. Oxford University Press, Oxford.

Ames, B.N., Profet, M., Gold, L.S. (1990a). "Nature's chemicals and synthetic chemicals: comparative toxicology". Proceedings of the National Academy of Sciences 87, 7782–7786.

Ames, B.N., Profet, M., Gold, L.S. (1990b). "Dietary pesticides (99.99% all natural)". Proceedings of the National Academy of Sciences 87, 7777–7781.

Anderson, K., Burkhauser, R. (1985). "The retirement-health nexus: a new measure of an old puzzle". Journal of Human Resources 20 (3), 315–330.

Arnould, R., Nichols, L.M. (1983). "Wage risk premiums and workers' compensation: a refinement of estimates of compensating wage differentials". Journal of Political Economy 91 (2), 332–340.

Bartik, T.J. (1987). "The estimation of demand parameters with single market data: the problems caused by unobserved tastes". Journal of Political Economy 95, 81–88.

Bartik, T.J. (1988). "Measuring the benefits of amenity improvements in hedonic price". Land Economics 64 (2), 172–183.

Berger, M.C., Blomquist, G.C., Kenkel, D., Tolley, G.S. (1987). "Valuing changes in health risks: a comparison of alternative measures". Southern Economic Journal 53 (4), 967–984.

Beron, K.J., Murdoch, J.C., Thayer, M.A., Vijberberg, V. (1997). "An analysis of the housing market before and after the 1989 Loma Prieta earthquake". Land Economics 73 (1), 101–113.

Biddle, J.E., Zarkin, G. (1988). "Worker preferences and market compensation for job risk". Review of Economics and Statistics 70 (4), 660–667.

Blomquist, G.C. (1988). The Regulation of Motor Vehicle and Traffic Safety. Kluwer Academic Publishers, Boston.

Blomquist, G.C. (1991). "Motorist use of safety equipment: expected benefits or risk incompetence". Journal of Risk and Uncertainty 4 (2), 135–152.

Brookshire, D.S., Thayer, M.A., Tschirhart, J., Schulze, W.D. (1985). "A test of the expected utility model: evidence from earthquake risks". Journal of Political Economy 93 (2), 369–389.

Brown, C. (1980). "Equalizing differences in the labor market". Quarterly Journal of Economics 94 (1), 113–134.

Brown, J.N. (1983). "Structural estimation in implicit markets". In: Triplett, J.E. (Ed.), The Measurement of Labor Cost. University of Chicago Press, Chicago.

Burmaster, D.E., Harris, R.N. (1993). "The magnitude of compounding conservatism in superfund risk assessments". Risk Analysis 13 (2), 131–134.

Chapman, K.S., Hariharan, G. (1994). "Controlling for causality in the link from income to mortality". Journal of Risk and Uncertainty 8 (1), 85–93.

Chay, C.Y., Greenstone, M. (2003). "The impact of air pollution on infant mortality: evidence from geographic variation in pollution shocks induced by a recession". Quarterly Journal of Economics 118 (3), 1121–1167.

Chemical Manufacturers Association (1991). "Analysis of the impact of exposure assumptions on risk assessment of chemicals in the environment". Prepared by Risk Focus, Versar, Inc.

Chestnut, L.G., Ostro, B.D., Vichit-Vadakan, N. (1997). "Transferability of air pollution control health benefits estimates from the United States to developing countries: evidence from the Bangkok study". American Journal of Agricultural Economics 79, 1630–1635.

Chirikos, T., Nestel, G. (1991). "Occupational differences in the ability of men to delay retirement". Journal of Human Resources 26 (1), 1–26.

Combs, B., Slovic, P. (1979). "Newspaper coverage of causes of death". Journalism Quarterly 56 (4), 837–843.

Crandall, R.W., Gruenspecht, H.K., Keeler, T.E., Lave, L.B. (1986). Regulating the Automobile. Brookings Institute, Washington.

Cropper, M.L. (1977). "Health, investment in health, and occupational choice". Journal of Political Economy 85 (6), 1273–1294.

Cropper, M.L. (1981). "Measuring the benefits from reduced morbidity". American Economic Review 71 (2), 235–240.

Cropper, M.L., Simon, N.B., Alberini, A., Arora, S., Sharma, P.K. (1997). "The health benefits of air pollution control in Delhi". American Journal of Agricultural Economics 79, 1625–1629.

Cullen, A.C. (1994). "Measures of compounding conservatism in probabilistic risk assessment". Risk Analysis 14 (4), 389–393.

Duleep, H.O. (1986). "Measuring the effect of income on adult mortality using longitudinal administrative record data". Journal of Human Resources 20, 238–251.

Duleep, H.O. (1989). "Measuring socioeconomic mortality differential over time". Demography 26 (2), 345–351.

Duleep, H.O. (1991). "Occupational experience and socioeconomic variations in mortality". Paper presented at the 1991 Annual Meeting of the Population Association of America.

Ellsberg, D. (1961). "Risk, ambiguity, and the Savage axioms". Quarterly Journal of Economics 75, 643–669.

Environmental Protection Agency (1987). The risk assessment guidelines of 1986. EPA-600/8-87/045. (Guidelines for carcinogen risk assessment; Guidelines for mutagenicity risk assessment; Guidelines for the health risk assessment of chemical mixtures; Guidelines for the health assessment of suspect developmental toxicants; Guidelines for estimating exposures.) U.S. EPA, Office of Health and Environmental Assessment, Washington.

Environmental Protection Agency (1992). Guidelines for exposure assessment. Federal Register 57, 22888–22938.

Environmental Protection Agency (1996). Proposed guidelines for carcinogen risk assessment. Federal Register 61, 17960–18011.

Epple, D. (1987). "Hedonic prices and implicit markets: estimating demand and supply functions for differentiated products". Journal of Political Economy 95, 59–80.

European Commission (1996). Technical Guidance Document in Support of Commission Directive 93/67/EEC on Risk Assessment for New Notified Substances and Commission Regulation No. 1488/94 on Risk Assessment for Existing Substances. Office for Official Publications of the European Communities, Luxembourg.

Evans, W.N., Viscusi, W.K. (1991). "Estimation of state-dependent utility functions using survey data". Review of Economics and Statistics 73 (1), 94–104.

Finkel, A.M. (1989). "Is risk assessment really too conservative?". Columbia Journal of Environmental Law 14, 427–467.

Finley, B., Paustenbach, D. (1994). "The benefits of probabilistic exposure assessment: three case studies involving contaminated air, water, and soil". Risk Analysis 14 (1), 53–73.

Fischhoff, B., MacGregor, D. (1980). "Judged lethality". Decision Research Report 80-4, Decision Research, Eugene, OR.

Freeman III, A.M. (1993). The Measurement of Environmental and Resource Values. Resources for the Future, Washington, DC.

Gayer, T. (2000). "Neighborhood demographics and the distribution of hazardous waste risks: an instrumental variables estimation". Journal of Regulatory Economics 17 (2), 131–155.

Gayer, T., Hamilton, J.T., Viscusi, W.K. (2000a). "Private values of risk tradeoffs at superfund sites: housing market evidence on learning about risk". Review of Economics and Statistics 82 (3), 439–451.

Gayer, T., Hamilton, J.T., Viscusi, W.K. (2000b). "The market value of reducing cancer risk: hedonic housing prices with changing information". Working Paper, Georgetown Public Policy Institute.

General Accounting Office (1992). Risk–risk analysis: OMB's review of a proposed OSHA rule. Report to the Chairman, Committee on Governmental Affairs, U.S. Senate.

Gerking, S., De Haan, M.H., Schulze, W. (1988). "The marginal value of job safety: a contingent valuation study". Journal of Risk and Uncertainty 1 (2), 185–199.

Gold, L.S., Slone, T.H., Stern, B.R., Manley, N.B. (1992). "Rodent carcinogens: setting priorities". Science 258, 261–265.

Gold, L.S., Manley, N.B., Slone, T.H., Garfinkel, G.B., Rohrbach, L., Ames, B.N. (1993). "The fifth plot of the carcinogenic potency database: results of animal bioassays published in the general literature through 1988 and by the National Toxicology Program through 1989". Environmental Health Perspectives 100, 65–135.

Graham, J., Hung-Chang, B., Evans, J.S. (1992). "Poorer is riskier". Risk Analysis 12 (3), 333–337.

Grossman, M. (1972). "On the concept of health capital and the demand for health". Journal of Political Economy 80 (2), 223–255.

Harrington, W., Portney, P.R. (1987). "Valuing the benefits of health and safety regulations". Journal of Urban Economics 22 (1), 101–112.

Hersch, J. (1998). "Compensating differentials for gender-specific job injury rates". American Economic Review 88 (3), 598–607.

Hersch, J., Pickton, T.S. (1995). "Risk-taking activities and heterogeneity of job–risk tradeoffs". Journal of Risk and Uncertainty 11 (3), 205–217.

Hersch, J., Viscusi, W.K. (1990). "Cigarette smoking, seatbelt use, and differences in wage–risk tradeoffs". Journal of Human Resources 25 (2), 202–227.

Jakoby, W.B. (Ed.) (1980). Enzymatic Basis of Detoxification. Academic Press, New York.

Jones-Lee, M.W. (1976). The Value of Life: An Economic Analysis. University of Chicago Press, Chicago.

Jones-Lee, M.W. (1989). The Economics of Safety and Physical Risk. Basil Blackwell, Oxford.

Kahn, S., Kevin, L. (1988). "Efficient estimation of structural hedonic systems". International Economic Review 29 (1), 157–166.

Kahneman, D., Slovic, P., Tversky, A. (1982). Judgment Under Uncertainty: Heuristics and Biases. Cambridge University Press, Cambridge, UK.

Kahneman, D., Tversky, A. (1973). "On the psychology of prediction". Psychological Review 80, 237–251.

Kahneman, D., Tversky, A. (1979). "Prospect theory: an analysis of decisions under risk". Econometrica 47, 263–291.

Keeney, R.L. (1990). "Mortality risks induced by economic expenditures". Risk Analysis 10 (1), 147–159.

Kiel, K., McClain, K.T. (1995). "House prices during siting decision stages: the case of an incinerator from rumor through operation". Journal of Environmental Economics and Management 28, 241–255.

Kitagawa, E.M., Hauser, P.M. (1973). Differential Mortality in the United States: A Study in Socioeconomic Epidemiology. Harvard University Press, Cambridge, MA.

Kniesner, T.J., Leeth, J.D. (1991). "Compensating wage differentials for fatal injury risk in Australia, Japan, and the United States". Journal of Risk and Uncertainty 4 (1), 75–90.

Kohlhase, J.E. (1991). "The impact of toxic waste sites on housing values". Journal of Urban Economics 30, 1–26.

Krupnick, A.J. (1993). "Benefit transfers and valuation of environmental improvements". Resources 110, 1–7.

Krupnick, A.J., Cropper, M.L. (1992). "The effect of information on health risk valuations". Journal of Risk and Uncertainty 5 (1), 29–48.

Larson, B.A., Avaliani, S., Rosen, S., Shaposhnikov, D., Strukova, E., Vincent, J.R., Wolff, S.K. (1999). "The economics of air pollution health risks in Russia: a case study of Volgograd". World Development 27 (10), 1803–1819.

Lave, L.B., Seskin, E.P. (1973). "An analysis of the association between U.S. mortality and air pollution". Journal of the American Statistical Association 68, 284–290.

Lave, L.B., Seskin, E.P. (1977). Air Pollution and Human Health. Johns Hopkins University Press, Baltimore, MD.

Lichtenstein, S., Slovic, P., Fischhoff, B., Layman, U., Combs, B. (1978). "Judged frequency of lethal events". Journal of Experimental Psychology: Human Learning and Memory 4, 551–578.

Liu, J.-T., Hammitt, J.K. (1999). "Perceived risk and value of workplace safety in a developing country". Journal of Risk Research 2, 263–275.

Liu, J.-T., Hammitt, J.K., Liu, J.-L. (1997). "Estimated hedonic wage function and value of life in a developing country". Economics Letters 57, 353–358.

Lutter, R., Morrall III, J.F. (1994). "Health–health analysis". Journal of Risk and Uncertainty 8 (1), 43–66.

Lutter, R., Morrall III, J.F., Viscusi, W.K. (1999). "The cost per life saved cutoff for safety-enhancing regulations". Economic Inquiry 37 (4), 599–608.

Magat, W.A., Viscusi, W.K., Huber, J. (1996). "A reference lottery metric for valuing health". Management Science 42 (8), 1118–1129.

Mazurek, J.V. (1996). "The role of health risk assessment and cost–benefit analysis in environmental decision making in selected countries: an initial survey". Resources for the Future Discussion Paper 96-36.

Michigan Manufacturers Association (1993). "A comparison of Monte Carlo simulation-based exposure estimates with estimates calculated using EPA and suggested Michigan manufacturers association exposure factors". Prepared by ENVIRON Corporation.

Miller, T., Guria, J. (1991). The value of statistical life in New Zealand. Report to the Ministry of Transport, Land Transport Division.

Moore, M.J., Viscusi, W.K. (1988a). "Doubling the estimated value of life: results using new occupational fatality data". Journal of Policy Analysis and Management 7 (3), 476–490.

Moore, M.J., Viscusi, W.K. (1988b). "The quantity-adjusted value of life". Economic Inquiry 26 (3), 369–388.

Moore, M.J., Viscusi, W.K. (1990a). "Discounting environmental health risks: new evidence and policy implications". Journal of Environmental Economics and Management 18 (2), S51–S62.

Moore, M.J., Viscusi, W.K. (1990b). "Models for estimating discount rates for long-term health risks using labor market data". Journal of Risk and Uncertainty 3 (4), 381–401.

Morrall III, J.F. (1986). "A review of the record". Regulation 10 (2), 25–34.

Murdoch, J.C., Harinder, S., Thayer, M.A. (1993). "The impact of natural hazards on housing values: the Loma Prieta earthquake". American Real Estate and Urban Economics Association Journal 21 (2), 167–184.

Murray, C.J.L., Lopez, A.D. (1996). The Global Burden of Disease: Summary. World Health Organization, Geneva.

Nichols, A.L., Zeckhauser, R.J. (1986). "The perils of prudence: how conservative risk assessments distort regulation". Regulation 10 (2), 13–24.

National Research Council (1983). Risk Assessment in the Federal Government: Managing the Process. National Academy Press, Washington.

National Research Council (1994). Science and Judgment in Risk Assessment. National Academy Press, Washington.

National Research Council (1996). Carcinogens and Anticarcinogens in the Human Diet. National Academy Press, Washington.

Olson, C.A. (1981). "An analysis of wage differentials received by workers on dangerous jobs". Journal of Human Resources 16 (2), 167–185.

Office of Science and Technology Policy, Executive Office of the President (1985). "Chemical carcinogens: a review of the science and its associated principles". Federal Register 50, 10371–10442.

Ostro, B.D. (1994). "Estimating the health effects of air pollutants: a methodology with an application to Jakarta". World Bank Policy Research Working Paper no. 1301.

Ostro, B.D., Eskeland, G.S., Feyzioglu, T., Sanchez, J.M. (1998). "Air pollution and health effects: a study of respiratory illness among children in Santiago, Chile". World Bank Working Paper no. 1932.

Ostro, B.D., Sanchez, J.M., Aranda, C., Eskeland, G.S. (2000). "Air pollution and mortality: results from Santiago, Chile". World Bank Working Paper no. 1453.

Palmquist, R.B. (1992). "Valuing localized externalities". Journal of Urban Economics 31, 59–68.

Pearce, D. (1998). "Environmental appraisal and environmental policy in the European Union". Environmental and Resource Economics 11 (3/4), 389–501.

Pearce, D. (2000). "Cost–benefit analysis and environmental policy". In: Helm, D. (Ed.), Environmental Policy in the UK. Blackwell, Oxford, UK.

Peltzman, S. (1975). "The effects of automobile safety regulation". Journal of Political Economy 83 (4), 677–725.

Portney, P.R. (1981). "Housing prices, health effects, and valuing reductions in risk of death". Journal of Environmental Economics and Management 8, 72–78.

Portney, P.R., Stavins, R.N. (1994). "Regulatory review of environmental policy". Journal of Risk and Uncertainty 8 (1), 111–122.

Pugh, D.M. (1998). "Deciding on the regulatory limits which have ensured that exposures of people to chemicals were without unacceptable risk". In: Pugh, D.M., Tarazona, J.V. (Eds.), Regulation for Chemical Safety in Europe: Analysis, Comment and Criticism. Kluwer Academic Publishers, Dordrecht, The Netherlands.

Pugh, D.M., Tarazona, J.V. (Eds.) (1998). Regulation for Chemical Safety in Europe: Analysis, Comment and Criticism. Kluwer Academic Publishers, Dordrecht, The Netherlands.

Schelling, T. (1968). "The life you save may be your own". In: Chase, S. (Ed.), Problems in Public Expenditure Analysis. Brookings Institution, Washington.

Shanmugam, K.R. (1997). "Compensating wage differentials for work-related and injury accidents". Indian Journal of Labour Economics 40, 251–262.

Shilling, J.D., Sirmans, C.F., Benjamin, J.D. (1989). "Flood insurance, wealth redistribution, and urban property values". Journal of Urban Economics 26 (1), 43–53.

Simon, N.B., Cropper, M.L., Alberini, A., Arora, S. (1999). "Valuing mortality reductions in India: a study of compensating-wage differentials". World Bank Policy Research Working Paper no. 2078.

Sloan, F., Viscusi, W.K., Chesson, H.W., Conover, C.J., Whetton-Goldstein, K. (1998). "Alternative approaches to valuing intangible health losses: the evidence for multiple sclerosis". Journal of Health Economics 17, 475–497.

Smith, R.S. (1974). "The feasibility of an 'injury tax' approach to occupational safety". Law and Contemporary Problems 38 (4), 730–744.

Smith, R.S. (1976). The Occupational Safety and Health Act. American Enterprise Institute, Washington.

Smith, R.S. (1979). "Compensating age differentials and public policy: a review". Industrial Labor Relations Review 32 (3), 339–352.

Smith, R. (1994). "Use of Monte Carlo simulation for human exposure assessment at a superfund site". Risk Analysis 14 (4), 433–439.

Smith, V.K., Epp, D.J., Schwabe, K.A. (1994). "Cross-country analyses don't estimate health–health responses". Journal of Risk and Uncertainty 8 (1), 67–84.

Smith, V.K., Desvousges, W.H., Fisher, A., Johnson, F.R. (1988). "Learning about Radon's risk". Journal of Risk and Uncertainty 1 (2), 233–258.

Stokey, E., Zeckhauser, R.J. (1978). A Primer for Policy Analysis. Norton, New York.

Thaler, R., Rosen, S. (1976). "The value of saving a life: evidence from the market". In: Terleckyj, N.E. (Ed.), Household Production and Consumption. NBER, Cambridge, MA.

U.S. Congress, Joint Economic Committee (1984). Estimating the Effects of Economic Change on National Health and Social Well-Being. U.S.G.P.O., Washington.

U.S. National Institutes of Health (1992). A Mortality Study of 1.3 Million Persons by Demographic, Social, and Economic Factors: 1979–1985. Second Data Book. U.S. National Longitudinal Mortality Study, Washington.

Vincent, J.R., Ali, R.M., Associates (1997). Environment and Development in a Resource-Rich Economy: Malaysia under the New Economic Policy. Harvard University Press, Cambridge, MA.

Viscusi, W.K. (1978). "Wealth effects and earnings premiums for job hazards". Review of Economics and Statistics 10 (3), 408–416.

Viscusi, W.K. (1979). Employment Hazards: An Investigation of Market Performance. Harvard University Press, Cambridge, MA.

Viscusi, W.K. (1981). "Occupational safety and health regulation: its impact and policy alternatives". In: Crecine, J. (Ed.), Research in Public Policy Analysis and Management, vol. 2. JAI Press, Greenwich, CT.

Viscusi, W.K. (1984). "The lulling effect: the impact of child-resistant packaging on aspirin and analgesic ingestions". American Economic Review 74 (2), 324–327.

Viscusi, W.K. (1992). Fatal Tradeoffs: Public and Private Responsibilities for Risk. Oxford University Press, Oxford, UK.

Viscusi, W.K. (1993). "The value of risks to life and health". Journal of Economic Literature 31, 1912–1946.

Viscusi, W.K. (1994). "Mortality effects of regulatory costs and policy evaluation criteria". Rand Journal of Economics 25 (1), 94–109.

Viscusi, W.K. (1995). "Carcinogen regulation: risk characteristics and the synthetic risk bias". American Economic Review 85 (2), 50–54.

Viscusi, W.K. (1996). "Economic foundations of the current regulatory reform efforts". Journal of Economic Perspectives 10 (3), 119–134.

Viscusi, W.K. (1998). Rational Risk Policy. Oxford University Press, Oxford, UK.

Viscusi, W.K. (2000a). "The value of life in legal contexts: survey and critique". American Law and Economics Review 2 (1), 195–222.

Viscusi, W.K. (2000b). "Jurors, judges, and the mistreatment of risk by the courts". Journal of Legal Studies, in press.

Viscusi, W.K., Chesson, H. (1999). "Hopes and fears: the conflicting effects of risk ambiguity". Theory and Decision 47 (2), 153–178.

Viscusi, W.K., Covallo, G.O. (1994). "The effect of product safety regulation on safety precautions". Risk Analysis 15 (6), 917–930.

Viscusi, W.K., Evans, W.N. (1990). "Utility functions that depend on health status: estimates and economic implications". American Economic Review 80 (3), 353–374.

Viscusi, W.K., Hakes, J.K. (1998). "Synthetic risks, risk potency, and carcinogen regulation". Journal of Policy Analysis and Management 17 (1), 52–73.

Viscusi, W.K., Hakes, J.K., Carlin, A. (1997). "Measures of mortality risks". Journal of Risk and Uncertainty 14, 213–233.

Viscusi, W.K., Hamilton, J.T. (1999). "Are risk regulators rational? Evidence from hazardous waste cleanup decisions". American Economic Review 89 (4), 1010–1027.

Viscusi, W.K., Hamilton, J.T., Dockins, P.C. (1997). "Conservative versus mean risk assessments: implications for superfund policies". Journal of Environmental Economics and Management 34, 187–206.

Viscusi, W.K., Hersch, J. (2000). "Cigarette smokers as job risk takers". Review of Economics and Statistics, in press.

Viscusi, W.K., Magat, W.A. (1987). Learning about Risk: Consumer and Worker Responses to Hazard Information. Harvard University Press, Cambridge, MA.

Viscusi, W.K., Magat, W.A., Forrest, A. (1988). "Altruistic and private valuations of risk reduction". Journal of Policy Analysis and Management 7 (2), 227–245.

Viscusi, W.K., Magat, W.A., Huber, J. (1987). "An investigation of the rationality of consumer valuations of multiple health risks". RAND Journal of Economics 18 (4), 465–479.

Viscusi, W.K., Magat, W.A., Huber, J. (1991). "Pricing environmental health risks: survey assessments of risk–risk and risk–dollar trade-offs for chronic bronchitis". Journal of Environmental Economics and Management 21 (1), 32–51.

Viscusi, W.K., Moore, M.J. (1989). "Rates of time preference and valuations of the duration of life". Journal of Public Economics 38 (3), 297–317.

Viscusi, W.K., O'Connor, C.J. (1984). "Adaptive responses to chemical labeling: are workers Bayesian decision makers?". American Economic Review 74 (5), 942–956.

Viscusi, W.K., Zeckhauser, R.J. (1994). "The fatality and injury costs of expenditures". Journal of Risk and Uncertainty 8 (1), 19–41.

Wildavsky, A. (1980). "Richer is safer". The Public Interest 60, 23–39.

Wildavsky, A. (1988). Searching for Safety. Transaction Books, New Brunswick.

Williams, S.F. (1993). "Second best: the soft underbelly of deterrence theory in tort". Harvard Law Review 106 (4), 932–944.

Wilson, R. (1979). "Analyzing the daily risks of life". Technology Review 81 (4), 40–46.

Wolfson, M., Rowe, G., Gentleman, J., Tomiak, M. (1992). "Career earnings and death: a longitudinal analysis of older Canadian men". In: Statistics Canada, Research Paper Series no. 45.

Xu, X., Gao, J., Dockery, D.W., Chen, Y. (1994). "Air pollution and daily mortality in residential areas of Beijing, China". Archives of Environmental Health 49 (41), 216–222.

Xu, X., Li, B., Huang, H. (1995). "Air pollution and unscheduled hospital outpatient and emergency room visits". Environmental Health Perspectives 103 (3), 286–289.

Zeckhauser, R., Shepard, D. (1976). "Where now for saving lives?". Law and Contemporary Problems 40, 5–45.

AUTHOR INDEX

n indicates citation in a footnote.

SUBJECT INDEX

HANDBOOKS IN ECONOMICS

1. HANDBOOK OF MATHEMATICAL ECONOMICS (in 4 volumes)
   Volumes 1, 2 and 3 edited by Kenneth J. Arrow and Michael D. Intriligator
   Volume 4 edited by Werner Hildenbrand and Hugo Sonnenschein

2. HANDBOOK OF ECONOMETRICS (in 6 volumes)
   Volumes 1, 2 and 3 edited by Zvi Griliches and Michael D. Intriligator
   Volume 4 edited by Robert F. Engle and Daniel L. McFadden
   Volume 5 edited by James J. Heckman and Edward Leamer
   Volume 6 is in preparation (editors James J. Heckman and Edward Leamer)

3. HANDBOOK OF INTERNATIONAL ECONOMICS (in 3 volumes)
   Volumes 1 and 2 edited by Ronald W. Jones and Peter B. Kenen
   Volume 3 edited by Gene M. Grossman and Kenneth Rogoff

4. HANDBOOK OF PUBLIC ECONOMICS (in 4 volumes)
   Edited by Alan J. Auerbach and Martin Feldstein

5. HANDBOOK OF LABOR ECONOMICS (in 5 volumes)
   Volumes 1 and 2 edited by Orley C. Ashenfelter and Richard Layard
   Volumes 3A, 3B and 3C edited by Orley C. Ashenfelter and David Card

6. HANDBOOK OF NATURAL RESOURCE AND ENERGY ECONOMICS
   (in 3 volumes). Edited by Allen V. Kneese and James L. Sweeney

7. HANDBOOK OF REGIONAL AND URBAN ECONOMICS (in 4 volumes)
   Volume 1 edited by Peter Nijkamp
   Volume 2 edited by Edwin S. Mills
   Volume 3 edited by Paul C. Cheshire and Edwin S. Mills
   Volume 4 edited by J. Vernon Henderson and Jacques-François Thisse

8. HANDBOOK OF MONETARY ECONOMICS (in 2 volumes)
   Edited by Benjamin Friedman and Frank Hahn

9. HANDBOOK OF DEVELOPMENT ECONOMICS (in 4 volumes)
   Volumes 1 and 2 edited by Hollis B. Chenery and T.N. Srinivasan
   Volumes 3A and 3B edited by Jere Behrman and T.N. Srinivasan

10. HANDBOOK OF INDUSTRIAL ORGANIZATION (in 3 volumes)
    Volumes 1 and 2 edited by Richard Schmalensee and Robert R. Willig
    Volume 3 is in preparation (editors Mark Armstrong and Robert H. Porter)

11. HANDBOOK OF GAME THEORY with Economic Applications (in 3 volumes)
    Edited by Robert J. Aumann and Sergiu Hart

All published volumes available

FORTHCOMING TITLES

HANDBOOK OF EXPERIMENTAL ECONOMICS RESULTS
Editors Charles Plott and Vernon L. Smith

HANDBOOK OF THE ECONOMICS OF GIVING, ALTRUISM AND
RECIPROCITY
Editors Serge-Christophe Kolm and Jean Mercier Ythier

HANDBOOK ON THE ECONOMICS OF ART AND CULTURE
Editors Victor Ginsburgh and David Throsby

HANDBOOK OF LAW AND ECONOMICS
Editors A. Mitchell Polinsky and Steven Shavell

HANDBOOK OF ECONOMIC FORECASTING
Editors Graham Elliott, Clive W.J. Granger and Allan Timmermann

HANDBOOK OF THE ECONOMICS OF EDUCATION
Editors Eric Hanushek and Finis Welch

HANDBOOK OF ECONOMICS OF TECHNOLOGICAL CHANGE
Editors Bronwyn H. Hall and Nathan Rosenberg